Alice Vittrant, Justin Watkins (Eds.)
The Mainland Southeast Asia Linguistic Area

Trends in Linguistics
Studies and Monographs

Editor
Chiara Gianollo
Daniël Van Olmen

Editorial Board
Walter Bisang
Tine Breban
Volker Gast
Hans Henrich Hock
Karen Lahousse
Natalia Levshina
Caterina Mauri
Heiko Narrog
Salvador Pons
Niina Ning Zhang
Amir Zeldes

Editor responsible for this volume
Hans Henrich Hock

Volume 314

The Mainland Southeast Asia Linguistic Area

Edited by
Alice Vittrant
Justin Watkins

DE GRUYTER
MOUTON

ISBN 978-3-11-076191-7
e-ISBN (PDF) 978-3-11-040198-1
e-ISBN (EPUB) 978-3-11-040213-1

Library of Congress Cataloging-in-Publication Data
Names: Vittrant, Alice, editor. | Watkins, Justin, editor. | Container of
  (work): Peterson, David A. (David August), 1968- Bangladesh Khumi.
Title: The mainland Southeast Asia linguistic area / [edited by] Alice
  Vittrant/Justin Watkins.
Description: Berlin ; Boston : Mouton, [2018] | Series: Trends in
  linguistics. Studies and monographs ; volume 314 | Includes
  bibliographical references and index.
Identifiers: LCCN 2018007425 | ISBN 9783110401769 (hardcover) | ISBN
  9783110401981 (pdf) | ISBN 9783110402131 (e-pub)
Subjects: LCSH: Southeast Asia-Languages.
Classification: LCC PL3501 .M33 2018 | DDC 495--dc23 LC record available at
  https://lccn.loc.gov/2018007425

Bibliographic information published by the Deutsche Nationalbibliothek
The Deutsche Nationalbibliothek lists this publication in the Deutsche Nationalbibliografie;
detailed bibliographic data are available on the Internet at: http://dnb.dnb.de.

© 2021 Walter de Gruyter GmbH, Berlin/Boston
This volume is text- and page-identical with the hardback published in 2019.
Typesetting: jürgen ullrich typosatz, Nördlingen
Printing and binding: CPI books GmbH, Leck

www.degruyter.com

James A. Matisoff
Preface

This book is a welcome addition to the literature on individual East and Southeast Asian languages, as well as an important validation of the concept of *linguistic area*. The 13 articles treat languages belonging to the five great families of the region (Sino-Tibetan, Mon-Khmer/Austroasiatic, Tai-Kadai [=Kradai], Hmong-Mien [=Miao-Yao], and Austronesian), with an explicit emphasis on the manifestation of particular areal features that have been discussed in the literature.[1]

By any criterion – sheer number of languages, significance for the history and culture of the world – East and Southeast Asia constitute one of the world's most important linguistic areas.[2]

- *Multilaterality, directionality, and concentric spheres of influence*

In a delightfully messy linguistic area like mainland Southeast Asia, where both lexical and grammatical homogenization have occurred on a grand scale, it is no simple matter to determine the genetic origin of such features as phonemic tone, quadrisyllabic "elaborate expressions", "psycho-collocations", classifier systems, emphatic sentence-final particles, adversative passives, grammaticalized verbs functioning as aspectual markers or prepositions, etc. The situation is reminiscent of a group of neighbors living cheek-by-jowl, who often squabble with each other, but who have nevertheless borrowed so many cups of sugar from each other over the years that they have lost track of who owes what to whom.[3]

---

1 The organization of this volume is thus quite different from that of Thurgood & LaPolla, eds. (2003), where some 40 Sino-Tibetan languages (30+ Tibeto-Burman and 7 dialects of Chinese) are featured, but all from a single great language family, and with few explicit references to cross-genetic similarities.
2 The discussion in this section roughly follows the presentation in Ch. VII (*Diffusional dynamics*) of the manuscript of my book *Languages of Mainland Southeast Asia* (still alas, "in progress"!).
3 Terms like *convergence, diffusion,* and *contact* are in themselves neutral with respect to directionality. On the other hand, there does exist a term *(parallel independent development)* which specifically denies that a certain phenomenon in Language A has been influenced by contact with Language B.

James A. Matisoff: University of California, Berkeley
E-Mail: matisoff@berkeley.edu

https://doi.org/10.1515/9783110401981-202

For millennia Mainland Southeast Asia (including China, especially the vast area south of the Yangtze) has been marked by voluntary migrations, forced displacements of populations by war or invasions, and intermarriage among different ethnic groups. One result has been widespread multilingualism, to the point where it is common to encounter people with little or no formal education who are fluent in several languages. Although one's mother tongue *(la lingua del cuore)* occupies a special place in people's hearts, the language one must speak in order to earn a livelihood *(la lingua del pane*[4]*)* is equally essential.

For not all languages are equal in terms of cultural and political prestige. The two most important cultural influences on the Southeast Asian linguistic area as a whole have been from India and China, domains of influence which are conveniently referred to as the *Indosphere* and the *Sinosphere*.[5] Of course these spheres overlap geographically, and the proportion of influence that each has had on a particular culture has sometimes greatly changed through time. Roughly speaking, the Southeast Asian Indosphere comprises northeast India, the Himalayan region, Burma, Cambodia, Thailand, and Indonesia (especially Java and Bali). The learned components of the lexicons of the "great" languages of this area (Mon, Burmese, Khmer, Cham, Thai/Lao, Javanese, Balinese) are from Sanskrit/Pali. The vast Sinosphere includes Korea, Japan, and large swaths of Inner Asia (Mongolia, Xinjiang), as well as regions where Southeast Asian languages are spoken: China south of the Yangtze ("Cisyangtzeana") and Vietnam. Southern China is a veritable "mother soup" of languages (W.L.Ballard, 1983),[6] a "corridor of peoples" (Sun Hongkai 1983),[7] that certainly witnessed the birth of Tai-Kadai and Hmong-Mien (Downer 1963),[8] and probably Austroasiatic and Austronesian as well. The learnèd components of the lexicons of Hmong-Mien and Vietnamese are from Chinese.

It is perhaps inevitable to distinguish between "great" languages, spoken by the majority populations of past or present nation-states, and "humble" languages, spoken by minority groups, and often well on the way to extinction. The present volume strikes a nice balance between these two categories, with eight chapters on "great" languages (Chinese, Burmese, Mon, Khmer, Vietnamese, Thai, Cham, Malay), and five on "humble" ones (Khumi, Na/Mosuo, Mong Leng,

---

4 In the Southeast Asian context *la lingua del riso* might be more appropriate.
5 These terms were first introduced in Matisoff 1978, "Tonogenesis in Southeast Asia".
6 "Mother soup – a south Chinese recipe for tonometamorphogenesis", *Computational Analyses of Asian and African Languages* (Tokyo) 22: 65–70.
7 [in Chinese] "The languages of the Corridor of Nationalities region of Western Sichuan." In *Research on the Peoples of the Southwest*, No. 1, pp. 429–454. Chengdu: People's Publishing Co.
8 "Chinese, Tai, and Miao-Yao." In Harry L. Shorto, ed., *Linguistic Comparison in South East Asia and the Pacific*, London: School of Oriental and African Studies, pp. 133–139.

Pwo Karen, Wa). Another important dichotomy is related to this distinction, but grounded in geographical/ecological factors: *plains languages* (spoken by majority populations in large contiguous geographical areas in the plains, where irrigated ricefields are possible) vs. *hill languages* (spoken by small relatively isolated groups of people in the hills, who live by practicing "slash-and-burn" agriculture in non-irrigated mountain fields or "swiddens").[9]

On the sociolinguistic level, great languages tend to reflect hierarchically stratified cultures, often with clearly distinguished formal vs. colloquial styles of speaking, including such features as elaborate pronominal systems that encode differences in age, gender, and social status. The languages of the hills are more "democratic", with simple pronouns and few euphemisms for embarrassing bodyparts or bodily functions.

The macro-distinction between Indo- and Sino-spheres is valid as far as it goes, but it is too simplistic when it comes to detailed examination of the influences exerted on particular modern languages. This is because there are a large number of regionally dominant languages that have developed spheres of influence of their own.[10] *Tibetan* has exerted a strong influence on the Tibeto-Burman languages of Nepal and southwest China. *Nepali*, the national Indo-Aryan language of Nepal, has had an even more powerful influence on the TB languages of the country. *Jingpho* (also called Kachin), itself influenced by Shan, Burmese, and Chinese, has strongly affected Burmish languages like Atsi/Zaiwa, Maru/Langsu, and Lashi/Leqi, to the point where they are considered in China to belong to the "Jingpho nationality". *Meithei* (also called Manipuri) is the dominant language of India's Manipur State, and is rapidly supplanting the other TB languages of the area. *Tai* languages (including standard Thai or Siamese, as well as closely related languages like Shan and Lue) have a wide area of influence on minority languages of Thailand, northern Burma, and southwest China.[11]

The languages represented in this volume may be differentiated according to the particular sphere(s) of influence that have affected them:

---

9 See Burling (1965) *Hill Farms and Paddy Fields*; New Jersey: Prentice Hall. This state of affairs has been called "vertical ecological zonation".
10 This is analogous to the situation with respect to Chinese dialects, where there is often a three-tiered system in a speaker's repertoire: the local "patois", spoken at home in intimate situations; the regional standard, used in more formal contexts outside the home; and the national language, used when communicating with people from other parts of the country.
11 SHINTANI Tadahiko (1998) has called this whole region the "Tai cultural area". See, e.g. "The zone of the Golden Quadrangle: the history, language, and ethnic groups of the Tai cultural area." Tokyo: Keiyusha. [in Japanese]

Sinosphere	Indosphere	Tibetosphere	Taiosphere
Chinese "dialects"	Burmese	Mosuo	Pwo Karen
	Cham		Wa
Mong Leng	Khmer		
Mosuo	Khumi Malay		
Thai	Mon		
Vietnamese	Pwo Karen		
	Thai		

Types of lexical borrowing situations

It is generally agreed that lexical borrowing involves the most superficial area of linguistic structure, yet it is by no means a simple matter. Several subtypes should be recognized:

(a) Unidirectional borrowing

Sometimes the direction of borrowing is clear. It is obvious that Japanese **pan** 'bread' is borrowed from Portuguese **pão**, rather than the other way around, since bread was not part of the Japanese diet before European contact. It is clear that Jingpho **yàk** 'difficult, distressful' is a loanword from Shan (cf. Siamese **jâak**), since no native Jingpho words end in **-k** (PTB *****-k** > Jg. **-ʔ**).

(b) Backloans

Much trickier are cases where Language B borrows a word from Language A at one historical period, then later A borrows the same etymon – which may meanwhile have undergone considerable change in the course of its history in Language B – back from B again. The case of the everyday condiment *ketchup* furnishes an interesting example. This word probably originated in a Cantonese compound **ke-chap** 茄汁 'eggplant [i.e. tomato] sauce', perhaps first borrowed into Malay as **kicap** 'fish sauce', whence to English *catsup* or *ketchup*, from where it was adopted as Japanese **kechappu**, then back into Taiwanese Chinese as **ket-chap-pu**, thus returning to its language of origin.

(c) Borrowing from related languages

In cases where the languages in contact are also genetically related, it may be particularly hard to distinguish true cognates from diffusional material. Lahu **ɔ̂-vɛ̂ʔ** 'screw' can easily be shown to be a borrowing from Burmese **wɛʔ-ʔu** (Written Burmese **wak-ʔu**), literally "pig intestine" (so called because of its spiral shape), although most Lahu are unaware of this, since the ordinary Lahu word for 'pig' is **vàʔ** (inherited from Proto-Lolo-Burmese *****wak**), and the head of the Burmese compound, **ʔu** 'intestine', has been dropped. The Lahu forms **và?** and **vɛ̀?** are thus doublets, one inherited and one borrowed.

(d) Borrowings from a common source
Lexical similarities between languages may be due to borrowing from a common source. Resemblant morphemes in Tai and Vietnamese are largely due to independent borrowings from Chinese. In psycho-collocations (one of the areal features emphasized in this volume), the "psycho-noun" for MIND derives from Pali **citta** in the literary languages of the Indosphere: Written Burmese **cit** (Mod. Bse. **sei?**), Khmer **ceut**, Mon **cɔt**.

(e) Reversibility of the directionality of influence
The vicissitudes of cultural and military history have sometimes led to striking reversals in the direction of influence between languages. English borrowed massively from French for centuries after the Norman Conquest (A.D. 1066), a situation which began to change in the 19th century, and which by now has reached alarming proportions as English words are flooding into the hallowed French lexicon. Japanese borrowed enormously from Chinese for hundreds of years, but this state of affairs changed radically in the latter half of the 19th century, when Japan was exposed to Western influence before China was. Many modern scientific and cultural terms were translated into Japanese by arranging Chinese morphemes (along with the characters used to write them) into novel combinations. Subsequently a good number of these were borrowed back into Chinese[12], e.g. 'university' Jse. **daigaku** > Chinese **dàxué** 大學; 'diabetes' Jse. **tōnyōbyō** > Chinese **tángniàobìng** 糖尿病. In Southeast Asia proper, a similar historical scenario affected the two principal Indospheric Mon-Khmer literary languages, Khmer and Mon. For centuries these two languages exerted strong influence on Thai and Burmese, respectively, only to have the directionality of influence reversed in recent times.

• *Scale of intensity of contact*
The publication of Thomason & Kaufman's seminal book *Language Contact, Creolization, and Genetic Linguistics* (1988), mentioned in the Editors' *Introduction* to this volume, went a long way toward making the study of degrees of language contact more precise. The authors established a scale from 1 to 5 according to the intensity of the contact involved, providing rich exemplifications of each point on the scale ranging from #1 (casual contact; only lexical borrowing) to #5 (very strong contact with heavy structural borrowing).

---

12 See section (b), *Backloans*, above.

• *Structural borrowing and metatypy*
In the not too distant past, the possibility of grammatical borrowing seemed like a rather daring notion. One of the questions on my doctoral orals (Fall 1964) was "Is structural borrowing possible?" The belief was widespread that morphosyntax is somehow the deepest level of linguistic structure, and thus virtually impervious to outside interference. Nowadays, careful study of borrowing patterns all over the world has shown that "While there may be some aspects of a language's syntax which, because of internal structural cohesion, are especially resistant to foreign interference, the evidence...indicates that syntactic interference is as common as phonological interference" (Thomason & Kaufman, *op. cit.*, p. 118).

The Southeast Asian linguistic area furnishes us with a number of especially striking cases of *metatypy*, i.e. typological change resulting from intensity of contact "to the fifth degree", such that areal influence has cut across genetic relationship. These cases include the following:

	Genetic	**Typological**
Karen	Tibeto-Burman	Tai; Mon-Khmer
Bai	Tibeto-Burman	Sinitic
Vietnamese	Mon-Khmer	Sinitic; Tai
Munda	Austroasiatic	Indo-Aryan
Cham, Rade	Austronesian	Mon-Khmer < Sinitic

Unlike the vast majority of Tibeto-Burman languages, the Karenic and Baic subgroups have acquired non-verb-final word order, under the influence of Tai/Mon-Khmer and Chinese, respectively. Vietnamese has changed from an atonal sesquisyllabic language to a fully tonal monosyllabic one, due to Chinese (and to a lesser extent, Tai) influence. The Austroasiatic Munda languages of eastern India have undergone a change from the non-verb-final syntax typical of AA/MK to a verb-final one, with the verb often accompanied by a string of suffixes alien to the rest of the family, suggesting some sort of Indo-Aryan substratum. The Chamic languages of southern Vietnam have changed from their earlier disyllabic or sesquisyllabic structure to a monosyllabic pattern, perhaps in part due to influence of Vietnamese (which had itself undergone monosyllabization under Chinese influence).

• *Some areal features emphasized in this volume, and the languages/articles which give the most information about them*

(1) Phonological
tone and register; monosyllabicity; sesquisyllabicity; profusion of vowels; relative paucity of syllable-final consonants

(2) Morphological
psycho-collocations; elaborate expressions; expressives; reduplication; compounding; lack of inflection; affixation

(3) Grammatical categories and syntax
classifiers; nominalization and relativization; pro-drop; emotive sentence-final particles; topic prominence; verb concatenation and serialization; grammaticalization of verbs to prepositions, auxiliaries, TAM particles, etc.; adversative passives

(4) Semantics/Pragmatics
proliferation of terms in certain semantic areas: *rice; cut; carry; dry*; politeness distinctions in pronouns; pronominal use of kin terms; literary vs. colloquial style

The extent to which each of the languages in this volume exemplify these features is roughly indicated in the following charts:[13]

	Tone (T) Register (R)	Mono-syllabic	Sesqui-syllabic	Vowel profusion	Paucity of codas
Min Chinese	(T) ++	+	–	+	+
Burmese	(T, R) +	+	+	–	+
Yongning Na	(T) +	+	–	+	+
Khumi	(T) ++	+	+	+	+
Pwo Karen	(T) +	+	+	+	+
Khmer	–	+	++	++	+
Mon	(R) +	+	+	+	+
Vietnamese	(T) ++	+	–	+	+
Wa	(R) +	+	+	+	+
Siamese	(T) +	+	+	+	+
Mong Leng	(T,R) ++	+	(+)	+	++
Cham	(R) +, (T) (+)	+	(+)	+	+
Malay	–	–	–	(+)	–

---

[13] A similar scheme of pluses and minuses is also followed in the Vietnamese paper by Do-Hurinville & Huy Linh Dao.

	Psycho-collocations	Elaborate expressions	Compounds	Redup-lication	Expressives	Affixation	Inflection
Min Chinese	+	+	+	+	–	–	–
Burmese	+	+	+	++	–	+	–
Yongning Na	+	+	+	+	–	+	–
Khumi	(+)	++	+	(+)	–	+	+
Pwo Karen	+	+	+	+	–	(+)	–
Khmer	+	–	–	+	++	+	–
Mon	+	(+)	(+)	+	+	+	–
Vietnamese	++	+	+	+	+	–	–
Wa	+	+	+	+	+	–	–
Siamese	++	+	+	+	+	–	–
Mong Leng	+	+	+	++	++	–	–
Cham	(+)	++	+	+	?	–	–
Malay	++	+	+	+	++	+	+

	Topic prominence	Classifiers	Nominalization & relativization	Pro-drop
Min Chinese	+	+	+	+
Burmese	+	+	+	+
Yongning Na	+	++	?	+
Khumi	+	(+)	+	+
Pwo Karen	+	+	+	+
Khmer	+	(+)	?	+
Mon	+	(+)	?	+
Vietnamese	+	+	?	+
Wa	+	(+)	?	–
Siamese	+	++	+	+
Mong Leng	+	++	?	+
Cham	+	(+)	?	+
Malay	+	++	?	+

	Grammaticalization of verbs[14]	Verb concatenation and/or serialization	Adversative passives	Emotive final particles
Min Chinese	+	+	+	+
Burmese	+	+	–	+
Yongning Na	++	++	?	?
Khumi	–	–	?	?
Pwo Karen	+	++	?	++
Khmer	+	+	+	?
Mon	+	+	+	–
Vietnamese	+	+	+	++

14 To prepositions, auxiliaries, TAM particles, etc.

	Grammatical-ization of verbs[14]	Verb concatenation and/or serialization	Adversative passives	Emotive final particles
Wa	++	+	?	−
Siamese	+	+	+	+
Mong Leng	+	+	+	++
Cham	+	+	?	++
Malay	(+)	+	+	+

	Literary vs. colloquial styles	Politeness distinctions in pronouns	Pronominal use of kinterms	Proliferation of culturally key words[15]
Min Chinese	+	+	+	+
Burmese	+	+	+	+
Yongning Na	−	−	+	+
Khumi	−	−	?	+
Pwo Karen	−	+	+	+
Khmer	+	+	+	?
Mon	+	−	+	+
Vietnamese	(+)	+	+	++
Wa	−	−	+	++
Siamese	+	++	+	+
Mong Leng	−	−	(+)	+
Cham	+	+	+	+
Malay	+	+	+	+

- *Other specially developed/interesting features of the individual languages*

Min Chinese (Chappell)
- complex tone sandhi
- voiced initial stops < older nasals (similar to Lahu)
- strong relationship between relativization and nominalization
- Southern Chinese dialects like Min share many features with Tai, while the Northern ones share features with Altaic

Burmese (Vittrant)
- interesting patterns of reduplication
- dozens of simplex/causative pairs distinguished by aspiration
- rich systems of pragmatic particles and classifiers
- strong Pali component in abstract lexicon and high style

---

15 For verbs like *cut, carry, dry* and nouns like *rice*.

Yongning Na/Mosuo (Lidz)
- strong contact with Bodic (Tibetospheric) languages: conjunct/disjunct system, emphasis on evidentiality, agentive marking/non-systemic ergativity
- speakers shifting to Mandarin
- basic tense distinction is between future and non-future
- three semantic types of possession: alienable, inalienable, and inabsoluble (the latter only for body-parts)

Bangladesh Khumi (Peterson)
- widespread use of tone for morphosyntactic purposes
- robust nominal case morphology
- semantically and syntactically complex sequences of post-verbal elements, divisible into several "zones" for analytic purposes
- reasonable amount of verbal inflection, including participant-coding prefixes

Pwo Karen (Kato)
- striking example of metatypy with respect to the rest of Tibeto-Burman: SVO syntax
- relative clauses may appear either before or after their head (as, e.g. in Lahu)
- elaborate systems of serial verbs, both concatenated and separated
- negation via a final particle rather than a pre-verbal adverb

Khmer (Haiman)
- register system has disappeared; infixation as well as prefixation
- a stronghold of sesquisyllabism; strong relationship between reduction of compounds and the creation of sesquisyllables, an ongoing process
- strong history of contact with Thai, which has led to much grammatical convergence as well as many lexical borrowings in both directions
- much word-play, rich ideophones, expressive onomatopoeia

Mon (Jenny)
- register survives, unlike in Khmer
- "class terms" appear as first elements in compounds for fruits, fish, plants, birds, etc. (as in Thai, Mong Leng, and Cham)
- in psycho-collocations there is a semantic difference according to the relative position of the psycho-noun and its mate (again as in Thai)
- many elaborate expressions, ideophones, euphonic compounds

Vietnamese (Do-Hurinville & Dao)
- huge phonological, lexical, and grammatical influence from Chinese, leading to tonogenesis and monosyllabization
- order of the elements in a classifier phrase is like Chinese: Num + Clf + N
- extensive repertoire of verbs for *cutting* and *carrying*
- rich psycho-collocations, especially with the favorite psycho-noun *lòng* 'entrails'

Wa (Watkins)
- variable word-order: VSO as well as SVO
- dual/plural and inclusive/exclusive distinctions in pronouns, as in many Himalayan TB languages
- tripartite compounds of the form *head-noun + transitive verb + object*, e.g. 'iron' ("machine-press-clothes"); just as in Thai, e.g. **phâa-chét-tua** 'towel' ("cloth-wipe-body")
- pro-drop is relatively rare

Thai (Jenny)
- very rich classifier system, although the younger generation is tending to lose some of the finer distinctions
- elaborate distinctions in pronouns, taking account of relative age, status, gender; the formal register of the language includes special locutions used for monks and royalty
- lexical influence from Pali, mediated by Khmer
- polite final particles, with compulsory gender distinctions for the first person

Mong Leng (Mortensen)
- extremely complex tonal system, involving both pitch and voice quality; many syllable onsets, but no codas (except **-ŋ** by one analysis)
- "class terms" in compounds (as in Thai, Mon, and Cham)
- classifiers play an important role in the syntax
- serial verb constructions are highly developed

Cham (Brunelle and Phu Van Han)
- becoming totally monosyllabized, perhaps because of Vietnamese influence
- long written tradition, but script is now rarely used
- Old Cham prefixes and infixes have been lost, replaced by compounds and other periphrastic structures
- has three implosives, including a palatal one (besides the usual labial and dental ones)

Malay (Nomoto & Hooi Ling Soh)
- no tones or registral differences
- highly developed systems of classifiers and psycho-collocations
- adversative passive (as in Thai, Vietnamese, Mon, Khmer, Mong Leng, Hokkien)
- mostly dissyllabic structure, with no sesquisyllabization

***

The expertise of many specialists has contributed to the excellence of this volume, which is destined to become a *livre de chevet* for everyone interested in the fascinating languages of the mainland Southeast Asian linguistic area.

Table of Contents

James A. Matisoff
Preface —— V

Alice Vittrant and Justin Watkins
Introduction: Languages of the Mainland Southeast Asia linguistic area – Grammatical Sketches —— 1
    1   Areal linguistics —— 1
    2   Establishing the existence of the Mainland Southeast Asian linguistic area —— 3
    3   Structure of the book —— 5
    References —— 8

David A. Peterson
Bangladesh Khumi —— 12
    Introduction —— 12
    1   Phonology —— 13
    2   Morphology —— 19
    3   Grammar and Syntax —— 24
    4   Semantics and pragmatics —— 42
    5   Summary —— 45
    Abbreviations —— 45
    References —— 47
    Appendix 1: Summary of linguistic features —— 48
    Appendix 2: Interlinearized Text —— 50

Alice Vittrant
Burmese —— 56
    Introduction —— 56
    1   Phonology —— 59
    2   Morphology —— 67
    3   Grammar and Syntax —— 81
    4   Semantics and pragmatics —— 109
    5   Summary —— 112
    Abbreviations —— 113
    References —— 114
    Appendix 1: Summary of linguistic features —— 121
    Appendix 2: Text interlinearized —— 123

Atsuhiko Kato
Pwo Karen —— 131
    Introduction —— 131
    1   Phonology —— 133
    2   Morphology —— 135
    3   Grammar and syntax —— 140
    4   Semantics and pragmatics —— 164
    5   Summary —— 167
    Abbreviations —— 168
    References —— 169
    Appendix 1: Summary of linguistic features —— 171
    Appendix 2: Text interlinearized —— 173

Hilary Chappell
Southern Min —— 176
    Introduction —— 176
    1   Phonology —— 181
    2   Morphology —— 187
    3   Grammar and Syntax —— 196
    4   Conclusion and summary —— 219
    Acknowledgements —— 221
    Abbreviations —— 222
    References —— 223
    Appendix 1: Summary of linguistic features —— 227
    Appendix 2: Text interlinearized —— 229

Liberty Lidz
Yongning Na (Mosuo) —— 234
    Introduction —— 234
    1   Phonology —— 236
    2   Morphology —— 238
    3   Grammar and Syntax —— 243
    4   Semantics and pragmatics —— 260
    5   Conclusion —— 264
    Abbreviations —— 265
    References —— 267
    Appendix 1: Summary of linguistic features —— 270
    Appendix 2: Text interlinearized —— 272
    Appendix 3: Map 1 —— 276

Mathias Jenny
Mon —— 277
  Introduction —— 277
  1 Phonology —— 279
  2 Word structure —— 283
  3 Syntactic structure —— 289
  4 Semantics and pragmatics —— 309
  5 Conclusion —— 312
  Abbreviations —— 313
  References —— 313
  Appendix 1: Summary of linguistic features —— 314
  Appendix 2: Text interlinearized —— 316

John Haiman
Khmer —— 320
  Introduction —— 320
  1 Phonology —— 321
  2 Morphology —— 327
  3 Grammar and syntax —— 344
  4 Verbal domain —— 352
  5 Semantics —— 369
  6 Summary and conclusions —— 372
  References —— 373
  Appendix 1: Summary of linguistic features —— 374
  Appendix 2: Text interlinearized —— 376

Danh Thành Do-Hurinville and Huy Linh Dao
Vietnamese —— 384
  Introduction —— 384
  1 Phonology —— 385
  2 Morphology —— 389
  3 Syntax —— 398
  4 Semantics and pragmatics —— 416
  Conclusion —— 420
  Abbreviations —— 421
  References —— 422
  Appendix 1: Summary of linguistic features —— 423
  Appendix 2: Text interlinearized —— 425

Justin Watkins
Wa (Paraok) —— 432
    Introduction —— 432
    1   Phonology —— 434
    2   Morphology —— 439
    3   Grammar and Syntax —— 448
    4   Semantics and pragmatics —— 460
    5   Conclusion/ summary —— 467
    References —— 468
    Appendix 1: Summary of linguistic features —— 469
    Appendix 2: Text interlinearized —— 471

Hiroki Nomoto and Hooi Ling Soh
Malay —— 475
    Introduction —— 475
    1   Phonology —— 476
    2   Morphology —— 480
    3   Grammar and Syntax —— 489
    4   Semantics and pragmatics —— 505
    5   Conclusion/ summary —— 509
    Abbreviations —— 510
    References —— 511
    Appendix 1: Summary of linguistic features —— 516
    Appendix 2: Text interlinearized —— 518

Marc Brunelle and Phú Văn Hẳn
Colloquial Eastern Cham —— 523
    1   Phonology —— 524
    2   Morphology —— 531
    3   Grammar and syntax —— 535
    4   Semantics and pragmatics —— 545
    5   Conclusion —— 548
    Acknowledgements —— 549
    Abbreviations —— 549
    References —— 550
    Appendix 1: Summary of linguistic features —— 552
    Appendix 2: Text interlinearized —— 554

Mathias Jenny
Thai —— 559
    1   Phonology —— 561
    2   Word structure —— 565
    3   Syntactic structure —— 574
    4   Semantics —— 597
    5   Conclusion —— 600
    Abbreviations —— 601
    References —— 602
    Appendix 1: Summary of linguistic features —— 602
    Appendix 2: Text interlinearized —— 604

David Mortensen
Hmong (Mong Leng) —— 609
    1   Phonology —— 610
    2   Morphology —— 613
    3   Grammar and Syntax —— 622
    4   Semantics and Pragmatics —— 639
    5   Conclusion —— 643
    Abbreviations —— 643
    References —— 643
    Appendix 1: Summary of linguistic features —— 645
    Appendix 2: Text interlinearized —— 647

Alice Vittrant and Justin Watkins
Appendix
Guidelines for the description of Mainland Southeast Asian languages —— 653
    1   Phonology —— 653
    2   Morphology —— 660
    3   Grammar and Syntax —— 664
    4   Semantics and pragmatics —— 675
    5   Summary —— 679
    Abbreviations —— 680
    References —— 681

Maps
Map of language families —— 687
Map of fieldwork locations —— 688
Maps of pervasiveness of the shared features —— 689

Language Index —— 711

Alice Vittrant and Justin Watkins
Introduction: Languages of the Mainland Southeast Asia linguistic area – Grammatical Sketches

1 Areal linguistics

Thomason and Kaufman's 1988 book *Language contact, creolization, and genetic linguistics* had a stimulating effect on the fields of comparative and descriptive linguistics and inspired a number of studies on various topics related to language contact: the relationship between typology and language contact; the effect of language contact on a language's genetically inherited characteristics, and work on mixed and endangered languages. More generally speaking, the increased availability of data relating to language contact has enabled wider-ranging discussion on the nature of language contact and its consequences (see Hickey 2010 for a more detailed account of these subjects).

Within this landscape, our book lies at the crossroads of the following themes:

(1) vulnerable and endangered languages, since some of the languages described here are minority languages losing ground under the linguistic influence of dominant neighbouring languages (see chapters on Cham, Wa); (2) areal typology, since our book is concerned with one area in particular: Mainland Southeast Asia (hereafter MSEA); (3) language contact and genetic affiliation, since the various grammatical sketches lay emphasis on characteristics shared by unrelated languages. This in turn raises the question of how such traits are acquired and how they spread, though neither of these two issues is addressed in this volume, at least from a typological perspective.

Specifically, we address here the issue of linguistic area or *Sprachbund*. This issue is closely associated with language contact and has been discussed extensively over the past fifteen years (see Thomason 2000, 2001; Muysken 2000; Stolz 2002; Heine & Kuteva 2005; Campbell 2006; Bisang 2006a; 2006b; 2006c; Matras et al. 2006; Matras & Sakel 2007; Muysken 2008; and Bisang 2010, *inter*

Alice Vittrant: Aix-Marseille Université / CNRS-DDL (UMR 5596)
E-Mail: alice.vittrant@cnrs.fr
Justin Watkins: SOAS, University of London
E-Mail: jw2@soas.ac.uk

alia). Linguistic area, or *Sprachbund* in German, is a concept which was introduced to linguistics in the 1930s by NS Trubetzkoy, in response to the need to account for the linguistic situation observed initially in the Balkans (Sandfeld 1930) and in India (Emeneau 1956; Masica 1976 etc.). In each of these regions both languages with a close genetic relationship and languages from different language families were found. However, despite lacking a common origin, these languages had surprising structural similarities, apparently acquired in part through contact with structural linguistic features that they did not originally possess.

This concept of linguistic area has triggered much debate among linguists interested in language contact. For some authors (e.g. Aikhenvald & Dixon 2001) the difficulty in distinguishing what is inherited through parentage from what is diffused through contact casts doubt on the possibility of establishing genetic parentage in language contact situations, for it may be impossible to determine whether shared traits arise through inheritance, distribution, independent parallel development or by accident.

For other linguists, the concept of linguistic area is viewed in the light of more general work on language change and the constraints on language change associated with language contact (e.g. Gilbers *et al.* 2000; Heine & Kuteva 2005; Aikhenvald & Dixon 2006b; Matras *et al.* 2006; Siemund & Kintana 2008). Studies in recent years concur on the idea that a linguistic area is not a purely linguistic phenomenon, but also brings into play history and culture (Aikhenvald & Dixon 2001: 11–13; Dahl 2001: 1458, Thomason 2001: 104).

> "[Linguistic areas] arise in any of several ways—through social networks established by such interactions as trade and exogamy, through the shift by indigenous peoples in a region to the language(s) of invaders, through repeated instances of movement by small groups to different places within the area." (Thomason 2001: 104)

In other words, the conditions which give rise to language contact (bilingualism, diglossia) are not sufficient in themselves to cause the emergence of a linguistic area. The linguistic communities involved must also share a common culture or a common history—and they are generally aware of this fact. Thus, even if it is not possible to determine when changes in languages occur, it may be possible to identify the factors which favour the emergence of a linguistic area, namely extralinguistic socio-linguistic factors such as culture or social organization, community type, history, politics, geography (for instance 'spread zone' vs. 'residual zone' – cf. Dahl 2001: 1461), population density and diversity, etc.

Finally, there is much published literature on the status of certain geographical areas where languages come to share common properties without being closely related to one another, such as the Balkans (van der Auwera 1998),

Meso-America (Stolz & Stolz 2001), the 'Baltic area' (Koptjevskaja-Tamm 2006), Africa (Heine et Nurse 2008), as well as South Asia (Masica 1994, Ebert 2001).

In recent decades a number of definitions of a linguistic area or Sprachbund have been proposed (see Campbell 2006; Stolz 2006: 33), all of which aim to describe the phenomena of linguistic convergence, common innovations or common retentions, or to identify the specific properties which set a *Sprachbund* apart from other language-contact situations. In general, such accounts invoke the same key concepts, namely (1) a geographical area; (2) the involvement of a number of languages (at least three); (3) shared linguistic characteristics; (4) convergence as a result of contact; (5) convergence not by accident; (6) convergence not as a result of shared heritage (Muysken 2008: 3). However, despite numerous attempts to define the concept precisely, a consensus emerges on the impossibility of identifying universal criteria (Stolz 2002, 2006; Bisang 2006c). Some linguists go so far as to suggest the outright abandonment of the term of *Sprachbund*, referring as it does not to a real object but to a projection by linguists (Stolz, 2002: 260), an *a posteriori* construction "based on the accumulation of residue and borrowed traits, regardless of how and when they came to be shared among the languages involved" (Campbell 2006: 14).

Meanwhile, faced with an unsatisfactory definition which is unlikely to produce a concrete generalization (see Dahl 2001: 1457–8), and because of the impossibility of distinguishing between a situation of linguistic borrowing and one of formation of a linguistic area (Sakel & Matras 2008), other linguists have favoured replacing the notion of linguistic area with less constraining concepts such as 'contact superposition zone' (Koptjevskaja-Tamm & Wälchli 2001) or 'zones of contact-induced structural convergence' (Bisang 2006c).

The problems encountered in seeking to define a linguistic area, however, do not detract from the relevance of studies of changes induced by contact between the languages spoken within a particular geographical area, i.e. areas of linguistic convergence. In the case of Southeast Asia, a region characterized by the presence of five language families and several millennia of contact between the area's linguistic communities, an areal approach is fruitful both for the description of undescribed languages and for typological studies.

2 Establishing the existence of the Mainland Southeast Asian linguistic area

Assessing the extent of our knowledge of the languages of Mainland Southeast Asia, we notice that recent publications on Asian languages are often genetically oriented, with the exception of Goddard (2005), a nice overview of the linguistic situation in Asia with partial information on each language. A number of recent publications do not address the MSEA *Sprachbund*, for instance Thurgood & LaPolla (2003) on Sino-Tibetan languages; Adelaar & Himmelmann (2005) on Austronesian languages; Diller, Edmondson & Luo (2008) on Tai-Kadai languages, and Jenny & Sidwell (2015) on Austroasiatic languages.

The Mainland Southeast Asian *Sprachbund* inhabits a geographical area stretching from the easternmost fringes of India in the west to China in the east, encompassing the peninsular Southeast Asian states of Burma, Thailand, Laos, Cambodia and Vietnam, as well as peninsular Malaysia. Five different language families are present in the area (Austroasiatic/Mon-Khmer, Tai-Kadai, Hmong-Mien, Sino-Tibetan and Austronesian). It is only relatively recently that this area has been described as a linguistic area or *Sprachbund* (Matisoff 1991, Bisang 1996, etc.), even though now the idea is firmly attested (and uncontroversial) since Enfield 2005.[1] Thus, new general publications on linguistic areas do cite the (M)SEA area as one of the recognized *Sprachbünde* (see for instance Heine & Kuteva 2005: 203), although it was not mentioned in previous works (see Campbell 1994, Feuillet 2001).

In the final analysis, we can say of a linguistic area that "in the absence of a universally valid numerical value of shared isoglosses, language contact situations lend themselves to a classification as a *Sprachbund* if the absolute number of shared isoglosses with no genetic basis among the members of the *Sprachbund* significantly exceeds the number of such isoglosses they have in common with languages outside the *Sprachbund*" (Stolz 2006: 36).

We have adopted an empirical and – we hope – more promising approach towards the study of the MSEA linguistic area. Previous studies such as Matisoff (1986), Migliazza (1996) and Enfield (2005) draw together features that cut across the genealogical phyla in many domains. These works cast light on phenomena or structural properties that cluster around this geographical area, offering an explanation for the distributional asymmetry that cannot be accounted for in terms of linguistic genealogy.

By adopting an approach that is similar to an isogloss approach rather than a geographical, historico-cultural or communicative approach (Stolz 2006: 36), we aim to determine the maximal distribution of single features. To put it in other words, one task of this book is to provide new information about the limits

---

[1] Enfield (2001, 2005) provides a very well-documented argumentation even though he is not alone in having pointed out the strange similarities between unrelated languages in the area. See also Henderson (1965), Matisoff (1986: 75–80), Matisoff (1991), Bisang (1996), Migliazza (1996).

of the contact-induced convergence area (see for instance the chapters on Yongning Na (Mosuo), Khumi or Southern Min) in Southeast Asia, examining the geolinguistic distribution of the given features (or zone of overlap of several such features) that shape the linguistic area.

3 Structure of the book

The structure of this book is intended to be in line with existing typological studies of specific grammatical phenomena such as Kahrel and van den Berg's (1994) work on negation, or cross-linguistic studies such as Aikhenvald & Dixon (2003, 2006), Zúñiga & Kittilä (2010), and Kopecka & Narasimhan (2012) *inter al.* Each of these publications is a collection of chapters which adopt a common format, structure and/or theoretical approach.

The present volume on languages of MSEA has been conceived in a similar way, to allow researchers to do cross-comparisons and to facilitate such comparisons by ensuring that all the chapters have a broadly similar organization and structure and use similar terminology. Our aim in adopting this common approach is to allow specific linguistic phenomena to be studied across a range of languages.

Each contributor was asked to compile a grammatical sketch of a MSEA language following the same guidelines, to allow the reader to navigate easily between and across chapters and languages. A copy of the guidelines which each author was asked to follow is included as an appendix at the back of the book.

Thus, the typological descriptions of the languages are intended to have a common structure to facilitate comparison and to highlight, on the one hand, the unique typological features of the language and, on the other, the features shared with other languages in the area.

Beginning with general information about the language — its affiliation, its geographical location, relevant ethno-linguistic information—the chapters then provide information on (I) phonology, (II) morphology, (III) grammar and syntax, (IV) semantics and pragmatics. Each section examines in turn the features known to be shared by the languages of the *Sprachbund*. Thus, in the section on Phonology, the stereotypical phonological features observed in languages of the area are as follows: complex vowel systems (diphthongs, a large number of vowels, contrastive vowel length), tone or register systems (or a combination of both), a restricted set of final consonants; a restriction on consonant clusters (see Enfield 2005: 186ff). Each contributor was asked to address the question: "To what extent does the language conform to this stereotype (or not)?" by providing a description of the phonological system and syllable structure, keeping in mind (as a secondary guideline) the correlation between the two as highlighted by Henderson (1965).

In the second section of each chapter, which is on Morphology, the contributors were asked to examine the morphological structure of words, the generally observed tendency toward monosyllabicity, the presence of sesquisyllables, the lack of extensive inflectional morphology, and the use of compounding (rather than derivation). Expressives (psycho-collocation, elaborate expressions) and reduplication are also phenomena examined as shared features across the MSEA area.

The third section, on Grammar and Syntax, is divided into three parts devoted, respectively, to (1) the nominal domain, (2) the verbal domain and (3) the clausal domain. Besides the basic structure of the NP, we also asked for a close investigation of classifier systems (see Grinevald 1999, 2000). Next, MSEA languages being famous for their lack of inflection, the description of the verbal domain relies on notional categories expressed in the verbal phrase, grammaticalization (see Matisoff 1991), and serial verb constructions (see Bisang 1991, Bisang 1996, Durie 1997, Aikhenvald & Dixon 2006, Vittrant 2006). In terms of sentence organization, the basic word order is (S)VO for MSEA languages, except for Tibeto-Burman languages in the area. All languages in the area show a characteristic information structure, being 'topic-prominent' rather than 'subject-prominent'. All languages in the area are also known for widespread ellipsis of definite arguments, regardless of grammatical role. These phenomena are investigated in each language.

Marybeth Clark (1985) also noticed that many MSEA languages share a similar device for asking questions that request an affirmative or negative response rather than other information, that is to say for wh-questions or yes-no-questions. Matisoff (1986: 78) noticed that MSEA languages have a penchant for nominalizing whole sentences without embedding them into any larger unit, typically via a particle, which is also used in citation-form verbs, and which has a relativizing/genitive function in other constructions. These two phenomena are examined by some contributors to the present volume (Chappell, Lidz, Peterson).

Regarding the last section on Semantics and Pragmatics (IV), MSEA languages seem to share basically similar conceptual frameworks about humans and nature (Matisoff 1986: 79). Thus the comparative semantics domain needs to be investigated. As for pragmatics, MSEA languages have systems of sentence-final particles as a basic mode of distinguishing illocutionary force (such as requesting, questioning, persuading, advising, reminding, instructing, etc.), but also for expressing 'propositional attitudes', that is to say emotions of the speaker (such as surprise, doubt, impatience, reluctance, hesitation, etc.). Lastly, some languages may have developed systems for encoding politeness (i.e. formality vs. intimacy with an interlocutor) and honorific systems (to express respect or reverence towards the referent). All these phenomena are explored in each of the thirteen languages described.

Each grammatical sketch ends with two appendices: a glossed text, and a table summarizing the features examined in the chapter. This glossed text offers a glimpse of the language used in more natural context and a demonstration of the broader expertise of the linguists who compiled them. A series of maps at the end of the book show the geographical distribution (in terms of the location of the language described in this book) of a number of the more linguistic features explored in the tables.

In conclusion, thirteen languages of MSEA are described in this collection. As with any linguistic survey, some explanation of why we chose that number and that particular selection of languages is required.

The languages in our sample were selected for a number of reasons. In part, languages such as Khmer, Wa, Vietnamese, Thai and Hmong are representative of the Mainland Southeast Asian peninsula, which is known to be the geographical core of this linguistic area, from which certain features diffused outwards. In contrast, languages such as Burmese, Khumi, Mosuo and Min are spoken on the periphery of the same area.

Any examination of the traits shared by the languages of Southeast Asia must also include some examples of languages which are representative of other contrasting phenomena, such as:

(a) size of speaker population – i.e. major or national languages (Malay) vs. minor or marginal languages (Cham);
(b) dominant lowland languages (Vietnamese or Khmer) vs. languages of highland minorities (Wa);
(c) languages with a long-established literary tradition (Burmese) vs. languages with a predominantly oral tradition or which are unwritten or seldom written (Mosuo).

These are also factors which have determined the choice of languages in this collection.

Finally, we would have preferred to be able to include, for each language family, at least one major and one minor language, which has unfortunately not been possible for two of the language families, namely Tai-Kadai or Hmong-Mien (a family whose very size makes an objectively major language difficult to identify).

The chapters are organized according to language family: five Sino-Tibetan languages; four Mon-Khmer (Austroasiatic) languages; two Austronesian and one each of Tai-Kadai and Hmong-Mien.

We might reasonably be accused of arbitrariness in our selection of languages; in fact our choice was intended to be neither comprehensive nor systematically representative of the area. Rather, we wanted to give an impression of the colours and flavour of the region, based on linguistic commonalities and differences. Given that MSEA is a recognized linguistic area (or, a zone of contact-induced structural convergence) in the literature on language contact and Asian languages more generally, our goal was not to prove its existence. Rather, it was an attempt to further explore the boundaries of the area and the path of diffusion of shared linguistic features.

At the same time, the diversity represented in our selection of languages entails a concomitant variability in the depth of the descriptions in the chapters of this book: for certain languages, the authors have the benefit of a wealth of previous linguistic investigations, while for others the authors are amongst the first linguists to describe the language in question. In all cases, however, the authors are actively involved in research on the languages they have described and the data is not taken from secondary literature.

On that note, we are very grateful to the consultants who have collaborated with the authors of each chapter. Without such collaboration or the readiness of linguists to engage in fieldwork on this kind, a book such as this would not have been possible. Lastly, we hope to inspire further work on the many languages of Southeast Asia which have yet to be described.

References

Adelaar, K. Alexander & Nikolaus Himmelmann. 2005. *The Austronesian languages of Asia and Madagascar*. London: Routledge.
Aikhenvald, Alexandra Y. & Dixon R. M. W. (eds.). 2001. *Areal diffusion and genetic inheritance: Problems in comparative linguistics*, Oxford: Oxford University Press.
Aikhenvald, Alexandra Y. & Dixon R. M. W. (eds.). 2003. *Studies in evidentiality*. Amsterdam/Philadelphia: Johns Benjamins.
Aikhenvald, Alexandra Y. & Dixon R. M. W. (eds.). 2006. *Grammars in contact: A cross-linguistic typology*. New York: Oxford University Press.
Aikhenvald, Alexandra Y. & Dixon R. M. W. (eds.). 2006. *Serial verb constructions: A cross-linguistic typology*. New York: Oxford University Press.
Bisang, Walter. 1991. Verb serialization, grammaticalization and attractor posi-tions in Chinese, Hmong, Vietnamese, Thai and Khmer. In Hansjakob Seiler & Waldfried Premper (eds.), *Partizipation*, 509–562. Tübingen: Gunter Narr.
Bisang, Walter. 1996. Areal typology and grammaticalization: Processes of grammaticalization based on nouns and verbs in East and mainland South East Asian languages. *Studies in Language* 20 (3). 517–597.
Bisang, Walter. 2006a. Contact-induced convergence: Typology and areality. In Keith Brown (ed.), *Encyclopedia of language and linguistics*, vol. 3, 88–101. Oxford: Elsevier.
Bisang, Walter. 2006b. South East Asia as a Linguistic Area. In Keith Brown (ed.), *Encyclopaedia of language and linguistics*, vol. 11, 587–595. Oxford: Elsevier.

Bisang, Walter. 2006c. Linguistic areas, language contact and typology: Some implications from the case of Ethiopia as a linguistic area. In Yaron Matras, April McMahon & Nigel Vincent (eds.), *Linguistic areas. Convergence in historical and typological perspective*, 75–98. Hampshire: Palgrave Mac Millan.

Bisang, Walter. 2010. Areal language typology. In P. Auer & J. E. Schmidt (eds.), *Language and space. An international handbook of linguistic variation – Vol. 1: Theories and methods*, 419–440. [Handbücher zur Sprach- und Kommunikationswissenschaft]. Berlin & New York: Mouton de Gruyter.

Campbell, Lyle. 1994. Grammar: Typological and areal issues. In R. E. Asher & J. M. Y. Simpson (eds.), *Encyclopedia of language and linguistics*, vol. 3, 1471–1474. London: Pergamon Press.

Campbell, Lyle. 2006. Areal linguistics: A closer scrutiny. In Yaron Matras, April M. S. McMahon & Nigel Vincent (eds.), *Linguistic areas: Convergence in historical and typological perspective*. New York: Palgrave Macmillan.

Clark, Marybeth. 1985. Asking questions in Hmong and other southeast Asian languages. Linguistics of the Tibeto-Burman area 8 (2). 60–67.

Dahl, Östen. 2001. Principles of Areal Typology. In M. Haspelmath, E. König, W. Österreicher & W. Raible (eds.), *Language typology and language universals*, vol. 2, 1456–1470. Berlin & New York: Mouton de Gruyter.

Diller, Anthony, Jerold A. Edmondson & Yongxian Luo (eds.). 2008. *The Tai-Kadai languages*. London & New York: Routledge.

Durie, Mark. 1997. Grammatical structures in verb serialization. In Alex Alsina, Joan Bresnan & Peter Sells (eds.), *Complex predicates*, 289–354. Stanford: CSLI Publications.

Ebert, Karen. 2001. Südasien als Sprachbund. In M. Haspelmath, E. König, W. Österreicher & W. Reible (eds.), *Language typology and language universals*, vol. 2, 1529–1539. Berlin & New York: Mouton de Gruyter.

Emeneau, Murray B. 1956. India as a linguistic area. *Language* 32. 3–16.

Enfield, Nick J. 2001. On genetic and areal linguistics in Mainland South-East Asian: Parallel polyfunctionality of 'acquire'. In Alexandra Y. Aikhenvald & R. M. W. Dixon (eds.), *Areal diffusion and genetic inheritance: Problems in comparative linguistics*, 255–290. Oxford: Oxford University Press.

Enfield, Nick J. 2003. *Linguistic Epidemiology: Semantics and Grammar of Language Contact in Mainland southeast Asia*, London: Routledge.

Enfield, Nick J. 2005. Areal linguistics and Mainland Southeast Asia, *Annual Review Anthropology* 34. 181–206.

Feuillet, Jacques. 2001. *Introduction à la typologie linguistique*. Paris: Honoré Champion.

Gilbers, Dicky G., J. Nerbonne & J. Shaeken (eds.). 2000. *Languages in contact*. Amsterdam & Atlanta: GA, Rodopi.

Goddard, Cliff. 2005. *The languages of East and Southeast Asia: An introduction*. Oxford & New York: Oxford University Press.

Grinevald, Colette. 1999. Typologie des systèmes de classification nominale. *Faits de Langue* 14, *La catégorisation dans les langues*. 101–122.

Grinevald, Colette. 2000. A morphosyntactic typology of classifiers. In G. Senft (ed.), *Nominal classification*, 50–92. Cambridge: Cambridge University Press.

Heine, Bernd & Tania Kuteva. 2005. *Language contact and grammatical change*. Cambridge: Cambridge University Press.

Heine, Bernd & Derek Nurse (eds.). 2008. *A linguistic geography of Africa*. Cambridge: Cambridge University Press.

Henderson, Eugénie J. A. 1965. The topography of certain phonetic and morphological characteristics of South East Asian language. *Lingua* 15. 400–434.

Hickey, Raymond (ed.). 2019. *Handbook of Language Contact*. Malden, MA: Blackwell Publishing.

Jenny, Mathias & Paul Sidwell. 2015. *The handbook of Austroasiatic languages* (2vols). Leiden: Brill.

Kahrel, Peter & René van den Berg (eds.). 1994. *Typological studies in negation*. Amsterdam: John Benjamins.

Kopecka, Anetta & Bhuvana Narasimhan. 2012. *Events of putting and taking. A crosslinguistic perspective*. Amsterdam: John Benjamins.

Koptjevskaja-Tamm, Maria. 2006. The circle that won't come full: Two potential isoglosses in the Circum-Baltic Area. In Matras Yaron, April McMahon & Nigel Vincent (eds.). *Linguistic areas: convergence in historical and typological perspective*. Hampshire: Palgrave.

Koptjevskaja-Tamm, Maria & Bernhard Wälchli. 2001. The Circum-Baltic languages: an areal-typological approach. In Östen Dahl & Maria Koptjevskaja-Tamm (eds.), *The Circum-Baltic languages: Typology and contact*, vol. 2: Grammar and typology, 615–750. Amsterdam: John Benjamins.

Masica, Colin P. 1976. *Defining a linguistic area: South Asia*. Chicago: University of Chicago Press.

Masica, Colin P. 1994. Some new perspectives on South Asia as a linguistic area. In A. Davison & F. M. Smith (eds.), *Papers from the 15th South Asian Language Analysis Roundtable 1993*, 187–200. Iowa City: University of Iowa.

Matisoff, James A. 1986. Linguistic diversity and language contact. In John McKinnon & Wanat Bhruksasri (eds.), *Highlanders of Thailand*. Singapore: Oxford University Press. 56–86.

Matisoff, James A. 1991. Areal and universal dimensions of grammatization in Lahu. In Elizabeth Closs Traugott & Bernd Heine (eds.), *Approaches to Grammaticalization: Focus on Theorical and Methodological Issues*. London: John Benjamins, vol. 2, 383–453.

Matisoff, James A. 2001. Genetic versus contact relationship: Prosodic diffusibility in South-East Asian languages. In Alexandra Y. Aikhenvald & R. M. W. Dixon (eds.), *Areal diffusion and genetic inheritance: Problems in comparative linguistics*, 291–327. Oxford: Oxford University Press.

Matras, Yaron & April McMahon & Nigel Vincent. 2006. *Linguistic Areas: convergence in Historical and Typological Perspective*, Hampshire: Palgrave.

Matras, Yaron & Jeanette Sakel (eds.). 2007. *Grammatical borrowing in cross-linguistic perspective*. Berlin & New York: Mouton de Gruyter.

Migliazza, Brian. 1996. Mainland Southeast Asia: A unique linguistic area. *Notes on Linguistics* 75. 17–25.

Muysken, Pieter. 2000. From linguistic areas to areal linguistics: a research proposal. In D. G. Gilbers, J. Nerbonne & J. Shaeken (eds.), *Languages in contact*, 263–275. Amsterdam & Atlanta: GA, Rodopi.

Muysken, Pieter (ed.). 2008. *From linguistic areas to areal linguistics*. Amsterdam: John Benjamins.

Norde, Muriel, Bob de Jonge & Cornelius Hasselblatt (eds.). 2010. *Language contact – New perspectives*. Amsterdam: John Benjamins.

Sandfeld, Kristian. 1930. *Linguistique balkanique: problèmes et résultats*. Paris: Librairie C. Klincksieck.
Sakel, Jeanette & Matras Yaron. 2008. Modelling contact-induced change in grammar. In Stolz Thomas, Bakker Dik & Palomo Roasa Salas (eds.), *Aspects of language contact – New theoretical, methodological and empirical findings with special focus on Romancisation processes*, 63–87. Berlin & New York: Mouton de Gruyter.
Siemund, Peter & Kintana Noemi. 2008. *Language contact and contact languages*. Amsterdam: John Benjamins.
Stolz, Christel & Thomas Stolz. 2001. Mesoamerica as a linguistic area. In M. Haspelmath, E. König, W. Österreicher & W. Reible (eds.), *Language typology and language universals*, vol. 2, 1–77. Berlin & New York: Mouton de Gruyter.
Stolz, Thomas. 2002. No *Sprachbund* beyond this line! On the age-old discussion of how to define a linguistic area. In P. Ramat & T. Stolz (eds.), *Mediterranean languages. Papers from the MEDTYP workshop*, 259–81. Tirrenia, June 2000. Bochum: Brockmeyer.
Stolz, Thomas. 2006. All or nothing. In Yaron Matras, April McMahon & Nigel Vincent (eds.), *Linguistic areas: Convergence in historical and typological perspective*, 32–50. Hampshire: Palgrave.
Thomason, Sarah G. 2000. Linguistic areas and language history. In Dicky Gilbers, John Nerbonne & Jos Shaeken (eds.), *Languages in Contact*, 311–327. Amsterdam & Atlanta: GA, Rodopi.
Thomason, Sarah G. 2001. *Language contact: An introduction*, Edimbourg: Edinburgh University Press.
Thurgood, Graham & Randy J. Lapolla (eds.). 2003. *The Sino-Tibetan Languages*. London: Routledge.
van der Auwera, Johan. 1998. Revisiting the Balkan and Meso-American linguistic areas. *Language Sciences* 20. 259–70.
Vittrant Alice. 2006. Les constructions des verbes en série. Une autre approche du syntagme verbal en birman. *Bulletin de la Société de Linguistique de Paris* 101 (1). 305–367.
Vittrant Alice. 2010. Aire linguistique Asie du Sud-Est continentale: le birman en fait-il partie ? *Moussons* 16. 7–38.
Zúñiga, Fernando & Seppo Kittilä. 2010. Benefactives and Malefactives. Typological perspectives and case studies. Amsterdam: John Benjamins.

David A. Peterson
Bangladesh Khumi*

Introduction

Bangladesh Khumi is a member of the Kuki-Chin branch of Tibeto-Burman spoken by around 2,000 people in the Chittagong Hill Tracts of Bangladesh. There are two mutually intelligible dialects of the language in Bangladesh, and there are closely related Khumi varieties with several tens of thousands of speakers in adjacent parts of Burma. This description is based on the northern dialect of Bangladesh Khumi, centered around Ruma Bazaar in the Bandarban Hill Tracts. The observations here are based primarily on an extensive text corpus with material representing a wide variety of discourse genres. Numbers following examples indicate location in the text corpus; examples without such indications are marked as elicited.

Members of this ethnolinguistic group are highly multilingual, many of them commanding near fluency in Marma, a local variety of Arakanese. They also show variable, but often advanced proficiency in Bawm, Mru, and Tripura. Of these, Marma is far and away the most significant from a linguistic standpoint, with a profound impact on lexicon and syntactic constructions, and probably ultimately on syllable structure and possibly even the tonal system and vowel allophony of the language; other languages the Khumi speak are not as influential.

The Khumi in Bangladesh, according to their oral record, migrated in a number of waves west from a more easterly point starting several generations ago. There is still a moderate degree of fluctuation in their location, with families drifting back and forth from one side of the border to the other as living conditions change.

---

* My research on Khumi has been sponsored by the Fulbright Foundation, The Max Planck Institute for Evolutionary Anthropology, and National Science Foundation grant BCS-0349021 Many thanks are due to Lelung Khumi and other members of the Khumi community in Bangladesh who have made this research possible. The contents and format of this paper have benefited greatly from comments provided by the editors and an anonymous reviewer.

David A. Peterson: Program in Linguistics, HB 6220, 307 Reed Hall, Dartmouth College, Hanover, NH 03755 U.S.A., E-Mail: david.a.peterson@dartmouth.edu

https://doi.org/10.1515/9783110401981-002

In terms of its position within Kuki-Chin, Khumi is usually regarded as belonging to a southern division of the family (Grierson 1904, So-Hartmann 1988, VanBik 2009). It is unclear that this subgrouping is warranted, however, and the language may instead represent an early branching from Proto-Kuki-Chin, as implied by Bradley's 1997 classification. Peterson 2017 alternatively suggests that Khumi belongs to a grouping, Khomic, or Southwestern, which together with the Southeastern and Northeastern groups forms a Peripheral Kuki-Chin branch. Khumi is nevertheless clearly a Kuki-Chin language, sharing, besides abundant lexical and grammatical cognates, diagnostic features like the change of Proto-Tibeto-Burman *s- to t^h-, the innovative 1s pronoun root *kaj, and probably even the system of verbal ablaut found elsewhere in the subgroup, although it has a distinct manifestation in Khumi. Otherwise, Khumi is not a prototypical Kuki-Chin language, especially given its relatively impoverished system of participant coding, its distinct nominal case morphology, and in unique paths of development for various verbal categories.

1 Phonology

As a Mainland Southeast Asian language, the phonological system of Khumi has a number of prototypical areal features: tonal contrasts (which involve quantity and phonation cues); a reasonably large number of vowel contrasts, including diphthongs; a usual array of consonantal contrasts; and typical restrictions on syllable structure.

1.1 Suprasegmental phonology: tone and register

Khumi exhibits standard sorts of suprasegmental distinctions for a tonal Southeast Asian language. There are five tones, which on monosyllables in isolation are phonetically realized as in (1), the only known minimal quintuplet:

(1) underlying tones:
  1   low falling $së^1$ 'scales'
  2   low checked $së^2$ 'kilogram'
  3   high checked $së^3$ 'pound rice for a second time'
  4   rising (with fall at end) $së^4$ 'begin, rise (of the sun)'
  5   high falling $së^5$ 'sound of seeds being scattered'

Tones 4 and 5 are clearly contour tones. Any of the five tones may occur with all syllable types, excluding the half-syllable associated with sesquisyllabic elements.

Two other things about the phonetics of these tones bear mentioning. First, syllables with checked tones are about half as long as those with the other three tones, so duration is an important aspect of tone in this language.[1] Also, the two checked tones are usually accompanied by glottalization towards the end of their syllables, meaning that phonation is also a significant tonal cue, alongside pitch and duration. Khumi might thus be viewed as exhibiting register phenomena to a certain extent, although the primary and most consistent tonal cue is pitch.

There is a further marginal tone, extremely high and long, which might qualify as a sixth lexical tone, but it also appears possible to describe it simply as an intonational phenomenon associated with intensification. See the discussion of demonstratives below (section 3.1.1) for a concrete example.[2]

Going beyond the basic tonal analysis, specific manifestations of the underlying tones and their interaction with each other yields a fairly convoluted system, but one which would appear to be typical for Kuki-Chin languages. (See, for instance, Hyman and VanBik 2004 and Watkins 2013 for some recent treatments of tonal interactions in other languages.) The instantiation of lexical tones in Khumi depends heavily on the morphosyntactic environment of nominal and verbal roots; furthermore, the tonal instantiation itself often is the sole indicator of particular high-frequency grammatical categories, to the exclusion of segmental material which might otherwise be involved in signaling those categories. For a fairly straightforward example, see (38), where the speaker marks 'locative' tonally on the first word rather than using the (also acceptable) segmental locative marker, $=a^l$. The second word in that example hypothetically has a tonal instantiation of 'negative', except that this predicate never occurs in the affirmative anyway.

Henderson 1965 discusses similar morphological uses of tone in other Southeast Asian languages (and see also Coupe 2007: 64–5 on the alternative tonal instantiation for Mongsen Ao's agentive case marker), but to my knowledge no other language of the area is reported to exhibit as widespread a use of

---

[1] An alternative analysis might therefore be to posit a vowel length distinction, and reduce the number of underlying tones to three (high falling, rising, low, but this would raise problems for the description of tonal variants, discussed in what follows.
[2] Solnit describes a highly comparable phenomenon in Kayah Li (1997: 27–28), suggesting this may have a wide areal spread. Several of Khumi's immediate neighbors also appear to exhibit it.

tone for marking morphosyntactic information as Khumi does. It seems likely that careful analysis of other Kuki-Chin languages will reveal comparable intricacies, however.

The phonetic characteristics of the tone variants for the basic tones 1–5 are summarized first, with phonetic descriptions, in (2). (2) also summarizes the morphosyntactic contexts where these variants appear for given nouns and verbs with particular underlying tones. There may be as yet undetected grammatical contexts which induce tonal variants, but these are the ones which have been identified so far.

(2) contextual variants of underlying tones:

tonal variant:	phonetic description:	morphosyntactic contexts:
6	checked low, but distinct from tone 2	genitive for nouns with underlying tones 1 and 2; negative for verbs with underlying tones 1 and 2
7	high checked, but higher than tone 3	genitive for nouns with underlying tone 3
8	high checked, but with less glottalization than other checked tones	imperative for verbs with underlying tones 3 and 4
9	rapidly rising (without a fall)	genitive for nouns with underlying tone 4
10	gradually rising (without a fall)	locative for nouns with underlying tones 1 and 4; irrealis for verbs with underlying tones 1 and 4
11	high level	locative for nouns with underlying tones 2, 3, and 5; irrealis for verbs with underlying tones 2 and 3
12	extremely high checked	genitive for nouns with underlying tone 5; negative for verbs with underlying tones 3 and 4

A conceptualization of the system focussing more specifically on underlying tones and their variants in particular morphosyntactic contexts is given in (3).

(3) underlying tones and their variants:

underlying	genitive	locative	V citation	negative	irrealis	imperative
1	6	10	1	6	10	2
2	6	11	3	6	11	2
3	7	11	3	12	11	8
4	9	10	4	12	10	8
5	12	11	n/a	n/a	n/a	n/a

As can be seen more clearly by the representation in (3), there are usually neutralizations for different underlying tones in the specific morphological categories. In fact, were it not for different behaviors of underlying tones 2 and 3 in the negative and imperative forms, the distinction between the high and low checked tones in verbs would be undetectable, as it is neutralized in verb citation forms (both are instantiated as tone 3). The lack of variants of tone 5 for negative, irrealis, and imperative, and the lack of a V citation form for that tone arises from the fact that no tone 5 words are verbs, and so never exhibit these verbal categories.

The tonal system exhibits further complexities when nouns are marked with other case and discourse clitics, or if verbal complexes have one or more postverbal element besides the negative and irrealis markers. Examples in the paper indicate essentially surface-level tones, which frequently deviate from underlying ones (and also from the non-lexical tones given in the chart above) due to the operation of a few tone rules which I will not attempt to illustrate in detail here.

To take one relatively simple example, though, in sentence (10) of the accompanying text, the nominalizer =$nö^3$ surfaces with tone 2 rather than tone 3 in the sequence niw^1-$thay^{11}$-$nö^2$ because it is preceded by the 'potential' element -$thay^3$, and a sequence of 3-3 undergoes a change to 3-2. A further complication in this form is the realization of tone 3 on -$thay^3$ as tone 11 due to its occurrence in non-final position (see the immediately following discussion).

The examples in this paper do not represent a surface-level process of peak-delay, whereby syllables with tones 1 (low falling) and 2 (low checked) preceded by a rising tone syllable (tone 10, which may result from underlying tone 4) are realized as tones 5 (high falling) and 3 (high checked), respectively. This peak delay is detectable instrumentally; speakers appear to hear such sequences in terms of their underlying tones, however. In non-final contexts, tone 1 surfaces as a relatively low unchecked tone without the normal fall that tone 1 has in final contexts. Tone 11 is similarly used for high-level tones in non-final contexts, which may be due to underlying tone 3 or tone 5; slight differences have been noted for these in some cases, which may suggest a further distinction needs to be made, ultimately, but I keep things as simple as possible here.

1.2 Segmental phonemes: consonants and vowels

Khumi's consonant inventory, seen in (4), is typical for Southeast Asia, although it differs from that of languages in the immediate vicinity in certain respects.[3] It has standard sorts of voicing and aspiration distinctions in its system of stops, but unlike many area languages (in particular, Marma), there is no voiced/voiceless distinction for sonorants. *k* and *kʰ* have a fairly uvular realization in contexts preceding low back vowels. *ʃ* is in free variation with *s*, a pattern also seen in a number of neighboring languages. *dʒ* and *j* are also in relatively free variation, except where *j* forms part of a consonant cluster.

(4) consonant inventory:

	bilabial	labio-dental	alveolar	palato-alveolar	velar	glottal
stops						
unaspirated	p		t		k	ʔ <'>
aspirated	pʰ <ph>		tʰ <th>		kʰ <kh>	
voiced	b		d			
nasals	m		n		ŋ <ng>	
fricatives	(f)	v		s~ʃ <s>		h
affricates			tɬ <tl>	tʃ <c>		
			tʰɬ <thl>	dʒ <j>		
approximants			r, l	j <y>		

In addition to the above consonants, original Proto-Kuki-Chin *u* has led to some interesting developments. In many instances this vowel has diphthongized to *iw* (e.g., PKC *bu?* > Khumi *biw²*). In most cases where the vowel has remained *u*, however, it has led to labialization of the immediately preceding consonant, and this labialization has further evolved into frication approximating *v* or *f*, depending on the voicing and other laryngeal characteristics of the associated consonant; this frication carries over into the vowel, yielding something quite distinct from a simple affricate. Even with only about two dozen instances *without* this frication, there are a handful of minimal pairs which show the distinction to have been phonemicized (e.g., *hu⁵* 'there' vs. *hfu⁵*

---

[3] Orthographic conventions used here for representing sounds where the relationship may not be clear are given in angled brackets following the sounds. Otherwise, these charts represent distinct phonemes with the symbol corresponding to their main phonetic variant.

'bamboo'), but exactly what phonemes should be recognized is problematic. Since this appears to be more a feature of the vowel at this point, one analysis would be to posit a separate vowel, resulting in two *u*-like vowels. A disadvantage of this is that there is a remarkably small number of words having a straightforward *u* phoneme, without the accompanying frication, but an overwhelming number exhibiting the variant with it. On the other hand, treating it as a feature of the consonant would nearly double the consonant inventory, with a skewed distribution resulting from the source of frication. Perhaps the best solution would be to treat these cases as *Cv* or *Cf* consonant clusters, reflecting their origin in labialization/affrication. However, in designing a practical orthography for Khumi, it is clearly more advantageous to treat this frication as automatic, and somehow signal its absence in the relatively small number of exceptions; for purposes of this paper, I will simply ignore the difference, as there are only a few instances where the frication is absent.[4]

There are also several interesting things to note about nasals in Khumi. First, one salient consonant sound not represented in the inventory above is a doubly-articulated bilabial-velar nasal. This occasionally occurs as a variant of a syllable final velar nasal reflecting an etymological bilabial nasal, e.g., the word 'house', *üng¹*, where *ng* reflects *-m*, sometimes occurs with this variant bilabial-velar nasal double articulation. Next, for unclear reasons, there are certain roots which optionally have nasals in one or more of their codas (cf. *biw¹tlëng⁵~blw¹tlë⁵* 'rice package', with an optional final nasal, and *ay¹tlëng¹* 'men's carry-basket', where the final nasal is obligatory.) Finally, Khumi has a number of forms which show an alternation between a final syllable *mu* or a syllabic bilabial nasal, e.g., the variants *mu³~m̩³* 'blow'.

The Khumi vowel inventory is given in (5).

(5) vowel inventory:

	front	central	back
high	i		u
high-mid	ẹ <ë>	ə <ö>	ɤ<ü>, o
low-mid	e		ɔ <å>
low	æ <ä>		a

diphthongs: iw, ew, əj <öy>, uj <uy>, aj <ay>, ɔj <åy>

Noteworthy in this chart is the richness of vowel and diphthong contrasts, including two non-front unrounded vowel qualities (approximating ə and ɤ). The

---

4 The word *Khumi*, in fact, also exhibits this frication: *khfu¹¹mi¹*.

only remarkable vowel allophony is found before syllable-final nasals; in this context non-low vowels (and diphthongs) tend to exhibit more lowered and lax phonetic realizations (e.g., *e* tends to be realized as *ɛ* or even *æ* and *u* tends to be realized as *ʊ*). Coda nasals do impart a certain amount of nasalization to preceding vowels, although the degree of nasalization varies according to speaker and word, and since there are clearly audible nasals for most speakers, it does not appear that the proper analysis of nasalization is as a property of vowels rather than syllable-final nasals.

1.3 Syllable structure

The Khumi syllable canon can be characterized as in (6):

(6) (C(v))C(C)V(N)+tone

Syllables have an underlying tone. The only possible final consonant (with the exceptions discussed earlier) is *ng*. The first (optional) *C(v)* portion of the schema in (6) represents the half-syllable found in sesquisyllabic forms. Orthographically, these half-syllables are indicated by an apostrophe between the half-syllable consonant and the following full syllable; no vowel is written in the half syllable: *p'liwng⁴* [pə¹liwŋ⁴] 'heart'. Rarely, these half syllables combine with a main syllable that has an initial consonant cluster. Initial consonant clusters themselves are also relatively rare and tightly constrained in terms of their composition: the first element must be a stop and the second must be *l*, *r*, or *j* (although not all combinations are attested in the available data.) By contrast, the consonants of the minor and major syllables of a sesquisyllable are largely unconstrained, though there is a clear tendency for them to have distinct places of articulation.

2 Morphology

The domain of morphology in Khumi and many other area languages is vexed by lack of coincidence between grammatical and phonological words (Dixon and Aikhenvald 2002, Hall et al. 2008). While the vast majority of morphemes in Khumi are monosyllabic, sesquisyllabic, or disyllabic, and could serve as independent phonological words, assuming a phrase-level analysis of tonal sandhi phenomena, many of them nevertheless are morphosyntactically bound, and so take on a highly structured, position class-like status; this is especially the case for post-verbal elements, as will be discussed further with the exposition of specific verbal categories below. While it would be possible to describe these as particles, it seems preferable, insofar as possible, to analyze them as morphosyntactic affixes or clitics, which may or may not constitute independent words from a phonological perspective, resorting to a separate category of particle only when absolutely required.

2.1 Word structure

With this background in mind, Khumi exhibits classic Mainland Southeast Asian monosyllabicity in the sense that it tends strongly to have monosyllabic or sesquisyllabic formatives (i.e., markers of inflectional information) which could be analyzed as standing alone as separate phonological words. It should be kept in mind, however, that a monosyllabic analysis belies the fact that the elements in question usually occur in highly fixed positions with respect to each other and from a morphosyntactic standpoint are bound: they may never occur in isolation, as free elements may, given an appropriate context.

Adopting Bickel and Nichols' (2007) approach to traditional morphological typology, many of the formatives Khumi has are isolating and agglutinative, and they typically have separative exponence: they tend not to encode multiple inflectional meanings simultaneously. Morphosyntactic word structure is highly complex, and given the semantic richness of grammatically bound adverbial elements to be discussed shortly, actually verges on polysynthetic.[5] The major deviation from these characterizations is the tonal variants of roots and other formatives used instead of discrete segmental expression for specific inflectional catetories discussed above (irrealis, locative, negative, etc.), which leaves the language with a decidedly less isolating and more fusional appearance.

Compounding is fairly standard for this part of the world. In Khumi, two-member compounds are typically right-headed (if endocentric) and are phonologically distinguished by the treatment of their first (and sometimes second) element. There are various possibilities, but typically, the first element bears less stress than the second and does not show the full array of tonal distinctions found on its last syllable compared to non-compound occurrences of that member; tonal distinctions on the last syllable of the first member are generally reduced to high vs. low, although tone 4 (rising) in compounds sometimes shows

---

5 Cf. Coupe 2007's category of 'lexical' suffixes in Mongsen Ao (298 ff.).

a peak delay that bleeds over into a following syllable, altering the tone of that syllable: e.g., kno^4+kho^4 'ear+hole' is realized as kno(rising with peak delay)-kho^5.

Besides exocentric and endocentric compounds, there are coordinate compounds (e.g., am^1-am^1po^1 'mother-father=parents', jay^{11}-$bä^5$ 'elder sibling-younger sibling=siblings'). More specialized compound types like psycho-collocations and elaborate expressions will be taken up in the next two sections.

2.2 Psycho-collocations

A handful of psycho-collocations have been recorded for Khumi, although the phenomenon does not appear to be as prevalent as it is in other area languages. There may be monomorphemic roots which come close to expressing some of these concepts, but they are probably not entirely equivalent. Most of the recorded psycho-collocations involve the word $p'liwng^4$ 'heart', as seen in (7), although there are a few for some other body parts (e.g., $möy^3$ 'eye' and $k'no^4$ 'ear').

(7) heart:
 $p'liwng^4\ bi^4$ lit. 'heart hot'='unhappy, sad, upset'
 $p'liwng^4\ håy^3$ lit. 'heart good'='generous'
 $p'liwng^4\ a^1dü^1$ lit. 'heart equal'='harmonious'
 $p'liwng^4\ a^1ngay^3$ lit. 'heart MID-like'='like, be pleased with'
 $p'liwng^4\ a^1pha^1$ lit. 'heart sufficient'='happy, contented, satisfied'
 $p'liwng^4\ khay^2$ lit. 'heart keep'='hold a grudge'
 $p'liwng^4\ dång^4$ lit. 'heart think.about'='pay attention, think'
 $p'liwng^4\ a^1ma^1$ 'sad, upset' (second element perhaps originally 'lost')
 $p'liwng^4\ a^1phöng^4$ lit. 'heart suspect'='worry'
 $p'liwng^4\ phra^2$ lit. 'heart destroyed'='worry, upset'
 $p'liwng^4\ khå^1$ lit. 'heart strong'='feel sure, certain, secure'
 (sometimes an elaborate expression for heart, $p'liwng^4$-$p'thüng^3$
 (='heart-liver') is used in these constructions rather than just 'heart')

(8) eye:
 $möy^3\ a^1dåy^2$ lit. 'eye MID.lure'='attracted to, interested in'

(9) ear:
 $k'no^4\ ha^2$ lit. 'ear porous'='able to hear easily'
 $k'no^4\ döy^6$-$lä^3$ lit. 'ear die-NEG'='lie awake, unable to fall asleep'

2.3 Elaborate expressions

Khumi makes extensive use of elaborate expressions (described in detail by Peterson 2010). These are quasi-reduplicative compound structures which are used in place of simpler structures for stylistic effect. The simpler structure is included in the more elaborate one. Use of elaborate expressions conveys the impression of speaking eloquence and is generally regarded as a desirable discourse feature. Given the performative nature of narrative, elaborate expressions are more likely to be encountered in storytelling than in procedural discourse or conversation, although they do occur with lower frequency in other text genres. Some typical examples are listed in (10).

(10) elaborate expressions
    a. *tu¹pli¹-tu¹pla¹* 'reduplicate elaboration-box'='box'
    b. *s'rung¹-s'rå¹* 'nonce elaboration-tobacco'='tobacco'
    c. *tuy¹-may¹* 'water-fire'='water'
    d. *mi¹-may¹* 'reduplicate elaboration-fire'='fire'
    e. *ka¹¹si¹-tå¹¹kë¹* 'star-nonce elaboration'='star'

Elaborate expressions in Khumi may differ from those found elsewhere in Southeast Asia (see Haas 1964 on Thai or Matisoff 1973 on Lahu for classic characterizations) in terms of their structure. While some elaborate expressions conform to a classic A-B-A-C type structure, as in (10a–b), others deviate from this pattern. (10c–e), for instance, either involve only two syllables, or involve four syllables which do not include a shared syllable.

2.4 Reduplication

The elaborate expressions just considered involve a reduplicative structure in the default case (i.e., when no more specific elaboration strategy overrides the default.) Besides this, there are certain verbal categories (adverbial elements and verbal classifiers, discussed in 4.2.2) which can occur in reduplicated form, with no readily discernible semantic effect. Next, the ideophone category (see Peterson 2013a) has numerous fully reduplicated elements (e.g., *kri¹kra¹-kri¹kra¹* 'sound of walking on a bamboo deck', *li¹lång⁵-li¹lång⁵* 'motion of bamboos waving in the breeze'.) Finally, there does appear to be limited use of reduplication for certain reciprocal (*lewng¹¹-lewng¹¹-rë¹*, lit. 'person-person-COUNT') or distributive contexts (as in (11), where *cung¹¹ngay¹* '100' is repeated, if not reduplicated.)

(11) k'ni¹¹bi¹¹   k'ni¹¹nay³   thiwng¹⁰=a¹   t'ko¹¹=nö²   alö¹-ngay¹¹=te¹
    sunshine.LOC   rain   inside=LOC   go.IRR=NMLZ   need-want=EVID

    n'='ë¹⁰   si¹'ewng¹¹=mö²   thuy¹¹-pë¹   tang¹ka²   cung¹¹ngay¹
    QUOT=REAS   (name)=FGD   say-BEN   money   100

    cung¹¹ngay¹   khay¹¹-pë¹-yo³
    100   leave-BEN-IMPV

'They said they needed them [umbrellas] for walking in the sunshine [speaker mistake], the rain, Si'ewng said, so I left them 100 taka each.' (41.128)

Otherwise, reduplication is not used for any established function in the language.

More important than reduplication proper is basic parallelism, which seems to be a driving force in Khumi as in many other Southeast Asian languages (see, for instance, Solnit 1995.) (12) below shows one such case for Khumi, where the speaker starts his sentence with two words meaning 'tomorrow'.

(12) vå¹khång¹¹=lö¹   kh'dang¹⁰=lö¹   ay¹¹ni²   måy¹-co¹
    tomorrow=TOP   tomorrow=TOP   1D.INCL   wild.boar-child

    lew¹¹=kh'=bo³   n'=pë¹=te⁵   am¹nå¹⁰=a¹
    catch=HORT=REAL   QUOT=say=EVID   younger.sibling=LOC

' "Tomorrow, tomorrow let's catch a wild boar piglet," he said, to his younger brother.' (34.86)

This does not have the structure of an elaborate expression, which usually would involve compounding of the two elements in question. Instead, the first word is from the northern dialect and the second is from the more southerly Thanchi Khumi variety spoken in Bangladesh, which speakers of the northern Ruma Khumi dialect also are familiar with. The second instance of 'tomorrow' really adds nothing to the content of the sentence, but by virtue of its parallelism, the repetition is stylistically more satisfactory to speakers.

3 Grammar and Syntax

In gross typological terms, Khumi is consistently verb-final with a highly complex verbal structure.[6] Rigid though it is in this ordering, as often is the case in verb-final languages, nominal expressions may occur fronted in a topicalization or left dislocation position, or post-posed as an afterthought. In addition to limited prefixal morphology, which may code S/A (=subject) participants, the verb root may be surrounded by an array of valence-affecting formatives (see Peterson 2013b), some of which clearly arose from historically independent verbs, a process reminiscent of verb serialization. Nevertheless, there is really nothing resembling the productive serialization type often found in Mainland Southeast Asian languages (see Aikhenvald 2005). The language also exhibits fairly limited numeral classifier phenomena. It has frequent argument ellipsis under appropriate discourse recoverability. In terms of alignment, Khumi displays roughly nominative-accusative and primative/secundative (Haspelmath 2005) case marking, regulated by considerations of P/R (=object) specificity. Relativization makes use of nominalization without relative pronouns. These and related topics will be taken up in more detail in this section.

3.1 Nominal domain

In terms of the types of things and order of elements within the noun phrase, Khumi is a typical Tibeto-Burman language for the most part. For nominals, there is collective marking rather than a strict plural, although the same marking indicates plural in the independent pronouns. Numeral classifiers occur but are limited in their coverage and distribution, and the language has a small set of clitic case-marking post-positions and discourse status indicators. In addition to the segmental case markers, however, a noteworthy tendency already mentioned above is that the two highest frequency case markers, genitive and locative, often are expressed by the tone of the last syllable of the case-marked NP (excluding discourse status markers, which are more peripheral).

---

6 In this section and in subsequent discussion, I make use of the by now familiar semantico-syntactic designations S (single participant of an intransitive clause), A (more agent-like participant of a transitive clause), and P (less-agent-like participant of a transitive clause). Less familiar is the designation R, used for the less-patient or more-recipient-like participant of a ditransitive clause (see Haspelmath 2005).

3.1.1 Basic structure of the NP

The structure of Khumi NPs is fairly complex, so I break this discussion into selected portions of it. A maximally schematic representation for the structure of Khumi NPs is given in (13); the subparts other than the head (premodifiers, post-modifiers, and clitics) will be discussed in more detail in what follows.

(13) overall NP structure:
 [premodifier(s)]   head N   [post-modifier(s)]=[clitics]

Of course, a noun phrase containing all or even most of these elements at once is relatively rare; (14) gives a few examples of some of the more complex NPs attested in our large text corpus.

(14) a. cǎng¹thing¹kiwng⁵   n'=pë¹=nö³   ha¹-rë¹=lö¹
        (name)   QUOT=say=NMLZ   one-COUNT=TOP
        '(as for) the one called Cawngthingkiwng' (2.3)

   b. c'po¹   lewng⁵   t'riw¹-rë¹⁰=ya¹
      son   CLF human   six-count=LOC
      'six sons [marked with a locative case clitic]' (3.28)

   c. a¹ke²   kang¹-tha⁵   ha¹-rë¹
      knife   NMLZ-new   one-COUNT
      'a new knife' (3.46)

   d. a¹vang⁶   üng¹   dewng¹   phay¹-rë¹
      village.GEN   house   CLF HOUSEHOLD   thirty-COUNT
      'thirty households of the village' (35.64)

The internal sequencing of the premodifier portion of the NP is as in (15), though there appears to be some flexibility in the positioning of the demonstrative.[7]

(15) premodifer(s):
     [demonstrative possessor relative clause]

---

[7] For instance, direct elicitation suggests that a particularly heavy relative clause can be preferentially dislocated, yielding a sequence relative clause-demonstrative-head N. So far no text data sheds light on this issue, however.

There are three basic demonstratives: *h'ni³* 'speaker proximal/addressee distal', *tu¹ni³* 'speaker distal/addressee proximal', *hu¹ni³* 'speaker/addressee distal', containing the deictic elements *hi²*, *tu²*, and *hu²*. To these could be added the super-distal *huuni³*, pronounced with a longer vowel and the tone that was mentioned earlier (section 1.1) as a possible sixth lexical tone; as noted before, though, this tone always involves a nuance of intensification, as in super-distal vs. merely distal, and perhaps might simply be regarded as an intonational contour applied in cases where such intensification is desired rather than as involving a distinct lexical tone.

Adjectival concepts are expressed in one of two ways in Khumi. First, there are verb-like roots which occur nominalized by the generalized nominalizer *=nö³* in prenominal position, constituting what is essentially a relative clause. (See section 3.3 below for examples of prototypical relativization.) Such relativizations technically also may occur in post-nominal position, although this is infrequent in natural discourse. This possibility is reflected in the (relative clause) portion of the post-modifier expansion seen in (16).

(16) post-modifer(s):
[adjective/(relative clause) classifier-numeral-count/quantifier(-count)]

Secondly, represented as 'adjective' in (16), there are a large number of verbal or adjectival concepts which have corresponding lexicalized nominalizations formed with a prefix *ka(ng)-*; if such a nominalization exists, it may serve as an adjectival modifier *following* the noun. (See (14c) above for an example.) The remaining post-modifer elements are classifiers and associated elements, or quantifiers, which will be discussed further in the next section.

Besides the collective marker, *=cë⁵*, NP clitics include case markers and various indicators of discourse status:

(17) clitics:
[collective=locative/genitive/other case markers=
foregrounder=topic/focus]

The high frequency case markers of Khumi are given in (18), along with some examples where they may be seen in context, where possible:

(18)

case marker:	meaning:	example:
=*'ë¹*, or tonal instantiation	genitive	(36b), (45)
=*a¹*, or tonal instantiation	locative	(12), (23)
=*håy¹*	comitative/instrumental	text, sentence 1

=*ma¹*	ablative	(19b)
=*ma⁴*	more restricted locative, often with allative sense	text, sentence 19

Members of this category with extremely low text-frequency include =*cang³* 'standard of comparison' and =*rö²* 'limitative', meaning 'up to N'. Other spatial notions are primarily encoded using relational nouns loosely compounded with a noun and marked by a locative or ablative case marker, as in (19a-b).

(19) a. N *teng¹⁰=a¹*
         N side=LOC
         'to/at/etc. N'

    b. N *thiwng⁴=ma¹*
         N inside=ABL
         'from inside N'

There are two primary members of the discourse status marker category, which will be introduced briefly here but are discussed more fully in a section 3.3.2. =*lö¹* is a high-frequency topic marker. =*mö³*, on the other hand, correlates highly with focus. However, since a different element, =*pö¹* 'also', has clearer focussing functions, and =*mö³* is more varied in its use, we treat the latter as a marker of foregrounding. Here, I assume notions of topic and focus along the lines of those assumed in Lambrecht 1994 and Van Valin and LaPolla 1997. The notion of foregrounding I assume, as distinct from focus, is similar to that developed in Chelliah 2009.

Compared to other Tibeto-Burman languages, Khumi is highly typical in terms of the word order attested at the basic level of the noun phrase. Its main clause word order being verb final, it has postposed case markers and postpositional relational noun phenomena, and since its marker for standard of comparison is a case marker, it also has standard-marker ordering, as usual for a verb-final language. It shows variability in placement of relative clauses and adjective-like expressions, but has genitives preceding the head noun internal to NPs. The only respect in which its NP-internal word order is somewhat atypical is with respect to numeral classifiers (see section 3.1.2 below).

Not surprisingly, noun phrases may also contain an independent pronoun in place of a noun. The paradigm of independent pronouns is given in (20).

(20) Independent pronouns:

	1st person inclusive/exclusive	2nd person	3rd person
singular	kay^1	$nang^1$	ni^3
dual	ay^{11}-ni^2/kay^1-ni^3	$nang^1$-ni^3	ni^{11}-ni^2
plural	a^1-$cë^5$/kay^1-$cë^5$	$nang^1$-$cë^4$	ni^{11}-$cë^5$

Noun phrase-internally, pronouns occur in the same position as the head noun, but there are generally restrictions on the remaining elements that may appear. Pronouns only co-occur with case markers and discourse-status markers. Demonstratives (illustrated above) are built from one of the deictic elements mentioned earlier and the third person pronouns; often demonstratives serve in place of a third person pronoun.

3.1.2 Classifier (CLF) device

Given general Kuki-Chin and also Mainland Southeast Asian languages' expected propensity to make use of numeral classifiers, Khumi has a surprisingly small inventory of true classifiers. The ones that exist are typical in terms of their semantics, such as $lewng^5$ 'humans', $jiwng^5$ 'long, thin things', $dång^3$ 'sheets of paper', $dewng^4$ 'houses', $kiwng^4$ 'trees', etc., but many typical classifier categories appear to be missing (such as a dedicated classifer for animals.) Many of the formal classifier elements are simply measure words (e.g., $së^2$ 'kilogram', pho^1 'basketful'), and so do not clearly contribute to the total, and a number of them are simply noun copies (e.g., $på^3$ 'flowers', a^ithay^3 'fruits'). In discourse, it is quite normal for numeral classifiers simply to be left out.

There are also some fundamental syntactic differences between the classifer constructions seen in Khumi compared to those found elsewhere in Mainland Southeast Asia (cf. the possible ordering of elements identified by Barz and Diller 1985). The basic template is given in (21).

(21) N   classifier   numeral-COUNT

This template may be illustrated by (22a). The element glossed here as 'COUNT' is a central element in the construction; it appears not only in classifer construction, but also in a number of adverbial contexts involving quantification (see below for further occurrences). In fact the element is not identical to the verb 'count', which is $rë^2$, but it seems probable that they are related.

(22) a.   *c'rang⁴*   *jiwng⁵*   *pang¹¹-rë¹*
       ceremonial.knife.type   CLF LONG   five-COUNT
       'five *c'rangs*' (elicited)

    b.   *c'rang⁴*   *pang¹¹-rë¹*
       ceremonial.knife.type   five-COUNT
       'five *c'rangs*' (elicited)

    c.   *c'rang⁴*   *ha¹-rë¹*
       ceremonial.knife.type   one-COUNT
       'one *c'rang*' (elicited)

    d.   *c'rang⁴*   *jiwng¹¹-rë¹*
       ceremonial.knife.type   CLF LONG-COUNT
       'one *c'rang*' (elicited)

    e.   **c'rang⁴ jiwng⁵ ha¹-rë¹*

The classifier element can generally be left out, as in (22b), such that it is really the element *rë¹*, which supports the numeral rather than the classifier. With the numeral *ha²* 'one' (and numbers including it), there is a further structural simplification in that either the numeral is present, with no classifier (22c), or the classifier is combined directly with *-rë¹*, without a numeral (22d), but not both: sequences like (22e) do not occur.

    Classifiers are used only with numerals; they are not usable anaphorically and they are also not generally used to form indefinites, except for *lewng⁵* 'person', which may sometimes have an interpretation of 'somebody'. The *rë¹* 'count' element, however, is used in a limited way to form indefinites (*h'tang¹-rë¹* 'to such an extent', *may¹¹dë¹-rë¹* 'a little bit') and occurs with some types of quantification, e.g., *lo²* (month) *tlöyng¹¹-rë¹* 'every month', or *vä¹-rë¹* 'every', although it is not obligatory in all such contexts.

    We may further note that while the numeral classifier appears to be a relatively poorly instantiated category in Khumi, and certainly one which is often ignored or simplified in discourse, there is a separate and prominent classification phenomenon in the language in the form of high-frequency *verbal* classifiers. These primarily concern the relative size of participants involved in an event. See Peterson 2008 for a full description; a brief example is given in (23).

(23) ...a¹cĕ⁵   h'ni¹¹   ĕ¹-bå¹=khö¹¹lö¹   pyå¹⁰=mi¹
     1P.INCL   PROX.DEM.LOC   push-AUGVCL=COND   ABLE=DUBIT
     '...if we push this (a large stone), perhaps we'll be able.' (28:28)

The post-verbal element -bå³ in (23), an augmentative verbal classifier, indicates that the stone (here not overtly expressed) is large in size, in addition to other complex semantic nuances that verbal classifiers often contribute. If the speaker were instead to use the corresponding diminutive verbal classifier, -bö³, they would be calling attention to the small size of the stone.

3.2 Verbal domain

3.2.1 No inflection

Unlike many other languages of Mainland Southeast Asia, there is a reasonable amount of verbal inflection in Khumi. Least controversially, the language exhibits participant coding (described in Peterson 2002) in the form of prefixes which cannot be analysed as unbound pronominals from either a phonological or a morphosyntactic standpoint.

The status of other marking as inflectional or not depends on whether other bound elements are counted as inflection. As discussed earlier, while an analysis of many morphosyntactically bound elements as independent phonological words is possible for this language, and so many potentially inflectional elements would not be phonologically bound and hence non-inflectional, this ignores the otherwise bound morphosyntactic behavior of the elements in question.

In this section, while recognizing that certain post-verbal elements have somewhat more mobility than other elements, I outline a model for the Khumi verbal complex that recognizes several zones and rigidly ordered positions within those zones. The approach sketched out here is inspired in part by Kari's 1989 analysis of Athabaskan prefixal morphology, as considered for Mongsen Ao by Coupe 2007, and Muysken's 1986 "mode" analysis of Quechua suffixal morphology.

In terms of semantics, some of the elements involved are highly lexicalized or restricted in conjunction with particular predicates, and so not strictly speaking inflectional. They nevertheless are interspersed with more clearly inflectional elements and must be treated in a unified manner with them.

Besides this intertwined nature of more derivational and clearly inflectional formatives, there are discontinuous dependencies between elements, suggesting that the morphological connections between them are tighter than simple concatenation. In particular, the negative marker, which always induces glottalization of an immediately *preceding* syllable, can have a *non-local* effect on the preceding verb root. This is most evident with certain roots having tone 1 in their citation form and the vowel -*a*, like the verbs *ca^1* 'eat' and *la^1* 'take'. When the negative is present, separate stem alternants, *co^6* and *lo^6*, or variants with non-final unchecked tones (see, for instance, example (29) below), are required; it does not matter whether the negative is immediately adjacent to or several formatives distant from the root.

3.2.2 Verbal categories

Minimally, a verb consists of a root, although more morphology often occurs in the verbal complex. Indicative verbs in either subordinate or main clauses can exhibit relatively complex structures. Other than indicative morphology, the verbal complex may contain elements marking categories like imperative, hortative, and optative. Interrogative sentences differ in form depending on whether they are polar or non-polar. Generally, interrogatives may contain indicative morphology embedded in them more readily than other non-indicative sentence types may.

The overall structure of the verbal complex requires the recognition of at least the zones seen in (24), which are described in more detail in A–E below. Following an introduction to the structure of these elements, I will make some observations about the types of elements which occur.

(24) prefixes-ROOT-invariably ordered suffixes-
transitional-variably ordered=clitics

A. The *prefix zone* includes participant coding, or middle – i.e., multi-purpose detransitivizer – (*a*-) elements, as well as a causative (*p*-/*t*-), treated in Peterson 2013b. These elements are rigidly ordered and the causative and middle are lexicalized in some cases.

(25) prefix zone:
    PARTICIPANT CODING-   CAUSATIVE-ROOT
    MIDDLE-

The following generalizations apply to participant marking, when it is used. If the S/A is first person, *ka(ng)*- is prefixed to the verb. Otherwise, *ang*- is used. It is clear that this participant marking ignores a number of the distinctions that are important for the independent pronouns seen earlier: number and inclusive/exclusive. This preverbal participant coding is also often omitted. It occurs fairly frequently in conversation and in reported speech, where first and second person participants are common. However, it only rarely appears in third-person narrative, where it has a subtle perspective-changing effect discussed in Peterson 2002. Participant coding is mutually-exclusive with the middle marker.

B. The *invariably ordered suffix zone* contains a group of ten or eleven bound, rigidly ordered positions situated closest to the verb root. Altogether these involve around 150 highly abstract elements, for the most part falling into several relatively specific semantic types.

(26) invariably ordered suffix zone:
ROOT   -BEN-   ASSOCIATIVE-DIR-VCL-PRIOR-ADV1-ADV2-ADV3-ADV4-IMPFV
       -CAUS-

- causative/applicative (CAUS -*hay³*)/benefactive/malefactive (BEN -*pë̈¹*)/ associative (-*hå̇y¹*) are all fairly standard in terms of their behaviour; possibly also -*vë̈⁴* 'substitutive applicative' (see Peterson 2013b.)
- directional (DIR): -*k'lå̇⁴* 'upwards' and -*k'thiw³* 'downwards'.
- (verbal) classifier (VCL): at least (perhaps significantly more than) 100 paired elements carrying all manner of idiosyncratic nuances, but with a central notion of largeness/smallness of a participant, usually S/P (Peterson 2008).
- prioritive (PRIOR): -*ma⁴* 'first'.
- adverbial: ADV1: usually associated with tightness or completeness, including -*thlöyng¹* 'tightly, fast, stuck', -*ceng¹* 'tightly, full', -*då̇⁴* 'incompletely, a bit, for a while', -*jö¹¹¹'ay²* 'randomly, haphazardly'. One might be tempted to analyze this and Adv2–4 as aspect; certainly aspect is involved, but often much subtler adverbial nuances are invoked, defying analysis in terms of simple aspectual distinctions.
- ADV2: -*prå̇¹* 'immediately, suddenly; desperately, with immediate need', -*bå̇y³* 'all', -*du⁴* 'in great number', -*lew²* 'at a distance', -*mä³* 'neatly, carefully', -*u¹* 'plural participant', -*tüng³* 'carefully, clearly'.
- ADV3: -*khö³* 'in the way', -*may³* 'a bit, partly', -*m'lä̇⁴* 'too much', -*sä¹* 'repeatedly, clearly'.
- ADV4: -*kä³* 'more, comparative', -*seng³* 'frustrative (due to a mistake)', -*hu³* 'frustrative (due to unexpected absence of something)', -*pay³* 'too much, excessively', -*play³* 'at all, ever, experiential perfect', -*vay³* 'experiential perfect', -*rüng³* 'in advance, already'.

- <u>imperfective</u> (IMPFV): highly ramified category whose members all have vaguely imperfective aspectual nuances; most can occur in a reduplicated form (*-ü⁴*, *-të⁴*, *-reng¹*, *-thüng³*, *-mu⁴*, *-hë¹*, *-lü⁴*, *-väng³*, *-r'sö³*, *-rü³*) (Note that a reduplicated form is not diagnostic for this class, as some elements from other classes – e.g., *-båy³* 'all', *-du⁴* 'in great number', and, most notably, verbal classifiers – may also show a reduplicated form.)

Direct elicitation suggests that for some of these groups, multiple members of a category may co-occur. If this is borne out by naturalistic data, further 'sub-zones' or additional positions may need to be recognized; e.g., the sequence benefactive-causative has been elicited directly, but does not occur in the text corpus; the opposite ordering may not be elicited and is likewise unattested.

C. The *transitional zone (free particles)* is a group of some of the elements just listed under the imperfective class which show a relatively less bound status than other such elements, especially in that they, or clearly related elements, may occur in preverbal position, in addition to their common post-verbal uses. The elements in question include *të⁴*, *väng³*, and possibly some others. For instance, consider (27a–b), where the postverbal element *-të⁴*, usually with iterative semantics, may be preposed to the verbal complex in circumstances where the speaker wishes to place some kind of emphasis on the iterativity, or to attach some kind of special attitude (e.g., annoyance) to the fact of the iterativity.

(27) a. *thuy¹¹-t'të¹*
   say-ITER
   'keep saying' (elicited)

   b. *t'të⁴*   *thuy³*
            say
   'keep saying' (elicited)

However, elements of the transitional zone are mutually incompatible with elements in the imperfective class, such that it would appear the imperfective class has arisen via the gradual accretion of suffixes at the end of the invariably ordered suffix zone. These elements therefore have a dual nature: they block the occurrence of other imperfective elements, but are themselves inherently more mobile than the other elements of the invariably ordered suffix zone.

D. The *variably ordered zone (bound particles)* includes a number of elements which are all apparently exclusively post-verbal, but which exhibit variable orders with each other, possibly with scopal differences. The basic elements are shown in (29), and an instance of scopal ordering differences is given in (28a–b), where the relative positioning of the inceptive aspect marker and the negative marker has clear consequences for the meanings of the forms.

(28) a. *co¹-rö¹²-lä²*
   eat-INCEPT-NEG
   'he didn't start eating' (elicited)

   b. *co⁶-lä¹¹-rö²*
   eat-NEG-INCEPT
   'he's started to not eat' (elicited)

- INTENSIFIER: *-ka¹¹mo¹*.
- ASPECT: *-yo³* 'generalized imperfective', *-vuy³* 'perfective, but with a frequent sense of surprise/irritation', *-pång¹* 'neutral perfective', *-rö³* 'inceptive', *-r'ra⁴* 'durative, keep on Ving', *-yo¹¹yo²* 'iterative', *-yå³* 'durative', *-råy⁴* 'perseverative'.
- ADVERBIAL: *-bë⁴* 'again, next', *-täng³~-t'läng³* 'again', *-vë⁴* 'almost' (homophonous but distinct from the substitutive applicative), *-yo¹¹ya²* 'reluctantly', *-ngöm¹* 'secretly', *-ngang³* 'with great difficulty'.
- NEGATIVE: *-lä³*.
- EVALUATION: *-vöyng¹* 'sympathy', *-lå³* 'surprise'.

(29) variably ordered zone:
   INTENSIFIER-ASPECT~NEGATIVE~EVALUATION

E. The *clitic zone* is a rigidly ordered group of elements which exhibit looser selectional restrictions in the sense that they can occur after nominals and other lexical categories in addition to their common post-verbal use. These elements co-occur quite readily.

(30) clitic zone:
   irrealis=nominalizer=adverbial=realis=evidential=deictic
- IRREALIS: =*a¹*, a high-frequency element mostly used for indicating future events, but also required marking in desiderative and purposive constructions. This marker evidently derives from the locative case clitic, as reflected in their identical tonal patterning.

- nominalizer: $=n\ddot{o}^3$.
- ADVERBIAL(S): a small number of items, including $=kh\ddot{u}^3$ 'just, only', $=pray^1$ 'intensivizer'.
- REALIS: $=bo^3$.
- EVIDENTIAL: $=te^5$, a straightforward hearsay evidential element.
- DEICTIC: $=he^1$, $=to^1$, $=ho^1$, clearly related to independent deictic elements (hi^2, tu^2, and hu^2); these also have subtle effects on evidentiality and tense interpretations, as typical of such elements in Kuki-Chin languages (cf. Barnes 1998).

(31) reiterates the main parameters distinguishing the elements of the verbal complex other than the root.

(31) summary of the combinatory characteristics of post-verbal elements:

	potential for displacement	variable position	non-selectivity
prefixes	–	–	–
invariable suffixes	–	–	–
transitional (free) particles	+	–	(–)
variably ordered (bound) particles	–	+	–
clitics	–	–	+

Displacement refers to the ability of the element to occur in a position other than post-verbally, illustrated above in (27). Items exhibiting variable position are able to be ordered in multiple ways with respect to each other, sometimes with semantic consequences. Such variability was seen in (29). Non-selectivity refers to the fact that certain items may show an affinity for more than just a verbal base; this applies most clearly to the elements regarded as clitics. The first two types of item are the most canonically affix-like. It would appear that there are certain items in the transitional (free) particle category which are on the verge of grammaticalizing into invariable suffixes, but these are nevertheless less bound. Variably ordered and clitic elements are also less bound for different reasons.

In a more abstract conceptualization, the verb complex might be viewed as containing a verbal core (comprising the verb root, prefixes and invariably ordered suffixes), and more peripheral auxiliary-like entities (the variably ordered elements); the transitional elements in between are more like free adverbs, and the clitic elements are not strictly part of the verbal complex, as indicated also by their ability to attach directly to nominal constituents.

To generalize in terms of verbal categories, it is first apparent that a large number of elements included here are more of a derivational nature, with richly adverbial semantics. Many of these adverbial elements, as well as the classifiers, are highly restricted in lexical terms. Although they are bound elements, this selectivity leaves them with a more lexical or derivational effect than an inflectional one. Similarly, clearly valence-affecting elements like the causatives and benefactive/malefactive are certainly to be treated as derivational.

Quite a few of the more peripherally-ordered elements, though, could be treated as inflectional in nature, including members of the imperfective class, the variably ordered aspect and adverbial elements, the negative marker, and many of the clitics (realis, irrealis, evidential, etc.) The participant coding prefixes are also clearly inflectional in nature, even though they aren't required for every occurrence of a verb.

In sum, then, while many of the morphosyntactically bound post-verbal elements do not appear to represent prototypical inflection in terms of their meaning and regularity, a good number of them do. Khumi thus does not fit the no-inflection Southeast Asian language prototype as well as other languages. However, since the more clearly affixal elements (the prefix zone and the invariably ordered suffix zone) are mostly more derivational in nature, and the elements occurring further to the periphery (the free and bound particles, as well as the clitics) are more inflectional in nature, in some sense Khumi does have a typical Southeast Asian treatment of such elements, which, as could be expected, are less bound.

3.2.3 Serial verb constructions (SVC)

Khumi exhibits only highly limited phenomena resembling verb serialization. This is different from other Kuki-Chin languages which by and large do allow for at least limited verb-verb compounds reminiscent of more prototypical serialization (see, e.g., Chhangte 1993 for Mizo).

The language does have numerous post-verbal elements which have evidently grammaticalized from formerly serialized verbs, however, such as the benefactive marker (-$pë^i$), which must have resulted from a serialized verb of giving (pe^i 'to give'), as most such markers do. In addition, there are a number of semi-bound modal elements, which have grammaticalized meanings distinct from their lexical usages:

(32) **element in bound usage:**   **source verb meaning:**
    -*thay³* 'general (internal) potential'   'hear'
    -*p'yå⁴* 'impeded (external) potential'   'finish'
    -*tla¹* 'obligative'   'fall'
    -*ngay³* 'desiderative'   'like'
    -*khëng¹* 'try'   'look'

A small number of similar elements have not undergone semantic shifts between their independent and bound uses: -*kå³* 'learned potential', -*nga¹* 'get (to)', -*håy³* 'be good to V', -*cung⁴* 'finish, perfective'. There is also a small, still more loosely bound category which can be regarded as a true auxiliary class (e.g., *a¹håy¹* 'do together with', *a¹say⁵* 'do again', etc.)

3.3 Clausal/sentential organization

Most non-main clauses in Khumi are loosely subordinated by means of clause final markers, expressing relations such as sequential (=*b'lö¹*, =*kha¹*), conditional (=*b'lö¹*), counterfactual/conditional (=*khö¹¹lö¹*), concessive (=*'ë¹⁰pö¹*, =*kha¹¹pö¹*), reason (=*'ë¹⁰*, =*nay¹¹dewng¹¹kho⁵wa¹*), anterior (=*ma¹b'lö¹*), and a few rarer elements. These bear a resemblance to chaining or converbial forms, but on the whole are not as invariant in form or bound as prototypical converbs are (e.g., as described for Mongsen Ao by Coupe 2007). In particular, the subordinate clause sometimes bears Khumi's general nominalizer, =*nö³* or =*nay³* (see the discussion immediately following), or this nominalizer may be absent, with only the marker of subordination present. The first of these possibilities is illustrated for the anterior marker by example (33), and the second is shown in (34).

(33) *niw¹*=***nö¹¹***=***ma¹b'lö¹***   *a¹ti³ k'sewng¹*=*mo⁴*   *p'nö¹¹-thay¹²-lä³*
    see=NMLZ=ANT   what flower=QUEST   know-POT-NEG

    tvåy¹¹ampo¹=*wö¹*   *do¹¹*=*khö¹¹lö¹*   *håy¹¹*=*a¹*   *n'*=*pë¹*=*te⁵*
    lover=ENDEARING   pick=COND   good=IRR   QUOT=say-EVID
    'When (after) she saw it, she didn't know what kind of flower it was, and she said, "Oh, love, if you pick it, it would be good."' (7.24)

(34) *nuy¹-bå¹*=***ma¹b'lö¹***   *ni¹¹cë⁵*   *thew¹-så¹*
    push-AUGVCL=ANT   3P   come out-AUGVCL
    'After they pushed it they came out.' (28.30)

Markers of adverbial subordination also may occur in conjunction with a dummy predicate (identical in form to the nominalizer, =nö³, or its variant form =nay³, or either of these combined with a deictic element) as clause-initial stand-alone conjunctions (see example (35)).

(35) h'nay¹¹ma¹b'lö¹   süng¹¹-yo²   c'nå¹⁰   kang¹⁰-p'yå⁶-lä¹¹=bo²
then   bring-IMPFV child.LOC forbid/prevent-POT-NEG=REAL
'Then, they took them along. They couldn't prevent the children [from coming].' (33.144)

Relative clauses are even more firmly grounded in nominalization, usually marked by the element =nö³. (36) gives examples where the target of relativization bears various roles (A vs. P vs. obliques) internal to the relative clause.

(36) a. A target:
    kay¹ h'ni³   ngo¹   abay¹=**nö³** s'ra¹⁰=a¹   niw¹
    1S DEM   fish   cut=NMLZ doctor=LOC see
    'I saw the doctor who cut the fish.' (elicited)

b. P target:
    kay¹ h'ni³ s'ra⁶='ë¹   abay¹=**nö³** ngo¹⁰=a¹   niw¹
    1S DEM doctor=GEN cut=NMLZ fish=LOC see
    'I saw the fish that the doctor cut.' (elicited)

c. instrument target:
    kay¹ h'ni³ s'ra⁶='ë¹   h'ni³   ngo¹   abay¹=**nö³** hay¹co¹⁰=a¹ niw¹
    1S DEM doctor=GEN DEM   fish   cut=NMLZ knife=LOC see
    'I saw the knife the doctor cut the fish with.' (elicited)

d. locative target:
    kay¹ h'ni³ s'ra⁶='ë¹   h'ni³   ngo¹   abay¹=**nö³** üng¹⁰=a¹   niw¹
    1S DEM doctor=GEN DEM   fish   cut=NMLZ house=LOC see
    'I saw the house the doctor cut the fish in.' (elicited)

Note the uniform treatment of the A participant in (36b-d) as a possessor. In addition, a couple of other nominalized forms are found less-frequently supporting relativization, including the dedicated locative nominalizer -ra¹ seen in (37), where it marks a headless relative.

(37) uh ne¹¹=yö¹   ngam¹ngampo¹ åm¹-ra¹=lö¹
  INTERJ old.sister=ENDEAR parents   exist-LOC. NMLZ=TOP

pnö¹¹=nö¹=cö⁴=ö¹
know=NMLZ=INSIST=ENDEAR
' "Oh elder sister, I know where your parents are living." ' (1.70)

3.3.1 Ellipsis of arguments

Like many other area languages, Khumi is extremely permissive when it comes to ellipsis of arguments which are recoverable from discourse context. As a simple example, (38) was spoken in response when someone had asked whether the speaker had any skewers of grilled pork on hand:

(38) hi¹¹   ø   bö⁶
  here.LOC (skewers of pork) exist.NEG
  'There aren't any here.'

In the following narrative text example, the consultant who assisted in translation amazingly identified the zero anaphor associated with the predicate 'exist' with s'i¹plang¹ 'sand bank', which had not been mentioned for about twenty intervening clauses!

(39) tläm³   khåy¹tewng⁵=mö³ p'yung¹¹-pë¹=pray¹=lö¹ nang¹pö¹
  suddenly (name)=FGD urinate-MAL=INTENS=TOP DISC.PART

bö⁶-lä¹¹=te¹   a¹yö¹ miwng² nüng² lüng¹¹-täng¹¹=te¹
exist-NEG=EVID man cubit two rise-AGAIN=EVID
'Suddenly Khåytewng peed a lot on her, you know; it (ø=the sandbank) didn't exist, man! It (ø=the water) rose again by two cubits.' (42.115)

However, zero anaphoric links are occasionally inadequate, as seen in the following exchange between a storyteller and a listener, in which there is apparently more than one possible referent for the zero.

(40) A: kang¹khüng¹¹-ka¹ngay¹¹=ma⁴ a¹tung¹-ka¹-t'nga¹¹=te¹
    finally-ELAB=LOC   pound-AUGVCL-AT.LAST=EVID
    'Finally he pounded him to death with difficulty.'

B: *tuy¹nang¹⁰=a¹*
　　water.spirit.LOC=INTERR
　　'The water-spirit?'

A: *tuy¹nang¹⁰=a¹*
　　water.spirit=LOC
　　'The water-spirit.' (42.133-5)

In this narrative context, a man is battling a water-spirit, and A's statement makes it unclear which participant is victorious. B asks if it was the water-spirit that was defeated in the second line, and A confirms B's intuitions.

3.3.2 Information structure

Besides the extensive argument ellipsis for discourse-recoverable entities just illustrated, Khumi has a dedicated topic marker, =*lö¹*, with a discourse use approximating that of well-known topic markers like Japanese =*wa*. This element occurs in one of the discourse marker slots already described above under basic noun structure (see section 4.1.1). In addition, the marker =*mö³*, which occurs in a less peripheral NP slot, serves to focus its NP in some cases. Since =*mö³* is actually compatible with =*lö¹*, and since different elements are responsible for focus under other circumstances (most notably, =*pö¹*, which otherwise means 'also'[8]), it is analyzed not as a focus marker, but as a marker of foregrounding. If both markers occur in a single NP, their order is invariably =*mö³*=*lö¹*.

The following sentences illustrate the basic focus types identified by Lambrecht (1994) in appropriate discourse contexts, and the occurrence of the markers in question. In the first sentence, we see a predicate focus structure, in response to a question like 'What did the hill doctor do?' As expected in such structures, a topic may be marked by the topic marker, as in (41).

(41) *s'ra¹(=lö¹)*　　　*biw²*　*ca¹-vuy³*
　　　hill.doctor(=TOP)　rice　eat-PFV
　　　'The hill doctor ate (rice).' (elicited)

In (42), the entire sentence is in focus, as in response to a question like 'What happened?'

---

8 This clitic is similar in at least certain respects to the particle treated in Konnerth 2012.

(42) s'ra¹=mö³   biw²   ca¹-vuy³
    hill.doctor=FGD   rice   eat-PFV
    'The hill doctor ate (rice).' (elicited)

Finally, in (43), the =mö³-marking and cleft-like structure allow narrow focus on a participant, in this case the hill doctor, as a contradiction to a hypothetical claim that someone other than the hill doctor ate.

(43) mhm,   s'ra¹=mö¹¹=tew²   biw²   ca¹-vuy¹¹=nö²
    interj   hill.doctor=FGD=COP   rice   eat-PFV=NMLZ
    'No, it was the hill doctor that ate (rice).' (elicited)

For further details on the use of these markers, the reader is directed to Peterson 2011, where they are given a more exhaustive treatment.

3.3.3 Other observations

Khumi has a robust use of so-called 'stand alone' nominalization commonly seen in Tibeto-Burman languages (see Matisoff 1972, Noonan 1997), where a nominalized clause appears as if it were independent, and at least in Khumi, often with special emphatic effect:

(44) a. nay¹¹b'lö¹   thang¹¹bë¹=te⁵   sam¹rüng¹   ka¹müng⁵
        then   nightingale=EVID   chili   red

        ca¹⁰   jew¹=nö³
        eat.IRR   come=NMLZ
        'Then a nightingale came to eat red chilis.' (1.75)

   b. lam¹phay²   ke³   në¹na¹   ke³   lam¹phay²   ke³   në¹na¹   ke¹=nö³
       weaving.belt bite skirt   bite   weaving.belt bite skirt   bite=NMLZ
       'They (dogs) bit the weaving belt and they bit her skirt, they bit the weaving belt and they bit her skirt.' (8.195a)

   c. a¹¹=mö²   klay¹⁰=nö²
       chicken=FGD   scratch=NMLZ
       'The chickens scratched her.' (8.195b)

In theory, this construction arose in Khumi via simplification of another commonly attested construction: V=nö³ tla¹, seen in (45), which has an interpretation basically indistinguishable from a simple past tense.

(45) nay¹¹b'lö¹   ca¹-vuy¹¹=b'lö¹   k'ni⁵   thung⁵   p'lü⁵=b'lö¹
      then   eat-PFV=SEQ   day   three   four=SEQ

   t'vöng¹¹=pö¹   a¹dång¹⁰=nö²   tla¹   ni³=mö⁶   c'niw¹⁰=a¹
   bear=ALSO   miss=NMLZ   happen   3S=REFL.GEN   daughter=LOC
   '...then, he (tiger) ate her (bear's daughter), and after three or four days, bear also, missed her, his own daughter.' (3.65)

In this more complex construction, *tla¹*, literally 'fall', appears to be used in a sense of 'happen', such that the entire construction means something like 'it happened that V'.

4 Semantics and pragmatics

4.1 Common semantic domains

4.1.1 Food terminology

In the food domain, there is a basic division between *biw²* 'cooked rice' and *ang¹* 'curry', or what accompanies the rice. As expected, there are many different rice-related terms. Aside from specific terms for different varieties of rice grown by the Khumi, which are quite numerous, the following are several relatively basic terms. However, some of these are obviously compounded.

(46) selected rice-related terminology:
   biw²   'cooked rice, food'
   co⁵   'uncooked, unpounded rice'
   co¹¹ngang⁵   'rice which is still wet but in the process of drying'
   co¹¹hung¹   'rice which still has its outer covering on it'
   co¹¹nöyng¹   'rice with the outer covering removed'
   co¹¹m(u)¹   'rice (seed)'
   cang¹tha⁵   'new rice, first rice harvested from the swidden'
   cang¹¹tlöyng¹   'sticky rice'
   cang¹hüng⁵   'old rice, rice carried over from one harvest to the following year'

ca¹liwng⁵	'sticky rice'
pew¹pew⁵	'puffed rice'

This hardly scratches the surface of the lexical domain related to rice.

4.1.2 Expressions for 'cutting', 'carrying', 'drying', 'directional'

Khumi differs from a number of closely related and certain other Mainland Southeast Asian languages in lacking a large number of directional elements (see DeLancey 1980, So-Hartmann 2009). However, for other lexical domains it is typical in having numerous clearly delineated actions. These include domains of cutting, carrying, wearing, hitting/beating, digging, and washing. I include just a couple of partial lists in (47) and (48):

(47) <u>carrying</u>:

pho³	'carry with a headstrap, in a basket, on the back'
süng³	'carry in the hand'
a¹pu¹	'carry over the shoulder'
a¹tläng⁴	'carry on the head or back, balance on the shoulder'
c'këng⁴	'carry or hold under the arm, at the side'
t'ke²	'carry behind the ear'
a¹jewng²	'carry on the shoulder (of two people)'
pew¹	'carry on the back (e.g., a child)'
t'pång⁴	'carry under or in the arm'
tång⁴	'carry on the back in a basket'
vä¹	'carry a hanging object'
t'va¹	'carry on the shoulder (e.g., a carry-bag)'

(48) <u>wearing</u>:

a¹na¹	'wear on the lower half of the body'
am¹co²	'wear in the ear (e.g., a flower or earring)'
åy⁴	'wear around the neck'
a¹jeng⁴	'wear on the head (e.g., a turban)'
a¹büng²	'stick or wear in the hair'
a¹khiw¹	'wear on the upper half of the body'
a¹diwng²	'wear on the head'
a¹t'ka¹	'wear on the face'
am¹cu²	'wear on the finger or wrist'

4.2 Pragmatics and discourse

4.2.1 Final particles

In keeping with its Southeast Asian areal status, Khumi is rich in final particles indicating all sorts of subtle subjective evaluations or emotional content. Glosses for most of these can only be tentative. They include: =mi^1 'dubitative', ='$ö^1$ 'endearing', =ba^1~=be^4~=$bä^4$ 'softening', =e^1 'affirmative', =$cö^4$ 'insistent', =$ma(ng)^1$ 'intensified affirmative', =$n'ang^5$ and =$l'o^5$, which are both roughly like an English tag question in which the speaker is not actually trying to get confirmation but rather to get the listener to believe what they are saying.

4.2.2 Politeness

Politeness is not expressed in Khumi by any of the usual means found in major Southeast Asian languages: there are no pronominal distinctions, special verbal morphology, or strict lexical choices used to indicate relative speaker status or deference.

Khumi discourse does exhibit the common South and Southeast Asian practice of using kinship terms in an extended manner for persons who are not members of one's actual family, e.g., 'grandson' used by an elderly person for males belonging to the generation of one's own grandchildren. The lexicon also distinguishes carefully between whether a person/addressee is a member of one's own clan or not. However, both of these are arguably separate phenomena from systems for grammatical encoding of politeness distinctions.

Imperatives are either bare (i.e., marked by a verb root or extended verb complex with the appropriate tonal variant on the final syllable of the complex), or they may involve a variety of further devices, such as a final particle (see section 4.2.1) for mitigating the abruptness of the imperative. This also is not a manifestation of politeness per se, but according to speakers an abrupt imperative rather than a more extended request form would be less likely to be used by persons of inferior social status towards those of a higher standing, or by a younger person to an elder.

5 Summary

All things considered, Khumi is clearly a prototypical Southeast Asian language closely allied with the Sinosphere in the vast majority of respects. Nothing shows this status better than its phonology, especially in terms of its sesquisyllabic structures, its fairly extensive vowel inventory, and its exceedingly complex system of contour tones and their interactions. While it has–albeit only minimal–participant-coding on its verbs, deviating from the Southeast Asian norm, it has ideophonic elements, widespread use of elaborate expressions and other parallel structures, a number of reduplication types, and at least a smattering of psycho-collocations and numeral classifiers.

Khumi has no true serialization, but it has structures which clearly arose from verb-verb compounding, which in turn presumably grew out of serial-like constructions. In terms of word structure, it clearly has monosyllabic or sesquisyllabic phonological words. It makes liberal use of argument ellipsis, and its lexicon is partitioned in ways that are familiar in the Southeast Asian context.

The ways in which Khumi deviates from the Southeast Asian prototype hinge clearly on its family membership more than its areal position. Its verb-final syntax making use of postpositional case markers and discourse status indicators, and converb-like clause combining strategies are squarely Tibeto-Burman in character. The more complex picture of word structure which consideration of the issue from the perspective of morphosyntactic wordhood reveals is highly typical for Kuki-Chin and other nearby portions of the family.

Given its position on the border between Southeast Asia and South Asia, and its central position within Tibeto-Burman, this generous mix of areal and genetic heritages is only to be expected.

Abbreviations

1	first person
2	second person
3	third person
ABL	ablative
AFFIRM	affirmative
AGR	agreement
ALL	allative
ANT	anterior
APPL	applicative
AUG	augmentative
AUGVCL	augmentative verbal classifier

AUX	auxiliary
BEN	benefactive
CAUS	causative
CLF	classifier
COLL	collective
COND	conditional
D	dual
DEM	demonstrative
DIMVCL	diminutive verbal classifier
DUBIT	dubitative
ELAB	elaboration (in an elaborate expression)
EMOT	emotive
ENDEAR	endearing
EVID	hearsay evidential
EXCL	exclusive
FGD	foregrounder
GEN	genitive
HORT	hortative
IDEO	ideophonic element
IMPER	imperative
IMPV	imperfective
INCL	inclusive
INSIST	insistent
INST	instrumental
INTENS	intensive
INTERJ	interjection
INTERR	interrogative
IRR	irrealis
MAL	malefactive
LOC	locative
NEG	negative
NMLZ	nominalizer
P	plural
PERS	perseverative
PFV	perfective
POT	potential
PROX	proximal
QUEST	question
QUOT	quotative
REAL	realis
REAS	reason
S	singular
SEQ	sequential
TOP	topic

References

Aikhenvald, Alexandra Y. 2005. Serial verb constructions in typological perspective. In Alexandra Y. Aikhenvald & R. M. W. Dixon (eds.), *Serial verb constructions: A cross-linguistic typology*, 1–68. Oxford: Oxford University Press.

Barnes, Jonathan. 1998. Tsuu khaa tii hla?: deixis, demonstratives and discourse particles in Lai Chin. *Linguistics of the Tibeto-Burman Area* 21 (1). 53–86.

Barz, R. K. & A. Diller. 1985. Classifiers and standardization: Some South and South-East Asian comparisons. in David Bradley (ed.), *Papers in Southeast Asian Linguistics No. 9, Pacific Linguistics*, 155–184. Canberra: Australian National University.

Bickel, Balthasar & Johanna Nichols. 2007. Inflectional morphology. In Timothy Shopen (ed.), *Language typology and syntactic description – Vol 3: Grammatical categories and the lexicon*, 2nd ed., 169–240. Cambridge: Cambridge University Press.

Bradley, David. 1997. Tibeto-Burman languages and classification. In David Bradley (ed.), *Papers in Southeast Asian linguistics No 14: Tibeto-Burman languages of the Himalayas*, 1–72. Canberra: Australian National University.

Chelliah, Shobhana. 2009. Semantic role to new information in Meithei. In Jóhanna Barðal & Shobhana Chelliah (eds.), *The role of semantics, pragmatics, and discourse in the development of case*, 377–400. Amsterdam: John Benjamins.

Chhangte, Lalnunthangi. 1993. *Mizo syntax*. PhD dissertation, University of Oregon.

Coupe, Alexander R. 2007. *A grammar of Mongsen Ao*. Berlin & New York: Mouton de Gruyter.

Delancey, Scott. 1980. *Deictic categories in the Tibeto-Burman verb*. PhD dissertation, Indiana University.

Dixon, R. M. W. & Alexandra Y. Aikhenvald. 2002. Word: A typological framework. In R. M. W. Dixon & Alexandra Y. Aikhenvald (eds.), *Word: A cross-linguistic typology*, 1–41. Cambridge: Cambridge University Press.

Grierson, G. A. (ed.) 1904. *Linguistic survey of India, vol. III: Tibeto-Burman family (3 parts)*. Calcutta: Office of the Superintendent, Government Printing.

Haas, Mary. 1964. *Thai-English student's dictionary*. Palo Alto: Stanford University Press.

Hall, T. A., K. Hildebrandt & B. Bickel. 2008. Introduction: Theory and typology of the word. *Linguistics* 46. 183–192.

Haspelmath, Martin. 2005. Argument marking in ditransitive alignment types. *Linguistic Discovery* 3 (1). https://journals.dartmouth.edu/cgi-bin/WebObjects/Journals.woa/1/xmlpage/1/article/280?htmlOnce=yes.

Henderson, E. J. A. 1965. The topography of certain phonetic and morphological characteristics of South East Asian languages. *Lingua* 15. 400–434.

Hyman, Larry & Kenneth VanBik. 2004. Directional rule application and output problems in Hakha Lai tone. *Phonetics and Phonology, Special Issue, Language and Linguistics* 5. 821–861.

Kari, James. 1989. Affix positions in the Athapaskan verb complex: Ahtna and Navajo. *International Journal of American Linguistics* 55 (4). 424–454.

Konnerth, Linda. 2012. Additive focus and additional functions of Karbi (Tibeto-Burman) =tā. *Berkeley Linguistics Society* 38. 206–221.

Lambrecht, Knud. 1994. *Information structure and sentence form*. Cambridge: Cambridge University Press.

Matisoff, James A. 1972. Lahu nominalization, relativization, and genitivization. In John P. Kimball (ed.), *Syntax and semantics* (1), 237–257. New York: Academic Press.
Matisoff, James A. 1973. *The grammar of Lahu*. Berkeley: University of California Press.
Muysken, Pieter. 1986. Approaches to affix order. *Linguistics* 24. 629–643.
Noonan, Michael. 1997. Versatile nominalization. In Joan Bybee, John Haiman & Sandra A. Thompson (eds.), *Essays on language function and language type*, 373–394. Amsterdam: John Benjamins.
Peterson, David A. 2002. (published 2006) On Khumi verbal pronominal morphology. *Berkeley Linguistics Society* 28 [special session]. 99–110.
Peterson, David A. 2008. Bangladesh Khumi verbal classifiers and Kuki-Chin 'chiming'. *Linguistics of the Tibeto-Burman Area* 31 (1). 109–138.
Peterson, David A. 2010. Khumi elaborate expressions. *Himalayan linguistics* 9 (1). 1–20.
Peterson, David A. 2011. Core participant case marking in Khumi. *Linguistics of the Tibeto-Burman Area* 34 (2). 73–100.
Peterson, David A. 2013a. Aesthetic aspects of Khumi grammar. In Jeffrey P. Williams (ed.), *The aesthetics of grammar: Sound and meaning in the languages of mainland South-east Asia*, 219–236. Cambridge: Cambridge University Press.
Peterson, David A. 2013b. Affecting valence in Khumi. In Balthasar Bickel, Lenore A. Grenoble, David A. Peterson & Alan Timberlake (eds.), *Language typology and historical contingency: In honor of Johanna Nichols*, 171–193. Amsterdam: John Benjamins.
Peterson, David A. 2017. On Kuki-Chin subgrouping. In Picus S. Ding & Jamin Pelkey (eds.), *Sociohistorical linguistics in Southeast Asia: New horizons for Tibeto-Burman studies in honor of David Bradley*, 189–209. Leiden: Brill.
So-Hartmann, Helga. 1988. Notes on the Southern Chin languages. *Linguistics of the Tibeto-Burman Area* 11 (2). 98–119.
So-Hartmann, Helga. 2009. *A descriptive grammar of Daai Chin*. STEDT Monograph 7, UC Berkeley.
Solnit, David. 1995. Parallelism in Kayah Li discourse: Elaborate expressions and beyond. *Berkeley Linguistics Society* 21 [special session]. 127–140.
Solnit, David. 1997. *Eastern Kayah Li: Grammar, Texts, Glossary*. Honolulu: University of Hawai'i Press.
Van Valin, Robert D. & Randy J. LaPolla. 1997. *Syntax: Structure, meaning, and function*. Cambridge: Cambridge University Press.
VanBik, Kenneth. 2009. *Proto-Kuki-Chin: A reconstructed ancestor of the Kuki-Chin languages*. Berkeley: STEDT Project, UC Berkeley.
Watkins, Justin. 2013. A first account of tone in Myebon Sumtu Chin. *Linguistics of the Tibeto-Burman Area* 36 (2). 97–127.

Appendix 1: Summary of linguistic features

Legend
+++ the feature is pervasive or used obligatorily in the language
++ the feature is normal but selectively distributed in the language
+ the feature is merely possible or observable in the language
− the feature is impossible or absent in the language

	Feature	+++/++/+/−	§ ref. in this chapter
Phonetics	Lexical tone or register	+++	§1.1, p.13
Phonetics	Back unrounded vowels	+	§1.2, p.18–19
Phonetics	Initial velar nasal	+	not discussed explicitly
Phonetics	Implosive consonants	−	not discussed explicitly
Phonetics	Sesquisyllabic structures	+++	§1.3, p.19
Morphology	Tendency towards monosyllabicity	++	§2.1, p.19
Morphology	Tendency to form compounds	+++	§2.1, p.20
Morphology	Tendency towards isolating (rather than affixation)	++	§2.1, p.20
Morphology	Psycho-collocations	+	§2.2, p.21
Morphology	Elaborate expressions (e.g. four-syllable or other set patterns)	+++	§2.3, p.22
Morphology	Reduplication generally	++	§2.4, p.22
Morphology	Reduplication of nouns	+	not discussed explicitly
Morphology	Reduplication of verbs	+	not discussed explicitly
Grammar	Use of classifiers	+	§3.1.2, p.28
Grammar	Classifiers used in counting	+	§3.1.2, p.28
Grammar	Classifiers used with demonstratives	−	−
Grammar	Adjectival verbs	+++	§3.1.1, p.26
Grammar	Grammatical number	+	§3 and §3.1.1, p.24
Grammar	Inflection of verbs	++	§3.2.1, p.30
Grammar	Use of tense/aspect markers	+++	§3.2.2, p.32–36
Grammar	Use of verb plural markers	+	§3.2.2, p.32
Grammar	Grammaticalization of GET/OBTAIN (potential mod. resultative/perfect aspect)	+	§3.2.3, p.37
Grammar	Grammaticalization of PUT, SET (completed/resultative aspect)	−	not discussed explicitly
Grammar	Grammaticalization of GIVE (causative, benefactive; preposition)	+++	§3.2.3. not discussed explicitly for causatives, though this is the probable source for prefixal causative, p.36
Grammar	Grammaticalization of FINISH (perfective/complete aspect; conjunction/temporal subordinator)	+	§3.2.3, p.37

	Feature	+++/++/+/−	§ ref. in this chapter
Grammar	Grammaticalization of directional verbs e.g. GO / COME (allative, venitive)	−	not discussed explicitly; Khumi has limited directional phenomena without clear grammaticalization sources; it also has fossilized remnants of a probably Proto-Kuki-Chin-level prefixal venitive, which had COME as its source
Grammar	Grammaticalization of SEE, WATCH (temptative)	+	§3.2.3, p.37
Grammar	Grammaticalization of STAY, REMAIN (progressive and continuous, durative aspects)	−	not discussed explicitly
Grammar	Serial verb constructions	−	§3.2.3, p.36
Syntax	Verb precedes object (VO)	−	−
Syntax	Auxiliary precedes verb	−	−
Syntax	Preposition precedes noun	−	§3.1, p.24
Syntax	Noun precedes adjective	+	§3.1.1, p.25
Syntax	Noun precedes demonstrative	−	§3.1.1, p.25
Syntax	Noun precedes genitive	−	−
Syntax	Noun precedes relative clause	+	§3.1.1, p.25–26
Syntax	Use of topic comment structures	+++	§3.3.2, p.40 & also p.27
Syntax	Ellipsis of arguments known from context	+++	§3.3.1, p.39
Lexical semantics	Specific terms for forms of rice	+++	§4.1.1, p.42
Pragmatics	Use of utterance-final pragmatic particles	+++	§4.2.1, p.44
Pragmatics	Encoding of politeness	−	§4.2.2, p.44
Pragmatics	Encoding of honorifics	−	−

Appendix 2: Interlinearized Text

Treeshrew and Owl

1. *tew^{11}su^1=håy^1*   *bew^{1}ku^{10}=håy^1*   *am^{1}nay^{11}=nö^1=te^1=ba^1*
   treeshrew=COM   owl=COM   be.friends=NMLZ=EVID=EMOT
   'Treeshrew and Owl were friends.'

2. *a¹håy¹=nö¹¹=te¹*
   hang.out=NMLZ=EVID
   'They hung out together.'

3. *ang¹lo¹¹-p'vay¹¹*   *ce¹=bo¹¹=te¹*
   girl-visit.IRR   go=REAL=EVID
   'They went visiting girls (=courting.)'

4. *ang¹lo¹¹-p'vay¹¹ ce¹=kha¹⁰ lang¹⁰ tko¹¹=kha¹⁰ a¹rung¹⁰=nö¹=te⁵*
   girl-visit.IRR go=time.LOC road.LOC go=time.LOC converse=NMLZ=EVID
   'When they went courting, when going along the road, they talked with each other.'

5. *tew¹¹su¹=mö³ (ö) bew¹ku¹⁰=wo¹ ay¹¹ni-² ay¹¹ni² ang¹lo¹¹-pvay¹¹*
   treeshrew=FGD uh   owl=VOC   1D.INCL   1D.INCL girl-visit.IRR

   ce¹=nö¹=a¹   nö¹=te⁵
   go=NMLZ=QUEST   QUOT=EVID
   'Treeshrew said, uh, "Oh, Owl, are we, are we going courting?"'

6. *ay¹¹ni²   m'nö¹=mö³   cång¹=nö¹¹=a¹   nö¹=te⁵*
   1D.INCL   how=FGD (mistake)   be.sold=NMLZ=INTERR   QUOT=EVID
   '"How will we be sold? (=are we going to be handsome enough?)" he said.'

7. *tew¹¹su¹=mö³ (ö) nang¹=lö¹ kay¹=lö¹ l'bewng¹ p'suy¹⁰-ka¹mo¹='e¹ vay¹⁰*
   treeshrew=FGD uh   2S=TOP   1S=TOP   mouth   pointy-INTENS=AFF   later.LOC

   ang¹lo¹¹=cë¹¹=mö² döyng¹¹=b'lö¹ thuy¹¹-pë²   kay¹=lö¹ k'lung⁴ kå¹¹=nö²
   girl=COLL=FGD   ask=SEQ   say-BEN.IMP   1S=TOP   song   POT=NMLZ
   'Treeshrew said, uh, "You, I have a very pointy mouth. Later, if the girls ask, say that I know how to sing songs."'

8. *(ö) a¹lung⁵   öyng¹¹-kå¹=nö² b'lüng⁴ öyng¹¹-kå¹=nö¹=nay¹ra⁴ l'bewng¹*
   uh   gourd.flute   play-POT=NMLZ   flute   play-POT=NMLZ=REAS   mouth

   p'suy¹⁰=nö¹=tew¹=ba¹   nay³   thuy¹¹-pë²=ba¹   bew¹ku¹⁰=wo¹ nö¹=te⁵
   pointy=NMLZ=COP=EMOT   QUOT   say-BEN.IMP=EMOT   owl=VOC   QUOT=EVID
   ' "Say that it's because I can play the gourd flute and the flute, that my mouth is pointy, Owl," he said.'

9. n'b'lö¹ bew¹ku¹⁰=mö² thuy¹¹-pë¹-bë¹⁰=bo¹=te¹   tew¹¹su¹⁰=wa¹   (ö)   kay¹=lö¹
   then   owl=FGD   say-BEN-NEXT-REAL=EVID   treeshrew=LOC   uh   1S=TOP

   möy³   lëng¹¹-ka¹mo¹=nö³   vay¹⁰   ang¹lo¹¹=cë¹¹=mö²   thuy¹¹=b'lö¹   nang⁶
   eye   big-INTENS=NMLZ   later.LOC   girl=COLL=FGD   say=SEQ   2S.GEN

   ahåy¹=lö¹   möy³   lëng¹¹-pray¹=ba¹   m'nö¹-m'nay¹¹=lew¹
   friend=TOP   eye   big-INTENS=EMOT   how-how=QUEST

   h'nay³   möy¹¹=lö¹   nö¹=te⁵
   thus   eye=TOP   QUOT=EVID
   'Then Owl said to Treeshrew, uh, "I have really big eyes. Later, if the girls say, 'Your friend has really big eyes. What's up with such eyes?'"'

10. nay¹¹b'lö¹ prë¹   vä¹   khu¹   vä¹-rë¹   niw¹-thay¹¹=nö² nay³   möy¹¹=nay¹ra⁴
    then   country   all   ELAB   all-count   see-POT=NMLZ   thus   eye=REAS

    kay⁶   möy³ lëng¹¹=nö² nay³ thuy¹¹-pë²=ba¹   tew¹¹su¹=wö¹   nö¹=te⁵
    1S.GEN   eye big=NMLZ   QUOT say-BEN.IMP=EMOT   treeshrew=ENDEAR   QUOT=EVID
    'Then he said, "They are such eyes that I can see all over the country. That's why my eyes are big, you say, Treeshrew."'

11. h'nay³   h'nay³   lew¹-a¹dew¹   kha¹⁰   tä¹-yo¹¹=bo¹=te¹
    thus   thus   word-agree   time.LOC   go-IMPFV=REAL=EVID

    ang¹lo¹¹=teng¹⁰=a¹   ang¹lo¹¹-p'vay¹¹=nö²
    girl=GOAL=LOC   girl-visit=NMLZ
    'When they agreed this way and that, they went to the girls' place, they went courting.'

12. nay³   ang¹lo¹¹=teng¹⁰   töng¹⁰=ma¹b'lö¹   ang¹lo¹¹-p'vay¹¹=nö²   (ö)
    thus   girl=GOAL.LOC   arrive=ANT   girl-visit.IRR=NMLZ   uh

    am¹rü¹=nö¹¹=bo²
    get.ready=NMLZ=REAL
    'So, when they arrived at the girls' place, they got ready to court them.'

13. ang¹lo¹¹=cë¹¹=teng¹⁰   a¹tä¹⁰=ma¹b'lö¹   ang¹lo¹¹=mö²   döyng¹¹=bo¹=te¹
    girl=COLL=GOAL.LOC   sit=ANT   girl=FGD   ask=REAL=EVID

    tew¹¹su¹=wa¹   tew¹¹su¹   (a)   bew¹ku¹⁰=teng¹¹   döyng¹¹=bo¹=te¹   bew¹ku¹⁰='ö¹
    treeshrew=LOC   treeshrew   er   owl=GOAL.LOC   ask=REAL=EVID   owl=ENDEAR

nang⁶   am¹nay¹¹=lö¹   l'bewng¹   p'suy¹⁰-pray¹=bä⁴   nö¹=te⁵
2S.GEN   friend=TOP   mouth   pointy-INTENS=EMOT   QUOT=EVID

'After they sat down at the girls' place, a girl asked Treeshrew, "Treeshrew-" er, she asked Owl, "Owl, your friend has a really pointy mouth." '

14. (*ö*) *kay⁶   am¹nay¹¹=lö¹   l'bewng¹ p'suy¹⁰=nö²*   (*ö*) *b'lüng⁴   öyng¹¹-kå¹-ra⁴*
    uh   1S.GEN   friend=TOP   mouth   pointy=NMLZ   uh   flute   play-POT-REAS

    k'lung⁴   thuy¹¹-kå¹-ra⁴   h'ni³   l'bewng¹   p'suy¹⁰=nö¹=tew²   nö¹=te⁵
    song   sing-POT-REAS   DEM   mouth   pointy=NMLZ=COP   QUOT=EVID

    'Uh, "About my friend's pointy mouth, uh, it's because he can play the flute and sing. His mouth's pointy," he said.'

15. *t'na¹=b'lö¹*   *ang¹lo¹¹=cë¹¹=mö²*   *döyng¹¹-bë¹⁰=bo¹=te¹*   *bew¹ku¹⁰=wa¹*
    little.while=SEQ   girl=COLL-FGD   ask-NEXT=REAL-EVID   owl=LOC

    (*ö*) *h'ni³   tew¹¹su¹=teng¹⁰=a¹*   *tew¹¹su¹='ö¹*   *nang⁶   am¹nay¹¹=lö¹*
    uh   DEM   treeshrew=GOAL=LOC   treeshrew=ENDEAR   2S.GEN   friend=TOP

    nang⁶   am¹nay⁵   bew¹ku¹⁰=lö¹   möy³   lëng¹¹-pray¹=bä⁴   m'nay¹¹-ra¹⁰=lew¹
    2S.GEN   friend   owl=TOP   eye   big-INTENS=EMOT   how-REAS=QUEST

    'After a little while, the girls asked Owl, uh, this treeshrew, "Treeshrew, your friend, your friend Owl has very big eyes. Why is that?" '

16. *kay⁶   am¹nay⁵   bew¹ku¹⁰=lö¹   s'thu¹=lö¹   seng¹pha¹¹=lö¹*
    1S.GEN   friend   owl=TOP   bad.sprit=TOP   bad.spirit=TOP

    nay¹¹ra¹⁰=n'ang¹   möy³   lëng¹¹=nö³   nö¹=te⁵
    therefore=INSIST   eye   big=NMLZ   QUOT=EVID

    ' "My friend Owl is a s'thu, he's a sengpha (types of spirits)! That's of course why his eyes are big," he said.'

17. *nay³   ang¹lo¹¹=cë¹¹=lö¹   nay³   nay³   thuy¹¹-pë¹=b'lö¹   jöy¹¹=nö²   tla¹=bo³*
    thus   girl=COLL=TOP   thus   thus   say-BEN=SEQ   afraid=NMLZ   occur=REAL

    ngay¹²-lä²=bo²   n'blö¹
    want-NEG=REAL   then

    'So the girls, when he said this, were afraid, and they didn't want him then.'

18. *h'ni³   bew¹ku⁴   nay¹¹b'lö¹   k'do¹¹thew¹=b'lö¹*
    DEM   owl   then   get.angry=SEQ

h'nay³   thuy¹¹-pë¹=b'lö¹   tä¹-yo¹¹=bo²
thus   say-BEN=SEQ   go-IMPFV=REAL
'This owl then got angry, when he said this way, and he left.'

19. lä¹⁰-yo¹=bo¹   öy¹nga¹¹=ma⁴   thew¹-yo¹¹=nö²   tla¹=bo³
    run.away-IMPFV=REAL   outside=ALL   go.out-IMPFV=NMLZ   occur=REAL

    ang¹lo¹¹=cë¹¹=mö²   ngay¹²-lä¹=b'lö¹
    girl=COLL-FGD   want-NEG=SEQ
    'He ran away, he went outside, because the girls didn't want him.'

20. nay¹¹b'lö¹   bew¹ku⁴   k'do¹¹thew¹-ra⁴   höy¹⁰   a¹pay¹¹nga¹¹
    then   owl   get.angry-REAS.LOC   here.LOC   village.entrance.LOC

    h'ni³   våy¹⁰=nö²   lang¹=ma⁴   a¹jöyng¹⁰-pö¹=b'lö¹   bäng-
    DEM   return=NMLZ   road=ALL   wait-DIMVCL=SEQ   (mistake)

    tew¹¹su¹   töng¹⁰-töng¹⁰=råy¹¹=sö²
    treeshrew   arrive-arrive=PERS=HORT
    'Then because Owl was angry, here, at the village entrance, at his return path, he waited for him. "Just let Tewsu come back!"'

21. töm¹⁰=b'lö¹   a¹mö¹=pö¹   p'nö¹¹=bo²   nö¹=te⁵   nö-   k'do¹¹-thew¹=nö²
    arrive=SEQ   3S.REFL=FOC   know=REAL   QUOT=EVID   (mistake) angry=NMLZ
    '"He knows what will happen if he comes back," he said, he was angry.'

22. nay³   tew¹¹su¹   ang¹lo¹¹-p'vay¹¹=cung¹   p'yo¹=cung¹⁰=b'lö¹   b'lüng⁴
    thus   treeshrew   girl-visit=FINISH   enjoy=FINISH=SEQ   flute

    öyng¹¹=t'råy¹   lang¹=ma⁴   t'ko¹¹=bo¹=te¹   tä¹=bo¹¹=te¹   våy¹⁰=nö¹=ma⁴
    play=CONTEMP   road=ALL   go=REAL=EVID   go=REAL=EVID   return.IRR=NMLZ=ALL
    'So Treeshrew finished courting, finished enjoying, and playing a flute, went on the road, set out on the path to return.'

23. nay³   bew¹ku¹⁰=mö²   a¹jöyng¹⁰='ö¹=b'lö¹   bew¹ku¹⁰=mö²   tläng¹¹mö³
    thus   owl=FGD   wait=ALREADY=SEQ   owl=FGD   suddenly

    h'ni³   a¹mö⁶   lu¹⁰=wa¹   ca¹-vuy¹¹=bo¹=te¹
    DEM   3S.GEN   head=LOC   eat-PFV=REAL=EVID
    'So Owl was already waiting, and suddenly Owl ate his head.'

24. *lu⁴   p'siw¹-vuy¹¹=nö²   tla¹=bo³   nay³   lu⁴   p'siw¹=cung¹⁰=b'lö¹*
    head suck.clean-PFV=NMLZ occur=REAL thus head suck.clean=FINISH=SEQ

    h'ni³   lu¹⁰ka¹kew²   a¹pay¹¹nga¹¹   biwng¹¹-pë¹-hä¹=te⁵
    DEM   skull   village.entrance.LOC   stick.in.ground-MAL-DIMVCL=EVID
    'He sucked the head clean, and when he thus sucked it clean, he stuck this skull into the ground at the village entrance way.'

25. *nay¹¹b'lö¹   tëng¹-vuy¹¹=bo²*
    then   finish-PFV=REAL
    'Then it's finished.'

26. *h'tang¹-rë¹=ya¹*
    to.this.extent-COUNT=LOC
    'Up to this point.'

Alice Vittrant
Burmese

Introduction

Burmese, the national language of Burma (or Myanmar), has been the official language of the country since 1948. Burmese is spoken as a mother tongue by two-third of a population[1] estimated at 52 million[2], that is to say, by around 35 million people (Bradley 1997, 2007, Watkins, 2007: 266). Burmese is spoken mainly[3] in Burma. The standard dialect, the one presented here, has evolved from a central dialect spoken along the lower valleys of the Irrawaddy and Chindwin rivers. It is the dialect taught in schools throughout Burma, and the one used on TV and radio. However, other varieties of Burmese[4] exist in outlying areas, some of them with scant mutual intelligibility, the best known of them being Arakanese or Rakhine (in Rakine State), Marma (west Burma, near the Bangladesh border), Intha (Shan state), Tavoyan (south coast, Tenasserim), and Yaw (west of the Irrawaddy). The dialects differ from the standard variety mostly in pronunciation, but also in lexis and grammar.

Beside Burmese, there are seven other officially-recognized languages in Burma, each of them being the language of a state: Arakanese, Chin, Kachin, Kayah, Kayin (or Karen), Shan and Mon. The first five are more or less closely related to Burmese (Tibeto-Burman language family), whereas Shan and Mon belong respectively to the Tai-Kadai and Mon-Khmer families.

---

1 The lastest complete census dates from 1931, providing information about the ethnicity and linguistic membership of the population. It stated that Burmese was the mother tongue of 67% of the population (Allott 1985: 131).
2 The results of the 2015 Myanmar population census shows a total population of 51, 486, 253. See *The Myanmar Population and Housing Census- Hightlights of the Main Results- Census Report Volume 2–A*, published by the Department of Population, Ministry of Immigration and Population, May 2015., p. 2. Accessible on line.
3 Burmese is not used to a significant extent outside of Burma other than by Burmese expatriates. According to Egreteau (2012: 304), more than 3 millions of Burmese live outside of Burma (Thailand, Singapore, Australia and other western countries).
4 On Burmese dialects other than Standard Burmese, see Lucien Bernot (2000: 60, 74), Denise Bernot (1958), Okell (1995), Bradley (1979: 72sq.).

Alice Vittrant: Aix-Marseille Université / CNRS-DDL (UMR 5596)
E-Mail: alice.vittrant@cnrs.fr

https://doi.org/10.1515/9783110401981-003

Other languages are spoken in Burma besides these official languages. Ethnologue lists more than one hundred individual languages for this country, most of them belonging to the Tibeto-Burman family. See also Bradley (2007a, b) on the endangered languages of Burma.

Burmese is classified as a Lolo-Burmese language within the Tibeto-Burman (henceforth TB) family (Sino-Tibetan *phylum*). Detailed classifications of TB languages are provided by Matisoff (1986), (1991), Bradley (1994), (2002), and Thurgood & Lapolla (2003). It is the most important TB language and one of the larger languages of the Sino-Tibetan family, along with Chinese dialects, in number of speakers.

Burmese is also one of the few TB languages with an original writing system and literacy tradition, alongside Tibetan, Manipuri (or Meithei) and Naxi. It is documented since the twelfth century[5]. Burmese script, adopted through Mon, is originally derived from *Nâgari* — or *Devanâgari*, a script of *Brâhmi*, used to transcribe the Indo-European languages of India, such as Sanskrit or Pali, and therefore not well suited for transcribing a tonal language like Burmese.

Burmese script is an abugida (or alphasyllabary)[6] script, with each unit denoting a consonant with a particular vowel (an [a] in Burmese). Burmese script contains 33 consonants of that type, some of which are only used for transcribing mainly Pali loanwords. Tones may also be indicated in the script, combined with vowel quality.

Pali, an Indian language used for Buddhist texts, was introduced to Burma through the Mon culture. When King Anawratha (AD 1044–77) established Buddhism as the official religion of his new state, it became the language of religion and literature (Allott, 1985: 133), a prestigious language favoring the unification of the emerging kingdom.

Burmese inevitably borrowed heavily from Pali. However the influence of Pali was not limited to the religious and philosophical domains: it also served as a model in elaborating legal codes (Pruitt, 1994: 25) and grammars. Finally, loanwords from Pali are found in several domains, such as poetry, astrology, medicine and daily life (Hla Pe 1961; Yanson 1994). Examples of Pali loanwords will be given in section § 2.1.3. on loanwords.

---

5 The earliest dated forms of Burmese script are found in Pagan on the Myazedi quadrilingual pillar (1112 A.D), which consists of an inscription related to Prince Rajakumar, in four languages: Pali, Mon, Pyu and Burmese.
6 Abugida (or alphasyllabary) is a writing system in which vowels are represented by subsidiary symbols, as opposed to a regular alphabet, where consonants and vowels have equal status. See Swank (2009) on the two terms and the relevancy of their definitions.

A general presentation of Burmese language would not be complete without mentioning the diglossia between the spoken (vernacular) and written (literary) registers. Westerners based in Burma in previous centuries (19th and 20th centuries) reported a marked difference between the two styles. Indeed, the relative stability of literary Burmese has to be compared to the rapid evolution of vernacular Burmese between the 15th and the 20th centuries (Allott, 1985: 135). However, the diglossia is now decreasing: the emergence and development of new media (newspapers, magazines, websites, blogs) has compelled literary Burmese to become more like vernacular Burmese. Today, the main differences lie in functional-grammatical morphemes (verbal markers, nominal markers, connectors, etc.) as shown in examples (1) and (2), where the difference between markers is highlighted in bold.

(1) a. လူကြီးများသည် ယဉ်ကျေးသောကလေးများကို ချစ်သည်။ [Written Burmese]
   lu². Ci³ **mya³** =**θi²** yiN². Ce³ =**θɔ³** kəle³-**mya³** =Ko² Chi? **θi²**
   adult PLUR S polite REL child-PLUR OBJ love REAL

   b. လူကြီးတွေက ယဉ်ကျေးတဲ့ ကလေးတွေကို ချစ်တယ်။ [Spoken Burmese]
   lu².Ci³-**Twe²** =**Ka¹** yaN².Ce³ **Tɛ¹** kəle³-**Twe²** =Ko² Chi? =**Tɛ²**
   adult-PLUR S polite REL child-PLUR OBJ love REAL
   Adults love polite kids. (lit. Adults love children who are polite.)

(2) a. မိုးရွာလျှင် ကျွန်မ၏အခန်းသို့လာ၍ ဖတ်တတ်ပါသည်။ [Written Burmese]
   mo³ ywa²=**lyiN²** cəma¹ =**ʔi¹** ʔəkʰaN³ =**θo¹** la² =**ywe¹** pʰaʔ taʔ =Pa² =**θi²**
   rainfall SUB 1SG POSS room DIR come SUB.TPS read HABIT POL REAL

   b. မိုးရွာရင် ကျွန်မ(ရဲ့)အခန်းလာပြီး ဖတ်တတ်ပါတယ်။ [Spoken Burmese]
   mo³ ywa²=**yiN²** cəma¹ (=**ye¹**) ʔəkʰaN³Ø la² =**Pyi³** pʰaʔ taʔ =Pa²=**Tɛ²**
   rain fall SUB 1SG (POSS) room (DIR) come SUB.TPS read HABIT POL REAL
   If/When it is raining, (he) is used to come to (/and) read in my room.

In this chapter, we will study vernacular or spoken Burmese and we will make little reference to literary or Written Burmese (WB). Our fieldwork has been conducted mainly in Yangon and Pagan (Central Burma). Therefore our examples will be utterances of the standard variety of Burmese (SB), although we may occasionally mention variations found in other dialects.

1 Phonology

The common phonological features observed in languages of the area are: a complex vowel system (diphthongs, large numbers of vowels, contrastive vowel length), tones or register (or mixed) systems, a restricted set of final consonants; and a restricted set of consonant clusters (Enfield, 2005: 186 sqq). The extent to which these features are found in Burmese will be discussed in the following sections.

1.1 Segmental phonemes: consonants and vowels

The Burmese phonological system has already been described in many works, some general studies such as Min Latt 1962, Okell 1969, Bernot 1980, Wheatley 1982, and some specific papers (Sprigg 1957, Bernot, 1963, Bradley 1982, Watkins 2000, 2001, Dubach Green 2004). Burmese dialect phonologies have also been studied (see Bernot 1958 on Marma, Sprigg 1963, Bernot 1965), often within a comparative perspective (Bradley 1985b, Okell 1995).

1.1.1 Consonants

- **Onset consonants**

Burmese consonants may be divided into three series: plain, voiced and aspirated. In word-initial position voiced consonants are less common than plain or aspirate consonants, and occur mainly in nouns. Table 1 shows the full inventory of Burmese consonants that surface as initials of main syllables.

Table 1: Burmese Consonants

stops/affricates					nasales				fricatives				Approximants			
p	t	tɕ	k	ʔ	m̥	n̥	ɲ̊	ŋ̊	θ	s	ʃ	h				
pʰ	tʰ	tɕʰ	kʰ							sʰ			ʍ	(ɹ)	ɬ	
b	d	dʑ	g		m	n	ɲ	ŋ	ð	z			w		l	j

- **Coda consonants**

As in most of the SEA languages described in this book, the coda consonants consist of a small subset of the initial consonants although Written Burmese shows that it was not always the case — see Bradley (1985b: 191ff.) on the evolution of Burmese dialect rhymes.

As stated by Matisoff (1973b: 80), on the general evolution of syllables in Asian languages, tones appear with the decay and the loss of initial and final consonants in languages that have a predisposition (monosyllabicity) to develop tones.

"It was only when the old consonantal system had decayed through cluster simplification, losses, mergers that the daughter languages were forced to exploit [those] pitch-differences for contrastive purposes." (Matisoff, 1973b: 79)

Thus, changes have occurred in the Burmese syllable structure, with a clear consonantal decay for final nasals and stops. For instance, the four-way contrast among the nasal stops reduced to a simple nasal feature that has lost its point of occlusion and is realized according to the phonological context, e.g. it tends to assimilate to the position of the following initial consonant as in (3). While the contrast between final stops has been reduced to a glottal stop, giving rise to checked syllables (see example (4)).

Today, the Burmese coda consonant inventory is reduced to two items: a nasal consonant (with various realizations) transcribed with a capital /N/, and a glottal stop /ʔ/.

(3) a. ဆင်း   [sʰiːn⁵²]   /shiN³/   to go down, descend
       ဆင်းပါ   [sʰiːm⁵² ba²²] /shiN³ Pa²/   Please go down
       ဆင်းတာ   [sʰiːn⁵² da²²] /shiN³ Ta²/   (the fact) X go/went down
       ဆင်းခဲ့   [sʰiːŋ⁵² gɛ⁵⁵] /shiN³ Khɛ¹/   went down (+ change of situation)

   b. ဓာတ်   [daʔ]   /daʔ/   element, mineral, essence, force
       ဓာတ်ပုံ   [dap pon²²]   /daʔ PouN²/   photograph
       ဓာတ်ခဲ   [dakʰkʰɛ⁵²]   /daʔ Khɛ³/   battery

(4)   a. တပ်   b. တတ်   c. တက်   d. လပ်   e. လတ်   f. လက်
    WB   <tap>   <tat>   <tak>   <lap>   <lat>   <lak>
    Transc. taʔ   taʔ   tɛʔ   laʔ   laʔ   lɛʔ
         fix, attach be skilled go up   be vacant be fresh   hand

• **Clusters**

Onset consonants may be followed by a glide, either [j] or [w], that may be realized "as a secondary labialization or palatalization of the first position consonant" (Watkins 2001: 292), as shown by example (5).

(5) a. ရွာ   'village'   /ywa²/   > [jwa²²]
but b. သွား   'to go'   /θwa³/   > [θʷaː⁵²]
     c. များ   'many' (PL)   /mya³/   > [mʲaː⁵²]

However, no cluster is uttered in Standard Burmese (SB), although they were present in old Burmese (Matisoff, 1973b)[7] and are still present in some dialects. Thus, Arakanese is well known for its conservative use of the approximant [ɹ], realized as a glide or a palatalization in SB.

For instance, the words meaning 'to like' or 'to fear' are pronounced with the cluster [kɹ] (transcribed /kr/) in Arakanese, and with an affricate consonant in Burmese. Intha and Tavoyan, on the other hand, have kept a cluster with the approximant [l], again realized as a glide in modern Standard Burmese (6c) (see Okell 1995 for details). Example (7) illustrates cluster pronunciations in four dialects.

(6) a. ကြိုက် 'to like'   WB <kruik> Arakanese [kɹaɪʔ] SB [tʃaɪʔ]
    b. ကြောက် 'to fear'   WB <krok>   Arakanese [kɹaʊʔ] SB [tʃaʊʔ]
    c. ခြောက် 'to frighten' WB <khrok> Intha   [klɔʔ]   SB [tʃʰaʊʔ]

(7)	Old Written Burmese	WB	SB	Arakan.	Intha	Tavoyan
be full	plañń	prañń. ပြည်	pye¹	pre¹	ple¹	plɛ¹
between	('a)krā	('a)krā (အ)ကြား	ca³ [tʃa⁵²]	kra³	kla³	kla³
be fast		mran မြန်	myaN	mrɛn	mlan	byan

Adapted from Okell 1995 & Nishi 1998

1.1.2 Vowels

The Burmese vowel system shows four degrees of openness as shown by table 2. However the roundness feature is not relevant to distinguishing phonemes, unlike what is found in many other languages of the area such as Hmong and Khmer (See Mong Leng rhymes p. 612 and Khmer syllabic Nuclei p. 322).

---

[7] Matisoff (1973: 78): "Written Burmese (WB) syllables may have initial consonant clusters of up to three members, but no more than a single consonant in final position: <mrwe> 'snake', <krwat> 'leech', <krwak > 'rat'.

Table 2: Simple Burmese vowels

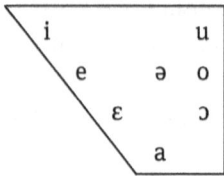

Notice also that vowel values vary according to whether the syllable is open or closed: diphthong correlate with coda consonants and do not appear in open syllables (Bradley 1982)[8]. This makes it possible to describe the vowel system using nine vowels only, the realizations depending on the syllable structure (see Watkins 2000 for details). Table (3) presents the different vowel realizations in different contexts.

Finally length is not a feature relevant to distinguish phonological vowels. However and as we will see in next section, it may be used to describe tones.

Table 3: Nine Burmese vowels and their realizations in different contexts

Syllable ending								
-V	i	e	ɛ	a/ɑ	ə	ɔ	o	u
-VN	ɪ	eɪ		a		aɪ	aʊ	oʊ	ʊ
-Vʔ	ɪ	eɪ	ɛ	a		aɪ	aʊ	oʊ	ʊ
Transcription	*i*	*e/ei*	*ɛ*	*a*		*ai*	*ɔ/aɔ*	*o/ou*	*u*

To summarize, simple vowels appear in open syllables and only /i, ɛ, a, u/ may appear in close syllables. The consonant coda may trigger a change in the vowel value, leading to diphthongs in checked and nasalized syllables.

1.1.3 Tones

- **Emergence of Tones**

It is generally admitted that tones emerged from syllabic reduction under certain conditions (e.g. monosyllabicity). Tonogenesis is best explained as a compensatory mechanism for the loss of consonantal contrasts either in initial or fi-

---

[8] Bradley (1982: 121): "The 'killed' type occurs only with a final stop. [...] Burmese orthography still represents the positions of these stops, but in modern spoken dialects the features of the stop have been 'shuffled' into the vocalic nuclei. As a result, the vowel system in killed syllables (and in nasalized syllables, [...]) is radically different from that of open syllables."

nal position (see section § 1.1.1 on final consonants). Tonogenesis in the Lolo-Burmese branch is well understood (Matisoff 1999, Abramson 2004, Michaud 2011) despite a complex interaction of initials, syllable-types (complex syllables with cluster or prefix) and codas (open or close syllables). It is beyond the aim of this grammatical sketch to draw a complete picture of the origin of tones in Burmese. However, tonal correspondences between languages of the family are fairly good, and Burmese tones can be traced back to proto-Lolo-Burmese reconstructed tones as shown in table 4.

- **Burmese, how many tones?**

Although authors working on Burmese language agree on its tonal nature, the consensus does not go far. Suprasegmental systems of SEA languages are hardly ever described in terms of one parameter only, and a comparison of the Burmese tonal system descriptions as provided by Watkins (2000: 140) shows the lack of consensus on important issues such as pitch characteristics, phonation and glottalization. Burmese tone descriptions vary according to what is understood as 'tone', what is considered as part of the syllable structure, and what is due to context (sandhi phenomena).

Regarding the number of tones, some authors have analyzed the language as having up to five opposed suprasegmentals (Bradley 1982), whereas other authors postulate either 4 or 3 contrastive tones (respectively Cornyn 1944, Wheatley 1987, Okell 1969, Watkins 2000 for the former proposal and Bernot 1963, 1980 for the latter). In this study, we will consider Burmese tonal system as having a four-contrast system, as illustrated in (8). Syllables that are not reduced (see § 1.2 on syllabic structure) carry one of these four tones, which may be described more accurately in terms of pitch (contour), phonation type, length and intensity (see table 4).

(8) စ /sa/ Tone 1 (high, creaky, short) 'start, begin'
    စာ /sa/ Tone 2 (low, long) 'letter'
    စား /sa/ Tone 3 (high-falling, breathy) 'eat'
    စပ် /saʔ/ Checked Tone (glottal stop) 'hot, spicy'

Table 4: Burmese tones description
Adapted from Bradley (1982: 122), Matisoff (1999: 17)

tone name	pitch	contour	phonation	duration	intensity	transcription	Proto-Lolo-Burmese Tone
'even'/low	low	level	normal	long	low	2	*1
'heavy'/high	fairly high	sharp fall	breathy	long	high	3	*2
'creaky'	high	slight fall with weak glottal stop[9]	creaky	short	high	1	*3
		with different vowel nucleus possibilities, and a final stop					
'killed' (or checked)	high	variable with glottal stop	normal	very short	high	?	

To summarize, the first three tones are found in either open or nasalized syllables. The 'killed' or checked tone is only found in syllables ending with a (glottal) stop, sometimes realized as homorganic stops.

1.1.4 Juncture or sandhi

The realization of the initial consonant (as well as the coda) is often conditioned by the degree of tightness (or juncture) between syllables. In connected speech or within compounds (9)b, assimilatory processes are at work.

(9) a. ဟင်းခတ် b. ဟင်းခတ် c. ဟင်းခတ်မှုန့်
    hiN³ kha?   hiN³-Kha?   hiN³-Kha?- mouN¹
    [hiŋ³ kʰa?]   [hiŋ³-ga?]   [hiŋ³-ga?- m̥õ(n)¹]
    curry (n.) + put in (v.)   curry-put.in (n.)   curry-put.in-powder (n.)
    to add condiment to dishes   condiment   sodium glutamate

For instance, the voiced quality of a consonant depends on the previous (or following) consonant. We have already mentioned the relatively low proportion of

---

9 On creaky tone and differences between creaky and checked tones, see Thurgood 1981, Bradley 1982, Watkins 2000.

voiced consonants in Burmese (see § 1.1.1.) However, an unvoiced consonant may be realized as voiced in close juncture, as in example (10).

(10) a. ဖြည်း   b. ဖြည်းဖြည်း   c. ငါး   d. ငါးထုပ်
     phye³   phye³-**PH**ye³   ŋa³   ŋə- THɔʔ
     [pʰje³]   [pʰje³.**bje³**]   [ŋa³]   [ŋə. **doʔ**]
     slow   slow (x2)   fish   fish-wrap
     slow   slowly (adv)   fish   fish fritters

Other assimilatory processes may:

(i) assign the point of articulation to a nasalized final consonant (see example 3 above),

(ii) realize a (glottal) stop as an homorganic stop, i.e. articulated similarly to the initial consonant of the following syllable as in (4) or (11).

(iii) replace a syllable with an unstressed and tonally non-contrastive one as in (12): for instance, the disyllabic word 'thief' in (a) is composed with /θu²/ (3sg pronoun or agent-nominalizer) and /kho³/ 'to steal'; it is however uttered with a reduced first syllable, i.e. creating a sesquisyllabic word (see sections § 1.2 and § 2.1 respectively on syllable structure and word structure).

Notice that in the case of sesquisyllabic words, the assimilatory process may affect the entire word: the consonant of the reduced syllable may become voiced (see (13) a), although this voicing process often does not occur when the initial consonant of the major syllable is aspirated (13)c.[10]

(11) သစ်   [θiʔ]   / θiʔ/   wood[11]
     သစ်ခိုင်း   [θikʰ kʰain⁵²]   / θiʔ KhaiN³/   branch
     သစ်သီး   [θiθ θi⁵²]   / θiʔ θi³/   tree's fruit
     သစ်ပင်   [θip pin²²]   / θiʔ PiN²/   tree
     သစ်တော   [θit tɔ⁵²]   / θiʔ Tɔ³/   forest

(12) a. သူခိုး   b. လူတစ်ယောက်
        θu² + kho³ > θə.kho³   lu²+ tiʔ + yaɔʔ > lu. tə. yaɔʔ
        3SG/NMLZ steal   man one CLF
        thief   one man

---

10 The image is more complex than that we described here. See Bernot (1958: 198 ff.) for details.
11 Adapted from Bernot (1958: 209).

(13) a. စားပွဲ b. ငါးဆုပ် c. ပုဆိုး
sa³+pwɛ³>[zə.bwɛ⁵²]   ŋa³+shoʔ>[ŋə.sʰoʔ]   puˡ+sho³>[pə.sʰo⁵²]
eat festival   fish handful   ??short dye
table   fish ball   men's sarong

One way to represent these phonetic variations or realization relying on the context (close juncture, compounding) is to use a capital letter to show when a phoneme may be subject to voicing, that is to say as an archiphoneme symbol.

1.1.5 Summary

In this section, we have described the phonological system of SB, which contains 34 consonants (most of them used only in initial position) and 9 phonological vowels (their realization depending of the syllable structure and/or the tone). In this system, aspiration is a much more relevant feature than voicing as generally observed in SEA languages. However, no uvular-velar distinction nor pre-glottalized or pre-nasalized consonants, are found in SB, all features often said to be shared by MSEA languages. The onset is simpler in Burmese than in other languages of the area. The Burmese vowel system is far less complex than those of other SEA languages (compare Hmong or Vietnamese), but it does have a mixed supra-segmental system, properly described in terms of pitch, contour and phonation.

1.2 Syllable structure:

Two syllable types need to be distinguished in Burmese: full major syllables and reduced minor syllables.

Minor syllables are unstressed and tonally neutral. Their distinctive phonological features are confined to the onset consonants, the vowel quality being reduced to a schwa (14).

Major syllable structure is given in (15). It can be characterized by the following properties:
- it contains any vowel except the schwa
- it bears tone except in checked syllables
- it may have a simple (C) or a complex onset (CG)

Notice also that a vowel cannot appear in initial position, and that consonant clusters are not found in Standard Burmese, as seen in § 1.1.1.

(14) a. ပုခက်   b. ငါးပိ
    pə.kʰɛʔ   ŋə.pi¹
    Cə.CVC   Cə.CVᵀ
    cradle   fermented fish paste

(15)   (Tone)
    Cᵢ   (G)   V   (C)

2 Morphology

2.1 Word structure

2.1.1 General facts

- **Monosyllabicity**

Burmese, like the other languages of the area, lacks extensive morphology and shows a greater tendency to monosyllabicity compared with other Tibeto-Burman languages such as Jinghpo (Matisoff, 1999: 14). Although most Burmese words are made of one syllable, looking at Burmese data gives the impression of multi-syllabic words. This is due to a great use of compounding (§ 2.1.2.), which offsets the low proportion of sesquisyllabic and disyllabic words. Sesquisyllabic structures, i.e. "morphemes that are a syllable and half in length" (Matisoff, 1973b: 86), appear both in the lexicon (16) and also in tight collocations (17). Disyllabic words on the other hand are often loan words from Pali, Mon or other languages (see § 2.1.4). Disyllabic words of Burmese origin may be compounds with an unpredictable meaning (18) or with a meaningless rhyming[12] syllable (19).

(16) a. စားပွဲ   (Written Burm.) sa: (eat)+pwɛ: (party) > **[zə bwɛ⁵²]** 'table'
     b. ကစား:   (WB) ka + sa: > **[gə za⁵²]** 'to play'
     c. ငါးမန်း   (WB) ŋa: (fish)+ man: > **[ŋə mɛ̃⁵²]** 'shark'
     d. ပုဇွန်   (WB) pu' + swan   > **[bə zõ(n)²²]** 'shrimp'

(17) a. လူနှစ်ယောက်   b. တစ်ခါ   c. သူကြီး
     lu²   ɲiʔ   yaɔʔ   tiʔ   kha²   θu²   Ciʸ
     [lu²² nə   yaɔʔ]   [tə   kha²²]   [θə   dʑi⁵²]
     person two CLF:hum   one   moment   3SG   big
     'two persons'   'once'   'village head-man'

---

12 On rhyming and chiming syllables in Burmese, see Wheatley (1985: 35–36).

Disyllabic words in (18) are idiomatic expressions: the meaning of the whole does not correspond to the meaning of the components, as shown by the gloss.

(18) a. ဆုံးဖြတ် b. စဉ်းစား c. ပြုစား
     shouN³ phya?   siN³ Sa³ [sĭn⁵²za⁵²]   pyu¹ Sa³ [pju⁵⁵za⁵²]
     conclude cut   mince eat/consume   act eat
     'to decide'   'think'   'bewitch, captivate'

In each word presented in (19), rhymes are identical in both syllables, but only the first one is meaningful.

(19) a. ခေါ်ဝေါ် b. ခင်မင် c. လှပ
     khɔ² wɔ²   khiN² miN²   la¹ pa¹
     call EUPH   friendly EUPH   pretty EUPH
     'call, name'   'be friendly with/ fond of'   'be beautiful'

- **Analytic or agglutinative language?**

Burmese is generally held to be a non-inflectional language (Min Latt 1962: 103), although the 'induced creaky tone' phenomenon — change of tone fulfilling several grammatical and pragmatic functions (Allott 1967)[13]—, can be considered as inflectional. While most words are monomorphemic, productive processes of compounding and lexicalization often create polysyllabic words. Due to its one-to-one correspondence of morphemes to words, Burmese can be seen as an isolating or analytic language (ex (9)). It is, however, also considered as an agglutinative language by some authors (Wheatley 1990[14], Delancey (1990: 78), Bernot 2010) given its use of some derivational morphology, illustrated in (10) (see section § 3.4.2 on nominalization processes). Compounding seems, however, more widespread than derivation.

(20) a. လှောင်ကန် b. လှောင်အိမ် c. မျက်လှည့်ဆရာ
     laɔn².KaN²   laɔn².ʔeiN²   myɛʔ- lɛ¹-sʰəya²
     store up.pool   store up.house   eye – twist/rotate – master
     'tank'   'cage'   'magician'

---

13 Delancey (1987: 120) sums up the various functions of the creaky tone upon words with low or high tones: abruptness and urgency (pragmatic function), repeated words, possession or attribution, grammatical dependency mainly with human referent objects.
14 In a previous work, Wheatley (1985: 28) analyses Burmese as an isolating language, thereby confirming the difficulty of deciding on a morphological type for Burmese.

(21) a. အလုပ်   b. ပြောကြားချက်   c. ကစားစရာ
       ʔə-loʔ   pyɔ³-Ca³-Chɛʔ   gəza³-Səya²
       NMLZ- work (v.)   talk-hear-NMLZ   play-NMLZ
       'work (n.)'   'speech'   'toys'

Although some morphemes may be considered as real affixes i.e. bound morphemes, others are better analysed as clitics, as they behave syntactically as free morphemes but show evidence of being phonologically bound. Clitics in Burmese are functional elements such as syntactic / pragmatic particles (/nɛ¹/, /Ka¹/, /Ko²/, /Ma²/...), negation, politeness and TAM operators (/Tɛ²/...), etc.

(22) ခွေးနဲ့လူက အိပ်ပျော်တဲ့အချိန်မှာ ဖားလေးကအပြင်ကို ထွက်သွားတယ်။   [MoMo, 05_frog2]

khwe³ = nɛ¹	lu² = Ka¹	ʔeiʔ.pyɔ²	= Tɛ¹	ʔəcheiN² = Ma²
dog=with	man=TOP	sleep	=REL.REAL	moment = LOC
pha³-le³ = Ka¹	ʔəpyiN² = Ko²	thwɛʔ	θwa³	= Tɛ²
frog-DIM =S. /TOP	outside=DIR	go out	CTFG	= REAL

'As the dog and the man [boy] were sleeping, the little frog 'went-out' outside.'

2.1.2 Compounding and class terms

As stated earlier, compounding is a frequent device in Burmese[15]. However, the line between lexical and syntactic compounds is not always easy to draw (see (23)a although some lexical compounds are easily distinguishable in particular when the compound items are semantically related: synonymous or similar terms (24)a & b, opposite terms (c), or superordinate terms (25). Notice that 'pleonastic' compounds such as (24)a & b, are mainly used in formal and literary styles to add weight and colour to regular monosyllabic forms.

(23) a. မြွေအရေခွံအိတ်   b. စာတိုက်   c. စားပွဲခင်း
       mwe² ʔəye² KhuN² ʔeiʔ   sa² Taiʔ   Sə Pwe³ KhiN³
                                                      [zəbwɛgin]
       snake skin peel/skin bag   letter building   eat.festival [table]
                                                      spread
       'tortoiseshell-plastic bag' 'post office'   'tablecloth'

---

15 See Wheatley (1985: 40sq) and Bernot (2005) on Burmese compounds.

(24) a. ပြောဆို b. ဖြူဖွေး c. ရောင်းဝယ်
     pyɔ³ sho²   pyu² phwe³   yaɔN³ wɛ²
     say say/sing white white   sell buy
     'say'   'be white'   'trade'

(25) a. ရိုက်နှိပ် b. ကျိုးပဲ့ c. ဝေလငါး
     yai? ɲei?   co³ pɛ¹   we² la¹ ŋa³
     hit/strike press break break off/chip 'whale' fish
     'stamp, imprint' 'chip'   'whale'

Compounding is a favorite way of coining new technical vocabulary in Burmese (26)[16]. It is also used extensively in some semantic domains such as wildlife and plants, according to typological studies (Grinevald 2000: 59). Fruits, plants and flowers are therefore designated by the name of the species followed by a generic term indicating the part of the plant in question, i.e. the class term (table 5)[17].

(26) a. ချက်လက်မှတ် b. ယာဉ်မောင်းလိုင်စင်   b. အဝတ်လျှော်စက်
     cɛ? lɛ?.m̥a?   yaN² maɔN³ laiN²siN²   ʔəwaʔ ʃɔ² Sɛ?
     'check'-note   yāna (vehicle) drive 'license' cloth wash machine
     'check (n.)'   'driving license'   'washing machine'

Table 5: CLASS TERMS in the botanical domain (fruits, plants and flowers)

	FRUIT			PLANT	
1a	ငှက်ပျော သီး: ŋəpyɔ³ -θi³ specie - FRUIT	banana	1b	ငှက်ပျော ပင် ŋəpyɔ³ -PiN² specie - PLANT	banana tree
2a	သရက် သီး: θəyɛʔ - θi³ specie - FRUIT	mango	2b	သရက် ပင် θəyɛʔ - PiN² specie - PLANT	mango tree
3a	သံလွင် သီး: θaN²lwiN² - θi³ specie - FRUIT	olive	3b	သံလွင် ပင် θaN²lwiN² - PiN² specie - PLANT	olive tree

---

16 On Burmese lexicon, see Bernot & Pemaungtin (1966), Bernot (1994), Kasevitch (1994).
17 Burling (1984: 14): "... *noun compound constructed from a categorizing initial portion to which is added one or more syllables that indicate the specific member of the category*". See also Jacquesson (1998).

	Fruit		**Plant**	
4a	စံပယ် ပန်း zəPɛ² - PaN³ specie - FLOWER	jasmine (flower)	4b	စံပယ် ပင် zəPɛ² - PiN² specie - PLANT	jasmine plant
5a	ဒေလီယာ ပန်း de² li² ya² - PaN³ specie - FLOWER	dahlia (flower)	5b	ဒေလီယာ ပင် de² li² ya² - PiN² specie - PLANT	dahlia plant
6a	ဒေစီ ပန်း de²si² - PaN³ specie - FLOWER	daisy (flower)	6b	ဒေစီပင် de²si² - PiN² specie - PLANT	daisy plant

Class terms are restricted to lexical composition; unlike classifiers (see § 3.2.3), they have no functional use. They characterize the noun and co-occur with it; they also correlate with inherent semantic features of the noun, and often display a generic-specific relationship with it (Vittrant 2005:138).

Class terms may be used as general nouns. They therefore appear with a nominalizing prefix as in (27)b.

(27) a. ... အသီးတွေ လျှောက်ခူးနေတယ် ။ [AA/08, 55_001]
       ?ə-θi³   =Twe²   ʃɔɔʔ   khu³   ne²   =Tɛ²
       NMLZ-fruit = PLUR walk>at random pick stay>INACC =REAL
       '(He) is picking fruits at random.'

   b. ကောင်မလေးက ငှက်ပျောသီး ပေးတယ် ။ [HNTH/08, 29_011]
      kɔɔN²ma²-le³   =Ka¹   ŋəpyɔ³-**θi³**   pe³   =Tɛ²
      woman-DIM   =S/top banana-**fruit** give   =REAL
      'The young lady, (she) gives/ gave (him) banana(s).'

Vittrant (2005) shows that Burmese has superimposed strata of noun classification systems:
(1) an old stage of classifying prefixes, similar to those found in other languages of the family such as Naga or Lushai, (Matisoff 1999: 16), with possibly a phonetic erosion of the classificatory prefix leading to sesquisyllabic word (see fish compounds),
(2) a new stage following the syntactic determination construction with categorizing morphemes (superordinate or generic nouns) ending the compound, similar in position to head nouns appearing in final position in the Noun Phrase (§ 3.2), and based on taxonomy.

Subsequently, the second categorizing structure may enter into competition with the old structure, as shown by the doublets shaded in table 6. However, while this second process is productive (see names for imported flowers *dahlia* and *daisy* in table 5 above), it seems restricted to the usual fields in which languages of the world categorize, i.e. the plant and animal realms.

Finally, notice that the same morpheme occurs either as a categorizing prefix or as a suffix, but that it does not match the usual numeral classifier used for those nouns (Vittrant, 2005: 146–47).

Table 6: Two structures for noun classification

prefixed class term (1)			suffixed class term (2)		
1.	ငါး မန်း	shark	3.	ဝင်ပေါင်စာ ငါး	white bellied opsarion
	ŋə – maN³			yiN² paɔN² sa² – ŋa³	
	FISH – *name*			*name* – FISH	
2.	ငှက် ခါး	jay	4.	သိမ်း ငှက်	falcon
	ŋɛʔ – kha³			θeiN³ – ŋɛʔ	
	BIRD – *name*			*name* – BIRD	
5a.	ငါး ဝေလ	whale	5b.	ဝေလ ငါး	whale
	ŋə – waN²			we² la¹ – ŋa³	
	FISH – *name*			*name* – FISH	
6a.	ငှက် ကြီးဝန်ပို	pelican	6b.	ဝန်ပို ငှက်	pelican
	ŋɛʔ – Cl³ waN² po¹			waN² po¹ – ŋɛʔ	
	BIRD *name*			*name* BIRD	

To sum up, Burmese like other languages in the area (Thai, Vietnamese), displays a class term device, partly related to its classifier device[18] (cf. § 3.2.3).

2.1.3 Loanwords

Loanwords[19] constitute the majority of dissyllabic words (other than compounds) in Burmese lexicon. The more ancient and numerous ones are from Pali, the language of Buddhist scriptures and a highly esteemed language in the area (Hla Pe 1961, Yanson 1994). Most of these loanwords concern abstract vocabulary, philosophy and religion (28)a, b.

---

18 DeLancey, in his history of the Tai classifier system, says that *'lexically the two categories overlap to a considerable degree'* (1986: 442), and suggests that CLASS TERMS [*class nouns in De Lancey's terms*] provide a source for Numeral Classifiers (1986: 445–46).
19 On loanwords and neologisms in Burmese, see Hla Pe (1961), (1967), Bernot (1979), Bernot & Pemaungtin (1966), Wheatley & Hnin Tun (1999), Bernot & al (2001: 67sq). On political and religious vocabulary, see Kasevitch (1994).

(28) a. စက်   < Pali *cakka* (wheel)   b. ပညာ   < Pali *paññā* (wisdom)
sɛʔ
'machine'
pyiN²ɲa²
'knowledge'

c. ရုပ်ရှင်   < Pali *rupā*[20] (form)   d. မှန်ဘီလူး   < Burmese မှန် /maN²/ (glass)

     + Burmese ရှင် /ʃiN²/   + Pali *bīruka* bhīru
     (alive)   (ogre)
yoʔ ʃiN²   maN² biʔlu³
'movies'   'microscope'

Moreover, Pali has been the main source for new lexical material throughout Burmese history as Latin and Greek were for European languages, and specialized words in Burmese often contain Pali material, frequently compounded with native stock (28)c, d.

Beside Pali, two other languages have given significant linguistic material to Burmese: chronogically, the first is Mon, and the more recent is English. Mon loanwords are mainly cultural (architecture, artistic, customs, etc.), whereas English provides new words related to technical innovations, fashion and politics (29).

Loanwords from other languages like Chinese, Persian, Arabic, Hindi, Malaysian, Shan and French are also found in Burmese (30).

(29) c. ဖိနပ်   a. ဆိုက်ကား   b. ဒီမိုကရေစီ
pənaʔ   shaiʔ ka³   di² mo² kə re² si²
khanap < MON   side-car < ENG   democracy < ENG
'shoes'   'Burmese trishaw'   'democracy'

(30) a. လုံချည်   b. ခေါက်ဆွဲ   c. အရက်
louN² Chi²   khaɔʔ shwɛ³   ʔəyɛʔ
long skirt < PERSIAN   noodles < SHAN, THAI   arak < ARABIC
'Burmese sarong'   'noodles'   'alcool'

---

20 The transliteration of the Burmese term pronounced /yoʔ/ is <rup>.

2.2 Psycho-collocations and elaborate expressions

'Expressives' are one of those striking similarities between Southeast Asian languages, at the crossroad of the phonetic, morphosyntactic and semantic domains that are regularly omitted or neglected in grammars, maybe because they are extremely difficult to elicit in the field. They rarely appear in declarative and neutral speech, as they represent an attempt by the speaker to transmit a sensation to the hearer.

Nonetheless, expressives constitute yet a fundamental word class in many of these languages. These idiomatic forms — sometimes also known as ideophones, 'onomatopoetic' forms or 'phonaesthetic' words — express emotional phenomena and display special phonological and structural properties with often a 'direct' or 'unmediated' relation to meaning (Vittrant, 2013: 255–56). In Burmese, these are of two kinds: psycho-collocations and elaborate expressions.

2.2.1 Psycho-collocations

The human body is frequently used as a metaphorical source domain across languages. Thus, body parts, either internal or external, are easily conceptualized as the locus of emotions and mental states. As such, they are regularly invoked in the description of these states and processes.

MSEA languages make a great use of polymorphemic expressions known as 'psycho-collocations'[21], and described for a number of MSEA languages (Matisoff 1986; Jaisser 1990; Clark 1996; VanBik 1997; Vittrant 2013). They involve metaphorical uses of high-frequency adjectives (or verbs) explicitly collocated with body-part terms to refer to psychological phenomenon (emotional and mental states or processes, physical and emotional feelings). These psycho-collocation constructions are also peculiar in terms of their structure: the psycho-nouns generally do not have argument status, the noun and the verb being semantically tight and working as single predicate[22].

---

[21] The term 'psycho-collocation' was coined by Matisoff (1986a: 7): *"Psycho-collocation [is] a polymorphemic expression referring as a whole to a mental process, quality, or state, one of whose constituents is a psycho-noun, i.e. a noun with explicit psychological reference (translatable by English words like heart, mind, spirit, soul, temper, nature, disposition, mood). The rest of the psy[cho]-collocation contains morphemes (usually action verbs or adjectives) that complete the meaning. This element we call the psycho-mate".*

[22] Psycho-collocation constructions raise the question of the relationship between the verb and the body-part term and the status of the latter as being incorporated into the verb. See Vittrant (2013: 271 sq) on syntactic properties of these constructions.

Although these 'body part-adjective' expressions may be seen as part of a universal metaphorical tendency, there seems to be a qualitative difference in the extremes to which MSEA languages carry this tendency: most of these languages cannot express mental activities, emotion, or character features without referring to a body part. However, beside the cross-cultural or universal status of the metaphors involved in these psycho-collocations, there are culture-specific ways of combining psycho-nouns and psycho-mates, i.e. body-part terms and predicates: every language has its favorite location for psychological states and feelings, either the heart as in English and Thai (cf. p. 566–67), the liver as in Malay and Hmong (cf. p. 484 and p. 617), or the guts or the stomach as in Vietnamese (cf. p. 395).

Burmese preferred body-part term for psycho-collocations is စိတ် *sei?* 'mind'[23], although other internal organs such as 'heart', 'liver', 'belly' also appear in collocation with stative verbs[24], as shown by examples (31) and (32).

(31) a. ... သူ့အဖေ သူ့အပေါ်မှာ စိတ်ကုန်သွားပြီ ။
... θu^1 $?\text{\textipa{e}}phe^2$ θu^1 $?\text{\textipa{e}}-p\text{\textipa{O}}^2$ =Ma^2 **sei? -kouN² θwa^3** =Pyi^2
3SG.GEN father 3SG.GEN NMLZ-top =LOC   **mind run**   ACC =CRS
                                                          out

'His father is fed up with him [because....].'

b. စိတ် ပေါက်   c. စိတ်တို   d. စိတ်ရှုပ်
   sei? pɔ?   *sei? to²*   *sei? ʃo?*
   mind + explode   mind + be short   mind + be complex
   '*become angry*'   'to be short-tempered'   'be confused'

(32) ကျမ အသည်းကို မခွဲပါနဲ့ ။
     cəma¹ *?əθɛ³*   =$Ko²$ *mə*= $k^hw\varepsilon^3$ =Pa^2 =$n\varepsilon^1$
     1SG   **liver** =OBJ   NEG=   **break/split**   =POL   =INJ
     '(Please), don't break my heart.'

2.2.2 Elaborate expressions

In many Asian languages, expressives appear in a specific form, intermediate in structure between an ordinary compound and reduplication. They are known as

---

23 The word စိတ် /sei?/ (transliterated *cit*) comes from Pali *citta*, via Mon. Interestingly, the same etymon is found as a psycho-noun in other Southeast Asian languages, such as Mon (See example (3), p. 286) or Khmer (See Table 2, p. 335).
24 See Vittrant (2013: 267 ff) for a more detailed list of psycho-nouns in Burmese.

'elaborate expressions' (Haas 1964), and have been described by Matisoff (1973: 81) as "a compound containing four (usually monosyllabic) elements, of which either the first and third or the second and fourth are identical (A-B-A-C or A-B-C-B) [and that] characteristically convey a rather formal or elegant impression.". The two non-reduplicated elements of the quadrisyllabic expression (bold terms in (33)) are usually referred to as an 'elaborate couplet,' i.e. pair of phonologically different but roughly synonymous or antonymic morphemes that conventionally appear together.

(33) a. မနီး မဝေး
    mə - ni³-   mə - we³
    NEG **close** NEG **far**
    'not so far, (to be) at a good distance'

b. ခြေစ လက်စ
    che² - Sa¹-   lɛʔ - Sa¹
    foot begin **hand** begin
    'aptitude, qualification'

These expressions usually function as adverbials (34), but, as shown by the Burmese example (33)b), they may form nominal compounds or other parts of speech (Wheatley 2013: 237).

(34) a. ကိုကိုမောင်သည် ... ခုတင်ပေါ် တွင် ခြေပစ်လက်ပစ် လဲနေလေသည်။
    [literary Burmese][25]
    ko²ko²maɔN² =θi² ...   KəTiN²   Pɔ²=TwiN²   **che²-Piʔ-lɛʔ-Piʔ**
    Ko Ko Maung =S./TOP   bed   top =LOC   <u>foot-throw-hand-throw</u>
    lɛ³   ne²   le²=θi²
    lie   INACC   EUPH =REAL
    'Ko Ko Maung [after...] lay down on the bed without a care in the world [in the state of exhaustion]'

2.3 Reduplication

Reduplication in Burmese concerns mainly the major parts of speech, i.e. the noun and the verb, and two kinds of reduplication are distinguished here[26]:
1. **simple reduplication** corresponds to a simple copy (total or partial) of a lexical root associated with a change of meaning or value

---

[25] From Bernot (1989–88), vol. 3: 131.
[26] Stolz et al (2011) provides an excellent review of works (and definitions) on reduplication. For a more detailed list of reduplication processes in Burmese, see Okell & Allott (2001: 274–75), Vittrant & Robin (2007).

2. **complex reduplication** involves, beside the lexical root and its copy, another item inextricably linked to the process of reduplication, either morphologically or syntactically.

2.3.1 Simple reduplication

Simple reduplication may occur with nouns, although the process is more frequent with verbs. A reduplicated nominal form unsurprisingly means plurality of the referent designated by the noun. However, it differs from the sequence [noun + plural morpheme တွေ /Twe^2/] (see § 3.2 on Noun Phrase). While this sequence means several occurrences of the N, the reduplicated form specifies sequential occurrences that have to be considered as a whole, as shown in (35).

(35) နင် မိုးမိုးရဲ့ဦးလေးနဲ့ ခဏခဏ တွေ့ဖြစ်(သ)လား ။
　　 niN^2　mo^{3}mo^3　=yɛ^1　ʔu^{3}le^3　=nɛ^1　**khəna^1-khəna^1**　twe^1　phyiʔ　(θə)　　　=la^3
　　 2SG　Moe Moe　=GEN uncle　=with **often**　　　　　　　　meet POSSIB (QST.REAL) =QST
　　 'Do you often have the opportunity to meet Moe Moe's uncle?'

Verb reduplication is more frequent and has two different values depending on the type of verb and the context: quantification (repeated actions) or qualification (modifying actions).
– The quantification carried by the reduplication process may be iterative, habitual (36)(a), continuative (b) or distributive (37). In all these cases, the reduplicated form keeps its verbal properties, being the head of the verbal phrase. It however must have an auxiliary following.

(36) a.　ဝယ်ဝယ် ပေးလာတယ် ။
　　　　 wɛ^{2}wɛ^2　　pe^3　　　la^2　　　　=Tɛ^2
　　　　 buy (x2)　　 BENEF　　come/CPETE　=REAL
　　　　 (He) came and bought (things) for me several times or
　　　　 '(He) used to buy and bring me (things).'

　　 b.　ကျမ ရှင့်ကို ပြောပြောနေတာပေါ့ ။
　　　　 cəma^1　　ʃiN^1　　　=Ko^2　　pyɔ^3 pyɔ^3　ne^2　　　=Ta^2　　=Pɔ^1
　　　　 1SG.FEM　 2SG.DAT　　=OBJ　　tell (x2)　　　INACC　 =REAL.NF　=DM
　　　　 'I am telling (it) to you constantly! (or I tell (it) to you again and again).'

In (36)(b) above, the repeated verb ပြော /pyɔ³/ indicates an action occurring several times, while the auxiliary နေ /neˀ²/ carries the continuity of this repetition, rather than the repetition itself.

Example (37) shows the distributive value of verb reduplication. These sentences refer to sequential actions implying different participants, either the agents (a) or the beneficiaries (b) of the action. In (a), several persons do the same action while in (b) one person does the same action once for each child. Thus, the distributive interpretation requires the presence of a plural argument in the sentence.

(37) a. ကျမကလေး အလုပ်ရဖို့ သူတို့ဘဲ ပြောပြောပေးနေတယ် ။
cəma¹   khəle³   ʔəloʔ   ya¹   =Pho¹ θu²-To¹   bɛ³   pyɔ³ pyɔ³   pe³
1SG.FEM child work obtain =SUB 3-COLL only tell (x2) BENEF

ne²   =Tɛ²
INACC =REAL
'They were the ones who kept intervening to help my child get a job.'
(lit. Only they intervened on behalf of me to help my child to get a job.)

b. ကျမကလေးတွေ အလုပ်ရဖို့ သူတို့ဘဲ ပြောပြောပေးနေတယ် ။
cəma¹   khəle³ =Twe²   ʔəloʔ   ya¹   Pho¹ θu² -To¹   bɛ³   pyɔ³ pyɔ³
1SG.FEM child =PLUR work obtain SUB 3SG =PLUR only tell (x2)

pe³   ne²   =Tɛ²
BENEF INACC =REAL
'It was he who kept intervening to help my children get a job.'
(lit. Only he intervened on behalf of me to help my **children** to get some job.)

- In qualifying reduplication, the repeated verb modifies another verb, i.e. the head verb (in bold). The process often adds intensification. The reduplicated form may be either mono-morphemic or a compound as shown respectively in (38)a & b. In colloquial speech, the repeated form may undergo slight changes, the rhyme becoming /-ɛʔ/ as in (39) (See Okell & Allott, 2001: 273).

(38) a. ကောင်းကောင်း စောင့်ရှောက် ခံရတဲ့ကလေးက ...
KaɔN³ KaɔN³   saɔN¹ ʃaɔʔ   KhaN²   ya¹   =Tɛ¹   khəle³   =Ka¹ ...
be good (x 2) look.after suffer GET =REL:R. child =TOP
'A child that is looked after very well... [will be happy].'

b. ပြေပြေ ပြစ်ပြစ် လက်ခံကြိုဆို ပါတယ် ။[27]
   pye² Pye² pyiʔ Pyiʔ   lɛʔ khaN²   co²Sho²   =Pa²   =Tɛ²
   adapted, smooth (x 2)   harbour.sb   welcome   =POL   =REAL

   < ပြေ ပြစ်
   [pye²pyiʔ]
   [be smooth, adapted]
   '(She) welcomed and hosted (him) smoothly.' (Fr. *Elle l'accueillit sans difficulté*).

(39) a. ခဲတံကို အမြန် ကောက်ကက် ယူတယ်။
   khe³TaN²   =Ko²   ʔə-myaN²   **kɔʔ kɛʔ**   yu²   =Tɛ²
   pencil   =OBJ   NMLZ-fast   **pick.up-(x2)**   take   =REAL
   '(He) swiftly snatched up the pencil].'

  b. ကြည့်ကြက်လည့် သွားအုံး ။
   Ci² Cɛʔ   lɛ³   θwa³   =ʔouN³
   look (x2)   also   go   =ITER.PROSP
   'Look carefully while going.'   or   'Be careful when going (there).'

2.3.2 Complex or constructional reduplication

Complex reduplication involving another item inextricably linked to the process of reduplication appears in both the nominal and verbal domains.

Within the nominal domain, the reduplication process is typically a morphological process, involving a nominalizing prefix, or other phonologically reduced syllables. In (40), the prefix အ /ʔə-/ appears with a repeated noun adding the meaning of genericity. In (41), an indefinite NP is created by reduplicating the classifier with the reduced form of the numeral 'one'.

(40) a. မြို့   b. အမြို့မြို့
   myo¹   ʔə-   myo¹ myo¹
   town   NMLZ   town (x2)
   'town'   'towns in general, various towns'

---

27 Adapted from Bernot (1978–88), vol. 10, p. 85.

(41) တစ်ယောက်ယောက် လာမယ် ။
    tə-   yaɔʔ yaɔʔ   laˀ   =mɛˀ
    one-   CLF:HUM (x2)   come   =IRR
    'Someone will come.'

Two types of complex verbal reduplication are illustrated below. One is a morphological process similar to the nominal one above, involving prefixes and creating verbal modifiers as in (42) and (43)[28]. Example (44) compares different verbal modifiers from the same verbal root[29].

(42) ဒီမနက်လေ တဖြူးဖြူး တိုက်နေတယ် ။
    diˀ   mənɛʔ   leˀ   tə-   phyu³ Phyu³   taiʔ   ne²   =Tɛ²
    DEM   morning wind   PFX-   **sprinkle (x2)** blow   INACC   =REAL
    'The breeze blows gently this morning.'

(43) a. ခပ်ဟောင်းဟောင်းပဲ ။   b. တဖြေးဖြေးစား ။
        khəʔ-   haɔN² haɔN²   be³   tə -   phye³Phye³   sa³
        PRF (adv)- be old (x2) DM:excl   PFX-   be slow (x2) eat
        'It is pretty old!'   'Eat slowly.'

(44) a. မြန်   b. အမြန်
        myaN⁴   ʔə-myaN⁴
        be fast, quick   NMLZ-fast
        'fast'   'quickly'

     c. မြန်မြန်   d. ခပ်မြန်မြန်
        myaN² myaN²   khəʔ-myaN² myaN²
        fast (x2)   PFX(adv) - fast (x2)
        'quickly, rapidly'   'very fast, very quickly'

The second type of verb reduplication is better analyzed as part of a syntactic process. For instance, the reduplication of the verb is triggered by the use of the subordinator ချင်း /ChiN³/ in (45). Other syntactic structures conveying meanings such as goal, concession (46), epistemicity (47)b, emphasis or intensification (47)a, require repeating the verb, the two occurrences being sometimes separated by various morphemes (conjunction, subordinator, discourse marker, etc.). See Okell & Allott (2001: 151), Vittrant (2004: 347 ff).

---

[28] See Bernot & *al.* (2001: 122sq), Okell & Allott (2001: 257) for more examples.
[29] See Vittrant & Robin (2007: 84) for other similar examples.

(45) အကြော်သည်း အော်သံကြားကြားချင်း သူ ပြေးထွက်တယ် ။
    ʔə-cɔ²-θɛ³   ʔɔ²-θaN²   ca³ Ca³   =ChiN³   θu²   pye²   thwɛʔ   =Tɛ²
    NMLZ-fry-AGENT shout-cry   **hear(x2)** SUB   3SG   run   go.out =REAL
    'He runs out as soon as he hears the cry of the fried-food seller.'[30]

(46) နင် ဘာပြောပြော ငါကြည့်ကြည့်နေတယ် ။
    niN²   ba²   **pyɔ³ pyɔ³**   ŋa²   ci¹ ci¹   ne²   =Tɛ²
    2SG   QST   **tell (x2)**   1SG   look (x2)   INACC   =REAL
    '**Whatever** you say, I am watching you constantly.'[31]

(47) a. စားတော့ စားတယ် ၊ ဒါပေမဲ့ မဝဘူး ။
    sa³   =Tɔ¹   **sa³**   =Tɛ²   da²Pe²mɛ¹   mə=   wa¹   =Phu³
    eat(1) DM:even **eat(2)** =REAL   but   NEG=   be fat   =NEG
    'As for eating, (he) is eating; but (he) does not become fat.'

    b. မနက်ဖြန် သူ လာရင်လာမယ် ။[32]
    mənɛʔphyaN²   θu²   **la²**   =yiN²   **la²**   =Mɛ²
    tomorrow   3SG   **come**   =SUB   **come**   =IRR.
    'He may come tomorrow [but I am not sure].'

3 Grammar and Syntax

Burmese has been studied by Western scholars since the 18th century (Pruitt, 1994: 35). Missionaries wrote the first grammars and dictionaries in Western languages, including the English-Burmese dictionary by the American Baptist Judson in (1852), followed by other language studies by both Western and Burmese scholars – Saint-John (1936), Cornyn (1944), Stewart (1936), Pe Maung Tin (1956) and Min Latt (1962-63-64).

More recent works also contain good descriptions of the language that avoid the Latin-Greek framework imposed by Western grammatical traditions. See Allott (1965), Okell (1969), Bernot (1980), Wheatley (1982), Bernot & al.

---

30 From Allott & Okell (2001: 38).
31 This structure is similar in meaning to the nominal reduplication used to create indefinite nouns. It also carries an indefinite meaning.
32 This reduplication expression may be analyzed as a merging of two clauses : လာချင်ရင် /la² CiN² =yiN²/ come-desire-if "If you wish to come", and လာမယ် /la²=Mɛ²/ come-IRREALIS/ "you could come".

(2001), Okell & Allott (2001), Vittrant (2004) Watkins (ed.) (2005) and Jenny & Hnin Tun (2016) among others.

The influence of Pali on Burmese grammar is substantial and started in the early Burmese kingdom (Esche, 1994: 395)[33], with a continuous attempt to adapt Burmese to Pali grammatical rules[34]. For instance, contemporary Burmese grammars analyze the language in terms of the Pali tradition, with inherited grammatical categories whose existence may be doubtful in Burmese. Pali was an Indo-European language, structurally distant from Tibeto-Burman.

3.1 General facts word classes

3.1.1 Parts of speech in traditional Burmese grammar

Traditional Burmese grammar distinguishes nine parts of speech (ဝါစင်္ဂ/ waziŋga/) comprising lexical (ပုဒ် /po?/) and grammatical categories[35]. Lexical categories include ကြိယာ /kəri²ya²/ 'verb' and နာမ် /naN²/ 'noun'. The adjective and adverb categories, whose statuses are controversial (Wheatley 1982: 87, Bernot 1983, Vittrant 2004: 119) are related to the verb and noun categories and respectively called ကြိယာ-ဝိသေသန /kəri²ya² – wi¹θe²θəna¹/ and နာမ်-ဝိသေသန /naN² – wi¹θe²θəna¹/, where the second term means ' qualifiying'.

Regarding grammatical categories, Burmese, based on the Pali tradition, distinguishes 3 types of function word : ဝိဘတ် /wi¹ba?/ from Pali '*vibhatti*' (division, grammatical inflection), ပစ္စည်း /pyi?si³/ from '*paccaya*' (cause, means) and သမ္ဗန္ဓ /θaN²baN²da¹/ from '*sambandha*' (connection).

These unsuitable transplanted categories are quite heterogeneous, including morphemes with various functions. For instance, the modal verb morpheme လိမ့် /leiN¹/ conveying probability, and also case markers က /Ka¹/ or ကို /Ko²/, are all described as ဝိဘတ် /wi¹ba?/ in the Burmese dictionary published by the Ministry of Education in Yangon (1991). By contrast, ပစ္စည်း /pyi?si³/ (a word which also means 'thing, item') includes nominalizing affixes, but also auxiliary verbs such as နေ /ne²/ 'to stay' > INACC (progressive or stative aspect).

---

[33] Esche (1994: 395): "Already during the Bagan times the strictly regulated grammar of Pali and Sanskrit was highly appreciated and therefore regarded as a shining example for the compilation of original works."
[34] See for instance the study of Burmese grammar within a Pali framework by Aung San Hta Sayadaw (1748).
[35] Bernot & al (2001: 16) gives a table of Burmese traditional grammatical and lexical categories with approximate corresponding terms in French grammar.

Thus next section presents a list of word categories based on the interactional and functional properties they can assume in modern Burmese.

3.1.2 Defining parts of speech in contemporary Burmese

A tentative list of part of speech comprises the lexical categories noun, verb, pronoun and classifier, and the grammatical categories postposition, demonstrative and subordinator (or conjunction). The categories adjective and adverb categories may be added to this list although these lexical categories contain very few members.

- **Noun**

Nouns are generally mono-morphemic (apart from the compounds). However, there is a small set of complex nouns that consist of a noun (or a root) preceded by a nominalizing prefix (48) or another noun it modifies (49). They are called 'Relator nouns' (RN) by DeLancey (1997) — a category that comprises Okell's 'Subordinate-nouns' and 'Location-Nouns' (also known as 'Internal Localization Nouns'[36]) (Okell, 1969: 141–144).

RNs are defined by their ability to follow a lexical noun with no genitive marking, and by their use of the nominalizing prefix အ /ʔə-/ when appearing as a lexical noun as in (49)b.

Nouns can be followed by a quantifier or a postposition associated to nominal functions.

(48) စားပွဲ ၊ ကုလားထိုင်အစား ဖျာခင်းမယ်။ [from Bernot & al, 2001: 93]
SəPwɛ³   kəlɑ³.thaiN²   **ʔə.sa³**   phya²   khiN³   =Mɛ²
table   Indian.seat   **instead.of** mat   spread =IRR
'We will put a mat instead of tables and chairs.'

(49) a. ဂူပေါက်ထဲကို ဝင်လာတယ် ။
gu² . pɔʔ $t^hɛ^3$=Ko²   wiN²   la²   =Tɛ²
cave. opening   **interior**=DIR   go.in   come/CPETE   =REAL
'(She) enters [towards DC] **in** the cave.'

---

[36] 'Internal Localization Nouns' (ILN) may be viewed as a kind of NR. They are lexical items which refer to a portion of an entity as opposed to a whole entity, for instance: top, front, edge, interior, corner, etc. They form a sub-class of nouns that exhibit spatial relational features. They also tend to form frozen complex postpositions. On ILN, see Borillo 1988, Aurnague 1989, and Aurnague & al 2000.

b. ဂူအပြင်ကို ထွက်သွားတယ် ။
   gu² **ʔə.pyiN²**= Ko²   tʰwɛʔ   θwa³   =Tɛ²
   cave **NMLZ-exterior** = DIR   go.out   go/CFUGE   =REAL
   '[She] went out to the **exterior** of the cave (away from DC).'

- **Pronoun**

Burmese pronouns are of nominal origin. Following the cross-linguistic tendency in SEA languages (Ishiyama, 2008: 205), (Cooke, 1968), Burmese first and second person pronouns originated from the words meaning respectively 'slave, servant' and 'master, lord, king' (see table 7). Unsurprisingly, while the lexical source of these pronouns expresses the social relationship between the speaker and the addressee, that of the third person pronoun is rather different. It simply denotes a 'person', a 'human' and rarely an 'object'.

As shown by table (7), first and second person pronouns are numerous. They differ in the degree of respect and politeness appropriate to the relationship between the speaker and hearer, reflecting their relative status and age. They are also differentiated by the sex of the speaker.

Table 7: Burmese Pronouns adapted from Bernot & al (2001: 100–102), Okell (1969: 100–101)

FIRST PERSON: I (WE)			
Burmese form	sex of the speaker	original meaning	degree of politeness
ငါ	ŋa²	male & female	< *proto-TB	familiar
ကျုပ်	coʔ	male	slave	fairly polite
ကျွန်တော်	cənɔ²	male	royal slave	polite
ကျွန်မ	cəma¹	female	female slave	polite
တို့ / ဒို့	to¹ / do¹	plural (we)		familiar
တပည့်တော်(မ)	təpi¹Tɔ²(ma¹)	male (female)	honorable disciple	speaking to monks
SECOND PERSON: YOU			
Burmese form	sex of the speaker	original meaning	degree of politeness
နင်	niN²	male & female		familiar
မင်း	miN³	male & female	king	familiar
ခင်ဗျား	kəmya³	male	lord, master	polite
ရှင်	ʃiN²	female	lord, master	polite
ညည်း	ɲiN³	female (to female)		familiar
အရှင်ဘုရား	ʔəʃiN² pʰəya³	male & female	lord Buddha	speaking to monks
THIRD PERSON: HE, SHE, (IT)			
Burmese form	sex of the speaker	original meaning	degree of politeness
သူ	θu²	male & female	person	

Moreover, relational terms such as kinship terms (အဖေ /ʔəphe²/ 'father', အမေ /ʔəme²/ 'mother', ဒေါ် /dɔ²/ 'aunt', ...), proper names and titles (ဆရာ /səya²/, ...) may be used as pronouns, referring to first or second person. In these cases, the context will indicate to which grammatical person the term refers. In (50), the expression အမေတို့ /ʔə.me²-To¹/ 'mother-COLL' refers to a first person singular despite the collective marker: the author, a sixties-year-old woman, wrote for young people. She refers to herself as a mother, as a member of the mother class.

(50) မင်းတို့က အမေတို့ ဆဲတဲ့အဆဲကို နားလည်ကြရဲ့လား။ [B2/11]
miN³-To¹ =Ka¹ ʔə.me²-To¹ shɛ³ =Tɛ¹ ʔə.shɛ³ =Ko²
2P-COLL =TOP mother-COLL [> 1P] insult(v.) =REL.REAL NMLZ.insult =OBJ.

na³.lɛ² =Ca¹ =yɛ¹ la³
understand =PLUR =REAL QST
'Eh you! Do you understand the insults that I [of the mother class] was using?'

Pronouns differ from common nouns in several syntactic respects. They may not be determined by a demonstrative, nor may they be reduplicated. Finally, pronouns are frequently omitted in natural speech, as they generally refer to accessible referents.

• **Adverb**
As mentioned before, the 'adverb' category is questionable: almost all the expressions that appear in the adverbial function as modifiers of verbs are transparently derived from verbs by processes of reduplication (44), prefixation (42), (43), (44), rhyme or chime (i.e. elaborate expressions).

There are few adverbs that are not derived from a verb: a few monomorphemic words borrowed from pali (51) alongs with frozen expressions that have become institutionalized enough to be considered as true adverbs such as လုံးဝ /louN³.wa¹/ 'totally' (from <'be round' + 'be full') (52) or တခါတလေ /təkʰa² təle²/ 'sometimes' (from < အခါ /ʔə.kʰa² / 'moment' + ?).

(51) a. မုချလာမယ်။ b. ကောင်မလေးကလဲ တကယ်ချစ်တယ်။ [SSN_3]
 moʔcha¹ la² =mɛ² kaɔN²ma²-le³ =Ka¹ lɛ³ **tə-gɛ²** chiʔ =Tɛ²
 certainly come =IRR woman-DIM =TOP also **really** love =REAL
 '(I) will **certainly** 'The young lady, she also **really** loved
 come.' [him].'

(52) သူ မိတ်ဆွေ လုံးဝ မရှိတာ ... [HP-10]
θu² mei?shwe² **louN³.wa¹** mə= ʃi¹ =Ta² ...
3SG friend ADV [be round. be full] NEG= have =REAL.NF
[Maybe] he *didn't have any friends* [at Hogwarts].
(lit. ... he totally did not have friends)

Lastly, onomatopoeic expressions such as ideophones that refer to noise, animal cries, mental states and the like, could also be classified as adverbs. These elaborate expressions[37], generally formed by reduplication of an element (cf. § 2.2.2), display acoustic symbolism and function as verb modifiers.

(53) ဒီစကားကြားတာနဲ့ သူတခစ်ခစ်ရယ်တော့တယ် ॥ [DB/6, p.84]
di² SəKa³ ca³ =Ta² =nɛ¹ θu¹ **tə-kʰi?-kʰi?** yei²
DEM speech hear =NMLZ.REAL =with 3SG sound.of.discreet.laugh laugh

=Tɔ¹ =Tɛ²
=ASP =REAL
Hearing that, he starts to giggle.

- **Adjective**

Adjectives are not a universal linguistic category: many languages have no separate class of words referring to properties and qualities, whereas other languages only have a small, closed set of adjectives at their disposal. Burmese belongs to the second type. Beside a rather small set of adjectives — mostly loans from Pali —, adjectival words are better analyzed as a subclass of verbs, i.e. stative verbs. When used predicatively, they function like intransitive verbs, and they generally cannot directly modify or qualify a following noun.

Notice, however, that a few common stative verbs, used within a large semantic domain and referring to fundamental qualities (i.e. 'big, good, bad, etc...), may be used attributively without a relator term (see လူကြီး /lu²-Ci³/ human-big > 'adult' in example 1). They are closely associated with the noun they modify and their initial consonant becomes voiced (table 8).

---

[37] On expressives and elaborate expressions, see Vittrant (2013) and Wheatley (2013).

Table 8: Burmese adjectives

Position	Burmese form		Meaning
– N	ပထမ –	pətʰəma¹-	first
– N	ဒုတိယ –	du¹ti¹ya¹-	second
– N	သာမန်-	θa²maN²-	ordinary
– N	အဓိက	ʔədi¹ka¹-	principal
– N	ယာယီ	ya²yi²-	temporary
N–	ကြီး	-Cî³	big
N–	ကောင်း	-KɔN³	good
N–	လှ	-l̥a¹	beautiful, pretty
N–	နီ	-ni²	red[38]

- **Classifier**

Classifiers may be viewed as a sub-class of nouns as in Vietnamese (cf. this volume, p. 398). They may also be considered as a grammatical category rather than a lexical one, given the functional properties associated with these words (numeration, individuation...). However, given their large numbers, and the fact that they are not a closed category (see repeater CLFs in section § 3.2.3), we list them within the lexical categories, and they will be examined in detail in section § 3.2.3.

- **Grammatical categories or function words**

Different classes of function word must be distinguished in Burmese, based on form, semantics and distributional properties. Thus, according to the grammatical level at which the words are used (sentential, clausal or phrasal), we distinguish the following subclasses, of which only the 'clause final particle' subclass will be detailed here:
– sentence particles (discourse markers): cf. § 4.2 *on pragmatics and discourse*
– clause-final particles (subordinating conjunctions)
– nominal particles: cf. § 3.2.2 *on relators*
– verbal particles: cf. § 3.3.2 *on verbal categories*

---

[38] Color terms, as often in languages, constitute a sub-class of stative verbs with particular syntactic properties. Thus for instance, beside ကားနီ /ka³ ni²/, "red car", it is possible to get ကားနီနီ /ka³ ni² ni²/ or ကားအနီ /ka³ ʔəni²/ with equivalent meanings.

In these subclasses, the term *'particle'* designates an invariable morpheme that is not syntactically autonomous and generally functions as a bound (or clitic) grammatical morpheme without lexical meaning, at least synchronically.

Clause-final particles are function words used to mark a dependency between a head constituent (the main clause, the head noun) and its modifiers (subordinating clauses, relative clauses), in other terms 'subordinating conjunctions' at clausal level[39]. For instance, the marker တဲ့ /Tɛ¹/ in example (38) relates the head noun 'child' to the preceding relative clause (cf. also (22), (50), (65), (66) and (73)).

Example (54) shows two clause-final particles, the conditional subordinating marker ရင် /yiN²/ and the causal marker လို့ /lo¹/. As *clause-final particles*, they appear at the end of the clause in place of a *Verb-Final Particle* (VFP) that indicates the status of the event and the finiteness of the clause (see Vittrant *to appear*).

Table 9 gives a list of the main clause final particles with their semantics[40].

(54) ဒါပေမယ့် ဒီအတိုင်း ဆက်သွားရင် သူငတ်လို့သေနိုင်တယ် ။ [HP/22–24]
 da²pe²mɛ¹ di² ʔə-TaiN³ sʰɛʔ θwa³ =yiN² θu² ŋaʔ =lo¹
 but DEM pattern go.on ASP =SUB:if 3SG starve =SUB:cause

 θe² nuiN¹ =Tɛ¹
 die CAN =REAL

 ... but the way things were going, he'd probably starve to death anyway.
 (lit. ... but **if** this pattern goes on, he could die **because** he will starve)

Table 9: Burmese main Clause final particles

	Clause final particle	Meaning
ရင်	yiN²	Conditional : 'if'
လို့	lo¹	Causal : 'because, like'
		Quotation
တုံး(က)	TouN³ (=Ka¹)	Temporal: 'when' (past event)
တော့	Tɔ¹	Temporal: 'when' (future event)
မ... ခင်	mə -V- KʰiN²	Temporal : 'before'

---

[39] Co-ordinating conjunctions will be treated with Relators as they mainly operate at phrasal level.

[40] For an extensive list of Final Clause Particles, see Bernot & al (2001: 136 ff), Okell (1969: 173 ff).

	Clause final particle	Meaning
ရင်	yiN³	Simultaneity : 'while'
ပြီး	pyi³	Consecutive (and simultaneity) : 'after, as'
ဖို့	pʰo¹	Goal : 'for, in order to'
အောင်	ʔaɔN²	Goal: 'in order to, so that'

Some nouns, such as 'sound' ((အ) သံ) /(ʔə)θaN³/), 'image' ((အ) ပုံ /(ʔə)pouN²/) or 'place' (နေရာ /nəya²/) may fulfill the function of a clause-final particle while partly keeping their original meaning, as shown by example (55) (Bernot & al 2001: 147–48).

(55) သူနားလည်ပုံ မရဘူး ။
   θu²   na³.lɛ²   -pouN²   mə=   ya¹   =Pʰu³
   3SG   understand   -SUB:image   NEG=   get   =NEG
   'It doesn't seem that he understands.'
 (lit)   'We don't get the image of him understanding.'

3.2 The nominal domain

3.2.1 Basic structure of the NP

A noun phrase (NP) is minimally constituted of a bare noun, to which modifiers can be added in a certain order. In some rare and restricted cases, the N may be omitted (See section on CLF). Within a slot — corresponding to a syntactic position—, elements are exclusive. Semantic constraints may also prevent the use of modifiers from different slots from appearing in the same NP.

Here is the schema for the Burmese NP. (*Small Brackets stand for optional items, large brackets stand for slot positions in the NP.*)

Figure (1): NP Component order for Colloquial Burmese

{ (Demonstrative) (subordinate clause) (possessives) (genitive complements) (Pali adjectives) } SLOT 1	{ Noun (compound with stative Verb, diminutive MRK, superlative MRK,) ... } SLOT 2	{ QFT₁ (Num + CLF) (plural, each, collective) } SLOT 3	{ QTF₂ (approximation QTF) (collective) } SLOT 4	{ (case / disc MRK) } SLOT 5

[slot 1]: Modifiers precede the head noun as expected in a verb-final language.

Table 10: Illustration of current pre-nominal modifiers

Burmese form		Meaning
ဒီ	di^2 + N	deictic proximal (this one)[41]
ဟို	ho^2 + N	deictic distal (that one)
ဘယ်-	$bɛ^2$ + N	interrogative or indefinite expressions
ပထမ	$pəthəma^1$ + N	cardinal (first)
တခြား	$təcha^3$ + N	other

[slot 2]: The noun may be a mono-morphemic word or a lexical compound. It may also be followed by a restricted set of stative verbs with attributive function.

[slot 3]: Nominal plural is not a compulsory grammatical category. It is rather pragmatically constrained, plural morphemes appearing with specific nominal reference.

[slot 4]: Indefinite quantifiers are morphemes that modify a quantifying expression and they convey a numeral approximation ('about, exactly, less than, both, together, all', etc.). They follow the first quantifier without a pause.

[slot 5]: Relators or postpositions have syntactic or pragmatic functions: they indicate arguments of the process but also reinforce their status (emphasis) in the discourse. Some postpositions are complex, compounded with 'relator nouns', as shown by (56)a (cf. also § 5.1.2).

(56) a. အခင်းလေးပေါ်မှာ b. အဲဒီစာအုပ်ကြီး ၂အုပ်
 $ʔə\text{-}khiN^3\text{-}le^3$ $pɔ^2$ =Ma^2 $ʔɛ^3di^2$ $sa^3ʔoʔ\text{-}Ci^3$ $ṇə\text{-}ʔoʔ$
 NMLZ-spread-DIM top =LOC DEM.ANAPH book-big 2 CLF:bound obj.
 'On the small tablecloth' 'These two big books'

3.2.2 Case-markers, postpositions or relators

In Burmese, syntactic functions are expressed by morphemes postponed to NPs and thus are usually considered as 'postpositions'. However, following Hagège 1997, we will refer to *'relators'*, a term that subsumes adpositions and case-markers under a single concept that relies on syntactic rather than morphological criteria. It shows the dependency of a constituent (generally a complement) on a head (generally a verb).

---

[41] Notice that demonstratives may also be used as nouns and are directly followed by a case marker in expressions meaning 'here','there'.

Burmese relators are multifunctional; they mark certain grammatical functions, pragmatic functions and basic locational relations. As clitics, they undergo voicing of the initial consonant according to general phonological rules. The most frequent ones are listed in table 11.

Notice, however, that they are not systematically expressed (see 52). They are used sparingly: their presence depends on the properties of the verbs (transitive, intransitive, motion...), on the number of arguments expressed, and on the amount of 'sharedness': the greater the shared context or the shared cultural background is, the less necessary it is to specify grammatical relations. Often, the markers appear to disambiguate relations between arguments. For instance in (36)b, the marker ကို /Ko²/ helps to identify the argument recipient of the talk.

Table 11: Relators (or Postpositions) in Burmese

Relator		Functions
ကို	=Ko²	Syntactic[42]: object (accusative)(1), (36), (39), (50), direction, (allative), destination (22), (49), distributive, recipient, future time
		Pragmatic: focus, emphasis
က	=Ka¹	Syntactic: subject (nominative), source (ablative), 'giver', past time
		Pragmatic: topic, delimit constituent in nominal predicates
မှာ	=Ma²	Syntactic: location, experiencer, possessor (22), (31)
နဲ့	=nɛ¹	Syntactic: instrumental, comitative (22), (53)
ရဲ့	=yɛ¹	Syntactic: Possession (genitive)
သ	=ha²	Syntactic/Pragmatic: Subject topicalizer

As noticed in table 11, some of the Burmese relators have not only a syntactic function but also a pragmatic function, namely topicalization and focalization of the host constituent to which they attached. For instance, က /Ka¹/ attached to the single argument of a predicate, designates the referent it refers to as the topic of the discourse. See examples (22) and (51)b.

On the other hand, the relator ကို /Ko²/ is required when the goal argument of the event has been moved from its expected position (preverbal). In that case, it denotes an emphasis on this argument, focalizing it.

ကို /Ko²/ may also be attached to other kinds of constituent (adverbial, clausal) with the same pragmatic functions (57).

---

[42] Sawada (1995) examines in detail the usages and functions of postpositions က /Ka¹/ and ကို /Ko²/. He also reviews previous descriptions of these two relators (p. 154–57), and discusses the adequacy of the concepts of 'subject' and 'object' in Burmese (p. 175ff). See also Okell & Allott (2001: 2, 7) on the same markers.

(57) a. ပြောကိုမပြောချင်ပါဘူး။ [from Okell & Allott (2001: 9)]
    pyɔ³ =**Ko²** mə=   pyɔ³   ChiN² =Pa²   =Phu³
    say   =EMPH   NEG= say   want   =POL   =NEG
    '(I) don't **even** want to say it!'

b. သိပ်ကိုတော်တာဘဲ။
    θei? =**Ko²** tɔ²   =Ta²   bɛ³
    very =EMPH   be skill =REAL.NF DM:excl
    '(He) is **incredibly** skilled.'

Finally, some derived nouns such as အတွက် /ʔə.Twɛ?/ (from တွက် /twɛ?/ 'to calculate') or အတိုင် /ʔə.TaiN²/ (from တိုင် /taiN²/ 'to measure') with purposive and similar (like, as) meanings respectively, may also function as relators, keeping some of their nominal properties (Wheatley 1982: 92, Bernot & al, 2001: 92).

One final relator should be mentioned here: the 'induced creaky tone', the function of which clusters around genitive, dative and related subordination constructions. Formally, certain types of syllable shift to creaky tone (tone 1), indicating dependency of the constituent bearing the tonal shift. It is usually analysed as a relic or a reflex of an old genitive postposition (Thurgood 1981, Delancey, 1997: 62). See examples (31) and (78).

3.2.3 Classifier device

The Burmese Classifier (henceforth CLF) device is quite well known in the literature (Haas 1951, Burling 1965, Hla Pe 1965, Becker 1975, Goral 1978, Vittrant 2005a, Simpson 2005[43]). All of the surveys mentioned deal with various aspects of the Burmese NUMERAL CLF system, such as morpho-syntactic patterns, semantic features, pragmatic uses and lists of the classifiers— the most extensive list can be found in Burling's article.

- **Form and Nature**

According to Hla Pe (1965: 167-68), the use of CLF is attested in Burmese from the earliest records of the language, i.e. 12th-13th centuries. At that time these morphemes were not systematically used: they became more consistent later.

---

[43] See Vittrant (2005: 131) for a more detailed survey of previous studies of Burmese classifiers.

Burmese numeral CLFs are divided into two semantic subcategories: classifiers and quantifiers, also called sortal and mensural classifiers[44]: sortal CLF individuate whatever they refer to in terms of the kind of entity that it is. In other words, they categorize referents in terms of their inherent characteristics, such as animacy, humanness, shape, social status or function. Repeater or 'unique' CLFs are a sub-class of sortal CLF (Hla Pe 1965: 166; Okell 1969: 213; Vittrant 2005: 134). Mensural CLFs, on the other hand, individuate in terms of quantity. They group objects in a unit of measure that can be understood as being countable. For instance, they occur in structures of measuring mass nouns or non-discrete physical entities, but also in the arrangement of units of countable nouns.

Some quantified sequences remain in need of explanation: units of time or dimension are commonly quantified without any apparent classifier. But a better examination of those sequences reveals that units of measure like dimensions and lengths of time (such as 'year' and 'time') in fact consistently appear to the right of the numeral (Num) in the CLF position, and not in the N- position which occurs to the left of Num in surface word order.

- **Syntax**

Languages of East and Southeast Asia fall into two large groups according to the structure of noun phrases involving classifiers. Jones (1970) noticed that word order within the NP follows an areal pattern. In the North, represented by Chinese, Vietnamese and Hmong[45], the head noun follows the numeral and the classifier ([NUM-CLF]-N). Whereas in the South, represented by Thai and Khmer, the head noun precedes the numeral-classifier group (N- [NUM-CLF]). Unsurprisingly, the Burmese NUMERAL CLF construction belongs to the second group.

Numbers and CLFs in a quantified NP commonly occur together as a single unit, a phonologically and syntactically *uninterrupted* sequence.

- **Function**

The basic function of a CLF is to encode a counting unit, when used with numerals. Thus, they are known as numeral classifiers. However, underlying quantification is the primary semantic function of *individuating* NPs, i.e. to conceive of NPs as discrete, individuated entities.

---

44 On the distinction between sortal and mensural classifiers, see Craig (1992: 279) and Aikhenvald (2000: 115–18).
45 On classifier devices in these languages see also Bisang (1999: 118) and Simpson (2005).

CLF in many languages may be used beyond counting. Functional expansions of CLFs have been studied by Bisang (1999), Craig (1982), Grinevald (2000) inter al.

Burmese CLFs, beside their occurrence with numerals, appear in indefinite expressions (58), and anaphoric expressions, i.e. referentialization function (59). They are not, however, used with demonstratives, or to indicate singulative, specificity or definiteness of the noun as in Hmong (this volume, p. 624–27) or Vietnamese (this volume, p. 399–405).

Indefinite expressions such as 'someone' or 'something' are formed by reduplication of the CLF following the numeral 'one', whereas negative indefinite expressions ('none', 'no one', 'nothing') require also the numeral 'one' followed by respectively the appropriate CLF and the particle မှ /m̥a¹/ 'only' (Vittrant 2005: 136). See examples in (60).

(58) a. တအုပ်အုပ် ယူပါ ။
 tə-ʔoʔ-ʔoʔ   yu²   =Pa²
 one-CLF:book (x2) take   =POL
 'Take any (book).'

 b. တယောက်ယောက် ဖြေးနိုင်မလား ။
 tə-yɔʔ-yɔʔ   phye²   naiN²   =mə   la³
 one-CFL:hum (x2)   answer CAN   =IRR   QST
 'Could someone answer [this question]?'

(59) ကောင်မလေးက ငှက်ပျောသီးလေးလုံးထဲကနေ နှစ်လုံးကိုဖြတ်ပြီး ကောင်လေကို ပေးတယ် ။ [AA/08, 66_011]
 kaɔN²ma¹-le³ =Ka¹   ŋəpyɔ³θi³ le³-louN³   thε³   =Ka¹-ne²
 woman-DIM   =S/TOP banana   4-**CLF:rond** inside   =S.(FROM)

 ŋə-louN³   Ko²   phyaʔ =Pyi³   kaɔN²-le³   =Ko²   pe³   =Tε²
 2-**CLF:round** =OBJ cut   =SUB:TPS man-DIM   =OBJ   give   =REAL
 'The young lady gave two bananas to the young man, after cutting them off the four.'

(60) တောင်းတာ တခုမှမပေးဘူး ။
 taɔN³   =Ta²   tə-khu¹-m̥a¹   mə=   pe³   =Phu³
 ask   =NMLZ.REAL   **one-CLF:general-only** NEG=   give   =NEG
 'He gives nothing of what has been asked.'

3.3 The verbal domain

This section is organized as follows: after a brief overview of the Burmese verb phrase structure, we examine the notional categories expressed in the verb complex[46], and try to distinguish between all the verbal morphemes that appear in the verb complex, before dealing with serial verb constructions.

3.3.1 Verb phrase structure

- **Minimal structure**

The Verb Phrase in Burmese minimally contains a verb and a *Verb Final Particle* (henceforth VFP), to which aspectual and modal morphemes and the like may be added. These modifiers are analyzed as *Verb Particles (VP)* or *Auxiliary verbs*. The former cannot be used as a head verb, although they are often from verbal origin. In the latter case, the morpheme conveying a grammatical notion may also appear as a head verb synchronically.

(V_{AUX})   -**V**-   (VP)   (V_{AUX})   (VP)   - **VFP**

(61) ... ဆက်မသင်နိုင်တော့ဘူး ။
    shɛʔ   mə=   **θiN²**   naiN²   Tɔ¹   =Phu³
    V_{AUX}:join   NEG=   **V_H: learn** V_{AUX}:can   VP:ASP   =NEG
    '(I) cannot go on learning....'

The verb phrase may also include a NP_{OBJ} (see for instance the psycho-collocation expressions in § 2.2.1).

- **No inflection, no agreement, no tense marking**

SEA languages are mostly isolating, that is to say words do not vary according to grammatical roles, as these languages lack inflection.

Unsurprisingly, Burmese lacks verbal cross-referencing (agreement). It also lacks tense markers, and expressing number is optional (or only required under specific pragmatic conditions).

To sum up, apart from the status (REALIS, IRREALIS, etc. cf. table 12 below) expressed by the VFPs, no grammatical category is compulsory in the VP.

---

46 On 'verb complex', see footnote 50 or Vittrant (2010: 104).

Nevertheless, Burmese speakers may use optional particles and auxiliaries for aspectual, modal and causal specifications. See next section.

Notice, however, a vestigial inflection in the verbal domain that originates from a causative prefix in Proto-Tibeto-Burman (Maspero 1947). Burmese, like many other Tibeto-Burman languages (Vittrant 1998: 5–15), possesses over a hundred pairs of verbs that are semantically and formally related[47]. Each pair consists of a transitive (or causative) member and an intransitive (or stative) one. In most cases, the former has an aspirated (or voiceless) consonant whereas the latter has a plain (or voiced) one. Other pairs have deviations in tone as in (62)c.

This phenomenon, however, is no longer alive in Burmese.

(62) a. ဖွင့်   ပွင့်   b. ခြောက်   ကြောက်   c. ကော်   ကော့
       phwiN¹ pwiN¹   chaɔʔ   caɔʔ   kɔ²   kɔ¹
       'open' 'be opened' 'frigthen' 'be afraid'   'lever up' 'curl up'

- **Verb Final Particles**

The *Verb-Final Particle* (VFP) is the only grammatical element required in a verbal predication. It is the final element in the verb phrase and it indicates the status of the event, that is to say whether the event is realized, unrealized, potential or refers to a new situation. Burmese has a set of 5 main[48] particles (Vittrant 2005: 158) of which the REALIS တယ် /Tɛ²/ (with its allomorphs) is the most used. The lack of a VFP in a verbal predicate stands for injunction when it occurs with an active verb in main clause. This is summarized in table 10.

The allomorphs of the VFP are used under specific syntactic and grammatical conditions: in complement clause, headless relative clause, sentential nominalization, expressive sentences (တာ /Ta²/, / မှာ Ma²/) and relative clauses (တဲ့ /Tɛ¹/, မဲ့ /Mɛ¹/) (Vittrant 2001, Simpson 2008).

---

[47] Exhaustive lists of 'simplex-causative' pairs of verbs in Burmese may be found in Okell (1969: 205 ff) and Vittrant (1998: 113 ff).

[48] Apart from these 5 main VFP, a few other miscellaneous particles or idiomatic expressions could be added, such as ရဲ့/yɛ¹/, ကဲ့ /kɛ¹/ (considered here as allomorphs of the REALIS VFP) or ရော/yɔ³/ (statement + speaker's point of view), သလိုလိုပဲ /θəlo²lo²bɛ³/ (speaker doubt) (Vittrant, 2004: 360, 374).

Table 12: Verb Final Particles

Burmese form (and allomorphs)		Prototypical Meaning	
သည် (တ - ရ့ - သ)	Tɛ² - (Ta², yɛ¹...)	REAL	Realis (past event, present event, realized event, habitual event ...)
မည် (မှာ - မ)	Mɛ² - (Ma²,...)	IRR	Irrealis (potential event, future event, unrealized or hypothetical event ...)
ပြီ:	Pyi²	CRS	Current Relevant State or New Situation (realized event)
မ ... ဘူး	mə ... Phu³	NEG	Negation of realized and non-realized event
မ ... နဲ့	mə ... nɛ¹	INJ	Negative injunction (prohibitive)
-	Ø	IMP	Imperative (order)

3.3.2 Verbal Categories

Previous descriptions of Burmese verb phrase (Allott 1965; Okell 1969; Bernot 1980; Wheatley 1982 and Vittrant 2005) show great variations in the definition of grammatical verbal morphemes, in particular the optional ones. The number and the functions of these morphemes vary depending on the criteria used by the author for the analysis. For instance, the classification given by Okell & Allott (2001) based on semantic criteria, leads to a list of 60 verbal morphemes, whereas the Bernot (1980) and Wheatley (1982) classifications, which are based on phonological, syntactic and semantic criteria, distinguish between "auxiliaries" and "verbal particles", although they do not list exactly the same morphemes.

So-called auxiliaries and optional verbal particles express mainly aspectual and modal notions (Vittrant 2005)[49]. Most of them are postponed to the main verb, but pre-verbal auxiliaries exist (cf. (61) or appendix 2/n°35). However, the status of auxiliary — roughly defined as a subordinated verb or a grammatical element of verbal origin — of these preverbal elements is questionable. They belong to an open class and above all, they have not undergone a change of meaning from lexical to grammatical. Thus they may be simply seen as the first element of a 'verb complex', that is to say a combination of bare verbs that

---

[49] Whereas Vittrant (2005) lists all these verbal morphemes with their main grammatical meanings, the following papers are dedicated to particular verbal morphemes: see for instance Myint Soe (1994), Romeo (2009) on grammaticalization of motion verbs, Jenny (2009), van Auwera & al (2009) and Vittrant & Auwera (2010) on modal morphemes, Allott Romeo (2009), Vittrant (2013) on aspectual morphemes, Okano (2005) on 'give'.

functions as a morpho-syntactical unit[50], a kind of Serial Verb Construction (see next section).

- **Verbal particles**

The term "verbal particle" is here used to refer to bound morphemes that convey grammatical information. Often originating from verbs, they never occur as main verbs synchronically. Vittrant (2005: 154) lists around twenty items, some of which are rare or literary. The plural morpheme က /Ca¹/ (50), the aspectual marker တော့ /Tɔ¹/ 'imminence', the spatio-temporal particle ခဲ့ /khɛ¹/ (Vittrant 2013), the modal particles ချင် /ChiN²/ 'desire' (57)a or လိမ့် /leiN¹/ 'probability' are common (optional) Verbal Particles.

- **Auxiliaries**

Auxiliaries, that is to say verbs that have undergone a semantic change and are used as modifiers of another verb, are numerous in Burmese. Following universal grammaticalization clines (Heine, 1993), non-specific motion verbs ('go', 'come', 'come back', 'follow') have been grammaticalized to several degrees, becoming aspectual markers (Romeo, 2008). Other common grammaticalizations include the change of နေ /ne²/ 'to stay, to dwell' and ပေး /pe³/ 'to give' toward respectively an aspect marker (progressive or stative), and an applicative or benefactive marker.

Less prototypical and universal verb changes (Heine & Kuteva, 2002) are also found in Burmese. For instance, the verb ထား /tha³/ 'to put' used with an active verb conveys a RESULTATIVE meaning, a grammaticalization path found with similar aspectual meanings in other Tibeto-Burman languages (Lahu, Lalo, Akka, Thangkul, Karen, Kachin, Tibetan, Newar, Kham).

Notice also the 'temptative' value conveyed by the verb ကြည့် /ci¹/ meaning 'to look at', a grammaticalization labelled under different terms, such as 'connative', 'experimentative' (Vittrant 2004: 208), and often translated by 'try/test V' (Voinov, 2013).

(63) ဒိန်ခဲကိုခဏခဏ နမ်းကြည့်ပါ ။
    deiN²gɛ³   =*Ko²*   *khəna¹ khəna¹*   *naN³*   ***ci¹***   =*Pa²*
    cheese   =OBJ   often   smell   **look** >TRY   =POL
    'Smell the cheese often, [so you know when it gets old].'

---

[50] The *complex verb* notion is first found in Hagège (1975) and his study of Chinese prepositions that originate from verbs. It must be distinguished from a compound verb (idiomatic expression) and from a 'complex predicate' that contains verbs with different status, i.e. head verb plus dependent verbs.

Unlike other MSEA languages and likely related to its syntactic type (SOV language, modifier-head), Burmese uses mainly the post-verbal position for auxiliary verbs.

The pre-verbal position is not very common, which may be partly due to language contact (cf. Mon 'to give', preV: permissive, 'postV: benefactive, p. 297.

Table 13: Common Verb grammaticalizations in Burmese (from Vittrant 2005: 150 ff)

Verb form		Lexical meaning	Grammaticalized meaning
သွား	/θwa³/	go	PstV: (1) directional/deixis (away from DC); (2) aspect (accomplishment, perfective, instantaneous change of state) (3) detrimental
လာ	/la²/	come	PstV: (1) directional/deixis (toward DC); (2) aspect (inchoative, leading to a change of state) (3) laudative
လိုက်	/laɪʔ/	follow	PstV: (1) aspect (accomplishment, action undertaken precipitately) (2) exclamation (with the REALIS VFP) PreV: (3) sequential or distributive action
နေ	/ne²/	to stay, to dwell	PstV: aspect (unaccomplished: progressive or stative)
ပြန်	/pyaN²/	to come back	PstV: simple iteration PreV: reverse action or iteration
ပေး	/pe³/	to give	PstV: applicative (benefactive) PreV: modal (permissive)
ရ	/ya¹/	to get, to obtain	PstV: modal (deontic, possibility)
ကြည့်	/ci¹/	to watch, to look	PstV: attemptive
ထား	/tha³/	to put	PstV: resultative aspect
ပစ်	/pyiʔ/	to throw (away)	PstV: completive aspect
ပြီး	/pyi³/	to finish	PstV: (1) aspect (accomplishment, perfective) (2) sequential subordinator: 'after P' *With modification in the form/ tone:* (3) CRS (current relevant state), new situation

Some verbs have been completely grammaticalized while others have not undergone a complete change, retaining some of their lexical meaning and verbal properties (cf. ထား /tha³/ 'to put', ပြန် /pyaN²/ 'to come back') as shown by syntactic tests such as negation.

3.3.3 Serial verb constructions

Burmese verbal predicates exhibit strings of verbs that (i) are not separated by a connector, (ii) share the same grammatical information and sometimes the same arguments, and (iii) describe a single event. These sequences are known as Serial Verb Constructions and are regularly found in SEA languages, as noticed by Matisoff (1983), (1991), DeLancey (1991), Clark (1989), (1992) and Bisang (1996). The phenomenon, which has been described extensively in Burmese by Vittrant (2006, 2012)[51] is illustrated by examples (64) to (66). Notice that, while the verb strings are identical on the surface, their underlying structures differ: consecutive or simultaneous actions in (64), characterization of an event in (65), adding grammatical information in (66). Thus SVC is far from being a uniform phenomenon, and most authors, after agreeing on a core set of properties, propose sub-types of SVC. Two types of SVC are generally distinguished, labeled respectively 'Symmetrical SVC class' (co-ranking predicates) and 'Asymmetrical SVC class' (implying a head-modifier hierarchy). See Bril (2004), Aikhenvald and Dixon (2006) for details.

Examples (64) and (65) illustrate a Symmetrical SVC in Burmese, whereas (66) and (67) illustrate an asymmetrical one.

(64) ခြင်္သေ့ဟာ သိုးကလေးကို ကိုက်စားလိုက်တယ် ။
  $chiN^?\theta e^1 = hu^2$ $\theta u^3 K \partial le^3 = K o^2$ $kai?$ sa^3 $lai?$ $=T \varepsilon^2$
  lion = TOP lamb = OBJ **V1:bite** **V2:eat** TERM = REAL
  'The lion devoured the lamb.'

(65) စလေမှာ ဘုန်းကြီးရှင်းပြတဲ့လိပ် ၊ ...
  $sa^1 le^2$ $= Ma^2$ $phouN^3 Ci^3$ $\int iN^3$ pya^1 $=T\varepsilon^1$ $lei?$ ...
  Sale = LOC monk **V1:clear** **V2:show** = REL.R. turtle
  '... the turtle about which the monk, in Sale, tells [the story]...'
lit. ... the turtle to which the monk shows clearly [the story]....

(66) ဝင်းဝင်းမော်က ကျမကို ထူးဆန်းတဲ့နေရာတွေကို လိုက်ပို့ပေးတယ်။
  $wiN^3 \ wiN^3 \ mɔ^2$ $=Ka^1$ $cəma^1$ $=Ko^2$ $thu^3 \ ShaN^3$ $=T\varepsilon^1$ $ne^2 \ ya^2$ $=Twe^2$ $=Ko^2$
  Win Win Maw =S 1SG =DAT be strange =REL:R place =PLUR =DIR

---

51 On SVC containing motion verbs in Burmese, see Vittrant 2015.

laiʔ	*po¹*	*pe³*	*=Tɛ²*
[V1:follow	V2:send off]	V3:give/BENEF	=REAL

'Win Win Maw, she took me to strange places.'

Finally, diachronic studies of verb serialization show a tendency for verbs to shift from isolation (serial verbs) to boundness. To put it in other words, serial verbs tend to lexicalize or to grammaticalize, with common cross-linguistic changes, leading synchronically to different types of serial verb constructions corresponding to different stages of the process.

3.4 Sentence organization

3.4.1 General facts

Although basic word order for SEA languages is (S)VO, Burmese, like the majority of Tibeto-Burman languages, is an SOV or verb final language. However, sentences are often reduced to OV or simply V, with the referents of the SoA not being represented by referential expressions or agreement. Zero referential form or zero anaphora is particularly typical of East and Southeast Asia languages, where referential choice is cognitively determined, and relies on the notion of topic continuity or accessibility of the referents (Lambrecht 1994). To put it in other words, a focally attended referent in clause *n*, stays the topic (or theme) in clause *n+1*. As such, it does not need to be expressed. Moreover, some referents, such as the ones present in the speech situation or animate referents, are easily accessible, and so are often not represented by referential expressions.

Sentence (67) illustrates the absence of referential expressions: the arguments of the V are omitted, recoverable from the context.

(67) ပြင်ပေးလိုက်မယ်။
pyiN² *pe³* *laiʔ* *=mɛ²*
repair give/BENEF follow/TERM =IRR
'[I] will repair [it] for [you].'

Beside uncluttered verbal clauses, Burmese makes great use of nominal clauses of the form NP₁- NP₂, where no copular verb is expressed, as in (68). See also (79)a and (84).

(68) a. မဆလာက မှုန့်ဘဲ ။ b. အလုပ်သမား သူ ။
    mashəla² =Ka¹ moṇN¹ (bɛ³)   ʔə-loʔ-θəma³ θu²
    [curry masala]ₙₚ =TOP [POWDER]ₙₚ DM:excl   NMLZ-work-NMLZ 3SG
    'Masala, [it is] a powder.'   'The worker, [it is] him.'

3.4.2 Clause types

Independent (verbal) clauses are characterized by the use of a VFP, whereas in dependent clauses VFPs have been replaced by a subordinating marker or a VFP reduced form marked for dependency, as in a relative clause.

- **Citation**

A citation is an independent or finite clause embedded in a matrix clause containing a *dicendi* verb and optionally closed off by a quotative particle, generally လို့ /lo¹/[52], that appears after the VFP. However, reported speech may be indicated by an evidential marker, the discourse particle တဲ့ /Tɛ¹/ (or ဆို /sho²/) appearing after the VFP as in (70).

(69) မနေ့က တို့သူငယ်ချင်းလာတယ်လို့ (သူက)ပြောတယ် ။
    məne¹Ka¹ To¹ θəŋɛ²ChiN³ la² =Tɛ² lo¹ (θu² =Ka¹) pyɔ³ =Tɛ²
    yesterday 1SG.COLL friend come =REAL QUOT (3SG =S.) say =REAL
    'He says that his friends came yesterday.'
or He says: "My friends came yesterday."

(70) အမ မသွားနိုင်ဘူး ၊ မသွားနဲ့တဲ့။ [A4/38]
    ʔəma¹ mə= θwa³ naiN² =Phu³ mə= θwa³ =nɛ¹ Tɛ¹
    older sister NEG= go can =NEG NEG= go =INJ.NEG QUOT
    'You (sister) cannot go (there). Don't go there, they said.'

- **Coordination and subordination**

Burmese, as a typically WITH-language[53] (Stassen 2000), does not have any dedicated coordinating marker either at the phrasal level or at the clausal level.

---

52 The other citation particles are *dicendi* verbs such as ဆို /sho²/ 'tell, say' in colloquial Burmese or ဟု /hu¹/ a verb meaning 'say' in literary Burmese.
53 WITH-languages take the comitative encoding to express either 'John and Mary left' vs. 'John left with Mary', although they tend to differentiate the comitative and coordinate strategies by changing one or more features, i.e. 'doubling' the comitative marker in coordination (Stassen 2000).

Connecting nominal phrases[54] is done by the comitative marker နဲ့ /nɛ¹/. At the clausal level, on the other hand, conjunction may be realized by juxtaposition of independent and finite clauses, the only indication of the link being the intonation, and sometimes the use of the discourse marker လဲ /lɛ³/ 'also'. Clauses may also be linked by weakly subordinating particles such as the 'conjunctive' marker ပြီး /pyi³/, or the simultaneous marker ယင်း /yiN³/. In the following examples, the first constituent of both sentences is a subordinated clause ending with a Clause Final particle (cf. § 3.1.2) and followed by the matrix clause.

(71) a. ရေချိုးရင်း သီချင်းဆိုတယ် ။
   yɛ²-cho³ ***yiN³*** *θi²chiN³* *sho²* =*Tɛ²*
   water-wash SUB song say =REAL
   '(She) bathes and sings.'
or   '(She) sings while bathing.'

 b. ပြုံးပြီး နားထောင်နေတယ် ။
   pyouN³ ***Pyi³*** *na³-thaɔN²* *ne²* =*Tɛ²*
   smile SUB listen INACC =REAL
   '(He) was smiling and listening.'
or   '(He) was smiling while listening.'

- **Complement clauses**

Complement clauses are embedded as arguments of the matrix clause through the use of a VFP displaying a dependant form similar in function to nominalizers, or through the replacement of the VFP with an appropriate member of the nominalizing nouns set (cf. § 3.1.2, example (55)). In the former case, the clauses may be considered as nominalized clauses although keeping the grammatical information that anchors the process (i.e. TAM, status), a phenomenon common in the area (DeLancey, 2011). See also Sawada (1994) and his review of complement clause types in Burmese.

(72) မတို့လုပ်တာကို ပြောခိုင်းတာလေ ။   [A5/14]
  ma¹-To¹ *loʔ* =*Ta²* =*Ko²* *pyɔ³* *khaiN²* =*Ta²* *le²*
  older.sister-COLL work =NMLZ.REAL =OBJ say order =REAL.NF DM
  'She asked us (sister & co) to say what we have done.'

---

[54] It is also possible to connect two noun phrases A and B using the structures A-ရော B- ရော /A-yɔ³ B-yɔ³/ or A- ရော B- ပါ /A-yɔ³ B-pa²/.

- **Relative clauses**

Unsurprisingly, relative clauses precede the modified noun and are closed off by a VFP marked for dependency by the induced creaky tone 1 (Allott 1967). The induced creaky tone may indicate dependency in other situations, being similar in function to the genitive marker ရဲ့/$y\varepsilon^1$/. Thus, the morphemes glossed 'relative marker' also carry information on the status (realis, irrealis) of the process expressed in the relative clause.

(73) ကျမ မပိုင်တဲ့အိမ်ဖြစ်လို့ မရောင်းနိုင်ဘူး ။
 $cama^1$ $m\partial$= $paiN^2$ =$T\varepsilon^1$ $ʔeiN^2$ $phyiʔ$ lo^1 $m\partial$= $ya\mathupsilon N^3$ $naiN^2$ =Phu^3
 1SG NEG= possess =REL.R house be SUB NEG= sell CAN =NEG
 'I cannot sell this house because it is a house **that does** not belong to me.'

(74) အိမ်ဝယ်မဲ့လူ ရှိတယ် ။
 $ʔeiN^2$ $w\varepsilon^2$ =$m\varepsilon^1$ lu^2 $ʃi^1$ =$T\varepsilon^2$
 house buy =REL.IRR (hu)man have, be =REAL
 'There is someone **who could** buy the house.'

3.4.3 Sentence types and Nominalization

- **Interrogative and exclamative sentences**

Burmese distinguishes polar questions and wh-questions. The former are formed by the addition of a question marker, i.e. the Sentence Particle လား /la^3/ after the VFP – which might be reduced or omitted in realis context (cf. (35)) – see examples (50) and (58).

Content questions, on the other hand, contain beside the (final) Sentence Particle လဲ /$l\varepsilon^3$/, an indefinite phrase indicating the element to be supplied. The indefinite phrase consists of the Wh-morpheme ဘယ်-ဘာ /$b\varepsilon^2$ ~ba^2/ in combination with a postposition, a classifier or other element such as a noun.

(75) ဘယ်လမ်းက သွားရမလဲ ။
 $b\varepsilon^2$-laN^3 =Ka^1 θwa^3 ya^1 =$m\partial$ $l\varepsilon^3$
 QST.INDEF-road = S go GET =IRR QST
 'Which road should we take?'

(76) ဒီမှာ အလုပ်လုပ်တာ ဘယ်လောက်ကြာပြီလဲ ။ [B4/51]
 di^2-ma^2 $ʔ\partial$-$loʔ$ $loʔ$ =Ta^2 $b\varepsilon^2$ -$laɔʔ$ ca^3 =Pyi^2 $l\varepsilon^3$
 here NMLZ-work work =NMLZ.REAL QST.INDEF. -amount last =CRS QST

'How long have you been working here?'
lit. 'The fact you are working here, how long has it lasted?'

Exclamative sentences express the speaker's attitude towards a certain state of affairs that is not in accordance with his expectations. Unlike declarative sentences that supply information, exclamatives have a propositional content assumed by the speaker to be true (Potsdam, 2011). Formally, Burmese exclamative sentences are typically associated with a syntactically-determined clause-type, i.e. nominalized clauses, and are often marked by discourse markers (see also next section on Pragmatics). However, other syntactic means exist such as the collocation of the verb လိုက် /laiʔ/ 'to follow' and the reduced form of realis VFP as in (77).

(77) နေရာလေးက ကောင်းလိုက်တာ ။
  ne²ya²-le³ =*Ka¹* *kaɔN³* *laiʔ-Ta²*
  place-DIM =TOP good follow-REAL.EXCL
  'What a nice (little) place!'

- **Nominalization**

Nominalization in Burmese applies at two different levels of the grammar, both lexical and clausal levels as regularly observed in Asian languages.
  – At lexical level, nouns are derived by the addition of an affix, usually a suffix. For instance, သူ /θu²/ — also functioning as the third person pronoun— သည် /θɛ³/ and သမ /θəma¹/ are agentive nominalizers (see respectively examples (78), (45), (68)). Burmese however also possesses a derivational and very productive prefix အ /ʔə-/, inherited from Proto-Tibeto-Burman (Maspero, 1947: 155–56, 167–68), (Matisoff, 2003: 104 ff, 112), which can combine with nouns (40), (49), (50), class terms (27) or verb roots (45), (56), (76).

(78) သူ့သား ဖြစ်ဟန်တူသူ၊
  θu⁽²˃¹⁾ *θa³* *pyiʔ* *haN²* *tu²* *-θu²*
  3SG.GEN son be attitude look.like -AGENT
  'A person who appears to be her son.' (Okell & Allott, 2001: 238)

  – At clausal or sentence level (Simpson 2008), the nominalizer has scope over the entire clause and may exhibit verbal features, encoding for instance TAM or status. The resulting nominalized-event has the same morphosyntactic characteristics as non-derived nouns, i.e. followed by adpositions/relators (see (53) and (72)).

In this second class of nominalizers, subtypes must be distinguished between (i) morphemes that bear some verbal features (REALIS/IRREALIS) as in (79) and (ii) those that simply nominalize actions.

The former are allomorphs of VFP (cf. § 3.3.1), whereas the latter are dedicated morphemes or may be generic nouns (or nominal roots) such as 'business', 'sound', 'place' as in example (80) a & b (Vittrant 2002: 343ff)[55].

(79) သူရန်ကုန်မှာဝယ်မှာက စာအုပ်နဲ့ ခဲတံပါ ॥
θu² Yan²gon² =Ma² wɛ² =Ma² =Ka¹ sa²ʔo? =nɛ¹ khɛ³daN² =Pa²
3SG Yangon =LOC buy =NMLZ.IRR =TOP book(s) =with pencil(s) =POL
'What he is going to buy in Yangon is book(s) and pencil(s).'

(80) a. ဒီအသံက စိတ်တိုစရာကောင်းတယ် ॥
di² ʔə-θaN² =Ka¹ sei?.to² -Səya² kɔN³ =Tɛ²
DEM noise (NMLZ-sound) =TOP mind.short NMLZ.'able' good =REAL
'This noise is irritating.'
lit. 'This noise, it is good at making one feel 'short-tempered.'

b. ကပျာကယာလုပ်ပုံရတယ်॥
Kə Pya² Kə ya² lo? pouN² ya¹ =Tɛ²
hurriedly work NMLZ.IMAGE obtain =REAL
'It seems that (they) they work hurriedly.'

3.4.4 Information Structure

Information structure is understood here as the *packaging* of information that meets the immediate communicative needs of the participants of the discourse situation (Krifka 2006).

Some languages indicate preferentially the informative status of the constituents in terms of background, new, presupposed or alternative information. Their clause structure is based on pragmatic relations, organized according to the communicative goal rather than grammaticalizing semantic roles. These languages are known as 'topic-prominent' rather than 'subject-prominent', or pragmatic languages rather than syntactic languages (Huang 2000). Burmese, like many other SEA languages makes great use of grammatical devices for focusing, defocusing, or topicalizing (see § 3.2.2 on relators).

---

[55] See also Bernot & al (2001: 134,135, 146), Wheatley (1982: 280ff).

- **Topic and topicalization**

Sentences are generally structured in two parts, the topic and the comment. The topic roughly corresponds to the information mutually shared by the discourse participants. As such, the topic constituent may be omitted, a situation often encountered in Burmese. Zero marking guarantees that the referent intended is maximally salient in the immediate Common Ground, that is to say the most accessible one (given the speech situation, background knowledge).

If not omitted, the topic constituent may be marked as the protagonist of the discourse either by syntactic particles, dedicated expressions or simply by being fronted as in (81).

In (22) for instance, the particle က /Ka¹/ marks the single referential expression of the clause as the topic, either in the first subordinated clause or the matrix. See also (50), (51)b, (68)a, (77), which contain a nominal phrase marked as the discourse topic by က / Ka¹/.

Sentences (82) and (81) exhibit another way of indicating a constituent as the topic. Using a topicalizing expression of the form < X say-(if)> , i.e. ဆို(ရင်) /... sho² (yiN²)/ equivalent in meaning to "about X", reinforces the status of a referent as the topic or given information. Similarity between topicalization and conditional structures has already been noticed cross-linguistically (Haiman, 1978).

(81) အလုပ်မစသေးတာက အလုပ်ခေါင်း မလာသေးလို့ ။
Pə-loʔ mə= sa¹ θe³ =Ta²   =Ka¹ Pə-loʔ- KhaɔN³ mə= la²   θe³
[work NEG=start YET NMZL.REAL]ₜₒₚ =TOP NMZL-work-head NEG= come yet
=lo¹
SUB.cause
'The fact that we haven't yet started work, it is because the foreman hasn't come yet.'

(82) လိပ်စာအရဆိုရင် ဒီခြံနဲ့ ဒီတိုက်ဘဲ ။
lei²sa²   Pə-ya¹   sho² yiN²   di²   chaN² =nɛ¹   di²
[address about]ₙₚ   say   if[TOP] [DEM garden =with DEM

taiʔ   bɛ³
construction]ₙₚ DM:excl
'(According to) the address, [it is] this ground and this building!'
lit. 'If (we) speak (according to) the address, this ground with this building!'

(83) အဲဒီမိန်းမကြီး ကျွမအတွက်စိုးရိမ်တယ်။ အဲဒါဆိုတော့ သူတို့လိုက်ပို့ပေးတယ် ၊
    တောင်ပေါ် မှာ ။
Pɛ³- di²   meiN³ma²-Ci³ =Twe² cəma¹ Pə-Twɛʔ so³yeiN² =Tɛ²
ANAPH-DEM woman-adult   =PLUR 1SG   FOR   worry   =REAL

[ʔɛ³- da²		sho²	=Tɔ¹]TOP	θu²-To¹	laiʔ-po¹	pḁ³	=Tɛ²
ANAPH-DEM.thing		say	CONTRAST	3-COLL	accompany	BENEF	=REAL

taɔN³	Pɔ¹	=Ma
montain	top	=LOC

'These mature women were worried about me. And so [saying that], they accompanied [me]. On the mountain.'

- **Focus and focalization**

The classical pragmatic use of focus is to highlight a constituent, a clause (81) or a sentence.

When focusing a constituent, the speaker indicates that in a set of alternative propositions, he picks out one of them, either to correct or confirm information, or to highlight parallel propositions.

Subtypes of focus are usually distinguished, such as (i) sentence focus, (ii) predicate (or 'broad') focus and (iii) argument (or 'narrow') focus (Lambrecht, 1994). Burmese differs in the way it marks these foci. The third type is often marked by a cleft construction[56] as shown by sentence (b) in (84). Predicate focus, on the other hand, refers generally to sentences with a topic-comment structure, the focus corresponding to the comment.

(84) a. ဒီခွေး ကျမကို ကိုက်တယ် ။
di²	khwe³	cəma¹	=Ko²	kaiʔ	=Tɛ²
DEM	dog	1SG.FEM	=OBJ	bite	=REAL

'This dog bit(e) me.'

b. ကျမကို ကိုက်တာ ဒီခွေးတဲ့ ။
[cəma¹	=Ko²	kaiʔ	=Ta²]	[di²	khwe³]FOC	bɛ³
1SG.FEM	=OBJ	bite	=NMLZ.REAL	DEM	dog	DM:EXCL

'It's THIS DOG who bit me !'

(85) အခုအလုပ်လုပ်တာက ပဲခူးမှာ ။
ʔəkhu¹	ʔə-loʔ	loʔ	=Ta²	[Pəgu³	=Ma²]FOC
now	work	(to) work	=NMLZ.REAL	Pegu	=LOC

'Now, I work IN PEGU. [It is IN PEGU that I work now].'

---

[56] On cleft (and pseudo-cleft) constructions in Burmese, see Wheatley (1982: 172ff), Sawada (1994b) and Vittrant (2002).

As noticed in other verb final languages (Simpson and Watkins, 2005:43), pre-verbal position is preferred for the focused constituent, regardless of its syntactic function or semantic role.

The particles meaning 'only, also and 'even' should be mentioned here: they are commonly associated with focus as they generally refer to the notion of alternatives, central in focus.

Table 14: Some pragmatic particles associated with information structure

Burmese		Meaning	Reference
သဲ(ဲ)	bɛ³	1. just, only – even, very (argument marker) [2. really, indeed (sentence final marker)]	Okell & Allott (2001: 121–22)
လည်း	lɛ³	1. also, as well, too, in addition, both/neither XP₁ and/nor XP² [2. content question (sentence final marker)]	Okell & Allott (2001: 217–18)
တောင်	tɔN²	even, as much as	Okell & Allott (2001: 81)

4 Semantics and pragmatics

4.1 Common semantic domains

As mentioned by Matisoff (1983: 79) on the subject of areal features of SEA languages, there is another domain that needs to be investigated, namely comparative semantics, given that these languages seem to share basically similar conceptual frameworks concerning man and nature.

4.1.1 Food terminology

Rice, first cultivated 2000 years ago in Southeast Asia (Bernot, 2000: 106), is intimately related to the Burmese (and Southeast Asian in general) way of living. It is the staple crop in Burmese agriculture, produced in large quantities — thanks to the monsoon rains —, and also the staple food[57] of the Burmese peo-ple. The central position of rice in Burmese culture is evident in the language.

---

[57] Before World War II, Burma was one of the biggest rice exporters, producing more rice than needed to feed the Burmese people, although a Burmese consumer eats up to 300 kg per year. Compare with the European consumer who eats around 3 kg of rice per year (Bernot, 2000: 101).

Like Hmong (cf. Mong Leng, p. 638), the Burmese lexicon is rich in expressions for talking about rice and its transformations, with different terms according to the stage in the crop's production. It is also the default object of the verb စား /sa³/ meaning 'to eat' (cf. Mon, p. 286).

Table 15: Burmese Rice terms
    Adapted from L. Bernot (2000: 103), and Myanmar English Dictionary (1993)

English	French	Burmese	
rice plant seedling	plant de riz à repiquer	ပျိုး	pyo³
paddy, rice in the field	riz sur pied	စပါး	zəba³
unhusked rice, paddy	grain vêtu	ကောက်	kɔʔ
husked rice (grain with husks removed)	riz blanchi	ဆန်	shaN²
cooked rice	riz cuit	ထမင်း	thəmiN³

- **Carrying in Burmese**

SEA languages tend to show fine lexical distinctions in certain particular semantic domains such as carrying. In Burmese, carrying lexemes specify the part of the body involved in the action of carrying (hand, shoulder, back, arm(s), etc...)

Table 16: Burmese expressions for carrying

English	Burmese	
carry with the hand, carry off	ဆွဲ	shwɛ³
carry on the shoulder or on the back	ထမ်း	thaN³
carry on one's head (or with a headband)	ရွက်	ywɛʔ
carry something slung across one's shoulder	သိုင်း	θaiN³
carry hanging from the shoulder	လွယ်	lwɛ²
carry on the back	ပိုး	po³
carry over there, transport	သယ်	θɛ²

4.2 Pragmatics & discourse

4.2.1 Pragmatic particles

Discourse particles provide instructions for understanding the referential message in the speech context. They anchor the clauses in the discourse by expressing notions such as surprise, certainty, doubt, ask for confirmation (question tag) as shown by example (86).

Syntactically, these particles may occur in different positions: (1) at the end of the sentence, or (2) linked to a constituent in order to bring it out and signal it as important in the discourse situation.

- **Sentence-final particles**

Burmese, as other SEA languages, has a sentence-final particle device as a basic mean of distinguishing illocutionary force (requesting, questioning, persuading, advising, reminding, instructing...) (cf. § 3.4.3), but also for expressing 'propositional attitudes', emotions of the speaker (surprise, doubt, impatience, reluctance, hesitation, ...) in face-to-face interactions.

Example (86) is adapted from Hnin Tun (2006: 40); the request has different values depending on the sentence final-particle used.

(86) a. ဒီကိုလာနော် ။   Come (here), OK?
       di^2=Ko^2 la^2 **nɔ²**   *soften the request; solicit the addressee agreement*
       [> from a nurse to old people, from an adult to a kid]

   b. ဒီကိုလာလေ ။   Please, come! (or Come along!)
       di^2=Ko^2 la^2 **le²**   *soften the order while giving a feeling of being impatient*
       [> intimate friendly conversation]

   c. ဒီကိုလာကွာ။   Come (here)! (or Come on, won't you?')
       di^2=Ko^2 la^2 **Kwa²** *compelling attention, informal request*
       [> to inferior or equal]

   d. ဒီကိုလာစမ်း။   Please come (here)! (or Get over here!)
       di^2=Ko la^2 **SaN³** *peremptory request, conveys urgency, abrupt command*
       [> to inferior person]

   e. ဒီကိုလာဆို ။   Come (here) (I already called you, so please do come!)
       di^2=Ko^2 la^2 **sho²** *Reiterating a request, impatiently.*
       DEM=DIR come DM

Some of these sentence-final particles may be combined and co-occur together at the end of a sentence in a relatively restricted order, leading to some expressive combinations.

(87) ညစာ မစားရဘူးဆိုတော့ သိပ်ဆာမှာပေါ့နော် ။ [adapted from Bernot & Pasquet (1991)]
    $\eta a^1 Sa^2$ mə= sa^3 ya^2 =Phu^3 sho^2=$Tɔ^1$
    dinner   NEG= eat   CAN   =NEG   say   =TOP

| θei? | sha² | =Ma² | **Pɔ¹** | **nɔ²** |
| very | hungry | =NMZL.IRR | DM:emph | DM:soften+approval |

'Well, if (we) cannot eat dinner, we will be starving, won't we!?'

- **Other pragmatic particles**

Other pragmatic particles in Burmese help to interpret correctly the propositional content of a discourse. They occur in various syntactic positions, following the constituent they highlight. Their functions are merely similar: bringing out a constituent (ကို /ko²/ in (57), တော့ /Tɔ¹/ in (47) and (81)) either for reference maintenance in discourse, anaphora (လဲ /lɛ³/ in (39), (51)) or signaling alternative referents (ဘဲ /bɛ³/ in (37), (43), (57), (68) and (82)).

4.2.2 Politeness and honorifics

Languages spoken by large and hierarchical communities usually have devices to indicate respect for the addressee and/or for the referent, that is to say, politeness and honorifics devices. Burmese systems are not highly developed compared to Japanese or Korean ones. Apart from a good set of sentence-final particles that help to soften requests and orders (cf. previous section), Burmese expresses politeness through the use of the particle ပါ /Pa²/, that may appear either in verbal and nominal sentences. See examples (32), (38)b, (57), (58), (63), and (80).

As for expressing deference toward the referent, Burmese, like the languages of other Buddhist communities, has special lexicon to refer to monks, lords and kings. Here again, Burmese device is not as developed as Tibetan.

Deference may also be seen in the pronoun set, which contains honorific and self-humbling forms (cf. § 3.1.2, table 7, p. 84).

5 Summary

Although spoken on the border of the Mainland Southeast Asian area, Burmese shares most of the prototypical features of a Southeast Asian language, the main deviation being word order.

With its complex tones, its vowel system with four levels of aperture and the presence of sesquisyllabic structures, Burmese phonology conforms to what is expected for a SEA language. As for morphology, Burmese is less isolating than its neighbors, with a few affixes besides a great use of compounding. It has, however, developed a rich classifier system, and makes use of verb serialization like the majority of SEA languages.

As regards word-order, Burmese is a verb-final language, with postpositions, i.e. mainly a modifier-head language due to its family membership: Burmese syntax is in accordance with the syntax of Tibeto-Burman languages.

In summary, and as we have already shown in Vittrant 2010, Burmese, beyond its position on the edge of Southeast Sprachbund, close to South Asia, is undeniably a Southeast Asian language.

Abbreviations

ACC	accomplished (aspect)
AGENT	agentive nominalizer
ANAPH	anaphoric
ASP	aspect
ASS	assertive
AUX	auxiliary
BENEF	benefactive
CLF	classifier
COLL	collective
CFUGE	motion away from deictic center
CPETE	motion toward deictic center
CRS	current relevant state, new situation
DAT	dative
DEM	demonstrative
DIM	diminutive
DM	discourse marker
DIR	directional
EMPH	emphatique
EUPH	euphonique
EXCL	exclamative
FEM	feminine (or woman speaking)
GEN	genitive
HUM	human
IMP	imperative
INACC	inaccomplishment (aspect)
INCHOAT	inchoative (aspect)
INDEF	indefinite
IRR	irrealis
ITER	iterative (aspect)
LOC	locative

NEG	negation
NF	non-finite form
NMLZ	nominalizer
OBJ	object
PFX	prefix
POL	politeness
POSSIB	possibility (modality)
PLUR	plural
PROSP	prospective (aspect)
QUOT	quotative
QST	question
R. OR REAL	realis
REL	relative marker
RESULT	resultative (aspect)
S	source of the action (« ablative » or « nominative »)
SG	singular
SUB	subordinator
SPT	spacio-temporal,
TAM	tense, aspect, modality
TERM	terminative (aspect)
TOP	topic
TPS	temporal (consecutive, sequential)
VFP	verb final particle
VP	verb particle

References

Aikhenvald, Alexandra Y. & Dixon R. M. W. (eds.). 2001. *Areal diffusion and genetic inheritance: Problems in comparative linguistics.* Oxford: Oxford University Press.

Aikhenvald, Alexandra Y. & Dixon R. M. W (eds.). 2006. *Serial verb constructions: A cross-linguistic typology.* Oxford: Oxford University Press.

Abramson, Arthur S. 2004. The plausability of phonetic explanations of tonogenesis. In G. Fant, H. Fujusaki, J. Cao & Y. Du (eds.), *From traditional phonology to modern speech processing: Festschrift for professor Wu Zongji's 95th birthday*, 17–29. Beijing: Foreign Language & Research Press.

Allott, Anna. 1965. Categories for description for verbal syntagma in Burmese. *Lingua* 15. 283–309.

Allott, Anna. 1967. Grammatical tone in modern spoken Burmese. *Wissenschaftliche Zeitschrift der Karl-Marx Universität Leipzig, Gesellschafts- und Sprachwissenschaftliche Reihe* 16 (1–2). 151–161.

Allott, Anna. 1985. Language policy and language planning in Burma. In The Australian National University (ed.), *Papers in South East Asia Linguistics* 9, 131–154. Canberra: Research School of Pacific and Asian Studies.

Aung, San Hta Sayadaw (Pahtama). 1962. [1st ed. 1748] *Kəwilɛʔ khənā mjānma ṭədā* [A Burmese Grammar Systematically Arranged]. Rangoon.

Aurnague, Michel. 1989. Catégorisation des objets dans le langage: Les noms et les adjectifs de localisation interne. *Cahiers de Grammaire* 14. 1–21. Toulouse: UTM.

Aurnague, M., K. Boulanouar, J.-L. Nespoulous, A. Borillo & M. Borillo. 2000. Spatial semantics: the processing of Internal Localization Nouns. *Cahiers de Psychologie Cognitive/ Current Psychology of Cognition* 19 (1). 69–110.

Becker, A. J. 1986. The figure a classifier makes: describing a particular Burmese classifiers. In C. Craig (ed.), *Noun classes and categorization: Proceedings of a symposium on categorization and noun classification*, 327–343. Amsterdam: John Benjamins.

Bernot, Denise. 1958. Rapports phonétiques entre le dialecte marma et le birman, 273–294. Paris: Bulletin de la Société de Linguistique de Paris LIII.

Bernot, Denise. 1963. Esquisse d'une description phonologique du birman. *Bulletin de la Société de Linguistique de Paris* N°58-1, 164–224. Paris: Klincksieck.

Bernot, Denise. 1965. The vowel systems of Arakanese and Tavoyan. In G. B. Milner & E. J. A. Henderson (eds.), *Indo-Pacific linguistic studies*, vol. 2, 463–474. Amsterdam: North Holland Publishing Co.

Bernot, Denise. 1971. L'épithète en birman. Contribution à l'étude des langues sans catégorie adjectivale. *La Linguistique* 7 (1). 41–53.

Bernot, Denise. 1979. Néologismes en birman formel et birman quotidien. In Alice Cartier (ed.), *Journee d'etude: Langue formelle – langue quotidienne, quelques langues d'asie*, 5–14. Paris: Sorbonne, Université René Descartes.

Bernot, Denise. 1978–1988. *Dictionnaire birman-français*, vol. 1–11. Paris: Société d'Études Linguistiques et Anthropologiques de France.

Bernot, Denise. 1989–1992. *Dictionnaire birman-français,* vol. 12–15. Louvain & Paris: Editions Peters.

Bernot, Denise. 1980. *Le Prédicat en Birman Parlé*. Paris: Société d'Etudes Linguistiques et Anthropologiques de France.

Bernot, Denise. 1983. Y a-t-il des catégories adjectivales et adverbiales en birman? *Cahiers de l'Asie du Sud-Est* 13–14. 67–78. Paris: INALCO.

Bernot, Denise. 1994. Evolution of contemporary Burmese language – some features. In *Tradition and modernity in Myanmar*, Proceedings of an international conference held in Berlin, 7–9 May 1993, 379–392. Berlin: Lit Verlag.

Bernot, Denise. 2005. Usage de la composition en birman. In *Bulletin d'Arch'Asie* 1 (1). 5–12. http://archasie.free.fr/dossiers/cat.php?idcat=17 (accessed 29 May 2018).

Bernot, Denise. 2010. Le birman. In E. Bonvini, J. Busuttil & A. Peyraube (eds.), *Dictionnaire des langues*, 1050–1056. Paris: PUF/Quadrige.

Bernot, Denise & Brenda Pemaungtin. 1966. Le vocabulaire concret du birman et les notions abstraites. *Revue des Langues Orientales* 3. 1–18.

Bernot, Lucien. 2000. *Voyage dans les sciences humaines: Qui sont les autres?* Paris: Presses Universitaires de Paris-Sorbonne (CREOPS).

Bernot, Denise & Sylvie Pasquet. 1991. Les bonzillons. Deux petits birmans au monastère. *Cahiers de l'Asie du Sud-Est* 29/30. 111–131.

Bernot, Denise, Cardinaud Marie-Hélène & Yin Yin Myint Marie. 2001. *Grammaire Birmane – manuel du Birman*, vol. 2. Paris: L'Asiathèque (Langues et Mondes).

Bisang, Walter. 1999. Classifiers in East and Southeast Asian languages: counting and beyond. In Jadranka Gvozdanovic (ed.), *Numeral Types and Changes Worldwide*, 113–185. Berlin & New York: Mouton de Gruyter.

Borillo, Andrée. 1988. Le lexique de l'espace: les noms et les adjectifs de localisation interne. *Cahiers de Grammaire* 13. 1–22. Toulouse: Université de Toulouse le Mirail.

Bradley, David. 1979. *Proto-Loloish*. (Scandinavian Institute of Asian Studies, Monograph series 39.) London: Curzon.

Bradley, David. 1980. Phonological Convergence between languages in Contact: Mon-Khmer Structural Borrowing in Burmese. *Proceedings of the Sixth Annual Meeting of the Berkeley Linguistics Society, BLS* 6, 259–267. Berkeley: Berkeley Linguistics Society.

Bradley, David. 1982. Register in Burmese. In D. Bradley (ed.), *Tonation* (Pacific Linguistics Series A-62), 117–132. Canberra: Australian National University.

Bradley, David. 1985. Arakanese vowels. In G. Thurgood, J. A. Matisoff & David Bradley (eds.), *Linguistics of Sino-Tibetan area: The state of the art*, 180–200. Canberra: Pacific Linguistics (C-87).

Bradley, David. 1994a. Pronouns in Lolo-Burmese. In Hajime Kitamura, Tatsuo Nishida & Yasuhiko Nagano (eds.), *Current issues in Sino-Tibetan linguistics*, 556–563. Osaka: The Organizing Committee, 26th International Conference on Sino-tibetan Languages and Linguistics.

Bradley, David. 1994b. The subgrouping of Proto-Tibeto-Burman. In Hajime Kitamura, Tatsuo Nishida & Yasuhiko Nagano (eds.), *Current Issues in Sino-Tibetan Linguistics*, 59–78. Osaka: The Organizing Committee, 26th International Conference on Sino-tibetan Languages and Linguistics.

Bradley, David. 1997. Tibeto-Burman languages and classification. In D. Bradley (ed.), *Papers in Southeast Asian Linguistics No. 14: Tibeto-Burman languages of the Himalayas*. Camberra: Dept. of Linguistics, The Australian National University.

Bradley, David. 2002. The sub-grouping of Tibeto-Burman. In C. Beckwith (ed.), *Medieval Tibeto-Burman Languages*, 73–112, Leiden: Brill.

Bradley, David. 2007. Language endangerment in China and mainland Southeast Asia. In M. Brenzinger (ed.), *Language diversity endangered*, 277–301. Berlin & New York: Mouton de Gruyter.

Bradley, David. 2007. East and Southeast Asia. In C. Moseley (ed.), *Encyclopedia of the World's Endangered Languages*, 349–422. London: Routledge.

Bril, Isabelle. 2004. Complex nuclei in Oceanic languages: Contribution to an areal typology. In I. Bril, F. Ozanne-Rivierre (eds.), *Complex predicates in oceanic language: Studies in the dynamics of binding and boundness*, 1–48. Berlin & New York: Mouton de Gruyter.

Burling, Robert. 1965. How to choose a Burmese numeral classifier. In Melford E. Spiro (ed.), *Context and meaning in cultural anthropology*, 243–264. New York: The Free Press.

Cooke, Joseph Robinson. 1968. *Pronominal reference in Thai, Burmese, and Vietnamese*. Berkeley, CA: University of California Press.

Cornyn William. 1944. Outline of Burmese grammar. *Language* 20 (4) [suppl.]: 3–34. Baltimore: Waverly Press.

Craig, Colette. 1992. Classifiers in a functional perspective. In M. Fortescue et al. (ed.), *Layered structure and reference in functional perspective*, 277–301. Amsterdam: John Benjamins.

DeLancey Scott. 1990. Sino-Tibetan languages. In Bernard Comrie. *The major languages of East and Southeast Asia*. London: Routledge. Pp. 69–82.

DeLancey Scott. 1991. The origins of verb serialization in modern Tibetan. *Studies in Language* 15 (1). 1–23. Amsterdam: John Benjamins.

DeLancey Scott. 1997. Grammaticalization and the gradience of categories: Relator nouns and postpositions in Tibetan and Burmese. In Joan L. Bybee, John Haiman & Sandra A. Thompson (eds.), *Essays on language function and language type dedicated to Talmy Givón*, 51–69. Amsterdam: John Benjamins.

DeLancey Scott. 2011. Finite structures from clausal nominalization in Tibeto-Burman. In F. H. Yap, K. Grunow-Harsta & Wrona Janick (eds.), *Nominalisation in Asian languages, diachronic and typological perspectives*, 343–359. Amsterdam: John Benjamins.

Egreteau, Renaud. 2012. Birmanie, la transition octroyée. *Etudes* 416 (3). 295–305.

Esche, Annemarie. 1994. Some problems of hybridity in the Myanmar language. In *Tradition and modernity in Myanmar*, Proceedings of an international conference held in Berlin, 7–9 May 1993, 393–398. Berlin: Lit Verlag.

Goral, Donald R. 1978. Numerical classifier systems: A Southeast Asian cross-linguistic analysis. *Linguistics of the Tibeto-Burman Area* 4 (1). 1–72.

Grinevald, Colette G. 2000. A morphosyntactic typology of classifiers. In G. Senft (ed.), *Nominal Classification*, 50–92. Cambridge: Cambridge University Press.

Haas, Mary R. 1951. The use of numeral classifiers in Burmese. In W. Popper (ed.), *Semitic and oriental studies*, 191–200. Berkeley & Los Angeles: University of California Press.

Hagège, Claude. 1975. *Le problème linguistique des prépositions et la solution chinoise*. Collection Linguistique de la SLP, n° LXXI, Paris-Louvain: Peeters.

Hagège, Claude. 1997. Les relateurs comme catégorie accessoire et la grammaire comme composante nécessaire. In *La préposition: une catégorie accessoire? Faits de langues* 9. 19–27.

Haiman, John. 1978. Conditionals are topics. *Language* 54 (3). 564–589.

Heine, Bernd. 1993. *Auxiliaries: Cognitive forces and grammaticalization*. Oxford: Oxford University Press.

Heine, Bernd & Tania Kuteva. 2002. *World lexicon of grammaticalization*. Cambridge UK: Cambridge University Press.

Huang, Yan. 2000. *Anaphora: A cross linguistic study with special reference to Mandarin*. Cambridge UK: Cambridge University Press.

Hla Pe. 1961. Some adapted Pali loan-words in Burmese. *Fiftieth Anniversary Publications* 1. 71–99. Rangoon: Burma Research Society, University Estate.

Hla Pe. 1965. A re-examination of Burmese classifiers. *Lingua* 15. 163–185.

Hla Pe. 1967. A tentative list of Mon loan words in Burmese. *Journal of the Burma Research Society* L/i, 71–94. Rangoon: Burma Research Society, University Estate.

Hnin Tun San San. 2006. *Discourse marking in Burmese and English: A corpus-based approach*. PhD thesis, University of Nottingham, UK.

Ishiyama, Osamu. 2008. *Diachronic perspectives on personal pronouns in Japanese*. PhD dissertation, State University of New York at Buffalo.

Jacquesson, François. 1998. L'évolution et la stratification du lexique. Contribution à une théorie de l'évolution linguistique. *Bulletin de la Société de Linguistique de Paris* 93 (1). 77–136.

Jenny, Mathias. 2009. Modality in Burmese: 'may' or 'must' – grammatical uses of yá 'get'. *Journal of the SouthEast Asian Linguistic Society* 1. 111–126.

Jenny, Mathias & Hnin Tun San San. 2016. *Burmese, a comprehensive grammar*. London & New York: Routledge.

Judson, Adoniram. 1852 [1893]. *Judson's Burmese-English dictionary. Revised and enlarged by Robert C. Stevenson*. Rangoon: Printed by the superintendent, Government printing, Burma.

Kasevitch, Vadim B. 1994. Buddhist tradition and some aspects of the Burmese political vocabulary. In Uta Gärtner & Jens Lorenz (eds.), *Tradition and modernity in Myanmar*.

Proceedings of an international conference held in Berlin, 7–9 May 1993, vol. 3 (2), 373–78, Münster & Hamburg: Lit Verlag.

Krifka, Manfred. 2006. Basic notions of informational structure. In C. Fery & M. Krifka (eds.), *Interdisciplinary studies of information structure* 6, Potsdam.

Lambrecht, Knud. 1994. *Information structure and sentence form. Topic, focus, and mental representations of dicourses referent*. Cambridge UK: Cambridge University Press.

Maspero, Henri. 1947. Notes sur la morphologie du tibéto-birman. *Bulletin de la Société de Linguistique de Paris* 44. 155–185.

Matisoff, James A. 1973a. *The grammar of Lahu*. Berkeley: University of California Press.

Matisoff, James A. 1973b. Tonogenesis in Southeast Asia. In Larry M. Hyman (ed.), *Consonant types and tones*, 71–96. Los Angeles: Linguistic program of UCLA.

Matisoff, James A. 1983. Linguistic diversity and language contact in Thailand. In John McKinnon & Wanat Bhruksasri (eds.), *Highlanders of Thailand*, 56–86. Kuala Lumpur & New York: Oxford University Press.

Matisoff, James A. 1986. Hearts and minds in Southeast Asian languages and English: An essay in the comparative lexical semantics of psycho-collocations. *Cahiers de Linguistique Asie Orientale* 15 (1). 5–57.

Matisoff, James A. 1991. Endangered languages of Mainland Southeast Asia. In R. H. Robins & E. M. Uhlenbeck (eds.), *Endangered languages*, 189–228. Published with the authority of the Permanent International Committee of Linguists. Oxford & New York: Berg Publishers Ltd.

Matisoff, James A. 1991. Areal and universal dimensions of grammatization in Lahu. In Elizabeth Closs Traugott & Bernd Heine (eds.), *Approaches to grammaticalization: Focus on theorical and methodological issues*, vol. 2, 383–453. London: John Benjamins.

Matisoff, James A. 1999. Tibeto-Burman tonology in an areal context. In Shigeki Kaji (ed.), *Proceedings of the symposium 'Cross-linguistic studies of tonal phenomena: Tonogenesis, typology, and related topics'*, 3–32. Tokyo: Institute for the Study of Languages and Cultures of Asia and Africa, Tokyo University of Foreign Studies.

Michaud, Alexis. 2011. Les systèmes de tons en Asie orientale: typologie, schémas évolutifs et modélisation. *Faits de langues* 37. 247–261.

Min, Latt. 1962. First report on studies in Burmese grammar. *Archiv Orientalni*, 49–115. Prague: Czechoslowak Academy of Sciences.

Min, Latt. 1963. Second report on studies in Burmese grammar. *Archiv orientalni*, 230–273. Prague: Czechoslowak Academy of Sciences.

Min, Latt. 1964. Third report on studies in Burmese grammar. *Archiv orientalni*, 265–292. Prague: Czechoslowak Academy of Sciences.

Myint, Soe. 1994. A semantic study of deictic auxiliaries in Burmese. *Linguistics of the Tibeto-Burman Area* 17 (1). 125–139.

Myanmar-English Dictionary မြန်မာအင်္ဂလိပ်အဘိဓာန်. 1993. Department of Myanmar Language Commission, Ministry of Education, Union of Myanmar.

Nishi Yoshio. 1998. Old Burmese: Toward the history of Burmese. *Bulletin of the National Museum of Ethnology* 23 (3). 659–692. [reprinted 1999 in 'Four papers on Burmese'].

Okano Kenji. 2005. The verb 'give' as a causativiser in colloquial Burmese. In Justin Watkins (ed.), *Studies in Burmese linguistics*, 97–104. Canberra: Pacific Studies.

Okell, John. 1969. *A reference grammar of colloquial Burmese*. London: Oxford University Press.

Okell, John. 1995. Three Burmese Dialects. In D. Bradley (ed.), *Papers in Southeast Asian Linguistics* 13, *Studies in Burmese languages*, 1–138. Canberra: Pacific Linguistics, The Australian National University.

Okell, John & Anna Allott. 2001. *Burmese / Myanmar: A dictionary of grammatical forms.* Richmond: Curzon Press.

Potsdam, Eric. 2011. Expressing exclamatives in Malagasy. In Foong Ha Yap, Karen Grunow-Hårsta, Janick Wrona (eds.), *Nominalization in Asian languages: Diachronic and typological perspectives*, 659–684. Amsterdam: John Benjamins.

Pruitt, William. 1994. *Etude linguistique de nissaya birmans. Traduction commentée de textes bouddhiques*, vol. 174. Paris: Presses de l'Ecole Française d'Extrême-Orient (Monographies).

Romeo, Nicoletta. 2008. *Aspect in Burmese: Meaning and function.* Amsterdam: John Benjamins.

Romeo, Nicoletta. 2009. The grammaticalised use of Burmese verbs la 'come' and θwà 'go', In L. Hogeweg, H. De Hoop & A. Malchukov (eds.), *Cross-Linguistic Studies of Tense, Aspect, and Modality*, 131–154. Amsterdam: Benjamins.

Sawada, Hideo. 1994a. On the complement sentences in Modern Colloquial Burmese. In Hajime Kitamura, Tatsuo Nishida & Yasuhiko Nagano (eds.), *Current issues in Sino-Tibetan Linguistics*, 749–755.Osaka: The organizing committee, 26th international conference on Sino-Tibetan languages and linguistics.

Sawada, Hideo. 1994b. Significance of pseudo-cleft construction in Burmese. In Hajime Kitamura, Tatsuo Nishida & Yasuhiko Nagano (eds.), *Current issues in Sino-Tibetan linguistics*, 723–729. Osaka: The organizing committee, 26th international conference on Sino-Tibetan languages and linguistics.

Sawada, Hideo. 1995. On the usages and functions of particles -kou-/-Ka in Colloquial Burmese. In Yoshio Nishi, James A. Matisoff & Yasuhiko Nagano (eds.), *New horizons of the Tibeto-Burman morphosyntax*, 153–187. Osaka: National Museum of Ethnology.

Saint-John, Rev. A. 1936. *Burmese self-taught (in Burmese and Roman characters) with phonetic pronunciation.* London: E. Marlborough & Co. Ltd.

Simpson, Andrew. 2005. Classifiers and DP structure in Southeast Asia. In Guglielmo Cinque & Richard Kayne (eds.), *The Oxford Handbook of Comparative Syntax*, Oxford: Oxford University Press, 806–838.

Simpson, Andrew & Justin Watkins. 2005. Constituent focus in Burmese: a phonetic and perceptual study. In Justin Watins (ed), Studies in Burmese Linguistics, 27–66. Canberra: Pacific Studies.

Sprigg, Richard K. 1957. Junction in spoken Burmese. In *Studies in linguistic analysis* (special volume of the *Transaction of Philological Society*), 104–138. Oxford: Blackwell.

Sprigg, Richard K. 1963. A Comparison of Arakanese and Burmese Based On Phonological Formulae. In Harry L. Shorto (ed.), *Linguistic comparison in South East Asia and the Pacific*, 109–132. London: School of Oriental and African Studies, University of London.

Stassen, Leon. 2000. *and*-languages and *with*-languages. *Linguistic Typology* 4. 1–54.

Stolz, Thomas, Cornelia Stroh & Aina Urdze. 2011. *Total reduplication. The areal linguistics of a potential universal.* (Studia Typologica 8.) Berlin: Akademie-Verlag.

Stewart, John A. 1936. *An introduction to colloquial Burmese.* Rangoon: British Burma Press.

Swank, Heidi. 2009. A response to Peter T. Daniels. In *Written Language & Literacy* 12 (2). 282–285.

Thurgood, Graham. 1981. Notes on the origins of Burmese Creaky tone. Institute for the study of Languages and Cultures of Asia and Africa, *Monumenta Serindica 9*.

Thurgood, Graham & Randy J. Lapolla (eds.). 2003. *Sino-Tibetan languages*, London: Routledge.

van der Auwera, Johan, Peter Kehayov & Alice Vittrant. 2009. Acquisitive modals. In L. Hogeweg, H. de Hoop & A. Malchukov (eds.), *Cross-linguistic studies of tense, aspect, and modality*, 271–302. Amsterdam: Benjamins.
Vittrant, Alice. 1998. *Sémantique et syntaxe des paires verbales en birman. Dans une approche contrastive avec d'autres langues tibéto-birmanes,* Maîtrise en Sciences du Langage. Université Paris 8, Saint-Denis.
Vittrant, Alice. 2002. Les marques de la prédication en birman. *Actes du colloque jeunes chercheurs praxiling*, Montpellier, Septembre 2001.
Vittrant, Alice. 2004. *La modalité et ses corrélats en birman, dans une perspective comparative.* Doctoral dissertation, Sciences du Langage, Université Paris 8, Saint-Denis. http://halshs.archives-ouvertes.fr/docs/00/18/50/69/PDF/2007_THESE.pdf (accessed 1 June 2018).
Vittrant, Alice. 2005a. Classifier systems in Burmese. *Proceedings of twenty-eighth annual meeting of Berkeley Linguistic Society 2002* (BLS 28), Berkeley, CA.
Vittrant, Alice. 2005b. Burmese as a modality-prominent language. In Justin Watkins (ed.), *Studies in Burmese Linguistics*, 143–161. Canberra: Pacific Studies.
Vittrant, Alice. 2010. Epistemic modality or how to express likelihood in Burmese. *Cahiers de Linguistique Asie Orientale* 39 (1). 41–80.
Vittrant, Alice. 2012a. How typology allows for a new analysis of the verb phrase in Burmese. *Lidil* 46 (Typologie et description linguistiques. Interfaces et interactions). 101–126.
Vittrant, Alice. 2012b. Définir la modalité: vers une théorie linguistique de la modalité à partir de son expression dans les langues. In C. Maury-Rouan (ed.), *Recueil en hommage à Robert Vion*, 107–133. Aix-en-Provence: Presses Universitaire de Provence.
Vittrant, Alice. 2013. Modalité et temporalité en birman vernaculaire: L'exemple du développement modal du morpheme spacio-temporel /Khs'/. *Cahiers Chronos T.* 269–291.
Vittrant, Alice. 2013. Psycho-collocational expressives in Burmese. In Jeffrey P. Williams (ed.), *The aesthetics of grammar*, 255–279. Cambridge: Cambridge University Press.
Vittrant, Alice. 2015. Expressing motion: The Contribution of Southeast Asian languages – with reference to East Asian Languages. In N. Enfield & B. Comrie (ed.), *Languages of Mainland Southeast Asia. The state of the art*, 587–632. Berlin & New York: Mouton de Gruyter.
Voinov, Vitaly. 2013. 'Seeing' is 'trying': the relation of visual perception to attemptive modality in the world's languages. *Language and Cognition* 5 (1). 61–80.
Watkins, Justin. 2001. Burmese. *Journal of the International Phonetic Association* 31 (2). 291–295.
Watkins, Justin. 2007. Burma/Myanmar. In Andrew Simpson (ed.), *Language and national identity in Asia*, 263–287. Oxford: Oxford University Press.
Watkins, Justin (ed.). 2005. *Studies in Burmese linguistics*. Canberra: Pacific Studies.
Wheatley, Julian K. 1982. *Burmese: A grammatical sketch*, PhD dissertation, Berkeley: University of California.
Wheatley, Julian K. 1990 [1987]. Burmese. In B. Comrie (ed.), *The major languages of East and South-East Asia*, 106–126. London: Routledge.
Wheatley, Julian K. 2003. Burmese. In Graham Thurgood & Randy J. Lapolla (eds.), *Sino-tibetan Languages*, 195–207. London: Routledge.
Wheatley, Julian K. & San San Hnin Tun. 1999. Languages in contact: The case of English and Burmese. *The Journal of Burma Studies* 4. 61–99. Center for Southeast Asian Studies, Northern Illinois University.
Yabu, Shiro. 1994. Case particles *-kà* and *-kou* in Burmese. In Hajime Kitamura, Tatsuo Nishida & Yasuhiko Nagano (eds.), *Current issues in Sino-Tibetan linguis-tics*, 730–736. Osaka:

The Organizing Committee, 26th international conference on Sino-Tibetan languages and linguistics.

Yanson, Rudolph. 1994. Mon and Pali influence on Burmese: How essential was it? In Uta Gärtner & Jens Lorenz (eds.), *Tradition and modernity in Myanmar*, Proceedings of an international conference held in Berlin, 7–9 May 1993, 365–372. Münster & Hamburg: Lit Verlag.

Department of Population, Ministry of Immigration and Population. 2015. *The 2014 Myanmar population and housing census, Hightlights of the main results, census report*, vol. 2A.

Appendix 1: Summary of linguistic features

Legend
+++ the feature is pervasive or used obligatorily in the language
++ the feature is normal but selectively distributed in the language
+ the feature is merely possible or observable in the language
− the feature is impossible or absent in the language

Language studied: Burmese

Area/countries where it is spoken: BURMA (Myanmar)

	Feature	+++/++/+/−	§ ref. in this chapter
Phonetics	Lexical tone or register	+++	§1.1.3, p.63
Phonetics	Back unrounded vowels	−	−
Phonetics	Initial velar nasal	+++	§1.1.1, p.59
Phonetics	Implosive consonants	−	−
Phonetics	Sesquisyllabic structures	+(+)	§1.2, p.66
Morphology	Tendency towards monosyllabicity	+++	§2.1.1, p.67 & also p.62
Morphology	Tendency to form compounds	+++	§2.1.2, p.69 & also 67–68
Morphology	Tendency towards isolating (rather than affixation)	++	§2.1.1, p.68
Morphology	Psycho-collocations	+++	§2.2.1, p.74
Morphology	Elaborate expressions (e.g. four-syllable or other set patterns)	++	§2.2.2, p.75
Morphology	Reduplication generally	+++	§2.3, p.76
Morphology	Reduplication of nouns	+++	idem
Morphology	Reduplication of verbs	+++	idem
Grammar	Use of classifiers	+++	§3.1.2, p.87 & §3.2.3, p.92
Grammar	Classifiers used in counting	+++	§3.2.3, p.93
Grammar	Classifiers used with demonstratives	−	−

	Feature	+++/++/+/−	§ ref. in this chapter
Grammar	Adjectival verbs	+++	§3.1.2, p.86
Grammar	Grammatical number	+	§3.1.1 & 3.3.1, p.95
Grammar	Inflection of verbs	−	§3.3.1, p.95
Grammar	Use of tense/aspect markers	+++	§3.3.1, p.95 & 3.3.2, p.97
Grammar	Use of verb plural markers	+	§3.3.2, p.98
Grammar	Grammaticalization of GET/ OBTAIN (potential mod. resultative/perfect aspect)	++	§3.3.2, p.99 & p.104
Grammar	Grammaticalization of PUT, SET (completed/resultative aspect)	+++	§3.3.2, p.98–99
Grammar	Grammaticalization of GIVE (causative, benefactive; preposition)	++	§3.3.2, p.98–99
Grammar	Grammaticalization of FINISH (perfective/ complete aspect; conjunction/temporal subordinator)	+++	§3.3.2, p.99
Grammar	Grammaticalization of directional verbs e.g. GO / COME (allative, venitive)	+++	§3.3.2, p.98–99
Grammar	Grammaticalization of SEE, WATCH (temptative)	+++	§3.3.2, p.98
Grammar	Grammaticalization of STAY, REMAIN (progressive and continuous, durative aspects)	+++	§3.3.2, p.98
Grammar	Serial verb constructions	+++	§3.3.3, p.100
Grammar	Converbs	−/+	+
Syntax	Verb precedes object (VO)	−	§3.4 & §3.4.1, p.101
Syntax	Auxiliary precedes verb	−/+	§3.3.1, p.98
Syntax	Preposition precedes noun	−	§3.2.1, p.89
Syntax	Noun precedes adjective	−/+	§3.2.1, p.89
Syntax	Noun precedes demonstrative	−	−
Syntax	Noun precedes genitive	−	−
Syntax	Noun precedes relative clause	−	−
Syntax	Use of topic-comment structures	+++	§3.2.2, p.91, §3.4.3, p.101 & §3.4.4, p.106–08
Syntax	Ellipsis of arguments known from context	+++	§3.4.1, p.101
Lexical semantics	Specific terms for forms of rice	+++	§4.1.1, p.109–10
Pragmatics	Use of utterance-final pragmatic particles	++	§4.2.1, p.111

	Feature	+++/++/+/−	§ ref. in this chapter
Pragmatics	Encoding of politeness	++	§4.2.2, p.112
Pragmatics	Encoding of honorifics	+	§3.1.2, table 7, p.84 & also §4.2.2, p.112

Appendix 2: Text interlinearized

Dialogue between Daw Pu and her sister. Yangon (Burma), 1999.
　[Recording accessible online : https://cocoon.huma-num.fr/exist/crdo/meta/crdo-MYA-001_SOUND]

N°1 −　Speaker A (Daw Pu)
Burm　အဲဒီ လီယို Express ကို သွားဝယ်ရော လက်မှတ်။
phono　$?\varepsilon^3$　　　di^2　　li^2yo^2　$\varepsilon kpr\varepsilon s$ $=Ko^2$ θwa^3 $w\varepsilon^2$ yo^3 $l\varepsilon?.Ma?$
gl　　　DEM.anaph　DEM　Leo　　express　　DIR　　go　　buy　REAL　ticket
transl　We went to buy it at that 'Leo express', the ticket.

N°2
Burm　အဲဒီ အဲဒီဆိုင်လည်း သူသိတယ်၊ လီယို Express ကို။
phono　$?\varepsilon^3.di^2$　　$?\varepsilon^3.di^2$　　$shaiN^3$　$l\varepsilon^3$　θu^2　θi^1　$=T\varepsilon^2$　li^2yo^2
gl　　　DEM.anaph　DEM.anaph　shop　also　3SG　know　REAL　Leo

phono　$\varepsilon kpr\varepsilon s$　$=Ko^2$
gl　　　express　　OBJ
transl　And that... that shop, she knew it, (this) 'Leo Express'.

N°3
Burm　ဝယ်ဝယ်လည်း ပြီးလည်းပြီးရော ငါတို့လို့ အခု စကော့ဈေး သူက စကော့ဈေးသွား မယ်တဲ့။
phono　$w\varepsilon^2-w\varepsilon^2$　$l\varepsilon^3$　$pyi^3.l\varepsilon^3.pyi^3.yo^3$　ηa^2-To^1　lo^1　$?\partial-khu^1$　$s\partial Ko^1$
gl　　　buy-REDUPL　also　SUB.tps　　　　　　　　1SG-PLUR　QUOT　now　Scott

phono　ze^3　　θu^2　$=Ka^1$　$s\partial Ko^1$　ze^3　　θwa^3　$=m\varepsilon^2$　$=T\varepsilon^1$
gl　　　market　3SG　S./TOP　Scott　market　go　IR　QUOT
transl　When we were all done buying [the ticket], she said, 'Now we are going to Scott Market.'
lit :　After also buying, we, now, scott market, she said : (we) should go to Scott market.

N°4

Burm	အကျီချုပ်တာ သွားယူမယ်တဲ့॥						
phono	ʔiN²Ci²	cho?	=Ta²	θwa³	yu²	mɛ²	=Tɛ¹
gl	shirt	sew	NMLZ.REAL	go	take	IR	QUOT
transl	She said that (she) was going to pick up a blouse she'd had made.						

N°5

Burm	ဘယ်လမ်းကသွားရမလဲ॥						
phono	bɛ²	laN³	=Ka¹	θwa³	ya¹	=mə	lɛ³
gl	PR:QST	road	S.	go	AUX:GET	QST.IR	QST
transl	Which way should we go?						

N°6

Burm	ငါရပ် စဉ်းစားတယ် သိလား॥					
phono	ŋa²	ya?	siN³ za³	=Tɛ²	θi¹	la³
gl	1SG	stop	think	REAL	know	QST

Burm	ကုန်းကပဲ သွားရမလား॥					
phono	gouN³	=Ka¹	bɛ³	θwa³	ya¹	mə= la³
gl	footbridge	S.	DM:EXCL.	aller	AUX:GET	IR. QST
transl	I stopped to think about it, you know: should we go over the footbridge?					

N°7

Burm	လာ၊ လာတဲ့॥		
phono	la²	la²	=Tɛ¹
gl	come	come	QUOT
transl	'Come on,' she said.		

N°8

Burm	ငါလမ်း သိတယ်တဲ့॥				
phono	ŋa²	laN³	θi¹	=Tɛ²	=Tɛ¹
gl	1SG	road	know	REAL	QUOT
transl	'I know the way,' she said.				

N°9

Burm	သူက ရှေ့ ကနေ ခေါ် သွားလိုက်တာ॥						
phono	θu²	=Ka¹	ʃe¹	=Ka¹.ne²	khɔ²	θwa³	laiʔ-Ta²
gl	3SG	S./TOP	front	FROM	call	go	follow-REAL.EXCL
transl	She was in front, calling me to go with her.						

N°10								
Burm	Traders ဟိုတယ် ရှေ့ ကနေ စကော့ဈေးကို အတူ သွားကြတာ။							
phono	'Traders'-ho²Tɛ²	ʃe¹	=Ka¹.ne²	səKɔ¹	ze³		=Ko²	ʔə-Tu²
gl	Traders hotel	front	FROM	Scott	market		DIR.	together

phono	θwa³	=Ca¹	=Ta²
gl	go	PLUR	REAL.NF

transl   From in front of Traders Hotel, we went to Scott Market together.

N°11							
Burm	အဲဒါ ပြီးလည်းပြီးရော အပေါ်ထပ်ကို သူ ဆိုင်က						
phono	ʔɛ³-da²		pyi³.lɛ³.pyi³.yɔ³	ʔə-pɔ²	thaʔ	=Ko²	θu¹
gl	DEM.ANAPH.-that		SUB.TPS	NMLZ-top	floor	DIR	3SG.GEN

phono	shaiN²	=Ka¹
gl	shop	TOP

Burm	အပေါ်ထပ်မှာ သူက ရှေ့က ငါက နောက်က လိုက်တာ။							
phono	ʔə-pɔ²	thaʔ	=Ma²	θu²	=Ka¹	ʃe¹	=Ka¹	ŋa² =Ka¹	nɔɔʔ
gl	NMLZ.-top	floor	LOC.	3SG	TOP	front	S.	1SG S./TOP	behind

phono	=Ka¹	laiʔ-Ta²
gl	S.	follow-REAL.EXCL

transl   So then in the end, this shop of hers was upstairs, and we went up, her in front and me following behind.

N°12 – speaker B (sister)
Burm   သူ တစ်ခါတည်း ရောက်ဖူးတာ မှတ်လား။

phono	θu²	tə-kha²-Tɛ³	yɔɔʔ	phu³	=Ta²	maʔ	=la³
gl	3SG	one-time-only	arrive	EXPER	REAL.NMLZ	remember	QST

transl   Was it that she'd remembered it from just going there one time ?

N°13 – Speaker A
Burm   သူ မနှစ်ကလည်း ရောက်ဖူးတယ်။

phono	θu²	mə ɲiʔ.Ka¹	lɛ³	yɔɔʔ	phu³	=Tɛ²
gl	3SG	last year	also	arrive	EXPER	REAL

transl   She had been there last year as well.

N°14
Burm   အဲဒီ မိုးမိုးနဲ့လည်း သူငယ်ချင်း ဖြစ်နေတာ။
phono   ʔɛ³.di²   mo³mo³ =nɛ¹ lɛ² θəŋɛ²ChiN³ phyi? ne²   =Ta²
gl   DEM.anaph.   Momo   with also friend   be   AUX:INACC REAL.NF
transl She is friends with this Moe Moe as well.

N°15
Burm   အေး ဒါပေမဲ့ သူ မှတ်မိနေတယ်။
phono   ʔe²   da²pe²mɛ¹   θu²   ma?.mi¹   ne²   =Tɛ²
gl   EUPH. but   3SG   remember AUX:INACC REAL
transl Yes – but she remembers it.

N°18
Burm   ဝန်းသိုကနေ လာပြီးတော့ အကျီ ချုပ်တာတဲ့။
phono   waN³θo² =Ka¹.ne² la² pyi³-Tɔ¹   ʔiN²Ci² cho? =Ta²   =Tɛ¹
gl   Wantho   FROM   come SUB.tps-EMPH   shirt   sew   REAL.NF   QUOT
transl She [Momo] told (her) that she came from WanTho and she is a dress-maker.
lit.   She said she had sewn shirts after she came from Wantho.

N°19
Burm   ကောင်မလေးက တော်တယ် သိလား။
phono   kaɔN²ma¹le³   =Ka¹   tɔ²   =Tɛ²   θi¹   =la³
gl   young woman   TOP   be smart   REAL   know   QST
transl She's a clever girl, you know?

N°20
Burm   တော်တော်လေးလေ ဟို nice ဖြစ်တယ်လေ။
phono   tɔ²-Tɔ²-le³   le²   ho²   nice   phyi? =Tɛ²   le²
gl   smart-x2-DIM   DM:insist   EUPH   <nice>[Engl.] be   REAL   DM
transl Really quite clever, erm, well she's nice, you see.

N°21
Burm   အဲဒါ အန်တီရယ်တဲ့။
phono   ʔɛ³- da²   ʔaNti²-yɛ²   =Tɛ¹
gl   DEM.anaph.- that   Aunty-AFFECT.   QUOT
transl Moreover, [she called] me 'Aunty'.
lit.   So s.o. called [her] 'Aunty'.

N°22

Burm	သူ့နဲ့ မနှစ်က သူငယ်ချင်း ဖြစ်တာတဲ့။						
phono	θu²	=nɛ¹	məṇi?.Ka¹	θəŋɛ²ChiN³	phyi?	=Ta²	=Tɛ¹
gl	3SG	with	last year	friend	be	REAL.NF	QUOT
transl	She said they became friends last year.						

N°23

Burm	ဘယ်သူ သွားပို့လဲတော့ မသိဘူး မိုးမိုးကို။								
phono	bɛ²θu²	θwa³	po¹	lɛ³	=Tɔ¹	mə	θi¹	=Phu³	mo³mo³	=Ko²
gl	WHO	go	carry	QST	TOP	NEG	know	NEG	Momo	OBJ
transl	I don't know who took her there. To Moe Moe's place.								

N°24

Burm	သူ့နဲ့ မနှစ်က သူငယ်ချင်း ဖြစ်တာ၊ မနှစ်က သူ့ကို လျှောက်ပို့နိုင်တယ်။							
phono	θu²	=nɛ¹	məṇi?.Ka¹	θəŋɛ²ChiN³	phyi?	=Ta²	məṇi?.Ka¹	
gl	3SG	with	last year	friend	be	REAL.NF	last year	

phono	θu¹	=Ko²	ʃaɔ?	po¹	naiN²	=Tɛ²
gl	3SG.OBL.	OBJ	AUX:at random	accompany	can	REAL
transl	She became friends with her last year, so she could have taken her around with her.					
lit.	(She) is friend with her (since) last year ; last year, (she) could take her around anywhere.					

N°25

Burm	လျှောက်လည်နိုင်တယ်တဲ့။				
phono	ʃaɔ?-lɛ²	naiN²	=Tɛ²	=Tɛ¹	
gl	walk-visit	can	REAL	QUOT	
transl	They were able to go around [together].				

N°26

Burm	အဲဒါနဲ့ သူ အကျႌ ချုပ်တယ်။						
phono	ʔɛ³-da²	=nɛ¹	θu²	ʔiN²Ci²	cho?	khaiN³	=Tɛ²
gl	DEM.anaph.-that	with	3SG	shirt	sew	order	REAL
transl	And so she had some blouses made.						

N°27

Burm	ချုပ်ခိုင်းလည်း ပြီးလည်းပြီးရော၊ အဲဒီ အပေါ် ကို သူတက်သွားမပေါ့။							
phono	cho?	khaiN³	lɛ³	pyi³.lɛ³.pyi³.yɔ³	ʔɛ³di²	ʔə-pɔ²	=Ko²	θu²
gl	sew	order	also	SUB.tps	DEM.anaph	NMLZ-top	DIR	3SG

phono	tɛʔ	=Ta²	pɔ¹
gl	go.up	REAL.NF	DM:EXCL.
transl	When she'd done with asking to have the blouses made, she went right upstairs.		

N°28
Burm	အဲဒီ အပေါ်မှာတဲ့ အသစ်နေရာမှာ။						
phono	ʔɛ³- di²	ʔə-pɔ²	=Ma²	=Tɛ¹	ʔə-θiʔ	ne²ya²	=Ma²
gl	DEM.anaph.-DEM.	NMLZ.-top	LOC.	QUOT	NMLZ-be.new	place	LOC
transl	She said it was upstairs, in a new place.						

N°29
Burm	အဲဒါ တက်လည်း ပြီးလည်းပြီးရော။			
phono	ʔɛ³- da²	tɛʔ	lɛ³	pyi³-lɛ³-pyi³-yɔ³
gl	DEM.anaph.-that	go.up	also	SUB.tps
transl	So up we went, and that was it.			

N°30
Burm	အပေါ် လည်း ကျလည်းကျရော အကျီတွေဘာတွေ ချုပ်ချက်လည်း ပြီးလည်းပြီးရော။						
phono	ʔə-pɔ²	lɛ³	ca¹	lɛ³	ca¹	yɔ³	ʔiN²Ci²-Twe²
gl	NMLZ.-top	also	happen	also	happen	REAL	shirt-PLUR

phono	ba²-Twe²	choʔ - chɛʔ	lɛ³	pyi³-lɛ³-pyi³-yɔ³
gl	PR.QST-PLUR:some	sew-REDUPL.	also	SUB.tps
transl	So once we got upstairs, and we were all finished with having the blouses and what not made.			

N°31
Burm	အောက်ပြန်၊ ငါတို့ဆို၊ ခါတိုင်းဆို အောက်ကိုဆင်းပြီး						
phono	ʔaɔʔ	pyaN²	ŋa²-To¹	sho²	kha²-TaiN³	sho²	ʔaɔʔ	=Ko²
gl	below	back	1SG-PLUR.	say	time-each	say	below	DIR.

phono	shiN³	pyi³
gl	go.down	SUB.tps

Burm	အောက်ကနေ သွားတာ သူက မဟုတ်ဘူးတဲ့။							
phono	ʔaɔʔ	=Ka¹	ne²	θwa³	=Ta²	θu²	=Ka¹	mə hoʔ	=Phu³	=Tɛ¹
gl	below	S.	place	go	REAL.NF	3SG	TOP	NEG be true	NEG	QUOT
transl	To go back down, normally we go down the bottom way, but she said 'No'.									

N°32
Burm	သူက အပေါ် က သွားမယ်တဲ့။						
phono	θu²	=Ka¹	ʔə-pɔ²	=Ka¹	θwa³	=mɛ²	=Tɛ¹
gl	3SG	S./TOP	NMLZ-top	S.	go	IR	QUOT
transl	She said : 'We'll go the top way.'						

N°33
Burm	အပေါ် ကဆိုင်တွေကနေ ဖြတ်ဖြတ်ဖြတ်ဖြတ်ပြီး ထွက်တာ				
phono	ʔə-pɔ²	=Ka¹	shaiN²-Twe²	=Ka¹.ne²	phyaʔ phyaʔ phyaʔ phyaʔ
gl	NMLZ-top	TOP	shop-PLUR	FROM	(cross.REDUPL).REDUPL

phono	pyi³	thwɛʔ	=Ta²
gl	SUB.tps	go.out	REAL.NF

Burm	ဟို အရှေ့ ဝရံတာနား ရောက်သွားရော ။						
phono	ho²	ʔə-ʃe¹	wə-raN²da²	na³	yaɔʔ	θwa³	yɔ³
gl	DEM.distal	NMLZ.-front	corridor	nearby	arrive	go	REAL
transl	We went all the way right past the shops upstairs to get out, and ended up near the front balcony.						

N°34
Burm	နင် အဲဒီနေရာ သိလားလို့ ငါ တစ်ခါမှ မသိဘူးလို့။								
phono	niN²	ʔɛ³.di²	ne²ya²	θi¹	la³	lo¹	ŋa²	tiʔ	kha²	ma¹
gl	2SG	DEM.anaph.	place	know	QST	QUOT	1SG	one	time	only

phono	mə=	θi¹	=Phu³	lo¹
gl	NEG	know	NEG	QUOT
transl	'Do you know that place?' I asked; 'I've never known it,' I said.				

N°35
Burm	အဲဒီကနေ သွားပြီးမှ လှေကားကနေ ပြန်ဆင်းပြီးမှ သူဟာ ဘာ ဝယ်လဲ သိလား။							
phono	ʔɛ.di²	=Ka¹.ne²	θwa³	pyi³	ma¹	lɛ² ka³	=Ka¹.ne²	
gl	DEM.anaph	FROM	go	finish/SUB.	only	stairs	FROM	

phono	pyaN²	shiN³	pyi³	=M̥a¹	θu²	ha²	ba²	wɛ² lɛ³	θi¹	la³
gl	AUX:back	go.down	SUB.tps	only	3SG	TOP	PR.REL	buy QST	know	QST
transl	So after we'd gone back down the staircase from there, do you know what she bought then?								

N°36
Burm မြွေအရေခွံအိတ် ဝယ်တယ်။
phono mywe²-ʔəye²KhuN³   ʔeiʔ   wɛ²   =Tɛ²
gl   snake-skin.animal   bag   buy   REAL
transl She bought a 'snakeskin' bag.

Atsuhiko Kato
Pwo Karen

Introduction

Pwo Karen belongs to the Karenic branch of the Tibeto-Burman language family. Most Tibeto-Burman languages are of the SOV type, but the basic word order for Karenic languages is SVO. The change from OV to VO is believed to have occurred in the proto-language of the Karenic languages (see Matisoff 1991a: 481–482, 2000: 346–347), most likely through contact with some Mon-Khmer language(s). Matisoff (2000) suggests heavy contact with Mon in the late first millennium AD. Manson (2009) observes that Mon-Khmer loanwords in Karenic languages imply a greater connection with the Palaungic branch of Mon-Khmer rather than the Monic branch.

The Karenic branch includes various languages in addition to Pwo Karen, such as Blimaw, Bwe, Geba, Gekho, Kayah, Kayan, Kayo, Manu, Monebwa, Mopwa, Paku, Pa-O, Sgaw Karen, Thalebwa, Yeinbaw, and Yintale[1]. Although Jones (1961) argued that Pwo Karen and Sgaw Karen are only remotely related, one of the genealogically closest languages to Pwo Karen in the Karenic branch is Sgaw Karen. Manson (2003) and Shintani (2003), two of the most recent studies on the classification of the Karenic languages, both classify Pwo Karen as having a relatively close relationship to Sgaw Karen.

According to an estimate of the Myanmar government in 1993, the total population of the Karen people was 2.86 million. Nearly half of this number is most likely Pwo Karen. There are also tens of thousands of Pwo Karen in Thailand. In Myanmar, only Pwo Karen and Sgaw Karen are occasionally considered ethnically Karen.

The Pwo Karen language is widely spoken in the Irrawaddy Delta, Mon State, Karen State, Tennasserim Division, West-Central Thailand, and Northwestern Thailand. Given findings reported in the studies of Kato (1995, 2009b), Phillips (2000), and Dawkins & Phillips (2009a, 2009b), Pwo Karen dialects can

---

[1] According to Shintani, Tadahiko (p.c.), the number of Karenic languages can be near fifty.

Atsuhiko Kato: Keio University
E-Mail: atsuhiko@icl.keio.ac.jp

be classified into four preliminary groups, as shown in Table 1. The criterion for this grouping is mutual intelligibility, that is, dialects in each group are unintelligible to speakers from other groups. However, degrees of intelligibility between dialects can vary, even within the same group. Thus, these classifications might need to be revised after more consideration. For intelligibility between the dialects in Thailand, see the findings reported by Dawkins & Phillips (2009a, 2009b).

Table 1: Pwo Karen dialect groups

Dialect	Location
Western Pwo Karen	Irrawaddy Delta, Myanmar
Htoklibang Pwo Karen	Bilin Township, Mon State, Myanmar
Eastern Pwo Karen	Karen State, Myanmar; Mon State, Myanmar; Tennasserim Division, Myanmar; West-Central Thailand[2]
Northern Pwo Karen	Northwestern Thailand

This chapter focuses on one of the dialects in the Eastern Pwo Karen group, which is spoken around Hpa-an (ဘားအံ /phă?àn/ in Burmese and ထုံအင် /thə?àn/ in Pwo Karen), the capital of Karen State. I call this variety the Hpa-an dialect. This dialect has been influenced by its neighboring languages, including Mon, Burmese, and Thai, and there are a number of loanwords from these languages in the Hpa-an dialect. The name for ethnic Pwo Karen in the Hpa-an dialect is /phlòuɴ/. The majority of the speakers of the Hpa-an dialect are Buddhists, but there are also a few Christians. Buddhists and Christians use different writing systems (see Kato 2006); this chapter uses the Buddhist writing system. This system appeared in the second half of the 18th century at earliest through the influence of the Mon writing system. It is now more widespread than the Christian writing system in Karen State.

---

[2] The West-Central Thailand Pwo Karen people are a politically distinct group from the Pwo Karen people of Myanmar who speak Eastern Pwo Karen dialects. They are Thai citizens who came to Thailand over 200 years ago at the invitation of King Rama I (Renard 1980).

1 Phonology

1.1 Suprasegmental phonology

The Hpa-an dialect has four tones:

High-level	ဃː	má	[ma55]
Mid-level	ဃ·	mā	[ma̤33 ~ 334]
Low-level	ဃ	mà	[ma11]
Falling	ဃʔ	mâ	[ma51]

Mid-level is pronounced with breathy phonation, and may be pronounced with a rising pitch in utterance-final position and before a pause.

Haudricourt (1946) reconstructed three tones for Proto-Karen, and later added another tone in Haudricourt (1975). Hpa-an tones correspond to the Proto-Karen tones, as shown in Table 2. The numbers 1, 2, 2', and 3 represent the Proto-Karen tones. Tone1, Tone2, and Tone3 were first reconstructed in 1946, and Tone2' was added in 1975. Tone1, Tone2, and Tone2' are plain tones while Tone3 is a checked tone. The capital letters H, M, and L represent the classes of Proto-Karen initial consonants: H=voiceless aspirated stops, voiceless fricatives, voiceless sonorants; M=voiceless unaspirated stops, implosives (or preglottalized stops); L=voiced stops, voiced fricatives, voiced sonorants. Haudricourt (1975) assumes that Tone2' merged with Tone2 in syllables beginning with L-series consonants at the Proto-Karen stage.

Table 2: Tonal correspondence with Proto-Karen

	1 (plain)	2 (plain)	2' (plain)	3 (checked)
H	Falling [51]	High-level [55]	High-level [55]	Low-level [11]
M	Low-level [11]	High-level [55]	High-level [55]	Low-level [11]
L	Low-level [11]	Mid-level [33]		High-level [55]

Kato (1995) reports that some dialects of Pwo Karen, such as Tavoy (Eastern Pwo) and Kyonbyaw (Western Pwo), have a final glottal stop in the syllables which used to have Tone3 at the Proto-Karen stage, for example, /thòʔ/ 'pig' in Tavoy. Thus, Proto-Pwo must have had a final glottal stop, but it no longer appears in the Hpa-an dialect.

According to Shintani (2003), the Proto-Karen voiced stops *b, *d, *g are conserved in four Karenic languages, that is, Bwe, Geba, Monebwa, and Paku.

Detailed data for Bwe are presented in Henderson (1997) and Geba is discussed in Kato (2008a). In the other Karenic languages, Proto-Karen *b, *d, *g have changed to [p], [t], [k] or [pʰ], [tʰ], [kʰ] (see Jones 1961, Shintani 2003, and Manson 2009). In Pwo Karen dialects, *b, *d, *g have changed to [pʰ], [tʰ], [kʰ].

1.2 Syllable structure and segmental phonemes

The syllable structure of the Hpa-an dialect can be represented as C1(C2)V1(V2)(N)/(T). 'C' stands for a consonant, 'V' a vowel, and 'T' a tone. 'T' is bracketed because Pwo Karen has atonic syllables, which always end with the vowel /ə/, and I transcribe these syllables as *Cə* without a tonal diacritic. Atonic syllables cannot appear in an utterance-final position.

The transcriptions used in this chapter are phonemic. There are 26 consonant phonemes and 11 vowel phonemes, as shown in Table 3. Phonetic values to notice are: /θ/[t̪~θ], /c/[tɕ], /ph/[pʰ], /th/[tʰ], /ch/[tɕʰ], /kh/[kʰ], /b/[ɓ], /d/[ɗ], /j/[j~ʝ], /r/[ɾ], /i/[ᵊi], /i̱/[ɪ]³, /ɯ/[ᵊɯ]. Similar to the neighboring language Burmese, there are contrasts between aspirated and unaspirated stops; however, /b/ and /d/ are implosives, unlike egressive /b/ or /d/ in Burmese. There are no voiceless sonorants, even though, Proto-Karen used to have these sound types. The consonants /ɲ/, /ŋ/, and /r/ occur mostly in loanwords from Mon or Burmese.

Table 3: Consonants and vowels

Consonants							Vowels		
p	θ	t	c	k	ʔ		i	i̱	ɯ
ph		th	ch	kh			ɪ		ʊ
b		d					e	ə	o
			ɕ	x		h	ɛ	a	ɔ
				ɣ	ʁ				
m		n	(ɲ)	(ŋ)	ɴ				
w			j						
		l							
		(r)							

---

3 I usually use the symbol "ı" for the vowel phoneme that is represented as /i̱/ (underbarred "i") in this article. However, "ı" and the symbol "i" representing another vowel phoneme are difficult to distinguish from each other when they are with a tone mark and in italic. Compare, for example, "*ı̀*" (ı̀) to "*ì*" (ì). Thus, in this paper the symbol "i̱" is employed for the former, and these are represented respectively as "i̱" and "i".

All of the consonants except /ɴ/ can occur as C1. Four consonants can occur as C2: /w, l, r, j/. Table 4 displays all of the possible combinations of C1 and C2.

Table 4: Possible combinations of C1 and C2

		p	θ	t	c	k	ʔ	ph	th	ch	kh	b	d	x	h	m	n	j	l
C2	w	+	+	+	+	+		+	+	+	+	+	+	+	+	+	+		
	l	+			+		+		+	+		+	+			+			
	r	+		+	+														
	j	+				+						+				+			+

The part of the syllable labeled -V1(V2)(N) is called the rhyme. There are 21 types of rhymes in Hpa-an, as shown in Table 5.

Table 5: Rhymes

Rhymes

i	ɨ	ɯ		ai	aʊ	(iɴ)	əɴ	eiɴ	əɯɴ	oʊɴ
ɪ		ʊ				aɴ	oɴ	aiɴ		
e	ə	o								
ɛ	a	ɔ								

The uvular nasal /ɴ/, which can only occur syllable-finally, often does not form a closure and may only nasalize the preceding vowel, especially in rapid speech. Moreover, the final consonant /ɴ/ of /eiɴ/, /əɯɴ/, /oʊɴ/ is frequently totally dropped. /iɴ/ is only found in Burmese loanwords.

The vowel of the rhyme /aɴ/ is phonetically realized as a diphthong. The entire rhyme is pronounced as [ăɔɴ]. This diphthong is different from the diphthongs of /eiɴ/, /əɯɴ/, /oʊɴ/, and /aiɴ/ because it is a rising diphthong, while the first and second elements of the diphthongs in /eiɴ/ [ei(ɴ)], /əɯɴ/ [əɯ(ɴ)], /oʊɴ/ [oʊ(ɴ)], and /aiɴ/ [aiɴ] are of equal prominence.

2 Morphology

2.1 Word structure

Pwo Karen is a highly isolating language; its words do not inflect at all. However, there are three productive word formation processes: compounding (2.1.1), affixation (2.1.2), and reduplication (2.1.3). Pwo Karen words are classified into five classes: nouns, verbs, adverbs, particles, and interjections (Kato 2004).

Typical Pwo Karen morphemes are monosyllabic, and many of them can stand on their own as a word. Thus, Pwo Karen has a lot of monosyllabic words. Examples of monosyllabic words are as follows: ခေါဟ် *khú* 'head', ၃း *cuí* 'hand', ခင်း *khán* 'leg', နိဝ် *nò* 'mouth', နှာ *nâ* 'nose', နှာ· *nā* 'ear', လေဝ် *lḭ* 'go', ဟှယ့် *yê* 'come', မ့ိ *mî* 'sleep', အင်း *ʔán* 'eat', အဝ် *ʔɔ̀* 'drink', မာ *mà* 'do', and သိ့ *θî* 'die'. Some Pwo Karen words are polysyllabic, and many of them are formed through compounding, affixation, and reduplication.

Pwo Karen also has a lot of 'sesquisyllabic' words, that is, disyllabic words with an atonal first syllable. (The term 'sesquisyllabic' was first introduced by Matisoff 1973b: 84 ff.) Sesquisyllabic words may be monomorphemic or have an atonal prefix. Monomorphemic examples include: ကံ့ဆင် *kəchân* 'elephant', ပှ· *pənā* 'buffalo', တံ့ကဝ် *təkɔ̀* 'lotus', အံ့ယှက် *ʔəjáʊ* 'age', စံ့ယှာ *cəxwà* 'king', ပံ့အင် *pəʔòn* 'white ant', and သိ့ဝါ် *θəwài* 'to suck'. Examples with atonal prefixes အံ့ *ʔə-* and ဆံ့ *chə-* are shown in 2.1.2.

Below are the word formation processes in Pwo Karen.

2.1.1 Compounding

Compounding is a highly productive process of word formation in Pwo Karen. Only nouns and verbs are involved in compounding, and the resultant words are also nouns or verbs. The possible compounding patterns are described below.

[A] There are four patterns in the formation of compound nouns:
- N+N > N   There are many instances of this pattern in my data. In most cases the latter element is the semantic head as in (1), (2), and (3).
(1) မဲ *mé* 'eye' + ထံ့ *thî* 'water' > မဲထံ့ *méthî* 'tear'
(2) သီး *θí* 'medicine' + တဝ် *tàʊ* 'building' > သီးတဝ် *θítàʊ* 'hospital'
(3) ၃း *buí* 'rice' + ဖင် *phân* 'storehouse' > ၃းဖင် *buíphân* 'granary'

The former element may be the semantic head as in (4) and (5), but this is relatively rare. The reason for this irregularity is unknown; however, it could be the result of influence from Mon.
(4) လာင်း *láɪn* 'cart' + မ့ *mḭ* 'fire' > လာင်းမ့ *láɪnmḭ* 'train'
(5) ဖှင် *phə̀n* 'pot' + ထာ *thà* 'iron' > ဖှင်ထာ *phə̀nthà* 'Chinese pot made of iron'

- N+V > N There are many instances of this pattern in my data. The syntactic relationship of the noun and the verb varies: the 'N' may be the subject of the 'V' as in (6), the object as in (7), or the adjunct as in (8) and (9). In many cases, the semantic head is the 'N', but sometimes resultant nouns are headless as in (9): a 'handle' is not a kind of 'hand'.
(6) လုံး *lōʊN* 'stone' + ယှဲ့ *jḭ* 'to be green' > လုံးယှဲ့ *lōʊNjḭ* 'jade'
(7) သိၣ် *θâN* 'side dish' + အဓ် *ʔɔ̀* 'to drink' > သိၣ်အဓ် *θâNʔɔ̀* 'soup'
(8) ထာ *thà* 'iron' + ဆာ *chà* 'to sew' > ထာဆာ *thàchà* 'sewing needle'
(9) စုး *cúɪ* 'hand' + ဖိံး *phóN* 'to hold' > စုးဖိံး *chúɪphóN* 'handle, grip'

- V+V > N There are a few instances of this pattern in my data:
(10) ဝဲ *bàN* 'to be yellow' + အွာ *ʔwà* 'to be white' > ဝဲအွာ *bàNʔwà* 'curtain'
(11) ကဲၣ် *kòN* 'wear (as sarong)' + သိဲ့ *θò* 'wear (as shirt)' > ကဲၣ်သိဲ့ *kòNθò* 'clothes'

- V+N > N Only one instance of this pattern has been found in my data:
(12) အိဖွဲ့ *ʔɔ́phlé* 'to be born' + မု•ကီ *muīnì* 'day' > အိဖွဲ့မု•ကီ *ʔɔ́phlémuīnì* 'birthday'

[B] There are three patterns for the formation of compound verbs:
- V+V > V There are many instances of this pattern in my data. Compounding of quasi-synonymous verbs as in (15) and (16) results in more formal words.
(13) နိၣ် *nâN* 'to smell' + အူး *ʔuí* 'to be rotten' > နိၣ်အူး *nâNʔuí* 'to have rotten smell'
(14) ပျာ့် *cû* 'to bump' + ကိုလဲၣ် *kəlôN* 'to hurry' > ပျာ့်ကိုလဲၣ် *cûkəlôN* 'to hurry'
(15) ယှီ့ *xî* 'to be beautiful' + ပျာဓ် *yḭ̀* 'to be good' > ယှီ့ပျာဓ် *xîyḭ̀* 'to be beautiful'
(16) ဟိၣ် *yòN* 'to be finished' + ထက် *tháʊ* 'to end' > ဟိၣ်ထက် *yòNtháʊ* 'to be finished'

- N+V > V There are many instances of this pattern, and most of these have a body-related noun as the first element. (See also 3.2 below.)
(17) သာ *θà* 'heart' + ခဲဓ် *khū* 'to be hot' > သာခဲဓ် *θàkhū* 'to worry'
(18) နာ• *nā* 'ear' + ဟှိၣ် *yân* 'to hear' > နာ•ဟှိၣ် *nāyân* 'to hear'

- V+N > V A few instances including the verbs below have been found in my data:
(19) ဧး *bá* 'to hit' + သာ *θà* 'heart' > ဧးသာ *báθà* 'to want (something)'
(20) ကော် *kè* 'to write' + ပြိၣ် *pərâN* 'news' > ကော်ပြိၣ် *kèpərâN* 'to write (a letter)'

2.1.2 Affixation

Pwo Karen has affixes; however, only a limited number of morphemes function as affixes. These morphemes are all derivational as there are no inflectional affixes in Pwo Karen. Kato (2004) lists 10 derivational affixes, and the following affixes are the most productive ones.

အ့် *ʔə-* is prefixed to verbs mainly denoting states, and derives nouns. This morpheme is related to the Proto-Tibeto-Burman prefix **a-* (Benedict 1972: 121–123; see also Matisoff 2003: 104–117), which has various functions in Tibeto-Burman languages, including nominalization.

(21) အ့် *ʔə-* + ခိုင်း *khléiɴ* 'to be cold' > အ့်ခိုင်း *ʔəkhléiɴ* 'cold thing'
(22) အ့် *ʔə-* + ဆာင်း *cháiɴ* 'to be sour' > အ့်ဆာင်း *ʔəcháiɴ* 'sour food'
(23) အ့် *ʔə-* + အွာ *ʔwà* 'to be white' > အ့်အွာ *ʔəʔwà* 'white color'

ဆ့် *chə-* is prefixed to various kinds of verbs, and derives nouns. It originates from the noun ဆ့ *chā*, which means 'thing'. Compared to အ့် *ʔə-*, nouns derived with ဆ့် *chə-* tend to have more abstract meanings.

(24) ဆ့် *chə-* + ခိုင်း *khléiɴ* 'to be cold' > ဆ့်ခိုင်း *chəkhléiɴ* 'coldness'
(25) ဆ့် *chə-* + အဲ *ʔé* 'to love' > ဆ့်အဲ *chəʔé* 'love (n.)'
(26) ဆ့် *chə-* + မာ *mà* 'to do' > ဆ့်မာ *chəmà* 'job'

အေ *ʔè-* is prefixed to stative verbs, and derives adverbs.
(27) အေ *ʔè-* + ဂျံဝ် *yì* 'to be good' > အေဂျံဝ် *ʔèyì* 'well'

ဖ *phà-* is prefixed to stative verbs, and emphasizes the meaning of the verb.
(28) ဖ *phà-* + ဒွဟ် *dʊ́* 'to be big' > ဖဒွဟ် *phàdʊ́* 'to be quite big'

ဖျောဟ် *-phʊ́* (also pronounced *wʊ́*) is a diminutive which is suffixed to nouns. It originates from the noun ဖျောဟ် *phʊ́* 'child'.
(29) ယး *já* 'fish' + ဖျောဟ် *-phʊ́* > ယးဖျောဟ် *jáphʊ́ (jáwʊ́)* 'little fish'

2.1.3 Reduplication

Reduplication applies only to verbs; nouns cannot be reduplicated. Reduplication derives an adverb from a stative verb. Derived adverbs are more colloquial than those with အေ *ʔè-* shown in 3.1.2 above.

(30) အး *ʔá* 'to be many' > အးအး *ʔáʔá* 'much'
(31) ဖျဲ *phlé* 'to be fast' > ဖျဲဖျဲ *phléphlé* 'fast'

(32) ကၠဲ *xè* 'to be slow' > ကၠဲကၠဲ *xèxè* 'slowly'
(33) ဟောၟ *yì* 'to be good' > ဟောၟဟောၟ *yìyì* 'well'

Disyllabic words are reduplicated in the form of AABB (A and B stand for each syllable) when they are bimorphemic, as shown below.

(34) ထီၟဆာ *thîchà* 'to be exact' > ထီၟထီၟဆာဆာ *thîthîchàchà* 'exactly'
(35) ယှူၟယုၟၚ် *xuîxàn* 'to be united' > ယှူၟယှူၟယုၟၚ်ယုၟၚ် *xuîxuîxànxàn* 'unitedly'
(36) ယှူးမုက် *ɕuíɕmáʊ* 'to be peaceful' > ယှူးယှူးမုက်မုက် *ɕuíɕuíɕmáʊmáʊ* 'peacefully'

However, monomorphemic disyllabic words are reduplicated in the form of ABAB, as in the following example.

(37) ဗဒၟ *bádà* 'to be moderate' > ဗဒၟဗဒၟ *bádàbádà* 'moderately'

2.2 Psycho-collocations

Pwo Karen has psycho-collocations (Matisoff 1986). Many of these are N-V or V-N compound verbs that have သာ *θà* 'heart' as the noun, as shown in examples (38) to (43) (see also (19) above). Other body-related nouns also appear in psycho-collocations, as shown in (44) and (45).

(38) သာခေါ်ၟ *θàkhū* 'to worry' < သာ *θà* 'heart' + ခေါ်ၟ *khū* 'to be hot' (=17)
(39) သာယွဲၟ *θàxwî* 'to be glad' < သာ *θà* 'heart' + ယွဲၟ *xwî* 'to be light'
(40) သာလၚ် *θàlàn* 'to be sad' < သာ *θà* 'heart' + လၚ် *làn* 'to descend'
(41) သာထာၚ်း *θàthán* 'to be angry' < သာ *θà* 'heart' + ထာၚ်း *thán* 'to ascend'
(42) သာမဲ *θàmé* 'to fear' < သာ *θà* 'heart' + မဲ *mé* 'to sprout'
(43) ကးသာ *káθà* 'to be shy' < ကး *ká* 'to be difficult' + သာ *θà* 'heart'
(44) နာ•ကာၚ်း *nākáin* 'to be dishonest' < နာ• *nā* 'ear' + ကာၚ်း *káin* 'to be bent'
(45) မဲခေါ်ၟ *mékhū* 'to be ashamed' < မဲ *mé* 'face' + ခေါ်ၟ *khū* 'to be hot'

Below is a sample sentence with သာမဲ *θàmé* 'to fear':

(46) ကိုဗး သာမဲ အံၟဝေ့ အေးး
       nə   *bá*   *θàmé*   *ʔəwê*   *ʔé*
       2SG   must   fear   3SG   not
       'You don't have to be scared of him.'

2.3 Elaborate expressions

Pwo Karen has many elaborate expressions (Kato 2005; for the concept of elaborate expressions, see Haas 1964:xvii-xviii, Matisoff 1973a: 81–86, 297–301, Matisoff 1991b). Elaborate expressions are quadrisyllabic words or phrases where either the first and third, or the second and fourth, syllables are either identical or similar in that they have several phonemes in common. The following are examples of these types of expressions.

(47) သုင်းဃ္ဒဲ့ သာဃ္ဒဲ့ *θə́ɯɴ-xwî-θə̀-xwî* (liver-light-heart-light) 'to be glad'
(48) သုင်းတဒ်သာလိင် *θə́ɯɴ-tɔ̀-θə̀-lòɴ* (liver-honest-heart-straight) 'to be honest'
(49) ထောဟ်ဖောဟ်လိဖောဟ် *thʉ́-phʉ́-lí-phʉ́* (bird-child-squirrel-child) 'small animals'
(50) မာဆိက်မာက္ဍိ၀် *mà-chái-mà-klò* (make-rice.field-make-alluvium) 'to make rice fields'
(51) သိင်းဖိင်းဝးဖိင်း *θéiɴ-phōɴ-wá-phōɴ* (tree-explode-bamboo-explode) 'forest fire happens'

3 Grammar and syntax

As previously mentioned in 2.1, Pwo Karen words can be grouped into five classes: nouns, verbs, adverbs, particles, and interjections. There is no need to posit the category of 'adjectives' because semantically adjective-like words are verbs (Kato 2008b).

The basic construction of clauses with a single verb, that is, those without serial verb constructions, can be schematized as in Figure 1:

Figure 1: Basic construction of Pwo Karen clause

(NP_1) (verb particle(s)) verb (verb particle(s)) (NP_2) (NP_3) (adverbial elements)

NP_1 is the subject. NP_2 and NP_3 are the objects when a transitive verb is present; two objects can occur only when the verb is ditransitive (see (56) below). Verb particle(s) (so-called "auxiliaries") can occur immediately before and after the verb and function to modify the verb. 'Adverbial elements' include adverbs, adpositional phrases, adverbial particles, and other forms. The verb is the only required element in a Pwo Karen clause, thus it is not bracketed. There are no non-verb predicates such as noun predicates or adpositional phrase predicates (see (55)). For example, the following sentence contains a monotransitive verb.

(52) သာအ္ဝါ   မ့   အင်း   ဝး   မေဝ်   အးအး   လ့ ဟိုင်းဖိင်   ဆော်။
     θàʔwà   mə   ʔán   bá   mì   ʔáʔá   lə́ yéin phə̀n   ɕī
     Thawa   IRR   eat   get.to rice much   L house inside also
     ⏟   ⏟   ⏟   ⏟   ⏟   ⏟   ⏟   ⏟
     NP₁   VPT   verb   VPT   NP₂   adverb adpositional   adverbial
                                              phrase   particle

'Thawa will also get to eat much rice at home.'

3.1 Basic sentences and word order

The basic word order for Pwo Karen is SVO. Sentence (53) is an example of an intransitive sentence. The single argument of an intransitive verb always appears before the verb, and this is also true of existential or phenomenal sentences.

(53) သာအ္ဝါ ဆိုကင်။
     θàʔwà chînàn
     Thawa sit
     'Thawa sat down.'

Below is an example of a monotransitive sentence.

(54) သာအ္ဝါ ဒှော်ဟ် သာခ္လိုင်း။
     θàʔwà dʉ́   θàkhléin
     Thawa strike Thakhlein
     'Thawa struck Thakhlein.'

A copular verb sentence, shown in (55), is also considered a transitive sentence. The copular verb မ္ဝဲ *mwē* cannot be omitted. Pwo Karen does not have any sentences where predicates contain only a noun phrase or adpositional phrase (see Kato 2013).

(55) သာအ္ဝါ မ္ဝဲ ဖ္လို။
     θàʔwà mwē phlòun
     Thawa COP Karen
     'Thawa is a Karen.'

In the case of a ditransitive verb, the two objects are arranged in the order of Recipient - Theme.

(56) သာအွာ ဖဲ့လင့် သာခွိုင်း နွဲ့သး॥
θàʔwà phílân θàkhléin nwēēθá
Thawa give Thakhlein jackfruit
'Thawa gave Thakhlein a jackfruit.'

Adjuncts are introduced into sentences with 'adpositional particles' (defined in Kato 2004), which I will hereafter call 'adpositions'. Adpositions occur before the noun, that is, they are prepositions, with the exception of the circumposition ေဘ *bê* ... သိုဝ် *θò* 'like' (see (60) for an example). Sentences (57) and (58) are examples of လ့ *lə́* 'at; to; from'[4]. This adposition indicates the semantic roles of Location, Goal, and Source. Which role that လ့ *lə́* expresses in a particular clause depends on various factors including the meaning of the verb and context, as discussed in Kato (2010). When the verb is not a motion verb, the noun preceded by လ့ *lə́* is generally interpreted as the Location, as in (57). On the other hand, when the verb is a motion verb as in (58), the noun preceded by လ့ *lə́* can denote either the Goal or Source, and the semantic role is mainly determined by the context of the utterance. For example, in (58), if Hpa-an is the location where the utterance was made, it is interpreted as the Goal; otherwise, it would be interpreted as the Source.

(57) သာအွာ မာ ဆိုမာ လ့ ထို့အင်॥
θàʔwà mà chəmà lə́ thəʔàn
Thawa do work L Hpa-an
'Thawa works at Hpa-an.'

(58) သာအွာ ဟ့ယဲ့ လ့ ထို့အင်॥
θàʔwà yê lə́ thəʔàn
Thawa come L Hpa-an
'Thawa came to Hpa-an,' or 'Thawa came from Hpa-an,'

Sentences (59) and (60) are examples of ေဒ့ *dē* 'with' and ေဘ *bê* ... သိုဝ် *θò* 'like', respectively.

---

[4] The Pwo Karen spelling လ့ can be read as *lə́* or *lə*. Thus, many morphemes such as *lə́* 'adposition indicating Location, Goal, and Source', *lə́* 'relativizer', *lə* 'negative particle', and *lə* 'one' are written in the same way.

(59) သာအွာ လေဝ် ဆုံယာင် ဒေ့ သာခှိုင်း။
    θàʔwà lḭ chəjàin dē θàkhléin
    Thawa go far.place with Thakhlein
    'Thawa traveled with Thakhlein.'

(60) သာအွာ မာ ငွေ့သာခှိုင်းသိုဝ်။
    θàʔwà mà bê θàkhléin θò
    Thawa do like Thakhlein like
    'Thawa did it like Thakhlein.'

Negation is indicated by placing အေး ʔé in the clause-final position when the clause is a main clause, as shown in (61).

(61) သာအွာ ဒွောဟ် သာခှိုင်း အေး။
    θàʔwà dṳ́ θàkhléin ʔé
    Thawa strike Thakhlein NEG
    'Thawa did not strike Thakhlein.'

On the other hand, if the negated clause is a subordinate clause, two morphemes, လှ် lə and ဧး bá, have to be used at the same time. လှ် lə appears immediately before the verb, and ဧး bá appears in the clause-final position, as shown in (62). Neither of these usually are not omitted, but ဧး bá may occasionally be dropped in a highly informal speech.

(62) သာအွာ လှ် ဒွောဟ် သာခှိုင်း ဧး အံခေါဟ်ကျိုင်၊ ယှ် ဒွောဟ် အံဝေ့။
    θàʔwà lə dṳ́ θàkhléin bá ʔəkhúcòn, jə dṳ́ ʔəwê
    Thawa NEG strike Thakhlein NEG because 1SG strike 3SG
    'Because Thawa did not strike Thakhlein, I struck him.'

လှ် lə is related to the Proto-Tibeto-Burman negative affix *ta (Benedict 1972: 97; see also Matisoff 2003: 162, 172)[5]. I posit *tə for Proto-Karen (cf. Sgaw Karen tə); however, the etymology of ဧး bá is unknown.

Pwo Karen does not have a passive voice, as is often the case for languages in mainland Southeast Asia. However, as discussed by Kato (2011), agent-defocusing effect (see Myhill 1997), which is a significant functional role of the passive voice in many languages, is fulfilled in Pwo Karen by the indefinite pro-

---

[5] Benedict (1972: 97) says that The Proto-Tibeto-Burman *ta is an element for 'imperative negative'. In Karenic languages, its reflexes are used as general negative markers.

noun ဆ့် *chə* which originates from the noun meaning 'thing'[6]. The indefinite pronoun ဆ့် *chə* occurs only in the subject slot. One of the important functions of this pronoun is to show that an animate actor is unknown to the speaker, that is, the subject noun is indefinite. Examples of this construction are presented in (63) and (64).

(63) ဆ့် ဘောဟ် ယှ့်॥
    chə   dʉ́   jà
    INP   strike 1SG
    'I was struck by somebody.' (not 'struck by something')

(64) ဆ့် ခ့ိုင် ဖ့ို လ့ ထ့်အင်॥
    chə   khlàɪN   phlòʊN   lá   thəʔàN
    INP   speak   Karen   L   Hpa-an
    'The (Pwo) Karen language is spoken in Hpa-an.'

3.2 Nominal domain

3.2.1 Basic structure of the NP

The order of the constituents in the Pwo Karen noun phrase is shown in Figure 2. Brackets denote optional items.

Figure 2: The order of components within the Pwo Karen NP

{(RC) / (NM)}	(PRON)	HEAD NOUN	(RC)	(ADP)	{(NUM + CLF) / (PLUR)}	(DEM)
SLOT1	SLOT2	SLOT3	SLOT4	SLOT5	SLOT6	SLOT7

The slots represent locations for the following elements in the NP: SLOT1 is for the relative clause and nominal modifier; SLOT2 is for the pronoun expressing a possessor; SLOT3 is for the head noun; SLOT4 is for the relative clause; SLOT5 is for the adpositional phrase; SLOT6 is for the 'numeral + classifier' (see 3.2.2) and

---

6 The noun ဆ့် *chə* 'thing' is also used as the "formal subject" in sentences that denote natural phenomena. Examples include: ဆ့်ဆ့ိုင်॥ *chə chàN* (thing / rain) 'It is raining'; ဆ့်ခေါဝ်॥ *chə khō* (thing / hot) 'It is hot'; ဆ့်ခ့ှိုင်း॥ *chə khléɪN* (thing / cold) 'It is cold'; and ဆ့်ခါ်॥ *chə khàɪ* (thing / dark) 'It is dark'.

particle denoting plurality; and SLOT7 is for the demonstrative particle. The following examples illustrate this structure.

(65) ယး ဖာဘော့ဟ် သိင့်ခိင်း ယှိဝ်
    já   phàdʉ́   θə̄N   béiN   jò
    fish   big   three   CLF   this
    {SLOT3} {SLOT4} {SLOT6}   {SLOT7}
    'these three big fishes'

(66) ယှိုသိုဝ် ဒွေ ခေါဟ်လုက် သယ် ကို
    jə   θò   dē   khʉ́láʊ   θɛ̀   nɔ́
    my   friend   with   cap   PLUR   that
    {SLOT2} {SLOT3} {SLOT5}   {SLOT6} {SLOT7}
    'those friends of mine with a cap'

A noun that modifies the head noun, that is, the nominal modifier, appears in SLOT1. Below is an example:

(67) ဖျူ ဆိုယှို့.ဆိုလာ
    phlòʊN   chəxîchəlà
    Karen   culture
    {SLOT1}   {SLOT3}
    'Karen culture'

The noun that denotes the possessor of the head noun is one type of nominal modifier. Sentence (68) is an example. In a possessive expression, the pronoun referring to the possessor may occur before the possessed noun, which has the effect of marking the expression as more formal.

(68) မင်စဝ် (အှိ) ဟှိင်း
    màNcɔ̀   (ʔə)   yéiN
    uncle   his   house
    {SLOT1}   { SLOT2}   { SLOT3}
    '(my) uncle's house.'

Relative clauses in Pwo Karen are externally headed relative clauses, and occur in SLOT1 or SLOT4. In Pwo Karen, some relative clauses do not use any marker and others use the relativizer လှ် *lə́*. In colloquial speech, relative clauses without any marker are preferred. There are two types of relative clauses without any marker: the postnominal type occurring in SLOT4 and the prenominal type occurring in SLOT1. Generally speaking, when the relativized noun is the subject of the verb in the clause, the postnominal type is used, as shown in (69). On the other hand, when the relativized noun is not the subject, the prenominal type is used, as shown in (70). A single verb, such as ဟသောဟ် *phàdʊ́* 'very big' that occurs in SLOT4 in (65), can be regarded as a relative clause of the postnominal type.

(69) ဖှိ| သောဟ် ယှ် ကို ဟှုယှ် အေး॥
    phlòʊN   *[dʊ́*   *jà]*   *nɔ́*   *yê*   *ʔé*
    person   strike 1SG   TOP   come   NEG
    {SLOT3}   {SLOT4}
    'The person who struck me didn't come.'

(70) ယှ် သောဟ် ဒှေလဲ ဖှိ| ကို မွာ် အံ့ဝေ॥
    [jə   *dʊ́*   *dē*   *lé]*   *phlòʊN*   *nɔ́*   *mwē*   *ʔəwê*
    1SG   strike   with   stick   person   TOP   COP   3SG
    {   SLOT1   }   {SLOT3}
    'The person whom I struck with a stick is he/she.'

In formal speech, the relative clause with the relativizer လ့ *lə́* is preferred. The relative clause with လ့ *lə́* always appears in SLOT4. The relative clauses in (69) and (70) can be paraphrased with လ့ *lə*, as shown in (71) and (72) below. In the relative clause with လ့ *lə́*, the 'resumptive pronoun' (see Comrie 1989: 147) must appear when the head noun is the subject of the relative clause, as in (71). However, when the head noun is not the subject as in (72), the resumptive pronoun appears only when the head noun is animate, and the pronoun may be omitted in this case.

(71) ဖှိ| လ့ အံ သောဟ် ယှ် ကို ဟှုယှ် အေး॥
    phlòʊN   *[lə́*   *ʔə*   *dʊ́*   *jà]*   *nɔ́*   *yê*   *ʔé*
    person   REL   3SG   strike   1SG   TOP   come   NEG
    {SLOT3}   {   SLOT4   }
    'The person who struck me didn't come.'

(72) ဖှိ| လ့ ယှ် သောဟ် (အံ) ဒှေလဲ ကို မွာ် အံ့ဝေ॥
    phlòʊN   *[lə́*   *jə*   *dʊ́*   *(ʔə̀)*   *dē*   *lé]*   *nɔ́*   *mwē*   *ʔəwê*
    person   REL   1SG   strike   3SG   with   stick   TOP   COP   3SG
    {SLOT3}   {   SLOT4   }
    'The person whom I struck with a stick is he/she.'

3.2.2 Classifiers

Pwo Karen has numeral classifiers. Kato (2004) lists 31 numeral classifiers, and some examples are presented below. The final two are mensural classifiers, and the others are sortal classifiers (for the terms mensural and sortal classifiers, see Vittrant 2002).

၂ၠ	*duì*	used for mammals other than human beings; also used as a general classifier
ဟၠာ	*yà*	used for human beings
ဘိင်း	*béin*	used for flat things; also used for birds, fish, insects
ဖိၠုး	*phlóun*	used for round things
ဘင်	*bòn*	used for long things
ဒိင်း	*dón*	used for a group of people or animal
ဘိင်း	*bón*	used for a package of something

Classifiers in Pwo Karen must be used in enumeration and appear with a numeral, as shown in (73). 'Numeral + classifier' occurs in SLOT6 in terms of the NP structure illustrated in Figure 2.

(73) ထိုး ယဲ ၂ၠ ယိုဝ်
    thwí   jē   duì   jò
    dog   five CLF:animals this
    'these five dogs'

If there is no numeral, the phrase with a classifier is ungrammatical, for example, *ထိုး၂ၠယိုဝ် *thwí duì jò* (dog / CLF / this). Numerals also cannot occur without a classifier, for example, *ထိုးယဲယိုဝ် *thwí jē jò* (dog / five / this).

The head noun can be omitted in which case the 'numeral + classifier' would function anaphorically, as shown below:

(74) အံယိုဝ် မွဲ ယိုထိုး။ လၠ၂ၠယိုဝ် အဲယိုဝ် ဆာမာ။
    ʔəjò mwē jə thwí. lə   duì   jò   ʔέ jà   châ mā
    this COP my dog one CLF:animal this love 1SG much very
    'This is my dog. He (this one) loves me very much.'

Classifiers are also used in indefinite expressions. The form 'လၠ *lə* + CLF + CLF', where လၠ *lə* means 'one', indicates 'some ~'. Thus, လၠဟၠာဟၠာ + CLF:human + CLF:human' in (75) can be glossed as 'somebody'. Classifiers also occur in a negative sentence with တင် *nān* 'any' in the form of 'တင် *nān* + CLF' to indicate 'no ~', as shown in (76). These indefinite expressions occur in the position of 'adverbial elements' in Figure 1.

(75) ဖှိ့ ဆှုဟ် ယှ့ လှုဟှာဟှာ။
    phlòuɴ dʊ́   jə̀   lə-γà-γà
    person   strike 1SG   one-CLF:person-CLF:person
    'Somebody struck me.'

(76) ဖှိ့ ဆှုဟ် ယှ့ ကင်. ဟှာ အေး။
    phlòuɴ dʊ́   jə̀   nāɴ   γà   ʔé
    person   strike 1SG   any   CLF:person   NEG
    'Nobody struck me.'

3.3 Verbal domain

3.3.1 Verbal inflections and categories

Pwo Karen verbs are not inflected and do not mark tense, either obligatorily or optionally. In addition, number or person is not marked in the verb phrase.

On the other hand, modality and aspect are expressed by various particles. One of the most important particles denoting modality is the irrealis marker မှ̀ *mə*, which occurs before the verb[7]. This marker indicates that an action, event, or state that is denoted by the verb is 'non-actual'. There is a general pattern in use of this marker. When it is used with an active verb, that is, a verb indicating an action or event, a clause with မှ̀ *mə* refers to the future, as in (77), and a clause without မှ̀ *mə* refers to the past or present, as in (78).

(77) အ့်ဝေ့ မှ̀ ဟှုယှဲ။
    ʔəwê   mə   γê
    3SG   IRR   come
    'He will come.'

---

[7] According to my impression, the irrealis marker မှ̀ *mə* has considerable similarity in function to the Burmese irrealis verb sentence marker မယ် *mὲ*. For the details of modality-marking devices including မယ် *mὲ* in Burmese, see Vittrant & van der Auwera (2010).

(78) အ်ိဝ့ေ ဟုယ့်॥
    ʔəwê   ɣê
    3SG   come
    'He came. / He comes (e.g., every day).'

However, when used with a stative verb, မ့ *mə* can appear in a clause referring to the past or present when the speaker is not sure about the situation described in the clause. Notice that sentence (79) can refer to a past or present situation. In (79), the speaker is not sure whether 'he' is/was a farmer.

(79) အ်ိဝ့ေ မ့ မွဲ့ ဆိက်ဖောဟ်ဆာ•॥
    ʔəwê   mə   mwē   cháiphúchā
    3SG   IRR   COP   farmer
    'Maybe he is a farmer,' or 'Maybe he was a farmer.'

Moreover, မ့ *mə* does not occur in clauses with stative verbs that refer to the future if the speaker is sure that the situation denoted by the verb will be true. Therefore, in the sentence below, မ့ *mə* does not occur because the speaker is sure that the 'boxing game' will be held.

(80) ကေခိုင်း စုံးပို့မေဝ် အ်ိ॥
    kèkhó   bóʊɴpwèmè   ʔɔ́
    tomorrow   boxing.game   exist
    'There is a boxing game tomorrow.'

Etymologically, မ့ *mə* is considered to have meant 'want to (do something)' at an earlier stage, since the West Pwo Karen verb particle *mó* and the Sgaw Karen verb particle *mó* both mean 'want to' and are cognates with မ့ *mə* (Kato 2009b). In Western Pwo, the irrealis marker is *kə*, and in Sgaw Karen, the irrealis marker is also *kə*. Therefore, we can posit the form *kə* for the Proto-Pwo Karen irrealis marker. In Eastern Pwo, the form meaning 'want to' became an irrealis marker, and the form *kə has been lost.

Next, we will discuss the aspect-marking particle ယုဂ် *jàʊ*, which appears in the clause-final position. When used with a verb denoting a momentary event, this particle expresses that the event has occurred, as in (81).

(81) အ်ိဝ့ေ ထင် ထုံအင် ယုဂ်॥
    ʔəwê   thòɴ   thəʔàɴ   jàʊ
    3SG   arrive   Hpa-an   PERF
    'He has arrived in Hpa-an.'

When ယုာ် *jàʊ* is used with a verb denoting a durable action, the clause expresses that the action has been completed, or that the action has begun, that is, an inchoative meaning, as shown in (82).

(82) အံၣ်ဝ့ အင်းဖမိ ယုာ်။
 ʔəwê   ʔáɴ   mì   jàʊ
 3SG   eat   rice PERF
 'He has eaten,' or 'He has begun eating.'

When ယုာ် *jàʊ* is used with a stative verb, the meaning is always inchoative, as shown in (83).

(83) ယး ဃာၣ့် ယုာ်။
 já   xâɪɴ   jàʊ
 fish to.be.dry PERF
 'The fish is already dry.'

It is most likely the case that ယုာ် *jàʊ* indicates perfectivity. Note that the equivalent Sgaw Karen perfective marker is လံ *lí*. Thus, ယုာ် *jàʊ* probably had a lateral consonant [l] as its initial at an earlier stage. Etymologically, this form could be related to Chinese *liǎo* 'finish' or Thai *lɛ́ɛw* 'finish; perfective marker', but this point would need further clarification from future studies.

Pwo Karen does not have a form to indicate progressive aspect. Unlike the neighboring languages Burmese or Thai, where verbs meaning 'to stay' or 'to live' have been grammaticalized to indicate progressive aspect, no verb has been grammaticalized to have this kind of function in Pwo Karen. Instead, verbs can express a progressive action without the help of additional forms, as shown in (84).

(84) လ်ဟုာ်ဝယိဝ် အံၣ်ဝ့ အင်း ဖမိ။
 ləyɔ̀jò   ʔəwê   ʔáɴ   mì
 this.morning 3SG   eat   rice
 'He had a meal this morning,' or 'He was having a meal (when I arrived) this morning.'

3.3.2 Serial verb constructions (SVCs)

There are two types of serial verb constructions in Pwo Karen: the 'concatenated type' and 'separated type'. These terms were introduced in Kato (1998). The concatenated and separated types of serial verb constructions respectively correspond to the contiguous and non-contiguous SVCs of Aikhenvald & Dixon (2006). For the separated type, a noun phrase or an adpositional phrase can intervene between V1 (the first verb) and V2 (the second verb). However, for the concatenated type, these elements cannot intervene.

The definitions of these types of serial verb constructions are as follows. The negative particle လှ့ *lə*, which is used in the subordinate clauses (see sentence (62) in 4.1), occurs before V1 in the concatenated type, as in (85), and before V2 in the separated type, as in (86). Negatability as a syntactic test is widely used in studies of Southeast Asian languages for the purpose of classifying verb-related phenomenon (see Matisoff 1991c: 393–394, for example). Note that the negative particle အေး *ʔé* (see sentence (61) in 4.1) cannot be employed for the definition because it appears in the clause-final position.

(85) ယှ့ လှ့ ယှိုအင်း ကောဟ် ဝး အိုခေါဟ်ကျှိင် ...
    jə   lə   xwè   ʔán   kú   bá   ʔəkhúcòn ...
    1SG NEG V1:buy V2:eat cake NEG because
    'Because I did not buy and eat the cake ...'

(86) ယှ့ အင်း မေဝ် လှ့ ၃ယ် ဝး အိုခေါဟ်ကျှိင် ...
    jə   ʔán   mì   lə   blè   bá   ʔəkhúcòn ...
    1SG V1:eat rice NEG V2:full NEG because
    'Because I ate rice but did not get full ...'

The fundamental difference between the concatenated type and the separated type is whether the event denoted by V2 can be controlled or not. For the concatenated type, both events denoted by V1 and V2 are more or less controllable by the referent of the subject. However, for the separated type, the event denoted by V2 is always uncontrollable while the event denoted by V1 can be either controllable or uncontrollable by the subject.

- **Concatenated type**

The two verbs in this type express a sequence of events linked by particular semantic relationships, including Means (V1) – Purpose (V2), Manner (V1) – Action (V2), and Cause (V1) – Result (V2). The order of the verbs reflects the temporal sequence of the events.

There are four possible combinations of intransitive and transitive verbs; each combination is discussed in [A] to [D] below. Combined verbs function like a single verb in the clause.

[A] intransitive + intransitive => intransitive
This whole construction functions as an intransitive verb. Both verbs are volitional verbs. The subject arguments of V1 and V2 are the same (S=S).

(87) အံဝ့ ဆိၣ်ကၣ် ကိဝ်ယှၢႊ
    ʔəwê   chînàN   kòɕà
    3SG   sit   shout
    'He sat and shouted.'

[B] intransitive + transitive => transitive
This whole construction functions as a transitive verb. Both verbs are volitional verbs, and the subject arguments of V1 and V2 are the same (S=A). The object argument of V2 occurs as the object of the whole construction.

(88) ယ့ ဆိၣ်ကၣ် ပဒ် လိက်အုၣ်ႊ
    jə   chînàN   pɔ̄   lái?àʊ
    1SG   sit   read book
    'I sat and read a book.'

[C] transitive + transitive => transitive
This whole construction functions as a transitive verb. Both verbs are volitional verbs, and the subject arguments of V1 and V2 are the same (A=A). The object arguments of V1 and V2 are usually the same, as in sentence (89), but sometimes they are not the same, as in (90) where the object argument of V1 is 'window' and the object argument of V2 is 'mountain'. In (90), only the object argument of V2 can appear as the object of the whole construction; the object argument of V1 cannot appear. Thus, (91) is ungrammatical.

(89) ယ့ ဃဲ့အၣ်း ကောဟ်ႊ
    jə   xwè   ʔáN   kʊ́
    1SG   buy   eat   cake
    'I bought a cake and ate it.'

(90) ယ့ ပုၣ်ထၣ်း ယောဝ် ခေါဟ်လၣ်ႊ
    jə   pàʊtháN   jŏ   khʊ́lòn
    1SG   open   look mountain
    'I open (the window) and looked at the mountain.'

(91) *ယှၣ် ပုဂ်ထၣ်း ယောဝ်. ပါတြၣ်ႋ
    jə   pàuthán   jŏ   pàitərân
    1SG   open   look   window

[D] transitive + intransitive => transitive
This whole construction functions as a transitive verb. V1 is a volitional verb, while V2 is a non-volitional verb. The object argument of V1 and the subject argument of V2 are the same (O=S), and the shared argument occurs as the object of the whole construction.

(92) ယှၣ် ဒော့ဟ် သီ ထွဲးႋ
    jə   dʊ́   θî   thwí
    1SG   strike   die   dog
    'I struck the dog to death.' (More exactly: I struck the dog intending to kill it.)

In this combination, if V2 is a volitional verb, the concatenated verbs become ungrammatical. For example, ဒော့ဟ်ဆိၣ်ကၣ် *dʊ́ chînàn* (strike / sit) is ungrammatical and cannot mean '(I) struck (the dog) to made him sit' or '(I) struck (the dog) and sat down'.

Of the four combinations discussed above, in the combination [D] 'transitive + intransitive', the event denoted by V2 does not have to actually happen, because it is merely an intended event by the actor of V1.[8] Thus, (93) is acceptable. This characteristic is also found in the serial verb construction in Kayah Li (Solnit 1997: 68).

(93) ယှၣ် ဒော့ဟ် သီ ထွဲး လာ.ကၣ်သီး သီ အေးႋ
    jə   dʊ́   θî   thwí   lānânθí,   θî   ʔé
    1SG   strike   die   dog   although   die   NEG
    'Although I struck the dog intending to kill it, but it did not die.'

For the combinations other than 'transitive + intransitive', however, this feature does not hold. For example, in (89) above, negation of V2 renders the sentence semantically odd. Thus, sentence (94) is not acceptable.

---

8 In terms of pragmatics, if sentence (92) is not followed by a clause which negates the verb သီ *θî* 'die', the 'dog' is usually interpreted to have been dead.

(94) *ယှၢ် ယွံၢ်အၢင်း ကောဟ် လာ·ကဂ့်သီး အၢင်း အေးး॥
　　　*jə　　xwè　　ʔáɴ　　kɯ́　　lānânθí,　　ʔáɴ　　ʔé
　　　1SG　　buy　　eat　　cake　　although　　eat　　NEG
　　　Literal meaning: 'Although I bought a cake and ate it, but I did not eat it.'

In this case, V2 in the serial verb construction ယွံၢ်အၢင်း *xwè ʔáɴ* (buy / eat) is not merely a intended event of the actor. That is, the action denoted by V2 has to have been performed in order for this serial verb construction to be semantically true.

In addition, the order of V1 and V2 follows the temporal sequence of events, with the exception of the five motion verbs: လေဝ် *lḭ* 'go', ဟှယ့် *yê* 'come', ထာင် *thàiɴ* 'return', ထင်း *tháɴ* 'ascend', and လင် *làɴ* 'descend'. Pwo Karen mandates that these motion verbs appear as the first verb in the concatenated type of serial verb construction. Thus, even if the motions 'go', 'come', 'return', 'ascend', and 'descend' occurred after another action, these five verbs have to appear in the V1 slot. Thus, (95) can express not only the situation 'I came and bought a fish', but also the situation 'I bought a fish and came (with it)'.

(95) ယှၢ် ဟှယ့် ယွံၢ် ယး॥
　　　jə　　yê　　xwè　　já
　　　1SG　　come　　buy　　fish
　　　'I came and bought a fish,' or 'I bought a fish and came (with it).'

- **Separated type**

In the separated type of serial verb construction, a noun phrase or an adpositional phrase can intervene between V1 and V2. In this type, V2 is usually an intransitive verb, while V1 can be either intransitive or transitive.

There are two cases of the separated type constructions in terms of the semantic relationship between V1 and V2. The first case is when V2 is the result or effect of the action or event denoted by V1, as seen in (96), (97), and (98):

(96) အံၣ်ဂွေ လၢင်ထေဲ သွီ॥
　　　ʔəwê　　lànthé　　θí
　　　3SG　　fall　　die
　　　'He fell and died.'

(97) အံၣ်ဂွေ အၢင်း မေဝ် ၉ယ်॥
　　　ʔəwê　　ʔáɴ　　mḭ̀　　blè
　　　3SG　　eat　　rice　　full
　　　'He ate rice and got full.'

(98) မီယဝ် ဝး ကား သီ။
    mìjɔ̀   bá   kā   θî
    cat   hit car die
    'The cat collided with a car and died.'

The second case is when V2 denotes ability, possibility, or permissive. See (99) and (100):

(99) အံ့ဝေ့ ကင့် ကား သေ့။
    ʔəwê   nâɴ   kā   θḭ
    3SG   drive car capable
    'He can drive a car.'

(100) နဂို လေဝ် ဆိုယာင် ကော်။
    nə   lḭ   chəjàiɴ   nḭ
    2SG   go   far.place   get
    'You can travel. (You are permitted to travel.)'

The verb ကော်. *nḭ* 'get', when used in this position, denotes permissive as in (100). A semantic change of the verb, i.e. GET to PERMISSIVE, has occurred here, but the verb has not been grammaticalized into a grammatical marker.

As previously mentioned, in the separated type, the event denoted by V2 is always uncontrollable. Thus, V2 must always be a non-volitional verb, while V1 can be either volitional or non-volitional. For example, the sentence below in (101) is ungrammatical because the second verb အင်း *ʔáɴ* 'eat' is volitional:

(101) * ယို့ အင်းဖင့် မေဝ် အင်း။
    *jə   ʔáɴphôɴ   mḭ   ʔáɴ
    1SG   cook   rice eat
    Intended meaning: 'I cooked rice and ate it.'

If a speaker wants to construct a sentence with the meaning 'I cooked rice and ate it', the concatenated-type serialization has to be used, as shown in (102) below:

(102) ယို့ အင်းဖင့် အင်း မေဝ်။
    jə   ʔáɴphôɴ   ʔáɴ   mḭ
    1SG   cook   eat   rice
    'I cooked rice and ate it.'

Serial verb constructions like (101), where a noun phrase intervene between the two volitional verbs, are often observed in SVO languages in Southeast Asia. For example, Thai *hŭŋ khâaw kin* (cook / rice / eat) 'I cooked rice to eat'[9] is grammatical. However, serialization like this is not acceptable in Pwo Karen. Solnit (1997: 56–57) points out that Karenic languages show a preference for immediate concatenation of verbs. Pwo Karen is no exception. Solnit (2006: 159) also suggests that this preference is a legacy of the old Tibeto-Burman verb-final typology.[10]

In terms of argument sharing, there are two cases in the separated type. The first case is when the subject arguments of V1 and V2 are the same, as can be seen in (96), (97), (98), (99), and (100) above (S=S, A=S, A=S, A=S, and probably A=S, respectively). V2 in the separate type is usually an intransitive verb, as mentioned above; however, if V1 is a transitive verb, V2 also may be a transitive verb, although this is rare. Sentence (103) below is such an example. In this case, the object arguments of V1 and V2 are the same, as well as the subject arguments (A=A).

(103) ယှ် အင်းယှူ။ ခင်းဖၟ် ၃း ယုဂ်။
     jə   ʔánxuî   khánphài   dá   jàʊ
     1SG look.for   sandal   find PERF
     'I was looking for a pair of sandals and have found one.'

The second case is when the object argument of V1 and the subject argument of V2 are the same (O=S), as seen in (104). This type of serial verb construction is called a 'pivotal serial verb construction' in Jarkey (2010: 118)

(104) ယှ် ဒှော်ဟ် ထဲး သှီ ယုဂ်။
     jə   dʊ́   thwí   θî   jàʊ
     1SG strike dog   die PERF
     'I hit the dog, and it died.'

Finally, it is worthwhile to compare the semantic characteristics of (104) and (92), which are semantically similar to each other. As previously mentioned, in

---

9 As an English translation for this Thai serial verb construction, 'I cooked rice to eat' is more suitable than 'I cooked rice and ate it' because putting the clause 'but, I did not eat' afterwards makes no discrepancy (Prof. Marasri Miyamoto, p.c.).
10 Generally, serial verb constructions in verb-final languages do not allow a noun phrase to intervene between the verbs (see Foley & Olson 1985).

(92), the event denoted by V2 does not have to actually happen. However, in (104), a separated construction, the event denoted by V2 has actually happened. Thus, (105) is semantically unacceptable. Compare this with sentence (93).

(105) * ယှ် ဒျှော်ဟ် ထုံး သှ့် လာ.ကင့်သီး သှ့် အေး॥
   *jə dú thwí θî lānânθí, θî ʔé
   1SG strike dog die although die NEG
   Literal meaning: 'I struck the dog and it died, but it did not die.'

- **Versatile verbs**

Some verbs in concatenated serial verb constructions have changed their meanings into more abstract ones and are therefore more flexible in terms of co-occurrence with other verbs. I call these verbs 'versatile verbs' here, following Matisoff's (1969) terminology, although Kato (2004) treats them as verb particles. Aikhenvald & Dixon's (2006) 'asymmetrical serial verb constructions' are serial verb constructions which contain this type of verbs. Some of the Pwo Karen versatile verbs can be pronounced differently from the main verbs. This fact suggests that these verbs have been grammaticalized and function as particles.

  The verb ယှော်. *jū* 'look at' functions as a versatile verb which indicates tentativeness. (See Burmese parallel examples, p. 98).

(106) ယှ် အင်း ယှော်. ခေါ်ိသး॥
   jə ʔán jū khòθá
   1SG eat look mango
   'I ate a mango to taste it.'

The verb ထင်း *thán* 'ascend' can be used as a versatile verb to indicate that V1 is performed with upward movement. As a versatile verb, it can be pronounced either *thán* or *ʙán*.

(107) အ်ိဝေ့ ယှော်. ထင်း ခေါ်ဟ်လင်॥
   ʔəwê jū thán khúlòn
   3SG look ascend mountain
   'He looked up the mountain.'

Similarly, the verb လင် *làn* 'descend' functions as a versatile verb to indicate that V1 is performed with downward movement. As a versatile verb, it can be pronounced either *làn* or *ʙàn*.

(108) အံၣ်ဝေ ယောဝ်· လင် သိင်း ခင်းထၢ်॥
     ʔəwê   jʊ̃   làɴ   θéiɴ   kháɴthài
     3SG   look   descend tree   root
     'He looked down the root of the tree.'

Note that, in Pwo Karen, the verbs လေဝ် *lḭ* 'go' and ဟ့ၣယ့် *yê* 'come' are not used as versatile verbs.

The verb ခွါက် *khwái* 'throw', as a versatile verb, indicates thoroughness of an action. It can be pronounced either *khwái* or *wái* as a versatile verb. (See Burmese, table 13, p. 99).

(109) အဝ် ခွါက် သၢ် အေလုက်॥
     ʔɔ̃   khwái   θài   ʔèláʊ
     drink throw   liquor all
     'Drink up all the liquor.'

ဗးသာ *báθà* 'want' can occur as a versatile verb expressing desire to perform V1. It can be pronounced either *báθà* or *wáθà* as a versatile verb.

(110) ယ့် မ့ ယောဝ်· ဗးသာ ဆုိဟွၣင်မိၣ်॥
     jə   mə   jʊ̃   báθà   chəyàɴmâɴ
     1SG IRR look want   movie
     'I want to see the movie.'

ဖှဲ့လၣ် *phḭ̂lâɴ* 'give', a ditransitive verb, can occur as both V1 and V2 as a versatile verb. See also sentence (56) in 3.1, where ဖှဲ့လၣ် *phḭ̂lâɴ* occurs as the main verb. When the versatile verb ဖှဲ့လၣ် *phḭ̂lâɴ* appears in the V1 position, it functions as a causative auxiliary (see Kato 2009a for more detail):

(111) အံၣ်ဝေ ဖှဲ့လၣ် ပဝ်· ယ့ လိက်အုၣ်॥
     ʔəwê   phḭ̂lâɴ pɔ̃   jə   láiʔàʊ
     3SG   give   read 1SG book
     'He had me read a book.'

On the other hand, when ဖှဲ့လၣ် *phḭ̂lâɴ* appears as a versatile verb in the V2 position, it expresses benefactivity (see Kato 2009a for more detail). In this position, it can be pronounced either as *phḭ̂lâɴ* or *wḭ̂lâɴ*.

(112) အဲ့ဝေ့ ပဒ်• ဖေ့လင့် ယှ် လိက်အုဂ်॥
    ʔəwê   pɔ́   phílân   jə̀   láiʔàʋ
    3SG   read   give   1SG   book
    'He read a book for me.'

As Matisoff (1991c) discusses, many Southeast Asian languages have grammaticalized the verb 'to give' as a causative or benefactive marker, and Pwo Karen is no exception.

3.4 Clausal/sentential organization

3.4.1 Ellipsis of arguments

In Pwo Karen, arguments can be omitted if their identity is inferrable from the context. The next example presents two sequential sentences in context. The subject အဲ့ဝေ့ ʔəwê '3SG' in (b) refers to Thawa, and it is omittable.

(113) a.   လှ်ကီယှိဝ် သာအွာ ဟှုယှ့် လှ် ယှ်ဟှိုင်းယှိဝ်॥
    lənìjò   θàʔwà   yê   lə́   jə   yéin   jò
    today   Thawa   come   L   1SG   house   this
    'Thawa came to my house today.'

    b.   (အဲ့ဝေ့) မာစိုဝ် ဖေ့လင့် ယှ် သိဉ်ကီခွဲင်॥
    ʔəwê   màbò   phílân   jə̀   θèiɴnìkhlòɴ
    3SG   help   give   1SG   all.day
    '(He) helped me all day.'

3.4.2 Topicalization

Pwo Karen has a syntactic topicalizing process whereby the topicalized constituent appears in sentence-initial position followed by a topic marker. The topic marker is usually required. A topicalized constituent is given an explanation about it in the rest of the sentence. Topicalization occurs frequently in Pwo Karen. Kato (2004) lists five topic markers, among which ကှ် nɔ́ is used most frequently. ကှ် nɔ́ is grammaticalized from the demonstrative particle ကှ် nɔ́ 'that'.

Consider (114) below as an example. When the subject သာအွာ θàʔwà is topicalized, we get (115), and when the object သာခွိင်း θàkhléiɴ is topicalized, we get (116).

(114) သာအွာ ဆှောဟ် သာခှိင်း။
     θàʔwà   dʊ́   θàkhléin
     Thawa   strike   Thakhlein
     'Thawa struck Thakhlein.'

(115) သာအွာ ကှို ဆှောဟ် သာခှိင်း။
     θàʔwà   nɔ́   dʊ́   θàkhléin
     Thawa   TOP   strike Thakhlein
     'As for Thawa, he struck Thakhlein.'

(116) သာခှိင်း ကှို သာအွာ ဆှောဟ်။
     θàkhléin   nɔ́   θàʔwà   dʊ́
     Thakhlein TOP   Thawa   strike
     'As for Thakhlein, Thawa struck him.'

Constituents that can be topicalized are not limited to arguments of a verb. Sentence (117) is an example where an adpositional phrase is topicalized, and (118) is an example where a subordinate clause is topicalized.

(117) ဒှေ နှုောတ်ထှုံ ကှို ယှုံ အင်း မေဝ် အေး။
     dē   nʊ́thòʊɴ   nɔ́   jə   ʔáɴ   mḭ   ʔó
     with spoon   TOP   1SG eat   rice NEG
     'With a spoon, I don't eat rice.'

(118) သာခှိင်း အေ အှိ ကှို ယှုံ မှု ဟှုယှို့ ကှိုဝ် ကောဝ် အှိ။
     θàkhléin ʔè   ʔɔ́   nɔ́   jə   mə   yê   kò   nī   ʔà
     Thakhlein if   exist TOP 1SG IRR come call get 3SG
     'If Thakhlein is there, I will bring him here.'

3.4.3 Interrogative sentences

Interrogative sentences in Pwo Karen can be defined as sentences that have an interrogative particle ဟှ ɓâ or လယှ် lê, as disucussed in Kato (2013). There are two types of interrogative sentences: polar interrogative sentences (yes-no questions) and content interrogative sentences (wh-questions).

A polar interrogative sentence is formed by placing the particle ဟှ ɓâ at the end of the sentence. See (119) and (120) for examples.

(119) ကိုｰ မုံ လေဝ် ဟှ၁॥
　　　nə　mə　lì　ʁâ
　　　2SG　IRR　go　PQ
　　　'Will you go?'

(120) မူဟုး အံ့ဝေ့ လေဝ် ဖျ၁ ဟှ၁॥
　　　muìyá　ʔəwê　lì　phjâ　ʁâ
　　　yesterday　3SG　go　market　PQ
　　　'Did he go to the market yesterday?'

A content interrogative sentence is formed by using an interrogative word and placing the particle လယ့် *lê* at the end of the sentence. The occurrence of လယ့် *lê* seems semantically redundant, but it is a required element and cannot be omitted. Interrogative words include ဆိုကှံ *chənɔ́* 'what', ဖှ၂ *phlòN* 'who', ထံင်ခှံ *thòNkhɔ́* 'where', ဆ၁်ယဲဒ် *chàijái* (ယေ့ဝ်ယေ့ *èìɕí*) 'when', ဗးကှံ *bánɔ́* 'why', and ခဲ့ခှံ *khɔ̀khɔ́* 'which one'. Movement of interrogative words does not take place in the formation of content interrogative sentences. They appear in the same positions as equivalent elements in declarative sentences. Sentences (121) and (122) present examples of content interrogative sentences:

(121) ကိုｰ မုံ အင်း ဆိုကှံလယ့်॥
　　　nə　mə　ʔáN　chənɔ́　lê
　　　2SG　IRR　eat　what　CQ
　　　'What will you eat?'

(122) ဖှ၂ အင်း ဆင့်ယး လယ့်॥
　　　phlòuN　ʔáN　chânjá　lê
　　　who　eat　fowl　CQ
　　　'Who ate the chicken?'

Note that interrogative sentences in Pwo Karen cannot be formed by using a particular intonation pattern, which is the same case in Bwe Karen as discussed by Henderson (1978). Additionally, in some languages in the area, interrogative sentences can be made by juxtaposing the positive form and the negative form of the same verb; however, Pwo Karen does not have such a procedure for making an interrogative sentence.

In addition, လယ့် *lê* is phonologically similar to the colloquial Burmese particle လဲ *lé*, which has a similar function. Whether it was borrowed from Burmese is unknown. The Sgaw Karen equivalents of Pwo Karen ဟှ၁ *ʁâ* and လယ့် *lê* are, respectively, ဒါ *ɦá* and လဲ့ *lê*, and they are cognates with the Pwo Karen forms. Thus, if လလ့ *lê* is a borrowing from Burmese, the period of borrowing must date back to a time before the split of Pwo and Sgaw.

3.4.4 Complement clauses

Complement clauses are embedded in the matrix clauses without any marking, such as a nominalizer or complementizer. Sentences (123) and (124) contain complement clauses embedded in the subject position, and (125) is one embedded in the object position.

(123) အဲ့ဝေ့ အင်း မေဝ် ဖွဲ့။
     [ʔəwê ʔáN mì]   phlé
     3SG   eat   rice fast
     'He eats rice quickly.'

(124) ပှၤ ခလဲင် ဖွဲ့ ကး။
     [pə khlàiN phlòʊN] ká
     1PL speak   Karen   difficult
     'It is difficult for us to speak Pwo Karen.'

(125) ယှ့ ၃း အဲ့ဝေ့ ကၠီး။
     jə   dá   [ʔəwê klí]
     1SG see 3SG   run
     'I saw him running.'

Interrogative sentences can also be embedded in the object position. In this case, the entire embedded clause has to be moved to the clause-initial position as shown in (126). This sentence can be translated with 'whether'.

(126) အဲ့ဝေ့ ကၠီး ဟှၣ် ယှ့ သဲ့ယှၢ် အေး။
     [ʔəwê klí ʁâ] jə   θíjâ   ʔé
     3SG   run PQ   1SG know NEG
     'I do not know whether he ran.'

Sentence (123) above is similar to the separated serial verb construction in (127), but their sentence structures are different.

(127) အဲ့ဝေ့ အင်း မေဝ် ၉ယ်။ (=97)
　　　 ʔəwê　ʔán　mì̱　blè
　　　 3SG　eat　rice　full
　　　 'He ate rice and got full.'

One of the differences between (123) and (127) is that the embedded clause in (123) can be clefted, but the equivalent part that seems like an embedded clause in (127) cannot be clefted, as shown in (128) and (129).

(128) ဖဲ့ ကို့ မွဲ့ အဲ့ဝေ့ အင်း မေဝ် လှ။
　　　 phlé　nɔ́　mwē　[ʔəwê　ʔán　mì̱]　lɔ́
　　　 fast　TOP　COP　3SG　eat　rice　EMP
　　　 'What is fast is his eating rice.'

(129) *၉ယ် ကို့ မွဲ့ အဲ့ဝေ့ အင်း မေဝ် လှ။
　　　 *blè　nɔ́　mwē　ʔəwê　ʔán　mì̱　lɔ́
　　　 full　TOP　COP　3SG　eat　rice　EMP

Interestingly, northern Karenic languages such as Kayah and Geba use concatenated serial verbs to express similar meanings to (123), as shown in (130) and (131).

(130) ʔa　ʔe　phrē　dī　　　　[Kayah Li; Solnit (1997: 65)]
　　　 3SG　eat　fast　rice
　　　 'He eats quickly.'

(131) ja　ʔā　plá　dī　　　　[Geba; Kato (2008a: 174)]
　　　 1SG　eat　fast　rice
　　　 'I eat quickly.'

However, in Sgaw Karen, which is one of the closest Karenic languages to Pwo Karen in terms of genealogy and geography, a meaning similar to (123) is expressed with the same word order, as illustrated in (132).

(132) အဝဲ အီဉ် မှၢ ချ့.　　　　　[Sgaw Karen; my data (cf. Kato 1993)]
　　　 ʔəwé　ʔɔ́　mē　khlé
　　　 3SG　eat　rice　fast
　　　 'He eats quickly.'

In order to more fully understand the history of the Karenic languages, it is important to take such syntactic differences among the Karenic languages into consideration.

4 Semantics and pragmatics

4.1 Common semantic domains

4.1.1 Food terminology

In Pwo Karen, food is divided into two categories: 'rice' and 'food eaten with rice'. 'Rice' is called ေမ့ *mḭ* and 'food eaten with rice' is called သၟိၣ် *θàN*. The former term, ေမ့ *mḭ*, specifically means 'cooked rice', complemented by two other words for 'rice', as shown below.

Pwo Karen		English	cf. Corresponding Burmese words[11]	
ၿု:	*buí*	'paddy'	စပါး, ေကာက်	*zăbá, kau?*
ဟ္ျုဆော:	*yûchá*	'uncooked rice'	ဆန်	*shàn*
ေမ့	*mḭ*	'cooked rice'	ထမင်း	*thămín*

4.1.2 Expressions of "cutting", "carrying", and "washing"

Southeast Asian languages tend to show fine verbal distinctions for particular actions such as 'cutting'. Below are some examples of Pwo Karen verbs for 'cutting', 'carrying', and 'washing'.

- Verbs of cutting

၎င်:	*dáN*	'to cut vertically with a knife or a sword'
ေဖ	*phé*	'to cut horizontally with a knife or a sword.'
ထိတ်	*thái*	'to cut with scissors'
က်တတ်	*kətài*	'to cut with a saw'
က်ၣင်:	*klóN*	'to cut powerfully with a knife or a sword'

---

[11] See Table 15 (p. 110) in the Burmese chapter for a complete list of rice terms in this language. See also corresponding forms in other SEA languages (Yongning Na, p. 260, Mon, p. 310, Vietnamese, p. 417, Wa p. 460, Malais, p. 505, Cham, p. 546, Hmong, p. 639).

- Verbs of carrying
ေဆာတဲ်	chó	'to carry with hand(s) or arm(s)'
ယှိၥ်	jò	'to carry on the shoulder'
တၢၣ်	tàɴ	'to carry on the head'
ဖုး	phuí	'to carry on the back'

- Verbs of washing
သွီယာ	θîjà	'to wash hands, legs, dishes and general things'
အၣ်းဆူယွာ	ʔáɴchuȋjwà	'to wash clothes'
အၣ်းဖျူ	ʔáɴphluī	'to wash one's head'
ဖျာ.	phlā	'to wash one's face'

4.2 Pragmatics & discourse

4.2.1 Sentence-final particles

Pwo Karen has a group of particles that appear sentence-finally and show the speaker's attitudes towards the propositions expressed in the sentences. These items are called sentence-final particles in Kato (2004). The most significant feature of sentence-final particles in terms of syntax is that they cannot appear in subordinate clauses. In other words, they appear outside the schema shown in Figure 1. The reason for this is that their functions are related to discourse-level features. Kato (2004) lists 22 sentence-final particles, and the interrogative particles ဟွာ ʁâ and လဲ lê, which we have seen in 3.4.3, are also included. It is, however, debatable whether the interrogative particles should be regarded as sentence-final particles because they can also appear in certain types of subordinate clauses, as shown in (126) in 3.4.4 above. The most frequently used sentence-final particles are discussed in turn below.

ကနဲ့ nê is used when the speaker expects the hearer's approval, as in (133).

(133) ဆ့ ခေါ်. ဆ္ပမာ. ကနဲ့။
    chə   khʊ̃   châ   mā   nê
    thing hot   much   very SFP
    'It is very hot, isn't it?'

ယွဲ. xɔ́ is used when the speaker wants the hearer to understand his/her intention, as in (134).

(134) ယှၩ် မ့ ထာင် လၣ့် ယှဝ်.॥
    jə   mə   thàɪN   lɔ̂   xɔ̄
    1SG   IRR return imminently   SFP
    'I am going now. OK?'

ယာ.စိဝ် *jābò* is used when the speaker has a conviction, as shown in (135).

(135) အံဝေ့ လေဝ် ယာ.စိဝ်॥
    ʔəwê   lḭ̀   jābò
    3SG   go   SFP
    'Of course, he went.'

4.2.2 Politeness

Pwo Karen does not have a grammatical device for politeness, but politeness can be expressed using a vocative expression after the sentence. Vocative expressions include kinship terms such as ပါပါ, *pàpâ* 'father' and မောဝ်.တုၣ် *mōtôʊN* 'mother'; professional terms such as ဆရာ *chərâ* 'teacher' and မၣ်နၤ *màNNē* 'Buddhist novice'; and other relationship terms such as သောဝ် *θʊ́* 'friend'. Sentence (136) presents an example.

(136) ယှၩ် လေဝ် လှိင် အေး သောဝ်॥
    jə   lḭ̀   làN   ʔé, θʊ́
    1SG   go   anymore   NEG friend
    'I won't go anymore, my friend.'

The Hpa-an dialect has borrowed honorific verbs from Mon that indicate respect to Buddhist monks. Three verbs have been noted so far in my fieldwork: ကိုၣ်ညာ *kəɲà* 'go; come', ပဝ်. *pɔ̄* 'die', and ပုတၢိၣ် *pətêIN* 'inform'. They all are borrowings from Mon listed in Shorto's (1962) dictionary as <kña> 'honorific prefix used for verbs denoting movements when referring to monks', <patim> 'inform', and <paw> 'die (honorific)'.

The verbs ကိုၣ်ညာ *kəɲà* 'go; come' and ပဝ်. *pɔ̄* 'die' are used when the subject of the verb refers to a monk, as in (137) and (138).

(137) သင်ယာ့ ကိုၣ်ညာ ယှဝ်॥
    θàNkhâ   kəɲà   jàʊ
    monk   go;come   PERF
    'The monk has gone,' or 'The monk has come.'

(138) သင်ယှၣ် ပဝ်• ယုၵ်ⅲ
 θàɴkhâ pɔ́ jàʊ
 monk die PERF
 'The monk has died.'

The verb ပုံတီၣ် *pətêiɴ* 'inform' is used to describe speaking to a monk, as shown in (139).

(139) အဲ့ဝေ့ ပုံတီၣ် ထင်း သင်ယှၣ်ⅲ
 ʔəwê pətêiɴ tháɴ θàɴkhâ
 3SG inform up monk
 'He spoke to the monk'

There is no particular honorific verb that describes the action when a monk speaks. When the monk speaks, the verb လဝ် *lɔ́* 'tell' is used, which is the most common word for denoting speaking. Sentence (140) provides an example of this case.

(140) သင်ယှၣ် လဝ် အဲ့ တိုၵ်ကာ ⅲ
 θàɴkhâ lɔ́ ʔə təkà
 monk tell his disciple
 'The monk spoke to his disciple.'

ကိုညာ *kənà* 'go; come' and ပဝ်• *pɔ́* 'die' can be called 'honorific expressions', while ပုံတီၣ် *pətêiɴ* 'inform' is 'humilific'.

5 Summary

Pwo Karen is a language with the following characteristics. In terms of its phonology, it has four tones and implosives. It is an isolating language, and its morphemes are monosyllabic and also sesquisyllabic. It also has many compound words. The basic word order is SVO, it has no tense marker, the nominal modifier precedes the head noun, and it has both postnominal and prenominal relative clauses. There are many numeral classifiers. Two types of serial verb constructions have been identified. Arguments can be omitted, topicalization frequently occurs, and complement clauses are embedded without any marking. There are also a number of sentence-final particles.

Although Pwo Karen is a language that has basic SVO word order, some of its features are aberrant from the characteristics common to VO-type languages in mainland Southeast Asia. These include the following: (a) existence of prenominal relative clauses (as shown in (70), 3.2.1); (b) nominal modifiers preceding the head nouns (as shown in (67) and (68), 3.2.1); and (c) a preference for concatenated-type serial verb constructions (see the discussion following (101), 3.3.2). Through my contrastive observation with other Pwo Karen dialects such as Western Pwo Karen, and other Karenic languages including Sgaw Karen and Geba, I propose that (a) can be attributed to the recent influence of Burmese, and that (b) and (c) have been followed from the Proto-Karen stage.

The history of the Karenic languages is still full of many mysteries. In order to more fully understand what happened that caused the proto-language of this linguistic group to change from SOV to SVO, we need to continue studying and analyzing these languages, one by one in detail.

Abbreviations

1	first person
2	second person
3	third person
ADP	adpositional phrase
CAUS	causative verb particle
CLF	classifier
COP	copular verb
CQ	particle indicating content question
DEM	demonstrative particle
EMP	particle indicating emphasis
EXP	particle indicating experience
INP	indefinite pronoun
IRR	irrealis marker
L	particle *lə̀* indicating Location, Source, and Goal
NEG	particle indicating negation
NM	nominal modifier
NP	noun phrase
NUM	numeral
PERF	particle indicating perfectivity
PL	plural
PLUR	particle indicating plurality
PQ	particle indicating polar question
PRON	pronoun
RC	relative clause
REL	particle that introduces a relative clause

SFP   sentence-final particle
SG   singular
TOP   particle indicating a topic
VPT   verb particle

References

Aikhenvald, Alexandra Y. & R. M. W. Dixon (eds.). 2006. *Serial verb constructions: A cross-linguistic typology*. Oxford: Oxford University Press.
Benedict, Paul K. 1972. *Sino-Tibetan: A conspectus*. Cambridge: Cambridge University Press.
Comrie, Bernard. 1989. *Language universals and linguistic typology: Syntax and morphology*. Chicago: The University of Chicago Press.
Dawkins, Erin & Audra Phillips. 2009a. *A sociolinguistic survey of Pwo Karen in Northern Thailand*. Chaing Mai: Linguistic Department, Payap University.
Dawkins, Erin & Audra Phillips. 2009b. *An investigation of intelligibility between West-Central Thailand Pwo Karen and Northern Pwo Karen*. Chaing Mai: Linguistic Department, Payap University.
Foley, William A. & Mike Olson. 1985. Clausehood and verb serialization. In Johanna Nichols & Anthony C. Woodbury (eds.), *Grammar inside and outside the clause*, 17–60. Cambridge: Cambridge University Press.
Haas, Mary R. 1964. *Thai-English student's dictionary*. Stanford: Stanford University Press.
Haudricourt, André-G. 1946. Restitution du karen commun. *Bulletin de la Société de Linguistique de Paris* 42 (1). 103–111.
Haudricourt, André-G. 1975. Le système des tons du karen commun. *Bulletin de la Société de Linguistique de Paris* 70 (1). 339–343.
Henderson, Eugénie J. A. 1978. Notes on yes-or-no questions and allied matters in Karen and Chin. In S. Udin (ed.), *Spectrum: Essays presented to Sutan Takdir Alisjahbana on his 70th birthday*, 452–468. Jakarta: Dian Rakyat.
Henderson, Eugénie J. A. 1997. *Bwe Karen dictionary: With texts and English-Karen word list*. (2 vols). London: School of Oriental and African Studies, University of Amberber, Brett Baker & Mark Harvey (eds.), *Complex predicates: Cross-linguistic perspectives on event structure*, 110–134. Cambridge: Cambridge University Press.
Jones, Robert B. 1961. *Karen Linguistic Studies*. Berkeley & Los Angeles: University of California Press.
Kato, Atsuhiko. 1993. Verb serialization in Sgaw Karen. *Journal of Asian and African Studies* 45. 177–204. (In Japanese).
Kato, Atsuhiko. 1995. The phonological systems of three Pwo Karen dialects. *Linguistics of the Tibeto-Burman Area* 18 (1). 63–103.
Kato, Atsuhiko. 1998. On head verbs of serial verb constructions in Pwo Karen. *Journal of the Linguistic Society of Japan* 113. 31–61. (In Japanese).
Kato, Atsuhiko. 2004. *A Pwo Karen grammar*. PhD dissertation, University of Tokyo. (In Japanese).
Kato, Atsuhiko. 2005. Parallelism in Pwo Karen. In Nakayama Toshihide & Shiohara Asako (eds.), *Kijutsubunpoo kara Akiraka ni Naru Bunpoo no Shomondai*, 145–159. Tokyo: Research Institute for Languages and Cultures of Asia and Africa. (In Japanese).

Kato, Atsuhiko. 2006. Difference in prevalence of writing systems in the same language – a case of Pwo Karen. In Shiohara Asako & Kodama Shigeaki (eds.), *Hyooki no Syuukan no Nai Gengo no Hyooki* [Writing unwritten languages], 89–110. Tokyo: Research Institute for Languages and Cultures of Asia and Africa. (In Japanese).

Kato, Atsuhiko. 2008a. Basic materials in Geba. *Asian and African Languages and Linguistics* 3. 169–219. Tokyo: Research Institute for Languages and Cultures of Asia and Africa. (In Japanese).

Kato, Atsuhiko. 2008b. Is the category 'adjective' necessary in Pwo Karen? *Asian and African Languages and Linguistics* 3. 77–95. Tokyo: Research Institute for Languages and Cultures of Asia and Africa. (In Japanese).

Kato, Atsuhiko. 2009a. Valence-changing particles in Pwo Karen. *Linguistics of the Tibeto-Burman Area* 32 (2). 71–102.

Kato, Atsuhiko. 2009b. A basic vocabulary of Htoklibang Pwo Karen with Hpa-an, Kyonbyaw, and Proto-Pwo Karen forms. *Asian and African Languages and Linguistics* 4. 169–218. Tokyo: Research Institute for Languages and Cultures of Asia and Africa.

Kato, Atsuhiko. 2010. 'Case' in Pwo Karen. In Sawada Hideo (ed.), *Grammatical phenomena of Tibeto-Burman languages* 1: *Case-marking and related matters*, 311–330. Tokyo: Research Institute for Languages and Cultures of Asia and Africa. (In Japanese).

Kato, Atsuhiko. 2011. The agent-defocusing function of a Pwo Karen noun that means 'thing'. Paper presented at 17th Himalayan Languages Symposium, Kobe City University of Foreign Studies.

Kato, Atsuhiko. 2013. Classification of sentences in Pwo Karen. In Sawada Hideo (ed.), *Grammatical phenomena of Tibeto-Burman languages* 2, 81–114. Tokyo: Research Institute for Languages and Cultures of Asia and Africa. (In Japanese).

Manson, Ken. 2003. *Karenic language relationships: A lexical and phonological analysis*. Chiang Mai: Dept of Linguistics, Payap University.

Manson, Ken. 2009. Prolegomena to reconstructing Proto-Karen. *LaTrobe Working Papers in Linguistics* 12.

Matisoff, James A. 1969. Verb concatenation in Lahu: The syntax and semantics of 'simple' juxtaposition. *Acta Linguistica Hafniensia* 12 (1). 69–120.

Matisoff, James A. 1973a. *The grammar of Lahu*. Berkeley & Los Angeles: University of California Press.

Matisoff, James A. 1973b. Tonogenesis in Southeast Asia. In Larry M. Hyman (ed.), *Consonant types and tone* (Southern California Occasional Papers in Linguistics 1), 71–96. Los Angeles: University of California Press.

Matisoff, James A. 1986. Hearts and Minds in South-East Asian languages and English: An essay in the comparative lexical semantics of psycho-collocation. *Cahiers de Linguistique d'Asie Orientale* 15 (1). 5–57. Paris.

Matisoff, James A. 1991a. Sino-Tibetan linguistics: Present state and future prospects. *Annual Review of Anthropology* 20. 469–504.

Matisoff, James A. 1991b. Syntactic parallelism and morphological elaboration in Lahu religious poetry. In Jorge Hankamer & Sandra Chung (eds.), *Festschrift for William F. Shipley*, 83–103. Santa Cruz, CA: Syntax Research Center.

Matisoff, James A. 1991c. Areal and universal dimensions of grammatization in Lahu. In Elizabeth Closs Traugott & Bernd Heine (eds.), *Approaches to Grammaticalization*, vol. 2, 383–453. Amsterdam & Philadelphia: John Benjamins.

Matisoff, James A. 2000. On the uselessness of glottochronology for the subgrouping of Tibeto-Burman. In Colin Renfrew, April McMahon & Larry Trask (eds.), *Time depth in historical linguistics*, 333–71. Cambridge: The McDonald Institute for Archaeological Research.

Matisoff, James A. 2003. *Handbook of Proto-Tibeto-Burman: System and philosophy of Sino-Tibetan reconstruction*. Berkeley, Los Angeles & London: University of California Press.

Myhill, John. 1997. Toward a functional typology of agent defocusing. *Linguistics* 35. 799–844.

Phillips, Audra. 2000. West-Central Thailand Pwo Karen phonology. *33rd ICSTLL Papers*, 99–110. Bangkok: Ramkhamhaeng University.

Renard, Ronald D. 1980. *Kariang: History of Karen-T'ai relations from the beginnings to 1923*. PhD dissertation, University of Hawai'i at Manoa.

Shintani, Tadahiko. 2003. Classification of Brakaloungic (Karenic) languages in relation to their tonal evolution. In Shigeki Kaji (ed.), *Proceedings of the symposium cross-linguistic studies of tonal phenomena: Historical development, phonetics of tone, and descriptive studies*, 37–54. Tokyo: Research Institute for Languages and Cultures of Asia and Africa.

Shorto, Harry L. 1962. *A dictionary of modern spoken Mon*. London: Oxford University Press.

Solnit, David. 1997. *Eastern Kayah Li: Grammar, texts, glossary*. Honolulu: University of Hawai'i Press.

Solnit, David. 2006. Verb serialization in Eastern Kayah Li. In A. Y. Aikhenvald & R. M. W. Dixon (eds.), *Serial verb constructions: A cross-linguistic typology*, 144–159. Oxford: Oxford University Press.

Vittrant, Alice. 2002. Classifier systems and noun categorization devices in Burmese. In *Proceedings of the twenty-eighth annual meeting of the Berkeley Linguistics Society: Special session on Tibeto-Burman and Southeast Asian linguistics*, 129–148.

Vittrant, Alice & Johan van der Auwera. 2010. Epistemic modality or how to express likelihood in Burmese. *Cahiers de Linguistique Asie Orientale* 39 (1). 41–80.

Appendix 1: Summary of linguistic features

Legend
+++ the feature is pervasive or used obligatorily in the language
++   the feature is normal but selectively distributed in the language
+   the feature is merely possible or observable in the language
−   the feature is impossible or absent in the language

	Feature	+++/++/+/−	§ ref. in this chapter
Phonetics	Lexical tone or register	+++	§1.1, p.133
Phonetics	Back unrounded vowels	+	§1.2, p.135
Phonetics	Initial velar nasal	+	§1.2, p.134

	Feature	+++/++/+/−	§ ref. in this chapter
Phonetics	Implosive consonants	+++	§1.2, p.134
Phonetics	Sesquisyllabic structures	++	§2.1, p.136
Morphology	Tendency towards monosyllabicity	+++	§2.1, p.136
Morphology	Tendency to form compounds	+++	§2.1.1, p.136
Morphology	Tendency towards isolating (rather than affixation)	+++	§2.1, p.135
Morphology	Psycho-collocations	+++	§2.2, p.139
Morphology	Elaborate expressions (e.g. four-syllable or other set patterns)	+++	§2.3, p.140
Morphology	Reduplication generally	++	§2.1.3, p.138–39
Morphology	Reduplication of nouns	−	§2.1.3, p.138
Morphology	Reduplication of verbs	+++	§2.1.3, p.138–39
Grammar	Use of classifiers	++	§3.2.2, p.147
Grammar	Classifiers used in counting	+++	§3.2.2, p.147
Grammar	Classifiers used with demonstratives	−	not discussed explicitly
Grammar	Adjectival verbs	+++	§3, p.140
Grammar	Grammatical number	−	§3.2.1, p.144 & §3.3.1, p.148
Grammar	Inflection of verbs	−	§3.3.1, p.148
Grammar	Use of tense/aspect markers	++	§3.3.1, p.148
Grammar	Use of verb plural markers	−	not discussed explicitly
Grammar	Grammaticalization of GET/OBTAIN (potential mod. resultative/perfect aspect)	+	§3.3.2, p.155
Grammar	Grammaticalization of PUT, SET (completed/resultative aspect)	−	−
Grammar	Grammaticalization of GIVE (causative, benefactive; preposition)	+++	§3.3.2, p.158
Grammar	Grammaticalization of FINISH (perfective/ complete aspect; conjunction/temporal subordinator)	+	not discussed
Grammar	Grammaticalization of directional verbs e.g. GO / COME (allative, venitive)	−	§3.3.2, p.154
Grammar	Grammaticalization of SEE, WATCH (temptative)	+++	§3.3.2, p.157

	Feature	+++/++/+/−	§ ref. in this chapter
Grammar	Grammaticalization of STAY, REMAIN (progressive and continuous, durative aspects)	−	§3.3.1, p.150
Grammar	Serial verb constructions	+++	§3.3.2, p.150 ff
Syntax	Verb precedes object (VO)	+++	§3.1, p.141
Syntax	Auxiliary precedes verb	++	§3, p.140–41
Syntax	Preposition precedes noun	+++	§3.1, p.142
Syntax	Noun precedes adjective	+++	§3.2.1, p.144
Syntax	Noun precedes demonstrative	+++	§3.2.1, p.144
Syntax	Noun precedes genitive	−	not discussed
Syntax	Noun precedes relative clause	++	§3.2.1, p.146
Syntax	Use of topic-comment structures	+++	§3.4.2, p.159–60
Syntax	Ellipsis of arguments known from context	+++	§3.4.1, p.159
Lexical semantics	Specific terms for forms of rice	+++	§4.1.1, p.164
Pragmatics	Use of utterance-final pragmatic particles	+++	§4.2.1, p.165
Pragmatics	Encoding of politeness	−	§4.2.2, p.166
Pragmatics	Encoding of honorifics	+	§4.2.2, p.166

Appendix 2: Text interlinearized

Folk tale: **TAMARIND TREE** (Recorded in Hpa-an, November 2000)

(1) ကဲ၊ ဖျာ•ခွာ့ အံ့ လုံဟှာ။
    ké   *phjākhwâ*   *ʔɔ́*   *lə*   *yà*
    well   male   be   one   CLF:person
    'There was a [young] man.'

(2) ဖျာ•ခွာ့ လုံဟှာ ကုံတာ•
    phjākhwâ   *lə*   *yà*   *nɔ́tā,*
    male   one   CLF:person   TOP

    ဆုံ ဖါန်ထင်း ဆုံ ဖါန်ထင်း
    chə   *phàɴ*   *tháɴ,*   *chə*   *phàɴ*   *tháɴ,*
    thing   bright   ascend   thing   bright   ascend

ယောဝ်·ထင်း မင်ခွံင်· ထာင်လံင် ကို
jɯ̄   thán   màNkhlōN thàiN   lòN   nɔ́
look ascend tamarind branch upside TOP

ဖျာ·ဖွယုာ· ကို ခူး တာ·
phjāphu̯ɕā   nɔ́ dá   tā,
old.man   TOP find and

မွဲ ဖောဟ်သး ဖျာ· ကို အံခုံညာန့် အံ မာန့် ယုက် လဝ်ဝေ॥
"mwē phɯ́θá   phjā nɔ́ ʔə chənân ʔɔ́ mân jàʊ" lɔ̄ wê
COP bachelor guy that his wisdom exist exact PERF tell EMP
'An old man saw the young man [thoughtfully] looking up a tamarind branch every time when the sun rises, and said, "Absolutely this bachelor has wisdom!".'

(3) ဒေ ယုံ ဖောဟ်မူး ကို ယုံ မံ့ ဘုံခဲ့ ကင်·ထီး
    "dē jə phɯ́muí nɔ́ jə mə dàikhâ   nī"
    with my daughter TOP 1SG IRR make.marry for.a.while
    ' "I'll make him marry my daughter." '

(4) ယိက်ယိက် အံဝေ ဘုံခဲ့ ခွိုက် ဝေ ယာ·စိုဝ်॥
    jaıjaı ʔəwe dàikhâ   khwái wê jābò
    soon   3SG   make.marry throw EMP SFP
    'After a while he made them married.'

(5) ဘုံခဲ့ ဝေ သယ်ဟုံင် ကို
    dàikhâ   wê θèyòN   nɔ́,
    make.marry EMP after   TOP

    လုံ ဆိုဖာန် ဖျာ·ဖောဟ်သး ကို ယောဝ်· မင်ခွံင်· ထာင်လံင် ကို
    lá chəphàN phjāphɯ́θá nɔ́ jɯ̄   màNkhlōN   thàiN   lòN   nɔ́,
    L   dawn   bachelor   that look   tamarind   branch   upside because

    မွဲ ညာန့် ဆိုလယ့် ဆိုလယ့် ကို သေ့ယာ့ အေး॥
    mwē ɲân chəlê   chəlê   nɔ́ θíjâ   ʔé
    COP wisdom what   what   TOP know   NEG
    'After he made them married, he wondered what wisdom the young man had because the young man [kept] looking up the tamarind branch at dawn.'

(6) ဖျာ.ဖွူယှာ. ထေန့် ကၠို မ္ၚဲ အံၣ်ညာန့် ဖာဘော်ဟ်။
phjāphuîɕā thîɲ   nɔ́   "mwē ʔə   ɲân   phàdʉ́"
old.man   think   TOP   COP   his wisdom   huge
'The old man thought, " He is a very wise man." '

(7) ယိက်ယိက် ဖျာ.ဖွူယှာ. ကၠို အင်းစာ အံၣ်မး ဖဝ်။
jáijái   phjāphuîɕā   nɔ́   ʔáncà   ʔə   má   phɔ́
soon   old.man   TOP   ask   his   son.in.law PERF
'Soon, the old man asked his son-in-law.'

(8) မ္ၚဲ ဆိုလယ့် နာန်.ဝါ ၊ ဆို ဖါန်ထင်း ဆို ဖါန်ထင်း
"mwē   chəlê, nān   wà,   chə   phàn thán,   chə   phàn thán,
COP   what   daughter husband thing bright ascend thing bright ascend

ကၠို ယောဝ်. မင်ခွံင်. ထင်လံင် ကၠို
nə   jū   màNkhlōn thàin   lòn   nɔ́"
2SG   look   tamarind branch upside TOP
' "Why do you look up the tamarind branch every time the sun rises?" '

(9) ပး ပါ ပါ ၊ အံၣ်ဝေ လဝ် ဝေဒူး မ္ၚဲ ကျုၟစိုဝ်။
pápàpà,   ʔəwê   lɔ̀   wêdá   mwē   câbò
Oh!   3SG   tell EMP   COP   like.this
'Oh! The son-in-law answered like this.'

(10) မင်ခွံင်.ထင် ဖျာ. ကၠို ကယ့်
"màNkhlōn   thàin   phjā   nɔ́   nê
tamarind   branch thing   that   TOP

မ္ၚဲ အေ တာင် ယျုၚ် ထံင်း ကင်.ထီး
mwē   ʔè   tàin   ɕàʊ   thón   ní
COP   if   make   happen.to   top   for.a.while

မှ ဟုင်း ဖူ ယုးပှျော်။
mə   ɣáNphuì   xáxı̣̀
IRR   make.sound   surely
' "That tamarind branch, if you make a top from it, it will surely make a lot of sound!" '

Hilary Chappell
Southern Min

Introduction

Southern Min is a major Chinese language of wider communication in many countries of Southeast Asia with a conservative estimate of seven million speakers in this region, the result of a gradual, centuries-long diaspora from China.[1] This estimate includes the three main varieties of Hokkien, Teochew and Hainanese.

Historically, the core of the Min languages is located in modern day Fujian, a coastal province in the southeast of China. It represents one of the ten branches of the Sinitic taxon within the Sino-Tibetan language family, and accounts for approximately 4%–5% of Sinitic speakers in China, that is, approximately 52 million speakers (Zhang 2012). Southern Min, is in fact, the largest and most widely distributed subgroup of dialects within the Min supergroup, as it is known, extending south into Guangdong province, and over the straits to Taiwan. There are 27 million speakers of varieties of Southern Min on the mainland and a further 15 million in Taiwan.

In Southeast Asia, sizeable communities of the three main varieties of Southern Min speakers are located principally in the countries of Thailand, Malaysia, Singapore, Indonesia, and the Philippines. Hokkien or *Fújiànhuà* 福建话 has traditionally been the main overseas Chinese language in all these countries, except for Thailand, where the Chaozhou 潮州 or Teochew speakers predominate, reportedly making up more than 80% of the Chinese community.[2]

---

[1] This is a crude estimate based on data from Ethnologue (2017, see Simons & Fennig), the CIA World Factbook (2013) and on-line access to the relevant statistics from official government censuses. Many censuses do not or have not posed questions on language use, at home or in education, so that we have recourse only to statistics on ethnicity which evidently does not correlate perfectly with linguistic competences. In addition to this, the census data on language use is often out-of-date where particular governments have ceased asking questions about this. The estimate according to these same sources for ethnic Chinese populations in Southeast Asia comes to over 27 million.
[2] The latest census carried out in Thailand was in 2010. According to the National Statistical Office's report, *The 2010 Population and Housing Census*, http://popcensus.nso.go.th/file/popcensus-10-01-56-E.pdf , accessed on 23 August 2017, 95.9% of the population of 65.9 million in Thailand are Thai, 2.0% are Burmese' and 2.1% are classified under 'Others'. It does not provide any information on ethnicity.

Hilary Chappell: Ecole des Hautes Etudes en Sciences Sociales, Paris
E-Mail: hilary.chappell@ehess.fr

https://doi.org/10.1515/9783110401981-005

In this chapter, we thus present an overview of the main features of the grammar of Hokkien, focusing on aspects of its phonology, morphology and syntax which are distinct from standard Mandarin, while highlighting features that it shares with other languages of the Southeast Asian area.

Demography of Southern Min speakers

In China, Southern Min is largely spoken in the region of Zhangzhou 漳州, Quanzhou 泉州 and Xiamen 厦门 along a coastal strip in the south of Fujian province. Over the border from the Min homeland, two important dialects of the Southern Min subgroup are found in northeastern Guangdong, these being Shantou 汕頭 (Swatow) and Chaozhou 潮州 (Teochew), communities which live in close proximity to varieties of Hakka and Cantonese.[3]

Large communities of Min speakers are also found as far south as the Leizhou peninsula 雷州半島 in southern Guangdong and on Hainan Island 海南島, a province thirty kilometres off the southeastern coast of China. Here they live side by side with the Li and the Yao peoples, speakers of non-Sinitic languages belonging respectively to the Kra-Dai and Hmong-Mien families. On the basis of dynastic records, the forebears of these two outlier communities forming the Leiqiong subgroup are believed to have come mainly from Putian county in northern Fujian, beginning in the period of the late Song and early Yuan, that is, from the 13th century (Li & Yao 2008).

Across the Taiwan Strait from Fujian province, Southern Min flourishes as the first language of the majority of the population with approximately 15 million speakers (67% of the population of 22 million) (S. Huang 1993, Simons & Fennig 2017). The variety of Taiwanese Southern Min has evolved from a fusion and neutralization of the dialects spoken in Zhangzhou and Quanzhou and consequently belongs to the Quanzhang subgroup. Migrations began in the early 17th century from these two prefectural towns in southern Fujian province to the island of Formosa, as it was first named by the Portuguese, as well as to many neighbouring countries in Southeast Asia. Consequently, the Hokkien or Quanzhang subgroup (泉漳片) of Southern Min is spoken by Chinese communities living in particularly Malaysia, Singapore, Indonesia, Brunei, Cambodia and the Philippines.[4] In Vietnam, Laos and Myanmar, smaller communities of Chinese speak varieties of Mandarin and Yue.

---

3 Linguistic maps and the latest classification of the Min branch of Sinitic can be consulted in the second edition of the *Language Atlas of China* (Zhang 2012).
4 In the late 20th century, T'sou (1987) estimated there there were 9 million Southern Min speakers in the Indo-Pacific basin, including, however, second language speakers in the latter case. However, according to the most recent statistics from both *Ethnologue* (2017, see Simons

Dialect classification

The Min group is a very diverse group of dialects whose subdivisions are generally not mutually intelligible. For example, speakers of the Fuzhou dialect in northern Fujian cannot converse easily with speakers of the Chaozhou dialect in the south, or even Putian speakers with their distant relatives in Hainan. Min is reputed to be the most highly divergent group within Sinitic. Fujian province was, in fact, one of the last to be completely colonized and settled by the Han people in the 7th century. It remained for many centuries one of the most geographically inaccessible areas of China with its high mountain ranges and few major rivers suited to the typical north-to-south migration pattern in China's history. In the view of Norman (1988), this may partially explain the heterogeneous nature of the Min dialect group.[5]

In Chinese dialectology, the traditional division of Min dialects has been into Northern and Southern types (Yuan Jiahua et al, 1960). The Fuzhou 福州 dialect was generally used as the representative dialect for Northern Min while the Xiamen 廈門 or Amoy dialect was used for Southern Min. More recently, Jerry Norman proposed a new primary division into Inland (or Western) Min and Coastal (or Eastern) Min (see Norman 1988, 1991, You 1992, Wurm et al 1987: Map B12). Inland Min comprises the three subgroups of Northwestern and Far Western on the one hand, and Central on the other, which correspond in fact to the two main routes of migration taken in the third century AD, from Jiangxi in the west and Zhejiang in the north (Bielenstein 1959, Chappell 2001a). In chronological terms, the formation of Coastal Min also neatly matches the seventh century migration down the coast from these same two provinces and in-

---

& Fennig) and the relevant government censuses for each Southeast Asian country which have supplied figures on ethnicity and/or home language, this adds up to the rough estimate of seven million, excluding Papua New Guinea and the South Pacific islands which T'sou had included in his larger survey. Note also that the Hokkien dialects are far less common in the Americas, Europe, Australia and New Zealand, where Cantonese dialects predominate among established Chinese communities (Wurm et al, 1987: Maps B16a and 16b).

5 Some of the main toponyms and dialects of this group are listed below as a point of orientation for the reader:

Standard Mandarin (pinyin)	Anglicized (Historical names)	Min-Xiamen (IPA)	Characters
Fujian province	Hokkien	[Hok.kien]	福建
Fuzhou	Foochow	[Hok.tsiu]	福州
Xiamen	Amoy	[E.bng]	廈門
Quanzhou	Ch'uanchou	[Tsʰuan.tsiu]	泉州
Zhangzhou	Changchou	[Tsiang.tsiu]	漳州
Shantou	Swatow	[Suã·tʰau]	汕頭
Chaozhou	Teochew	[Dio.tsiu]	潮州

corporates Northeastern dialects such as Fuzhou and Southern dialects such as Xiamen and Teochew. To this classification, for the historical reasons adumbrated above, we need to add a separate subgroup for the Min dialects spoken on Hainan Island and the Leizhou peninsula, due to their evolution in isolation from the rest of Min. The list below includes some representative varieties for each subgroup.

(i) Inland Min
   a. *Northwestern*: Jian 建 dialects
   b. *Far Western*: Shaowu 邵武, Jingle 靜樂
   c. *Central*: Yong'an 永安

(ii) Coastal Min
   a. *Northeastern*: Fuzhou 福州, Fu'an 福安
   b. *Puxian*: Putian 莆田
   c. **Southern**: Xiamen 廈門(Amoy), Taiwanese 台語, Zhangzhou 漳州, Quanzhou 泉州, Chaozhou (Teochew) 潮州, Shantou 汕頭 (Swatow)

(iii) Leiqiong 雷瓊
   a. Dialects of the Leizhou peninsula 雷州話
   b. Hainanese 海南話

Literary versus colloquial registers
Within Sinitic, the Min dialects stand out for the striking contrast between literary and colloquial pronunciations of words, known as *wén-bái yì-dú* 文白異讀 in Mandarin. The literary or reading pronunciation tends to be closer to that in Mandarin, reflecting earlier diglossia with the language of the imperial court as the 'High' language. For example, the character 行 has the literary reading /$hing^5$/ and the colloquial reading /kia^{n5}/, pronunciations which are realized according to function: /$hing^5$/ is used in the more elevated literary lexicon for abstract words such as 行為 /$hing^5 ui^5$/ 'behaviour' and 行动 /$hing^5 tong^7$/ 'deeds, action' while /kia^{n5}/ is used in its colloquial and concrete sense of 'to walk' (Yang 1991: 10–14; 118–134). For the contemporary language, the different pronunciations cannot in fact be explained simply as two different stylistic levels used in different contexts but reshape the entire lexicon, due to their function in distinguishing senses of the same word and in creating families of words and compounds. The historical reason for these chronological strata in the Min dialects is treated in Mei & Yang (1995), while certain of the synchronic outcomes for the lexicon are discussed in Lien (2001) in terms of the interaction between the two types of pronunciation.

This description of Southern Min uses Taiwanese as the representative variety with examples transcribed in the revised Church Romanization, in wide use in Taiwanese linguistic circles.[6]

Popular literature and historical documents concerning the Southern Min language
Documents written in Min go back to at least the sixteenth century and include many different local styles of opera including the southern style or *nányīn* 南音 opera, songs, and Taoist liturgical material. For Southern Min, an important work is the popular Ming dynasty (1368–1644) play, the *Li Jing Ji* 荔鏡記 (Romance of the Litchi and Mirror, 1566), written in a mixture of the Quanzhou and Chaozhou dialects. These make use of the specially created demotic characters for Southern Min words for which a standard Chinese character does not exist, for example, 勿會 *bue⁷* 'cannot'; 亻因 *in¹* 3PL 'they'.[7]

Other pedagogical and religious materials from the same period have been traced to the Philippines, and even to Spain. These include a translation into Southern Min from Spanish of a Catholic catechism, *Doctrina Christiana en letra y lengua china* (1597–1605), two Southern Min–Spanish dictionaries, *Dictionarium Sino-Hispanicum* (Chinese-Spanish Dictionary)(c. 1604) and *Bocabulario de la lengua sangleya* (Lexicon of the Sangley Language) (c. 1617), not to mention an early grammar of the Southern Min dialect of Zhangzhou, *Arte de la lengua chiõ-chiu* (Grammar of the Chiõ Chiu language) (1620). These were all compiled and written by Spanish missionaries in collaboration with native speakers in Manila and Cebu where Chinese communities had been set up in the wake of established trade routes between southern Fujian and the Philippines.[8] The term 'Sangley'

---

6 The modifications of the Church Romanization originally devised by Carstairs Douglas (1873) are as follows : The symbols, *ts* and *tsʰ*, are not used since they represent sounds which are no longer phonemically distinct from *ch* and *chh* respectively in modern Southern Min. Open *o* and closed *o* are represented as *oo* and *o*. Vocalic nasalization is indicated by a superscript *n*. An empty box, □, is used wherever the Chinese character is not known, which is not infrequent in the case of the special Southern Min lexemes. We base this chapter on Taiwanese Southern Min for the practical reason that there are no comprehensive reference grammars of Southeastern Asian varieties of Hokkien available (nor of mainland Fujian varieties for that matter), while Taiwanese has been the subject of a great deal of research.
7 The writing system and the methods adopted for representing Southern Min in terms of characters are both discussed in more detail in Chappell and Lien (2011).
8 The 'Sangley' Chinese traders settled on the outskirts of Manila, in the Philippines, in an area known as the *parián* during the late 16th century. The Spanish missionaries of the Dominican order in Manila proselytized not only to the majority of Tagalog speakers but also to this Chinese community. For more information, see Klöter (2011) and Chappell and Peyraube (2006).

refers in fact to these Hokkien Chinese traders in the Philippines and is likely related to the Southern Min word which means 'commerce': $seng^1$-li^2 生理.

1 Phonology

Southern Min is an exclusively tonal language, without the use of any register differences.[9] It exhibits a complex system of tone sandhi, based on its seven citation tones. For a Chinese language, it possesses a reasonably standard size inventory of 18 consonants, two semi-vowels and six cardinal vowels which combine to form the syllable rhymes of Southern Min including eight diphthongs and two triphthongs (see Tables 2 and 3 below). Its inventory of syllables is quite expansive with over 2,200 combinations compared with standard Mandarin, which has approximately 1,100 different syllable types (Cheng 1997: 93). As for most Sinitic languages, Southern Min does not permit any consonant clusters in syllable-initial position, while it has a restricted set of consonants permitted in syllable-final position.

Min dialects show the main division common to the consonant inventory in most Sinitic languages of an aspirated versus unaspirated distinction for obstruents. Strikingly, however, Min dialects also possess a voiced series of stops that occur in syllable-initial position, having evolved from an earlier series of nasal phonemes. Admittedly, there is also a voiced series of consonants in many Wu and Xiang dialects. In the Wu dialects, however, this may be only realized intervocalically, as in Shanghainese, but murmured initially.

1.1 Suprasegmental phonology: tone and register

While phonation types are not recognized for Min dialects, in contrast to this, tone sandhi or tone change is a complex and well-known feature of the entire Min supergroup of dialects.[10]

Thus, in Southern Min, each syllable can be realized in its citation tone and in a sandhi (or changed) tone. The citation tone, also known as its 'isolation' tone refers to the pronunciation of any stressed syllable preceding a pause, such

---

9 See, however, Chen (2000: 74-76) on register spread in Chaozhou polysyllabic words.
10 Phonation may however be a secondary feature of tone systems in Chinese languages (e.g. creaky voice) and certainly played a role in tonogenesis. Shanghainese is considered to be a phonation register language with the feature of breathy or murmured voice.

as at the end of a tone group, or in a position before a following unstressed syllable. Table 1 uses the traditional classification system for Chinese tones into four categories and two registers, upper and lower (which, however, we note, no longer function as true register differences).

The four categories of tones are known as *píngshēng* 平聲 'level tone', *shǎngshēng* 上聲 'ascending tone', *qùshēng* 去聲 'departing tone' and *rùshēng* 入聲 'entering tone'. Due to tone merger, there is no lower register tone value for the Ascending Tone, that is, there is no Tone 6. Tone values are a case of relative pitch, and subject to both dialectal and individual speaker variation. The entering tone tends to be a clipped tone of short duration in most Sinitic languages, due to the fact that it occurs largely in closed syllables with the plosive codas: -p, -t, -k or -ʔ. To represent the relevant pitch values, Yuen Ren Chao's scale from the lowest value, 1, to the highest, 5 is used in this description of Hokkien, while the transcription known as the modified Church Romanization has been adopted. The tone sandhi values are given in italic numbers to the right of the citation values, and, in general, will not be given in the transcription of examples used in the present description.[11] See also Lin (2015: 68–80) on tonal properties.

Table 1: Tone inventory of Southern Min

	Level tone 平聲	Ascending tone 上聲	Departing tone 去聲	Entering tone 入聲
Upper Register	**Tone 1** 陰平 High level 55 *33*	**Tone 2** 陰上 High falling 51 *55*	**Tone 3** 陰去 Low falling 21 *51*	**Tone 4** 陰入 Low checked 2 *5*
Lower Register	**Tone 5** 陽平 Mid rising 25 *21/33*		**Tone 7** 陽去 Low level 33 *21*	**Tone 8** 陽入 High checked 5 *2*

Tone sandhi rules in Southern Min have been described in terms of a tone cycle by Robert Cheng (1972). For tones in the non-checked syllables, a cyclic effect is produced whereby the High Falling Tone (陰上51) changes to the same pitch value as High Level (陰平 55); High Level Tone (陰平 55) changes to Low Level Tone (陽去 33), the Low Level tone (陽去 33) changes to Low Falling (陰去 21) and Low Falling Tone (陰去 21) changes to High Falling (陰上 51), thereby completing the cycle. The two checked or entering tones also perform a similar kind of flip-flop: High Checked (陽入 5) becomes Low Checked (陰入 2) and vice-

---

11 Note that the tonal values vary widely from dialect to dialect of Southern Min and also from author to author, depending on a variety of factors including, for example, the region in Taiwan and whether it is predominantly Quanzhou-based or Zhangzhou-based. I refer to Chappell & Lien (2011) for these values. Yang (1991: 34-35) gives the following values for Taiwanese Southern Min which differ somewhat from ours: Tone 1 High Level, 陰平: 44; Tone 2 陰上: 53, Tone 3 陰去: 31; Tone 4 陰入: *32* or *22*; Tone 5 陽平: 13; Tone 7 陽去: 22 and Tone 8 陽入: *33*.

versa. Finally, the Mid Rising tone (陽平25) changes to a low tone: either Low Falling (陰去 21) or Low Level (陽去33). In Southern Min, syllables with the neutral or unstressed tone are less common compared with standard Mandarin Chinese where the phenomenon is widespread, that is, the loss of the full tonal value on unstressed syllables in compound words, in addition to affixes and clitic-like elements.

A paradigm of tonal syllables in reading pronunciation is next presented, according to the traditional numbering:

Open syllables:
Tone 1: su^{55} 私 'secret'   Tone 5: su^{25} 詞 'an expression'
Tone 2: su^{51} 使 'to cause'   Tone 7: su^{33} 事 'business'
Tone 3: su^{21} 思 'be anxious'

Checked syllables:
Tone 4: sut^{2} 率 'to lead'
Tone 8: sut^{5} 述 'to recite'

1.2 Segmental phonemes : consonants and vowels

1.2.1 Initial and final consonant patterns

There are 18 consonants and two semi-vowels in Southern Min which are characterized by aspiration and voicing. While the nasal consonants, /m/ and /ŋ/ may act as syllables, consonant clusters in either initial or final position are not permitted, at least at the level of the syllable. While all consonants may occur in syllable-initial position, syllable-final position is restricted to the nasals /m n ŋ/, the voiceless unaspirated plosives /p t k/ and the glottal stop /ʔ/.

There are two series of obstruents comprising plosives, fricatives and affricates: (1) a voiceless series, and (2) a voiced series. In addition to this, there is a contrast in aspiration in the voiceless series: the unaspirated class (p, t, k, ʔ, ts) and the aspirated class (pʰ, tʰ, kʰ, tsʰ). Voiced series of obstruents are uncommon in Sinitic languages. Notwithstanding this, through a process of denasalization, Southern Min has acquired a voiced series (b, l, g) noting that in Southern Min, the phoneme /l/ has an apical place of articulation, close to /d/ (Zhou 1991: 13–14). In some dialects, there is also free variation for the phoneme /dz/ with /l/, for example, the word for 'day' 日 may be pronounced as jit^{8} [$dzit^{8}$] or lit^{8}. The Xiamen or Amoy variety only has /l/, as is also the case in Quanzhou (Zhou 1991: 14, Yang 1991: 25).

Table 2: Consonants of Taiwanese Southern Min

		Bilabial	Dental	Velar	Glottal
Plosives	voiceless unaspirated	p	t	k	ʔ
	voiceless aspirated	p^h	t^h	k^h	
	voiced	b		g	
Affricates	voiceless unaspirated		ts		
	voiceless aspirated		ts^h		
	voiced		dz		
Fricatives	voiceless		s		h
Nasals		(m)	(n)	(ŋ)	
Lateral			l		

The voiced series of plosives is in partial complementary distribution with their homorganic nasals in Southern Min. Synchronically, /b/, /l/ and /g/ are realized as their nasal allophones, /m/, /n/ and /ŋ/, respectively, when they occur in the initial position of syllables with the nasalized finals -i^n, -a^n, -$ɔ^n$, -ia^n, -iu^n, ai^n, -au^n, -ua^n, ui^n etc. Some examples are (i) /bia^{n5}/ 名 'name' which is realized phonetically as [mia^{n5}], (ii) /liu^{n5}/ 娘 'woman' which is realized phonetically as [niu^{n5}] and (iii) /gi^{n7}/ 硬 'hard' which is realized phonetically as [$ŋi^{n7}$] (see Yang 1991: 26–27, Zhou 1991: 31 for more examples).[12] Historically, under certain conditions, the three nasal phonemes in Southern Min /m n ŋ/ all lost their nasality in initial position, producing /b l g/ (Zhou 1991: 14, 31, Baxter & Sagart 2014: 92ff). Examples of words that have voiced plosives or the voiced lateral initial in combination with non-nasalized syllable rhymes are [be^2] 馬 'horse', [lam^5] 南 'south' and [go^5] 鵝 'goose'.

1.2.2 Vowel patterns

In Southern Min, there are basically six vowels, with much dialectal variation, it should be added.[13] Vowels can be classified as either: (1) monophthongs (single vowels), or (2) diphthongs. In addition to this basic division, Southern Min also possesses two triphthongs.

---

12 Here an implicit reference to the literary pronunciation and the reconstructed forms is being made by Yang (1991). For more details of the development of the nasal and plosive series of initial consonants, see Baxter & Sagart (2014).
13 The Quanzhou dialect has two extra vowels : /ə/ and /ɯ/ according to Yang (1991) and Wei-rong Chen (2011).

Table 3: Monophthongs of Southern Min

	front	central	back
high	i		u
high-mid	e		o
mid			
low-mid			ɔ
low		a	

There are eight diphthongs possible in Southern Min, formed by combinations of the medial vowels and offglides /i/ and /u/ with 5 of the cardinal vowels. Only the open-mid back vowel /ɔ/ does not participate in such combinations:

Table 4: Inventory of diphthongs and triphthongs in Southern Min

Onglides \ Vowels	i	e	a	o	u	au	ai
i-	–	–	ia	io	iu	iau	–
u-	ui	ue	ua	–	–	–	uai

There are also two triphthongs: these are *–iau* and *–uai*, as observable in the last two columns of Table 4. For an in-depth treatment of Southern Min phonology, see Cheng (1972), Zhou (1991) and Yang (1991).

1.3 Syllable structure :

According to traditional Chinese phonology, the structure of each syllable consists of two parts: an initial and a final. The final is composed of a medial and a rhyme, while the rhyme is further divided into a nucleus and a coda. We can represent this by the following diagram:

Table 5: Syllable structure in Southern Min

INITIAL	FINAL			
	MEDIAL	RHYME		
		NUCLEUS	CODA

Except for the nucleus, there is no obligatory element in the syllable, nor is there any restriction on consonants that occupy the initial position, apart from the impossibility of voiced stops to co-occur with nasalized finals. The glottal stop is not, however, phonemically distinct in this position. Bilabial and velar nasals may be syllabic, as in /m⁷/ 伓 'not want' and /ŋ5/黃 'yellow' or act as finals, as in /hm⁵/ 媒 'matchmaker' and /mŋ⁷/ 問 'to ask'. As mentioned earlier, the coda position allows the three nasals /m n ŋ/, as well as the voiceless unaspirated plosives /p t k/ and /ʔ/.

Southern Min does not possess sesquisyllables in the sense of Matisoff (1991), although a small number of subsyllables can be recognized (R. Cheng 1997). Affixes and the allomorphy in which they take part are discussed in §2.1.2.

1.4 Morphophonology

Fusion of grammatical and derivational morphemes is a common process in Min dialects, evident for the plural forms of the personal pronouns (§2.1.1), many negated forms of modal verbs (§3.4), and prepositional markers when followed by generic and third person pronouns : ka^7 + i^1 共伊 → kai^1 OM-3SG '3rd person fused form of object marker ; 'her, him, it, them'; hoo^7 + $lang^5$ 與 儂 → $hong^5$ PASS-GENERIC PRONOUN 'by someone'. More examples may be found in Huang (1988) and Lin (2015: 399).

The diminutive suffix and nominal marker $-a^2$ 仔 (< kia^{n2} 囝 'child') exhibits a diverse array of morphophonemic alternations which can in the main be neatly accounted for by four simple rules according to Lien (1998). Given that there is just a restricted number of possibilities for syllable codas in Southern Min, namely /p t k ʔ m n ŋ/ or else a vowel nucleus, the following processes take place. First, in a process of gemination, the coda of the first syllable, is copied onto the suffix $-a^2$ and then voiced in the case of the finals /p t k/.[14] This copied element consequently becomes the initial consonant of the newly created suffix. Second, only in the case of voiceless codas, and by means of regressive assimilation, the original /p t k/ coda of the first syllable also takes on the voicing feature (see examples 1,2,3 in Table 6).

Third, for root syllables with nasal codas or nasalized vowel nucleii /m n ŋ Vⁿ/, after their gemination, the nominal suffix $-a^2$ is nasalized to $-ã^2$ in a process of progressive assimilation (examples 4,5,6,7). Fourth, for open syllables and for syllables with a glottal stop final, the resultant form simply preserves the underlying or overt suprasegmental glottal feature: V+a(ʔ) → V+aʔ (8,9). Table 6 illustrates these processes.

---

[14] Recall here that the voiced counterpart of /t/ in Southern Min has merged with /l/.

Table 6: Morphophonemic alternations for the nominal suffix $-a^2$ in Southern Min (adapted from Lien 1998: 475)

	Template	(i) Gemination	(ii) Voicing	Characters	Translation
1.	Vp+a²	ap⁸+ba²	ab⁸+ba²	盒仔	'box'
2.	Vt+a²	tsʰat⁸+la²	tsʰal⁸+la²	賊仔	'thief'
3.	Vk+a²	tek⁴+ga²	teg⁴+ga²	竹仔	'bamboo'
4.	Vm+a²	kam¹+maⁿ²		柑仔	'tangerine'
5.	Vn+a²	gin²+naⁿ²		囡仔	'child'
6.	Vŋ+a²	aŋ¹+ŋaⁿ²		翁仔	'doll'
7.	Vⁿ+a²	iⁿ⁵+aⁿ²		圓仔	'meat ball (in soup)'
8.	V+a²	bi²+a?²		美仔	(girl's given name)
9.	V?+a2	hio?⁸+a?²		箬仔	'leaf'

Furthermore, as Wang and Lien (1993) and Lien (1998: 476–477) both observe, after the general rules for tone sandhi have been applied, as explained in §1.1 above, a second special set of tone sandhi for diminutive suffixation goes into action. Essentially, while the diminutive suffix remains invariant as Tone 2, that is, High Falling (51) after the first stage has taken place, a low- (21) or mid-tone (33) first syllable becomes a rising tone (25 or 35), and a high tone syllable (High Level 55, High Falling 51, High Checked 5), remains high with a 55 pitch. Note that, in the case of person's names taking the $-a$ suffix, a completely different set of rules is followed for tone sandhi (Lien 1998: 475).

The semantics of the diminutive suffix is discussed in §2.1.2.5.

2 Morphology

2.1 Word structure

In overall terms of its typology, Southern Min appears to behave like Sinitic languages in general, being analytic in tendency. Thus, it does not possess inflectional paradigms for case, gender, tense, number or person. Nonetheless, it also shows agglutinative features, including a substantial inventory of affixes and clitics used on nouns and verbs, a proclivity for compounding and reduplication, but also a propensity for fusion through syllable contraction. Case roles are coded by adpositions.

Structurally speaking, there are many word types, starting with words constituted of a simple monomorphemic monosyllable and moving through combinations of root + affix to polysyllabic compounds and reduplicated forms. Fusional features are represented by the contraction of words, particularly the high frequency markers of grammatical function (see §1.4 above and the sections on negation, passives and object-marking) while assimilation of phonetic features at syllable edges results in complex allomorphy, as we saw in the case of the diminutive suffix –a^2 仔, discussed in §1.4.

2.1.1 Nominal categories: coding of case, gender, number

Case, gender and number are not marked inflectionally in Southern Min, nor in Sinitic as a whole. Apart from the use of syntactic position in the clause to indicate the role of a noun phrase referent, for example, as subject or direct object of the verb, other means to code such roles require the use of prepositions to designate case relations, for example, *hoo^7* 與 to mark oblique roles including indirect objects, but also the agent noun in passive constructions, and either *chiong^1* 將 or *ka^7* 共 to mark direct objects that precede the main predicate.

The category of gender is lexically coded for a subset of animate nouns (domestic animals, fowl) by means of the suffix –*kang^1* 公 for male of the species and suffix –*bu^2* 母 for a reproductive female of the species: *ti^1–kang^1* 豬公 'boar', *ti^1–bu^2* 豬母 'a sow that has produced a litter'. This is an interesting distinction from standard Mandarin which makes use of prefixes in this function.

Number can also be explicitly coded by means of plural classifiers such as *koa^2* in *chit^8 koa^2 lang^5* 一寡儂 one-CLF_PL-people 'some people' or by plural adverbs such as *long^2* 攏 'all'. The plural pronouns all end in suffix –*n* which represents a trace of *lang^5* 儂 'person, people' according to Mei Tsu-lin (1999), who observes that the evidence is found in the fact that the full form is used in other Min dialects as the plural suffix. Note that this does not occur elsewhere in the lexicon as a plural marker on common nouns. There is also an inclusive–exclusive distinction for first person plural. Compare the singular and plural forms in the Southern Min pronominal paradigm:

Table 7: Personal pronouns of Southern Min (Taiwan)

	Singular		Plural	
1.	*goa^2*	我	*gun^2*	阮
			lan^2 (inclusive)	咱
2.	*li^2*	汝	*lin^2*	恁
3.	*i^1*	伊	*in^1*	亻因

The reflexive form is *ka¹ki⁷* 家己 'self' while the generic pronoun 'one' is *lang⁵* 儂 < 'person'.

From Table 7, it can be observed that there is no polite form for the 2ⁿᵈ person pronoun, as found in Mandarin which uses the opposition of *nǐ* 你 2SG versus *nín* 您 2SG:POL. Politeness is lexically expressed in Southern Min with forms coding respect. These may include kin terms involving an age hierarchy: for example, younger versus older brothers, sisters, aunts and uncles; or titles of professions as a vocative form of direct address. These forms are either politer or more culturally-appropriate than using the person's name or a pronoun on its own. The polite classifier *ui⁷* 位 may be used instead of the general classifer *e⁵* 個 with human nouns. Along this conceptual dimension, Southern Min does not differ from other Sinitic languages.

Plural forms of the personal pronouns tend to be used in zero-marked genitive noun phrases, even where only one person is involved as the possessor. This could be viewed as a 'sociative' kind of pronominal marking since relations within a family are not viewed individualistically as one-to-one between parents and children but rather, shared, as part of the family.

(1) 我想欲見阮阿公。
    goa²   *siu^{n2}*   *beh⁴*   *ki^{n3}*   *gun³*   *a²-kung¹*.
    1SG   think   want   see   1PL   PREF.-grandfather
    'I want to see my grandfather.' (literally: our grandfather')

2.1.2 Derivational morphology

Derivation in Southern Min essentially involves the process of affixation whereby a prefix or a suffix is attached to the root, or more rarely, the insertion of an infix. Suffixing predominates as the main strategy in derivational morphology.

2.1.2.1 Prefixes in Southern Min

The main prefix in Southern Min is used on kin terms and given names as a hypocoristic prefix:

(2) *a¹-* 阿 as a hypocoristic prefix on kin terms and given names:
    a¹-ma² 阿媽 'grandma', *a¹-i⁵* 阿姨 'aunty',

a^1-$khing^3$ 阿慶 (affixed to the syllable for the second character in a person's given name)

2.1.2.2 Suffixes in Southern Min

Many of the suffixes used in Southern Min have a quite specific nominalising function to denote different kinds of persons, occupations and professions. These are the suffixes –*e* 的, –*thau*^{5} 頭 < 'head', –*sai*^{1}*(hu)* 師(傅)< 'master' (colloquial register) or –*su*^{1} 師 < 'master' (literary register), *jin*^{5} 人< 'person' (literary register), *lang*^{5} 儂 < 'person' (colloquial register), –*sien*^{1} 先 < 'sir', –*sien*^{1}<仙 'immortal' and –*kui*^{2} 鬼 < 'demon'. Five of these are described and illustrated below:

1. The nominalising suffix –*e* 的 in Southern Min may be attached to simple verbs, compound verbs and even clauses. It serves to convert these phrases into nominals, a feature which is widespread in Southeast Asian languages for this type of particle that typically possesses genitive, relative clause and other modifying functions as well (Matisoff 1986b).

The nominalizer –*e* 的 in combination with a verb (or a clause) could thus be translated approximately as 'the one who + VERBS' or 'that which + VERBS':

(3) i. Simple verb + –*e* 的
    chiah^8-*e* 食的 'what is eaten', *chhing*^{1} *e* 穿的 'what is worn'
 ii. V-O verb compound + –*e* 的
    liah^8 *hi*^{5}–*e* 掠魚的 'fisherman' (catch-fish-suffix), *phoa*^{3} *pi*^{n7}–*e* 破病的 'sick person' (fall-sick-suffix)
 iii. Clause + –*e* 的
    thau^5 *mng*^{5} *tng*^{5} *e* 頭毛長的 hair-be.long-suffix 'the long-haired one'

It may also be used as a suffix to form a respectful term of address, as *Ong*^{5}-*e* 王的 'Mr Wang'.

2. Suffix –*thau*^{5} 頭 < 'head'
This suffix is a pure nominal marker and, interestingly, covers a largely different set of nouns from its Mandarin cognate, *tóu* [tʰoʊ^{35}] (Cheng 1997: 92).

(4) *jit*^{8}-*thau*^{5} 日頭 'sun', *chioh*^{8}-*thau*^{5} 石頭 'stone', *lo*^{5}–*thau*^{5} 路頭 'journey', *hoe*^{3}–*thau*^{5} 歲頭 'age'

3. Suffixes –sai¹(hu) 師(傅) and su¹ 師

Lien (2001) has argued for the complementary distribution of such pairs of suffixes arguing that colloquial register –sai¹(hu) forms agentive nouns for crafts and trades while literary register su¹ forms agentive nouns for professions that require more intellectual skills:

Although the cognate shīfu 師傅 'master' exists in Mandarin, it is not used as a suffix.

(5) –sai¹(hu) 師(傅): thou⁵chui²-sai¹ 塗水師 'bricklayer', iu⁵chhat⁴-sai¹hu 油漆師傅 'painter (of buildings)', bak⁴-chhiu^{n7}-sai¹hu 木匠師傅 'carpenter'
  –su¹ 師: i¹-su¹ 醫師 'doctor', ui⁷-su¹ 畫師 'artist', kau³-su¹ 'teacher'

4. Suffix –sien¹ 仙 < 'immortal', 'adept'; suffix for professions; suffix for addicts of various vices (humorous). The lexeme sien¹ 仙 is similarly not used as a suffix in Mandarin.

(6) siao³kui⁷sien¹ 數櫃仙 'book-keeper', kun⁵thau²-sien¹ 拳頭仙 'boxer'
  sio¹-chiu² sien¹ 燒酒仙 'drunkard', a¹-phien² sien¹ 鴉片仙 'opium smoker',
  poah⁸kiao² sien¹ 博繳仙 'gambler', thit⁴-thou⁵-sien¹ 口口仙 'an idler'

5. In Taiwanese Southern Min, the diminutive formed with the suffix -a² 仔 can be diachronically related to the lexeme for 'son, child', kia^{n2} 囝, in contemporary Taiwanese and Xiamen (Amoy), albeit in a much reduced form (Yang 1991, Chappell 2000).[15] From the expressive, diminutive usage, the suffix further evolves into a nominalizer and then into a simple marker of nominals. Some further examples of the broad range of usages of –a² in contemporary Southern Min are given below. (See also §1.4 on the morphophonemic alternations and special tone sandhi pertaining to this suffix).

There are three main functions of -a² 仔 as a suffix:

(7) Non-productive use as a diminutive marker for smaller versions of objects (= fossilized invariant use): thng⁵-a² 糖仔 'candy' (< thng⁵ 糖 'sugar'), chhia¹-a² 車仔 'sewing machine' (< chhia¹ 'vehicle' 車); liap⁸-a² 'ulcer' 瘡仔 (< liap⁸ 'grain' 粒)

(8) Nominalizer
  Deverbal nouns: that⁴ 塞 'to fill, plug (Verb)' → that⁴-a² 塞仔 'stopper, cork'

---

[15] Note that the stem of the word used for 'child' –囝仔 gín-á ~ gín-ná in contemporary Taiwanese – cannot be the source for this diminutive on phonological grounds (see Lien 1998).

Occupations: *thai⁵-ti¹-a²* 治豬仔 slaughter-pig-suffix 'butcher'; *poaⁿ¹hi³-a²* 搬戲仔 act-play-suffix 'actor'
(9) Noun marker
hi⁵-a² 魚仔 'fish', *chiao²-a²* 鳥仔 'bird'; *tiu⁷-a²* 稻仔 'rice plant, paddy'

More examples can be found in Table 6 above.

2.1.3 Compounding processes in Southern Min

Compounding is an important process in Southern Min for producing new disyllabic and polysyllabic word forms. Compounds may be created from combinations of bound and free roots which hold a variety of semantic relationships to one another, including coordination, subordination, verb-object and subject-verb relationships. In their turn, coordinate compounds may be composed of either synonyms or antonyms.

a. Coordinate compounds : *sio¹loah⁸* 燒熱 hot+hot 'hot' *hoan⁵lo²* 煩惱 troubled+anxious 'anxious' *hiaⁿ¹ti⁷* 兄弟 older brother+younger brother 'brothers'
b. Subordinate compounds : *toa⁷lang⁵* 大人 big+person 'adult', *kiam⁵lng⁷* 鹹卵 salt+egg 'salted egg', *tian⁷hue²* 電火 electric+fire 'lamp'
c. Subject-verb compounds : *te¹tang¹* 地動 (earth+move) 'earthquake', *cheng⁵goan⁷* 情願 feeling+be:willing 'be willing to'
d. Verb-object compounds : *thai⁵thau⁵* 治頭 cut:off head 'behead' ; *sng³biaⁿ³* 算命 tell-fate 'to tell someone's fortune'; *piⁿ⁷ kiaⁿ²* 病囝 fall:ill child 'fall pregnant'

2.2 Psycho-collocations

Southern Min is no different from other Sinitic and Southeast Asian languages in possessing special expressions, including compounds, that have been labeled 'psycho-collocations' by Matisoff (1986a). These collocations, for the main part, all involve body part terms and the expression of inalienability which is subject to metaphorical extension into the realm of emotions and subjective evaluations (Clark 1996). The inalienable expressions may occur as N-V compounds in double nominative and SV sentences, or as V-N expressions in unaccusative constructions (Chappell 1996, 1999). These are each illustrated in turn below:

Noun_Topic − [Noun_Body part − Verb_Intransitive/Stative]_Comment
(10) 汝目孔赤（大）啊。
  li² bak⁸-khang¹   chhiah⁴ (toa⁷) a.
  2SG eye:socket   red   (big) CRS
  'You're jealous.'   (literally: 'As for you, eye sockets red.')
  'You're proud.'   (literally: 'As for you, eye sockets big.')

[Noun_Possessor − GEN − Noun_Possessed body part]_Subject − Verb_Intransitive/Stative
(11) 我的耳孔輕。
  goa² e⁵   hi^{n7}khang¹   khin¹
  1SG GEN   ear:channel   light
  'I'm gullible.'   (literally: 'My auditory channel is light.')

Noun_Subject − Verb_Intransitive/Stative − Noun_Body part
(12) 伊跛着倒脚。
  I¹ pai² tioh⁸ toh⁸ kha¹.
  3SG lame ACH   left leg
  'He has gone lame in the left leg.'

There are many compound adjectives formed on the basis of body part terms. Noteworthy is the fact that they are all based on the similar grammatical relationships to the above of either S-V, V-O, or ADJ-NOUN.

(13) Subject_Body Part − Predicate_Stative → Predicative adjective
  sim¹-sek⁴ 心適 heart-fit 'interesting'; bin⁷-sek⁸ 面熟 face-ripe 'be familiar with'; chhui³-ta¹ 喙焦 mouth-dry 'thirsty'; sim¹-sng¹ 心酸, heart-sour 'sad'; phi⁷ sng¹ 鼻痠 nose-aching 'mean, stingy'

(14) Subordinate type compounds
  kek⁴-kut⁴ 激骨 provoke-bone (V-O) 'to be contrary'; toa⁷-chih⁸ big-tongue (ADJ-N) 大舌 'to lisp, stutter' 'someone who stutters'; thih⁴-khi² iron-tooth (ADJ-N) 鐵齒 'to be uncompromising'

This striking property of using body part terms to code emotions and inherent physical and personality characteristics, whose expression makes use of several construction types, appears to be an areal feature of Southeast Asia (Clark 1996).

2.3 Elaborate expressions

In Southern Min, a productive process for creating polysyllabic adjectives is the use of the common reduplication pattern ABB. Such alliterative expressions, also known as 'ideophones', possess either a common syllable across the reduplicated section, as in (15), if not a common syllable component, as in (16):

(15) *ang⁵-chu¹-chu¹*　　紅口口　　'rosy red'
　　 kim¹-siak⁴-siak⁴　　金口口　　'glossy, glittering'
　　 tam⁵-ka³-ka³　　　氵昝口口　　'drenched, dripping wet'

This is based on onomatopoeia and intensifies the meaning of the first morpheme and adjective (S. Cheng 1981: 58–62). Such constructions are one of the patterns distinguishing adjectives from verbs, which cannot in the main be modified by intensifiers.

A second pattern involves partial reduplication of the syllable, either the initial consonant or the rhyme, that is, the nucleus vowel combined with the syllable coda, if any:

(16) *san²-pi¹-pa¹*　　嗽口口　　'thin as a rake'
　　 khin¹-bang²-sang²　　輕口口　　'light as a feather'

These elaborate expressions have an emotive element in expressing vividness. The reduplicated syllables do not have any independent lexical use as free morphemes.

As regards quadrisyllabic expressions, Southern Min is no exception among Sinitic languages in making use of four-character idiomatic phrases which contribute to a lively and expressive style in both speech and writing. Furthermore, a large number of these four-character phrases are unique to Southern Min and without word-for-word equivalents in Mandarin.

(17) *chhui³-chhio³-bak⁸-chhio³*　　喙笑目笑　　mouth-smile-eye-smile
　　 'beaming radiantly'
　　 chiah⁸-kong¹-khng³-su¹　　食公口私　　eat-public-store:up-private
　　 'hoard personal savings while making use of public funds'

2.4 Reduplication

Reduplication is a morphological process in which a root is wholly or partially copied.

There are quite distinct forms and meanings for adjectival and verbal reduplication in Southern Min which do not correspond fully to those in standard Mandarin.

First of all, verbs are reduplicated VV to code the aspectual meaning of short duration of an action 'to Verb for a little while', that is, the delimitative, but not the tentative aspect of 'just try to Verb' as in Mandarin. Second, when adjectives are reduplicated, they code the approximative meaning 'sort of $X_{quality}$'. A further contrast with Mandarin is that monosyllabic adjectives also permit triplication to express an intensity reading 'extremely $X_{quality}$' as predicative adjectives, an operation which is not permitted however for verbs in Southern Min:

Monosyllabic adjectives thus possess two possibilities of derivation:

AA 'sort of $X_{quality}$' and AAA 'extremely $X_{quality}$'

(18) Reduplication of monosyllabic adjectives: AA
 ang^5-ang^5 紅紅 'sort of red, reddish'
 sui^2-sui^2 美美 'rather beautiful'

(19) Triplication of monosyllabic adjectives: AAA
 ang^5-ang^5-ang^5 紅紅紅 'extremely red'
 sui^2-sui^2-sui^2 美美美 'very beautiful'

whereas disyllabic adjectives have, in general, just one main structure for reduplication which again contrasts with the Mandarin AABB form:[16]

AB-AB 'sort of $X_{quality}$'.

(20) 憨面 憨面
 $gong^7bin^7$ – $gong^7bin^7$
 'kind of stupid-faced'

---

[16] The reader is referred to detailed studies on reduplication in Taiwanese Southern Min including S. Cheng (1981) and F. Tsao (2001). The discussion in §2.4 is based partly on these analyses. Due to contact with Mandarin, the form AABB is also possible for some disyllabic adjectives with the intensity reading (S. Cheng 1981: 62-63).

Finally, adjectives, but not verbs, freely allow derivation of new adverbs by means of another reduplication pattern using the suffix –a^2 仔. These express manner:

(21) *chhian² -chhian² –a² kong²* 淺淺仔講 shallow-shallow-ADV say 'says very superficially (to me)'; *ban⁷-ban⁷-a²* 慢慢仔 'slowly'

Table 8: Comparison of Southern Min adjectives and verbs in reduplication processes

	ADJECTIVES	VERBS
REDUPLICATION: AA Mono- and disyllabic forms	YES: approximative	YES: short duration
TRIPLICATION: AAA	YES: intensification	NO
ABB pattern: intensification of quality with onomatopoeic effect	YES	NO
ADVERBIAL USE	YES: manner AA-a^2-Verb pattern	NO

These patterns of reduplication also serve to differentiate adjectives from verbs as two different grammatical categories in Southern Min.

3 Grammar and Syntax

3.1 Word order

Although Southern Min has the word order of (S)V(O) as one of its basic orders, as seen in example (22) below, many permutations are possible due to topicalization, particularly the kind which involves patient or direct object fronting, as in (23): OSV. OV word orders are in fact often accompanied by subject noun ellipsis as in (45) and (57) below. Furthermore, they have a purportedly very high frequency in Southern Min and are claimed to represent a syntactic characteristic which distinguishes the language clearly in terms of word order from standard Mandarin (Yang 1991: 269–276, Li Rulong 2007: 13).

(22) SVO: 阿瑛咧拭卓仔。
 　　 A¹ Ing¹　leh⁴　chit⁴　toh⁴a²
 　　 A-Ing　PROG　wipe　table
 　　 'A Ing is wiping the table.'

(23) Object topicalization: OSV
這件代誌，我考慮真久呀。
chit⁴-kiaⁿ⁷   tai⁷chi³   goa²   kho²li⁷   chin¹   ku²   a.
this-CLF   matter   1SG   consider very   long:time   PRT
'This matter, I thought about it for a long time.'

Sinitic languages, in general, display *head-final* characteristics for their NP structure but a *mixture of head-initial and head-final* ordering for their VPs and Southern Min is again no exception to this rule. Hence, all the constituents of the noun phrase, including relative clauses, precede the head noun (see §3.3.1. and Figure 1 below) whereas the majority of adverbs and prepositional phrases precede the main verb (for more details, see Chappell 2015).

In conformity with this tendency for dependent-head typology in Sinitic languages, for complex sentences, temporal, causal, conditional and concessive clauses typically precede the matrix clause. The comparative construction also has the comparative marker preceding the standard noun in one of its subtypes (§3.5.2).

The main parts of speech in Southern Min are nouns and pronouns, verbs, adjectives (attributive and predicative), adverbs and adverbial adjuncts, demonstratives, quantifiers, conjunctions, classifiers (nominal and verbal), localizers, aspect markers and grammatical function words, not to mention the modal or attitudinal discourse markers occurring in clause-final position.

3.2 Syntactic functions

As typical of Sinitic languages, there appears to be a certain fluidity as to which grammatical categories may fill which syntactic functions: For example, verbs may act as nouns without requiring any explicit morphological marking in Southern Min, and in a similar vein, both nouns and 'small' SV clauses may act as predicates. However, these possibilities are all subject to quite specific syntactic and semantic constraints: for example, once a verb is used as a noun, it may no longer be reduplicated in its new function as a deverbal noun.[17]

---

17 Note that it is possible for a certain number of monosyllabic nouns to be reduplicated with the sense of 'every': *lang⁵ lang⁵* 儂儂 'every person', 'everyone'.

(24) Verb   >   Deverbal noun
     變更設定   住所變更
     pìan-keng   siat-tēng   chū-sóo   pìan-keng
     update   setting   address   update
     'to update a setting'   'an address update'

Adjectives may be used as predicates without requiring the copula but they do not form a subclass of verbs in Southern Min due to their different syntactic patterning and constraints on usage (§2.4). There is no morphological distinction for voice on verbs to signal active versus passive mood. Instead, prepositions are used to signal different case-like roles (§3.5.1) as part of special grammatical construction types including object-marking, dative and passive constructions.

3.3 Nominal domain

3.3.1 Basic structure of the NP

The basic structure and constituents of the noun phrase in Southern Min are represented by the diagram in Figure 1.

3.3.1.1 NP Component order for Southern Min

Figure 1:

$$\left\{ \begin{array}{l} \text{(Possessive pronoun)} \\ \text{(DEM+CLF) (Relative clause)} \\ \text{(DEM+CLF) ((Ints) Adjective)} \end{array} \right\} \begin{array}{c} e^5 \\ 其 \end{array} \left\{ \begin{array}{l} \text{(DEM+(Num)+ CLF)} \\ \text{(DEM+(QF + (CLF))} \end{array} \right\} \left\{ \text{NOUN} \right\} \left\{ \text{Postpositions} \right\}$$

$$\;\;\;\;\;\text{SLOT 1}\;\text{SLOT 2}\;\;\;\;\;\;\;\;\;\text{SLOT 3}\;\;\;\;\;\;\;\;\;\;\;\text{SLOT 4}\;\;\;\;\;\;\;\;\;\;\text{SLOT 5}$$

The diagram in Figure 1 can be decompressed into two main types of noun phrase in Southern Min, simple and complex:

i. Basic noun phrase structure
                     (DEM–NUM–CLF)
    (POSS. PRO– e^5) – (DEM–(CLF)) – (ADJECTIVE$_{\text{CORE}}$) – NOUN
                     (NUM–CLF)
                     (QF–CLF)

ii. Complex noun phrase structure

(POSS. PRO– e^5) – (NUM–CLF)   – (INTENSIFIER–) ADJECTIVE – e^5 – (NOUN)
                 (DEM–NUM–CLF)
                 (DEM–CLF)   – CLAUSE – e^5 – (NOUN)
                 (QF–(CLF))

[e^5 = marker of linkage and dependency; nominalizer]

The NP in Southern Min can be minimally realized as just the head noun on its own, such as the bare noun *toh⁸-a²* 卓仔 'table' in (22), or by the use of a nominalizing construction with either an *Adjective* + e^5 個 or a *Relative clause* + e^5, as in *soe³- e^5* 細個 small-LNK 'the one that is small', a headless NP. Apart from this nominalizing function, the grammatical function word, e^5, is a linker or, more technically, a marker of ligature for a variety of syntactic relationships involved in modification.[18] Thus, it links modifiying elements such as relative clauses and adjectives with the head noun, and also serves as the genitive marker and the general default classifier. This function word is claimed to be historically derived from the particle *qī* 其 of Archaic Chinese which had genitive, demonstrative and interrogative uses, developing additional uses as a classifier and attributive marker during the Medieval Chinese period (Li Rulong 2007: 128–130).

There is a simple bipartite distinction in Southern Min for **demonstratives**, distinguishing proximal from distal: *chit⁸* 這 'this' and *hit⁴* 彼 'that' in determiner function and *che¹* 遮 'this' and *he¹* 遐 'that' in pronoun function, mainly serving as subjects (see example 56). In simple NPs, demonstratives generally occur in Slot 3 position with a following classifier but may also be used in the position of Slot 1, where they can precede a relative clause or an adjectival phrase in a complex NP. Their use with a classifier is on the whole obligatory, apart from a special discourse use which highlights a (singular only) referent (see example 28 below). Combined with the individuating type of classifier, demonstratives similarly exclusively code the singular (§3.3.2).

With respect to information structure, demonstratives also serve to provide an overt morphological means for coding the definiteness of the head noun. Some typical examples are provided below with descriptive labels for the different combinations of constituents. These are all extracts from a narrative text in Taiwanese Southern Min.

---

18 Despite the fact that the etymology of e^5 is the morpheme *qī* 其(Li Rulong 2007), the Chinese character 個 is generally used to represent the particle e^5 in its classifier function while the character 的 is used for its other modifying functions as a genitive and attributive marker. This is for ease of comprehension of the examples.

3.3.1.2 Simple NPs with adjectival phrases

That the **attributive adjective** may directly precede the head noun is particularly common with the core set of basic adjectives, including evaluative adjectives for 'good' and 'bad' but also those for size: 'big', 'little' and, generally speaking with monosyllabic adjectives. This type of adjective has a predilection for lexicalization with the following noun to code generic or classificatory nominals for kinds of persons and objects: cf. se^3-han^3 小漢, literally 'little chap' → 'small, in childhood'; $phai^{n2}$-$lang^5$ 歹儂 'evil person'; $sian^7$-su^7 善事 'good deeds'.

(25) MONOSYLLABIC ADJECTIVE_CORE—NOUN

好儂客　　　　　　足濟歹儂客
ho^2　$lang^5kheh^4$　　chiok-che^7　$phai^{n2}$　$lang^5kheh^4$
good　customer　　　many　bad　customer
'good customers' (J602)　'many bad customers' (J470)

In contrast, for disyllabic adjectives and adjectival phrases that incorporate an intensifier, the ligature marker e^5 is generally required as in (26):

(26) INTENSIFIER—ADJECTIVE – $e5$ – NOUN

上占早的方法
$siong^7$　$kou^2cha^2e^5$　　$hong^1hoat^4$
most　ancient　　LNK　method
'a most ancient method' (J750)

3.3.1.3 Simple NPs with classifier phrases

The next set of examples illustrates various combinations of numerals, demonstratives and classifiers with a head noun:

(27) NUM – CLF – NOUN

伊着與汝蜀枝竹仔。
i^1　$tioh^8$　hoo^7　li^2　**$chit^8$-ki^1**　tek^4-a^2.
3SG　then　give　2SG　one-CLF　bamboo-DIMN
'He then gives you a bamboo stick.' (J38)

(28) DEM – Ø – NOUN
啊彼竹仔口牢下
a **hit⁴** **tek⁴-a²** *gia⁵* *tiau⁵-e⁷*
PRT that bamboo-DIMN carry stay-down
'Eh, that bamboo stick, (you) keep it held down' (object topicalization clause) (J39)

(29) NUM – CLF – ADJECTIVE – NOUN
…找一個大樹腳，
chhoe⁷ **chit⁸-e⁵** *toa⁷* *chhiu-kha¹*,…
search one-CLF big tree.foot
'(I) looked for a tree with a large base …' (J695)

3.3.1.4 Complex NPs with relative clauses

What equates or translates from an English **relative clause** into Southern Min is not structurally different, in fact, from attributive modification, since the same particle e^5 is used.

(30) 啊挾來的便當啦，
ah **chah⁴-lai⁵** *e⁵* **pian⁷tong¹** *la*,
PRT bring-come LNK lunchbox PRT
攏食完啊。
long² *chiah⁸-oan⁵* *a*.
all eat-finish PRT_CNF
'The bento (lunchbox) I'd brought along had all been eaten up.' (J697–698)

3.3.2 Classifier system of Southern Min

Southern Min dialects generally possess 30 or 40 true individuating classifiers, if we exclude measure words and collective nouns that occur in the same prenominal modifier slot but which do not share any salient cognitive or perceptual features with the classified noun. The main parameters in Sinitic languages for classifier systems are

Animacy: humans versus animals versus plants
Shape: length, cylindricity, flatness, roundness

Let us highlight some distinguishing features of Southern Min classifier systems. The general classifier is e^5 個 and is used with nouns for humans, in addition to its default function : $chit^4$ -e^5 $lang^5$ this-CLF-person 遮個儂 'this person'. In contrast, for prototypical animal nouns (mammals, domestic animals), and also for fowl, the classifier is $chiah^4$ 隻, for example, oxen and pigs, nouns which normally take *tóu* 'head' 頭 [t^hou^{35}] in Mandarin. However, within the animal kingdom, an extremely interesting distinction is made between fish, reptiles and amphibians as opposed to all other creatures by means of boe^2 尾 < 'tail': sa^{n1}-boe^2 hi^5 三尾魚 three-CLF-fish 'three fish'. The classifier 欉 $tsang^5$ < 'bush' is used for plants and trees in general while, lui^2 蕊 'core of flower' is another special Southern Min classifier used for flowers, eyes, and mushrooms. These last three classifiers are not used as individuating classifiers in standard Mandarin.[19] Some of the other main shape classifiers shared with other Sinitic languages are given in the following brief list. We remark on differences in usage with standard Mandarin, where relevant:

(31) ki^1 枝 < 'branch'   long, cylindrical objects – brushes, quills, columns, sticks

$tiau^5$ 條 < 'strip'   objects with a long, one-dimensional profile such as roads, railway lines, streets, belts (a more restricted usage than in Mandarin)

tiu^{n1} 張 < 'extend'   objects with a flat, two-dimensional part such as sheets (of paper), pictures, tickets

te^5 塊 < 'piece'   non-round objects with a chunky shape such as stones, cakes of soap, table, chair, sugar, biscuit, house (a wider in usage than in Mandarin)

$liap^8$ 粒 < 'grain'   is used in many Sinitic languages, including Mandarin, for small, round objects including seeds, beads and pearls. In S. Min, it has generalized in use with a large variety of round-shaped objects, regardless of size: round fruits including melons; also balls, hand grenade

As mentioned earlier, classifiers are obligatory with numerals and certain quantifiers, but may be omitted under special discourse conditions with demonstratives (as in example 28 above). Unlike Cantonese and many Wu dialects, specific classifiers cannot be used as markers of the genitive construction in Southern Min which uses the invariant form e^5, if not zero-marking with kin

---

[19] It is true however that wěi 尾 can be used just for the one noun 'fish' in Standard Mandarin.

terms and other inalienable categories. Nonetheless, it can be observed that the genitive is homophonic with the general classifier e^5 to which it is very likely historically related, as observed above. The **demonstrative (+ classifier)** possesses an important function in anaphora and the information structure of discourse, as exemplified by (27) and (28) above, consecutive utterances from the same text where the information status changes from new in (27) to given in (28) for tek^4-a^2 竹仔 'bamboo stick', being coded with the help of a demonstrative on its own in the latter instance.

Unlike many Southeast Asian and other Sinitic languages including Yue, Hui, Southern Jianghuai Mandarin and Wu dialect groups, Min dialects located in Fujian province do not allow omission of the demonstrative to code **definiteness** by means of simply the CLF + Noun. This takes place in the relevant dialects under the condition that the head noun represents given or 'old' information in the particular discourse context, specifically when occurring in a preverbal position (Wang Jian 2015). By way of contrast, the Southern Min dialects located in neighbouring Guangdong province to the south including Chaozhou (Teochew), Shantou (Swatow) and dialects of the Leizhou peninsula may do exactly this, under contact influence from the Yue dialects (Li Rulong 2007: 77, his example).

(32) Shantou dialect of Southern Min, Guangdong province
支筆無用了。
ZHI   BI   WU   YONG   LE.
CLF   pen   NEG   use   CRS
'This pen is broken.'

3.3.2.1 Restrictions on adjectives preceding the classifier

As shown above in §3.3.1, adjectives typically are linked to head nouns with the marker of ligature, e^5. Unusually, in many Min, Yue (Cantonese) and most Wu dialects, classifiers can be used in a highly restricted way to link certain attributive adjectives to the head noun. These adjectives are, interestingly, typically confined to 'big' and 'small'.

DEM – [**big/small**] – CLF (–(ADJ) – NOUN)

(33) 有彼大粒的大石頭佇遐
u^7 hit^4 **toa^7** $^\wedge liap^8$ e^5 toa^7 $chioh^8 thau^5$ ti^7 hia^1. –
have   that   **big**   CLF   LNK   big   stone   LOC   there
'There were large-sized boulders there.' (J 760)

3.4 Verbal domain

The verb in Southern Min does not undergo any inflectional changes, as is typical of SEA languages in general (Clark 1989). There is no obligatory category of tense, person or number marked on the verb. Even compared with other Sinitic languages such as Cantonese and standard Mandarin, the verbal aspect system in Southern Min is in an early developmental stage with few grammaticalized markers (Li Rulong 2007). *En revanche*, the use of a diverse number of phase markers and verbal complements of result, manner and extent in V_2 position is lexically rich.

3.4.1 Verbal categories and the predicate in Southern Min

3.4.1.1 Aspect

Southern Min possesses the grammatical category of aspect, but not of tense. This is, without a doubt, a pan-Sinitic feature and is common across Southeast Asian languages. Unlike most other major Sinitic languages (standard Mandarin, Cantonese, Shanghainese), however, its grammaticalized markers of aspect tend to occur in the preverbal position for adverbs. In fact, this reflects a strategy used in earlier stages of Chinese for which a huge corpus of written documents attest to the fact that aspectual meanings are typically coded in this position (see Chappell 1992).

The main verbal aspect markers of Southern Min are given in the table below:

	BOUNDED	UNBOUNDED
(34)	u^7 有 + Verb Affirmative or perfect	$((ti^7)\text{-}(leh^4))$ + Verb ((佇)(咧)) Progressive
	bat^4 捌 + Verb Experiential perfect	Verb + .*leh* 咧 Continuous

As can be seen from the table, Southern Min does not possess a highly grammaticalized perfective aspect marker equivalent to Mandarin –*le* 了 or Cantonese –*jo* 咗. The cognate to Mandarin-*le* 了 which is *liau²* in Southern Min is used as a phase marker, meaning 'to finish' (see (37) below).

The common markers are the affirmative (or perfect) u^7 有–Verb which makes use of the verb 'to have', in a similar fashion to many European languages for this same aspectual category: $u^7\text{-}be^2$ 有買 'have bought, did buy'; the past experiential bat^4 捌–Verb (alternatively coded as a verbal suffix by the Mandarin borrowing: Verb–koe^3 過) and the use of the same aspect marker for both the progressive *leh⁴* 咧–VERB and the durative, VERB–.*leh* 咧. Note that these two aspectual functions are distinguished by their placement in different positions, the first preverbally and the second postverbally, not to mention also by the fact that the postverbal use is typically atonal.

For the two imperfective aspect markers, *leh⁴* 咧–Verb (progressive) and Verb +.*leh* 咧(durative), some claim that both have their source in the highly polysemous verb *tioh⁸* 着 whose basic meaning is 'to adhere, to stick to' but also 'to be at' as a verb (Yang 1991: 235, 258), while others claim it is related to the compound verb *ti⁷ leh⁴* 佇口 'to be at (a place)' formed from the combination of *ti⁷* 佇, a locative verb 'to be at' and *leh⁴*, a locative preposition (Li Rulong 2007: 8; W. Chen 2011: 374–383) whereby *leh⁴* is gradually taking over the functions of the compound form.²⁰ In either case, Southern Min has a semantically similar, but not identical, source to Mandarin *zài* 在 'be at' which has also developed into a preverbal progressive marker, equally the case in many Southeast Asian languages for verbs meaning 'to dwell, to stay' (Matisoff 1991). The progressive and the perfect (in its less grammaticalized affirmative use) are both illustrated in the next example:

(35) 伊彼陣仔抵好佇唱歌。　我有聽着。
 I^1　　 hit^4　 $chun^7$-a^2　tu^2ho^2　ti^7　 $chhiu^{n3}$-koa^1. –　Goa^2　u^7　 $thia^{n1}$-$tioh^8$.
 3SG　that　time　just　PROG　sing-song　　1SG　PFT　listen-ACH
 'She was singing then. – I did hear it.'

For the experiential aspect, the Quanzhou dialect group makes use of a postverbal marker, *tioh⁸* 着 'touch, be in contact with' (Li 2007: 1–13), based on a sensory verb while the preverbal marker in Taiwanese Southern Min has developed from a cognition verb: *bat⁴* 捌 < 'to know, to distinguish' (see Chappell 2001c for a pan-Sinitic treatment of experiential aspect markers as evidentials).

(36) 伊捌死無去。
 I^1　 bat^4　si^3　bo^5　khi^3.
 3SG　EXP　die　NEG　go
 'He had a near-death experience.'

Reduplication of the verb is used to code the short duration of an action or event, that is, the delimitative aspect: Verb₁-Verb₁ *che⁷-che⁷* sit-sit 坐坐 'to stay a little

---

20 Consequently, I adopt the use of the character 咧 to provisionally represent this aspect marker since the actual source has not yet been ascertained. My informant could also use the locative verb, *ti⁷* 佇, on its own as a progressive aspect marker, as seen in example (35).

while'. This aspect can also be coded by means of a verbal classifier phrase: Verb *chit⁸-e⁷-a²*, as in *che⁷ chit⁸-e⁷-a²* 坐一下仔 sit-one-time_CLF-DIMN 'to stay a little while'.

3.4.1.2 Phase markers in V₁V₂ concatenations

In reality, the aspect system in Southern Min is complemented by a variety of verbs used directly after the main verb in V₂ position, and which are grammaticalized to varying degrees. These have evolved from historically earlier serial verb constructions and may code aspect-like meanings, if not result and direction, manner, extent and intensification (Lien 1994, 1995). Phase markers, resultative and directional verb complements are discussed in turn below.

Phase markers are less grammaticalized than the aspect markers of Southern Min and retain a generalized lexical meaning associated with the stage to which an event is implemented, for example, completion (but not perfectivity), achieving an activity, or termination of an event, including the disappearance of any objects connected with it. This set of semi-grammaticalized markers includes the cognate of standard Mandarin *–le* 了, *liau²* in Southern Min, which is still used in its original lexical sense of '(able to) finish', as in: *chiah⁸-liau²* 食了 'to finish eating' (and not *'to have eaten'), *tioh⁸* 着 'to hit (the target)', an achievement phase marker in *thia^nl-tioh* 聽着 'to (successfully) hear' (< listen-achieve) and *khi³* 去 'away' (< 'to go, depart', a phase marker denoting completion of a process that carries the negative connotation of disappearance as in *ta¹-khi³* 焦去 'to dry up' (< dry-away).

Most of these phase markers form complex predicates that require the direct object noun to be fronted into clause-initial position, particularly if it is given and referential. These include *liau²* 了 'to finish', *khi³* 去 'away', *ho²* 好 'properly, completely ' < 'well, good', and *oan⁵* 完 'finish' as in (30) above with *chiah⁸-oan⁵* 'finish eating' (Yang 1991, Lien 1994).

(37) 伊工作做了就走啊。
    I⁷   *khang¹khoe³*   *cho³-liau²*   *tioh⁸*   *chau²*   *a⁰*.
    3SG   work   do-finish   then   leave   PRT_CNF
    'When he'd finished work, he left.'

Note that phase markers, in many cases, are unstressed and lose their full tonal value, which distinguishes them from the highly lexical nature of resultative and directional complements, discussed in the next section. In addition to this, their more restricted combinatorial possibilities with verb classes and retention of lexical features, albeit generalized in meaning, also act as identifying criteria.

3.4.1.3 Resultative and directional verb constructions

Resultative verb compounds (RVCs) and directional verb compounds (DVCs) are $V_1V_2(V_3)$ constructions that represent a special feature of Sinitic languages. They have the following structure:

RVC: $V_{1[Action/Event]} - V_{2[State/Phase\ marker]}$
DVC: $V_{1[Action/Event]} - (V_{2[Spatial\ orientation]}) - (V_{3[来\ lai5\ 'come'/去\ khi3\ 'go']})$

RVCs are productively formed by two verb constituents $V_1\ V_2$ where V_1 is an action or event verb and V_2 is typically filled by adjectives and some intransitive verbs, that code the state which results after V_1 has occurred, for example, *kong³-phoa³* 敲破 hit-break 'to break by hitting' and similarly *hoan²-ng⁵* 'turn yellow' in (38) and *long⁵-phoa³* 'cause-break' in (45) below.

(38) 所以規個骹攏**反黃**按呢。
   soo²i²   *kui¹-e⁵*   *kha¹*   *long²* **hoan²-ng⁵**   *an²ni*.
   therefore whole-CLF   foot   all   **turn-yellow** in.this.way
   'so your whole foot turned yellow like this.' [from working in the paddy fields all day] (J71)

A second major type of verb complex involves directional verb compounds or DVCs. Unlike most RVCs, they can be composed of up to three verb constituents $V_1 (V_2) V_3$ where V_1 is a frequently a motion verb in the concrete use of these DVCs (but can also be an action or event verb in more abstract uses) and V_2 is a directional verb. V_3 is usually one of two main deictic verbs, either 來 *lai⁵* 'come, motion towards speaker' or 去 *khi³* 'go, motion away from speaker', for example, 挾來 *chah⁴-lai⁵* bring-come 'to bring along' in (30) above, which is a V_1V_3 combination. The trisyllabic DVCs, composed of $V_1V_2V_3$, include as V_2 six different verbs of orientation used as directional complements: *khi²* 起 'up', *loh⁸* 落 'down', *tng²* 轉 'back', *kue³* 過 'over', *jip⁸* 入 'in' and *tshut⁴* 出 'out' in combination with one of the two deictic verbs as V_3. One such disyllabic directional complement is exemplified in (39) by *sin³-khi²-lai³* 'pick up (towards speaker):

(39) 卡緊閣 **承起來** 按呢。
 khah⁴ kin² koh⁴ **sin⁵-khí²-lai⁵** an²-ni.
 more fast again **pick-up-come**_DEIC_ in.this.way
 'and I quickly picked them up again. [plates dropped while waitering]'
 (J232)

3.4.1.4 Potential verb compounds

Both RVCs and DVCs can also form what are called 'potential verb compounds' by means of an infix e^7 會 in its affirmative form: V_1 會 $(V_2)V_3$ or by means of the infix boe^7 勿會 in the negative potential form: V_1 勿會$(V_2)V_3$. These two variants of the potential verb compound allow for the interpretation of 'able to V_1 so that V_2' or alternatively, 'unable to V_1 so that V_2'. Here are some examples:

(40) 我看會清。
 goa² khoa^{n3}-e⁷-chheng⁷.
 1SG look-able-clearly
 'I could see clearly.'

(41) 我看勿會清。
 goa² khoa^{n3}-boe⁷-tshin⁷ chheng⁷.
 1SG look-NEG.able-clearly
 'I couldn't see clearly.'

Some dialects of Southern Min, such as Quanzhou even allow a doubled-up infix with V_1-e^7lit^4-$(V_2)V_3$ or the negated form V_1 boe^7 lit^4 $(V_2)V_3$ where 得 lit^4 (the weakened form of tit^4) is an infix derived from a modal verb, similarly meaning 'to be able', which in its turn is related to a transitive verb meaning 'to get, to obtain' (see Sun 1996 for details).

(42) Double marking of 'can': $V_1 e^7lit^4$ V_2
 汝食會得落去勿會。
 li² chiah⁸-e⁷lit⁴-loh⁸-khi boe⁷?
 2SG eat-can-down-go_DEIC_ NEG.can
 'Can you eat it all up?' (e.g. a large bowl of rice)

Another potential construction in Southern Min, which is used to express a judgement as to whether an action is allowed or not (Li Rulong 2007: 133–135), reflects a conservative form in that it is attested from the Medieval Chinese period up until the 13th century when it began to decline in use in Early Mandarin, being gradually ousted by the V_1-*de* 得-V_2 potential form (Sun 1996: chapter 2). The construction formed by e^7 VERB lit^0 is still in use in Southern Min:

(43) Potential construction: e^7 VERB lit^0 ~ 會 VERB 得
 伊會食得。
 I^1 e^7 $chiah^8$-lit^0.
 3SG   can   eat-able
 'He is allowed to eat it (i.e. it's not forbidden to him).'

These two potential constructions exemplify another common process of semantic change in Southeast Asia from *get* > *able* (Matisoff 1991, Enfield 2003).

3.4.1.5 Modality

The irrealis and future contexts are expressed with modal verbs such as beh^4 卜 'want', ai^3 愛 'wish, like'. By semantic extension of meaning, the latter verb can thus be used to express the future. E^7 會 'able, can' may serve both as a dynamic modal verb expressing capability and an epistemic modal expressing possibility. The latter sense is uppermost in e^7 koa^{n5} boe^7? 會寒勿會 able be:cold NEG:able 'Is it going to be cold?'. Some verbs have undergone dramatic semantic change to evolve into modal verbs as exemplifed by $tioh^8$ 着 'hit the mark', 'to be right' which is used as a deontic modal verb of obligation 'should, must', so too $thang^1$ 通 'to go through, to succeed' which has evolved into a modal verb of permission 'may, to be allowed' or in its negative form m^7 $thang^1$ 伓通 'must not'. There is also a large number of disyllabic or compound modal expressions, including e^7sai^2 lit^0 會使得 'may', $tioh^8$ ai^3 着愛 'ought to' and e^7hiau^2 會曉 'can' in the sense of 'to know how to'.

3.1.4.6 Negation

Southern Min dialects possess a well-developed set of highly semantically diversified negative markers, finely nuanced as to the type of negation. Structurally, this plethora of markers has largely arisen from fusion of the two main negators bo^5 'existential and perfective negative' and m^7 'general negative' with the commonly occurring modal verbs in Southern Min. Some of the main negative adverbs are presented in the following table.

Table 9: Taiwanese Southern Min negative markers

bo⁵ 無+ V	Negation of both perfective & habitual contexts, most predicative adjectives, negative possessive verb 'to not have', negative existential verb 'there is not'
m⁷ 唔+V	Negative marker for copular verb, modal verbs, imperfective contexts, irrealis, unwillingness to V
(la⁵) be⁷ (猶)未+ V	Negation of expectation or presupposition: 'have not (yet) V-ed'
boe⁷ 勿会+ V	Negation of ability or possibility to V: 'unable to V'
mai³ 莫+ V	Negative imperative: 'Don't V!'
(m⁷)bien² (唔)免+ V	Negation of necessity: 'You don't need to V'

Southern Min, as for many non-Mandarin Sinitic languages, also possesses a negative existential verb 'to not have, there is not' which can be used directly before a noun phrase: *bo⁵hoat⁴to⁷* 無發度 'there is no way, no method'. The negative imperative is formed by the use of *mai³* 莫, among other possibilities with compound modal forms such as *(m⁷)bien²* 唔免 'Don't VERB (there is no need)' and *boe⁷-sai³* 勿会使 'Don't VERB (it is not allowed)':

(44) 汝莫受氣。
 Li² mai³ siu¹khi³.
 2SG NEG.IMP get.angry
 'Don't get angry!'

For a detailed discussion of both simple and fused negative adverbs in Southern Min, see Li (2007: 144–153).

3.4.2 Serial verb constructions (SVCs)

Serial verb constructions of several different types can be found in Sinitic languages which belong the core serialization type (Foley & Van Valin 1984): S V₁ (N₁) V₂ (N₂) (...). Historically, this syntactic configuration has led to the creation of the asymmetrical type of SVC, producing both preverbal or postverbal prepositional adjunct phrases from former V-N concatenations, a strong tendency for this type of SVC. These prepositional phrases in turn serve to express different case roles (see Durie 1997 and Vittrant 2006 for details on SVC types.).

Hence, the first main outcome of this grammaticalization process for the type S V₁ N₁ V₂ (N₂) is the formation of major syntactic constructions in Sinitic languages – including dative, object-marking, passive, locative and instrumental types, several of which are discussed in §3.5. A second outcome is the formation of complex verbs including resultative and directional verb compounds where the second verb in a V_1V_2 series gradually grammaticalizes from a lexical verb into a resultative or directional complement, thence into a phase marker where it ultimately faces the possibility of developing into a highly bleached aspect marker (§3.4.1.1).

3.5 Clausal and sentential organization

3.5.1 Word order

As noted in §3.1, while SV(O) is one of the basic word orders in Southern Min, there are several other highly frequent patterns available, whose use depends on certain syntactic features of the clause. Alternation in the basic word order is, thus, not simply a function of pragmatics and discourse in Southern Min but is determined by the given syntactic constraints in operation. For example, certain constructions with verb complexes may obligatorily require the object noun to be fronted: OV_1X, due to the use of specific phase markers (X) which do not allow a postverbal object to follow them (Lien 1994, Li 2007). The following example is from a narrative text and shows a clear OV order with the use of an RVC and ellipsis of the subject noun, goa^2 '1SG'. The topic of the discourse is the narrator's fear of dropping and smashing a tray of soup bowls that he is carrying upstairs to give to a wedding party, since superstition dictates that this would bring bad luck. The noun oa^{n2} 'bowl' is thus both the discourse and syntactic topic in (45).

(45) 差一點彼塊碗規個弄破。
 $chha^1$-$chit^8$-$diam^2$ hit^4-te^5 oa^{n2} kui^1-e^5 $long^5$-$phoa^3$.
 nearly   that-CLF bowl whole-CLF cause-break
 '(I stumbled up the stairs and) nearly broke the whole lot of bowls.' (J221)

3.5.2 Clause types

In this section, we discuss clause types which have historically evolved from fixed sequences of serial verbs, including ditransitives, benefactives, passives, object-marking and comparative constructions in addition to some other basic types such as conditionals and questions.

3.5.2.1 Give constructions

A pan-Southeast Asian feature involves the grammaticalization of *give* verbs into dative, benefactive and causative markers. This applies equally well to Sinitic languages. In Southern Min, the **dative** marker may have evolved from the verb *hoo^7* 與 'give' and introduces the indirect object in ditransitive constructions in a postverbal position. Compare the so-called 'double object' construction in (46) whose main verb is a ditransitive verb of transferral, *sang^3* 'to offer as a present', with the dative construction which uses the same lexeme *hoo^7*, grammaticalized as a preposition marking the indirect object. In both, the indirect object precedes the direct object but there is no prepositional marker in the double object construction. (See example (27) for the verbal use of *hoo^7* as a verb 'to give'.)

(46) Double object construction in Southern Min: Subject–Verb$_{Transferral}$ – IO – DO
我送伊一領衫。
Goa^2 sang^3 i^1 chit^8-nia^{n2} sa^{n1}.
1SG   give   3SG   one-CLF   shirt
'I gave him a shirt (as a present).'

(47) Ditransitive construction in Southern Min:
Subject–Verb$_{Transferral}$ – [*hoo^7* 與 – IO]   DO
閣加與我一寡。
koh^4 ke^1 hoo^7 goa^2 chit^8-kua^2.
again   add   DAT   1SG   one-CLF$_{PL}$
'Give some more (food) to me!'

Nonetheless, the **benefactive** preposition in Southern Min is not derived from this source, unlike standard Mandarin which uses *gěi* 給 'for' < 'to give'. Rather, it has evolved from the comitative marker *ka(ng)^7* 共 which underwent a secondary grammaticalization into a marker of oblique case roles.

(48) 儂攏會共咱送來。
*lang^5 long^2 e^7 **ka^7**   **lan^2**   sang^3-lai.*
people   all   able   for   1PL$_{INC}$ deliver-come
'(Usually when we run out of goods), they'll deliver **for us**.' (J428)

A distinctive feature of Sinitic languages which is quite rare in the SEA linguistic area is the use of a **passive** marker derived from a *give* verb, in the case of Southern Min, the same postverbal marker of the dative, *hoo^7* 與 'to give'. This is a typical feature of Southern and Central Sinitic languages while it is much less common in Northern Mandarin dialects, including the standard language (Chappell 2015). Its use is restricted to adversative events, such as *i¹ bo⁷ thang⁴ hoo⁷ lang⁵ kong²* 伊無通與儂講 3SG-NEG.allow PASS-3GENERIC-criticize 'She isn't willing to be criticized by others'. This development is possible via a stage where *hoo⁷* is used as a permissive causative verb meaning 'to let' (Chappell & Peyraube 2006, for Southeast Asia, see Yap & Iwasaki 2003):

(49) Taiwanese *hoo⁷* ambiguous between passive and causative meanings:
啊 我伓與汝管。
a   goa²   m⁷   hoo⁷   li²   koan²
PRT   1SG   NEG   CAUS/PASS   2SG   rule
'I won't let you rule me.' OR: 'I don't want to be ruled by you.' (JT 677)

Another important syntactic constraint is that the agent may *not* be omitted. In the case of indefinite agents, a fusion and contraction of *hoo⁷ lang⁵* 與儂 'by someone' to *hong⁵* is frequent in colloquial speech to minimally fulfil this syntactic requirement for a dummy agent NP:

(50) Taiwanese *hoo⁷* passive with contracted agent NP:
轉來著 與侬拍甲欲 死。
tng⁵-lai   toh⁸   hong⁵   <F ^phah⁴   kah   beh⁴   si³ F>.
return   then   PASS:3INDEF   hit   EXT   want   die
'[When I] returned home, I really got a terrible beating [from my parents].' (J 142)

Other Min languages use cognates of the verb *khit⁴* 乞 in this function, which also means 'to give', including the Northeastern Fuzhou dialect (see Chappell 2000, Lien 2002).

3.5.2.2 Object-marking constructions

Object-marking constructions, known as the **'disposal'** or **'pretransitive'** form in Chinese linguistics, employ *ka⁷* < *kang⁷* 共) to introduce the direct object which is placed before the main verb. This corresponds to the use of *ba³* 把 in Mandarin. However, the source is different as the marker *ka⁷* has grammaticalized from earlier comitative and oblique functions, one of which is illustrated in (48) above, the benefactive (Chappell 2000, 2006; Chappell, Peyraube & Wu 2011).

(51) Taiwanese Southern Min object-marking construction with *kā*:
(NP_SUBJECT) – [*KĀ*_OM+ NP_DO] – VERB PHRASE
所以阮 攏共 褲 褪起來。
soo²-i²	*gun²*	*long²*	*ka⁷*	*khoo³*	*tng³-khi²-lai⁵*
therefore	1PL	all	OM	trousers	take.off-come_DEIC

'So we all took our trousers off (to go swimming).'
(J 116; summertime activities of a mischievous group of boys)

Also highly frequent is a variant of the *ka⁷* construction where the direct object is placed in clause-initial position or, if absent and thus 'zero-marked', is to be found in the preceding text, as in (52). In this subtype, a co-referential 3SG pronoun *i²* 伊 follows the marker *ka⁷*, which in its turn may be contracted in fast speech to *kai⁷* or *kah⁴*.

(52) Taiwanese Southern Min *KĀ* with a clause-initial object and an anaphoric pronoun: (NP_DO(i))– [*KĀ*_OM+ PRO_DO(i)] – VP
耳朵 … 共伊封起來！
(*ěrduo*…)	*ka⁷*	*i¹*	*hong¹-khi²-lai*	
(ears …)	OM	3SG	seal-INCT	(F101–102)

'(Best to fill your ears with wax) and seal them up! (so as not to hear the nagging).'[21]

3.5.2.3 Comparative constructions

The most common way of forming the **comparative** construction in Taiwanese Southern Min is with a hybrid form composed of *pi²* 比 (<'compare'), cognate with the Mandarin comparative marker *bi³*, and the 'native' comparative marker *khah⁴* 較 'more', as in the next example:

(53) A [Comparee] *pi²* B [Standard] *khah⁴* Verb
阿輝比汝較早出生。
A¹ Hui¹	*pi²*	*li²*	*khah⁴*	*cha²*	*chhut⁴-seⁿ*.
NAME	COMP	2SG	more	early	be.born

'A Hui was born before you.' (literally: A Hui was born earlier than you.)

---

[21] In this conversational text, the speaker begins in Mandarin and then switches back to Southern Min, which explains why the subject noun, *ěrduo* 'ears', is given in Mandarin.

In more conservative Southern Min dialects, such as Hui'an, the predicative adjective precedes the standard noun.

(54) A [Comparee] *khah⁴* Verb B[Standard]
                                 in the Hui'an dialect (Quanzhou subgroup)
   伊較大我。
   i³³   k'aʔ⁴   toa⁴²   goa⁵⁵.
   3SG   COMP   big   1SG
   'She is older than me.' (literally: 'She more olds me.')

For more details on comparatives of inequality in Hui'an Southern Min, see Chen (2015).

3.5.2.4 Conditional constructions

Conditional constructions make use of the conjunction *na⁷* 若 'if', with the condition clause preceding the consequence clause.

(55) 暝仔載若是落雨，我久勿會來。
   bin⁵-na²-chai³   na⁷   si³   loh⁸   hoo⁷,   goa²   boe⁷   lai⁵.
   tomorrow   if   be   fall   rain   1SG   NEG.can come
   'If it rains tomorrow, I won't come.'

A compound conjunction *na⁷ kong²* if.say 'if' is also common in conversational texts, making use of the verb 'to say' as one of its components (see Chappell 2008 for an analysis of the grammaticalization of *say* verbs in Sinitic).

(56) 古早 *hon*...若講 讀國民學校，這是卡普遍。
   koo²-tsa²   hon   ...na⁷-kong²   thak⁸...   kok⁴-bin⁵   hak⁴-hau⁷
   earlier   PRT   if:SAY_COND   study   state   school

   che¹   si³   khah⁴   pho²-phian³ (...).
   this   be   more   common
   'Earlier, if you completed elementary school education, this was more common. (...). (JT 246–250)

3.5.3 Ellipsis of arguments

Ellipsis of arguments is a widespread phenomenon in Sinitic languages. It can be viewed as a form of zero anaphora, in particular for 1st and 2nd person participants universally present in the context of a dialogue, and in general for the referent of any noun found in the immediately preceding context. This process takes place when there is a change of status for the referent in the specific discourse from new into given information. This can be seen in the textual material provided in the appendix and in examples (29), (30), (39), (45), (50) and (57).

3.5.4 Information Structure

In general, given information precedes the verb phrase in Southern Min while new information follows the main verb. In this, Southern Min is no different from other Sinitic languages. For example, in the object-marking construction with ka^7, the preverbal direct object introduced by this preposition typically represents given information. This explains why it is often pronominalized. See examples (48), (51) and (52).

3.5.4.1 Topicalization and topic markers

Topicalization of patient nouns is a common syntactic process in Southern Min whereby the noun representing the direct object of a transitive verb is 'fronted' into clause-initial position (see example (57) below, (45) and (37) above).

(57) 今仔日生意勿愛做。
  Kim^1-a^2-jit^8 $seng^1$-li^2 $buai^3$ cho^3.
  today   business   NEG.want   do
  'Today (I) don't want to do trading.' (J542)

As earlier remarked, this is in fact obligatory for certain structures composed of complex predicates with phase markers (Yang 1991, Lien 1994, R. Li 2007) and distinguishes Southern Min from other Sinitic languages. Other topic markers are based on discourse markers that can occur post-nominally and mark this noun as a topic, including *ne* 呢 in Taiwanese, exemplified in (58).

(58) 彼個稻稿頭**呢**，有佇水的外口。
 *Hit⁴ e⁵ tiu⁷ko²thau² **ne,** u⁷   ti⁷ chuí² e⁵   goa⁷-khau².*
 that CLF rice.stalk.head PRT_{TOP} have at water GEN outside
 '(After the harvest), as for those rice stalk heads, they were right above the water.' (J17–18)

It is not accurate to claim however that Southern Min is essentially a topic-prominent language, if this refers to purely its syntactic structure. Many constructions illustrated in §3.5.2 show that the grammatical subject can be identified, even in the double nominative pattern discussed in §2.2 which involves a topic and an SV comment. The topical value of nouns in terms of discourse flow and information structure is undoubtedly a question that may only be answered by means of a detailed discourse analysis of a large corpus of oral texts.

3.5.5 Questions

A special form of polar questions, which require either 'Yes' or 'No' as the response, was early remarked upon by Marybeth Clark (1985) as a feature of many SEA and Chinese languages, as opposed to information or 'Wh-' questions. She observed that there are two main patterns for polar questions, both involving positive and negative counterparts of the same verb:

(59) VERB-NEG-VERB
 VERB-NEG

In Sinitic languages, the first pattern is typical of standard Mandarin, while Cantonese and Hakka can use both types.

(60) VERB-NEG-VERB construction in standard Mandarin
 Nĭ   qù   bu   qù? 你去不去？
 2SG go NEG go
 'Are you going?'

In contrast to this, one of the most frequently occurring **interrogative** constructions in Southern Min is the second pattern, formed by simply attaching the main negative markers, including *bo⁵* 無 or *m⁷* 唔, to the end of a declarative statement (see also Yue-Hashimoto 1991). Hence, it is in fact, more accurate to describe the construction as CLAUSE-NEG:

(61) CLAUSE-NEG polar question in Southern Min
伊卜來唔？
i¹ beh⁴ lai⁵ m⁷?
3SG want come NEG
'Is he going to come?'

Other strategies are the use of the paradigm of interrogative pronouns *in situ* within the clause and disjunctive questions.

3.6 Pragmatics & discourse

3.6.1 Final particles

As for Southeast Asian and Sinitic languages in general, Southern Min uses a set of clause-final particles to code different kinds of modality including the associated subjective attitudes of the speaker. Some of the clause-final particles in Southern Min are presented in Table 10 and given authentic discourse examples below:

Table 10: A selection of Taiwanese Southern Min clause-final particles

Clause-final particle	Character	Function
e^0	的	Assertion of a state of affairs
a^0	啊	Confirmation of a situation, slightly insistent
bo^0	無	Non-neutral polar question marker (general)
m^7	唔	Non-neutral polar question marker (intention)
boe^0	燴	Non-neutral polar question marker (likelihood)
$kong^1$	講	Newsworthiness, exclamations, warnings, rebuttals
$o^5 \sim o$	喔	Exclamatory value
la^1	啦	Draws hearer's attention to topic at hand; directive

This grammatical sketch of Southern Min closes with a final three examples to illustrate some of the modal values for four of the discourse markers listed in Table 10:

(62) 我足驚的。
  Goa² chiok⁸ kia^{n1} e⁰.
  1SG very scared PRT$_{ASST}$
  'I was *very* scared.' (J557) (assertion of how narrator felt on finding himself lost on a mountain at night)

(63) 嘛勿會使睏啊。
  Ma¹   bue⁷   sai³   khun¹   a⁰.
  also   NEG: allow   sleep   PRT_CNF
  'You mustn't take a nap either (while looking after the shop).' (J538)

The use of the clause-final particle kong¹ 講 in Southern Min, derived from the verb 'say' kong² (which undergoes tone sandhi), has a newsworthy, exclamatory value in threats and rebuttals (see Chappell 2017), similar to old-fashioned English *I say (old chap)!* or French *Dis-donc!* 'How about that!'. The following example shows the rebuttal use of kong¹ 講 and relies on the context that A is on a strict diet and cannot indulge in any treats. CM's offer of chocolate therefore challenges her determination to stick to her diet.

(64) Strict diet
  CM: 你 愛   <L2 巧克力 L2>   無?
      Li²   beh⁴ai³   <M qiǎokèlì M>   bo⁰
      2SG   like   chocolate   PRT_Q <NEG

  A: 無在痟**講**。
      bo⁵   teh⁴   siao²   **kong¹**
      NEG   PROG   crazy   PRT_SAY

  CM: 'Would you like some chocolate?'
  A: 'I'm not going crazy!' (literally: '*I'm telling you*: it's not the case that I'm crazy.')²²

The reader is referred to Cheng (1977), Lien (1988), Yang (1991), Chappell & Peyraube (2016) and Chappell (2017) for further details and discussion of these discourse markers.

4 Conclusion and summary

Matisoff (1991: 386) divides the larger Southeast Asian zone into two main areas: the Sinospheric and the non-Sinospheric. The Sinospheric area includes Southern Sinitic (basically Sinitic languages south of the Yangzi) and all the

---

22 See Chappell (2017) for source details.

language families which have been in close cultural contact with China such as Hmong-Mien, Tai-Kadai, Vietnamese in the Mon-Khmer branch of Austroasiatic, and certain branches of Tibeto-Burman such as Lolo-Burmese. The non-Sinospheric languages include Austronesian languages, many Mon-Khmer languages, and Tibeto-Burman languages, for example, those found in Northeastern India and Nepal.

This division in fact meshes with the classic and fundamental division made by Mantaro Hashimoto (1976, 1986) for Sinitic languages into Northern and Southern groups, which however has been much debated in recent literature in Chinese linguistics (q.v. the discussion in Chappell, Li & Peyraube 2007). The essence of Hashimoto's hypothesis on contact-induced language change is that Chinese languages in the south have been subject to Taïcization while those in the north have been subject to Altaïcization. Hence, language contact influences from Tai (Kra-Dai), but also from Austroasiatic, should be theoretically observable amongst the Southern Sinitic languages, including the Min group of dialects.

This hypothesis can be tested out in a preliminary fashion by considering some of the grammatical features presented by Matisoff (1991) which he views as unifying the Southeast Asian area into a linguistic zone:
1) modal verbs > desiderative markers, 'be likely to'
2) verbs meaning 'to dwell' > progressive aspect markers
3) verbs meaning 'to finish' > perfective aspect markers
4) verbs meaning 'to get, obtain' > 'manage', 'able to', 'have to'
5) verbs of giving > causative and benefactive markers
6) verbs of saying > complementizers, topic and conditional markers
7) formation of resultative and directional compound verbs through verb concatenation

With respect to Sinitic, all these pathways of grammaticalization apply to both Northern and Southern Sinitic languages, albeit the use of *give* verbs as causatives is less well-developed in Northern Chinese (Chappell 2015). It also needs to be noted that little is known about the use of *say* verbs as conditional markers, apart from Southern Min (§3.5.2.4.) where the main *say* verb, *kong*² 講, shows just this development. Beijing and Taiwanese Mandarin as well as Hong Kong Cantonese also have complementizers introducing subordinate clauses which are grammaticalized from *say* verbs but along a different grammaticalization pathway from the conditional and topic marker use (Chappell 2008).

With respect to just Southern Min, all these pathways have been illustrated or discussed in this grammatical sketch while observing that two pathways are less well-developed, namely (i) *finish > perfective*, which is still at an early stage of grammaticalization, and (ii) *get > able* which has not remained the main strategy for coding potential verb compounds, nor a high frequency modal verb. In pan-Sinitic terms, however, all these pathways can be illustrated.

In conclusion, there are strong grounds for treating most of continental East Asia including the Sinitic languages, as forming a linguistic area with Southeast Asia on this basis of broadly defined traits. A more precise identification of linguistic micro-areas will depend on further detailed research by specialists in the languages of East and Southeast Asia.

Acknowledgements

This research has been supported by funding from two grants accorded by the *Programme blanc* – blue sky programme – of the Agence Nationale de la Recherche, France: ANR-08-BLAN-0174 DIAMIN (2009–2011) and ANR-11-ISH2-001-01 TYSOMIN (2012–2015), both part of an international collaborative project on the diachronic syntax of Southern Min carried out with the teams directed by Professor Lien Chinfa of National Tsing Hua University, funded by the National Science Council of Taiwan. A third source of support was provided by a grant from the European Research Council (ERC Advanced Grant Project FP-7 SINOTYPE N° 230388, 2009–2013). I express my gratitude to these organizations.

I would also like to thank Dr Imogen Yu-Chin CHEN 陳玉琴 for her dedicated research assistance in collecting and transcribing the Southern Min narratives and conversations in Taipei used in this research and also for the elicitation and analysis of Southern Min grammar which we carried out together during many enjoyable sessions. I am similarly grateful to both Song Na (宋娜) and Lai Yun-fan (賴雲帆) at the CRLAO in Paris for their work in updating and finalizing these transcriptions.

Table 11: Southern Min corpus

Title	FATE (F)	JAPANESE TALES (JT)	JESSE (J)	TOTAL
Length in minutes	14:06	26:23	17:48	58:17
N° Intonation units	796	1216	831	2843
Genre	Family conversation in Taipei	Narrative by Fang Laoshi (Other interlocutors make remarks)	Narrative by Jesse Chen (A second interlocutor makes remarks)	

Title	FATE (F)	JAPANESE TALES (JT)	JESSE (J)	TOTAL
Length in minutes	14:06	26:23	17:48	58:17
N° of interlocutors	6	4	2	
Content	*Various*: 1. *Principal subject* News on the latest fortune-telling results for members of the family, based on divination carried out by the youngest uncle; 2. *Also discussed*: sister and her family in Australia, stockmarket losses, changing jobs	1. *Japanese history*: Rise of General Toyotomi; 2. *Also discussed*: life in Taiwan under the Japanese occupation	*Reminiscences* 1. Childhood stories: summer holidays, running a family business, waitering experiences 2. As an adult: Lost overnight on a mountain	

Abbreviations

ACH	achievement phase marker
ASST	assertive use of sentence-final particle
CAUS	causative marker
CLF	classifier
COMP	comparative marker
CNF	confirmation use of sentence-final particle
COND	conditional marker
CRS	currently relevant state marker
DAT	dative preposition
DEIC	deictic
DIMN	diminutive marker or nominalizer
EXP	experiential aspect marker
EXT	extent marker 'so that'
GEN	genitive marker
IMP	imperative marker
INC	inclusive form, inct inchoative phase marker
INDEF	indefinite reference
LOC	locative preposition
LNK	linker (genitive, relative clause or attributive marker)
NEG	negative adverb
OM	object marker
PASS	passive marker

PREF	prefix
PRT	discourse particle
PFT	perfect aspect marker
PL	plural
PROG	progressive aspect marker
PRT	discourse particle
Q	question particle for polar questions
SG	singular
SAY	verbal source of grammaticalized marker

References

Baxter, William H. & Laurent Sagart. 2014. *Old Chinese: A new reconstruction*. Oxford: Oxford University Press.

Bielenstein, Hans. 1959. The Chinese colonization of Fukien until the end of the T'ang. in Søren Egerod & Else Glahn (eds.), *Studia Serica Bernhard Karlgren Dedicata: Sinological studies dedicated to Bernhard Karlgren on his 70th birthday*, 98–122. Copenhagen: Ejnar Munksgaard.

Central Intelligence Agency. 2013. *The world factbook 2013-14*. Washington, DC: Central Intelligence Agency. https://www.cia.gov/library/publications/the-world-factbook/index.html (accessed on 1 June 2018).

Chappell, Hilary. 1992. Towards a typology of aspect in Sinitic languages. *Zhongguo Jingnei Yuyan ji Yuyanxue: Hanyu Fangyan* [Chinese Languages and Linguistics: Chinese dialects] 1 (1). 67–106. Taipei: Academia Sinica.

Chappell, Hilary. 1996. Inalienability and the personal domain in Mandarin Chinese discourse. In H. Chappell & W. McGregor (eds.), *The grammar of inalienability. A typological perspective on body part terms and the part-whole relation*, 465–527. Berlin & New York: Mouton de Gruyter.

Chappell, Hilary. 1999. The double unaccusative in Sinitic languages. In Doris L. Payne & Immanuel Barshi (eds.), *External possession and related noun incorporation constructions*, 197–232. (Typological Studies in Language Series 39). Amsterdam: John Benjamins.

Chappell, Hilary. 2000. Dialect grammar in two early modern southern Min texts: A comparative study of dative *khit4* À˜, comitative *cang* ÕÏ and diminutive *–guia* Î®. *Journal of Chinese Linguistics* 28. 247–302.

Chappell, Hilary. 2001a. Synchrony and diachrony of Sinitic languages: A brief history of Chinese dialects, In H. Chappell (ed.), *Sinitic grammar: synchronic and diachronic perspectives*, 3–28. Oxford: Oxford University Press.

Chappell, Hilary. 2001b. Language contact and areal diffusion in Sinitic languages: Problems for typology and genetic affiliation. In Alexandra Aikhenvald & R. M. W. Dixon (eds.), *Areal diffusion and genetic inheritance: problems in comparative linguistics*, 328–357. Oxford: Oxford University Press.

Chappell, Hilary. 2001c. A typology of evidential markers in Sinitic languages. In H. Chappell (ed.), *Sinitic grammar: Synchronic and diachronic perspectives*, 56–84. Oxford: Oxford University Press.

Chappell, Hilary. 2006. From Eurocentrism to Sinocentrism: The case of disposal constructions in Sinitic languages. In Felix Ameka, Alan Dench & Nicholas Evans (eds.), *Catching language: The standing challenge of grammar writing*, 441–486. Berlin & New York: Mouton de Gruyter.

Chappell, Hilary. 2008. Variation in the grammaticalization of complementizers from *verba dicendi* in Sinitic languages. *Linguistic Typology* 12 (1). 45–98.

Chappell, Hilary. 2015. Linguistic areas in China for differential object marking, passive and comparative constructions. In H. Chappell (ed.), *Diversity in Sinitic languages*, 13–52. Oxford: Oxford University Press.

Chappell, Hilary. 2017. From verb of saying to attitudinal discourse marker in Southern Min: (inter)subjectivity and grammaticalization. In Hubert Cuyckens, Lobke Ghesquière & Daniël Van Olmen (eds.), *Aspects of grammaticalization: (Inter)subjectification, analogy and unidirectionality*, 139–165. (Trends in Linguistics Studies and Monographs). Berlin & Boston: Mouton de Gruyter.

Chappell, Hilary & Chinfa Lien. 2011. Le Min. In E. Bonvini, Joëlle Busuttil & A. Peyraube (eds.), *Encyclopédie des sciences du langage : Dictionnaire des langues*, 1025–1036. Paris: Presses Universitaire de France.

Chappell, Hilary & Alain Peyraube. 2006. The analytic causatives of Early Modern Southern Min in diachronic perspective. In Dah-an Ho, H. S. Cheung, W. Pan & F. Wu (eds.), *Shan gao shui chang. Linguistic studies in Chinese and neighboring languages*, 973–1011. Taipei: Academia Sinica.

Chappell, Hilary & Alain Peyraube. 2016. Mood and modality in Sinitic languages. In Johan van der Auwera & Jan Nuyts (eds.), *Oxford Handbook of Mood and Modality*, 296–329. Oxford: Oxford University Press.

Chappell, Hilary, Alain Peyraube & Li Ming. 2007. Chinese linguistics and typology: the state of the art. *Linguistic Typology* 11 (1) 187–211.

Chappell, Hilary, Alain Peyraube & Yunji Wu. 2011. A comitative source for object markers in Sinitic languages: 跟 *kai55* in Waxiang and ÖÏ *kang7* in Southern Min. *Journal of East Asian Linguistics* 20 (4). 291–338.

Chen, Matthew Y. 2000. *Tone sandhi: Patterns across Chinese dialects*. Cambridge: Cambridge University Press.

Chen, Weirong. 2011. The Southern Min dialect of Hui'an: Morphosyntax and grammaticalization. PhD thesis, University of Hong Kong.

Chen, Weirong. 2015. Comparative constructions of inequality in the Southern Min dialect of Hui'an. In H. Chappell (ed.), *Diversity in Sinitic languages*, 248–272. Oxford: Oxford University Press.

Cheng, Robert L. 1972. Some notes on tone sandhi in Taiwanese. *Linguistics* 100. 5–25.

Cheng, Robert L. 1977. Taiwanese question particles. *Journal of Chinese Linguistics* 5 (2). 153–185.

Cheng, Robert L. 1997. Taiwanese and Mandarin structures and their developmental trends in Taiwan. *Book II: Contacts between Taiwanese and Mandarin and the restructuring of their synonyms*. Taipei: Yuan-Liou Publishers.

Cheng, Susie S. 1981. *A study of Taiwanese adjectives*. Taipei: Student Book Co. Ltd.

Clark, Marybeth. 1985. Asking questions in Hmong and other southeast Asian languages. *Linguistics of the Tibeto-Burman area* 8 (2). 60–67.

Clark, Marybeth. 1989. Hmong and areal Southeast Asia. In D. Bradley (ed.), *Papers in Southeast Asian Linguistics 11: Southeast Asian syntax*, 175–230. Canberra: Pacific Linguistics.

Clark, Marybeth. 1996. Where do you feel? – Stative verbs and body-part terms in Mainland Southeast Asia. In H. Chappell & W. McGregor (eds.), *The grammar of inalienability. A typological perspective on body part terms and the part-whole relation*, 529–564. Berlin & New York: Mouton de Gruyter.

Douglas, Rev. Carstairs. 1873 [1990]. *Chinese-English dictionary of the vernacular or spoken language of Amoy with the principal variations of the Chang-chew and Chin-chew dialects.* London: Trubner & Co. Reprinted 1990 by Southern Materials Center, Taipei.

Durie, Mark. 1997. Grammatical structures in verb serialization. In Alex Alsina, Joan Bresnan & Peter Sells (eds.), *Complex Predicates*, 289–354. Stanford: CSLI Publications.

Enfield, N. J. 2003. *Linguistic epidemiology: Semantics and grammar of language contact in mainland Southeast Asia*. London: Routledge Curzon.

Foley, William & Robert D. van Valin Jr. 1984. *Functional syntax and universal grammar.* Cambridge: Cambridge University Press.

Hashimoto, Mantaro. 1976. Language diffusion on the Asian continent: Problems of typological diversity in Sino-Tibetan. *Computational Analyses of Asian and African Languages* 3. 49–65.

Hashimoto, Mantaro. 1986. The altaicization of Northern Chinese. In John McCoy & Timothy Light (eds.), *Contribution to Sino-Tibetan Studies*, 76–97. Leiden: Brill.

Huang, Shuanfan. 1988. Taiwanese morphology. In Robert L. Cheng & Shuanfan Huang (eds.), *The structure of Taiwanese: A modern synthesis*. 121–144. Taipei: Crane.

Huang, Shuanfan. 1993. *Yuyan, Shehui yu Zuquan Yishi (Language, Society and ethnic identity)*. Taipei: Crane.

Klöter, Henning. 2011. *The language of the Sangleys: a Chinese vernacular in missionary sources of the seventeenth century*. Leiden: Brill.

Li, Rulong 李如龙. 2007. *Minnan fangyan yufa yanjiu* (The grammar of Southern Min dialects). Fuzhou: Fujian Renmin Publishers.

Li, Rulong & Yao Rongsong. 2008. *Minnan fangyan* (Southern Min dialects). Fuzhou: Fuzhou Renmin Chubanshe.

Lien, Chinfa 連金發. 1988. 'Taiwanese Sentence-Final Particles', in Robert L. Cheng and Shuanfan Huang (eds.), *The Structure of Taiwanese. A Modern Synthesis*. Taipei: Crane Publishing, 209–233.

Lien, Chinfa. 1995. 'Táiwān Mǐnnányǔ cízhuì a de yánjiū' 台湾闽南语词缀'仔'的研究, in *Dì Èr Jiè Táiwān Yǔyán Guójì Yántǎohuì Lùnwén Xuǎnjí* 第二届台湾语言国际研讨会论文選集 [Proceedings of the Second International Symposium on Languages in Taiwan], Institute of Linguistics. National Taiwan University, 3–4 June, 227–42.

Lien, Chinfa. 1994. The order of 'Verb - complement' constructions in Taiwan Southern Min.(台灣閩南語'動補'結構的語序) *Tsing Hua Journal of Chinese Studies*. New Series. 24: 193–215.

Lien, Chinfa. 1995. 'Táiwān Mǐnnányǔ de wánjié shíxiāngcí shìlùn' 台湾闽南语的完结时相词试论, in *Táiwān Mǐnnányǔ lùnwénjí* 台湾闽南语论文集. Taipei: Wenhe Chubanshe, 121–40.

Lien, Chinfa. 1997. Aspects of the evolution of *tit* 得 in Taiwan Southern Min. *Studies on the History of Chinese Syntax*, ed. by Chaofen Sun, 167–190. Journal of Chinese Linguistics Monograph Series 10. Project on Linguistic Analysis, University of California at Berkeley.

Lien, Chinfa.1998. 台灣閩南語詞綴'仔' 的研究 (A study of the affix 'a' in Taiwan Southern Min). 第二屆台灣語言國際研討會論文選集 (*Selected Papers from the Second International Symposium on Languages in Taiwan)*. 465–483. Taipei: The Crane Publishing Co., Ltd.

Lien, Chinfa. 2001. Competing morphological changes in Taiwanese Southern Min. In H. Chappell (ed.) *Sinitic grammar: synchronic and diachronic perspectives*. 309–339. Oxford: Oxford University Press.

Lien, Chinfa. 2002. Grammatical function words *khit⁴, thoo³, kang⁷, kah⁴, chiong¹* and *liah⁸* in *Li⁴ Jing⁴ Ji⁴* and their development in Southern Min. In *Papers from the Third International Conference on Sinology: Linguistics section. Dialect variations in Chinese*, ed. by Ho, Dah-an. 179–216. Taipei: Institute of Linguistics, Preparatory Office, Academia Sinica.

Matisoff, James A. 1986a. « Hearts and Minds in South-East Asian languages and English : an essay in the comparative lexical semantics of psycho-collocation», in *Cahiers de Linguistique d'Asie Orientale* 15.1.

Matisoff, James A. 1986b, « Linguistic Diversity and Language Contact », in *Highlanders of Thailand*, Singapore : Oxford University Press

Matisoff, James A. 1991, « Areal and Universal Dimensions of Grammatization in Lahu », In: *Approaches to grammaticalization : Focus on Theorical and Methodological Issues*, Elizabeth Closs Traugott & Bernd Heine (eds), Londres: John Benjamins, Vol.2, p. 383-453.

Mei, Tsu-lin 梅祖麟. 1999. Jige Taiwan Minnanhua changyong xuci de laiyuan 幾個臺灣閩南話常用虛詞的來源 (The etymologies of some grammatical particles in Southern Min). In Panghsin Ting (ed.) *Contemporary Studies on the Min Dialects. Journal of Chinese Linguistics Monograph* No. 14: 1–41. Project on Linguistic Analysis, University of California at Berkeley.

Mei, Tsu-lin & Yang, Hsiu-fang 梅祖麟,楊秀芳. (1995). 'Jǐgè Mǐnyǔ yǔfǎ chéngfèn de shíjiān céngcì' 几个闽语语法成分的时间层次 [Stratification in the Grammatical Elements of Several Min Dialects], *The Bulletin of the Institute of History and Philology* 66: 1–21.

Norman, Jerry. 1988. *Chinese*. Cambridge: Cambridge UP.

Norman, Jerry. 1991. The Min Dialects in Historical Perspective, in William S.-Y. Wang (ed.), *Languages and Dialects of China* (Journal of Chinese Linguistics Monograph Series No. 3). Berkeley: Project on Linguistic Analysis (University of California), 325–60.

Simons, Gary F. and Charles D. Fennig (eds.). 2017. *Ethnologue: Languages of the World, Twentieth edition*. Dallas, Texas: SIL International, Online version: http://www.ethnologue.com. (consulted 16 August 2017).

Sun, Chaofen. 1996. *Word-Order Change and Grammaticalization in the History of Chinese*. Stanford: Stanford University Press.

Tsao, Fengfu. 2001. Semantics and syntax of verbal and adjectival reduplication in Mandarin and Taiwanese Southern Min. In Hilary Chappell (ed.) *Sinitic Grammar: Synchronic and Diachronic Perspectives*. Oxford: Oxford University Press. 285–308.

T'sou, Benjamin K. (Zou Jiayan). 1988. Chinese Dialects Overseas: Indo-Pacific and other parts of the world. In Stephen Wurm and Li Rong (eds.), text for Maps B16a and B16b.

Vittrant, Alice. 2006, « Les constructions verbales en série, une nouvelle approche du syntagme verbal birman », *Bulletin de la Société Linguistique de Paris*.

Wang Jian. 2015. Bare classifier noun phrases in Sinitic languages: a typological study, in H. Chappell (ed.), *Diversity in Sinitic languages*. Oxford: Oxford University Press, pp. 110–133

Wang, William S-Y and Chinfa Lien. 1993. Bidirectional diffusion in sound change. In Jones, Charles (ed.) *Historical Linguistics: Problems and Prospectives*. 345–400. London: Longman Group Ltd.

Wurm, Stephen and Li, Rong (eds.) (1987). *Language Atlas of China*. Hong Kong: Longman.

Yang, Hsiu-fang.1991. *Taiwan Minnanyu Yufagao* 台灣閩南語法稿 [A grammar of the Minnan language of Taiwan]. Taipei: Ta An Press.

Yap, Foong Ha & Shoichi Iwasaki. 2003. From causative to passive: A passage in some East and Southeast Asian languages. *Cognitive linguistics and non-Indo-European languages* [Cognitive Linguistics Research 18]. Eugene Casad & Gary Palmer (eds.), 419–446. Berlin: Mouton de Gruyter.

You Rujie 游如杰. 1992. *Hànyǔ Fāngyánxué Dǎolùn* 汉语方言学导论 [Chinese Dialectology]. Shanghai: Shangyai Jiaoyu Chubanshe.

Yue-Hashimoto, Anne. 1991. Stratification in comparative dialectal grammar: A case in Southern Min, *Journal of Chinese Linguistics*, 19–2, pp. 172–201.

Yuan, Jiahua 袁家骅 (comp.) (1960, repr. 1989). *Hanyu fangyan gaiyao* 汉语方言概要 [An outline of Chinese dialects]. Beijing: Wenzi Gaige Chubanshe.

Zhang Zhenxing 张振兴 (ed.). 2012. *Zhongguo Yuyan Dituji Di'er ban* 中国语言地图集: 第二版 (Language Atlas of China, 2nd edition). Beijing: Commercial Press.

Zhou Changji 周长楫. 1991. *Minnan-hua yu putonghua* 闽南语与普通话 (Southern Min and Putonghua). Beijing : Yuwen Chubanshe.

Appendix 1: Summary of linguistic features

Legend
+++ the feature is pervasive or used obligatorily in the language
++ the feature is normal but selectively distributed in the language
+ the feature is merely possible or observable in the language
− the feature is impossible or absent in the language

	Feature	+++/++/+/−	§ ref. in this chapter
Phonetics	Lexical tone or register	+++	§1.1, p.181
Phonetics	Back unrounded vowels	−	§1.2.2 Tables 3 & 4, p.184–85
Phonetics	Initial velar nasal	++	§1.1.1, p.183
Phonetics	Implosive consonants	−	−
Phonetics	Sesquisyllabic structures	−	§1.3: subsyllables, p.186
Morphology	Tendency towards monosyllabicity	+	not discussed explicitly
Morphology	Tendency to form compounds	+++	§2.1.3, p.192
Morphology	Tendency towards isolating (analytic)	+	§2.1, p.187
Morphology	Psycho-collocations	+++	§2.2, p.192
Morphology	Elaborate expressions (e.g. four-syllable or other set patterns)	+++	§2.3, p.194
Morphology	Reduplication generally	+++	§2.4, p.195–96
Morphology	Reduplication of nouns	(+)	Footnote 16, p.195
Morphology	Reduplication of verbs and adjectives	+++	§2.4, p.195–96
Grammar	Use of classifiers	+++	§3.3.1.3, p.200 & also §3.3.2, p.201ff
Grammar	Classifiers used in counting	+++	§3.3.2, p.202

	Feature	+++/++/+/−	§ ref. in this chapter
Grammar	Classifiers used with demonstratives	++	§3.3.2, p.202–03
Grammar	Adjectival verbs	+++	§3.2, p.194, p.198, §3.3.1.2, p.200, §3.3.2.1, p.203
Grammar	Grammatical number	−	§2.1., p.187–88, §3.4, p.204
Grammar	Inflection of verbs	−	§2.1., p.187, §3.4, p.204
Grammar	Use of tense/aspect markers	++ (aspect)	§2.1., p.187, §3.4.1, p.204
Grammar	Use of verb plural markers	−	not discussed
Grammar	Grammaticalization of GET/ OBTAIN (potential mod. resultative/perfect aspect)	+	§3.4.1.4, p.208 & also p.220
Grammar	Grammaticalization of PUT, SET (completed/resultative aspect)	+	§3.4.1.1, p.205 'stick, adhere to' > 'be placed' > accomplishment phase marker
Grammar	Grammaticalization of GIVE (causative, benefactive; preposition)	+++ also passive, but not benefactive	§3.5.2.1, p.212
Grammar	Grammaticalization of FINISH (perfective/ complete aspect; conjunction/temporal subordinator)	+ partial grammaticalization; not a conjunction	§3.4, p.204, 206 & p.220
Grammar	Grammaticalization of directional verbs e.g. GO / COME (allative, venitive)	+++	§3.4.1.3, p.207ff
Grammar	Grammaticalization of SEE, WATCH (temptative)	+	not discussed
Grammar	Grammaticalization of STAY, REMAIN (progressive and continuous, durative aspects)	+	§3.4.1.1, p.205
Grammar	Serial verb constructions	+++	§3.4.1, p.206ff & §3.4.2, p.210
Syntax	Verb precedes object (VO)	++	§3.5.1, p.211
Syntax	Auxiliary precedes verb	+++	§3.4, p.204
Syntax	Preposition precedes noun	+++	§3.1, p.197 & also §3.5.2.1, p.212
Syntax	Noun precedes adjective	−	§3.3, p.198
Syntax	Noun precedes demonstrative	−	§3.3, p.198
Syntax	Noun precedes genitive	−	§3.3, p.198
Syntax	Noun precedes relative clause	−	§3.3, p.198–99 & p.201
Syntax	Use of topic-comment structures	+ (object fronting)	§3.5.4, p.216 §3.1, p.196–97

	Feature	+++/++/+/−	§ ref. in this chapter
Syntax	Ellipsis of arguments known from context	+++	§3.5.1, p.216
Lexical semantics	Specific terms for forms of rice	+++	not discussed explicitly
Pragmatics	Use of utterance-final pragmatic particles	+++	§3.6, p.218
Pragmatics	Encoding of politeness	+	§2.1.1, p.189
Pragmatics	Encoding of honorifics	+	not discussed

Appendix 2: Text interlinearized

我
1. *goa²-* -- ((NOISE OF MIC & VOICE))
   1SG
   "I - --

   我細 漢的時陣,
2. *goa²* ^*se³-han³* *e⁵* *si⁵chun⁷,* /
   1SG little LNK time
   When I was little,

   是蹛 佇庄腳的所在,
3. *si⁷* *toa³* *ti⁷* *chng¹-kha¹* *e⁵* *soo²chai⁷,* \
   be live LOC country LNK place
   I lived in a country area.

   彼當時
4. .. <F *hit⁴* *tong¹* F> *-si⁵=* , /
   that exact -time
   At that time,

   厝裏真散赤。
5. .. *chhu³-li* *chin¹* ^*san³* - ^*chhiah⁴*. \
   house-inside really poor
   My family was really poor.

啊所以，
6. ... a   soo²i²= , –
       PRT   therefore
   Therefore,

   學校歇睏的時陣,
7. .. hak⁸hau⁷   .. hioh⁴khun³   e⁵   si⁵sun⁷ (chun⁷),
      school   rest   LNK   time
   during the school break,

   攏愛去做一寡工,
8. long²   ai³   khi³   ^cho³   chit⁸-koa²   kang¹= , –
   all   need   go   do   one-CLF_PL   labour:work
   I always had to do some work

   來補貼。
9. lai⁵   ^poo²thiap⁴. \
   come_PURP   supplement
   to supplement the income.

   我上會記下,
10. .. goa²   ^siong⁷   e⁷   ^ki³-he⁷, –
       1SG   most_SUP   able   remember-down
    I can remember best of all –

    啊有一個
11. a   ^u⁷   chit⁸-e⁵   = --
    PRT   have   one-CLF   =
    one time when there was --

    eh 歇熱的時陣。
12. .. eh   ... ^hioh⁴^joah⁸   e⁵   si⁵chun⁷. –
       PRT   rest-heat   LNK   time
       eh   ... the summer holidays.

    啊
13. .. a = --
       PRT
    .. Ah

彼陣仔抵抵
14. .. hit⁴-chun⁷-a²   ^tu² - ^tu² --
       at:that-time   just
   At that time,

稻仔置收割。
15. .. ^tiu⁷- a² ..   ti⁷   siu¹koah⁴. \
       rice   DUR   collect-cut
   the rice was just being harvested.

啊收割了咧,
16. a   siu¹^koah⁴   liau²   leh , –
    PRT   collect-cut   finish   PRT_CRS
   After the harvest,

彼個稻稿頭呢,
17. hit⁴-e⁵   tiu⁷-^ko²   ^ thau⁵   neh⁴, –
    that-CLF   rice-stalk   head   PRT_TOP
   the tops of the rice stalks

有佇水的外口。
18. ... u⁷   ti⁷   ^chui²   e⁵   goa⁷ khau². \
        have   LOC   water   LNK   outside
   were right above the water.

汝知影彼陣仔攏愛落 水,
19. Li²   chai¹-ia^n²   hit⁴-chun⁷-a²   long²   ai³   ^lau³-chui², \
    you   know   at:that-time   all   need   let:fall-water
   You know at that time it was necessary to let out the water,

落在田裏。
20. ^lau³   e⁷   chhan⁵   le⁵ . \
    let:fall LOC   rice-field   inside
   to fill the rice-fields.

然後呢,
21. <MSC ránhòu   ne   MSC> , –
         then   PRT
   So,

伊著無 法度犁 - 犁田咧,
22. <EXH .. (5.0) EXH>   i¹   toh⁸ ..   ^bo⁵   hoat¹to⁷   le⁵- le⁵
                         3SG   then   NEG   method   plough-plough-

    chhan⁵   leh,
    rice:field   PRT_CRS
    he had no way of ploughing, ploughing the rice fields,

    無 法度共這個稻稿頭呢,
23. ^bo⁵   hoat¹tou⁷   kah⁴   chit⁴ – e⁵   tiu⁷-ko²   thau⁵   neh, –
    NEG   method   OM   this-CLF   rice:stalk   head   PRT_TOP
    no way to soak the tops of the rice stalks

    浸在水裏底。
24. ^chim³   e⁵   chui² lai⁷te² . \
    drench   LOC   water-inside
    in the water.

    啊所以,
25. .. a   soo²i, –
       PRT   therefore
    Therefore,

    伊著愛請一寡囝仔工咧,
26. i   tioh⁸-ai³   ^chhia^n3   chit⁸-koa²   'gin²-a²-kang¹   leh , –
    3SG   need   hire   one-CLF_PL   childworker   PRT_CRS
    he needed to hire some child-workers

    來-來踏稻稿頭。
27. la-   lai⁵   ^ tah⁸   tiu⁷-ko²   thau⁵. \
    co-   come_PURP   trample   rice:stalk   head
    for trampling down the tops of the rice stalks.

    啊彼陣仔我會記下,
28. .. a   hit⁴-chun⁷-a²   goa²   e⁷   ki³-he⁷ --,
       PRT at:that:time   1SG   able   remember-down
    At that time I can remember,

我會記下一工是差不多
29. .. goa² e⁷ ki³-he⁷ chit⁸-kang¹ si⁷ chha¹-put⁴-to¹
    1SG able remember one-day be about
    I can remember one day was about

是十五箍啊。
si⁷ ^chap⁸-goo⁷ khou¹ a. \
be ten-five dollar PRT
15 dollars.

但是上好是食五頓。
30. tan³si⁷ siong⁷ ho⁷ si⁷ chiah⁸ goo⁷-tng⁷. \
    but most_SUP good be eat five-meal_CLF
    But the best of all was eating five meals.

會用食五頓的所在
31. e⁷-eng⁷ chiah⁸ goo⁷-tng⁷ e⁵ ^soo²chai⁷ . –
    may eat five-meal_CLF LNK place
    It was a place where we were allowed to eat five meals.

啊彼陣仔置歇睏,
32. a hit⁴-chun⁷-a² ti⁷ ^hioh⁴khun³, \
    PRT at:that:time DUR rest
    I was on holidays then,

無代誌
33. bo⁵ ^tai⁷chi³, –
    no business
    and had nothing to do.

啊著去
34. a toh⁸ ^khi³ = --
    PRT then go
    So I went –

去參加踏稻稿頭。
35. khi³ cham¹ka⁷ ^tah⁸ tiu⁷-ko² thau⁵. \
    go participate trample rice-stalk head
    I went to take part in trampling the tops of the rice stalks.

Liberty Lidz
Yongning Na (Mosuo)

Introduction

This work[1] discusses the Yongning variety of Na (also known as Mosuo), a Tibeto-Burman language spoken in southwestern China. The three varieties of Na (Yongning Na, Ninglang/Beiqu Na, and Guabie Na), along with Laze and Naxi, form the Naish branch of the Naic subgroup of Tibeto-Burman; this wider Naic group also includes Namuyi and Shixing/Xumi (Jacques and Michaud 2011, Chirkova and Chen 2013, Michaud 2017). Within Tibeto-Burman, Naic is close to Lolo (Yi)-Burmese (Bradley 1975, Matisoff 1986b, and Thurgood 2017). The Na varieties are spoken in the foothills of the Himalayas in northern Yunnan, southwestern Sichuan, and southeastern Tibet. The location of the fieldsite for this research, Lugu Lake, is shown in Appendix 3.

Geographically, Na is spoken on the very northerly edge of the Mainland Southeast Asia linguistic area. Although much of Na material culture reflects a strong Tibetan influence, Na is a language of Mainland Southeast Asia, as can be seen in its tone system, analyticity, morphological patterns, elaborate classifier system, prolific grammaticalization, serial verb constructions, zero anaphora, and information structure. Na also is well within the Sinitic and Himalayan linguistic areas. In many respects, it is difficult to distinguish the effects of Sinitic and Mainland Southeast Asian language contact on Na, as Sinitic and Mainland Southeast Asian languages have long been in contact and share many typological attributes. An additional factor complicating the analysis is that

---

[1] This chapter is based upon my dissertation, the fieldwork for which was supported by the National Science Foundation under Doctoral Dissertation Improvement Grant No. 0345862 (PI Tony Woodbury), as well as a grant from the National Science Foundation Office of International Science and Engineering. I am extremely grateful for this support.
I would like to thank native speaker consultant Geze Dorje for his extraordinarily thoughtful and incisive discussion and long hours of work. I would also like to thank Yang Zhenhong, Lamu Gatusa, Awu Daba, Dibi Daba, Mupha Daba, Yongzhutser Daba, Zhao Hua'er, Tseren Dorje, and Erqing. James Matisoff contributed very helpful comments. Any remaining misanalyses, inaccuracies, and mistakes are mine alone.

Liberty Lidz: E-Mail: libertylidz@gmail.com

https://doi.org/10.1515/9783110401981-006

some of the features so distinctive of the Mainland Southeast Asia linguistic area are not independent variables. Bradley notes that analytic languages which permit zero anaphora may be more likely to develop serial verb constructions because the verbs concatenate without any intermediary agents, objects, or inflectional marking (2003: 231). Likewise, analyticity and the presence of serial verb constructions may contribute to a propensity for the grammaticalization of TAM marking, as post-head verbs can so easily undergo reanalysis to TAM markers (Bradley 2003: 231, Aikhenvald 2006: 30). Na differs from many Mainland Southeast Asian languages in that Na shows significant effects of language contact with Himalayan languages. One of the most striking examples of Himalayan language contact is the unusual egophoric system in Na, which will be discussed in §3.3.4.

A variety of geographic, cultural, socioeconomic, and political factors shape Na life and influence language use among the Na. The Na live in the foothills of the Himalayas, a mountainous area with low population density. There is significant linguistic variation, even between adjacent villages, and speakers often can identify which village another speaker comes from by linguistic variants in his or her speech. These variants include: rhotacization on vowels, variation between $twæ^{13}$ and $zwæ^{13}$ for the intensifier, head-modifier versus modifier-head word order with the intensifier, variation between the high back vowels /u/ and /ɣ/, frequency of the high tone, variation between the nasals /ɲ/ and /ŋ/, and frequency of use of nu^{33} EMPH, in addition to lexical differences. A number of other ethnolinguistic groups live in the Na areas, including Han, Pumi, Yi, Bai, Tibetans, Naxi, and Lisu, and intermarriage is not uncommon. The Na also tend to look down upon mercantilism as slightly unseemly, so village shops often are owned and run by people from other ethnolinguistic groups. Some Na speak Yunnanese or Sichuanese, and/or know liturgical Tibetan. In recent years, there has been pronounced language shift to Mandarin in some areas, particularly among younger Na. This shift is due to Mandarin-medium education and media, infrastructure development, dramatic increases in tourism, an exodus of youth to work for months at a time in the cities, and the significant socioeconomic benefits to speaking Mandarin.

An important cultural difference between the Na and the ethnolinguistic groups of the Mainland Southeast Asia linguistic area is that the Na are Buddhists of the Vajrayana tradition, taking Lhasa as the religious capital, while most of Mainland Southeast Asia adheres to Theravada Buddhism. The Na retain the sacred geography of Indo-Tibetan Buddhism, with the Potala Palace and Mount Kailash as pilgrimage sites, and send a significant number of their sons to study in Tibetan lamaseries. The Na also have a shamanic tradition of Indo-Tibetan origin called Dabaism.

1 Phonology

Yongning Na adheres closely to the phonological profile of Mainland Southeast Asian languages. It has a complex vowel system, including nine simplex vowels, three diphthongs, and two nasalized vowels; however, unlike many Mainland Southeast Asian languages, Na does not have contrastive vowel length. Na has a tone system. Syllable structures are CVT and CGVT.

1.1 Suprasegmental phonology: Tone and register

The tone system of Na has three tone levels, high, mid, and low, which yield four primary tones at the surface level: a high tone (55), a mid tone (33), a low falling tone (31), and a rising tone (13). The high tone is noticeably less common than the other tones, especially in monosyllables. The high tone also is less common in Luoshui, the village on Lugu Lake where this fieldwork was conducted, than in Yongning proper. The basic prosodic domain for tone is word-level, although tonal association rules are extremely complex (cf. Michaud 2017 for a highly detailed description and analysis). When verbs with rising tone reduplicate (see §2.4 for the semantic correlates of reduplication), tonal dissimilation occurs:

(1) *bæ^{31} bæ^{13}*   'runs (refers to water)'   *t^{h}æ^{31} t^{h}æ^{13}*   'to mutually bite'
     ɢɑ^{31} ɢɑ^{13}   'to help'   *dzɑ^{31} dzɑ^{13}*   'to tremble; to shiver'
     gwɤ^{31} gwɤ^{13} 'to roam'   *tʂæ^{31} tʂæ^{13}*   'to mutually grab'

1.2 Segmental phonemes: Consonants and vowels

As can be seen in Table 1, Na has a large number of consonants in its inventory, including retroflex fricatives and affricates, as well as retroflex allophones of the alveolar series. It also has a uvular stop series, which is contrastive with the velar stop series in only a small number of lexical items, and is thus somewhat peripheral. Local varieties of Chinese spoken in the area show /h/ appearing as [f] in certain phonological environments, and it may be that Na has, at least partially, adopted this alternation. Na makes a three-way obstruent distinction and has a voiceless lateral fricative. Although Lijiang Naxi has a series of prenasalized stops, Yongning Na does not.

Na bilabials /p^h p b m w/ appear as the allophones [ʙ^h ʙ ʙ m̥ ɣ] preceding high back vowels. This phonological process is remarkably similar to the spirantization Matisoff finds for Lahu labials (Matisoff 1982 [1973]). The alveolars /tʰ t d n l/ appear as the retroflex allophones [tʰ ʈ ɖ ɳ ɭ] preceding /ɯ, u, ɣ, ʏ, æ, wʏ, wæ/. The palatal nasal /ɲ/ has the allophone [ŋ] preceding /u, ɣ, ʏ, wʏ/, and the velar fricative /ɣ/ has the allophone [ʁ] preceding the low vowels /æ, ɑ/. The uvular series /qʰ q ɢ/ is phonemic, but very minimally so, and appears to have developed fairly recently from the velar series /kʰ k g/ (Lidz 2010: 67–84, Lidz 2017: 841).

Table 1: Yongning Na consonant inventory (allophones are shown in parentheses)

	Bilabial	Labio-dental	Alveolar	Alveo-palatal	Retro-flex	Palatal	Velar	Uvular	Glottal
Stop	pʰ p b		tʰ t d		(tʰ ʈ ɖ)		kʰ k g	qʰ q ɢ	
Trill	(ʙʰ ʙ̥ ʙ)								
Nasal	m	(ɱ)	n		(ɳ)	ɲ	(ŋ)		
Fricative		f	s z	ɕ ʑ	ʂ ʐ		ɣ	(ʁ)	h
Affricate			tsʰ ts dz	tɕʰ tɕ dʑ	tʂʰ tʂ dʐ				
Lateral fricative			ɬ						
Approx	w					y²			
Lateral approx			l		(ɭ)				

Mainland Southeast Asian languages tend to have rich vowel systems, and Na shares this tendency. Na has nine monophthongs, including the high back unrounded vowel /ɤ/, plus [ə], a reduced vowel subect to vowel harmony, following Michaud (2008). Na also has three diphthongs, a nasalized monophthong, and a nasalized diphthong. The nasalized vowels are clearly secondary; [ĩ, ũ, ɔ̃] only occur through rhinoglottophilia following initial /h/ or /ʔ/, the automatic glottal shop that precedes any syllable-initial /ɛ, ʏ, ɔ, æ, ɑ/. /æ̃/ and /wæ̃/ are attested outside rhinoglottophilia environments, but are rare.

Table 2: Yongning Na vowel inventory

	Front	Central	Back
Close	i		ɯ, u, ɣ
Mid	ɛ	(ə)	ʏ, ɔ
	æ		

---

2 The symbol /y/ is used to represent the palatal approximant rather than the /j/ symbol of the IPA, as this is in accordance with the Chinese *pinyin* system of Romanization, and thus will be more intuitive for many readers.

	Front	Central	Back
Open			ɑ
Diphthongs		wɤ, wɔ, wæ	
Nasalized		æ̃, wæ̃, (ĩ), (ũ), (ɔ̃)	

1.3 Syllable structure

Na has only two possible syllable structures: CVT and CGVT. Na has initial consonant clusters, but the second position in the cluster is restricted to the glide /w/. Final consonants are unattested. Comparison of Na reflexes with reconstructed Proto-Tibeto-Burman (PTB) forms reveals that the nasalized vowels found in Na generally appear through rhinoglottophilia rather than through the loss of nasal finals. Sesquisyllables, although common in the Mainland Southeast Asian languages, are not found in Na. Vowel-initial syllables are not attested, with an automatic glottal stop appearing in what would otherwise be vowel-initial syllables, for example: $ɛ^{33}$ $k^hɯ^{31}$ [ʔɛ^{33} k^{h}ɯ^{31}] 'turnip,' æ̃^{31}-q^{h}ɣ^{33} [ʔæ̃^{31}-q^{h}ɣ^{33}] 'cave.'

2 Morphology

2.1 Word structure

Na is quite analytic, and does not have inflectional morphology. Na has minimal derivational morphology, but makes extensive use of compounding. The derivational morphology that exists tends to occur through grammaticalization processes initiated when a compound is reanalyzed. Thus, even in the derivational morphology of Na, compounding plays a central role.

Two examples of derivational morphemes obtained in this manner are -hĩ^{33}, a nominalizer used in general and agentive nominalizations, and -di^{33}, a nominalizer used in locative and purposive nominalizations (Lidz 2010: 182–185, Lidz 2017: 845). In the grammaticalization process of hĩ^{33} 'person' to -hĩ^{33} NOM$_{Agt}$, compounds of the type V + hĩ^{33} 'person who does V' are reanalyzed so that hĩ^{33} gains status as a productive nominal agentive marker, i.e. 'V-er.' This nominal agentive marker then undergoes semantic extension to become a general nominalizer, where the noun formed no longer needs to be animate, for example: lə^{33}-ʂu^{33} du^{33}-hĩ^{33} 'thoughts.' Na retains all three usages of hĩ^{33}: a lexical item meaning 'person,' agentive nominalizer, and general nominalizer.

The second example is di^{33} 'earth, place,' which grammaticalized to $-di^{33}$ NOM$_{Loc}$ and then further grammaticalized to $-di^{33}$ NOM$_{Purp}$. In the first step of this grammaticalization process, compounds of the type N + di^{33} 'earth, place' and V + di^{33} 'earth, place' are reanalyzed so that di^{33} gains status as a productive locative nominalizer, for example: the stative verb zu^{33} 'be warm' + $-di^{33}$ NOM$_{Loc}$ → zu^{33}-di^{33} 'warm area.' In the second step, locative nominalizer $-di^{33}$ undergoes semantic extension to become a purposive nominalizer where the noun created no longer has locative semantics, for example: dzi^{33} 'water' + $qwæ^{13}$ 'to ladle' + $-di^{33}$ NOM$_{Purp}$ → dzi^{33}-$qwæ^{13}$-di^{33} 'implement for ladling water.' Lexical di^{33} 'earth, place,' $-di^{33}$ NOM$_{Loc}$, and $-di^{33}$ NOM$_{Purp}$ all coexist in Na.

Compounding is the most robust morphological process in Na. The noun compounding processes in Na are [N N]$_N$, [N ADJ]$_N$, [N CLF]$_N$, [V N]$_N$, and [N V]$_N$ (Lidz 2010: 168–176, Lidz 2017: 846). The verb compounding processes are [V V]$_V$, [N V]$_V$, and [N SV]$_{SV}$, where [N SV]$_{SV}$ should be understood as a subclass of [N V]$_V$ (Lidz 2010: 346–349, Lidz 2017: 844). From a semantic standpoint, coordinate compounds include those where the coordinated elements are antonyms: a^{33}-$p^hγ^{33}$ 'grandfather' + a^{33}-$sɯ^{33}$ 'grandmother' → a^{33}-$p^hγ^{33}$-a^{33}-$sɯ^{33}$ 'ancestors,' and those where the coordinated elements are synonyms: $lə^{31}$-$yĩ^{33}$ 'to labor' + zu^{31}-$yĩ^{33}$ 'to work' → $lə^{31}$-$yĩ^{33}$-zu^{31}-$yĩ^{33}$ 'to work.' Although somewhat less common, Na also has compounds of the structure [generic N-specific N]$_N$, for example: ts^hi^{13} 'goat' + $pγ^{33}$ $lɔ^{33}$ 'breeding goat' → ts^hi^{31}-$pγ^{33}$ $lɔ^{33}$ 'non-castrated goat.' [N CLF]$_N$ compounds are extremely common, and can be thought of as somewhat akin to [generic N-specific N]$_N$ compounds, as the classifier specifies a characteristic of the noun such as shape, size, or consistency. Examples of [N CLF]$_N$ compounds are:

(2) $sɯ^{33}$ 'wood' + $dzɯ^{33}$ CLF.tree → $sɯ^{33}$-$dzɯ^{31}$ 'tree'
 pi^{13} 'bran' + $lγ^{33}$ CLF.kernel → pi^{31}-$lγ^{33}$ 'wine lees'
 ha^{33} 'rice, food' + $łu^{31}$ CLF.ball → ha^{33}-$łu^{31}$ 'ball of rice, ball of food'
 $dzɛ^{33}$ 'money' + $wγ^{33}$ CLF.stack → $dzɛ^{33}$-$wγ^{33}$ 'wealth'

2.2 Psycho-collocations

Psycho-collocation is an important morphological resource in mainland Southeast Asian languages (Matisoff 1986a), and Na makes ample use of this resource. Given in example (3) are several psycho-collocations based on Na nu^{31} mi^{13} 'heart.' Psycho-collocations based on body parts such as 'liver' and 'mind' do not appear in the extensive narrative texts collected during this fieldwork, and this area remains for future research.

(3) $nu^{31}\ mi^{13}$ 'heart' + fu^{33} 'happy' → $nu^{31}\ mi^{13}$-fu^{33} 'be happy'
$nu^{31}\ mi^{13}$ 'heart' + $kwɔ^{33}$ LOC + $hɯ^{33}$ 'go' → $nu^{31}\ mi^{13}$-$kwɔ^{33}$-$hɯ^{33}$ 'be pleased'
nu^{33} 'heart' + $gɔ^{33}$ 'hurt' → nu^{33}-$gɔ^{33}$ 'be pitiable'
$nu^{31}\ mi^{13}$ 'heart' + $kwɔ^{33}$ LOC + $k^hɯ^{13}$ 'place (v.)' → $nu^{31}\ mi^{13}$-$kwɔ^{33}\ k^hɯ^{13}$ 'memorize'
nu^{33} 'heart' + $tʂwæ^{33}$ 'insert' → nu^{33}-$tʂwæ^{33}$ 'trust'

A notable psycho-collocation is shown in (4), where $ʐ^{33}$ 'bone' is the seat for 'hope, strength,' rather than an internal organ such as 'heart,' 'mind/brain,' or 'liver.'

(4) $ʐ^{33}$ 'bone' + $mə^{33}$ NEG- + t^hu^{33} 'arrive' → $ʐ^{33}$-$mə^{33}$-t^hu^{33} 'have no strength'

Two common typological features attested in Na may be correlated with the presence of psycho-collocations: semantic extension of body parts and noun incorporation. In Na, semantic extension of body parts outside of psycho-collocations occurs frequently. For example, one finds body parts such as 'hand,' 'heart,' 'head,' 'skin,' 'eye', and 'tongue' in the examples given in (5), which are not psycho-collocations. The question remains open whether these two typological characteristics correlate with the presence of psycho-collocations in other Mainland Southeast Asian languages more generally.

(5) $lɔ^{31}\ k^hwɤ^{33}$ 'hand' is used metaphorically to mean 'technique'
$sɯ^{33}$ 'wood' + $nu^{31}\ mi^{13}$ 'heart' → $sɯ^{33}$-$nu^{31}\ mi^{13}$ 'heartwood'
$bæ^{31}\ bæ^{13}$ 'flower' + $wɔ^{33}$-$lɤ^{31}$ 'head' → $bæ^{31}\ bæ^{13}$-$wɔ^{33}$-$lɤ^{31}$ 'bud'
$sɯ^{33}$ 'wood' + $wu^{31}\ ku^{13}$ 'skin' → $sɯ^{33}$-$wu^{33}\ ku^{31}$ 'bark'
$ɲæ^{13}$ 'eye' + $dʑi^{33}$ 'ability' + di^{33} EXIST.P → $ɲæ^{33}$-$dʑi^{33}$-di^{31} 'artistic vision'
mu^{33} 'fire' + $ɕi^{31}$ 'tongue' → mu^{33}-$ɕi^{31}$ 'flame'

A number of verbs show noun incorporation in Na, which is notable in a language as typologically isolating as Na (Lidz 2010: 347–348, Lidz 2017: 844). Examples are provided in (6).

(6) ha^{33} 'rice, food' + $ʐwɤ^{33}$ 'starve' → ha^{33}-$ʐwɤ^{33}$ 'starve'
$mɤ^{33}$ 'name' + $tʂæ^{33}$ 'call' → $mɤ^{33}$-$tʂæ^{31}$ 'be named'
ha^{33} 'rice, food' + dzi^{33} 'eat' → ha^{33}-dzi^{33} 'eat'
$dʑi^{33}$ 'water' + $t^hɯ^{33}$ 'drink' → $dʑi^{33}$-$t^hɯ^{33}$ 'drink'

2.3 Elaborate expressions

Na has elaborate expressions, which are four word expressions with a canonical repeated element. As Mortensen (2003) points out, elaborate expressions are coordinate compounds. Examples are given in (7). Na also has constructions of the type named 'quasi-elaborate expressions' (Matisoff 1982 [1973]: 85) in which the compounded elements are clearly coordinate, both syntactically and semantically, but there is no repeated morpheme. For example, ha^{33}-dzi^{33}-dzi^{33}-t^hw^{33} meaning 'eat and drink,' which is composed of 'rice' + 'eat' + 'water' + 'drink'. One can analyze this expression either as being composed of four morphemes or as a verbal coordinate compound of the verbs 'eat' and 'drink' in which each verb has an incorporated noun.

(7) $\varsigma\varepsilon^{33}$-$\varsigma\jmath^{33}$-$ha^{33}$-$\varsigma\jmath^{33}$ 'meat' + 'clean' + 'rice' + 'clean' → 'clean meat and rice (for consecrating)'
dw^{33}-zw^{33}-dw^{33}-$ts^h\alpha^{13}$ 'one' + 'lifetime' + 'one' + 'era' → 'generations'
a^{31}-$\textipa{\textltailn}i^{33}$-$ts^hw^{33}$-$\textipa{\textltailn}i^{33}$ 'yesterday' + 'today' → 'now'
a^{31}-yi^{33}-ts^hw^{33}-yi^{33} 'last' + 'year' + 'this' + 'year' → 'now'

2.4 Reduplication

Reduplication is another important morphological resource in Na. Reduplication in Na fundamentally is iconic, though it both operates in several different morphosyntactic realms and conveys several different meanings. Reduplication occurs with nominals, adverbials, stative verbs, active verbs, and in aspect marking. The semantic correlates of reduplication in Na include increased intensity, reciprocal or back-and-forth movement (Yang 2009), and representation of aspectual movement. Reduplication also occurs with sound symbolic noises. This latter usage is not grammatical, but rather is a feature of narrative discourse. Examples (8)–(10) show reduplication denoting increased intensity. (8) shows nominals, while (9) gives adverbials, and (10) presents stative verbs of the A-A-B-B pattern.

(8) dw^{33} wu^{33} dw^{33} wu^{33} (lit.: ['one' + CLF.person] ~) 'every single person'
dw^{55}-dw^{55}-$t\varepsilon i^{31}$-$t\varepsilon i^{31}$ (lit. ['big' + 'small'] ~) 'everyone big and small'

(9) ta^{31} 'just' → ta^{31}-ta^{31} 'just now'
$ts^h w\alpha^{33}$ 'quickly' → $ts^h w\alpha^{33}$-$ts^h w\alpha^{33}$ 'very quickly'

(10) hwæ³³-hwæ³³-ta³¹-ta³¹ 'very comfortable and safe'
    fu³³-fu³³-sa³¹-sa³¹ 'very happy'

While a stative verb reduplicated indicates increased intensity, as shown above in (10), an active verb reduplicated indicates reciprocity or back-and-forth action (Yang 2009, Lidz 2010: 372–373, Lidz 2017: 844).

(11) wɤ³³ 'stack' → wɤ³³-wɤ³³ 'stack together'
    tʰæ¹³ 'bite' → tʰæ³¹-tʰæ¹³ 'bite each other'
    si³³ 'know' → si³³-si³³ 'meet each other'
    tɯ³³ 'pull' → tɯ³³-tɯ³³ 'pull back and forth'
    fu³³ 'like' → fu³³-fu³³ 'court (v.)'

The semelfactive and iterative aspects are iconic in that they employ reduplication to portray aspectual motion. The semelfactive aspect is created by reduplicating the delimitative aspect. The delimitative aspect, which indicates that an action takes place over a short period of time, takes the form dɯ³³ 'one' + V. Thus, the semelfactive aspect, which denotes that a brief action occurs again and again for a period of time, is derived by reduplicating the delimitative form, so that the semelfactive takes the form [dɯ³³ 'one' + V] ~, where ~ indicates reduplication. The iterative aspect, which indicates that an event that consists of many iterations of an action, takes the form dɯ³³ 'one' + [V]~.

Table 3: Iconicity in Na (from Lidz 2010: 441)

Name	Morph. form	Example	Semantics
Reciprocal	V~	tɯ³³-tɯ³³ ('pull' + 'pull')	'pull back and forth'
Delimitative	dɯ³³ 'one' + V	dɯ³³-lĩ³³ (dɯ³³ 'one' + lĩ³³ 'see')	'have a look'
Semelfactive	[Delimitative] ~	dɯ³³-ŋu³³-dɯ³³-ŋu³³	'sobbed and sobbed'
Iterative	dɯ³³ 'one' + [V]~	dɯ³³-ŋu³³-ŋu³³	'cry for a long time'

Sound symbolic noises tend to appear in reduplicated form, as can be seen in (12).

(12) ki³³ qwæ³¹ ki³³ qwæ³¹ 'sound of an axe cutting down trees'
    ṣü³³ ṣü³³ 'sound of whistling'
    wɔ³³ wɔ³³ 'sound of wind blowing'
    ʒ³¹ ʒ¹³ 'sound that a dog barking makes'
    tɤ³¹ tɤ³¹ tɤ³¹ 'sound of floodwater'
    ha³³ ha³³ kʰɯ¹³ 'to yawn' (ha³³ ha³³ + kʰɯ¹³ [light verb])

3 Grammar and Syntax

3.1 Nominal domain

3.1.1 Basic structure of the noun phrase

The structure of the noun phrase is given in Table 4. Constituent order in Na is (A)(O)V, which is prototypically Tibeto-Burman. Nouns, whether agent/subject or object, can be omitted if they can be understood from the discourse context (see §3.3.1). Na is postpositional, and has constituent orders of standard of comparison-COMP-ADJ, head-modifier, possessor-possessum, and N_H–NUM–CLF. NUM–CLF–N_H constituent order is not attested. Demonstrative and number are not crucially ranked; this may be because $dɯ^{33}$ 'one' also is used as a demonstrative to indicate indefinite reference.

Table 4: Structure of the noun phrase

N + REL + N_H + ADJ + INTS + DEM/NUM + CLF + CASE

3.1.2 Classifier devices

Na has a robust classifier system, which includes the generic classifier $lɯ^{33}$, as well as over forty classifiers which select for shape, measure, number, round number, quantity, time, and various categories of living things (Lidz 2010: 216–224, Lidz 2017: 848). Na also has echo classifiers, where the noun itself also is used as a classifier, appearing in the noun phrase twice: once as noun head and once as classifier. Many Na classifiers are transparent grammaticalizations, including the classifiers used for time, round numbers, $q^hwɤ^{13}$ CLF.bowlful/$q^hwɤ^{13}$ 'bowl,' $tɕʰɔ^{13}$ CLF.ladleful/$tɕʰɔ^{13}$ 'ladle,' as well as all of the echo classifiers. It may be that the echo classifiers simply are less easily extended semantically—for example, $tɕi^{31}$ CLF.whistle and $wɤ^{33}$ CLF.village—and thus have not come to be used with a class of nouns. The classifiers for time generally do not use noun heads, and thus may represent an intermediate stage in the process of grammaticalization. Na quantification classifiers, as in Lahu (Matisoff 2003a) and Mandarin, often have the structure $dɯ^{33}$ 'one' + CLF; this may due to semantic properties, or it may be an areal feature of languages of the Sinosphere or Mainland Southeast Asia linguistic area. Many Na classifiers have no clear origins, such as $lɯ^{33}$ CLF.generic, na^{33} for long, flat, and stick-shaped things, $dzɯ^{33}$

for trees and large plants, mi^{31} for birds and some animals, and ku^{13} for more than one person. These classifiers tend to be used with a wider range of items than those which are clear grammaticalizations.

Na classifiers are obligatory with numerals. However, note that noun heads are not obligatory with classifiers for time, as has been noted for other Mainland Southeast Asian languages such as Yao (Caron 1987) and Lahu (Matisoff 2003a). Classifiers are not obligatory with demonstratives, but commonly are found when demonstratives are employed, and constituent order may be non-canonical when a classifier is not used. For example, in (13), the constituent order is DEM-N$_H$-CASE rather than N$_H$-DEM-CLF-CASE. As Na does not have articles but rather indicates direct reference with demonstratives, classifiers also are not obligatory for definite reference.

(13) t^hw^{33} my^{33}-di^{33} $kwɔ^{33}$ $a^{31}\,yi^{33}\,sɛ^{33}$ na^{13} $dzæ^{33}$-pi^{13} t^hw^{33}-dzw^{31} $dzɔ^{33}$.
      this   earth   LOC   long, long ago   Na   lots   DUR-live   EXIST
      'On this land, long, long ago many Na lived.'

Na has alienable, inalienable, and inabsoluble possession.[3] Classifiers are not obligatory with any of these three types of possession. Classifiers can be used anaphorically, as can be seen in example (14), where the classifier dzw^{33} refers anaphorically to the tree where the birds Kunazo and Baenazo live.

(14) $tɕɔ^{31}$-$kw^{33}\,t^hu^{31}$ du^{33} dzw^{33} $ku^{31}\,na^{33}\,zɔ^{33}$ la^{33} $bæ^{33}\,na^{31}\,zɔ^{33}$
      first   one   CLF.tree   Kunazo   and   Baenazo
      'In the first tree, Kunazo and Baenazo

      ha^{13} ni^{33}.
      live   CERT.STR
      live.'

The construction du^{33} 'one' + CLF creates an indefinite expression in Na. Note, though, that because Na classifiers can be quite specific as to selection, indefinite reference in Na can incorporate more information about the referent than an indefinite pronoun does in a language such as English (Lidz 2010: 206). For example, in example (15), although du^{33} + $q^hwɤ^{33}$ CLF.bowlful creates an indefi-

---

3 In Na, alienable possession is used with items with which there is no natural relationship of possession, inalienable possession is used with items with which there is a natural relationship of possession, and inabsoluble possession is used solely with body parts, which have a very strong natural relationship of possession.

nite reference in Na, it literally means 'a bowlful,' which tells the listener more about the referent than in an indefinite pronoun such as 'something' in English does.[4]

(15) ɲa³³-tsi³¹   tæ³³-tæ³³   zɔ³³   tʰæ³³   nɯ³³
     eyes and eyebrows horizontal.INTS ADVB   often   EMPH
     'A horizontal-eyed (person) often (thinks),

ɲa³³   nɯ³³   mə³³-ni³³   nɔ³³   bu³³   dɯ³³   qʰwʁ³³
1SG.PRO   AGTV   NEG-COP   2SG.PRO POSS   one   CLF.bowlful
"Won't I eat a bowl of yours

dzi³³   zɔ³³   ni³³   nɔ³¹   tsʰɯ³³-ɲi³³   wu³³ la¹³   dɯ³³   qʰwʁ³³
eat   PERF   CERT.STR   then   today   business   one   CLF.bowlful
in order to do business

tʰɯ³³-yĩ³³   zɔ³³.
DUR-make   PERF
today?"'

3.2 Verbal domain

The structure of the verb phrase is presented in Table 5. Manner adverbs precede the verb head. Causative markers follow the verb head. If the verb head is stative, it often is followed by the intensifier ʐwæ¹³. Aspectual markers, modals, and auxiliaries take the next slot in the verb phrase, with evidential and epistemic marking taking scope over the full sentence.

As will be discussed in §3.3 on clausal and sentential organization, both agent and object can be ellipsed when they can be understood from discourse context. Thus, V_H is the only constituent that is obligatory for a sentence to be considered grammatical. Na, like other languages of the Mainland Southeast Asia linguistic area, does not have inflection marking person, number, gender, or tense on its verbs, though Na does have two Aktionsart prefixes.

---

4 In Na mythology, people can be divided into vertical-eyed people and horizontal-eyed people, where 'vertical-eyed' refers to someone whose eyes are aligned vertically on his/her face, and 'horizontal-eyed' refers to someone whose eyes appear normally. Horizontal-eyed people act out of self-interest, while vertical-eyed people do not. The fact that no one has found a vertical-eyed person is a metaphor for humans' self-interested nature.

Table 5: Structure of the verb phrase

$$\text{ADV} + V_h + \text{CAUS} + \text{INTS} + \begin{Bmatrix} \text{TENSE} \\ \text{ASPECT} \\ \text{MODAL} \\ \text{AUX} \end{Bmatrix} \begin{matrix} + \text{QUOT} & + \text{CERT.STR} \\ pi^{33} & ni^{33} \end{matrix} + \begin{Bmatrix} \text{REP} \\ tsi^{13} \\ \\ \text{INFR} \\ p^h æ^{33}\text{-}di^{33} \end{Bmatrix} \begin{matrix} + \text{CERT.M} \\ mæ^{33} \end{matrix}$$

$$\text{zwæ}^{13}$$

Na is rich in modal and aspectual distinctions. Modal and aspectual markers primarily appear as post-verb head auxiliaries, many of which are clear grammaticalizations. However, three of the aspects are marked through derivation (the delimitative, semelfactive, and iterative—see §2.4).

3.2.1 Modality

Na has three modality types: deontic, dynamic, and epistemic. Dynamic modality is the richest of these modality types, distinguishing four separate modalities: two abilitives, $wɔ^{33}$ and ku^{13}; a volitive, $ṣu^{33}\ du^{33}$, which has grammaticalized from $ṣu^{33}\ du^{33}$ 'think'; and a desiderative, $hɔ^{33}$. The deontic and epistemic modality types are simpler. The deontic modality has the obligative $zɔ^{33}$ and two modals which each are composed of the deontic modal plus a dynamic modal: $zɔ^{33}$-$hɔ^{33}$ should ($zɔ^{33}$ obligative + $hɔ^{33}$ desiderative) and $zɔ^{33}$-ku^{13} ought ($zɔ^{33}$ obligative + ku^{13} abilitive). The epistemic modality has possibility t^ha^{13}. The Na modals are shown in Table 6.

Table 6: Na modals (from Lidz 2010: 412)

Modality type	Modal	Form	Semantics
Deontic	OBLIGATIVE	$zɔ^{33}$	'must, need'
	SHOULD	$zɔ^{33}$-$hɔ^{33}$ (OBL + DES)	'should'
	OUGHT	$zɔ^{33}$-ku^{13} (OBL + ABLT)	'ought'
Dynamic	ABILITIVE	$wɔ^{33}$	'can, able to'
	ABILITIVE	ku^{13}	'can'
	VOLITIVE	$ṣu^{33}\ du^{33}$	'want'
	DESIDERATIVE	$hɔ^{33}$	'want'
Epistemic	POSSIBILITY	t^ha^{13}	'may'

3.2.2 Tense, aspect, and Aktionsart marking

Na is an aspectual language, and does not have obligatory morphemes marking tense, as is true for many Sinospheric languages. Smith and Erbaugh (2005) present an expansive account of the different strategies used to indicate temporal interpretation in Mandarin Chinese: aspectual marking, aspectual viewpoint, adverbials, lexical information, situation type, deixis, anaphora, and context. Na uses the same fundamental strategies for temporal representation, although with significant differences in the specifics, such as the particular aspects attested and the presence of Aktionsart marking in Na (Lidz 2007a: 48, Lidz 2010: 423).

Lexical aspect in Na is marked using the language's two derivational Aktionsart prefixes, $lə^{33}$- ACCOMP and $t^hɯ^{33}$- DUR, with slightly different results depending upon whether the verb has process, liminal, or stative lexical aspect, as can be seen in Table 7. They are formally distinct from the aspectual markers in that they are preverbal prefixes rather than postverbal particles; they can co-occur with aspectual markers; and they contribute to the lexical aspect of the verb. The origins of the two Na Aktionsart markers are unknown, but given their position as verbal prefixes, adverbial origins can be hypothesized.

Table 7: Aktionsart marking

Aktionsart marker	Verb's original lexical aspect	Change in lexical aspect	Example
$lə^{33}$- ACCOMP	Process	The process has been accomplished.	dzi^{33} 'eat' $lə^{33}$-dzi^{33} 'eat up'
	Liminal	Indicates acccomplishment	$wɔ^{13}$ 'turn' $lə^{33}$-$wɔ^{13}$ 'turned'
	Stative	State has been achieved; the verb will appear with the change of state marker $zɛ^{33}$, indicating that there has been a change of state.	$gɔ^{33}$ 'be sick' $lə^{33}$-$gɔ^{33}$ $zɛ^{33}$ 'became sick'
$t^hɯ^{33}$- DUR	Process	The process is ongoing.	$kɯ^{31}$ 'hide' $t^hɯ^{33}$-$kɯ^{31}$ 'hide (and stay hidden)'
	Liminal	The result of the action endures.	$k^hɯ^{13}$ 'put' $t^hɯ^{33}$-$k^hɯ^{13}$ 'put (and the item remains in that place)'
	Stative	Durative marking is rare on stative verbs, but frequently appears on existential verbs	di^{33} EXIST.P $t^hɯ^{33}$-di^{33} 'exist (for a long time)'

Aktionsart marker	Verb's original lexical aspect	Change in lexical aspect	Example
		(a subtype of stative verbs), where it gives the notion of a stable and continuing presence.	

Table 8 shows the full range of Aktionsart and aspectual marking in Na. The Aktionsart markers, which alter the verb's inherent lexical aspect, are prefixes, while the aspectual markers are particles or iconic derived forms.

Table 8a: Overview of Aktionsart and aspectual marking in Na (revised from Lidz 2010: 425–426)

Aspect/Aktionsart	Semantics	Form	Morph.	Abbr.
Accomplished	Indicates that the intended result of a process or activity has been achieved; for a verb with liminal lexical aspect, indicates accomplishment; for a stative verb, that the state has indeed been achieved	la^{33}-	Prefix	ACCOMP-
Durative	Indicates that a process is ongoing; for a verb with liminal lexical aspect, indicates that having achieved the expect result, the action continues or the result endures; attested with existential verbs (subclass of stative verbs), where it indicates that something continues to exist	t^hw^{33}-	Prefix	DUR-
Perfective/ Change of state/ Currently relevant state	Event is viewed in its entirety; may indicate that a change of state has occurred, in which case it often occurs in conjunction with the accomplished marker; may indicate that event is of ongoing relevance to discussion	$z\varepsilon^{33}/z\sigma^{33}$	Particle	PERF/CSM /CRS
Completive	Grammaticalized from the verb $s\varepsilon^{13}$ 'complete'; indicates that event has been completed	$s\varepsilon^{13}$	Particle	CMPL
Experiential	Event has been experienced	tci^{31}	Particle	EXPER
Progressive	Grammaticalized from EXIST/TOP $dz\sigma^{33}$; indicates that event is ongoing	$dz\sigma^{33}$	Particle	PROG
Delimitative	Event occurs for a short period of time	dw^{33} + V	Derived	DEL

Aspect/Aktionsart	Semantics	Form	Morph.	Abbr.
Semelfactive	Event is an extremely brief iteration of an action that occurs repeatedly for a period of time	$[dɯ^{33} + V]$ ~	Derived	SEM
Iterative	Event occurs repeatedly; may be an event that involves many iterations of an action for a short period of time	$dɯ^{33} + V_1V_1$	Derived	ITER

Table 8b: Overview of Aktionsart and aspecto-temporal marking in Na (cont'd)

Aspect/Aktionsart	Semantics	Form	Morph.	Abbr.
Immediate future	Grammaticalized from bi^{33} 'go'; indicates an immediate future	bi^{33}	Particle	FUT.IMM
Remote future	Grammaticalized from $hɯ^{33}$ 'go'; indicates a remote future	$hɯ^{33}$	Particle	FUT.REM
Predictive future (desire)	Grammaticalized from desiderative $hɔ^{33}$; indicates a predictive future, and retains some of its pre-grammaticalization semantics	$hɔ^{33}$	Particle	FUT.DES
Predictive future (ability)	Grammaticalized from abilitive ku^{13}; indicates a predictive future, and retains some of its pre-grammaticalization semantics	ku^{13}	Particle	FUT.ABL

The primary temporal distinction in Na is future/non-future. For the non-future, the following aspects are distinguished: perfective/change of state/currently relevant state, completive, experiential, progressive, delimitative, semelfactive, and iterative. For the future, there are four distinctions: immediate future, remote future, predictive future (desire), and predictive future (ability). The two predictive futures are grammaticalizations from modals, and each retains some of its pre-grammaticalized semantics, such that predictive future (desire) is distinct from predictive future (ability). The Na aspect markers primarily are post-verbal particles, although the delimitative, semelfactive, and iterative are derived forms (see Table 3 and §2.4). Of the post-verbal particles, nearly all are transparent grammaticalizations, with the exceptions of the perfective/change of state/currently relevant state marker $zɛ^{33}/zɔ^{33}$ and the experiential marker $tɕi^{31}$.

3.2.3 Grammaticalization

There is a considerable amount of grammaticalization in Na, particularly in modal, aspectual, evidential, and semantic role marking. Bradley (2003) views the presence of serial verb constructions within a language as a contributing factor to the grammaticalization of TAM markers, because a lexical verb in a set position in a serial verb construction can become reanalyzed into a TAM marker. As will be discussed in §3.3.5, evidential marking appears to be a fairly recent phenomenon in Na, and most of the evidentials are grammaticalizations from verbs which have increased scope to indicate source of knowledge for the sentence. The reasons why grammaticalization occurs with semantic role markers are less clear-cut, but include a propensity for semantic extension of spatial terms to temporal terms, as shown in (16), and extension of body part terms to role markers indicating spatial position, as shown in (17).

(16) $kwɔ^{33}$ LOC (spatial) → $kwɔ^{33}$ LOC (temporal), concern, source
gi^{13} 'following, behind' (spatial) → gi^{13} 'following, after' (temporal)

(17) $wɔ^{33}$ 'head' → $wɔ^{33}$ 'on'
$k^hɯ^{31} ts^hɯ^{13}$ 'foot' → $k^hɯ^{33}$ CIS

Table 9 shows common grammaticalization processes in Mainland Southeast Asian languages, as compiled in Vittrant & Watkins (this volume, p. 669). The following sections will discuss which of these grammaticalization processes have occurred in Na, giving examples from narrative texts recorded during fieldwork where possible.

Table 9: Common grammaticalization processes in Mainland Southeast Asian languages

Common MSEA grammaticalization pathway	Na
'get, obtain' → POT, RES/PERF	NOT ATTESTED
'put, set' → CMPL, RES	NOT ATTESTED
'give' → CAUS, BEN → ADPOSITION	YES
'go,' 'come' → ALL, VEN, LAUD/MAL	YES: ALL, VEN
'see, watch' → TEMPTATIVE & SUCCESS	NOT ATTESTED
'stay, remain' → PROG and CONT/DUR	NOT ATTESTED

- **'get, obtain'**

Although other Mainland Southeast Asian languages have a grammaticalization pathway of 'get, obtain' → potential modality, resultative/perfect aspect (Matisoff 1991, Enfield 2003, Vittrant 2008, van der Auwera et al. 2009), this does not seem to be the case in Na, where the relevant forms are unrelated: $dɯ^{33}$ 'obtain,' t^ha^{13} POSSIB, and $zɛ^{33}$ PERF/CSM/CRS.

- **'put, place'**

$k^hɯ^{13}$ 'put, place' and $tɕi^{33}$ 'put' grammaticalize into causatives, not completed/resultative aspect markers as in some other Mainland Southeast Asian languages (See Burmese, p. 98, Southern Min, p. 205 or Thai, p. 302).[5] $k^hɯ^{13}$ also appears as a light verb in expressions like mu^{33} $k^hɯ^{13}$ 'light a fire' and $tɕi^{31}$ $ɕi^{33}$ $k^hɯ^{13}$ 'make a whistling sound.'

- **'give'**

Na ki^{33} 'give' grammaticalized into a dative marker through the following grammaticalization pathway: ki^{33} 'give' → ki^{33} ALL → ki^{33} BEN → ki^{33} DAT (recipient, goal). Example (18) astonishingly contains three out of the four usages for ki^{33}: lexical ki^{33} 'give,' ki^{33} ALL, and ki^{33} DAT, where $dɯ^{33}$ wu^{33} 'each (person)' is the clear recipient for the dative. Example (19) shows ki^{33} BEN, where one receives a clear reading of benefaction because the shaman is creating dough idols for the benefit of an ill monk. ki^{33} is not a dative, because the dough idols are not given to the monk, but rather used in a healing rite.

(18) ni^{13} $t^hɯ^{33}$ ki^{33} $hɯ^{33}$ $dzɔ^{33}$ $dɯ^{33}$ wu^{33} ki^{33} ni^{33} $sɯ^{31}$
who   3SG.PRO   ALL   go   TOP   one   CLF.person   DAT   all
'Whoever went to visit her, to each (she) would

$dʑi^{31}$ ki^{33} $dɯ^{33}$ $k^hɯ^{31}$ $t^hɯ^{33}$-ki^{33}.
belt   one   CLF   DUR-give
give a belt.'

(19) t^hi^{13} $t^hɯ^{33}$ ki^{33} $ɣæ^{33}$ $mɤ^{33}$ $ʐu^{33}$ $ɲɤ^{33}$ mu^{33} la^{33} $dɯ^{33}$-pi^{13} $tɕ^hi^{13}$.
so   3SG.PRO   BEN   as one pleases   shape   and   some   throw
'So, (using flour) (he) made a few idols (to be used in a healing rite) as he pleased for him.'

- **'go, come'**

The grammaticalization of verbs meaning 'go' and 'come' into andative and venitive markers, respectively, represent a very simple grammaticalization process: when one of these lexical verb appears in secondary position in a verb concatenation, it is reanalyzed into an andative or venitive.

Na bi^{33} 'go' grammaticalized into an andative marker, and then further grammaticalized into a future marker. Grammaticalization occurred along the following pathway: bi^{33} lexical verb 'go' → bi^{33} AUX (AND/movement to a loca-

---

[5] Note that Na also has a third causative, yi^{33}, grammaticalized from a verb meaning 'do.'

tion) → bi^{33} FUT.IMM. All three usages of bi^{33} are attested in Na, as shown in examples (20)–(22). (20) shows lexical bi^{33} 'go,' where bi^{33} is a verb head. (21) shows bi^{33} AND, where bi^{33} appears as the second verb in a serial verb construction and adds directional semantics to the concatenation. In (22), bi^{33} has grammaticalized into an immediate future marker. In the narrative from which (22) is extracted, the speaker is directly facing the man whom he wishes to kill, so there is no notion of movement to a location indicated by bi^{33}.

(20) $t^h æ^{33}$ $t^h ɯ^{33}$-ni^{13} $mγ^{31}$-$tɕ^h ɔ^{33}$ bi^{33} $mə^{33}$-$tʂ^h wɤ^{33}$.
often   this way   below   go   NEG-allow
'Often in this way (she) did not allow (him) to go below (to earth).'

(21) $p^h æ^{31}$-$tɕ^h i^{33}$-mu^{31}-$zɔ^{33}$=$æ^{31}$ $\tilde{3}^{31}$-bu^{33} $l\tilde{3}^{33}$-yi^{33} bi^{33} $mə^{33}$-$zɔ^{33}$.
man-young woman=PL   REFL   labor   AND   NEG-OBL
'People don't need to go labor (in the fields) themselves.'

(22) $lə^{33}$-$sɯ^{13}$ bi^{33} $zε^{33}$ pi^{33} ni^{33}.
ACCOMP-kill   FUT.IMM   CRS   QUOT   CERT.STR
'(He) said, "I am going to kill him."'

Na $yɔ^{33}$ 'come' directly grammaticalizes into a venitive marker through the pathway: $yɔ^{33}$ lexical verb 'come' → $yɔ^{33}$ VEN. Example (23) shows $yɔ^{33}$ as a verb head meaning 'come.'

(23) $\tilde{3}^{31}$-$sɤ^{33}$ ku^{31} bu^{33} $mγ^{33}$-di^{33} $kwɔ^{33}$ $lə^{33}$-$yɔ^{33}$ bi^{33} $zε^{33}$
1INC.PRO   POSS   land   LOC   ACCOMP-come   FUT.IMM   CSM
'(He) said, "(I am) going to return

pi^{33} ni^{33}.
QUOT   CERT.STR
to our land."'

Example (24) shows $yɔ^{33}$ grammaticalized into a venitive marker. In this example, $yɔ^{33}$ VEN follows the verb head $pɔ^{13}$ 'take,' and contributes directional semantics to the verb concatenation.

(24) $bæ^{33}$ $pɔ^{31}$-$yɔ^{33}$.
rope   take-VEN
'Bring over the rope!'

- **'stay, remain'**

The progressive marker in Na, $dzɔ^{33}$, does not appear to have grammaticalized from a verb meaning 'stay, remain,' as in other Mainland Southeast Asian languages. In Na, $dzɔ^{33}$ EXIST → $dzɔ^{33}$ PROG, where $dzɔ^{33}$ EXIST appears to come from PTB *m-dzyaŋ 'be there/have' (Matisoff 2003b: 267). Additionally, although 'stay, remain' is found to grammaticalize into a durative marker in some Mainland Southeast Asian languages, it is unclear where the Na Aktionsart prefix $tʰɯ^{33}$- DUR comes from; given its pre-verbal position, it seems more likely to have originated as an adverbial than as a verb head.

3.2.4 Serial verb constructions

Na has symmetrical serial verb constructions, where verb choice is unrestricted; asymmetrical serial verb constructions, where verb choice is restricted (terminology per Aikhenvald 2006); and resultative/cause-effect serial verb constructions. There also are a number of complement-taking predicates in which the complement does not have an overt subject, so the verbs concatenate. An example of a symmetrical serial verb construction is given in (25).

(25) $tʰi^{13}$ $lə^{33}$-$wæ^{13}$ $zɔ^{33}$ $tʰɯ^{33}$ $ʐɯ^{33}$-mi^{33} $tʰɯ^{33}$ $lɯ^{33}$
      so   ACCOMP-call   CSM   this   hearth room   this   CLF.generic
      'So, having called (it), the hearth room

   $lə^{33}$-$wɔ^{13}$ $lə^{33}$-si^{31} $lə^{33}$-$yɔ^{33}$ $hɯ^{33}$.
   ACCOMP-return   ACCOMP-live   ACCOMP-come   FUT.REM
   will come return to life.'

In asymmetrical serial verb constructions in Na, the second verb in the concatenation is typically directional: $yɔ^{33}$ VEN, bi^{33} AND, $tsʰɯ^{33}$ 'come,' or $hɯ^{33}$ 'go.' $tsʰɯ^{33}$ 'come' and $hɯ^{33}$ 'go' differ from $yɔ^{33}$ VEN and bi^{33} AND, respectively, in that $tsʰɯ^{33}$ 'come' and $hɯ^{33}$ 'go' do not take the speaker as the deictic center.

(26) $bæ^{33}$ $pɔ^{31}$-$yɔ^{33}$.
      rope   take-VEN
      'Bring over the rope!'

(27) $lɤ^{33}$-yi^{33} bi^{33}
      labor   AND
      'go labor (in the fields)'

(28) di^{33} $lə^{33}$-$ts^hɯ^{33}$
follow   ACCOMP-come
'came following'

(29) $tɕ^hi^{33}$ $lə^{33}$-$hɯ^{33}$
enter   ACCOMP-go
'entered'

(30) shows a resultative/cause-effect serial verb construction, $ʂɛ^{33}\ dɯ^{33}$ 'look for and obtain; able to find.' The first part of this example also shows that one can indicate an unobtained result by marking V₂ with the negative marker; $ʂɛ^{33}\ mə^{33}$-$dɯ^{33}$ 'didn't find' can be translated literally as 'looked for but did not obtain.'

(30) $ɲa^{33}$-tsu^{33}-mi^{33} $dʐɔ^{33}$ $ʂɛ^{33}$ $mə^{33}$-$dɯ^{33}$ $ɲa^{33}$-$tæ^{33}$-mi^{33}
vertical-eyed woman   TOP   look for   NEG-obtain   horizontal-eyed woman
'(He) didn't find a vertical-eyed woman;

$t^hɯ^{33}$ wu^{33} $ʂɛ^{33}$ $dɯ^{33}$ $zɔ^{33}$.
this   CLF.person   look for   obtain   PERF
(rather) (he) found the horizontal-eyed woman.'

In example (31), the modal $zɔ^{33}$ OBL is a complement-taking predicate, and the complement has a non-overt subject, so the complement's verbs $ʂɛ^{33}\ bi^{33}$ 'go look for' concatenate with the $zɔ^{33}$ OBL.

(31) $t^hɯ^{33}$ q^ha^{33} k^hu^{13} $p^hæ^{31}$-$tɕ^hi^{33}$=$æ^{31}$ a^{33}-$p^hɔ^{13}$ $dʑɛ^{33}$
this   several   years   men=PL   outside   money
'These last few years, men don't need to go to the outside world

$ʂɛ^{33}$ bi^{33} $mə^{33}$-$zɔ^{33}$.
look for   AND   NEG-OBL
to find work.'

TAM marking is shared across Na serial verb constructions. Aspectual marking is shown in (32), and modality marking is shown above in (31). Example (32) shows the serial verb construction $lə^{33}$-$wɔ^{13}\ lə^{33}$-$si^{31}\ lə^{33}$-$yɔ^{33}\ hɯ^{33}$ 'come back to life,' where the construction is marked with the remote future marker $hɯ^{33}$. However, Aktionsart is marked at the morphological level, so each verb in a Na serial verb construction can either take the same Aktionsart marker as in (32), or take different markers as in (33).

(32) tʰi̠¹³ lə³³-wæ³³   zɔ³³   tʰɯ³³   ʐɯ³³-mi³³   tʰɯ³³   lɯ³³
     so   ACCOMP-call   CSM   this   hearth room this   CLF
     'So, having called (it), the hearth room

     lə³³-wɔ¹³   lə³³-sɯ³¹   lə³³-yɔ³³   hɯ³³.
     ACCOMP-return   ACCOMP-live   ACCOMP-come   FUT.REM
     will come return to life.'

(33) tʰi̠¹³ hɔ̃³³   pi³³   sɯ³¹-tʰi̠¹³   lə³³-wɔ¹³   tʰɯ³³-tʂʰwæ¹³   hɯ³³.
     so   INTERJ say   knife   ACCOMP-return   DUR-insert   go
     'So (he) said, "Huh!" (and) put his knife back (in its case).'

Clear instances of polarity differing across a serial verb construction are attested in Na resultative serial verb constructions where the result or effect is not achieved, as in (34).

(34) lə³³-dzi³³   mə³³-ɲi³³
     ACCOMP-eat   NEG-be full
     'did not eat to the point of being full'

3.3 Clausal and sentential organization

Na has a basic constituent order of (A)(O)V. The only grammatically required element in the sentence is the verb—either or both subject and object can be ellipsed if they can be understood from the previous discourse context. Agentive $nɯ^{33}$ appears in pragmatically-marked constituent orders, such as contrastive focus, shift in speaker, switch in subject, or for emphasis on the agent. Agentive marking (also sometimes referred to as non-systemic ergative marking) is common in Tibeto-Burman languages (LaPolla 1995). The agentive marker $nɯ^{33}$ grammaticalized from a seldom-used ablative marker. Na also has a patient marker $tɔ^{31}$, which grammaticalized from allative $tɔ^{31}$. Agentive marking in Na occurs with some frequency; patient marking is much more rare. It is possible for both agentive and patient marking to appear in the same sentence.

(35) tʰi̠¹³   hĩ³³   tɔ³¹   kʰu³³-pʰæ³³-tɕi¹³   tɔ³¹   fu³³-fu³³   la³³
     so   people   PAT   young people   PAT   like.RECIP   and
     'So, (she also protects) people, young people courting and such things

tʰɯ³³-ni¹³	a³³-wɔ³³	a³³-da³³-a³³-mi³³	dɯ³³-sɔ³³	ʐwɤ³³	mə³³-tsʰwɤ³³.
this way	home	father-mother	at all	say	NEG-permit

parents say (they) do not permit.'

3.3.1 Ellipsis of arguments

In example (36), both the agent and the direct object are ellipsed, as both can be understood from the discourse context of the narrative text in which the example appears. Such ellipses are quite common in naturalistic discourse in Na.

(36)   a³³-pʰɔ¹³   lə³³-bu³³   lə³³-dzi³³.
       outside   ACCOMP-roast   ACCOMP-eat
       '(Once) outside, (he) roasted (it) (and) ate (it).'

3.3.2 Information structure

Na has topic/comment information structure. The topic appears at the beginning of a clause and is marked with *dzɔ³³*, which is also the progressive marker and an existential verb. It can be difficult to distinguish between the existential and topic marker usages of *dzɔ³³*, as an existential verb serves to introduce a new referent into the discourse which will then be commented upon, while a topic marker, when used with a noun phrase, marks that referent as being under discussion, and is followed by a comment. It can also be difficult to distinguish between the progressive and topic marker usages when *dzɔ³³* appears following a verb phrase in a non-final clause, because one can receive the reading that an event is underway at the time another event in the main clause occurs (progressive reading), or the reading that the event is the topic and the main clause is the comment.

(37)
mỹ³³-di³³	tʰɯ³³	dzɔ³³	dɯ³³	kʰwɤ³³	ki³³	ni³³	tsi¹³.
land	this	TOP	one	CLF.strip	give	CERT.STR	REP

'As for land, it is said that (she) gave a strip (of it).'

3.3.3 Interrogatives

Na has an A-not A structure for yes/no questions, as can be seen in the elicited example shown in (38). However, this is not the preferred structure for such questions, and the A-not A structure may be due to language contact with Chinese. More commonly, yes/no questions are constructed with the question marker a^{31} in penultimate position of the question, as shown in the overheard example in (39). Questions generally also can be made with a^{31} QM in ultimate position, as shown in the elicited example (40).

(38) _____ dzɔ³³ mə³³-dzɔ³³?
                   EXIST NEG-EXIST
'Is there any _____?'

(39) nɔ³³ a^{31} kʰi¹³?
     2SG.PRO   QM   go
     'Where are you going?'

(40) tʰɯ³³   gɔ³³ a^{31}?
     3SG.PRO   sick   QM
     'Is s/he sick?'

3.3.4 Egophoricity: Person, evidence, and verbal semantics

Na has an egophoric system, in which the natural differential access to knowledge among first, second, and third persons has become grammaticalized (Lidz 2007a, 2007b, 2010, 2018). The Na system is somewhat different from other egophoric systems (also known as conjunct/disjunct systems) in the literature, although egophoric systems are a common areal feature of Himalayan languages (Hale 1980, Bickel 2000, Bickel 2008). Table 10 provides an overview of how person, evidence, and verbal semantics interact in the Na egophoricity system.

Table 10: Egophoricity: Person, evidence, and verbal semantics in Na (from Lidz 2010: 381)

Type of verb	Person	Qualified?	Form of qualification
Volitional	1SG.PRO/1EXC.PRO	No	
	2SG.PRO/1INC.PRO/2PL.PRO	Yes	Appears as question
	3SG.PRO/3PL.PRO	Yes	Takes hɔ³³ FUT
Internal state	1SG.PRO/1EXC.PRO	No	
	2SG.PRO/1INC.PRO/2PL.PRO	Yes	Appears as question
	3SG.PRO/3PL.PRO	Yes	Takes inferential evidential pʰæ³³-di³³

Type of verb	Person	Qualified?	Form of qualification
Observable state	1SG.PRO/1EXC.PRO	No	
	2SG.PRO/1INC.PRO/2PL.PRO	Yes	Appears as question
	3SG.PRO/3PL.PRO	Yes	Formally and functionally unmarked direct/visual evidential

As can be seen in Table 10, first person statements are unqualified, while second and third person statements are qualified. This is because for first person, the speaker has direct access to knowledge of his/her own actions and states, while for second and third persons, the speaker has only indirect access to knowledge of second and third persons' actions and states. Second person statements in Na require strong qualification, because not only does the speaker not have direct knowledge of a situation, but the second person is a speech act participant, and thus is directly addressed. Na second person statements are qualified by being phrased as questions. If a speaker does not phrase a second person statement as a question, a pragmatically-marked reading is received, such as the speaker is using an imperative, or is speaking in an insolent manner.

Third person statements also are qualified, but the form of qualification varies depending on verbal semantics. Three classes of verbs are distinguished based on verbal semantics in Na: volitional verbs such as 'go' and 'say,' internal state verbs such as 'be happy,' 'be tired,' and 'like,' and verbs denoting an observable state such as 'be sick/hurt.' These classes are similar, but not identical to those identified for other Himalayan languages, such as Amdo Tibetan (Sun 1993) and Newari (Hale 1980). Third person statements with a volitional verb are qualifed with $hɔ^{33}$ FUT.DES, while third person statements with an internal state verb are qualified with the inferential evidential $pʰæ^{33}$-di^{33}. Third person statements with a verb denoting an observable state are qualified with the formally and functionally unmarked direct/visual evidential.

3.3.5 Evidentiality

Na has a five-part system of evidentiality, with particles that distinguish reported, quotative, inferential, and common knowledge evidence, while direct/visual evidence is formally and functionally unmarked (Lidz 2007a, 2010). The evidential markers are presented in Table 11.

Table 11: Evidential markers

Type of Evidence	Marking	Source of marker
Direct/visual evidence	Formally and functionally unmarked	
Reported	tsi^{13}	Grammaticalized from the verb tsi^{13} 'say'
Quotative	pi^{33}	Grammaticalized from the verb pi^{33} 'say, is called'
Inferential	pʰæ^{33}-di^{33}	Grammaticalized from the verb pʰæ^{33}-di^{33} 'resemble, look like'[6]
Common knowledge	=a^{31} dʐɔ^{33}	QM =a^{31} + EXIST/PROG dʐɔ^{33}

The reported, quotative, and inferential evidentials are transparent grammaticalizations of verbs. Na has V-final consitutent order, and these evidentials are verbs which have increased scope, and thus appear even further to the edge of the sentence. LaPolla (2003a) views evidentiality in Tibeto-Burman as being recent and independently developed in different languages, which is consistent with the literature suggesting that languages can develop evidentiality fairly easily through language contact (Aikhenvald 2004: 21). The reported, quotative, and inferential evidentials appear at the end of the final clause in a sentence, while direct/visual evidence is unmarked and the common knowledge marker only can appear in non-final clauses. These evidentials are not simply lexical, but rather form a closed-class grammatical system, as per the definition of evidentiality given in Aikhenvald (2004). How can one know that an unmarked utterance receives a reading of direct/visual evidence? In examples such as (41), excerpted from a creation story, if tsi^{13} REP is not used, native speakers receive the reading that the narrator witnessed creation (Lidz 2007: 50–51, Lidz 2010: 479).

(41) ɕi^{13} tʰæ^{33}-kwɔ^{33} dʐɔ^{33} kʰɔ^{33} pʰy̥^{33} dɯ^{33} pʰæ^{13} dɯ^{33}-ta^{13} dʐɔ^{33}
lake   under-LOC   TOP   grassland   one   CLF.slice   all   TOP
'Underneath the lake, it is said everything was a field of

my̥^{33}-di^{33} ni^{33} tsi^{13}.
land   COP   REP
grass, earth.'

---

[6] Native speaker La Mingqing and Roselle Dobbs report pʰæ^{33}-di^{33} as a verb meaning 'resemble, look like.' I am very grateful to them both for noticing this and passing along this information.

4 Semantics and pragmatics

4.1 Common semantic domains

Data on food terminology, directionals, verbs of cutting and carrying, and metaphorical compounds are presented for comparison of semantic domains within the Mainland Southeast Asia linguistic area.

4.1.1 Food terminology

In contrast to most of Mainland Southeast Asia, rice in the Na areas is not an omnipresence. Most varieties of rice will not grow due to the fairly high elevation; Himalayan red rice is the only variety of rice grown natively in the area. As infrastructure has improved in the past fifteen years, rice is now imported from the rice-growing regions of southeastern China. The Na diet remains centered upon preserved pork, chicken, tsampa, and yak butter tea, with the substantial fats in pork and yak butter tea important for maintaining one's body warmth in the high altitude winters. Nevertheless, 'rice, food' appears as an incorporated noun in the verb ha^{33}-dzi^{33} 'eat,' and there are copious terms for rice, as shown in example (42).

(42) ha^{33} 'cooked rice, food' (饭)
　　　ha^{33}-ly^{33} 'grain of rice' ('rice' + CLF.kernel)
　　　ha^{33}-$tɤ^{33}$ 'uncooked rice'
　　　$ṣu^{33}$ $tṣ^hwæ^{33}$ 'rice' (米饭)
　　　$ɕi^{33}$, $ɕi^{33}$-lu^{33} 'paddy' (水稻) ('paddy' + 'land')
　　　$ɕi^{33}$-$yæ^{13}$ 'paddy seed' ('paddy' + 'seed')
　　　$ɕi^{33}$-$tɕi^{13}$ 'bran' (糠) ('paddy' + 'raw')
　　　$ṣu^{33}$ 'paddy' (稻谷)
　　　$p^hɔ^{13}$, tu^{33} 'to plant'

4.1.2 Expressions of 'cutting,' 'carrying,' 'drying,' 'directional' (upper ~ lower, from ~ toward)

As is common in the region, Na has multiple verbs to express different ways of cutting and carrying things. Directionals are common in Tibeto-Burman languages, and Na employs both adverbials and directionals to indicate direction.

(43) verbs of cutting:
   tsʰɯ¹³ 'cut down (as of a tree)'
   dɑ¹³ 'cut down (as of a tree)'
   hæ̃¹³ 'cut, slice'

(44) verbs of carrying:
   ʂu³³ 'carry'
   pɤ³³ lu³¹, pɤ³³ pɤ³³ 'carry on one's back'
   gɯ¹³ 'carry on one's shoulder (as of a hoe)'

gɯ³¹-tɕɔ³³ 'upwards' and my³¹-tɕɔ³³ 'downwards' are adverbials which appear preceding the verb, for example: my³¹-tɕɔ³³ kwɤ¹³ 'fall down' and gɯ³¹-tɕɔ³³ hɯ³³ 'go up.' bi³³ AND, yɔ³³ VEN, tsʰɯ³³ 'come,' and hɯ³³ 'go' are directionals which appear in asymmetical serial verb constructions, usually as the second verb in a two verb concatenation, as discussed in §3.2.4.

(45) directional morphemes:
   gɯ³¹-tɕɔ³³ 'upwards'
   my³¹-tɕɔ³³ 'downwards'
   bi³³ AND
   yɔ³³ VEN
   tsʰɯ³³ 'come'
   hɯ³³ 'go'

gɯ³¹-tɕɔ³³ can appear as the shortened form prefix gɯ³¹-, as in example (46). gɯ³¹ 'up' has aspectual-like semantics in a number of instances, such as gɯ³¹-tsɛ¹³ 'float up,' gɯ³¹-ʂu¹³ 'fill up,' and gɯ³¹-pu¹³ 'take out.' This is the case even though Na has an accomplished marker (lə³³-), a perfective marker (zɛ³³/zɔ³³), and a completive marker (sɛ¹³), all of which mark the finishing or completion of an action.

In other cases, however, gɯ³¹ 'up' has clear directional semantics, as in gɯ³¹-tsʰɔ⁵⁵ 'leap up,' gɯ³¹-tsʰwæ³³ 'wake up, get up,' gɯ³¹-ku³³ 'rise up, flourish,' and gɯ³¹-tɤ³³ 'stand up, get up.' my³¹-tɕɔ³³ is not attested as a shortened form prefix. This may be a gap in the textual data, but given the aspectual-like use of gɯ³¹- in addition to the directional usage, this asymmetry may be real.

(46) gɯ³¹-tsɛ¹³ 'float up'
   gɯ³¹-ʂu¹³ 'fill up'
   gɯ³¹-tsʰɔ⁵⁵ 'leap up'

gɯ³¹-ta³³ la³³ 'drop from above'
gɯ³¹-pɯ¹³ 'take out'
gɯ³¹-tʂʰwæ³³ 'wake up, get up'
gɯ³¹-kɯ³³ 'rise up, flourish'
gɯ³¹-tʁ³³ 'stand up, get up'

4.1.3 Metaphors in compounds

Na makes extensive use of metaphor in compounds. These metaphors include semantic extension of body parts, non-somatic metaphors, and explicit metaphors using *ni³³ kɯ³¹* 'be like.' Those metaphorical compounds which also are found in other languages of the region are duly noted. As discussed in §2.2, a number of expressions make use of semantic extension of body parts. These are given again in example (47) for ease of reference. Vittrant & Watkins (this volume, p. 677) notes that several Mainland Southeast Asian languages use a word for 'ankle' which is a compound of 'foot' and 'eye.' This is not attested in Na, where the word for 'ankle,' *kʰɯ³¹ tsʰɯ¹³-tʂæ¹³*, is a compound of *kʰɯ³¹ tsʰɯ¹³* 'foot' and *tʂæ¹³* 'joint.' Matisoff (2004: 5) notes 'fire' + 'tongue' → 'flame' is a common metaphor both in Southeast Asian languages and cross-linguistically.

(47) *lɔ³¹ kʰwʁ³³* 'hand' is used metaphorically to mean 'technique'
sɯ³³ 'wood' + *nɯ³¹ mi¹³* 'heart' → *sɯ³³-nɯ³¹ mi¹³* 'heartwood'
bæ³¹ bæ¹³ 'flower' + *wɔ³³-lʏ³¹* 'head' → *bæ³¹ bæ¹³-wɔ³³-lʏ³¹* 'bud'
sɯ³³ 'wood' + *wu³¹ ku¹³* 'skin' → *sɯ³³-wu³³ ku³¹* 'bark'
ɲa¹³ 'eye' + *dʑi³³* 'ability' + *di³³* EXIST.P → *ɲa³³-dʑi³³-di³¹* 'artistic vision'
mu³³ 'fire'+ *ɕi³¹* 'tongue' → *mu³³-ɕi³¹* 'flame'

Example (48) shows non-somatic metaphorical compounds in Na. Several of these are of particular interest because they or very similar compounds are found in other languages of the region. These are 'freckle,' 'meteor,' and 'cockroach.' In Na, 'bird' + 'excrement' → 'freckle,' while 'fly' + 'shit' → 'freckle/mole' is a common Southeast Asian compound, attested in Khmer, Mon, Thai, and Indonesian (Matisoff 2004: 19). In Na, 'star' + 'diarrhea' → 'shooting star, meteor,' which is highly similar to 'star' + 'shit' → 'meteor,' found in Hmong and Lahu (Matisoff 2004: 19). Matisoff (2004: 3–4) notes that Evans (1999) gives 'salt' + 'steal' → 'bat' in Qiang; by comparison, Na has 'rice' + 'steal' → 'cockroach,' which is an analogous metaphor even if the animal doing the stealing and the type of food being stolen are different.

(48) bæ³¹ bæ¹³ 'flower' + tsʰɯ³¹ tsʰɯ¹³ 'leaf' → bæ³¹ bæ¹³-tsʰɯ³³ tsʰɯ³¹ 'petal'
ʒ³³ 'bone' + mʁ³³ 'oil' → ʒ³³-mʁ³³ 'marrow'
ɕi³³ 'rain' + qʰa³³ 'angry' → ɕi³³-qʰa¹³ 'storm'
ɕi¹³ 'sea' + wʁ³³-wʁ³¹ 'mountaintop' → ɕi³³-wʁ³³-wʁ³¹ 'island'
qʰa³³ 'angry' + ʐwæ¹³ INTS → qʰa³³-ʐwæ¹³ 'bitter, overly salty'
qʰæ³³ 'excrement' + gɯ¹³ 'carry on one's shoulder' → qʰæ³³-gɯ¹³ 'meconium'
wu³¹ dzɛ¹³ 'bird' + qʰæ³³ 'excrement' → wu³¹ dzɛ¹³-qʰæ³³ 'freckle'
kɯ³³ 'star' + qʰæ³³-ʂwæ³¹ 'diarrhea' → kɯ³³-qʰæ³³-ʂwæ³¹ 'shooting star, meteor'
wu³³ 'pot' + la¹³ 'strike' → wu³³-la³¹ 'business'
wɔ³³ 'above' + dzɯ³¹ 'live' → wɔ³³-dzɯ³¹ 'Tibetans'
ha³³ tɕʁ³³ 'uncooked rice' + kʰu³¹ 'steal' → ha³³ tɕʁ³³-kʰu³¹ 'cockroach'
hæ³³ 'Han' + gɔ³³ 'sickness' → hæ³³-gɔ³³ 'sexually transmitted disease'
ʐɯ³³ 'building' + lu¹³ 'move' → ʐɯ³³-lu¹³ 'earthquake'
ʑi³¹ 'sleep' + wæ³³ 'call' → ʑi³¹-wæ³³ 'snore'

Na also has explicit metaphorical expressions using ni³³ kɯ³¹ 'be like'; several of these are presented in (49). Non-primary color terms in Na frequently are metaphors using ni³³ kɯ³¹.

(49) wu³³-tʰæ³³ 'underside of a pot' + ni³³ kɯ³¹ 'be like' → wu³³-tʰæ³³-ni³³ kɯ³¹
    'very black, ebony'
wu³¹ dzɛ¹³ 'bird' + ni³³ kɯ³¹ 'be like' → wu³¹ dzɛ¹³-ni³³ kɯ³¹
    (said of a pretty girl)
tsʁ³¹ pɔ³³ 'harness bells' + ni³³ kɯ³¹ 'be like' → tsʁ³¹ pɔ³³-ni³³ kɯ³¹
    (said of one who likes to talk)
mʁ³³-wɔ³³ 'sky' + ni³³ kɯ³¹ 'be like' → mʁ³³-wɔ³³-ni³³ kɯ³¹
    'blue'

4.2 Pragmatics and discourse

4.2.1 Final particles

Na has several phrase-final particles. Some of these are so semantically bleached that native speakers were not able to ascribe nuanced readings to them. However, mæ³³ CERT.M and tɛ³¹ EXCLM are fairly conceptually salient. The epistemic marker mæ³³ indicates that the speaker is certain of the statement, as illustrated in (50). tɛ³¹ is exclamatory, calling attention to or indicating surprise at a statement, as can be seen in (51).

(50) gɣ³³   ɲi³³   gɣ³³   ha³³   pi³³   gi³³   dʑɔ³³   la³³   tʰɯ³³   dzɔ³³
    nine   day   nine   night   snow   fall   PROG   tiger 3SG.PRO   TOP
    '(When) snow is falling for nine days and nine nights,

    la³³-qʰɣ³³   kwɔ³³   tʰɯ³³-kɯ³¹   ku¹³   tsi¹³   mæ³³.
    tiger den   LOC   DUR-hide   FUT.ABL   REP   CERT.M
    it is said the tiger, it will hide away in its den.'

(51) tʰi¹³   lə³³-tʰu³³   zɔ³³   tɛ³¹!
    so   ACCOMP-succeed   PERF   EXCLM
    'So, (he) succeeded, oh!'

4.2.2 Politeness

Na does not have the elaborate politeness registers found in languages such as Balinese, Javanese, and Burmese. However, native speaker intuitions suggest that politeness strategies are of significant importance in the language, particularly when speaking with elders, and this area requires further research.

5 Conclusion

Na has many of the features found in languages of Mainland Southeast Asia and the Sinosphere, including a fairly simple syllable structure; a complex tonal system; no inflectional morphology; a tendency toward analyticity; compounding as a primary resource; 'elaborate expressions' of four words with a canonical repeated element; 'quasi-elaborate expressions' of four syntactically and semantically coordinated words without a repeated element; reduplication as a common morphological resource; agent/subject and object nouns which can be ellipsed if understood from the discourse context; a large system of classifiers; temporal reference given through aspectual marking, adverbials, and a variety of discourse strategies rather than tense marking; grammaticalization as a key source of modal, aspectual, and semantic role marking; symmetrical and asymmetrical serial verb constructions; topic/comment information structure; and lexical semantic features such as psycho-collocations, numerous terms for rice and rice paddy, directionals, and particular distinctive metaphorical compounds. Na does not have breathy/creaky voice, sesquisyllables, or a politeness register from Sanskrit.

Na also has a number of features showing evidence of the influence of the Himalayan linguistic area on the language: a number of retroflexes in the sound system; loanwords from Tibetan due to the influence of Vajrayana Buddhism; an egophoric system linked to verbal semantics; agentive marking; evidentiality; and a shamanic tradition of Indo-Tibetan origin.

Abbreviations

1SG.PRO	1st person singular pronoun	ɲɑ³³
1INC.PRO	1st person plural inclusive pronoun	ɔ̃³¹-sɣ³³ ku³¹
1EXC.PRO	1st person plural exclusive pronoun	ɲɑ³³-sɣ³³ ku³¹
2SG.PRO	2nd person singular pronoun	nɔ³³
2PL.PRO	2nd person plural pronoun	nɔ³³-sɣ³³ ku³¹
3SG.PRO	3rd person singular pronoun	tʰɯ³³
3PL.PRO	3rd person plural pronoun	tʰɯ³³-sɣ³³ ku³¹
ABL	ablative	kwɔ³³, nɯ³³
ABLT	abilitive	wɔ³³, ku¹³
ACCOMP	accomplished	lə³³-
ADESS	adessive	tɔ³¹
ADV	adverb	(various)
ADVB	adverbializer	zɔ³³
ADVERS	adversative conjunctive coordinator	nɔ³¹, dʐɔ³¹
AGTV	agentive	nɯ³³
ALL	allative	ki³³, tɔ³¹
AND	andative	bi³³
ASSOC	associative	bu³³
AUG	augmentative	-mi³³
AUX	auxiliary	(various)
BACK AND FORTH	back and forth movement	V₁ -V₁
BEN	benefactive	ki³³
CAUS	causative	kʰɯ¹³, tɕi³³, yĩ³³
CERT.M	certainty: epistemic marker	mæ³³
CERT.STR	certainty: epistemic strategy	ni³³
CIS	cisative	kʰɯ³³
CLF	classifier	(numerous)
CMKN	common knowledge evidential	=ɑ³¹ dʐɔ³³
CMPL	completive	sɛ¹³
COM	comitative	ɢɑ³³
COMP	comparative	tɔ³¹
COMPL	complementizer	dʐɔ³³
CONJ	conjunctive coordinator	lɑ³³
CONTR	contrastive focus	nɯ³³
COP	copula	ni³³
CSM	change of state marker	zɛ³³/zɔ³³

CRS	currently relevant state marker	zɛ³³/zɔ³³
DAT	dative	ki³³
DEL	delimitative aspect	dɯ³³ + V
DES	desiderative	hɔ³³
DIM	diminutive	-zɔ³³
DISJ	disjunctive coordinator	nɔ³³
DUR	durative	tʰɯ³³-
EMPH	emphatic	nɯ³³
EXIST	existential: generic	dʑɔ³³
EXIST.C	existential: container	ʐɯ³³
EXIST.P	existential: used with items perpendicular to a plane	di³³
EXIST.T	existential: used with past existence of time	ku³³
EXPER	experienced aspect	tɕi³¹
FOC	focus	nɯ³³
FUT.IMM	future immediate	bi³³
FUT.REM	future remote	hɯ³³
FUT.DES	future predictive (desire)	hɔ³³
FUT.ABL	future predictive (ability)	ku¹³
IMP	imperative	(suppletive forms)
INESS	inessive	kwɔ³³ lɔ³¹
INFR	inference evidential	pʰæ³³-di³³
INSTR	instrumental	pɔ¹³
INTERJ	interjection	hæ³¹, kwæ³¹
INTS	intensifier	ʐwæ¹³
INTSF	intensified (of a stative verb)	SV₁- SV₁
ITER	iterative aspect	dɯ³³ + V₁ V₁
LOC	locative (temporal/spatial)	kwɔ³³
NEG	negative	mə³³-
NOM	nominalizer	-hĩ³³
NOM_Agt	agentive nominalizer	-hĩ³³
NOM_Loc	locative nominalizer	-di³³
NOM_Purp	purposive nominalizer	-di³³
NRA	non-relative attributive	bu³³
OBL	obligative	zɔ³³
PAT	patient	tɔ³¹
PERF	perfective aspect	zɛ³³/zɔ³³
PL	plural	=æ³¹
POSS	possessive	bu³³
POSSIB	possibility	tʰɑ¹³
PROG	progressive aspect	dʑɔ³³
PROH	prohibitive	tʰɑ³³
QM	question marker	ɑ³¹
QUOT	quotative evidential	pi³³
RECIP	reciprocal	V₁ - V₁
REFL	reflexive pronoun	ɔ³¹-bu³³
REL	relativizer	di³³

REP	reported/hearsay evidential	tsi¹³
SEM	semelfactive	[dɯ³³ + V] ~
SV	stative verb	(various)
SVC	serial verb construction	
TOP	topic marker	dʐɔ³³
VEN	venitive	yɔ³³
VOL	volitive	ʂu³³ du³³

References

Agha, Asif. 1993. *Structural form and utterance context in Lhasa Tibetan: Grammar and indexicality in a non-configurational language*. New York: Peter Lang.

Aikhenvald, Alexandra Y. 2006. Serial verb constructions in cross-linguistic perspective. In Alexandra Y. Aikhenvald & R. M. W. Dixon (eds.), *Serial verb constructions: A cross-linguistic typology*, 1–68. Oxford: Oxford University Press.

Aikhenvald, Alexandra Y. 2004. *Evidentiality*. Oxford: Oxford University Press.

Aikhenvald, Alexandra Y. & R. M. W. Dixon (eds.). 2006. *Serial verb constructions: A cross-linguistic typology*. Oxford: Oxford University Press.

Aikhenvald, Alexandra Y. & R. M. W. Dixon (eds.). 2003. *Studies in evidentiality*. Amsterdam: John Benjamins.

Bickel, Balthasar. 2008. Verb agreement and epistemic marking: A typological journey from the Himalayas to the Caucasus. In B. Huber, M. Volkart & P. Widmer (eds.), *Chomolangma, Demawend und Kasbek: Festschrift für Roland Bielmeier zu seinem 65. Geburtstag*, 1–14. Halle: International Institute for Tibetan and Buddhist Studies.

Bickel, Balthasar. 2000. Introduction: Person and evidence in Himalayan languages. *Linguistics of the Tibeto-Burman Area* 23 (2). 1–11.

Bickel, Balthasar. 1999. Nominalization and focus constructions in some Kiranti languages. In Yogendra P. Yadava & Warren G. Glover (eds.), *Topics in Nepalese linguistics*, 271–296. Kathmandu: Royal Nepal Academy.

Bradley, David. 2003. Lisu. In Graham Thurgood & Randy J. LaPolla (eds.), *The Sino-Tibetan languages*, 222–235. London & New York: Routledge.

Bradley, David. 1975. Nahsi and Proto-Burmese-Lolo. *Linguistics of the Tibeto-Burman Area* 2 (1). 93–151.

Bybee, Joan, Revere Perkins & William Pagliuca. 1994. *The evolution of grammar: Tense, aspect, and modality in the languages of the world*. Chicago: The University of Chicago Press.

Caron, Bruce R. 1987. A comparative look at Yao numerical classifiers. *Linguistics of the Tibeto-Burman Area* 10 (2). 151–168.

Chirkova, Katia & Yiya Chen. 2013. Xumi (part 1): Lower Xumi, the variety of the lower and middle reaches of the Shuiluo River. *Journal of the International Phonetic Association* 43 (3). 363–379.

DeLancey, Scott. 1992. The historical status of the conjunct/disjunct pattern in Tibeto-Burman. *Acta Linguistica Hafniensia* 25. 39–62.

DeLancey, Scott. 1986. *Relativization as nominalization in Tibetan and Newari*. Presented at the 19th International Conference on Sino-Tibetan Languages and Linguistics.

Dixon, R. M. W. 2006. Serial verb constructions: Conspectus and coda. In Alexandra Y. Aikhenvald & R. M. W. Dixon (eds.), *Serial verb constructions: A cross-linguistic typology*, 338–350. Oxford: Oxford University Press.

Dryer, Matthew S. 2007a. Word order. In Timothy Shopen (ed.), *Language typology and syntactic description*, vol. 1, 61–131. Cambridge: Cambridge University Press.

Dryer, Matthew S. 2007b. Noun phrase structure. In Timothy Shopen (ed.), *Language typology and syntactic description*, vol. 2, 151–205. Cambridge: Cambridge University Press.

Eliade, Mircea. 1964. *Shamanism: Archaic techniques of ecstasy*. Translated by Willard R. Trask. Princeton: Princeton University Press.

Enfield, Nick. 2003. *Linguistic epidemiology: Semantics and grammar of language contact in Mainland Southeast Asia*. London: Routledge/Curzon.

Evans, Jonathan P. 1999. An introduction to Qiang diachronic phonology: Synchrony and diachrony. PhD dissertation, University of California, Berkeley.

Goral, Donald R. 1978. Numerical classifier systems: A Southeast Asian cross-linguistic analysis. *Linguistics of the Tibeto-Burman Area* 4 (1). 1–72.

Hale, Austin. 1980. Person markers: Finite conjunct and disjunct verb forms in Newari. In Ronald L. Trail et al. (eds.), *Papers in South-east Asian linguistics* 7, 95–106. Canberra: Pacific Linguistics.

Heine, Bernd & Tania Kuteva. 2002. *World lexicon of grammaticalization*. Cambridge: Cambridge University Press.

Hopper, Paul J. & Elizabeth Closs Traugott. 2003 [1993]. *Grammaticalization*. Cambridge: Cambridge University Press.

Jacques, Guillaume & Alexis Michaud. 2011. Approaching the historical phonology of three highly eroded Sino-Tibetan languages. *Diachronica* 28 (4). 468–498 and appendix.

LaPolla, Randy J. 2003b. Overview of Sino-Tibetan morphosyntax. In Graham Thurgood & Randy J. LaPolla (eds.), *The Sino-Tibetan languages*, 22–42. London: Routledge Language Family Series.

LaPolla, Randy J. 2003c. Evidentiality in Qiang. In Alexandra Y. Aikhenvald & R. M. W. Dixon (eds.), *Studies in evidentiality*, 63–78. Amsterdam: John Benjamins.

LaPolla, Randy J. 1995. 'Ergative' marking in Tibeto-Burman. In Yoshio Nishi, James A. Matisoff & Yasuhiko Nagano (eds.), *New horizons in Tibeto-Burman morphosyntax*, 189–228. Osaka, Japan: National Museum of Ethnology.

LaPolla, Randy J. 1992. 'Anti-ergative' marking in Tibeto-Burman. *Linguistics of the Tibeto-Burman Area* 15 (1). 1–9.

Lahaussois, Aimée. 2003. Nominalization and its various uses in Thulung Rai. *Linguistics of the Tibeto-Burman Area* 26 (1). 33–57.

Li, Charles N. & Sandra A. Thompson. 1981. *Mandarin Chinese: A functional reference grammar*. Berkeley, California: University of California Press.

Lidz, Liberty. 2018. Egophoricity and differential access to knowledge in Yongning Na (Mosuo). In Simeon Floyd, Elisabeth Norcliffe, & Lila San Roque (eds.), *Egophoricity*, 153–172. Amsterdam: John Benjamins.

Lidz, Liberty. 2017. Yongning Na (Mosuo). In Graham Thurgood & Randy J. LaPolla (eds.), *The Sino-Tibetan languages*, 2nd ed., 840–855. New York: Routledge.

Lidz, Liberty. 2011. Agentive marking in Yongning Na (Mosuo). *Linguistics of the Tibeto-Burman. Area* 34 (2). 49–72.

Lidz, Liberty. 2010. A descriptive grammar of Yongning Na (Mosuo). PhD dissertation, University of Texas at Austin.

Lidz, Liberty. 2007a. Evidentiality in Yongning Na (Mosuo). *Linguistics of the Tibeto-Burman Area*. 30 (2). 45–87.
Lidz, Liberty. 2007b. Combinatorial complexity: An example from Yongning Na (Mosuo). Presented at the Workshop on Linguistic Typology and Language Documentation during the Association for Linguistic Typology VII conference.
Lord, Carol, Foong Ha Yap & Shoichi Iwasaki. 2002. Grammaticalization of 'give': African and Asian perspectives. In Ilse Wischer & Gabriele Diewald (eds.), *New reflections on grammaticalization,* 217–235. Amsterdam: John Benjamins.
Matisoff, James A. 2004. Areal semantics: Is there such a thing? In Anju Saxena (ed.), *Himalayan languages, past and present*, 347–395. New York: Mouton de Gruyter.
Matisoff, James A. 2003a. Lahu. In Graham Thurgood & Randy J. LaPolla (eds.), *The Sino-Tibetan languages*, 208–221. London & New York: Routledge.
Matisoff, James A. 2003b. *Handbook of Proto-Tibeto-Burman: System and philosophy of Sino-Tibetan reconstruction*. Berkeley: University of California Press.
Matisoff, James A. 1991. Areal and universal dimensions of grammaticalization in Lahu. In Elizabeth Closs Traugott & Bernd Heine (eds.), *Approaches to grammaticalization: Focus on theoretical and methodological issues*, vol. 2, 383–453. London: John Benjamins.
Matisoff, James A. 1986a. Hearts and minds in South-East Asian languages and English: An essay in the comparative lexical semantics of psycho-collocations. *Cahiers de Linguistique Asie Orientale* 15 (1). 5–57.
Matisoff, James A. 1986b. The languages and dialects of Tibeto-Burman: An alphabetic/genetic listing, with some prefactory remarks on ethnonymic and glossonymic complications. In John McCoy & Timothy Light (eds.), *Contributions to Sino-Tibetan studies*. Leiden: Brill.
Matisoff, James A. 1982 [1973]. *The grammar of Lahu*. Berkeley: University of California Press.
Matisoff, James A. 1978. Mpi and Lolo-Burmese microlinguistics. *Monumenta Serindica* 4. 1–36.
Matisoff, James A. 1972. Lahu nominalization, relativization, and genitivization. In John P. Kimball (ed.), *Syntax and semantics*, vol. 1, 237–257. New York & London: Seminar Press.
Mayhew, Bradley & Thomas Huhti. 1998. *Lonely Planet: South-West China*. Hawthorn, Australia: Lonely Planet Publications.
Michaud, Alexis. 2017. *Tone in Yongning Na: Lexical tones and morphology*. (Studies in Diversity Linguistics 13). Berlin: Language Science Press.
Michaud, Alexis. 2008. Phonemic and tonal analysis of Yongning Na. *Cahiers de Linguistique. Asie Orientale* 37 (2). 159–196.
Mortensen, David. 2003. Hmong elaborate expressions are coordinate compounds. Unpublished manuscript, University of California, Berkeley.
Newman, John. 1996. *Give: A cognitive linguistic study*. Berlin & New York: Mouton de Gruyter.
Noonan, Michael. 1997. Versatile nominalizations. In Joan Bybee, John Haiman & Sandra A. Thompson (eds.), *Essays on language function and language type*, 373–394. Amsterdam: Benjamins.
Smith, Carlota S. and Mary S. Erbaugh. 2005. Temporal interpretation in Mandarin Chinese. *Linguistics* 43 (4). 713–756.
Sun, Jackson T.-S. 1993. Evidentials in Amdo Tibetan. *Bulletin of the Institute of History and Philology Academia Sinica* 63. 945–1001.
Thurgood, Graham. 2017. Sino-Tibetan: Genetic and areal subgroups. In Graham Thurgood & Randy J. LaPolla (eds.), *The Sino-Tibetan languages,* 2nd ed., 3–39. New York: Routledge.

Timberlake, Alan. 2007. Aspect, tense, mood. In Timothy Shopen (ed.), *Language typology and syntactic description*, vol. 3, 280–332. Cambridge: Cambridge University Press.

van der Auwera, Johan, Petar Kehayov & Alice Vittrant. 2009. Acquisitive modals. In Lotte Hogeweg, Helen de Hoop & Andrej Malchukov (eds.), *Crosslinguistic semantics of tense, aspect and modality*, 271–302. Amsterdam: John Benjamins.

Vittrant, Alice & Watkins, Justin. 2018. Appendix: Guidelines for writing a Southeast Asian language description. In Alice Vittrant and Justin Watkins (eds.), The mainland Southeast Asia Linguistic area. Berlin: Mouton de Gruyter, 653–686.

Vittrant, Alice. 2008. Burmese as a language of the mainland South-East Asia *sprachbund*. Presented at the 21st International Conference on Sino-Tibetan Languages and Linguistics.

Yang, Zhenhong. 2009. An overview of Mosuo. *Linguistics of the Tibeto-Burman Area* 32 (2). 1–44.

Appendix 1: Summary of linguistic features

Legend
+++ the feature is pervasive or used obligatorily in the language
++ the feature is normal but selectively distributed in the language
+ the feature is merely possible or observable in the language
− the feature is impossible or absent in the language

Language studied: Yongning Na (Mosuo)
Area/countries where it is spoken: Yunnan/Sichuan border, People's Republic of China

	Feature	+++/++/+/−	§ ref. in this chapter
Phonetics	Lexical tone or register	+	§1.1, p.236
Phonetics	Back unrounded vowels	+	§1.2, p.237
Phonetics	Initial velar nasal	+	§1.2, p.237
Phonetics	Implosive consonants	−	−
Phonetics	Sesquisyllabic structures	−	§1.3, p.238
Morphology	Tendency towards monosyllabicity	++	§2.1, p.238
Morphology	Tendency to form compounds	++	§2.1, p.238
Morphology	Tendency towards isolating (rather than affixation)	+++	§2.1, p.338 & p.264
Morphology	Psycho-collocations	+++	§2.2, p.239
Morphology	Elaborate expressions (e.g. four-syllable or other set patterns)	+++	§2.3, p.241
Morphology	Reduplication generally	+++	§2.4, p.241

	Feature	+++/++/+/−	§ ref. in this chapter
Morphology	Reduplication of nouns	+	§2.4, p.241
Morphology	Reduplication of verbs	+++	§2.4, p.241–42
Grammar	Use of classifiers	+++	§3.1.2, p.243
Grammar	Classifiers used in counting	++(+)	§3.1.2, p.244
Grammar	Classifiers used with demonstratives	++	§3.1.2, p.244
Grammar	Adjectival verbs	+++	not discussed explicitly
Grammar	Grammatical number	+++	§3.2, p.271
Grammar	Inflection of verbs	−	§3.2, p.245
Grammar	Use of tense/aspect markers	+++	§3.2, p.245 & §3.2.2, p.247
Grammar	Use of verb plural markers	−	§3.2, p.245
Grammar	Grammaticalization of GET/OBTAIN (potential mod. resultative/perfect aspect)	−	§3.2.3, p.250
Grammar	Grammaticalization of PUT, SET (completed/resultative aspect)	−	§3.2.3, p.251
Grammar	Grammaticalization of GIVE (causative, benefactive; preposition)	++	§3.2.3, p.251
Grammar	Grammaticalization of FINISH (perfective/ complete aspect; conjunction/temporal subordinator)	++	§3.2.2 FINISH > completive aspect (not fully grammaticalized); also appears in phasal/aspectual complementation as an SVC. Not discussed explicitly
Grammar	Grammaticalization of directional verbs e.g. GO / COME (allative, venitive)	+++	§3.2.3, p.251–52
Grammar	Grammaticalization of SEE, WATCH (temptative)	−	−
Grammar	Grammaticalization of STAY, REMAIN (progressive and continuous, durative aspects)	−	§3.2.3, p.253
Grammar	Serial verb constructions	++	§3.2.4, p.253
Grammar	Converbs	−	−
Syntax	Verb precedes object (VO)	−	§3.3, p.255
Syntax	Auxiliary precedes verb	−	§3.2, Table 5, p.246
Syntax	Preposition precedes noun	−	§3.1.1, p.243
Syntax	Noun precedes adjective	+	§3.1.1, p.243
Syntax	Noun precedes demonstrative	++	§3.1.1, p.243
Syntax	Noun precedes genitive	++	§3.1.1, p.243

	Feature	+++/++/+/−	§ ref. in this chapter
Syntax	Noun precedes relative clause	++	§3.1.1
Syntax	Use of topic-comment structures	+++	§3.3.2, p.256
Syntax	Ellipsis of arguments known from context	+++	§3.3, p.255 & §3.3.1, p.256
Lexical semantics	Specific terms for forms of rice	+++	§4.1.1, p.260
Lexical semantics	Use of utterance-final pragmatic particles	+++	§4.2.1, p.263–64
Lexical semantics	Encoding of politeness	−	§4.2.2, p.264
Lexical semantics	Encoding of honorifics	−	−

Appendix 2: Text interlinearized

tsʰɔ³¹ du³³ lu³³ yi³³ zɔ³³   pi³³   jiushi (loan)   ɔ̃³¹-sɤ³³ ku³¹   na¹³   bu³³
Tsodeluyizo   be called   that is   1INC.PRO   Na   POSS
'Tsodeluyizo, that is, our Na Tsodeluyizo
Tsodeluyizo.1

tsʰɔ³¹ du³³ lu³³ yi³³ zɔ³³   la³³   tsʰɤ³¹ hɔ̃⁵⁵ tsɛ³³ tsɛ³³ mi³³
Tsodeluyizo   and   Tsuhodzedzemi
of Tsodeluyizo and Tsuhodzedzemi,

tsʰɔ³¹ du³³ lu³³ yi³³ zɔ³³   pi³³   dzɔ³³   zɔ³³   tʰɯ³³   du³³   wu³³   ni³³.
Tsodeluyizo   be called   TOP   boy   3SG.PRO one   CLF   COP
Tsodeluyizo, he was a boy.

tʰɯ³³   a³¹ yi³³ ʂɛ³³   dzɔ³³   ʐɯ³¹ mu³³ ku³³   la³³   du³³   ʐɯ³³   ni³³   tsi¹³.
3SG.PRO   long, long ago   TOP   Zhimuku   and   one   family COP   REP
It is said (that) a long time ago, he and Zhimuku were a family.
Tsodeluyizo.2

ʐɯ³¹ mu³³ ku³³   la³³   hĩ³³   dzɔ³³   du³³   ʐɯ³³   ni³³   tsi¹³.
Zhimuku   and   people   TOP   one   family COP   REP
Zhimuku and people were of one family, it is said.
Tsodeluyizo.3

ʐɯ³¹ mu³³ ku³³   dzɔ³³   hæ³³ qʰv̩³³   ta³¹   lɔ̃³¹-yi³³ hĩ³³   dzɔ³³   ɲi³³-łi³¹ ku³³   lɔ̃³¹-yi³³.
Zhimuku   TOP   evening   only   labor   people   TOP   daytime   labor
Zhimuku worked only at night, (but) people worked during the day.
Tsodeluyizo.4

mə³³-hɔ³³-hɔ³³   dzɔ³³   tʰɯ³³ kwɔ³³ ɲi³³...   ʐɯ³¹ mu³³ ku³³   dzɔ³³
incompatible   TOP   absolutely   Zhimuku   TOP
Completely incompatible...   as for 'Zhimuku,'
Tsodeluyizo.5

ɔ̃³¹-sʁ³³ ku³¹   pi³³   dzɔ³³   dʑi³³-qʰv̩³³   la³³   tʰæ¹³   ɲi³³.
1INC.PRO   say   COMPL   spring (of water)   and   such   COP
we say, "'spring' and such."

a³³-wɔ³³   a³¹ yi³³ ʂe³³   dzɔ³³   du³³   ʐɯ³³   ɲi³³   tsi¹³.   wɔ³³ ta³³   dzɔ³³
home   long, long ago   TOP   one   family COP   REP   before   TOP
It is said (that) a long time ago, (they) were one family.   Before,
Tsodeluyizo.6   Tsodeluyizo.7

du³³   ʐɯ³³   yi³³   dzɔ³³   hĩ³³   dzɔ³³   ɔ̃³¹-sʁ³³ ku³¹   hĩ³³   dzɔ³³
one   family   make   TOP   people TOP   1INC.PRO   people   TOP
(they) were one family, people, we humans,

pi³³ li³³ pi³³ tsʰɯ³¹ zɔ³³   dzɔ³³   tʰæ̃³³   ɲi³³-łi³¹ ku³³   lɔ̃³¹-yi³³
pilipitsizo⁷   TOP   often   daytime   labor
'pilipitsizo' would often labor during the day,

ʐɯ³¹ mu³³ ku³³   nɯ³³   dzɔ³³   tʰɑ̃³³   hæ³³ qʰv̩³³   ta³¹   lɔ̃³¹-yi³³.
Zhimuku   CONTR   TOP   often   night   only   labor
(but) Zhimuku would often labor only at night.

hæ³³ qʰv̩³³   lɔ̃³¹-yi³³   zɔ³³   tʰɯ³³ kwɔ³³ ɲi³¹   mə³³-hɔ³³-hɔ³³   zɔ³³
night   labor   OBL   absolutely   NEG-compatible   PERF
Having to work at night was absolutely incompatible,
Tsodeluyizo.8

---

7 'Pilipitsizo' is a term of humility used by the Na to refer to themselves. It can also be used as an insult.

ʐɯ³³-tʰu¹³		bi³³	pi³³	ni³³.	ʐɯ³³-tʰu¹³		nɔ³³	tʰi¹³
separate families		FUT.IMM	QUOT	CERT.STR	separate families		then	so

(so they) said, "(We) will split into separate families." In splitting families, Tsodeluyizo.9

ʐɯ³¹ mu³³ ku³³	tʰɯ³³	nɯ³³	dʐɔ³³	sɤ³¹ tʂʰɤ³¹	ʐɯ³¹-kwɔ³³	gɤ⁵⁵	dʐɤ¹³
Zhimuku	3SG.PRO	AGTV	COMPL	landscape	wherever	side	good

Zhimuku said, "(I) want for myself wherever the landscape is good...

dʐɔ³³...	wɤ³³	la³³	tʰæ¹³	sɤ³¹ tʂʰɤ³¹	ʐɯ³¹-kwɔ³³	dʐɤ¹³	dʐɔ³³
TOP	mountain	and	such	landscape	wherever	good	TOP

mountains and such, wherever the landscape is good,"

nɔ¹³	ɲi³³	pi³³.	tʏ³³-di³¹		yi³¹ ha¹³	nɔ¹³	ɲi³³	pi³³.
REFL	want	QUOT	wings-EXIST.P		all	REFL	want	QUOT

(they) say. (She) said (she) wanted for herself everything with wings. Tsodeluyizo.10

tʰɯ³³-ni¹³	ku³³	ni³³	tsi¹³.	tʏ³³-di³¹-hĩ³³		ʒ³¹-sɤ³³ ku³¹
this way	seem	COP	REP	wings-EXIST.P-NOM		1INC.PRO

It is said that it was like this. Things with wings, our Tsodeluyizo.11 Tsodeluyizo.12

dʑi³³ wɤ³³		gɤ⁵⁵	wu³¹-dzɛ³³	la³³	læ³¹ yæ̃³³	la³³	nu⁵⁵ ɕi³¹-hĩ³³	tʰæ¹³...
in the mountains		side	bird	and	crow	and	beautiful-NOM	such

birds and crows in the mountains, and beautiful things and such...

ʒ³¹-sɤ³³ ku³¹	pi³³ li³³ pi³³ tsʰɯ³¹ zɔ³³		ki³³	dʐɔ³³	æ̃¹³	la³³	tʰæ¹³
1INC.PRO	pilipitsizo		DAT	TOP	chicken	and	such

(Given) to us people, chickens and such, Tsodeluyizo.13

tʏ³³-di³¹-hĩ³³		tʰɯ³³-ni¹³	dɯ³³-pi¹³	ta³¹	ki³³	dzɛ³³	ku¹³	tʰɯ³³-ni¹³
wings-EXIST.P-NOM		this kind	some	only	give	fly	ABLT	this kind

(of) things with wings, only some of these (chickens) were given; (of) things that can fly,

dɯ³³-pi¹³	ta³¹	ki³³.	ni³³ zɔ³³	pʁ³³ tɔ³¹	ʐɯ³¹ mu³³	ku³³	bu³³	tʂʁ³³.
some	only	give	fish	all	Zhimuku		POSS	allot

only (chickens) were given All fish were allotted as Zhimuku's.
(to us). Tsodeluyizo.14

tʰɯ³³-ni¹³   ʐɯ³³-tʰu¹³.
this way   separate families
(They) split households in this way.'
Tsodeluyizo.15

Appendix 3

Map 1: Southwestern China in situ
Redrawn from Mayhew and Huhti 1998 (insert between pp. 16–17)

Mathias Jenny
Mon

Introduction

Mon (အရေိဝ်မန် *ʔərè mɔ̀n*, ဘာသာမန် *phèəsa mɔ̀n*), a member of the Monic branch of Mon-Khmer, is spoken today by about 800,000 to one million speakers (depending on the source) in southern Burma[1] and along the southern stretch of the Thai-Burmese border, besides a few communities in central and northern Thailand. The closest relative of Mon is Nyahkur, a language spoken by 1000–4000 speakers (different sources) in the region between central and northeastern Thailand. Nyahkur has convincingly been shown by Diffloth (1984) to be a direct offshoot of the Mon language spoken in Dvāravatī, which was separated from the bulk of Mon around the 10th century.

The areas where Mon is spoken today are the residue of a once large cultural area covering southern Burma, central Thailand and parts of north and northwestern Thailand up to the region of Vientiane in Laos. Mon apparently was the vernacular used in large parts of what has come to be known as the Dvāravatī cultural area that flourished in the region between the 4th and 10th centuries, before central Thailand became part of the Khmer empire of Angkor and later the Tai kingdom of Sukhothai and Ayudhya. The earliest inscriptions in Mon date back to the 6th century and were found in central Thailand, around Nakhon Pathom and Lopburi. In the 11th century, Mon was introduced as literary language in the Burmese empire of Pagán, together with Pali and the perhaps then already extinct Pyu, which probably had religious and ceremonial status. Mon was in use here for about a century, before being gradually replaced by Burmese.

While Mon was superseded in central and upper Burma by Burmese, its use as language of everyday conversation as well as commerce and culture continued in the southern parts of the country, which at different times formed inde-

---

[1] I use the terms Burma and Burmese throughout this paper, rather than Myanmar, as the latter seems still to be less commonly used in European languages and lacks the noun-adjective distinction of the former terms. Other Burmese place names are given in their most common spellings, which usually are the same as the traditional ones used in European sources.

Mathias Jenny: Department of Comparative Linguistics, University of Zurich
E-Mail: mathias.jenny@uzh.ch

pendent Mon kingdoms at Martaban and Pegu, also known as Haṁsāvatī. Smaller Mon communities were spread across the Irrawaddy Delta as far west as Bassein.

The history of the Mon language can be conveniently divided into three periods:
1. Old Mon: 6th–14th century
2. Middle Mon: 14th–17th century
3. Modern Mon: after 17th century

Modern Mon can be further divided into (classical) Literary Mon and Spoken Mon. The two varieties differ in vocabulary and sentence structure. Both are far from being a unified linguistic system, but consist of a number of varieties, depending on geographical region as well as register. It is probable that these distinctions existed in earlier periods of the language, but we do not have any records of the colloquial language prior to the modern period, and more research is needed to work out a historical dialectology of Mon from the inscriptions.

Today Mon does not have official status in the Union of the Republic of Myanmar, but it is used as the means of everyday communication and taught in some 300 Mon schools in Mon and Kayin (Karen) States and in Tanintharyi (Tenasserim) Region in Burma, which offer full instruction in Mon. Literacy in Mon is believed to be about 25% and increasing over the past few years, though accurate numbers are impossible to come by. A large number of popular songs in Mon are produced every year, mostly with accompanying karaoke videos. The few publications in Mon within Burma are mostly religious texts, though there are a number of reprints of literary and historical texts. Mon has recently been included in the Myanmar block of Unicode, which may allow Mon text to be digitized following internationally accepted standards. The few online journals publishing in Mon, run by overseas communities, will hopefully soon follow this development.

The linguistic situation of the Mon is far from clear. Given the number of speakers, Mon cannot be considered an endangered language, but two factors threaten its survival in the long term. Firstly, most Mon are bilingual, speaking also Burmese and/or Thai. In the case of the Mon in Thailand, known as Thai-Raman, Thai is clearly their first language in terms of proficiency, with many speakers being semi-speakers. In Burma, Mon is less threatened, as there are still villages where children grow up speaking Mon as their first language, learning Burmese only at school and in their dealings with state institutions. But here also there are very few monolingual speakers. Secondly, there is no generally accepted standard variety of the Mon language, either spoken or written. The dialects vary greatly in pronunciation, and the orthography is very inconsistent in many respects. In spite of these problems, Mon seems to be viable, and its use may even be increasing with the political reforms in Burma since 2010 allowing greater freedom for minority ethnic nationalities..

1 Phonology

Like several other Mainland Southeast Asian languages, Mon is written in an Indic-derived syllabic (or abugida-type[2]) script, which only approximately reflects the phonology of the spoken language. While the inventory of 35 consonant letters in the script is sufficient to represent the consonant sounds and clusters occurring in Mon, the script's provision for Indic vowels (a ā i ī u ū e o) does not cater for the vowel distinctions of spoken Mon. Even the invention of new signs and combinations still leaves room for ambiguity. Major changes occurred in the phonology of Mon between Old Mon and some time before Modern Mon[3], devoicing all voiced stops, giving rise to two distinct phonation types or registers. Different authors vary in the dating of these sound changes, but most agree that they occurred rather late, maybe as late as the 16th century. These changes are not reflected in the orthography, which means that the written language represents a pre-devoiced state. In other words, the voicing contrast in the voicedness distinctions in the orthography to express register distinctions, similar to the reading of the two vowel series in Khmer (see chapter on Khmer, this volume) or the tone rules in modern Thai (see chapter on Thai, this volume). Providing a description of the phonology of Mon is made difficult by the absence of a standard form of the language. The description below is based on the analysis of a number of dialects from different regions in Burma (see Jenny 2005 for details). It does not include the varieties of Mon spoken in Thailand.

1.1 Segmental phonemes

The inventories of both consonants and vowels are rather rich in Mon. While the set of initial consonants is straightforward, the vowels and final consonants are

---

[2] An abugida script contains symbols that denote a consonant accompanied by a specific vowel. See Daniel & Bright (1996: 4, 385–87) for details.
[3] Old Mon covers a period starting from 6th century AD up to 11th century; Middle mon correspond to the 12th to 20th century. And Moderne Mon refer to the language spoken these days.

harder to describe independently, as they influence one other. Syllable rhymes also exhibit the greatest variation between dialects. In initial position, there is at least one and at most two consonants, while only one final consonant is allowed. A syllable may end in a consonant or a vowel/diphthong.

The simple initial consonants are given in the following table. The aspirated sonorants (hɲ hn hm) are realized as partly voiceless sonorants [ɲ̥ɲ n̥n m̥m],. In older stages of Mon, aspirated stops they are best analysed as clusters of stop + h because of their behaviour in the context of various morphological processes, but this analysis is not possible in the modern language..

Table 1: Initial consonant phonemes and their orthographic counterparts

	k	kh	ŋ				က ဂ	ဒ ဃ	ç
ɕ	c	ch	ɲ	hɲ	ၜ	ၐ ဃ	ဆ ၛ	ၛ	ၛ
ɗ	t	th	n	hn	ၒ	ဘ ၃	ထ ၔ	ၒ ထ	ၒ
ɓ	p	ph	m	hm	ၑ ၕ	ပ ဗ	ဖ ဘ	မ	မ
y	r	l	hl	w	ဃ	ရ	ၐ ထ	လ	၀
hw	s	ʃ	h	ʔ	၀	သ	ၐ	ၐ	အ

Of the initials listed above, ɕ occurs only in very few words, and only with the rhyme -iəʔ (which, in turn, occurs only with this initial), so its phonemic status is not certain. It merges with ʃ in some dialects, and with palatal c in others. The initial ʃ on the other hand occurs only in loans from Burmese and English loan words. The voiceless bilabial approximant hw is variously pronounced as [xw], [w̥] or [ɸ ~ f]. The implosives ɗ and ɓ are pronounced as fully voiced implosive or preglottalized stops..

Initial clusters are allowed only with a velar or labial stop in first and a liquid in second position.

Table 2: Initial clusters

ky	kr	kl	kw	ကျ ကြ	ကြ ကြ	က ၀	က ၀
khy	khr	khl	khw	ၛ	ၐ	၀	၀
py	pr	pl		ပျ ပြ	ပ ပ	ပ ပ	
phy	phr	phl		ၛ	ၐ	ၐ	

The cluster *ky* merges with the palatal stop c in the northern dialects but is pronounced like [ky] or [cy] in the southern dialects, where its phonemic status is shown by the existence of minimal pairs like *kyac* 'Buddha, sacred object' vs. *cac* 'be torn'. The combination *khy* on the other hand is kept distinct from *ch* in only a few conservative dialects (and in the orthography).

Turning to the inventory of syllable rhymes, there are a number of vowel-final combinations which do not occur, accounting for the gaps in the table of syllable rhymes below. Furthermore, not all rhymes occur in both registers.

Vowels in Mon generally tend to be centralized and diphthongized. Thus *i* is pronounced rather like [ɨ] or [ɨi] and *u* like [ʉ] or [ɤʉ]. The mid front vowel *e* is pronounced very high, approaching [ɪ] or even [i], similarly *o* is [ʊ] or [u], in some dialects and contexts more like [ʊŏ] or [oŏ]. In many dialects *ɒ* approaches [ɔ], while *ɔ* is realized with an off-glide [ɔŏ]. In certain dialects the diphthongs *eə* and *ɛə* merge, while in some the merger includes also *iə*. A similar merger is true for the diphthongs *ɒə, ɔə, oə* and *uə*. As in other Mon-Khmer languages, final palatal consonants are preceded by a palatal off-glide after the vowel, so that *ac* is pronounced [aⁱc]. The rhymes *ɤk* and *ɤŋ* as well as *ak* and *aŋ* are pronounced with palatal finals a number of dialects, i.e. [ɤc], [ɤɲ] and [ɒc], [ɒɲ], the latter very close to [ac], [aɲ]. The rhyme *ɒəh* seems to occur only in one lexeme in some dialects, viz. *(pərɔc) həmɒəh* 'pepper'. Vowel quantity is not contrastive. Vowels in open syllables are phonetically longer than vowels in closed syllables. Syllables with final ʔ and h have particularly short vowels.

Table 3: Syllable rhymes

V	Vʔ	Vh	Vy	VC$_{velar}$		VC$_{palatal}$		VC$_{dental/labial}$
monophthongs								
i	iʔ	ih		iək	iəŋ			it in ip im
e	eʔ	eh						et en ep em
ɛ	ɛʔ	ɛh		ɛk	ɛŋ			ɛt ɛn ɛp ɛm
a	aʔ	ah	ay	ak	aŋ	ac	aɲ	at an ap am
ɒ	ɒʔ	ɒh						ɒt ɒn ɒp ɒm
ɤ	ɤʔ	ɤh	ɤy	ɤk	ɤŋ			ɤt ɤn ɤp ɤm
ɔ	ɔʔ	ɔh		ɔk	ɔŋ	ɔc	ɔɲ	ɔt ɔn ɔp ɔm
o	oʔ	oh	oy	ok	oŋ	oc	oɲ	ot on op om
u	uʔ	uh	uy					ut un up um
diphthongs								
iə	iəʔ							
eə								
ɛə								

V	Vʔ	Vh	Vy	VC_velar	VC_palatal	VC_dental/labial
ɒə	ɒəʔ	ɒəh				
ɔə						
oə						
uə						
ao	aoʔ	aoh				

1.2 Suprasegmental phonemes

Phrasal stress increases towards the end of a phrase, peaking with the last lexical word, which may be followed by postverbal auxiliaries and final particles, including the topic marker *kɔ̀h*.

Mon is not a tonal language, but each major syllable is assigned one of two registers, variously labelled 'clear' vs. 'breathy', 'head' vs. "chest", 'light' vs. 'heavy', or simply 'first' vs. 'second' register. While pitch may be involved especially in elicitation pronunciation, the main feature of the registers is phonation type. The first register is pronounced with a clear, modal or tense voice, while the second register is characterized by lax pronunciation and some breathiness throughout the syllable (but not resulting in the aspiration of the initial consonant). This often comes with a lower pitch, which is not phonemic and can be overridden by prosody. The second register is indicated (following Shorto 1962) with a grave accent over the vowel or the main part of a diphthong: *à, ùə*.

The rhymes including the vowel *ɒ* and the diphthong *ao* do not occur in second register syllables, neither does the rhyme *oə*. The diphthongs *eə* and *ɛə* on the other hand are found only in the second register. The asymmetrical distribution is a result of the role of register in the development of diphthongs.

1.3 Syllable structure

The syllable in Mon consists of at least an initial consonant and a rhyme. Minimal rhymes are either a long vowel or a diphthong, or a short vowel followed by a consonant, i.e. a rhyme must be two morae in length. A syllable may be preceded by a minor syllable, which consists of a single initial from a restricted set and the neutral vowel *ə*. The number of possible onsets of minor syllables varies somewhat with dialects and registers of language, but most commonly only *k, t, p, m, h,* and *ʔ* occur in this position. In formal pronunciation (or in formal words used in colloquial speech), *s, c, ch, n, r, l,* and *y* are also found. There is no register distinction in minor syllable or presyllables. The syllable structure can be summarized as follows:

CVV, CVC, CCVV, CCVC all with or without presyllable Cə-.

2 Word structure

2.1 Derivational morphology

Old Mon had a productive system of derivational morphology and at least one inflectional prefix, viz. *s-* for what Shorto calls "hypothetical" mode, probably irrealis or prospective. Derivation in Old Mon is achieved by means of prefixes and infixes, depending mainly on the syllable structure of the base lexeme. Phonetic reduction of the left periphery of the word led to a merger of many of these affixes ("affix syncretism") The result in modern spoken Mon is a restricted set of presyllables and a general derivational prefix *hə-* (examples 2, 3, 4, table 4). This general prefix *hə-* is the only partly productive prefix in the modern language, all other affixes surviving only in lexicalized forms. Otherwise, the Old Mon inflectional prefix remains only in the written language, but it is not pronounced in speaking. The following examples illustrate the development of derivational affixes from Old Mon to modern written and spoken Mon.

Table 4: Affixes in Old Mon, Middle Mon and modern Literary and Spoken Mon

	Old Mon	Middle Mon	Literary Mon		Spoken Mon	Gloss
1	gluṅ	glaṅ	ဂ္လိင်	glaṅ	klàŋ	be numerous
2	girluṅ	gralaṅ	ဂလိုင်	galaṅ	həlàŋ	quantity
3	gumluṅ	gamlaṅ	ဂမ္လိင်	gamlaṅ	həlàŋ	many
4	*guluṅ	*galaṅ	ဂလိင်	ga-laṅ	həlàŋ	increase
5	ñāc	ñāt	ညာတ်	ñāt	ɲàt	see
6	ñirñāc	?	လညာတ်	lañāt	kəɲàt	sight
7	tīt	tit	တိတ်	tit	tɛt	move out
8	ptīt	ptit	ပ္တိတ်	ptit	pətɛt	bring out

In the spoken language, the prefix *pə-*, which forms causatives of stative and dynamic base verbs, is replaced in some dialects by the general prefix *hə-*, which, among others, is derived from the original causative infix *-u-* after an original voiced initial. This prefix has retained some productivity in spoken Mon, as in the word *həpyrk* 'to ruin', apparently based on a recent loan from Burmese ပြုပ် *pyouʔ* 'fall off'. That the loan is recent is shown by the initial cluster for Burmese *py-*, written <pr->, which in older loans is retained as *pr-* in Mon (s. Jenny 2005: 122f). Nominalizations of the type of *ñirñāc* (example 6, table 4) with the nominalising infix inserted after reduplication of a single initial consonant led to a generalization of a prefix *la-* (< *r-*), which is used mostly in formal contexts, rarely in the spoken language. The pronunciation varies between *lə-* and *kə-/ʔə-*.

Nominalization in modern Mon is achieved by compounding, while the only fully productive causativising device is a periphrastic expression involving preverbal (*paʔ*) *kɒ* '(do) give' (see 3.2.3).

2.2 Compounding

Compounding is a frequent device in spoken Mon to derive new lexemes, both nominal and verbal. The the composition of the vast majority of compound words is transparent, but in some cases old compounds were phonetically reduced giving the appearance of monomorphemic sesquisyllabic words, e.g. *ləkyac* 'monk' from *kəlaʔ kyac* 'lord of the Sacred Being'.

More common are expressions combining a generic term with a more specific one, like *hʋəʔ-ɗac* 'bathroom', lit. 'house – water', where both elements are nouns. In other cases the modifier is verbal, as in *mənìh-hnòk* 'adult', lit. 'person-big'. In such compounds the modifying element follows the modified head. In loans borrowed from Burmese, the modifier-head order of Burmese may be reversed in the Mon version (like *ka-làɲ* 'bus' from Burmese *làin-kà*, from English 'line-car'), or else the Burmese word is imported whole and not internatlly reordered (like *mì-yətha* 'train' from Burmese *mi³-yətha³*, lit. 'fire + vehicle').

(1) a. *hʋəʔ-ɗac*   'house water'   >'bathroom'
    b. *mənìh-hnòk*   'person-big'   > 'adult'
    c. *ka-làɲ*   (Bur) laiN³-ka³ 'line-car'   > 'bus'
    d. *mì-yətha*   (Bur) *mi³-yətha³* –'fire-chariot'   > 'train'

One common type of head-modifier compounding has a general class term preceding a more specific term. These 'class terms' are used regularly in many semantic domains (see Grinevald 1999, Vittrant 2002 on class terms). If the referent of the specific term is taken to be common knowledge, the class term can in some cases be dropped. Examples of class term are *sɔt* 'fruit', *nɔm* 'plant, tree', *həcem* 'bird', *kaʔ* 'fish', *dɤŋ* 'town, country', etc. Class terms also have disambiguating function, as in *nɔm krɤk* 'mango tree', *sɔt krɤk* 'mango (fruit)' and *dɤŋ krɤk* 'China'.[4] The 'dummy nominal head' *ɓɛ̀ʔ* functions as referential marker in colloquial Mon and can occur before any noun. The nominal head *sɛ̀k* (sometimes *sɔ̀k*) forms nouns from verbs with the meaning 'something to V', as in *sɛ̀k ɕiəʔ* 'something to eat, food' and *sɛ̀k ʔa* 'a place/reason to go'.

In other compounds the component parts make up a new meaning by addition, rather than modification, as in *mìʔ-mɛ̀ʔ* 'parents', lit. 'mother-father' and *dɤŋ-kwan* 'country, land', lit. 'town-village'.

(2) a. *nɔm krɤk*   'plant-mango'   'mango tree'
    b. *sɔt krɤk*   'fruit-mango'   'mango (fruit)'
    c. *sɛ̀k ɕiəʔ*   NMLZ-'eat'   'something to eat, food'
    d. *sɛ̀k ʔa*   NMLZ-'go'   'a place/reason to go'
    e. *mìʔ-mɛ̀ʔ*   'mother-father' 'parents'
    f. *dɤŋ-kwan*   'town-village'   'country, land'.

Compounding is the only productive process available to form nouns from verbs. This process is observed to be especially common in formal registers like newspapers and translations from Burmese and English. Otherwise, many verbs have lexicalized nominal forms (like *klon* 'do' vs. *kəlon* 'work n.'). In most other cases a verbal expression is preferred in the spoken language.

Common nominal heads for deriving nouns from verbs are *pərao* and *pəriəŋ* 'story, affair'. Less frequent (and more formal) are expressions with *hətɔ̀h mə* V, lit. 'the fact that V', which is syntactically a complex phrase with a nominal head followed by a relative clause, rather than a simple compound.

Verbal compounds occur frequently, both indigenous and borrowed from Burmese. In many cases a distinction between verbal compounds and serialization cannot be easily made. The main criterion to assign an expression to the latter is the greater degree of productivity (see § 3.2.2). Examples of verbal compounds are given in the following table.

---

[4] The homonymy of 'mango' and 'Chinese' in modern Mon is a historical accident. While krɤk 'mango' is an inherited Mon-Khmer lexeme, krɤk 'Chinese' (originally 'Turk' > 'Mongol') is a more recent loan, ultimately from Sanskrit *turuṣka* 'Mongol', cf. Burmese တရုပ် ‹trut›.

Table 5: Verbal compounds

ချုတ်	khyʊt	die	ပိုတ်	plʊt	extinguished	ချုတ်ပိုတ်	khyʊt.plʊt	certain
ဖုံ	phuy	mix	ဖက်	phɛk	associate	ဖုံဖက်	phuy.phɛk	mix
ဂွံင်	kwòɲ	worry	ဖောက်	phɔc	afraid	ဂွံင်ဖောက်	kwòɲ.phɔc	worry
အလော်	halɤʔ	instruct	ဉ္ဇာန်	hətɔn	teach	အလော်ဇ္ဇာန်	halɤʔ.hətɔn	educate

2.3 "Psycho-collocations" and generic V-O expressions

Psycho-collocations as defined by Matisoff (1986) are compounds made up of a term designating the seat of emotions and a modifying element, usually verbal, to describe a certain feeling or emotional state. The normal centre of emotions in Mon is *cʊt* 'mind' (from Pali *citta*). This is not the same as the anatomical 'heart', which in Mon is called *kon kəmɔʔ* or *kon phyun krɤ̀h*. The noun *cʊt* can precede or follow the descriptive element, depending on whether a permanent trait or a passing feeling is expressed (see in example 3). Usually expressions with *cʊt* preceding the modifier express a permanent disposition, but this rule is not absolute as illustrated by the last three examples in (3):

(3) စိတ်ကေဲ့   *cʊt klɛʔ*   'short tempered'   lit. 'heart – short'
    မှပ်ရိုင်   *cʊt klòɲ*   'tolerant'   lit. 'heart – long'
    စိတ်ပြုဟ်   *cʊt prɔh*   'impulsive'   lit. 'heart – quick'

    စိတ်ရုက်   *cʊt ʃɤk*   'troubled'   lit. 'heart – trouble'
    စိတ်လျမ်း   *cʊt lɤ̀m*   'discouraged'   lit. 'heart – destroyed'
    စိတ်ထု   *cʊt thuy*   'at one's wits' end' lit. 'heart – disturbed'

    မိပ်စိတ်   *mìp cʊt*   'happy'   lit. 'happy – heart'
    အောန်စိတ်   *ʔon cʊt*   'sad'   lit. 'little – heart'
    ပေင်စိတ်   *pɔɲ cʊt*   'agree'   lit. 'full – heart'

Another type of psycho-collocation involves an active verb followed by *cʊt*. The interpretation here is usually that X does something which has an effect on Y's state of mind. In some cases the affectee is identical to the agent.

(4) ဖျေံစိတ်   *phyeh cʊt*   'make up one's mind' lit. 'put down - heart'
    ပရေစိတ်   *pəre cʊt*   'comfort, appease'   lit. 'appease - heart'
    တၟိုဟ်စိတ်   *kəmʊh cʊt*   'make happy'   lit. '(make) overflow - heart'

Some verbs require a generic object if no specific object is overtly expressed or present in the discourse context. After the first mention, the generic object is dropped. The choice of generic object is lexically determined, and the semantic connection is usually transparent. The generic object is not referential and cannot be modified or referred to by an anaphoric element later in the discourse, but generic objects can be (and often are) replaced by a specific, and sometimes referential, object as the discourse develops. The following examples illustrate verbs with generic objects.

(5) စပုင်   ɕiəʔ pɤŋ   'eat (rice)'   သုင်ဍၚ်   sɤŋ ɗac   'drink (water)'
     ဖျာန်လိက်   həton lòc   'study (text)'   ဗ္လိက်   pɔ̀h lòc   'read (text)'
     ချူလိက်   khyu lòc   'write (text)'   ဟုံဍၚ်   hum ɗac   'bathe (water)'

2.4 Elaborate expressions, ideophones and euphonic compounds

Elaborate expressions, usually consisting of four morphemes, are found largely in poetic language, though much less frequently in ordinary speech. The connection between the elements is not fixed: it can be purely phonetic, semantic, or syntactic. One common type of elaborate expressions consists of two semantically related and syntactically parallel phrases, which together make up a new meaning, like *thʊʔ krɤ̀p kɤ̀ʔ wèə* 'go through forests and fields', lit. 'abandon - forest - get - field'. In other cases one part is added for purely euphonic reasons, without adding semantic content. The difference between elaborate expressions and euphonic compounds (described below) lies in the fact that in elaborate expressions all parts occur as lexical items with their own semantics in other contexts. One example of this type of expression is *sɔt chuʔ sɔt tùn* 'fruit', lit. 'fruit - wood - fruit - bamboo', with *sɔt chuʔ* being the common word for 'fruit'.

Ideophones describing sounds or other perceptual impressions occur frequently in poetic language, but only rarely in everyday speech. They are usually made up of two identical, or rhyming or alliterating syllables[5]. Examples are *tèŋ-tèŋ* 'with a creaking, grating noise', *tìn-thin-tìn-thin* 'with a drumming noise', *phyi-phyi-phya-phya* 'with a flashing light, like lightening'.

Euphonic compounds are made up of a lexical element and a semantically empty element which shares the onset or the rhyme with the lexical part. Usu-

---

5 See Sidwell 2014 on expressives in Austro-asiatic languages.

ally the lexical element precedes the euphonic syllable, but this order is reversed in some cases. as in *hman-hmɤk* 'to question' (*hman* 'ask', alliteration *hmɤk*), *mìp-sìp* 'happy' (*mìp* 'happy', rhyme *sìp*), *ɲìʔ-ɲèʔ* 'a little bit' (*ɲìʔ* 'little', alliteration *ɲèʔ*), and *kəre-kərot* 'lament' (alliteration *kəre*, *kərot* 'complain, lament',). In some rhyming or alliterative compounds both syllables occur only in the compound and are not synchronically independent lexemes, as in *dʊp-dʿao* 'green, lush'.

(6) a. *hman-hmɤk* 'to question' *hman* 'ask' + *hmɤk*
    b. *mìp-sìp* 'happy' *mìp* 'happy' + *sìp*
    c. *ɲìʔ-ɲèʔ* 'a little bit' *ɲìʔ* 'little' + *ɲèʔ*
    d. *kəre-kərot* 'lament' *kərot* 'complain, lament' + *kəre*

2.5 Reduplication

Reduplication of whole words occurs mostly with verbs, and occasionally with pronouns or nouns, with different functions. One common function of the reduplication of verbs is the formation of adverbial expressions, often used in an imperative sentence.

(4) a. အာပြှပ်ဟ်။[6]   b. စၟိုင်င်။
    ʔa **prɔh-prɔh**   *ɕiəʔ* **klàŋ-klàŋ**
    go quick-RED   eat much-RED
    'Go quickly!'   'Eat a lot!'

    c. မင်သ္ဂုတ်တ်။   d. ဟီုခိုဟ်ဟ်။
    mɔ̀ŋ **hɛt-hɛt**   *hʊm* **khʊh-khʊh**
    stay calm-RED   speak good-RED
    'Stay quiet!'   'Speak well!'

Another function of reduplicated stative verbs is to turn them into attributives following a noun, usually reinforcing ('very ...') or attenuating ('rather ...; ...-ish') the force of the verb.

---

[6] In Mon orthography, reduplication of a word is indicated by repetition of the final consonant, or the repetition of the whole word if there is no final consonant.

(5) a. ကာဒေါ့တ်တ်　　　　　b. သွရိုင်ငိုင်
    ka   **ɗot-ɗot**   hwaʔ **rò̤ŋ-rò̤ŋ**
    car small-RED   curry spicy-RED
    'a very/rather small car'   'very/rather spicy (hot) curry'

Both stative and dynamic verbs are reduplicated in connection with interrogatives to form indefinite expressions as in Burmese (cf. ex. 46, p. 81):

(6) a. အဲလိုခွေ့အာအာ အဲဒးဗက်ရောင်ǁ
    hənày   lɔ   ɗəh   ʔa-ʔa,   ʔuə   tɛ̀h   pèk   noŋ.
    place   which   3   go-RED   1SG   HIT   follow ASRT
    'Wherever he goes, I have to follow him.'

  b. ဗုံလိုဗေုံဟီုဟီု ခွေ့ဟွံဏှံပုဟ်ǁ
    pɤ̀m   lɔ   pèh   hʊm-hʊm,   ɗɛh   hùʔ   pəteh   pùh.
    manner which   2   speak-RED 3   NEG   believe NEG
    'However you speak, he won't believe you.'

Pronouns can in some cases be reduplicated to express plurality. The most common cosntruction is *ɲèh-ɲèh-ʔuə-ʔuə* 'all of us', lit. 'he-he-I-I'. Less common are reduplicated nouns indicating plural referents, like *plày-plày* 'young men'. Some quantifiers, e.g. *hmɛ̀p* 'every', can be reduplicated for reinforcement of their meaning. Similarly the numeral *mùə* 'one' is reduplicated to mean 'any one'. Nouns only rarely occur in reduplication.

3 Syntactic structure

3.1 Nominal phrase

The noun phrase in Mon can consist of a bare noun or a noun with modifiers. The relative order of multiple modifiers within a noun phrase is fixed, though the quantifier expression has some freedom of movement within the complex nominal expression. A modifier usually has scope over all preceding elements in the noun phrase. The maximal extension of a nominal phrase includes function marking prepositions, one or more noun stems, modifying elements (nominal or verbal), a quantifier, demonstratives and the phrase final topic marker, in this order. These modifying elements will be discussed in the next sections.

Table 6: Maximal extension of noun phrase

ဒၟ	လိက်ဗွဟ်	တၟိ	ေၛံ	ကၠဳ	လဝ်	အဲ	ၜါ	ဏံ	ဂှ်
ɖɔə	lòc-hawɔ̀h	kəmʋəʔ	dɛh	kʋ	lɔ̀	ʔuə	ɓa	nɔʔ	kɔ̀h
LOC	book-reading	new	3	give	deposit	1SG	two	PROX	MEDL
PREP	nom. head	MOD	relative clause					QUANT	DEM	DET
'in these (aforementioned) two new reading books which he gave me'										

3.1.1 Determiners

Determiners in Mon can be classified as either interrogative or demonstrative. One interrogative *mùʔ* 'what (kind of)' precedes the noun while the other *lʋ* 'which' follows it.

Demonstratives, which always follow the noun, distinguish between proximal *nɔʔ*, medial *kɔ̀h* and distal *tɤʔ*. The presence of a demonstrative other than *kɔ̀h* implies singularity of the referent, unless the plural marker *tɔʔ* is added (see below). Unmodified nominals can have either singular or plural reference. The medial demonstrative *kɔ̀h* is also used as marker of known information, and functions in this regard as a topic marker. (see 7d). When used as a topic marker, *kɔ̀h* may follow another demonstrative, as in *hʋəʔ tɤʔ kɔ̀h* 'that house (which we're talking about)' or *lòc nɔʔ kɔ̀h* 'as for this book' (see Jenny 2009 for a detailed study). The following examples illustrate the use of determiners.

(7) a. မုသွ b. သွဏံ c. သွတေံ d. သွတေံဂှ်
    mùʔ hwaʔ   *hwaʔ nɔʔ*   *hwaʔ tɤʔ*   *hwaʔ tɤʔ kɔ̀h*
    what curry   curry PROX   curry DIST   curry DIST MEDL=TOP
    'what curry'   'this curry'   'that curry'   'that (known) curry'

3.1.2 Classifiers, quantifiers and number

Unlike most Mainland Southeast Asian languages, Mon only rarely makes use of nominal classifiers. Although a few classifiers exist, their use is never obligatory, with the possible exception of *həkaoʔ* 'body' for monks and novices. Other classifiers which are sometimes used in the spoken language in connection with numerals are *mɛ̀ʔ* 'seed' for various objects, including houses, cars, computers, etc., and *kənɤŋ* for relics and other sacred objects. The word *nɔm* 'tree, plant' may infrequently be used in counting trees.

Despite the fact that classifiers are not normally used in Mon, the word order in quantifier expressions is similar to the corresponding constructions in classifier languages like Thai and Burmese, with a gap where the classifier would be expected. The numeral follows the noun if it is a general noun, but precedes if it is a measure word, such as 'meter', 'bottle', 'hour' or 'day'.

(8) a. ရဲ၀ါ
    rɜ̀ə ɓa
    friend two
    'two friends'

b. ကားပိ (မဲ)
    ka pɒəʔ (mɛ̀ʔ)
    car three (CLF)
    'three cars'

c. သ္ၚိမွဲ (မဲ)
    hɒəʔ mùə (mɛ̀ʔ)
    house one (CLF)
    'one/a house'

d. ၀ါတ္ၚဲ
    ɓa ŋuə
    two day
    'two days'

e. ပိပလင်
    pɒəʔ pəlɛŋ
    three bottle
    'three bottles'

f. မွဲသၞာံ
    mùə hnam
    one year
    'one year'

The basic numerals in Mon are given in the following table. Compound numerals are made up from the basic numerals by regular processes of addition and multiplication. The word for 100,000 is the highest numeral in colloquial use, one million is expressed as '10×100,000'. The only irregularity that occurs in compound numerals is the use of *ʔiʔsɔn* for 'five' after multiples of ten. In this case the compound form of 'ten', *coh*, is dropped.

Table 7: Numerals

၀	သုည, သုန်	sun(ɲaʔ), tɤŋɲaʔ[7]	zero	၈မွဲ	cɔh-mùə	eleven
၁	မွဲ	mùə	one	၈သုန်	cɔh-sɔn	fifteen
၂	၀ါ	ɓa	two	၀ါစှော်	ɓa-coh	twenty
၃	ပိ	pɒəʔ	three	ပိက္ၜသုန်	pɒəʔ-ʔiʔsɔn	thirty-five
၄	ပန်	pɔn	four	ပန်စှော်ဒစါံ	pɔn-coh-həcam	forty-eight
၅	မသုန်	pəsɔn	five	က္ၜံ	klɔm	hundred
၆	တရဲ	kərao	six	မသုန်က္ၜံ	pəsɔn-klɔm	five hundred
၇	ထပှ်	həpɔh	seven	လ္ၚီ	ɲìm	thousand
၈	ဒစါံ	həcam	eight	လက်	lɛk	ten thousand
၉	ဒစိတ်	həcit	nine	ကိုတ်	kʊt	hundred thousand
၁၀	စှော်	cɔh	ten	စကိုတ်	cɔh-kʊt	million

---

7 Both words are versions of Pali *suñña* 'empty, void'. The form *tɤŋɲaʔ*, from Burmese *θouN²ɲa¹*, is common among Mon speakers in Burma. The English derived *sìrò* 'zero' is also common.

The interrogative quantifier, *mù?.ci?* means both 'how much' and 'how many' (See § 3.3.2 on questions). Like the numerals it occurs after general nouns (*hloə mù?.ci?* 'how much money') and before measure words (*mù?.ci? ŋuə* 'how many days'). The general indefinite quantifier *təŋʏ̀* 'some' is also used as an indefinite pronoun.

Plurality of nominal referents is optionally expressed by adding either the plural marker *tɔ?* or the attributive form of *klàŋ* 'be much/many', namely *həlàŋ*. The former expresses an inclusive (definite, complete) number, while the second is a more general plural marker. The two markers are not mutually exclusive. *tɔ?* can be added after an expression marked by *həlàŋ*, with no obvious change in meaning apart from a possible shift of emphasis. *tɔ?* occurs only after pronouns and personal names. After pronouns it marks plurality, as in *pèh tɔ?* 'you pl.' and *dɛh tɔ?* 'they', while it has associative function with personal names, as in *rɔ̀t.mòn tɔ?* 'Rot Mon and his friends' (compare with Burmese marker တို့ /toˀ/). When the plural marker *tɔ?* occurs with the adnominal demonstratives *nɔ?* 'this' and *tʏ?* 'that', the words merge into *tənɔ?* 'these' and *tətʏ?* 'those'.

3.1.3 Other modifiers

A noun can be modified by other nouns, pronouns, verbs or relative clauses. Noun modifiers may indicate possession or other association. Some nominal modifiers are better described as nominal compounds, like *hʋə? ɗac* 'bathroom, rest room', as the compound meaning is idiomatic (see section 2.2). If a pronoun modifies a noun, the relation is always one of possession. For general possession with no overt possessum expressed, the generic nominal head *krɔ̀p* 'thing' or the (synchronically opaque) possessive head *hmɛk/hmɔk* is used. The possessum almost always precedes the possessor, with the important exception of the interrogative 'whose', in which case the interrogative pronoun *ɲèh.kɔ̀h* 'who' precedes the possessum, as seen in (9).

(9) ညးဂံသ္ၚိ။ ညးေဂံကွန်။
    ɲèh.kɔ̀h   *hʋə?*   *ɲèh.kɔ̀h*   *kon*
    who   house   who   son
    'whose house?'   'whose son?'

In the answer to these questions, the constituent order is as expected, with the modifier following the head, as seen in (10).

(10) သို့ရ။ တွေန်အဲ။
    hʋaʔ   rɔ̀ə   kon   ʔuə
    house   friend   son   1
    'the friend's house'   'my son'

Verbs, both stative and dynamic, can modify a nominal head. In some cases the verb occurs in the (lexicalized) attributive form (cf. example (11)a–b), but usually the basic verb root can be used attributively (cf. example (11)c). Depending on the semantics of the noun and the modifying verb, the modified noun is understood as subject or object of the verb, as in the following examples.

(11) a. မ္ၚိဟ်ဇၞော်   b. လိက်ခိုဟ်   c. စၞစ
    mənìh hnòk   lòc   khʋh   kəna?   ɕiəʔ
    person be.big   text be.good   food   eat
    'adult'   'a/the good book' 'food (for eating)'

Relative clauses were common in Old and Middle Mon and occur regularly in Literary Mon, but they are less frequent in the spoken language. The old relativizer *mɛ̀ʔ/mə* has been almost completely lost in colloquial Mon, so that there is no overt relativizer in the spoken language. Relative clauses are added after the modified noun, frequently followed by the topic marker *kɔ̀h*, which in this case functions as noun phrase boundary marker as well as topic marker. The relative clause serves to anchor the referent in the discourse, making it more easily accessible and therefore a better candidate for topic-hood (see Lambrecht 1994: 109; Jenny 2009). With juxtaposition being the only means of building a relative clause, relative expressions are usually restricted to subject and object as relativized functions. More complex constructions, such as oblique relativized functions, are not found. The following examples illustrate the development of relative constructions in Mon from Old Mon to the modern spoken language. Notice the shift of position from clause initial position to preverbal position of the relativizer *mun/ma* from Old Mon to Middle Mon (and modern Mon), which may well have caused or facilitated the loss of the marker in the spoken language. As seen in (11a), the relativizer is sometimes realized as a weak proclitic before the verb. This form is hardly audible in normal speech and often disappears in elicited sentences (11b).

(12) a. Old Mon
    ဍေက်မုန်ဇုန်တကျာက်
    ḍek   **mun**   jun   ta   kyāk
    slave REL   make.over   to   sacred
    'the slaves which he made over to the shrine'

b. Middle Mon
ဂလာန်ဒေဝတာမဟှိမ်
galān   dewatau   **ma**   həm
word   god   REL   speak
'the words that the gods spoke'

(13) a. Spoken Mon
ဣၟဟ်ဗ္ၜိမအာ
hənày   pèh   mə=ʔa
place   2   REL=go
'the place you are going'

b. Spoken Mon
အရေဝ်ဗ္ၜိဟှုမ်(ကှဲ)
ʔərè   pèh   hʊm   (kɔ̀h)
language   2   speak   (MEDL)
'the things you said'

3.1.4 Prepositions

Mon makes regular use of a rather small number of prepositions which cannot be synchronically connected to verbs or nouns. The most common among these is *kɒ*, marking indirect objects of different types (recipient, benefactive) as well as peripheral functions like comitative and instrumental. This preposition is the result of a lexical conflation of the original oblique preposition (comitative, instrumental) OM/MM *ku* (formal pronunciation in SM *kaoʔ*) with the verb *kɒ* 'give'. It also combines with some other prepositions, such as *nù* 'from, out of, since' (general marker of source) and *dɔə* 'in, at' (locative marker). Other prepositions are restricted to the literary language, like *hwɛk/swɛk* 'for', *kom.kaoʔ* 'together with' and *nə̀ʔ kɒ* 'with'(instrumental). More specific prepositions, also used in colloquial Mon, are *hətaʔ* 'in front of', *ʔətao* 'on (top of)', *hmɔ/ʔəhmɔ* 'under', *kərao* 'behind, after', and others. They can also be used adverbially as 'ahead', 'up(stairs)', 'down', and 'back' respectively.

3.2 Verbal phrase

The verbal phrase[8] consists of at least one verbal element, and can be expanded to include a number of verbs and particles. There is no marker of finiteness, and verbal categories are optionally expressed. Traces of the Old Mon morphological system remain in spoken Mon, but the processes themselves are no longer productive. Some verbs require an overt object, as seen in section § 2.3 above. A large number of auxiliary verbs occur in Mon, expressing various functions (s. § 3.2.3). Verb phrase particles (i.e. verb phrase operators which are not themselves verbs) are rare in Mon, the most common being the negator discussed in the next section. A special subcategory of verbs are the two copulas *tɔ̀h* 'be something', an identificational copula, and *nùm* 'exist, be there, have', an existential copula. Both show irregularities in negation, (see section 3.2.1).

3.2.1 Verbal categories

Verbal categories such as tense-aspect-modality(-manner) and directionality, are expressed in Mon by auxiliary verbs. Number (subject agreement) is not usually expressed, but the verb *ʔʊt* 'all' can be added at the end of the verbal phrase to indicate the plurality of the subject, but depending on the context and semantic content of the clause it can also indicate plural objects, as the following examples show.

(12) ကောန်ၚာ်အာဘာအိုတ်ရ။
    kon.ŋàc   ʔa   phèə   **ʔʊt**   raʔ.
    child   go   school all   FOC
    'The children have (all) gone to school.'

(13) အဲဗှ်လိက်အိုတ်ကၠာရ။
    ʔuə   pɔ̀h   lòc   **ʔʊt**   yaʔ.
    1SG   read   text   all   NSIT
    'I have read (all) the books.'

The negation marker *hùʔ* (alternative pronunciations *hɤ̀ʔ* and *hə*) is placed directly in front of the verb that is to be negated as in (14), realized as labial infix -

---

8 I use 'verbal phrase' in the sense of Dixon's (2010: 108ff) 'verb phrase', which is different from the use of 'verb phrase' (including object NPs) in some syntactic theories, and similar to 'complex verb' used by Vittrant, this volume.

w- in a small number of frequent verbs with initial velar stop, such as *kɤʔ* 'get', *khʊh* 'good', *kʊ* 'give', and a few others (Jenny 2003: 185ff). *hùʔ* cannot occur with non-verbal predicates, which are negated using the dummy verb *hùʔ siəŋ* 'not to be so' is placed after the predicate (15). This verb occurs only in negative and interrogative contexts.

A special negated form is delete found with the existential copula *nùm* 'exist, there is, have' which is *hùʔ mùə* 'not to exist, there is not, not to have', lit. 'not one' (cf. 16). This is the only occurrence of *hùʔ* before a non-verbal element; it can be explained by the historical development of the negation particle from Old Mon *sak* 'not to be, not to exist', which could be combined with a reinforcing element like *moy* (> *mùə*) 'one'. After *sak* was weakened to *ha/hə* (which in turn was later strengthened to *hùʔ*), it lost its verbal character, with *sak moy* > *hùʔ mùə* being a relic of the original construction.[9] A negation reinforcing particle can (and often does) occur in sentence final position also in spoken Mon (cf. 14). While the old form *mùə* is still common in Mon varieties spoken in Thailand, the Myanmar/Burma dialects usually add the Burmese loan *pùh* (Burmese ဘူး *phu³/bu³*). The following examples illustrate negation in verbal and non-verbal predicates.

(14) တ္ၚဲဏံ ကောန်ၚာ်တံ ဟွံတိုန်ဘာပုဟ်။
  ŋuə nɔʔ   kon.ŋàc tɔʔ **hùʔ** tʊn   phèə   **pùh**.
  day PROX   child   PL   NEG   go.up   school   NEG
  'Today the children are not going to school.'

(15) တ္ၚဲဏံဟွံသေင်ပုဟ် ကောန်ၚာ်တံတိုန်ဘာ။
  ŋuə nɔʔ   **hùʔ** **siəŋ** **pùh** kon.ŋàc tɔʔ tʊn   phèə.
  day this NEG   be.so   NEG   child   PL   go.up school
  'It's not today that the children go to school.'

(16) သြ့ဲအဲဟွံမွဲ။
  hloə   ʔuə   **hùʔ.mùə**.
  money   1SG   not.exist
  'I don't have any money.'

---

9 The construction *hùʔ mùə* has led some authors to the conclusion that numerals are verbs in Mon, an analysis that is not supported by other data, e.g. no other numerals can be directly negated (cf. Bauer 1982: 164).

3.2.2 Serial verb constructions

Mon, like other Southeast Asian languages, makes frequent use of serial verb constructions, i.e. clauses containing more than one full lexical verb. Serial verb constructions typically describe a single event, rather than a series of independent events, and the verbs involved are of equal syntactic status, i.e. none is subordinate to the other(s) (see Aikhenvald & Dixon 2006 for details and definitions). Serial verb constructions in Mon can be either the root serialization or the core serialization type. In root serialization, verbs are always adjacent and have the same polarity and transitivity value (cf. 17–19), while in core serialization the verbs can be separated by intervening noun phrases and do not necessarily share polarity and transitivity value (cf. 20b, 21) (Bril, 2004: 2)[10]. Serial verbs can easily acquire different grammatical functions, depending on their semantic content and the type of serialization involved. Grammatical functions of verbs in serialization will be discussed in the next section.

Root serializations consist of two or more adjacent verbs with shared subject and, if transitive, shared object (cf. 17). Auxiliary verbs can be added, such as directional (cf. 19) or aspectual-modal markers. The position of these depends on their status as root or core operator. The following examples (17 to 19) illustrate serialization in transitive (17, 18) and intransitive (19) clauses.

(17) အဲကွက်အာရာန်စကွာင်ပို့ဖျာ။
 ʔuə   kwac   ʔa   ràn   ɕiəʔ   kwaɲ   dɔə   phya.
 1SG   walk   GO   buy   eat   sweets   LOC   market
 'I went to the market to buy some sweets to eat.'

(18) ဒြေဗက်ထဒြေင်ဏာကၠိ။
 dɛh   pèk   hədìəŋ   na   klʋ.
 3   drive   CAUS.flee   CAUS.GO   dog
 'He chased the dog away.'

(19) ကၠိဂြိပ်ဒတိတ်အာနုကၠိ။
 klʋ   krìp   tèə   tɛt   ʔa   nù   kʋ   klɔʔ.
 dog   run   run.away   go.out   GO   SRC   OBL   garden
 'The dog ran away out of the garden.'

---

10 The terms core serialization and nuclear serialization refer to the layered structure of the clause used in the Role and Reference Grammar approach. See Van Valin and LaPolla (1997: 25)

In the above examples, the verbs glossed with small caps are auxiliary verbs with grammatical function, in this case directionals. Example (17) shows the combination of an intransitive sequence *kwac ʔa* 'walk go' with a transitive serial construction *ràn ɕiəʔ* 'buy eat'.

A frequent verb in root serialization is *kɒ* 'give', which is easily extended from acts of giving to benefactive situations, as in (20).

(20) a. မိရာန်ကိုကောန်ငှ့်ကွာင်။
      mìʔ   **ràn**   **kɒ**   *kon.ɲàc*   *kwaɲ.*
      mother buy give child   sweets
      'The mother bought sweets for the children.' [intended action]

b. မိရာန်ကွာင်ကိုကောန်ငှ့်။
      mìʔ   **ràn**   *kwaɲ*   **kɒ**   *kon.ɲàc.*
      mother buy sweets give child
      'The mother bought sweets for the children.' [spontaneous action]

There is some variation in serial verb constructions between dialects and individual speakers, some perhaps reflecting influence from Thai and Burmese. The difference between sentences (20a) and (20b) is that the former expresses a benefactive action which is based on a wish or order of the beneficiary, while the latter expresses a "not-planned" act by the actor. The construction in (20b) is identical in structure to the Thai expression. Native Mon speakers in Burma tend to prefer prepositional expressions as (20c),[11] especially when two overt objects are involved.

(20) c. ဘိုအ်ကောန်ငှ့် မိရာန်ကွာင်။
      phɤʔ *kon.ɲàc* *mìʔ*   **ràn** *kwaɲ.*
      for   child   mother buy   sweets
      'The mother bought sweets for the children.'

In core serialization the juncture between the involved verbs is looser than in root serialization. Arguments and peripheral elements may intervene between the verbs, and the verbs may be negated individually. Semantically, core serialization is used especially in resultative constructions, which in turn may easily acquire grammatical function. The borderline between lexical and grammatical function is not always clear, and often both may be present. Both

---

[11] Notice that the preposition *phɤʔ* is a(n indirect) loan from the Burmese causative subordinator ဖို့ *pho¹*.

transitive and intransitive verbs occur in core serialization. Some examples are given below.

(21) အဲပုင်ဟွံစှ်ေ။
 ʔuə **ɕiaʔ** pɤŋ hùʔ **ceh**.
 1SG eat cooked.rice NEG go.down
 'I cannot (force myself to) eat.'

(22) ခဲှတံရပ်ကၠိုဟွံဂွံ။
 dɛh tɔʔ **rɔ̀p** klʊ hùʔ **kɤ̀ʔ**.
 3 PL catch dog NEG get
 'They (try to) catch the dog without getting it.'

The choice of root vs. core serialization when possible makes a semantic difference in the interpretation of an expression. While the subject of (23a) was explicitly shooting at a (specific) bird and hit it, in (23b) the activity involves only shooting with no specific goal in mind and the result (i.e. hitting a bird) is rather incidental. This difference in meaning has given rise to different grammatical functions of some serialized verbs, as illustrated in section 3.2.3 below.

(23) a. ခဲှပန်ဂစေံ။
 dɛh pɔn həcem tɛ̀h.
 3 shoot bird hit
 'He shot (and hit) a bird.'

 b. ခဲှပန်ဒးဂစဲ။
 dɛh pɔn tɛ̀h həcem.
 3 shoot hit bird
 'He hit a bird while shooting.'

3.2.3 Auxiliary verbs

An auxiliary verb is a verb with grammatical function which occurs in combination with one or more lexically full verbs. As stated above, the distinction between lexical and grammatical function is not always easily made, and may in many instances be irrelevant to the analysis. Auxiliary verbs occur before or after the main verb, sometimes with different functions in each of the two positions. The lexical sources of auxiliary verbs are always synchronically transparent and they are not generally reduced phonetically. The functional categories of auxiliary verbs are not clear-cut, with some verbs expressing a range of functions covering directionality, modality, manner and others. In some cases syntactic differences are indicative of one or another functional category. For example, as an auxiliary verb, the verb *ʔa* 'go' can be separately negated if it has resultative function but not if it is directional, as shown in (23.1).

(24) a. ဒခှေင်ဟွံအာ॥
     həd̀iəŋ   hù?   ʔa
     chase   NEG   go
     'Cannot chase away.'

   b. တွံဟွံအာ॥
     *kwac   hù?   ʔa
     *walk   NEG   go
     Intended: 'Cannot walk away.'

Auxiliary verbs do not always have full-verb counterparts. Again, the same verbs can occur as free or bound form in different contexts and functions, as the example of *tèh* 'come into contact with, touch, hit' shows. The instances of *tèh* in (25a) and (25b) are free forms, while in (25c) and (25d) they are bound forms as shown by the question tag test.

(25) a. ကောန်ငၞါးကၠိုက်ကိတ်ဟာ॥
     kon.ŋàc   **tèh**   klɒ   kit   ha?
     child   **hit**   dog   bite   Q
     'Was the child bitten by the dog?'

     ဟွံး(ကိတ်)ပုဟ်॥
     hù?   **tèh**   (kit)   pùh.
     NEG   **hit**   (bite)   NEG
     'No.'

   b. ဗမ်ှအာသွုင်ရဲဒှးဟာ॥
     pèh   ʔa   hɒaʔ   r̀ə   **tèh**   haʔ
     2   go   house   friend   **hit**   Q
     'Do you know the way to the friend's house?'

     (အာ)ဒှးရ॥
     (ʔa)   **tèh**   raʔ.
     (go)   **hit**   FOC
     'Yes.'

   c. အဲဒှးတိုန်ဘာဟာ॥
     ʔuə   **tèh**   tɒn   phɛ̀ə   haʔ
     1SG   **hit**   go.up   school   Q
     'Do I have to go to school?'

     ဒှးတိုန်ရ॥
     tèh   *(tɒn)   raʔ.
     hit   *(go.up)   FOC
     'Yes.'

   d. ခဲ့စဒှးဂျိုဟာ॥
     dɛh   ɕiəʔ   **tèh**   kyìʔ   haʔ
     3   eat   **hit**   poison   Q
     'Did he eat poison by accident?'

     စဒှးရ॥
     *(ɕiəʔ)   **tèh**   raʔ.
     *(eat)   **hit**   FOC
     'Yes.'

Another example of an auxiliary verb occurring before or after the main verb is *kɤʔ* 'get'. In preverbal position, it functions as a bound auxiliary indicating an event which is caused by some backgrounded prior (enabling) event (see Enfield 2003, van der Auwera & al 2009). In postverbal position it is a free form indicating a general deontic possibility for the subject to perform an event, i.e. a -situational modality (van der Auwera & Plugian 1998). The latter function can be seen as extension of the resultative reading seen in example (22), first from 'success in catching' to general 'success' of an attempted act, and then further to general deontic possibility.

Other resultative auxiliary verbs have modal functions like *màn* 'win' > 'be physically/mentally capable' and *lèp* 'be skilled > can, know how to V' (cf. analogous Burmese verbs).

Directional auxiliary verbs indicate the spatial or temporal direction of an activity. While the spatial use is straightforward, the interpretation in the temporal domain is less obvious and depends on the verbal semantics as well as the context. Directionals are always bound forms and cannot be separately negated. The directionals in Mon occur in two sets, basic spatial event and caused spatial event. The latter is used whenever the object is moved in some way by the subject and this movement is indicated lexically or morphologically in the main verb. Compare the following sentences:

(26) a. ၍ ဗက်အာ။
     dɛh **pèk** *ʔa.*
     3 drive GO
     'He drove off/followed.'

b. ၍ ဗက်ဏာ။
   dɛh **pèk** *na.*
   3 drive CAUS.GO
   'He chased [her] away.'

(27) a. ၍စအာသ္ဌိ။
     dɛh **cao** *ʔa* *hʋəʔ.*
     3 return GO house
     'He went back home.'

b. ၍ဖျဉ်ဏာသ္ဌိ။
   dɛh **phyao** *na* *hʋəʔ.*
   3 CAUS.return CAUS.GO house
   'He brought [her] back home.'

c. ၍ကောက်ဏာရဲအာသ္ဌိ။
     dɛh **kok** *na* *rɔ̀ə* *ʔa* *hʋəʔ.*
     3 call CAUS.GO friend go house
     'He brought his friend home.'

d. ၍အာကောက်နင်ရဲ။
     dɛh *ʔa* **kok** *nèŋ* *rɔ̀ə.*
     3 go call CAUS.COME friend
     'He went to fetch a friend.'

In (27c), the first directional verb (or orientation verb, see Bisang 1992: 67), *na*, occurs in root serialization with *kok* 'call', the second, *ʔa*, in core serialization. Only the first two verbs of the serialization share the causativity value and negation is only possible of the whole expression.

Other auxiliary verbs indicate aspectual values, frequently with an emotional, modal or manner connotation, like *thʋʔ* (often reduced to *hʋʔ* as an auxiliary) 'discard, throw' (example 28d), which indicates a spontaneous action carried out to the end (see Burmese ပစ် *pyiʔ* or *ɕiə?* 'eat', the exact function of which remains obscure: it can be used to mark habitual activities, but is not restricted to these. There is a sense of 'self-interest' or 'activity directed towards agent' (see example 28b), but not in all occurrences of this auxiliary verb. The verb *ket* 'take' as an auxiliary indicates that an activity is performed by or for the subject (ex. 28e); the verb *lɔ̌* 'put' (28d) as an auxiliary has a resultative function (like Burmese ထား *tʰa³*). The following examples cover only a small portion of possible auxiliaries and their functions (for a more detailed account see Jenny 2005: 152ff).

(28) a. ညဏံကော်စဗိုလို့။
    ɲɔʔ   **kok**   ***ɕiə?***   *pr̀m*   *lʋ*
    NMLZ.this   call   **eat**   manner   which
    'What is this called?'

b. အဲလုပ်စသွံဉာ်ကျာ။
    ʔuə   ***lùp***   ***ɕiə?***   *hʋəʔ.dac*   *kla.*
    1SG   enter   **eat**   room.water   before
    'I'm (just) going to the toilet for a second.'

c. ဖေံဖေ့တော်အာကဓာန်ဖေ့။
    pèh   **pliə**   ***thʋʔ***   *ʔa*   *kon*   *pèh.*
    2   abandon   **discard**   go   child   2
    'Get rid of your children (for good)!'

d. ကောတ်ဏာလဝ်မိတ်။
    ket   *na*   ***lɔ̌***   *mìt.*
    take   CAUS.GO   **put**   turmeric
    'They took along turmeric (for later use).'

e. မိက်ဂွံစတုံစေကတော်။
    məkɤ̀ʔ   *cao*   *teh*   *cao*   ***ket.***
    DES   return   TOP   return   **take**
    'If you want to go back, (find a way to) go back yourself.'

3.2.4 Valency

Transitivity distinctions are believed to be, in principle, a universal feature of the languages of the world. Transitivity in Mon is not easy to determine, as the distinction between core and peripheral participants is not a clear cut one. Verbs of motion, for example, can take a direct (unmarked) object if the motion is spatially orientated, that is if a directional auxiliary is present and if the object is a location, such as a place-names or a noun referring to a place like 'house', 'market', 'forest', etc. In all other cases a preposition is required.

While some verbs may be either transitive or intransitive in function, such as *pɔk* 'be open' ~ 'open' and *mat* 'be shut, closed' ~ 'shut, close', a large number of instransitive verbs have a derived causative transitive counterpart. Although the morphological processes available in Old and Middle Mon to derive causative transitive predicates from base verbs are no longer productive in the modern language, many pairs of base intransitive and causative transitive verbs have been lexicalized and the connection is still transparent synchronically in most cases. The most common causativising affix was the prefix *p-/pə-*, which survives in this form in many causative verbs.

The phonetic detail of this prefixation is complex in spoken Mon, although the prefixation is clear from the spelling. Before a single initial consonant, the prefix appears as p- if it can form a cluster with the initial, otherwise as pə-. Initial *c-* and *s-* fused with the prefix, resulting in *phy-*, as in *ceh* 'move down' - *phyeh* 'bring/put down', *sɤŋ* 'drink' - *phyɤŋ* 'give to drink'. In later formations, the prefix *pə- > bə- > hə-* is added, as in *cʊp* 'arrive' - *həcʊp* 'convey'. The prefix *hə-* replaced original derived causative forms also in other cases, e.g. *pətɛt ~ hətɛt* 'take out' and *pətɒn ~ hətɒn* 'bring up'. With initial clusters in the base verb, the vocalic infix *-ə-* (from Old Mon *-u-*) is used, often resulting in irregular phonetic realizations of the causative affix. In some cases analogy has created irregular forms, such as *payɛ* 'adorn, decorate' from the base *kyɛ* 'be beautiful'. The regular causative would be *kəyɛ*, with the vocalic infix.

Table 8: Causative prefixation

intransitive form			derived transitive verb		
ခှေ	ceh	'go down'	ဖှေ	phyeh	'bring/put down'
သုင်	sɤŋ	'drink'	ဖျုင်	phyɤŋ	'give to drink'
စိုပ်	cʊp	'arrive'	ဟစိုပ်	hə-cʊp	'convey, pass on'
တိတ်	tɛt	'go out'	ပိုတ်	pətɛt ~ hətɛt	'take out'
တိုန်	tɒn	'rise'	ပိုန်	pətɒn ~ hətɒn	'lift up'
ကျိုဝ်	kyɛ	'be beautiful'	မပျိုဝ်	payɛ	'adorn, decorate'

Some verbal bases cannot be prefixed to form causatives. In these cases the periphrastic construction with preclausal *kɒ* 'give' > 'let/cause' is used, often together with the verb *paʔ* 'do', as in *paʔ kɒ khɒh* 'make good, improve' from the base *khɒh* 'be good'.

Other valence increasing processes (applicative, benefactive) in Mon always involve the use of auxiliary verbs or verb serialization (cf. § 3.2.2). No derivational morphological processes are available for these.

There is no grammatical device for valence reduction in Mon. A quasi-passive construction using the lexical verb *tèh* 'come into contact, touch, (be) hit' can take nominal or phrasal/clausal complements. This does not involve agent demotion, and usually has an adversative connotation. Another possibility to promote the undergoer to subject position is by the more complex construction *tèh tɤ̀ŋ C*, lit. 'get accept C', where C denotes the event, which is syntactically embedded as complement of *tɤ̀ŋ*. In this case there is no negative connotation of the event. If the auxiliary verb *tèh* is dropped, *tɤ̀ŋ* indicates that the subject undergoes the event voluntarily. In both cases the agent is expressed in its normal position in the complement clause.

3.3 Clause structure

The basic constituent order in Mon is A V O and S V[12]. In natural language it is more common, though, for constituents to be fronted for pragmatic reasons. Fronting can signal topic or focus, either emphatic or contrastive. The only restriction that seems to apply to the fronting of constituents is that grammatical subject and object may not be fronted at the same time. The constituent orders A V O and O, A V are possible, but not A O V. Any part of the sentence can function as topic or comment, but by far the most common is for NPs to be topical and VPs to be the comment (ex. 29a), with the sentence organized in a topic + comment structure. Fronted topics may be marked by the topic marker *kɔ̀h*. The two principal markers employed for purposes of information structure are the topic marker *kɔ̀h* (originally a medial demonstrative) and the focus marker *raʔ*. Both follow the constituent they mark and are sufficient in themselves to indicate the pragmatic function of the constituents; there is not necessarily a change in word order.

---

[12] Transitive and Intransitive clauses are symbolized respectively by A V O and S V. A stands for the first argument (Agent) of a transitive clause while S stands for the unique argument of the intransitive clause.

(29) a. လိက်ဂူ ခေံမှ။   b. ခေံမှရ လိက်ဂူ။
    lòc   kɔ̀h dɛh pɔ̀h.   dɛh pɔ̀h raʔ, lòc kɔ̀h.
    text MEDL 3   read   3   read FOC   text MEDL
    'That book, he read.'   'He read it, that book.'

(30) a. အဲအာရ။   b. အဲရအာ။
    ʔuə   ʔa   raʔ.   ʔuə   raʔ   ʔa.
    1SG   go   FOC   1SG   FOC   go
    'I am going.'   'It's me who's going.'

3.3.1 Clause linkage

The distinction between subordinate and coordinate clauses is not clear in many cases in Mon, as there is no morphosyntactic marking of verbal finiteness. Various morphemes may be used to link clauses, or the linkage may be made implicit by simply juxtaposing the clauses. Spoken narratives frequently link clauses by 'tail-head linkage', where part of the previous sentence is repeated, followed by the linker *toə teh*, 'this being done', lit. 'finish TOPIC'[13], or simply the topic marker *teh* as in (31). The same linker *toə teh* can also occur in sentence initial position, implying a follow up on something stated earlier (see Burmese on similar functions of ပြီး *pyi³*, table 13, p. 99).

(31) ၄ဂ်ကေံ့အာ ၄ဂ်ကေံ့အာတေံ့ ...
    ŋèə kɔ̀h   klɛʔ   ʔa, ŋèə   kɔ̀h   klɛʔ   ʔa   **teh** ...
    frog MEDL disappear go   frog MEDL disappear go   TOP   ...
    'The frog had disappeared. When the frog had disappeared, ...'

Conditional clauses are either introduced by the conditional marker *yɔ̀.raʔ* 'if' or followed by the topic marker *teh*, or both. In speech, the version with the clause-final topic marker is preferred, unless the conditional value of the clause is to be emphasized. In the formal language, either clause-initial *yɔ̀.raʔ* or clause-final *məkɛ̀h* 'speaking of which, saying which', which may be a calque of Burmese ဆိုရင် *sʰoʔ.yiN²* 'speaking of which', with topicalising force.

Other adverbial clauses are introduced by a lexical or grammatical morpheme, indicating the relationship between the clauses. Causal clauses thus are preceded by *hʊt nù*, lit. 'reason from', purposive clauses by *ɲɔ̀ŋ kɤʔ*, *swɛk kɤʔ* or

---

13 See the similar structure of the Burmese linker *pyi³.Tɔ¹* ပြီးတော့ 'after'

phɤʔ kɤʔ all 'so that, in order to'. Temporal clauses are introduced by *laʔ* 'when'(from Pali *kāla* 'time'), *khɤ̀* 'while' or *nù* 'from > since' and *tɤ̀* (*thɤ̀ʔ*) 'until'.

Complement clauses can in formal Mon be introduced by *kɛ̀h* 'say', as in (32)[14]. In colloquial speech, juxtaposed complement clauses are preferred, frequently marked by *kɔ̀h*, indicating their non-predicative (topical) status, as in (33).

(33) ထင်းဍေံကလေင်စအာဖိုဟ်ရ။
    thiəŋ   **kɛ̀h**   *dɛh*   *kəliəŋ*   *cao*   *ʔa*   *phɤh*   *raʔ.*
    think   say   3   return   return   go   still   FOC
    'I thought he was going back.'

(33) အလိုဍေံအာဂှ် အဲဟွံတီ အဲဟွံပဍိုတ်။
    ʔəlɒ   *dɛh*   *ʔa*   **kɔ̀h**   *ʔuə*   *hùʔ*   *tɛm,*   *ʔuə*   *hùʔ*   *paʔ*   *cɒt*
    where   3   go   MEDL   1SG   NEG   know   1SG   NEG   do   mind
    'I don't know, I don't care where he went.'
lit.   Where he went/goes, I don't know, I don't care.

As seen above (section 3.1.3), relative clauses are usually unmarked in spoken Mon, tough the original relativizer *mə* may still occur cliticized to the verb.

3.3.2 Questions

Content questions consist of an interrogative pronoun, modifier, or adverb, such as *ɲèh.kɔ̀h* 'who', *mùʔ/mɔ̀ʔ* 'what', *ʔəlɒ* 'where', *lɒ* 'which', etc. The interrogative word occurs either *in situ* or is fronted. When fronted, the old relativizer *mə=* is sometimes placed before the verb, showing that the fronting of interrogatives is a reanalysis of cleft sentences (as in (34). Both positions are possible with adverbial interrogatives such as *ʔəlɒ* 'where', *chəlɔʔ* 'when' and others. 'What' is always fronted in attributive function ('what kind of...'), and can be fronted and pleonastically occur *in situ* as well when in object function. 'Who' *ɲèh.kɔ̀h* is fronted in attributive function before nouns, as in *ɲèh.kɔ̀h kon* 'whose child', never in object function. An interrogative sentence usually ends in *rao*, but this question particle is often dropped in colloquial speech. Content ques-

---

[14] On the complementizer function of verbs meaning 'say' in (Southeast) Asian languages, see Min chapter (§3.5) and Chappell 2008 on Sinitic languages.

tions can be pluralized by adding *kɒm* to the end of the question (before the particle *rao*), e.g. *mù? mə=nùm kɒm rao?* 'what is there?' (with more than one answer in mind). Interrogatives occurring in negated clauses express the corresponding negatives, i.e. *mù? hù? pa?* 'I'm not doing anything.', lit. 'what – not – do'.

Table 9: Interrogative forms and their position in the clause

Interrogative form	Meaning	In situ	Fronted
ɲèh.kɔ̀h	'who',	Yes	Yes (with restriction)
mù?/mɔ̀?	'what'	Yes	Yes (with restriction)
ʔəlɒ	'where',	Yes	Yes
lɒ	'which'	Yes	
chəlɔ?	'when'	Yes	Yes

(34) အလိုဒ္ဓေမအာ။   ဗွေရော။
    ʔəlɒ   dɛh   mə   ʔa?   pèh   rao?
    where   3   REL   go   2   Q
    'Where is he going?'   'And what about you?'

Polar questions both with verbal and non-verbal predicates are formed by adding the question particle *ha* in sentence-final position, or after the constituent questioned in the case of narrow interrogative focus (cf. 35). This particle *ha* can also be used in negative questions. For tag questions *siəŋ ha* 'is it so?' is added, which in rapid speech is often shortened to *siə?* or *se?*, spoken in a high pitch. The particle *ha* is also used to form alternative questions, as there is no direct translation equivalent of 'or' (see example 35).

(35) လမ္စက်ဟာ ပုဟာ။
    pəcɔk   ha,   pù?   ha
    black   Q   white   Q
    'Is it black or white?', (lit. 'is it black, is it white?').

Both content and polar questions can be "passed on" to a new addressee or referent with the formula *X rao*, where X is the new addressee or the new referent about which the question is asked (see example 34b).

3.3.3 Imperatives

The imperative can be formed by the bare verb, though is considered blunt and not appropriate in many contexts. Usually the attenuative auxiliary verb *ɲìʔ* 'little, few' is added. Indirect speech acts, such as questions like 'could you please...', to express orders are rarely used in colloquial Mon.

Hortative expressions use the sentence-final particle *coʔ* 'let's', a Burmese loan (စို့ *soˈ*). For optatives the pre-clausal auxiliary *kɒ* 'give > let' is used, as in *kɒ dɛh ʔa* 'let him go; may he go'. The prohibitive is expressed by the preverbal *paʔ*, homophonous (and historically connected) with the verb *paʔ* 'do'. The prohibitive marker in Old Mon was *lah* 'don't', which was combined with *paʔ* 'do'. This was later reanalysed as a single word and was shortened to *paʔ*. The modern spelling လ္ပ <lpa> as well as the reading pronunciation *ləpaʔ* still reflect this etymology.

3.3.4 Clause-final particles

Mon makes less frequent use of clause final particles than other languages in the area, such as Burmese and Thai. The politeness particle *ʔao* may be added to an utterance, but this is less regularly done than in neighbouring languages. The same particle may also be used to answer a question or call. When speaking with Buddhist monks, *kyac*, lit. 'sacred being' is used in both functions, i.e. expressing respect.

The focus marker *raʔ* is often used to end a sentence, though this is not the primary function of this marker. The sentence final particle *nah* is frequent; it puts emphasis on the truth of the statement and at the same time asks for consent of the addressee.

Some sentence particles are obviously borrowings from Burmese, like *nɔ* and *pɔʔ* (see Burmese နော် *nɔ²* and ပေါ့ *pɔˈ*). These are regularly used only in forms of Mon which have been Burmanized to some degree. More frequent is the Burmese loan *lèy* (Burmese လေ *le²*) indicating emphasis. Other sentence particles, viz. interrogative *ha* and *rao* and negative *pùh*, have been discussed above.

4 Semantics and pragmatics

4.1 Pronouns

The pronominal system of Mon is simple compared to other languages in the region (see Burmese or Thai). In spite of a long social tradition with different layers of society, Mon has not developed an elaborate hierarchical pronominal system, which may be indicative of the historically less institutionalized character of the hierarchical structure of Mon society as opposed to Thai and Burmese customs. There is only one form for the first person singular, viz. ʔuə, used by both men and women, irrespective of the social status of the speaker and the addressee. Only when speaking with monks the extended form ʔuə ɗoc, lit. 'I servant' is used. The plural of the first person is poy, equally socially neutral. Instead of second person pronouns, personal names or kinship or professional terms are normally used. The pronoun ɓèʔ 'you' is considered rude and mainly used among close friends or in contempt, while the form mənèh is in formal use only. A somewhat more neutral pronoun is pèh, used when speaking to friends or inferiors, as well as intimately among lovers. Third person pronouns are ɗɛh 'it; he, she', used colloquially for both human and non-human referents. In more formal contexts, ɲèh, lit. 'person', is used for human referents. The plural of second and third person pronouns is regularly formed by adding tɔʔ.

Table 10: Pronouns in Mon

Pronouns	Mon		Literal meaning
1sg (fam.)	အဲ	ʔuə	
1sg. (honor.)	အဲခိုက်	ʔuə ɗoc	'I servant'
1pl	ပို့	poy	
2sg. (fam)	ဗှ်	ɓèʔ	
2sg. (neutral)	ပေဲှ	pèh	
2sg. (formal)	မုး	mənèh	
3sg.	ဒၟံင်	ɗɛh	
3sg. (formal, human)	ညး	ɲèh	'person'
2–3pl	တံ	tɔʔ	

4.2 Semantic domains

Being a rice cultivating society, Mon naturally has a rich indigenous vocabulary for all aspects of rice cultivation. The rice plant itself is called *sɒʔ*, a term also denoting the unhusked rice grain. The husked, uncooked rice grain is *haoʔ*, and cooked rice is *pɤŋ*, which has also come to denote 'food' in general. Rice is planted in *ŋèʔ* 'rice field', while other crops, including *pəlɔɲ* 'sticky rice', are grown in *kù* 'field', *klɔʔ* 'orchard' or *wèə* '(open) field'.

Table 11: Terms for Rice

rice plant	unhusked rice grain	husked rice	cooked rice	'sticky rice'	'rice field'
သၞဴ *sɒʔ*,	သြုံ *haoʔ*	ပုၚ် *pɤŋ*	ဝါမဳၚ် *pəlɔɲ*	၃ *ŋèʔ*

While loanwords from Burmese are mostly basic vocabulary, Pali is the source language for most religious vocabulary. One noticeable exception is the use of the indigenous *kyac* 'sacred being/object' for the Buddha, including Buddha statues, as well as pagodas. Some Pali words have been naturalized, so that their Indian origin is now hardly visible, such as *phèə* 'monastery, school' from Pali *vihāra* 'Buddhist monastery'. A few Buddhist terms are from Sanskrit rather than Pali, like *thɔ̀* 'Law, Doctrine' from *dharma* (cf. *kɔm* 'karma, deed' from the Pali form *kamma*). Some basic words have special forms when referring to monks, like *kɒ pɒn* 'eat' (common language *ɕiəʔ*), lit. 'give merit', based on the belief that people attain merit by giving food to the monks, and the monks in turn give merit to the people by accepting the food.

The Mon lexicon allows for fine semantic distinctions in some daily activities, as is illustrated by the set of verbs used for wearing various items of clothing[15]. In younger speakers these differences tend to disappear, especially those whose speech is influenced by Thai which makes fewer distinctions in this domain. One term considered sufficiently neutral takes over the fields of all others, resulting in semantic bleaching (and impoverishment of the vocabulary).

---

[15] Notice that Khmer has similar distinctions.

Table 12: Verbs of 'wearing'

လွက် (ပလော်)	kətɛk (pəlɒʔ)	wear (a shirt)
စုတ် (ခရောပ်ဇိင်, ဒေၚာ်မတ်)	cut (hərop càŋ, kəhò mòt)	wear (socks)
ဒလိုံ (ခော်)	həlʏ̀ (həmok)	wear (a hat)
မိက် (ပင်မိ, ဂိုက်)	pàk (pɔŋmɒə, klòc)	wear (trousers, a waistcloth m)
ဟို (ဂိုန်)	hʏ (nìn)	wear (a waistcloth f)
လိုန် (ဒုပ်)	lʏ̀n (hənɔ̀p)	wear (shoes)
ဝက် (သွေက်)	wɛ̀k (hniək)	wear (earrings)
ပါတ် (နာဍိ)	pat (nədi)	wear (a watch)
လွက် (ပဝါ)	kəbɛk (kəwa)	wear (a shawl)
ကွက် (မဒ္ဒီ)	kwɛk (mɛ̀ʔ kwɛ̀a)	wear (a necklace)

The basic colour terms in Mon are monomorphemic and synchronically opaque. The class term *sac* 'type, kind, colour' is usually prefixed to all colour terms. The most common basic colour terms are listed in the following table.

Table 13: Basic colour terms

ပု	pùʔ	white	ဒ္ဒဴ	day	(bright) red	ဒုံ	dʊm	(dark) blue
လမ္ၚက်	pəcɔk	black	ဗကေတ်	həket	red	တေၚ်က်	ɲiək	green

Other colours are referred to using nouns, like *sac mìt* 'yellow' < 'turmeric colour' and *sac təkah* 'light blue'< 'sky colour', *sac limao* 'orange colour'.

In Mon kinship terminology both gender and relative age are important. The extended family is called *mɛ̀sa*ʔ. Other cover terms are compound forms, such as *mìʔ-mɛ̀ʔ* or *yày-ʔəpa* for 'parents'. It is noticeable that generally the female comes first in compounds of this kind, as can be seen also in the term for ancestors in general, *cùʔ cɛ̀ʔ pɛ̀a lɛ̀ʔ*. Apart from some kinship terms are borrowed from Burmese, most kinship terms are Mon. Note that the system is not symmetrical, showing many gaps especially in the generations above the parents. While there are specific terms for grandfather's younger siblings, there are none for his older siblings, nor for grandmother's. Cousins are not usually distinguished from siblings, though the technical term *kon-kao-kon-tɛ̀ʔ*, lit. 'child - older.brother - child - younger.brother' can be used. This compound is not specified for gender and relative age.

Table 14: Kinship terminology

1)	ကော, အဝေါ်	kao, ʔəwao	older brother	12)	ဣုစ်	ʔiʔci	younger aunt
2)	အမ, မဲ့	ʔəmaʔ, ɓɔ̀a	older sister	13)	အမူ	ʔəmù	younger uncle
3)	ဒေံ	tèʔ	younger sibling	14)	သီ	sʊa	parent's younger sister
4)	ကောန်	kon	child	15)	ဣုနဲ	ʔiʔnày	older aunt
5)	စဴ	cao	grandchild	16)	အနဲ	ʔənày	older uncle
6)	စိက်, စီက်	cak, coc	great grandchild	17)	ဣုနောံ, ပ	ʔiʔnòk, pèa	grandmother
7)	စေက်	ciək	great great grandchild	18)	အနောံ, လ	ʔənòk, lèʔ	grandfather
8)	စော်	cok	great great great grandchild	19)	မိနက်, စု	mìʔ nèk, cùʔ	great grandmother
9)	ကောန်ကွိန်	kon mɛn	nephew, niece	20)	အပါနက်, ခ	ʔəpa nèk, cèʔ	great grandfather
10)	မိ, ယဲာ	mìʔ, yày	mother	21)	ဣုစု	ʔiʔcùʔ	younger sister of grandfather
11)	မ, အပါ	mèʔ, ʔəpa	father	22)	အစု, လစု	ʔəcùʔ, lèʔ cùʔ	younger brother of grandfather

5 Conclusion

This chapter sets out some of the main characteristics of Mon, one of the languages at the heart of the Mainland Southeast Asian linguistic area. Like Thai, Burmese and other neighbouring languages, Mon has a system of psycho-collocations formed from the same Pali etymon *citta* 'mind', a developed classifier system, an elaborate pronoun set which encodes social relations. Serial verb constructions and TOPIC-COMMENT type sentences are common, and pragmatic detail is indicated with sentence-final particles.

Abbreviations

ASRT	assertive
CAUS	causative
CLF	classifier
DES	desiderative
DIST	distal demonstrative
FOC	focus
LOC	locative
MEDL	medial demonstrative
MM	middle mon
NEG	negation
NMLZ	nominalizer
NSIT	new situation
OBL	oblique
OM	old Mon
PL	plural
PROX	proximal demonstrative
Q	question
RED	reduplication
REL	relativizer
SG	singular
SRC	source
SM	spoken Mon
TOP	topic

References

Aikhenvald, Alexandra Y. 2006. Serial verb constructions in typological perspective. In Alexandra Y. Aikhenvald & R. M. W. Dixon. *Serial Verb constructions*, 1–68. London: Oxford University Press.

Bauer, Christian. 1982. *Morphology and syntax of spoken Mon*. PhD dissertation, School of Oriental and African Studies, University of London.

Bril, Isabelle. 2004. Complex nuclei in Oceanic languages: Contribution to an areal typology. In I. Bril & F. Ozanne-Rivierre (eds.), *Complex Predicates in Oceanic Language: Studies in the Dynamics of Binding and Boundness*, 1–48. Berlin & New York: Mouton de Gruyter.

Chappell, Hilary. 2008. Variation in the grammaticalization of complementizers from *verba dicendi* in Sinitic languages. *Linguistic Typology* 12 (1). 45–98.

Diffloth, Gérard. 1984. *Dvaravati Old Mon and Nyah Kur*. Monic Language Studies, vol. 1. Bangkok: Chulalongkorn University Press.

Daniels, Peter T. & William Bright. 1996. *The world's writing systems*. Oxford: Oxford University Press.

Dixon, R. M. W. 2010. *Basic linguistic theory – Vol. 1: Methodology*. Oxford: Oxford University Press.

Enfield, Nick J. 2003. *Linguistic epidemiology*. London: Routledge Curzon.

Jenny, Mathias. 2003. New infixes in spoken Mon. *Mon-Khmer Studies* 33. 183–194.
Jenny, Mathias. 2005. *The verb system of Mon*. Zurich: Arbeiten des Seminars für Allgemeine Sprachwissenschaft (ASAS).
Jenny, Mathias. 2006. Mon 'raʔ' and 'noŋ': Assertive particles? *Mon-Khmer Studies* 36. 21–38.
Jenny, Mathias. 2009. Deixis and information structure in Mon. The multifunctional particle kòh. *Journal of the Southeast Asian Linguistics Society* 2. 53–72.
Lambrecht, Knud. 1994. *Information structure and sentence form*. Cambridge: Cambridge University Press.
Sidwell, Paul. 2014. Expressives in Austroasiatic. In Jeffrey P. Williams (ed.), *The aesthetics of grammar*, 17–35. Cambridge: Cambridge University Press.
Shorto, Harry L. 1962. *A dictionary of modern spoken Mon*. London: Oxford University Press.
Shorto, Harry L. 1971. A dictionary of the Mon inscriptions from the 6th to the 16th centuries. London: Oxford University Press.
van der Auwera, Johan, Peter Kehayov & Alice Vittrant. 2009. Acquisitive modals. In L. Hogeweg, H. De Hoop & A. Malchukov (eds.), *Cross-linguistic studies of tense, aspect, and modality*, 271–302. Amsterdam: John Benjamins.
Van Valin, Robert D. & Randy J. LaPolla. 1997. *Syntax: Structure, meaning, and function*. Cambridge: Cambridge University Press.

Appendix 1: Summary of linguistic features

Legend
+++ the feature is pervasive or used obligatorily in the language
++ the feature is normal but selectively distributed in the language
+ the feature is merely possible or observable in the language
− the feature is impossible or absent in the language

	Feature	+++/++/+/−	§ ref. in this chapter
Phonetics	Lexical tone or register	+++	§1.2, p.282
Phonetics	Back unrounded vowels	+	§1.1, p.281
Phonetics	Initial velar nasal	+++	§1.1, p.280
Phonetics	Implosive consonants	+++	§1.1, p.280
Phonetics	Sesquisyllabic structures	+++	§1.3, p.282 & §2.2, p.284
Morphology	Tendency towards monosyllabicity	+++	not discussed explicitly
Morphology	Tendency to form compounds	+++	§2.2, p.284
Morphology	Tendency towards isolating (rather than affixation)	+(+)	§2.1, p.283 & see also color terms, p.311
Morphology	Psycho-collocations	+++	§2.3, p.286
Morphology	Elaborate expressions (e.g. four-syllable or other set patterns)	+++	§2.4, p.287

	Feature	+++/++/+/−	§ ref. in this chapter
Morphology	Reduplication generally	+++	§2.5, p.288
Morphology	Reduplication of nouns	+	§2.5, p.288
Morphology	Reduplication of verbs	+++	§2.5, p.288–89
Grammar	Use of classifiers	+	§3.1.2, p.290
Grammar	Classifiers used in counting	+	§3.1.2, p.290
Grammar	Classifiers used with demonstratives	−	§3.1.1, p.290
Grammar	Adjectival verbs	+++	not discussed explicitly
Grammar	Grammatical number	++	§3.1.2, p.295
Grammar	Inflection of verbs	−	−
Grammar	Use of tense/aspect markers	++	§3.2.1, p.295 & also §3.2.3, p.299
Grammar	Use of verb plural markers	−	§3.2.1, p.295
Grammar	Grammaticalization of GET/OBTAIN (potential mod. resultative/perfect aspect)	+++	§3.2.2, §3.2.3, p.301
Grammar	Grammaticalization of PUT, SET (completed/resultative aspect) 'keep, deposit' > completed/resultative marker	+++	§3.2.3, p.302
Grammar	Grammaticalization of GIVE (causative, benefactive; preposition)	+++	§3.2.1, p.298 §3.2.4, p.304
Grammar	Grammaticalization of FINISH (perfective/ complete aspect; conjunction/temporal subordinator)	+++	§3.3.1, p.305
Grammar	Grammaticalization of directional verbs e.g. GO / COME (allative, venitive)	+++	§3.2.2, p.297 & §3.2.3, p.301
Grammar	Grammaticalization of SEE, WATCH (temptative)	++	not discussed explicitly
Grammar	Grammaticalization of STAY, REMAIN (progressive and continuous, durative aspects)	+++	not discussed explicitly
Grammar	Serial verb constructions	+++	§3.2.2, p.297
Syntax	Verb precedes object (VO)	++	§3.3, p.295
Syntax	Auxiliary precedes verb	++	§3.2.3, p.299
Syntax	Preposition precedes noun	+++	§3.1.4, p.294
Syntax	Noun precedes adjective	+++	§3.1, p.289

	Feature	+++/++/+/–	§ ref. in this chapter
Syntax	Noun precedes demonstrative	+++	§3.1, p.289
Syntax	Noun precedes genitive	+++	§3.1.3, p.292
Syntax	Noun precedes relative clause	+++	§3.1.3, p.293 & also table 6, p.290
Syntax	Use of topic-comment structures	+++	§3.3, p.304 also §3.1, p.290 & p.312
Syntax	Ellipsis of arguments known from context	+++	not discussed explicitly
Lexical semantics	Specific terms for forms of rice	+++	§4.2, p.310
Pragmatics	Use of utterance-final pragmatic particles	++	§3.3.4, p.308
Pragmatics	Encoding of politeness	+	§3.3.4, p.308
Pragmatics	Encoding of honorifics	+	§4.1, p.309

Appendix 2: Text interlinearized

Memories of World War II in Monland

အေ နူကိုသက္ကရာတ် ၃၀၃ ဎား၊ ဂျပါနဲတံ့နံအာစုံပံကြုင်ံကင်ဂံ၊ ကာဂျပါနဂံနက်မံင်အဲဂံတဲ့တံေ ခွုံပလးနင်ကောန်စလဇ္ကြုံအံမ္ဂံ အင်ဂံလံက်ဂံ။

ʔe	nù	kɒ	sɛkkerât	pʋaʔ-klɔm-pʋaʔ		nah	cəpan	tʊn	ʔa
well	from	OBL	era	three-hundred-three		EMPH	Japanese	up	go

cʋp	krɤŋ-kɛŋ	kɔ̀h,	ka	cəpan	kɔ̀h	nɛ̀k	mɔ̀ŋ	hənày	kɔ̀h
arrive	Kroeng-Kang	MEDL	car	Japanese	MEDL	stuck	stay	place	MEDL

toə	teh	dɛh	həlɛ̀h	nɛ̀ŋ	kon.cao	ləcùʔ	krʋʔ	mùə
finish	TOP	3	CAUS.free	CAUS.come	grandchild	old.man	stout	one

ʔeŋkəlòc	kɔ̀h.
English	MEDL

'It was in the year 1303 [1941 AD], right, that the Japanese came up to Kroeng Kang village. Their car got stuck there, and they released the grandchild of a stout old man, that Englishman.'

ကာလဂို့ အင်္ဂလိက်န္တီမင်ပွဲကြက်ပိဂို့ ပိနုစာ ပွဲပုဂို့နိုင်စာ အေ ဂပဝ်ကျှိင်ခြိုက်ကွှင်ကြက်ပိဂို့ ဂပဝ်ကျှိင်နောကာစ်မှီကြှင်ကင်တောံသေင်၊ အေ ကျှိုင်ဂဗဆိုစုတ်ဂျပါန်အွဲဂို့နိုင်တ အင်္ဂလိက်တံဂို့လေဝ် အာလဂို့ ...

kalaʔ	kɔ̀h	ʔɛŋkəlòc	nùm	mɔ̀ɲ	ɗɔə	krʏk-pʊəʔ	pʊəʔ.coh,	ɗɔə	pəŋaʔ
time	MEDL	English	exist	stay	LOC	Kroek-Poi	thirty	LOC	Panga

kɔ̀h	pʊəʔ.coh.	ʔe	həpɔ	klʏŋ	ɗak	ɓɛŋ	krʏk-pʊəʔ	kɔ̀h,
MEDL	thirty	well	go.around	come	ride	ship	Kroek-Poi	MEDL

həpɔ	klʏŋ	kənot	ɓi	krʏŋ-kɛŋ	tʏʔ	siəŋ,	ʔe	klʏŋ
go.around	come	far.end	river	Kroeng-Kang	DIST	right?	well	come

həpɛ̀ʔ	chʏ	cut	cəpan	hənày	kɔ̀h	teh	ʔɛŋkelòc	tɔʔ	kɔ̀h	lɛ
meet	find	PUT	Japanese	place	MEDL	TOP	English	PL	MEDL	ADD

ʔa	ləkɔ̀h	...
go	then	...

'At that time there were thirty English at Kroek Poi, another thirty at Panga. They made a detour around [the Japanese], riding a ship to Kroek Poi. They came to the far end of the Kroeng Kang river, and here they bumped into the Japanese, and then the English went ...'

အင်္ဂလိက်ဂို့ မုခြိုက်ကျှိုင်မှု။

ʔɛŋkəlòc	kɔ̀h	mùʔ	ɗak	klʏŋ	mùʔʔ
English	MEDL	what	ride	come	what

'What did they ride coming here, the English?'

လ္ဂာ ... ချိုက်ကျှိုင်လ္ဂာ ချိုကဂကျှိုင်လ္ဂာတွဲတို့ လ္ဂာဂို့ထော်ထော်ဖအိုတ်။ ကြိပ်စကျှိုင်ကွာန်ပွတဲ့နိုင်တ စိတ်ထပို့နာခို့မို့ဂို့တော တိုန်အာချုင်မတ်မလိုတော်။ ဂုံနိုင်ကာကို့ထောန်မေဝ်မှုမ ဂုံနိုင်ကာကို့ဂျဝ်ဒေန်မှုမ။ အေ ကာလဂို့တို့ စိုပ်အာကန်ှိသင်လာတော်။ ပန်နာခိုပယျှီယးတော် ဂျပါန်တံမိုင်ဂွံလဂို့ ...

la,	ɗak klʏŋ	la	toə	teh la	kɔ̀h	thʊʔ	hʊʔ	həʔʊt.
donkey	ride come	donkey	FINISH	TOP donkey	MEDL	discard	DISCARD	ADV.all

krìp	cao	klʏŋ	kwan	pəŋaʔ	toə	teh	ɓʊt	həpɔh	nədì
run	return	come	village	Panga	FINISH	TOP	about	seven	hour

hətɔm	kɔ̀h	teh	tʊn	ʔa	ɗʏŋ	mòt.məlʏ̀m	tʏʔ	kʏʔ	nɛ̀ŋ	ka
night	MEDL	TOP	go.up	go	town	Moulmein	DIST	get	CAUS.come	car

kɤ-thon-mè	mùə	mὲʔ,	kɤʔ	nὲŋ	ka	kɤ-kyɔ̀-tὲn	mùə	mὲʔ.
Ko-Htun-May	one	CLF	get	CAUS.come	car	Ko-Kyaw-Tin	one	CLF

ʔe	kalaʔ	kɔ̀h	teh,	cʊp	ʔa	kyac-sɛŋ-làn	tɤʔ.	pɔn	nədî
well	time	MEDL	TOP	arrive	go	Kyaik-Than-Lan	DIST	four	hour

pəyʊ	yèh	tɤʔ	cəpan	tɔʔ	pàŋ	kɤʔ	ləkɔ̀h ...
border	dawn	DIST	Japanese	PL	surround	GET	then

'Donkeys, they came riding donkeys, and then they just got rid of them all. They ran back here to Panga village and then about seven o'clock that night they went up to Moulmein. They got one car from Ko Htun May, and they got another car from Ko Kyaw Tin. Well, then they went to Kyaik Than Lan pagoda. At four o'clock, before dawn, the Japanese had surrounded [the place] ...'

လွဟ်ခုံအလီတော်။

ləwɔ̀h	dɛh	ʔəlʊ	thʊʔʔ
weapon	3	where	discard

'Where did they put their weapons?'

ထော်ထော်ပဲကြိပ်ဂုံဖအိတ်ရ။

thʊʔ	hʊʔ	dɔə	kɤɤp	kɔ̀h	həʔʊt	raʔ.
discard	DISCARD	LOC	forest	MEDL	ADV.all	FOC

'They just threw them away in that forest.'

ကံဂုံထော်လဝ်ဘွဲ့ဂုံဖအိတ်။

kɔm	kɔ̀h	thʊʔ	lɔ̀	hənày	kɔ̀h	həʔʊt
bullet	MEDL	discard	deposit	place	MEDL	ADV.all

'The bullets too, they threw them all away there.'

ဂျပါန်ခြိုက်ဂွံတဲ့ အင်္ဂလိက်လက်လီအာ။

cəpan	dak	kɤʔ	toə,	ʔeŋkəlòc	lɛk	lʊ	ʔaʔ
Japanese	ride	GET	FINISH	English	side	which	go

'When the Japanese gained the upper hand, where did the English go?'

အေ ဂျပါန်ဂုံခြိုက်ဂွံ အာရပ်ဂွံအင်္ဂလိက်၊ ခုံရပ်ဂွံလဝ်ဖအိတ်။ အဲဂုံေ ပန်မင်သည်းသွဲဂုံပ်ပုံတဲ့ နုမတ္တမတော်ဗလးနှင် နင်္ကွဲမတ်မလီဟုံဗလးဏာ။ အေ လဂုံတဲ့တ အယောနရေဇင်မင်္ဂုံ လဂျပါန်တိုန် လိက်ဟာပင်တော် ဂျပါန်ေနက္ကာဏာဌာန်တိုက်တော်။ အေလဂုံတဲ့တ အင်္ဂလိက်ဆုတ်တ်အာ။

ʔe	cəpan	kɔ̀h	dak	kɤʔ	ʔa	rɔ̀p	kɤʔ	ʔeŋkəlòc,	dɛh	rɔ̀p	kɤʔ
well	Japanese	MEDL	ride	GET	go	catch	get	English	3	catch	get

lɔ̃	haʔʊt.	hənày	kɔ̀h	teh	pɔn	mɔ̀ŋ	ɲèh.həkɔʔ	pʋəʔ	hətɔm
DEPOSIT	ADV.all	place	MEDL	TOP	shoot	stay	each.other	three	night

pʋəʔ	ŋuə,	nù	mɔttemaʔ	tɤʔ	həlèh	nèŋ,	nù	kʋ	mòt.məlɤ̀m
three	day	from	Martaban	DIST	CAUS.free	CAUS.come	from	OBL	Moulmein

nɔʔ	həlèh	na.	ʔe	ləkɔ̀h	toə	teh	ʔəkhɤ̀	chɔ̀ɲ	mɔ̀ŋ	kɔ̀h
PROX	CAUS.free	CAUS.go	well	then	FINISH	TOP	while	fight	STAY	MEDL

laʔ	cəpan	tʊn	lɔ̀k-həplɛŋ	tɤʔ	cəpan	klʋʔ	na
when	Japanese	go.up	Lok-Haplang	DIST	Japanese	cross	CAUS.go

ɗan	tak	tɤʔ.	ʔe	ləkɔ̀h	teh	ʔɛŋkəlòc	chut	ʔa.
road	land	DIST	well	then	TOP	English	go.back	go

'Well, when the Japanese gained he upper hand they went and managed to capture English [soldiers]. They captured them all. At that place they kept shooting at each other for three nights and three days. From over there in Martaban they shot over here, and from here in Moulmein they shot there. Well, while they were still engaging each other in the fight, when the Japanese went up to Lok Haplang, they crossed that road. Well, then the English retreated.'

အေတဲ့လကၠဒ်ကျာကျၤင်အာကိုကၠံန္ထသင်ကပူ ...

ʔe	toə	laʔ	ɓɛŋ.kya	klɤŋ	ʔa	kʋ	klɔm	nù	sɛŋkəpu ...
well	FINISH	when	airplane	come	go	OBL	hundred	from	Singapore

'And when hundreds of airplanes came and went from Singapore ...'

အင်္သကၠရာတ် ၃၀၁ သင်ကပူဒကား အာယျ၊ ၃၀၃ ဂံ ဂျပါန်ဇိပ်ဍုင်ပိုဏံ။

ʔəkɔ̀h	sɛkkəràt	pʋəʔ-klɔm-mùə	sɛŋkepu	həkah	ʔa	yaʔ
NMLZ.MEDL	era	three-hundred-one	Singapore	break	go	NSIT

pʋəʔ-klɔm-pʋəʔ	kɔ̀h	cəpan	cʊp	ɗɤŋ	poy	nɔʔ.
three-hundred-three	MEDL	Japanese	arrive	land	1PL	PROX

'That was in 1301, Singapore had already fallen. In 1303 the Japanese reached our land.'

John Haiman
Khmer

Introduction

Location and number of speakers

Most of the speakers of Central Khmer live in present-day Cambodia, where it is the native language of 90% of the current population of 14 million. Outside Cambodia, there are communities speaking Northern dialects (Surin and Tatey), estimated at 200,00–500,000 people in the Dangrek and Cardamom mountain border regions of Cambodia and the southern third of Northeast Thailand (Prakorb 1992, Jenner 1974, Martin 1975) and a Southeastern dialect (Kiangkleang/ Kiengiang) spoken by no fewer than 600,000 people in the Mekong river delta region of what used to be Cambodia, but is now Vietnam (Thach 1999).

Surin Khmer retains: a) syllable-final [r], which Central Khmer has lost (Gorgoniev 1966: 14, Jenner 1974: 63, Martin 1975: 76), and, possibly, (b) phonemic register (Martin asserting its existence in Tatey, and Jenner 1974: 62 denying it in Surin).

Kiangkleang Khmer exhibits incipient phonemic falling or low tone, arising concomitant with the loss of syllable-initial [r], whether as the only consonant or as the second consonant in a cluster (Thach op.cit., Wayland and Guion 2007). Tone is nowhere else phonemic in Khmer. In contradistinction to most Mon-Khmer languages, Central Khmer no longer exhibits phonemic register (Gorgoniev 1966, Huffman et al. 1970, Lim et al. 1972, Vickery 1990, pace Henderson 1952 and Jacob 1968), although there are careful reading pronunciations where the clear/breathy contrast is maintained.

Khmer within Mon-Khmer

Khmer is now identified as the main language of the "Khmeric" group within Mon-Khmer, with no particularly close subgrouping ties to Mon (Sidwell 2010). A number of languages which were formerly identified as members of this subfamily, among them Stieng and Kuj (Jenner 1969: 1) are now no longer thought

---

John Haiman: Macalester College
E-Mail: haiman@macalester.edu

1 Phonology

1.1 Register: Orthography casts a long shadow

Khmer has been written since the 7th Century CE, and the written tradition is held in some reverence. This has had a number of consequences, among them the careful reading pronunciations. Although contrasting "clear/head" and "breathy/chest" registers are identified as phonological benchmarks of Khmer, the almost entirely moribund contrast is now one that is preserved mainly in careful reading pronunciations, because it is obligatorily represented in the orthography.

Another spelling pronunciation which hews to the writing system is the "retention" of word-final <s>, which is normally pronounced [h]. Hypercorrect final [s] is in fact sometimes provided for words in final orthographic <h> as well. So, not only can <nas> ណាស់ /nah/ "very" be spoken as [nas], so too can <nih> នេះ /nih/ "this" be pronounced [nis]. That said, it must be noted that not even spelling pronunciations "restore" word-final <r>. So, for example, written <khmaer> ខ្មែរ is always [khmae], and <thoarm> ធម៌ "the dharma" is spoken as [thoa].

Although "default vowels" are not written, the orthography still distinguishes between [CVC] which arises through the anaptyctic insertion of schwa between consonants in a underlying cluster /CC/, and an organic string [CVC] which corresponds to a sequence /CVC/. (Minimal contrast pairs arise where the default vowel is unwritten. The second consonant in an underlying C_1C_2 cluster is represented by a subscripted form, which is distinct from the full-size form of the same consonant.) Now the rule of anaptyxis clearly applies between /r/ and a following consonant[1], but it happens that the orthography recognizes no cases of underlying /rC/ clusters whatsoever. That is, all cases of [rVC] are treated orthographically as if they were underlying strings /r+ default V +C/. The result is that careful spelling pronunciations of hundreds of words like របស់ <robawh>

---

[1] As is made clear from derivational morphological facts. For example, the relationship between រលាយ /rliaj/ "melt, dissolve (intransive) and រំលាយ /r-um-llaj/ "melt, dissolve (transitive) is exactly parallel to that between ស្លាប់ /slap/ "die" and សម្លាប់ /s-am-lap/ "kill". In each case, the causativizing infix –Vm- is inserted between the first and second consonants of an initial cluster.

"thing, possession" (from រស់ /ruah/ "live") give the anaptyctic vowel an etymologically unwarranted independent vowel coloring which is lacking in structurally parallel words like ល្បែង <lbaeng> "game" (from លេង /lee:ng/ "play").

1.2 The segmental phonemic inventory

All transcriptions are presented in a practical orthography defended at length in Haiman (2011). For the most part, the IPA equivalents are straightforward.

1.2.1 Consonants

	Bilabial	Alveolar	Palatal	Velar	Glottal
Stop	p,b	t,d	c	k	ʔ
Fricative	f	s		h	
Nasal	m	n	nj	ng	
Liquid		l			
Rhotic		r			
Glide	v		j		

Voiced stops <b,d> are ingressive word-initially, egressive elsewhere.
The rhotic <r> is an alveolar flap or trill.

1.2.2 Syllabic Nuclei

Monophthongs:	Front	Mid	Back
High	i, i:	w, w:	u, u:
Mid	ee, ee:	eu, eu:	o, o:
Low-mid	e, e:	au,	au:
Low	ae	a, a:	aw, aw:

The high mid vowel <w> is phonetically [ɯ];
The mid front vowel <ee> is phonetic [e];
The mid mid vowel <eu> is phonetic [ɤ];
The low-mid mid vowel <e> is phonetic [ɛ];
The low-mid back vowel <au> is phonetic [ɔ];
The low front vowel <ae> is a long diphthong [ae:] or a long [æ:];
The low back vowel <aw> is phonetic [ɑ].

Schwa is represented by <a> in initial unstressed syllables and in offgliding diphthongs, and by <e> as a monophthong before palatals and glides. Thus បង្អួច <bang'uac> "window" is [bəŋ'uəc], and ដី <dej> "earth, land" is [dəj].

All monophthongs except <ae> (always long) occur in contrastive long and short forms.

Diphthongs: ia ([iə])   wa ([ɯə])   ua ([uə])
              ea ([ɛə])   oa ([oə])
                             aeu ([aɣ])
                             ao

All diphthongs except <ao> and <aeu> are schwa-offglides.

The apparent diphthongs
<ej> ([ej], [əj], [ɨj]), as in e.g. បី <bej> "three"
<ev> ([eɯ], [əɯ], [ɨɯ]), as in e.g. ទៅ <tev> "go"
<a(:)j> ([a(:)j]), as in e.g. ដៃ <daj> "hand, arm", បាយ <ba:j> "cooked rice", and
<a(:)v> ([a(:)ɯ]), as in e,g. ក្ដៅ <kdav> "warm", អាវ <a:v> "shirt",

are all phonemicized as V+C sequences (that is, as syllable rhymes, rather than nuclei), because unlike the true diphthongs, they cannot be followed by a tautosyllabic consonantal coda.

1.3 Word and syllable structure

Khmer has a high number of Pali loanwords (perhaps 40% of the entries in Headley et al. 1977), some of which are totally unassimilated to the canons of Khmer phonological structure.

The canonical native vocabulary is largely monosyllabic or bisyllabic. If bisyllabic, it is "sesquisyllabic", that is to say, iambically stressed with a highly reduced initial syllable. Based on the historical evidence, most sesquisyllabic words with a sharply reduced initial syllable derive from earlier bisyllabic words with full initial syllables, and the erosion of the initial syllable of such words is a still on-going historical process (Pinnow 1957, Huffman et al. 1970: 109 et passim). The typical Khmer native word is thus composed of an initial unstressed syllable plus a stressed second syllable, or of a single stressed syllable. But these two patterns cannot be reduced to a single formula:

*Word = (Initial syllable) + Main syllable

Rather, the main syllable of sesquisyllabics must be distinguished from the sole syllable of monosyllabic roots:

Sesquisyllabic word = Initial syllable + Main syllable, and Monosyllabic word = Monosyllable

The reason is that the syllable structure constraints on the main syllable in a sesquisyllabic word are much more restrictive than those on the typical monosyllable. While the rhyme portions of main syllables and monosyllables are identical (syllables are open or terminate with no more than a single consonant, which may be an unreleased stop, a glide, [h], or a nasal) their onsets differ. And the reason for this is that many presently monosyllabic words are themselves the maximally reduced remnants of earlier sesquisyllabic words, which derived from original bisyllabic words, typically via the elision of the rhyme portion of the initial syllable. Their (maximally biconsonantal) onsets may consist of the rubble (just the onset) of an eroded initial syllable followed by the regular onset of the main syllable. Monosyllables thus exhibit a huge variety of syllable-initial derived biconsonantal consonant clusters (Jenner and Pou (1982) enumerate over 120)[2] which do not arise in the main syllables of sesquisyllabics (where less than half a dozen clusters recur). Thus monosyllabic words like ផ្ទះ <pteah> "house", ល្មម <lmau:m> "comfortable", ថ្ងៃ <tngaj> "day", ក្បែរ <kbae> "close to", ល្ពៅ <lpev> "pumpkin", and ឆ្នាំ <cnam> "year" exhibit initial consonant clusters which do not arise in the main syllables of sesquisyllabic words. Typically there is an anaptyctic schwa between the initial and the second consonant of cluster onsets: e.g. ល្ពៅ <lpev> "pumpkin" → [ləpəɯ], ស្តេច <sdac> "king" → [səda'c˺], whose phonological status can be ambiguous. If the phonetic schwa is inserted by a rule, these words are underlying monosyllables; if the schwa is always there, the words are sequisyllables. (Sometimes, the history of such words is still transparent. Thus ផ្ទះ <pteah> derives from Sanskrit *pada* "place".)

The only consonant clusters which are frequent in main syllable onsets are stop + liquid (e.g. កន្ត្រៃ <kan.traj> "scissors"), stop + glide (e.g. កខ្វក់ ka.kvawk "dirty"), and stop + [h] (e.g. រកេង <ra.kheang> "tall and skinny"). This state of affairs is compatible with Pinnow's (1957) suggestion that the monosyllabism of

---

[2] The exact number of such clusters depends on the status of the anaptyctic vowel, which depends in turn (at least in part, for literate speakers) on the conventional orthography, cf. the preceding note.

Khmer is the result of the same ongoing process of erosion as sesquisyllabicity. Inherited permissible syllable onsets are then only those which occur in main syllables. All others arise through erosion.

As for the initial syllable of sesquisyllabic words, its onset is the most highly restricted of all. The only permitted syllable structures here are CV- (e.g. in ទទួល <ta.tual> "receive, accept"), CrV- (e.g. in ក្រពើ <kra.peu:> "crocodile"), and CVN- (e.g. in ដំរី <dam.rej> "elephant"). The final vowel V can only be schwa (written as <a> in unstressed syllables) or [u] (the latter possible only before bilabials or nasals as in e.g. ជប់លៀង <cup.liang> "celebration, party" or ទំព័រ <tum.poa> "page").

Erosion of the initial unstressed syllable of sesquisyllabics via reduction of the syllable rhyme is the most pervasive phonological process in the modern spoken language. (It does not occur in reading styles at all.) It optionally reduces

CrV- to C(V) (e.g. ប្រហែល <prahael> "approximately, about" → [pəhael]),
CVN- to C(V) (e.g. ដង្កូវ <dangkev> "worm" → [təkəɯ]), and
C to zero (e.g. ផ្ទះ <pteah> "house" → [tɛəh] ~[tɛə]).

The unstressed syllable rhymes so demolished by erosion in casual speech can be "restored". Whether or not they were ever there is indeterminate. Note that this indeterminacy as to the phonological status of syllable rhymes in general begins with the anaptyctic vowel between onset-initial consonants. Is the reduced vowel inserted as the result of a rule of anaptyxis? Or is it what is left via the erosion of a fuller syllable? In the former case, the underlying structure of word-initial [CəC] is /CC/. But in the latter case, it may be /CrVC/ or /CVNC/. The indeterminacy leads on the one hand to triplets of synonymous words, as below.

ទំនើរ <t-um-neu:> ~ ទ្រនើរ < t-ra-neu:> ~ ត្នើរ <tneu:> "shelf"
ចំពើស <c-um-peu:h> ~ ច្របើស <c-ra-peu:h> ~ ច្បើស <cpeu:h> "crooked"
សំដី <s-am-dej> ~ ស្រដី <s-ra-dej> ~ ស្តី <sdej> "speech"

Presumably, one of these forms (possibly the monosyllabic form, possibly one of the sesquisyllabic forms) is the originally inherited one, the others being plausibly attributable to either attrition of the unstressed initial syllable, or hypercorrect restoration or back-formation processes of the familiar variety. The causative prefix is subject to the same tug-of-war between erosion and restoration, and it exhibits the same alternation, being written as

p- (e.g. in ផ្ដែក p-dee:k "lay down" from ដេក dee:k "lie down") ,
bVN- (almost fully productive, e.g. in បង្រៀន bang-rian "teach", from រៀន rian "study"),
pVN- (e.g. in បង្ឮ pun-lw: "make heard", from ឮ lw: "hear")
pra- (the last being infrequent, as in e.g. ប្រដូច prado:c "compare", from ដូច do:c "like, similar").

In casual pronunciation, there is no real difference between bVN- and p-: both may be realized as [ph] ~ [pə].

This same etymologically unmotivated "restoration" of lost phonetic material may lead on the other hand to the exaptative creation of new morphemes: the common infixes –Vm- and –rV- may have arisen by a kind of reinterpretive morphologization named "secretion" by Otto Jespersen (1964: 384). See the discussion of derivational morphology below in Section 3.1.

1.3.1 Assimilation

Unassimilated Indic, i.e. Sanskrit (Skt.), Prakrit or Pali (P.), borrowings are recognizable from their pronunciation. If a Khmer word consists of more than two syllables (e.g. ព្យញ្ជនៈ pjaunjcineah "consonant"), it is definitely an Indic borrowing (< P. vyañjana "letter"). (If the syllables are open, there is a strong tendency to close them with a final glottal stop in formal speech, e.g. អវីចី a'vi'cej "a level of hell" (< P. avīci "a hell"). If the word contains only two syllables, but the initial syllable features a nuclear vowel other than schwa or [u] (e.g. ពិសេស piseh "special"), it is a borrowing (< P. visesa "distinction"). If it consists of only two syllables, but the initial syllable features any initial consonant cluster other than Cr- (e.g. ស្នេហា snee:ha: "love"), it is a borrowing (< Skt. sneha). If it consists of only two syllables, but the initial syllable has any consonant coda other than a nasal (e.g. ធរណី thaurni: "earth"), it is a borrowing (<Skt., P. dharaṇī "world"). If it consists of only two syllables, but the second one is unstressed (e.g. វត្ថុ va.tho' "object"), it is a borrowing (< P. vatthu "object"). In the written language, even more borrowings are recognizable since transliterations tend to retain word-final consonants and consonant clusters which do not occur in the spoken language. Among the most common phonetically assimilated borrowings are set out below.

Table 1: Borrowings in Khmer

Khmer		gloss		Skt/Pali	gloss
ទឹក	teuk	water	<	(u)daka	water
ថ្ពាល់	tpoal	cheek	<	kapola	cheek
ទិស	twh	direction	<	disā	direction, point
នាម	niam	name, noun	<	nāma	name
រោម	ro:m	body hair	<	roma	body hair
ត្រកូល	trako:l	family	<	gotrakula	family
តាបស	ta:bawh	anchorite,	<	tāpasa	hermit, ascetic
សភា	sophia	council	<	sabhā	judge
ក្បាល	kba:l	head	<	kapāla	skull
គាត់	koat	3SG pronoun	<	jagat	people, world
ព្រះ	preah	god; honorific prefix	<	vara	excellent
ឃ្លាន	klian	hungry	<	gilāna	ill

2 Morphology

2.1 Derivational morphology

There is no inflectional morphology: in this respect, Khmer is a typical mainland SEAsian language. In contradistinction to other mainland Southeast Asian languages outside the Mon-Khmer family, however, Khmer exhibits a fairly elaborate derivational morphology. Moreover, derivational morphology and compounding exist in both the Indic and the Mon-Khmer vocabulary. Indic derivation is both prefixing and suffixing. Native derivation is exclusively prefixing and infixing. Although much is made of them (Haiman 2011: chapter 3), traces of possible inherited suffixing are barely attested.

2.1.1 Indic derivation and compounding

- **Nominalizations**

The borrowed Pali morphemes which can act as independent words and as suffixes include the following.

state nominalizer ភាព phiap (< P. *bhāva* 'condition')

សេរីភាព > សេរីភាព
see'rej   *see'rej-phiap*
'free'   'freedom'

an agent nominalizer ករ *kaw:* (< P. *kara* 'doing')

កីឡា > កីឡាករ
kejla: *kejla:-kaw:*
'sport'   'athlete'

action nominalizer កម្ម *kam* (< P. *kamma* 'deed, action')

អនិច្ច > អនិច្ចកម្ម
a'ni'ca   *a'ni'ca-kam*
'impermanent' 'death'

action nominalizer ឋាន *tha:n* (< *thāna* 'place')

ការ > ការដ្ឋាន
ka:(r)   *ka:r(a)-tha:n*
'work'   'construction site'

Alone among these four nominalizers, ភាព *phiap* may act as a prefix, as in the compounds:

(2) ភាពប្រាកដប្រជា   *phiap prakaw:t pracia*   'accuracy'
    ភាពឈ្លាសវៃ   *phiap cliah vej*   'quickwittedness'
    ភាពលំបាក   *phiap lumba:k*   'difficulty'
    ភាពស្រើបស្រាល   *phiap sreu:p sra:l*   'desire, sexual excitement'
    ភាពងាយរំភើប   *phiap ngiaj rumpheu:p*   'overexcitement'

Invariably prefixed nominalization affixes include two nouns meaning "matter, affair"

ការ *ka:* and សេចក្តី *(sec)kdej-* . Both are extremely productive, the first somewhat more than the second:

(3) រាប់អាន *roap a:n* > ការរាប់អាន *ka:-roap a:n*
'count depend'   'friendship, relationship of trust'

គ្រប់គ្រង *krup kraw:ng* > ការគ្រប់គ្រង *ka:-krup kraw:ng*
'protect, govern'   'government, protection'

កែតម្រូវ *kae tamrev* > សេចក្តីកែតម្រូវ *sec kdej kae tamrev*
'correct'   'correction'

សង្កេត *sangkee:t* > សេចក្តីសង្កេត *sec kdej sangkee:t*
'notice, observe'   '(foot)note; NB'

2.1.2 "Inflectional" suffixes

Included in this category are those affixes which are fully productive in Indic, but are recognizably foreign and as unproductive as derivational affixes in Khmer.

- **Number**

(4) កំហុស នានា   កំហុស ផ្សេងៗ
kamhoh nania   *kamhoh psee:ngpsee:ng*
mistake PL   mistake PL
'various mistakes'

Judging by their syntax, the pluralizing suffixes នានា *nania* (< Skt/P. nānā 'different') and ផ្សេងៗ *psee:ng psee:ng* 'various' are apparently Pali. That is, if they are inflectional affixes, they are suffixes, in keeping with canonical Pali Root + Suffix morphology. However, both are equally compatible with canonical Khmer Head # Attribute word order. That is, if they are adjectives, they follow the head noun, as in Khmer. Here is a case where the problem of identifying a morpheme as a word or an affix can be resolved by etymological evidence from another language. While *nania* is impeccably Pali (Ménétrier 1933: 79), and suggests the analysis Root + Suffix, there is no apparent evidence that *psee:ng* occurs in Pali.

Hence កំហុសផ្សេងៗ *kamhoh psee:ngpsee:ng* may be a case of Khmer Head # Attribute word order, rather than Pali Root+ Suffix morpheme order.

- **Gender**

For a handful of words, the original gender suffixes have been borrowed into Khmer from Pali.

(5) Pali female suffix -*a:*.

ឧបាសក *o.ba:saw:k* (< P. upāsaka)   ឧបាសិកា *o.ba:si.k - a:* (< P. upāsikā)
'lay devotee'   'lay devotee (female)'

(6) Pali female suffix -*ej* (< P. -ī)

កុមារ *kuma:r* (< P. kumāra)   កុមារី *kuma:rej* (< P. kumārī)
'boy'   'girl'

Highly educated speakers are aware of both the meanings and the origins of these suffixes, in much the same way as highly literate English speakers recognize the plural suffixes of words like *medium/media* or *cherub/cherubim*.

- **The negative prefix *a'* -**

There are enough paired Pali borrowings with and without this prefix that Khmer speakers can parse many words that contain it (as English speakers can do with the cognate prefix in *a*-moral, possibly *a-gnostic*, but cannot generally do with *a-tom*, and so on).

(7.a) មនុស្ស → អមនុស្ស
manuh~mea.nuh   *a.mea.nuh*
(< P. manussa)   (< P. amanussa)
'human'   'non-human, supernatural'

(7.b) និច្ច → អនិច្ច
nicca   *a.nicca*
(< P. nicca)   (< P. anicca)
'eternal'   'impermanent'

2.1.3 Native derivational affixation

- **Nominalizations**

The prefix/infix *am-* ~ *aN-* is a largely purely decorative affix. Note that N represents a alveolar, palatal, velar, or labial nasal homorganic with the following obstruent. Phonologically, [h] [v], ['], and [r] pattern in the same way as velars.

(8) ឬក re:k "carry on a pole over one's → អំរែក am-re:k "burden so carried"
    shoulders"
    ចង caw:ng "bind; catch fish with a → អញ្ចង anj-caw:ng "fishing net, line"
    net"
    រឹង reung "tight"   → អង្រឹង ang-reung "hammock"

The nominalizing infix *-aN-* (clear register) ~ *-uN-* (breathy register). There are relatively few examples of this, and their meaning is not always entirely clear.

(9) ខ្ចប់ kcawp "wrap"   → កញ្ចប់ k- anj-cawp "package"
    ផ្ញើ pnjaeu "send, present, offer" → បញ្ញើ b-anj- njaeu "gift, messenger"

The nominalizing infix *-am(n)-* (with roots in the clear register) ~ *-um(n)-* (with roots in the breathy register). If this derivation is productive (and it is common enough to seem nearly so), then it provides one of the few pieces of evidence for the reality of a phonemic register distinction in Khmer.

(10) ច្រៀង criang "sing" (clear register) → ចម្រៀង c-am-riang "song"
     ជ្រាប criap "be informed" (breathy   → ជំរាប c-um-riap "being informed"
     register)

The [n] enlargement occurs if the infix (which follows the first consonant of the root) is prevocalic:

ឆ្លើយ claeuj "answer (verb)" → ចម្លើយ c-am-laeuj "answer (noun)"
កើត kaeut "be born"   → កំណើត k-am+n- aeut "birth".

Usually the derivations with all three of the affixes *am- ,-Vm(n)-* , and *–VN-* mean "(result of) act of doing". Their near-identity of form and meaning suggest the possibility that the prefix and the infixes have a common origin, and that therefore the infix may have arisen via metathesis.

- **Causative affixes**

There are five causative affixes, distinguished in the orthography: the infix -*am(n)*-, the prefixes *baN*-, *paN*-, *p(a)*-, and the rarer prefix *pra*-. The first three prefixes have already been dealt with in the treatment of erosion. It is most likely that they are all the same morpheme in different stages of reduction. The last prefix may be the result of a back-formation. The infix -*am(n)*- (clear register) ~ -*um(n)*- (breathy register) is homophonous with the nearly productive nominalizer infix discussed above.

(11) ស្លត់ *slot* "terrified, panic-stricken" → សំឡត់ *s-am-lot* "terrify, intimidate"
ជ្រុះ *cruh* "fall" → ជំរុះ *c-um-ruh* "drop"
ស្លាប់ *slap* "die" → សម្លាប់ *s-am-lap* "kill"

- **Instrumental**

The infix -*n*- may denote "instrument for", as in

(12) រាស់ *roah* "harrow (V)" → រនាស់ *ra-n-oah* "harrow(N)"
កើយ *kaeuj* "rest one's head" → ខ្នើយ *k-n-aeuj* "pillow"
សែង *saeng* "jointly carry on a pole" → ស្នែង *s-n-aeng* "a carrying pole"
ដល់ *dawl* "arrive" → ផ្លូវ *t-n-awl* "street"
ដាល *daol* "punt" → ត្នោល *t-n-aol* "punting pole"
ទាក់ *teak* "join" → ត្នាក់ *t-n-eak* "linking word"
(this is a neologism)
ដោះ *do:* "exchange" → ត្នោះ *t-n-o:* "means of exchange"
សិត *seut* "comb (V)" → ស្និត *s-n-eut* "comb (N)"

But other meanings are also attested for this infix:

(13) សូរ *so:* "a sound" → ស្នូរ *s-n- o:* "a sound"
បួស *bua:h* "undergo initiation as a monk" → ប្នួស *p-n-ua:h* "ordination"

- **The (usually) Agent infix - m -**

(14) ដើរ *daeu* "walk" → ដម្រើ *t-m-aeu* "walker, pedestrian"
លួច *luac* "steal" → លម្ចួ *l-m-uac* "thief" (archaic)
ចាំ *cam* "wait" → ឆ្មាំ *c-m-am* "guard"
សូន *so:n* "mold" → ស្មូន *s-m-o:n* "potter"
ជួញ *cuanj* "do business, trade" → ឈ្មួញ *c-m-uanj* "businessman, trader"

The *m*- formative also builds rare nominalizations as a prefix:

(15) ហូប *ho:p* "eat" → ម្ហូប *m-ho:p* "food"
    ចាស់ *cah* "old" → ម្ចាស់ *m-cah* "owner"

- **The nominalizing infix -*b*-.**

Pou (2004: 135–41), in an exhaustive catalog, lists 72 cases of this infix in Khmer. More frequently than not, it is phonetically irregular in that the vowel of the root is altered in unpredictable ways when the infix occurs:

(16) រស់ *ruah* "live" → របស់ *ro-b-awh* "thing"
    លេង *lee:ng* "play" → ល្បែង *l-b-aeng* "game"
    រីង *ri:ng* "dry" → របេង *r-b-ee:ng* "drought"
    រាំ *roam* "dance (V)" → របាំ *r-b-am* "dance (N)"
    ឮ *lw:* "hear" → ល្បី *l-b-ej* "famous"

2.1.4 Derivation via regular syntactic compounding

- **Prefix អ្នក *neak* "person"**

Nouns of agency in Khmer are totally regularly formed by the syntactic device of prefixing អ្នក *neak* "person" to a verb or noun:

(17) ទាយ *tiaj* "predict" → អ្នកទាយ *neak tiaj* "fortune teller"
    ទាស់ *toah* "disagree, have strife" → អ្នកទាស់ *neak toah* "wrongdoer"
    និពន្ធ *nipun* "write (literature)" → អ្នកនិពន្ធ *neak nipun* "writer"
    ណែនាំ *naenoam* "advise" → អ្នកណែនាំ *neak naenoam* "advisor"

- **Ordinalizer ទី *ti:* "place"**

As a prefix, this converts a cardinal numeral into the corresponding ordinal:

(18.a) ជ្រូកមួយ
    cru:k   muaj
    pig   one
    "a pig"

(18.b) ជ្រូកទីមួយ
    cru:k   ti: muaj
    pig   place   one
    "the first pig"

2.1.5 Possible Origins of Infixation in Khmer

All prefixes and infixes in Khmer create the favorite word structure: a sequisyllabic iambic foot. No sequisyllabic root (with the signal striking exception of ដំបូន្មាន *d-am-bo:nmian* "advice") tolerates the addition of an affix that would create a third syllable, cf. Haiman (1998: 600, 610), Pou (2004b: 25). It is as if many of the so-called derivational processes of Khmer existed to do no more than to restore a structure that is and constantly has been subject to phonetic erosion, specifically by undoing that erosion, most typically the loss of the rhyme portion of the anacrusic syllable.

It is also noteworthy that the optionally inserted and often meaningless strings /VN/, /Vm/, and /rV/ described by Gorgoniev 1966, Jenner 1969, Jacob 1976, Prakorb 1992, Pou 2004, and Haiman & Ourn 2003 for Central and Northern Khmer are exactly the strings that are most regularly eliminated by unstressed initial syllable reduction in casual speech, and that they occur in exactly the same position: between the first and second consonants in the onset of monosyllabic roots. In those cases where the inserted string is etymologically motivated, its pronunciation can be regarded as simply a careful restoration of an inherited underlying structure.

There is possibly no real difference between these strings and simple interconsonantal schwa in syllable onsets. Both are characterized by the same phonological indeterminacy. They may be there in the underlying representation of the word, and then eroded. Or they may be absent in the underlying representation, and then inserted by a generalized rule of "anaptyxis".

Haiman (1998, 2003) proposed that the nearly productive and generally meaningful derivational infix {-*Vm(n)*-}, apparently confined to Cambodian and Kammu, may owe its origin to exactly such an insertion process. An initially meaningless (possibly decorative but in any case purely phonetic) restoration – whether of a lost nasal in Central Khmer or of a lost rhotic in Surin Khmer (Prakorb 1992) – has been morphologized to create in some cases meaningful infixes denoting nominalization (in hundreds of words like កំណើត *k-amn-aeut* "birth"), causation (as in dozens of words like សម្លាប់ *s-am-lap* "kill"), and finally, apparently meaningless infixes in a number of other words that should be nominalizations or causatives by the look of things but are not (an ostensibly derivational procedure results in no derivational change of state, cf. Haiman and Ourn 2003). What looks like a nominalization is still a verb; what looks like a causative or transitive verb is still an intransitive one. This is the state of affairs we called "syntactic backsliding". But possibly there is no syntactic backsliding going on. Rather than undoing an apparent morphological derivation, the syntax simply treats the infixation as the meaningless insertion that it originally was.

If this hypothesis about the origin of -*Vm(n)*- is correct, then the most productive infixation process in Khmer is itself an iambic or sesquisyllabic phenomenon. In opposition to the processes of erosion, rather than reducing a sesquisyllabic word to monosyllabicity, it rebuilds a monosyllable and restores it to sesquisyllabicity. Like the quintessential rule of interconsonantal anaptyctic schwa insertion which converts monosyllabic words with complex consonant cluster onsets into sesquisyllables with a reduced vowel in their first syllable, it serves primarily to convert a monosyllabic word into a disyllabic one.

2.2 Psycho-collocations

Minds are hearts in Khmer as in many other SE Asian languages. Note that the expression ចិត្ត *ceut* "heart" is itself a Pali borrowing (< P. citta), which figures in the expressions below:

Table 2: 'Heart' psycho-collocations in Khmer

ចិត្តជា	ceut cia	good heart
ចិត្តច្រើន	ceut craeun	upset, offended
ចិត្តផ្អែត	ceut c'aet	to one's heart's content (literally "heart is full")
ចិត្តក្តៅ	ceut kdav	disappointed (literally "heart is hot")
ចិត្តខ្លាំង	ceut klang	upset, stressed (literally "strong heart")
ចិត្តធំ	ceut thom	pretentious, boastful (literally "big heart")
ចិត្តទូលាយ	ceut tuliaj	generous (literally "spacious heart")
ជូរចិត្ត	cu: ceut	harsh (literally "sour heart")
កំលាចិត្ត	kamla: ceut	encourage (literally, "make+brave heart")
ខកចិត្ត	khaw:k ceut	disappointed (literally "empty heart")
ខ្លោចចិត្ត	klaoc ceut	heartbroken (literally "burn heart")
ខ្លាចចិត្ត	kla:c ceut	embarrassed, shy (literally "afraid heart')
គាប់ចិត្ត	koap ceut	grateful, satisfied (literally "heart is satisfied")
ពេញចិត្ត	penj ceut	satisfied, happy, eager (literally "fill heart")
ផ្គាប់ចិត្ត	pkoap ceut	gladden (the causative of *koap ceut*)
ផ្លូវចិត្ត	plav ceut	feelings, mental illness (literally "road heart")
ត្រូវចិត្ត	trev ceut	get along well (literally "heart is correct")
ត្រជាក់ចិត្ត	traceak ceut	calm, serene (literally "cool heart")
ទឹកចិត្ត	teuk ceut	mood, state of mind (literally "water heart")
ផ្ចិត	p+ceut	pay careful attention, concentrate meticulously

2.3 Elaborate expression: Symmetrical compounds

Symmetrical or repetitive compounds are sometimes iconic: Repetition means repetition.

(19.a) ចប់ចុងចប់ដើម
cawp cong cawp daeum
stop treetop stop treetrunk
"exhaustive, from A to Z"

(19.b) ខួបប្រាំងខួបវស្សា
khuap prang khuap vassa:
cycle dry cycle rainy
"in all seasons, year-round"

(19.c) ម្ខាងពីរនាក់ពីរនាក់
mkha:ng pi: neak pi: neak
one-side two person two person
"two people on each side"

Decorative symmetry, which also occurs at the phrase and word level, is another matter. The impulse to create pumped-up expressive doublets like *last and final* exists in English, but the phenomenon is hypertrophied in Khmer, as in many other languages of Southeast Asia (cf. Nacaskul 1976, Watkins' chapter on Wa). It affects not only nouns and verbs, but conjunctions, prepositions, negative particles, and possibly even derivational affixes (cf. Schmidt 1916, who proposed that the nominalizing/causative infix *–Vmn-* , a phonotactically conditioned allomorph of *–Vm-*, may have originated as a symmetrical compound of synonymous *–Vm-* and *–n-*).

Four-word symmetrical constructions, often asyndetic coordinations of two NPs or VPs, consist of the same initial word repeated with different second words, in effect creating an ABAC "alliterating" pattern. Either B and C are synonyms, or one of them is nonsense.

(20.a) ដាក់ខ្លួនដាក់កាយ
dak kluan dak ka:j
put body put body (ka:j is a Pali borrowing)
"throw oneself into something energetically, enthusiastically"

(20.b) ខាតសព្វខាតគ្រប់
     kha:t   saw:p   kha:t   krup
     lose   everything lose   everything (saw:p is from Pali)
     "lose everything"

The nonsense word may be a word which cannot possibly have its usual meaning in the symmetrical expression:

(21.a) ងូតទឹកងូតភក់
     ngu:t   teuk   ngu:t   phuak
     wash   water   wash   mud
     "wash/shower" (in water alone: "mud" is decorative here)

(21.b) អី   ចេះ   អី   ចុះ
     ej   ceh   ej   coh
     what   know   what   descend/Q particle
     "vaguely, generally, indefinably"

In this case, ចេះ *ceh* and ចុះ *coh* are obviously not synonyms, nor is either of them meaningless, but they seem to be yoked together in this construction because of their common sound.

Alternatively the nonsense form may be a totally made-up word:

(22.a) ក្របីទាំងហ្វូងទាំងហ្វាយ
     krabej   teang   fo:ng   teang fa:j
     A   B   A   C
     buffalo whole herd whole   – (fa:j does not exist as a separate word)
     "whole herd of water-buffalo"

(22.b) យ៉ាងណាយ៉ាងណី
     ja:ng   na: ja:ng   nej
     kind   any   kind   – (nej does not exist as a separate word)
     "anything at all"

What is true of four-word expressions is also true of pairs. There are an enormous number of more or less lexicalized synonym pairs:

(23) កំយខ្លាច   phej kla:c   "fear"
    ខ្លាចផ្សា   klaoc psa: "burn"
    ស្អប់ខ្ពើម   s'awp kpeu:m   "loathe"
    ព្រួយបារម្ភ   pruaj baraum   "worry"
    ឮសូរ   lw: so: "hear, be audible"
    ចៀសវាង   ciah viang   "avoid"
    អាថិកំបាំង   a: kambang   "secret, arcane, mysterious"
    ដឹកជញ្ជូន   deuk canjcu:n   "transport"
    ខិលខូច   kheul kho:c   "depraved"
    ចែវអំ / អុំចែវ caev om (or om caev) "paddle, row"

And there are an even greater number of compounds one of whose members is meaningless:

(24.a) ប្រងប្រៀប
       prong   priap
       prepare –
       "prepare"

(24.b) រួចរាល់
       ruac   roal
       escape –
       "finish" (meaningful elsewhere as "every")

(24.c) កាត់កង
       kat   kaw:ng
       cut   –
       "cut, reduce"

The symmetrical pairing process may be mildly recursive, a coordination being conjoined with another word (or another coordinate compound) of the same general meaning:

(25.a) ចោទប្រកាន់   ចាប់ទោស
       caot prakan "accuse" + cap   toah "accuse"
       accuse resent   catch discord
       "accuse"

(25.b) រត់រាយ   ពាសវាលពាសកាល
       roat riaj "disordered" + piah vial piah ka:l "disordered"
       messy spread   messy field messy time
       "disordered"

(25.c) ស្ងប់ស្ងាត់   រសេះរសោះ
       sngawp snguat   + raseh   raso:h
       quiet dry   depressed –
       "depressed, dejected"

(25.d) ប្រុងប្រៀប   រៀបចំ
       prong priap   + riapcawm
       prepare –   prepare
       "prepare"

An extremely large special subclass of paired synonyms are those which happen to exhibit formal symmetry, whether through alliteration (like *kith and kin*), ablaut (like *flim flam*) or, more rarely, through rhyme (like *razzle dazzle*).

(26) រួបរួម   ruap ruam   "join, unite"
     ស្ទាបស្ទង់   stiap stung   "sound out, assay, test"
     រាយរៀវ   ruaj riav   "wither away"
     បំផ្លើសបំផ្លាយ   bamplaeuh bampla:j "exaggerate"
     បង្ហិនបង្ហោច   bangheun banghaoc "ruin, wear down, destroy"

Closely related to synonym compounds exhibiting formal symmetry are compounds of the *jibber jabber* or *higgledy piggledy* variety, in which one or both symmetrical morphemes are identified as either meaningless or incapable of standing alone. Such decorative words in symmetrical compounds are known to Cambodians as បរិវារសព្ទ *bo'ri'va: sap* "servant words" (Sisovat n.d., Chun-Leuh 2007, N. Ourn pers.com., V. Keat pers.com.). One can distinguish between compounds where
a) only one word is meaningful (cf. *jibber jabber*), and
b) both morphs are meaningless (cf. *helter skelter*)
c) both morphs are meangful (cf. *creepy crawly*)

Native speaker judgments will often differ on whether a symmetrical form is a synonym pair that happens to alliterate, a meaningful word plus a servant word, though it is not always clear which word in the pair is the meaningful one, or a single word made up of meaningless parts. The servant word can precede the meaningful root in some items:

(27.a) ជុនដាប
      don   da:p
      –   deteriorate

(27.b) ហិចហើរ
      hec   haeu
      –   fly

(27.c) ក្នីគ្នា
      kni: knia
      –   companion, each other

And follow it in others:

(28.a) ស្ងៀមស្ងាត់
      sngiam sngat
      quiet   –

(28.b) ប្រយ័ត្នប្រយែង
      prajat   prajaeng
      take.care –

(28.c) ម្ដេចម្ដា
      mdec   mda:
      how   –

(28.d) ត្អូញត្អែរ
      t'o:nj   t'ae
      complain –

The prime motivation for the creation of such decorative compounds is for the most part neither iconic nor pejorative (as in Anglo-Yiddish schm- reduplication, cf. Stolz 2007). It seems to be rather a drive to create symmetry for its own sake. The clearest evidence for this statement is the behavior of symmetrical compounds when they undergo iambic erosion (or any other alteration, but erosion, the most productive, is the only one described here). Both elements undergo erosion entirely, fail to undergo it at all, or undergo it to the same degree.

For example, we encounter many pairs like

(29) កន្តិញកន្តុញ *kantenj kantonj* (both conjuncts full) and
katenj katonj (both conjuncts reduced), but neither
*kantenj katonj (only the second reduced) nor
*katenj kantonj (only the first reduced) for
"short and squat"

Here the only issue is whether reduction takes place or not. But we also encounter triplets like

(30) តម្រែតម្រង់   តម្វែតម្វង់   តមែតមង់
tamrae tamrawng → *tamvae tamvawng* → *tamae tamawng*
"straighten"
(full form)   (partially reduced form)   (fully reduced form)

and never any of the following:
*tamrae tamnawng (no reduction of first conjunct, partial reduction of second)
*tamrae tamawng (no reduction of first conjunct, full reduction of second)
*tamvae tamawng (partial reduction of first conjunct, full reduction of second)
*tamvae tamrawng (partial reduction of first conjunct, no reduction of second)
*tamae tamrawng (full reduction of first conjunct, no reduction of second)
*tamae tamvawng (full reduction of first conjunct, partial reduction of second)

That is, no matter what happens to one element in a symmetrical coordination, the same change will also affect the other member.

The etymological origins of meaningless servant words are uncertain. Undoubtedly there must be some which were once meaningful words that have fallen out of use. Khmer-speaking scholars (Sisovat 1972, Chun-Leuh 2007) however believe that at least some of them have come into being via a rhyme-swapping word game (*piak kat kunlawh*) akin to the production which yields Spoonerisms, or portmanteaux like *smog* (from *sm-oke* and *f-og*).

The game as a word-producing engine works as follows. Initially, a word may appear in a symmetrical expression with a near synonym :

(31.a) ធំទូលាយ
     th-om   *tul-iaj*
     big   roomy

Then, by rhyme swapping, this expression may be transformed into the two nonsense syllables:

(31.b) ជាយទុលំ
      th-iaj   *tul-om*
      (nonsense) (nonsense)

Then, the nonsense forms (or more generally, just one of them) are now available to function as servant words. This novel function they now perform in derived decorative compounds like:

(31.c) ទុលំទុលាយ
      tulom   *tuliaj*
      (nonsense) roomy

In English some Spoonerisms can take on a life of their own as portmanteaux. In Cambodian, they do so as servant words. Speaking in favor of the rhyme-swapping hypothesis is the fact that the vast majority of servant words alliterate. This is typologically rather unusual: English conforms with the majority of the world's languages in having relatively many twin forms that are created via rhyme, like *helter skelter*, or ablaut, like *jibber jabber*, and hardly any that are created via simple alliteration, like *spic'n'span*. There are two possible explanations for this phenomenon, neither of them entirely convincing.

    First, alliteration of servant words is common in Southeast Asian languages other than Khmer, among them Vietnamese, Wa, Thai, Hmong, Sui, Tkong Amwi, and others. That is, alliteration may be plausibly explained as simply an areal phenomenon. Still, why in this area? A structural explanation is that many of these languages, to the extent that they have affixation at all, tend to be prefixing or infixing, while the vast majority of the world's languages favor suffixation. Ourn & Haiman (2000) suggested that suffixing languages would favor rhyme, inasmuch as stress tends to fall on the root, and that the phonetically highlighted and thus maximally contrastive portion of the word would correspond roughly to the part of the word included in the root, while the minimally contrastive portion of the word occurred in the suffix. Prefixing languages like Khmer would favor alliteration for the same reason.

    But the Sisovat hypothesis would account for the prevalence of alliteration quite simply: if the majority of servant words arise via rhyme swapping game, then their onsets will be unaffected: ទុលាយ *tuliaj* "roomy" will be transformed into the nonsense word ទុលំ *tulom* and not into some other nonsense word with a different onset or initial syllable. They will therefore alliterate with the word they accompany, if they are derived from alliterating synonyms.

Second, the hypothesis may account indirectly for a remarkable but undiscussed feature of the Khmer vocabulary : the existence of huge numbers of near synonyms which differ phonetically in their final syllable codas. Here, for example, is a single such set, a number of words which mean "curved":

(32) ក្ងង់ *kngong* curving
ក្ងៀង *kngiang* bent to one side
ក្ងក់ *kngok* bent like a hook
ក្ងង់ *kngawng* very curved (said of sticks)
ក្ងក់ *kngawk* bent, curving
ក្ងល់ *kngol* bent over, stooped
ក្ងេងក្ងង់ *kngeung kngang* bent out of shape

There are no rules of final-consonant ablaut which could generate such suspicious look-alikes.

It is plausible that some coincidences are only accidental, but it is also plausible that at least some of these similar forms derive from a common origin, by the same reasoning that leads us to set up family trees, both for cognate words and for the languages in which they occur. Moreover, it is at least conceivable that many of them were once servant words. Like statues coming to life, they have entered the world of meaning. It is plausible that initially, on coming to life in this way, they are servant words, or virtual synonyms of the words they once accompanied. But then via the familiar process of repartition (Bréal 1897, Bolinger 1975), once a form exists at all, it will eventually come to pay its way by having some meaning of its own, which may be what the various forms meaning "curved" are now slowly beginning to do. In the same way that *partner* and *pardner*, or *creature* and *critter* no longer mean the same thing in English, the constellations of similar words with almost entirely identical meanings are slowly separating out.

3 Grammar and syntax

3.1 Nominal domain

3.1.1 Noun Phrases

The only multi-word syntactic constituent which has been identified in the previous literature is the NP, which has been characterized by both Jacob (1968:83) and Huffman et al (1970:50) as having roughly the following structure:

NP → (Honorific) Noun (Adjectval Modifier) (Numeral) (Classifier) (Deictic)

Haiman (2011) proposes a revision of this rule, with a unit called the Nominal Clump (NC), consisting of

NC → (Honorific)(NP)(MeasurePhrase)(DeicticPhrase)

The claims made in this revized nomenclature are that none of the elements in the clump is any more or less obligatory than any of the others, and that although they may cooccur and when they do they do so typically in the order given, this arrangement is fortuitous, as each is perfectly capable of occurring alone. In particular, there is no compelling reason that the measure phrase (MP), which includes quantifiers such as the numerals, belongs to the same constituent as the NP, which consist of a head Noun and its modifiers. Both NP and MP have internal structure:

Noun Phrase → (Noun Phrase) (Modifier) (i.e. Modifiers follow Heads)
Measure Phrase → (Quantifier) (Measure Unit) (i.e. Quantifiers precede Heads).

The rule for NP is recursive (a noun may have a number of modifiers), while for MP it is not.
    Thus, minimally contrasting expressions like

(33.a) ជ្រូកល្អ
cru:k   l'aw:
pig   good
"good pig"

(33.b) ជ្រូកពីរ
     cru:k   pi:
     pig   two
     "two pigs"

will have a radically different structure. The first is an NP, with a modifier following the head noun. On the other hand, the second is actually two constituents, a NP consisting of only a noun, and a following MP consisting of only a numeral. A necessary distinction is thus made between NP in which a numeral acts as a modifier, and an MP in which the same numeral, acting as a quantifier, precedes a measure unit with an MP.

(34.a) ម៉ោងបួន
     maong   *buan*
     hour   four
     "the hour of four, four o'clock"

(This is an NP consisting of one N and a following modifier consisting of a numeral)

(34.b) បួន   ម៉ោង
     buan   *maong*
     four   hour
     "(for) four hours"

This is an MP consisting of a quantifier and a measure unit. All measure units are themselves nouns, as they mostly are in English. The word ម៉ោង *maong* as a measure unit may be thought of as "hourfuls".

There are three further arguments for thinking of MP as appositions to NP rather than part of NP. First: as recognized by Noss & Proum (1966: 358), Huffman et al. (1970: 268), Ehrman & Sos (1972: 20), and Headley & Neou (1991), the two constituents [NP] and [MP] of even an apparently simple expression like ជ្រូកពីរ *cru:k pi:* "two pigs" may be separated by other material and even appear to occupy separate clauses:

(35.a) ស្រា   ផឹក   មួយ   កូនកែវ
     [*sra:*] *pheuk* [*muaj ko:n kaev*]
     wine   drink   one   small glass
     NP   MP
     "drink a small glass of wine"

(35.b) លោក ជួយ ហៅ ស៊ីក្លូ អោយ ខ្ញុំ មួយ បាន ទេ
     lo:k   cuaj hav [siklo:] aoj knjom [muaj] ba:n tee:
     you help call cyclo   for me   one   manage not
                           NP   MP
     "Can you get me a cyclo?"

Second: Small NP and MP may occur independently of each other.

Measure phrases occur on their own in many expressions where no head can be imagined for them.

(36) ពីរ ដង
    [pi: daw:ng]
    two time
    "twice"

Third: NP and MP, even when contiguous, can cooccur in either order. Although the measure phrase typically follows the modified phrase, examples of the opposite order seem to be unexceptionable:

(37.a) ពីរ នាក់ បង ប្អូន នេះ
     pi: neak   baw:ng   p'o:n   nih
     two   person older.sibling younger sibling this
     MP   NP
     "the two brothers"

(37.b) ពីរ ដួស បាយ
     pi: duah   ba:j
     two   portion rice
     MP   NP
     "two portions of rice"

- **Pali Syntax: Modifier + Head Constructions**

The fundamental principle of NP word order is that all modifiers follow their heads.

There is one irregular exception to this principle, the use of កូន *ko:n* "child" as a prenominal modifier meaning "little, young" illustrated by examples like កូនក្របី *ko:n krabej*. "young buffalo". Another set of exceptions is provided by NP usually consisting entirely of Pali words, which observe Modifier + Head order.

(38.a) មហា   មិត្ត
       m(o)ha: meut
       great   comrade

(38.b) អនាគត   ជីវិត
       anakaut civeut
       future   life

(38.c) វិចិត្រសិល្ប
       vi'ceut seulpa.
       fine   art

(38.d)឵ន្ទ   ទំនាយ
       eun   tumniaj
       Indra   prophecy
       "prophecy of Indra"

(38.e) ទិព្វចក្ខុ
       teu:pa'   cak
       omniscient eye

3.2 Pronouns

3.2.1 Personal pronouns

As in European languages, person deixis is often accompanied by social status marking, and not just in the second person, with the familiar T/V distinction.

Table 3: Khmer pronominal device

	(Singular)	Plural	Approximate Social Status
1st.	ខ្ញុំ knjom		speaker is acting humble or polite
		យើង jeu:ng	
	អញ anj		speaker is arrogant or on intimate terms with addressee
	អាត្មា a:tma:		speaker is monk
2nd	អ្នក neak		addressee is younger or of lower status
	ឯង aeng		addressee is of much lower status
	លោក lo:k		addressee is older or of higher status
	ឆាន់ chan		speaker and addressee are both monks

3rd គាត់ koat   referent is respected other
     វា via   referent is disrespected other or inanimate
     គេ kee: referent may be any other (often plural)
     ទ្រង់ truang   referent is royalty

The only personal pronoun which is neutral with respect to social status marking is the 1pl., on which deference may be marked by the addition of following ខ្ញុំ *knjom* – which is thereby shown not to mark singularity in itself. In fact, the only personal pronouns which incorporate information on number are 1sg. អញ *anj* and 1pl. យើង *jeu:ng*. All others can be understood as either singular or plural. The optional disambiguating pluralizer ពួក *puak* can precede any one of these, including (redundantly) យើង *jeu:ng*.

(39) ពួកវាហាមប្រាមអ្នកស្រុកមិនអោយកប់ខ្មោចនោះទេ។
     puak via ha:m   pra:m   neak   srok   mwn   aoj   kawp
     PLU 3   forbid prohibit   person country not   so.that bury

     kmaoc   nuh   tee:
     corpse that   not
     "They [the Khmer Rouge] forbade the peasants to bury those corpses."

The pronoun table is seriously misleading, however, in two respects. First, because the number of words apparently used as pronouns is far larger than suggested by this listing: any honorific (including kin terms) can function as a first (self-referential), second (address), or third person form. Second, most of the pronouns listed above are in fact themselves common nouns not only in terms of their etymology, but in terms of their capacity for modification and quantification, and for themselves acting as modifiers.

- **Anaphoric Pronouns**

These are metalinguistic, in the sense that they anchor a referent not to a participant of the speech act stage (as personal pronouns ostensibly do), but relative only to another word in the text, its antecedent. Examples in English are reflexive and reciprocal pronouns, *former... latter,* and so on, for identity of reference, and *the ...one* for identity of sense. The main anaphors in Khmer are គ្នា *knia*, ឯង *aeng*, ខ្លួន *kluan*, (for reference) and អា *a:-* (for sense).

- ឯង **aeng**

This does function as a (very rude or intimate) pronoun of address, but it is not a "dedicated" second person pronoun, but rather a reflexive/emphatic (cf. the meaning of the same etymon in Thai). It occurs in both related senses in construction with ខ្លួន *kluan* "body", the unmarked reflexive/emphatic pronominal expression, and other words.

(40.a) រៀនភាសាថៃដោយខ្លួនឯង។
(rian   phiasa: thaj   daoj)   kluan   aeng
(study   language   Thai   by)   self   self
"(study Thai all by) himself" (Emphatic)

(40.b) ស្ទើយោងអាត្មាខ្លួនឯង(ពុំរួច)
(steu: jo:ng) atma: kluan   aeng   (pum   ruac)
(almost pull) body   self   self   (not   manage)
"(almost but not quite succeed in pulling) himself (along)" (Reflexive)

- **The reciprocal pronoun គ្នា *knia*.**

Another apparent anaphoric pronoun is the reciprocal, derived from the common noun គ្នា *knia* "companion".

(41.a) ជួបគ្នានឹងបងមួង
cuap   knia   nwng   baw:ng   Muang
meet   each.other   with   comrade   Muang
"meet comrade Muang"

(41.b) ដូចគ្នា
do:c   knia
like   each.other
"alike"

(41.c) ចាប់ដៃគ្នា
cap   daj   knia
strike   hand   each.other
"shake hands with each other"

- **The identity of sense anaphor អា *a:-* "the ... one"**

Unlike the other pronouns, this morpheme is a bound prefix incapable of standing alone as an NP. Like them, however, it has another syntactic function, in that it serves as a (dis)honorific, used in addressing social inferiors and animals, e.g. *a:campa:* "Champa! (said to an ox)".

(42.a) អាធំកន្ទុយក្រហមល្អជាង។
      a: 'thom   kantuj   krahaw:m   l'aw: ciang
      ANA   big   tail   red   good   exceed
      "The big one (fish) with the red tail is the best."

(42.b) ខ្ញុំមានកូនស្រីបីនាក់ជំនាន់នេះ។
      (knjom mian   ko:n   srej   bej   neak   cumnoan   nih)
      I   have   child   female 3   person   time   this
      ("I had three daughters at this time:")

(42.c) អាបងអាយុប្រាំបួនឆ្នាំ។
      A:-   baw:ng   aju'   9   cnam
      ANA   oldest   age   9   year
      "The oldest was nine years old"

(42.d) អាទីពីរអាយុប្រាំមួយឆ្នាំ។
      A:-   ti: pi: aju'   6   cnam
      ANA   place two   age   6   year
      "the second one was six"

(42.e) អាទីបីអាយុបីឆ្នាំ។
      A:-   ti: bej   aju'   3   cnam
      ANA   place three age   3   year
      "the third one was three."

3.3 Deictics

The definite deictics នេះ *nih* "this", នោះ *nuh* "that", and ហ្នឹង *nwng* "the (colloquial)" may occur as NP in their own right (e.g. ដូច្នេះ *do:c nih* "like this, thus") or after any nominal clump (e.g. ជ្រូកពីរក្បាលនោះ *cru:k pi: kba:l nuh* "those two pigs"), including even the bound dishonorific អា នេះ *a:-nih* "this lowlife". They correspond to indefinites/ interrogatives meaning "any, which", of which the most common is ណា *na:*.

(43.a) នាក់ណា
 neak   na:
 person which
 "who?"

(43.b) ឯណា
 ae   na:
 at   which
 "where?"

(43.c) ដូចម្ដេច
 do:c   mdec
 like   how
 "How?"

(43.d) ម៉ោងប៉ុន្មាន
 maong   ponma:n
 hour   how.many
 "What time(is it)?"

Table 4: Deictics in Khmer

Definite		Indefinite		
This	នេះ nih	Which / What	ណា na: / អ្វី, អី (av)ej	
That	នោះ nuh			
The (coll.)	ហ្នឹង nwng			
Here	នេះ nih	Where	ឯណា (ae) na:	
There	នោះ nuh			
Thus	ចឹង ceung / អ៊ីចឹង i ceung / អញ្ចឹង anjceung	How	ម្ដេច, ម៉េច m(d)ec	
This much	ប៉ុណ្ណោះ pon no:h / ប៉ុណ្ណឹង pon nwng / ឯហ្នឹង ae nwng	How much	ប៉ុន្មាន pon ma:n, ម្លឹង mleung, ម្លេះ mleh	

In colloquial speech, both definite and indefinite deictics in a nominal clump may be followed by another "shadow" deictic which apparently adds nothing to the meaning of the whole expression. Following definites, the only common shadow deictic is ឯង *aeng* "self", here with a novel function, while following indefinite/interrogative deictics, all of the following are attested. It is possible, though not certain, that the combination deictic + shadow deictic is an example of decorative doubling, the topic of Section 4.

គេ *kee*: "third person indefinite",
ប៉ុន្មាន *ponma:n* "any, how many" and
ហ្នឹង *nwng* "that/the" .

(44.a) វាហែកក្រដាសជក់ [អីចឹងឯង]
      Via   haek   krada:h   cuak   [i ceung   aeng]
      3   tear   paper   smoke   thus   self
      "They tear cigarette paper like that."

(44.b) មិត្តឯងនាំគ្នាទៅឯ[ណាហ្នឹង]
      Meut   aeng   noam knia   tev   ae [na: nwng] ?
      friend   you   together   go   at which that
      "Where are you folks going?"

4 Verbal domain

4.1 Verbs and auxiliaries

In Khmer, verbs may be strung together apparently without limit, in an order which reflects the order of events. Some partially conventionalized strings, however, clump together in accordance with rules that go beyond the demands of narrative iconicity. The predicate so defined consists of a sequence of AUXILIARY verbs, a main verb phrase and a much more limited sequence of SERIAL verbs.

    Predicate → (AUX) VP (SER)

While there may be more than one auxiliary verb and more than one serial verb flanking a main verb in a predicate, flanking verbs may not themselves have flanking verbs of their own. The only morphosyntactic trappings which they typically allow are negative particles. AUX often correspond to auxiliary verbs of tense, aspect, and mood; to verbs that take infinitival complements in English, like ចង់ *cawng* "want" and ខំ *khawm* "try, strive"; and also to a number of what in English are manner adverbs like មិនសូវ *mwn sev* "hardly", and លួច *luac* "furtively" (<លួច *luac* 'steal').

SER are more likely to correspond to separate clauses that can be thought of as describing actions that follow the main clause. There is only a porous line separating serial verbs within a predicate from non-initial predicate in a complex predicate verb clump. This line exists only to the extent that

a) the ordering of the constituents within a predicate has become conventionalized to some degree, while the order of Verbal Clumps within a narrative has not, that is, is still totally narrative-iconic;
b) flanking verbs within a predicate, as noted, cannot occur with the morphosyntactic trappings of separate main verbs, any of which may occur with their own flanking verbs. Subject to the constraints which are the substance of this section, the ordering of verbs in the AUX V SER predicate is still largely narrative-iconic. Whether a verb behaves as an auxiliary or a serial verb largely reflects whether the action that it describes precedes or follows that of the main verb:

(45) ចាប់ផ្ដើមធ្វើ
    cap pdaeum   tveu:
    begin +   do
    AUX   V
    "begin (to) do"

contrasts with

(46.a) ធ្វើហើយ
    tveu: haeuj
    do +   finish
    V   SER
    "finish doing"

and

(46.b) ធ្វើត
    tveu: taw:
    do +   continue
    V   SER
    "continue to do"

The ordering of auxiliary verbs within an auxiliary string is largely scope-iconic (an auxiliary will include following auxiliaries within its scope, as is the case with English complement-taking verbs. *Try to finish doing* is not the same as *finish trying to do*). But the iconic ordering of verbs in a predicate is limited.

4.1.1 Conventionalizations of AUX ordering

- **Some AUX may precede the subject Nominal clump**

The main transitive verb ចាំ *cam* "wait (for)" can be understood as a future auxiliary in colloquial utterances like

(47) ចាំខ្ញុំត្រឡប់មកវិញ។
     Cam [knjom tralawp mau:k venj]
     wait   I   return   come   back
     "I will be back"

NB: This cannot be translated as: "wait for me to come back", although some such gloss was the presumable origin of the construction.

The same preclausal position is possible (though not obligatory) for a handful of other AUX.

(48.a) គប្បីកូនខ្មែរចងចាំទុកជាមេរៀន។
      <u>kua'bej</u> ko:n   kmae   caw:ng   cam   tok   cia   mee:rian
      should   child Khmer bind remember keep   as   lesson
      "Khmer children should remember this as a lesson."

(48.b) ចង់ណាក៏ណាធ្វើអីក៏ធ្វើទៅ។
      <u>cawng</u>   neakna: tveu: ej   kaw: tveu: tev
      want   anyone   do   what   so   do   IMP/DIR
      "Anyone could do whatever they wanted."

Compare the regular word order:

(49.a) មនុស្សសម័យថ្មីគប្បីចេះរក្សា។
      Mnuh   sa'maj tmej   <u>kua'bej</u> ceh   reaksa:
      person era   new   should   know   guard
      "People of the modern era should know (how) to guard."

(49.b) ជ្រូកចង់ស៊ី។
      Cru:k   <u>cawng</u>   si:
      Pig   want   eat
      "Pigs want to eat."

- **The future auxiliary និង *nwng* precedes the negative particle**

The negative particles (most derived from verbs) precede the verb and whatever auxiliaries it occurs with. The future auxiliary alone must precede the negative particles.

(50) ពេលខ្ញុំចាស់ ខ្ញុំនឹងគ្មានកូនៗ
    pee:l   knjom¹ cah,   knjom   nwng   k-   mian   ko:n
    time   I   old   I   will   not-   have   child
    "When I am adult, I will not have children."

4.1.2 Conventionalizations of serial verbs

Serial verbs are in many cases indistinguishable from any asyndetically following clause. Four clear cases of partial grammaticalization (where they seem to be semantically slightly different from simple sequential VP) which therefore justify calling them something other than separate VP in multi-clause asyndetic predicates are the resultative constructions, directionals, pivot constructions and perfective aspect marking.

- **The resultative construction: Verb (action) + Verb (result)**

The resultative construction, also known as the completive, is a favorite construction not only in Khmer (Huffman et al 1970: 187–8), but in many other Southeast Asian languages (Bisang 1992, Enfield 2003), among them Vietnamese (Nguyen 1974: 9–10), Mandarin (Li & Thompson 1981: 56–8; 426–8), Lahu (Matisoff 1969: 75–7), Hmong, Lao (Enfield 2003), and Thai (Iwasaki & Ingkapirom 2005: 239). If neither the MV nor the SV is negated, the flavor of this construction approximates the perfective in Slavic languages[12]. The SV (here a perfectivizing .success. verb) signals that the operation attempted in the MV was carried out successfully; if the SV is negated, that it was not. The most commonly used "success verbs" are listed below.

បាន	ba:n	"get"
ផុត	phot	"exceed, go beyond",
រួច	ruac	"escape"
ចេញ	cenj	"exit"
ទាន់	toan	"be on time"
ត្រូវ	trev	"hit squarely"
ឈ្នះ	cneah	"win"
ដល់	dawl	"arrive"

ដាច់   *dac*   "cut"
កើត   *kaeut*   "be born, arise".

While it is understandable how these verbs can signal success through their specific intrinsic meanings, the differences among those meanings often cease to be significant in this construction. Therefore, when such popular semi-grammaticalized "success" verbs occur without any hint of their original specificity they can simply be translated as "succeed" or "manage" in the examples below.

(51.a) ត្រសក់នេះហូបកើត។
       trasawk   nih   ho:p   kaeut
       cucumber this   eat   succeed/manage
       "(One) can eat this cucumber; this cucumber is edible"

(51.b) លើកដៃជើងស្ទើរពុំរួច។
       leu:k   daj   ceu:ng   steu: pum   ruac
       raise   arm   leg   insufficient not   succeed/manage
       "(They) could hardly manage to raise arms and legs"

(51.c) ខ្ញុំទ្រាំលែងបាន។
       k'njom   troam   le:ng   ba:n
       I   endure   no.longer   succeed/manage
       "I could endure it no longer."

Whether or not a verb qualifies as a "success" verb is often simply through its appearance in this construction, rather than through its intrinsic properties. For example, the same verb *deung* "know" may be a neutral or attemptive verb of knowing in one phrase, but a success verb in another:

(52.a) រាប់ដឹងមិនឈ្នះ
       roap   deung   mwn   cneah
       count   know   not   win
       "can't know"

(52.b) ស្មានមិនដឹង
       sma:n   mwn   deung
       guess   not   know
       "guess but not know for sure"

- **Directional Verbs (DIR)**

Verbs of motion functioning as serial verbs can function like directional particles in English, indicating both the physical trajectory of some actions and sometimes more abstract properties. The simplest examples of a serial verb indicating the direction of a preceding main verb are

(53.a) វាដាក់ចានចុះ
    via   dak   ca:n   coh
    3   put   bowl descend
                                    DIR
    "S/he put the bowl down."

(53.b) ក្រោយពីយកសំបកវាចុះ។
    kraoj pi: jau:k   sambaw:k via   coh
    after from take   bark   it   descend
                                                       DIR
    "after taking the bark off..."

(53.c) រឹតតែឆ្ងល់ឡើង។
    reut tae   cngawl   laeung
    become   curious   rise/go.up
                                  DIR
    "became increasingly curious"

- **"Pivot" constructions ("See Spot run" constructions)**

This is not strictly speaking an Serial Verb construction, since the second verb can take a full panoply of verbal trappings. But it represents a partial conventionalization of the narrative-iconic sequence of predicates insofar as the verbs "see" and "run" are thought of as simultaneous rather than sequential. It can be called a "pivot" construction (Bisang 1992: 438), inasmuch as an NP simultaneously acts as the object of the MV, and as the subject of the SV. An extremely frequent example of this is the យក *jau:k* "take" + NP + មក *mau:k* "come" construction, best translated into English as "bring" (compare Tok Pisin *kisim i kam* "catch'em it come"). An example that looks like "see Spot run" (with the pivot NP underlined) is:

(54) អាជ្រើងតែងតែនាំក្មេងវត្តអើតក។

Acreung	taeng tae	noam	kmee:ng	voat	aeut	kaw:
A.	always	take	youth	temple	crane	neck

"A. always took the temple youths to crane their necks (looking down on congregants bringing alms to the temple)."

- **The serial verb as perfective aspect marker**

Enfield (2003: 41) carefully distinguishes between serial verbs marking "success" (an action has consequences, and results in another one) and "attainment" (an action is actually completed). The sequence *seek and find* is an example of success, while *seek + PAST* is an example of attainment or completion. Sometimes, there is conflation between the two, as when the same serial verbs mark both. The two verbs ហើយ *haeuj* "finish" and រួច *ruac* "escape" as well as being "success" verbs, can function simply to indicate the completion of an event.

(55) វាខានជឹកទឹកត្នោតយូរណាស់មកហើយ។

via	kha:n	pheuk	teuk	tnaot	ju:	nah	mau:k	haeuj
3	miss	drink	juice	palm	long.time	very	come	finish
							DIR	PERF

"He had missed drinking palm syrup for a very long time already."

The verb *haeuj* also functions as a sequential clausal conjunction, and can often be translated simply as "and then" or "thereafter."

(56) គាត់លូកដៃទៅក្នុងថង់យាមហើយដកលុយមួយរៀលមក។

koat	lu:k	daj	tev	knong	thawng jiam	haeuj	daw:k	luj
3	reach	hand	go	in	knapsack	finish	remove	money
						CONJ		

muaj	rial	mau:k
one	rial	come
		DIR

"He reached into his knapsack and took out a one-riel piece."

It is clear that this use of ហើយ *haeuj* as a clause conjunction is a grammaticalization of ហើយ *haeuj* as a verb (meaning "finished") marking attainment or perfectivity.

4.2 Clausal syntax

4.2.1 Constituent order

The normal order of sentential constituents is (S)V(O)(Adverb):

(57.a) ខ្ញុំស្គាល់ស្ទើរសព្វកន្លកកន្លៀតព្រៃ។
  k̇njom   skoal   sṫeu: sawp   kanlok   kanliat   prej
  I   know   almost all   corner   cranny   forest
  "I know almost every corner and every nook of the forest."

(57.b) គាត់ដាក់ខ្ញុំតែម្ដងគត់។
  koat   dȧk   knjom   tae   mdaw:ng   kaut
  3   put   me   only   once   exactly
  "He laid me down [on the ground] only once"

Presentative sentences (typically those with the existential verb *mian* "have") invariably exhibit (X)VS order:

(58.a) មានផែនការណ៍។
  mian   phaenka:
  have   plan
  "There is a plan."

(58.b) ប៉ុន្តែគ្មានឱសថអ្វីព្យាបាល។
  pontae   k-   mian   aosawt   avej   pjiaba:l
  but   not-   have   medicine   any   treatment
  "But there is no medicine for treatment."

(58.c) គ្រានោះមានប្ដីប្រពន្ធកំសត់ទុគ៌ត។
  kria   nuh   mian   pdej   prapun   kamsawt   turkaut
  time   that   have   husband wife   wretched   miserable
  "Once there was a poor, poor couple,"

4.2.2 Predicate Complements

As copula verbs, ជា *cia* and នៅ *nev* provide an unreliable distinction between verbal and nominal and locative predicates. Ideally there is:

- no copula for verbal-adjectival predicates (ជ្រូកធាត់ *cru:k thoat* "the pig is fat"),
- a copula ជា *cia* for nominal predicates in statements of identity:

(59) ជ្រូកជាអ្នកទាយ
    cru:k   *cia*   *neak*   *tiaj*
    pig   be   AGT   prognosticate
    "the pig is a prognosticator", and

- a copula នៅ *nev* with locative predicates:

(60) ជ្រូកនៅក្រោមផ្ទះ
    cru:k   *nev*   *kraom*   *pteah*
    pig   be.at   under   house
    "the pig is under the house".

4.2.3 Modification

Heads generally precede modifiers. This rule is far more general than that modifiers follow heads in NP. Subsumed under this rule are "tough predicate" structures like:

(61.a) ធ្ងន់ត្រចៀក
      tnguan   *traciak*
      heavy   ear
      "hard of hearing" (with Adjective + Noun order)

(61.b) ស្រួលមាត់
      srual   *moat*
      easy   mouth
      "easy to say" (again with Adjective + Noun/Verb order)

Adverb of manner phrases usually follow the verb they modify. Both they and adjectival phrases are frequently (but not always) marked with a preceding word like យ៉ាង *ja:ng* "kind" or របៀប *rabiap* "manner".

(62) និយាយរបៀបខឹង
 ni'jiaj   rabiap   khwng
 say   manner   angry
 "say angrily"

4.2.4 Coordination

Unmarked (asyndetic) parataxis of both phrases and clauses is almost always possible:

(63) ម្ដាយក្មេកវាជាមនុស្សអាក្រក់ណាស់ជេរកូនប្រសាមិនស្ងាង។
 mda:j   kmee:k   via   cia   mnuh   akrawk   nah   cee: ko:n   prasa:
 mother in-law   3   be   person   bad   very   curse   child in-law

 mwn   sva:ng
 not   cease
 "His mother-in-law was a very bad woman [and] swore at her son-in-law ceaselessly."

Generally, when coordination is explicitly marked at all, phrasal coordination is signalled by
 និង *nwng*, and asymmetric clausal coordination by ហើយ *haeuj* ("and then"), and by clause-final adverbial conjunctions ដែរ *dae/* ផង *phaw:ng* ("and also").

(64.a) អ្វីដែលអាចប៉ះពាល់បាននិងអ្វីដែលមិនត្រូវប៉ះពាល់បាន។
 avej   dael   a:c   pah   poal   ba:n   nwng   avej   dael   mwn   trev
 what   which can   touch manage   and   what   which   not   must

 pah   poal   ba:n
 hit   touch   manage
 "What can be touched and what can't be touched"

(64.b) កូនទាំងពីរនៅចាំម្ដាយក្នុងរូងហ្នឹងហើយកុំទៅណាមកណាអោយសោះណា។
 ko:n   teang   pi: nev   cam   mda:j   knong   ru:ng   nwng   aoj
 child   all   two   stay   wait   mother in   cave   this   so.that

	haeuj	kom	tev	na:	mau:k	na:	sawh	na:
	and	don't	go	where	come	where	at.all	any

"Both of you kids wait for me here in this cave and don't go anywhere at all."

Non-exhaustive disjunction of A and B, both phrasal and clausal, is expressed by A ឬ *rw:* B.

4.2.5 Negation

The word "no" is ទេ *tee:*, which can be reinforced by a preceding "not" word like អត់ *awt*.

(65) អត់ទេ!
(*awt*) *tee:!*
(not) no
"No!"

The normal word អើ *aeu* "yes" has a deferential version, បាទ *ba:t* (for males), ចាំះ *cah* (for females), but since both of these may also appear before ទេ *tee:*, it is clear that if they have an invariant meaning at all, they are signals of deference and politeness (the willingness to agree, perhaps) rather than of actual agreement.

- **Prohibitives**

Khmer distinguishes between constative "not" (expressed by the negative particles មិន *mwn (mee:n)*, ពុំ *pum*, ក់- *k-* "not", as well as by negative verbs such as លែង *le:ng* "do no longer, quit", អត់ *awt* "lack, (do) without"), on the one hand, and imperative/subjunctive prohibitive negation "don't!" (rendered by a prohibitive auxiliary កុំ *kom*) on the other.

(66.a) មិនប្រឡំ។
mwn cralawm
not confuse
"(S/he) is not confused"

(66.b) កុំប្រឡំ។
kom cralawm
don't confuse
"Don't be confused."

- **Clause-final negative reenforcers**

The word ទេ *tee:* "no" may appear clause-finally, co-occurring with constative, but not prohibitive negatives:

(67) មិនចាំបាច់ព្រឡានមកប្រាប់ខ្ញុំទេ។
    mwn   cambac   pru: la̱:n   mau:k   prap   knjom   tee:
    not   need   ticket   taker   come   tell   me   no
    "The ticket taker didn't need to come tell me."

Stronger reenforcers include សោះ *sawh*, ឯណា *aena:* and ឡើយ *laeuj* "at all".

4.2.6 Questions

- Polar questions

Polar questions are either unmarked, or followed by ឬ *rw:*+ ទេ/នៅ/អត់ *tee:/nev/awt* "or no/stay/lack".

(68) តើនាងមានគូឬនៅ?
    taeu   niang   mian   ku: rw: nev?
    Q PAR   she   have   partner   or   stay
    "Does she have a partner or doesn't she?"

- **Content questions**

Content question words (indefinite pronouns) occupy the same position in the sentence as the corresponding non-interrogative NP:

(69.a) ខ្ញុំប្រឹងដណ្តើមហូបធ្វើអ្វី?
    khawm   preung   dandaeum ho:p   tveu: <u>avej</u>?
    force   force.down   eat   do   what
    "Why(=with what intention) were you forcing it down (as if it were) food?"

(69.b) ពួកគាត់ចង់និយាយអ្វី និយាយទៅ។
    puak   koat   cawng   ni'jiaj   <u>avej</u>,   ni'jiaj   tev
    group   3   want   say   what   say   go
    "Let them say what they like./ I don't care what they say."
    (literally: Do they want to say what? Let them go right ahead and say it.)

(69.c) រឿងនោះយ៉ាងម៉េចទៅ។
     rwang   nuh   ja:ng   <u>mec</u>   tev?
     matter that   kind   how   go
     "What's going on?"

(69.d) តាបសនឹងត្រូវជាម៉េច។
     ta:bawh   n̈wng   trev cia   <u>mec</u>
     hermit   that   related   how
     "What relationship does that hermit have (to you)?"

- **Sentence-initial interrogative particles**

There are two such particles, which are mutually exclusive.

    ចុះ coh "how (about)..." (< ចុះ coh "descend", is colloquial, occurring only with content questions)

(70) ជី ចុះអ្នកឯងនិយាយអញ្ចឹង?
     Ji: <u>coh</u>   neak   aeng   ni'jiaj   anjceung
     Gee QPAR person you   say   thus
     "Gee, how can you say such a thing?"

The other is តើ taeu (with no apparent lexical source, the formal counterpart of coh, perhaps, occurring with both polar and content questions):

(71.a) តើ X ឆ្ងាយប៉ុន្មាន?
     <u>taeu</u>   X   cnga:j   ponma:n
     QPAR   X   far   how.much
     "How far is it to X?"

(71.b) តើខុច?
     <u>taeu</u>   kho:c   ej
     QPAR   go.wrong something/anything/what
     "Is something wrong?"

4.2.7 Imperatives:

Imperatives are typically unmarked, and the subject may be present:

(72) ហឺប្អូន ឯងនិយាយអ៊ីចឹង ដាប់ខ្ញុំហើយ!
(heu: p'o:n   aeng ni'jiaj i ceung,) ngoap knjom haeuj!
Uh   younger.sibling you say thus   kill me   for.sure
"(Uh, if you think so, young comrade, then) kill me."

The verb in prohibitives is preceded by កុំ *kom* "don't." Again, the subject may be present:

(73) កូនឯងកុំភ័យ។
ko:n   aeng kom   phej
child you   don't fear
"Don't you be afraid, child."

Hortatory imperatives and only these, are preceded by តស់ *tawh* "all right, let's":

(74) តស់ដើរជុំវិញថ្មនោះ។
tawh   daeu   cumvenj   tmaw: nuh
let's walk   around   stone   that
"Let's walk around that stone."

4.2.8 Information structure

- **Marking Topics**

A number of phrases, all optional, and all roughly translatable by "as for" mark topics (their topicalization is also indicated by fronting, as well as, optionally, by pronominal resumption). The most frequent seem to be ចំពោះ *campo:h* ...(វិញ *venj*), ចំណែក *camnaek* ... (វិញ *venj*), (រី *ri:*) ឯ *ae* ... (វិញ *venj*) and ឯណេះ *aeneh*.

(75) ឯនាងខ្ញុំវិញមានអាយុ ២៣ ឆ្នាំ។
<u>ae</u>   niang   knjom <u>venj</u> mian   aju' 23   cnam
as.for   missy   I   back   have   age 23   year
"As for my (humble female) self, I'm twenty three years old."

- **Marking Focus**
  គឺ *kw:*

This emphatic focussing word, glossed here as "namely", is probably from Thai *khww*, with roughly the same apparent functions), often accompanies and precedes the regular copula ជា *cia* or even replaces it entirely, and it is tempting to translate it as another copula.

(76) មនុស្សទាបដែលពាក់វ៉ែនតានោះគឺជាឪពុកខ្ញុំ។
  mnuh   tiap   dael   peak   vee:nta: nuh   kw: cia   aopuk   knjom
  person short which wear   glasses   that namely be father my
  "The short man wearing glasses is my father."

A purely "drumroll"/annunciatory translation without a copula translation is mandatory for:

(77) មានទុនវិនិយោគរបស់ ៤ ប្រទេស គឺអង់គ្លេស បារាំង អាល្លឺម៉ង់ និងអេស្ប៉ាញ។
  mian   tun   vi'ni'jo:k   robawh   4   pratee:h   *kw:*
  exist capital investment of   4   countries namely

  awnglee:s,   ba:rang,   aleumawng   nwng   espanj
  England,   France,   Germany,   and   Spain
  "Four countries have invested capital in this: namely, England, France, Germany, and Spain."

4.2.9 Explicit clause combining

Asyndetic clause combining is always possible in narratives. This section describes some of the means whereby clauses are combined with overt conjunctions and complementizers.

The first indicative Complementizer ថា *tha:* (< "say"). The complements of verbs of saying, knowing, thinking and perceiving (and the like) verbs can be introduced by ថា *tha:*

(80.a) ស្មានថាឈ្នះនឹងកណ្តុរហើ?
  sma:n   tha: cneah   nwng   kawndol   hej?
  guess   say   win   against rat   huh
          COMP
  "Do you reckon that we can beat the rats?"

(80.b) ឃើញថារហ័សជាសុខសប្បាយមែន។
      kheu:nj   tha: rahah   cia   sawk   sba:j   mee:n
      see   say   quick   heal   healthy well   really
              COMP
      "see that it had really healed quickly."

- **The second indicative complementizer *cia* "be"**

This has a number of idiomatic uses.

First: While the verb ដឹង *deung* know that....occurs with ថា *tha:* in the positive, in the negative ("not know whether/why/to...") the same verb typically occurs with ជា *cia*.

(81) មិនដឹងជាមកពីហេតុអ្វីសោះ។
     mwn   deung   cia   mau:k   pi: het   avej   sawh
     not   know   be   come   from   cause which at.all
                      COMP
     "don't know where this comes from at all."

Second: Another productive combination is interclausal បាន *ba:n* "get" (+ ជា *cia*), which means "cause S", or "that S" in sentences like

(82) អាសត្វហ្នឹងធំប៉ុណ្ណា បានជាវាហ៊ាននិយាយដូច្នេះ។
     a: sat   nwng   thom   pon na: ba:n   cia   via   hian
     HON   animal that   big   extent   what   get be   3   dare
                                                          COMP

     ni'jiaj   do:c neh?
     speak   like that
     "How big is that wretched animal, that he dares to speak like that?"

- **The verb បាន *ba:n* can function as a sentential conjunction**

It is basically restricted in this function to sentences whose subject and object are both themselves sentential. There is, however, one significant exception to this. A formal word "why" is

(83) ហេតុអ្វីបានជា
     het   (av)ej   ba:n   cia   (+S)
     cause what   get   be

as exemplified in:

(84) ហេតុអ្វីបានជាអាយុ ៥០០ ឆ្នាំហើយមិនទាន់ងាប់?
     het ej ba:n cia   aju. 500   cnam   haeuj   mwn   toan   ngoap?
     why   age 500   year   already not   yet   croak
     "How come he's 500 and still hasn't croaked?"

- **Clausal conjunctions**

Some dedicated clausal conjunctions that behave much the same as their English translations are:

(85) (ប្រ)សិន *(pra)seun*, បើ *baeu* "if; given that, since"
    ដូច *do:c* "like" (< "be like, resemble")
    ពីព្រោះ *pi: proh~pru(a)h* "because" (*pi:* < "from")
    តែ *tae* "but" (< "only")
    អោយតែ *aoj tae* "as soon as" (< "give" + "only")

And there are some cases where such a conjunction, like បាន *ba:n*, is followed by the complementizer ជា *cia*:

(86.a) របៀបដូចជាគ្រាសកន្លង
      rabiap   *do:c*   *cia*   *kriah*   *kanlaw:ng*
      manner like   be   eclipse pass.over
                           COMP
      "acted like/as if an eclipse had passed over (his mother while she was pregnant)"

(86.b) ប្រសិនជាអ្នកដំណើរណាមកវង្វេងផ្លូវ
      praseun *cia*   *neak*   *damnǎeu* *na:* *mau:k* *vaungvee:ng* *plav*
      if   be   person journey   any   come   get.lost   road
               COMP
      "If a traveler should lose his way...."

- **The purpose complementizer** អោយ *aoj* "so.that" (<"give")

This is almost entirely a change-of-subject marking complementizer (as opposed to ទៅ *tev*, "to", the same-subject purpose clause complementizer, and ដើម្បី *daeumbej* "in order to/that", which also marks purpose clauses, but without marking switch-reference).

(87) គេប្រើខ្មោចអោយភ្ជួរដី។
    kee: praeu   kmaoc   aoj   pcua   dej
    3   use   cadaver   so.that   plow   earth
                                          COMP
    "They use cadavers for plowing"

- **The Clause-internal conjunction ក៏ *kaw:***

The least that can be said of the ubiquitous narrative discourse particle ក៏ *kaw:* "accordingly, then, and so" within a clause is that it "introduces a predicate in some way related to what has gone before" (Ehrman & Sos 1972: 69). By this minimal definition its treatment already belongs in a section on explicit conjunction, since ក៏ *kaw:* marks a clause as part of something larger. The major single function of this particle is to mark foregrounded narrative clauses (often after the sequential coordinate conjunction ហើយ *haeuj* or after clause-initial ដល់អញ្ចឹង *dawl anjceung* "thus"). The sequences ហើយ *haeuj*/ ដល់អញ្ចឹង *dawl anjceung* (Subject Nominal Clump) ក៏ *kaw:* (the first pronominal chunk occurring extraclausally, the second like a clitic favoring clause-internal position) can be translated simply as "and so/then" in:

(88) ព្រះមេតាចេញមកដល់ក្នុងព្រៃហើយក៏ដើរទៅជួបនឹងអាស្រមព្រះមុនីឥសី
    preah   mee:ta: cenj   mau:k   dawl   knong   prej   haeuj
    HON.   old.man   exit   come   to   in   forest   and

    kaw: daeu   tev   cuap   nwng   asraw:m   preah   muni: ejsej
    then so   walk   to   meet   with   precinct   HON   hermit
    "The old man walked out into the forest and then walked towards the hermit's cottage."

It has at least a half dozen other functions as well, but all of them can be traced back to this one (Haiman 2011: chapter 10).

5 Semantics

5.1 Idiomaticity

The most striking feature of Khmer lexical semantics, once the initial questions have been dealt with, is not the proliferation of terms for any particular semantic domain, but the degree to which non-compositionality rules. Given words

A,B,C, combinations of these words (AB, ABC, BC) do not mean what they might be predicted to. For a very insufficient example the combination កប៉ាល់ *kapal* "boat" and ភ្លើង *pleu:ng* "fire" may mean "steamboat", but it may also mean "thoroughly unpleasant woman". More unnerving examples have already occurred in many of the sample sentences cited here, as in:

(89) តាបសហ្នឹងត្រូវជាម៉េច?
    ta:bawh   nwng   trev cia   <u>mec</u>
    hermit   that   must be   how
                              =related
    "What relationship does that hermit have (to you)?"

(90) របៀបដូចជាគ្រាសកន្លង។
    rabiap   do:c   cia   kriah   kanlaw:ng
    manner like   be   eclipse   pass.over
                          COMP (=retarded)
    "acted like/as if retarded (an eclipse had passed over (his mother while she was pregnant)"

5.2 Politeness mitigators

Explicit imperatives and prohibitives are rendered less brusque with different shades of meaning, by a number of words that have been grammaticalized from full verbs. Polite, but still peremptory imperatives, can be given to subordinates, using preclausal ចូរ *co:*.

(91) ចូរអ្នកកុំយកតម្រាប់តាមដំរី។
    <u>co:</u>   neak   kom   jau:k   tamrap   ta:m   dawnmrej
    IMP   you   don't   take   example follow elephant
    "Don't follow the elephant's example."

Polite imperatives and pious wishes (jussives) are expressed by preclausal សូម *so:m* (< "please"):

(92) សូមធ្វើតាមបណ្ដាំគាត់ទៅ។
    <u>so:m</u>   tveu: ta:m   bandam   koat   tev
    please do   follow instruction 3   go
    "Please follow his instructions."

Invitations are preceded by preclausal អញ្ជើញ *anjceu:nj* "invite."

(93) អញ្ជើញហូបទៅពិសាទៅ។
    <u>*anjceu:nj*</u> *ho:p* *tev* *pisa:* *tev*
    invite eat DIR eat DIR
    "Please, eat!"

A request for a favor is expressed by the auxiliary verb *cuaj* "help (me)":

(94) លោកតាជួយនិទានរឿងអា។
    lo:k *ta:* <u>*cuaj*</u> *nitian* *rwang* *A.*
    HON grandpa help tell story A.
    "Please grandpa, please please tell me the story of A., do!"

The laissez-faire "help yourself, go for it" imperative is expressed by the use of clause-final ចុះ *coh*, "descend", or ទៅ *tev* "go", functioning here as directive particles much like "away" in English:

(95.a) បើកូនឯងចង់ទៅក៏ទៅចុះ។
    Baeu *ko:n* *aeng* *cawng* *tev* *kaw:* *tev* <u>*coh*</u>
    if child you want go so go descend
    "If you want to go, child, then go."

(95.b) ទុកលុយចុះ។
    tuk *luj* <u>*coh*</u>
    keep money descend
    "Keep the change."

(96) ញាំទៅ!
    njam *tev!*
    eat go
    "Go ahead and eat!"

Wheedling humble entreaties can also be expressed by clause-final ផង *phaw:ng* "also":

(97.a) សួរថ្លៃអោយខ្ញុំផង។
    sua *tlaj* *aoj* *knjom* *phaw:ng*
    ask expensive for me also
    "Can you please find out how much it will cost?"

(97.b) ជួយផង!
     cuaj   *phaw:ng*
     help   also
     "Please help me !"

It is common to find imperatives with more than one softener:

(98.a) សូមចាំខ្ញុំផង។
     <u>*so:m*</u>   *cam*   *knjom*   <u>*phaw:ng*</u>
     please wait   me   also
     "Please wait for me."

(98.b) សូមជួយយកទឹកមួយដប។
     <u>*so:m*</u>   <u>*cuaj*</u>   *jau:k*   *teuk*   *muaj*   *daw:p*
     please help   bring   water one   bottle
     "Please, please bring me a bottle of water."

6 Summary and conclusions

Khmer is a typical MSEA language, exhibiting typical word order patterns: SVO, Head # Modifier, Preposition # NP, and a total lack of inflectional morphology. It exhibits sesquisyllabicity in its native vocabulary, and has a moderately rich derivational morphology which is largely prefixing or infixing. Like many SE Asian languages, Khmer exhibits a predilection for decorative symmetrical compounding. Finally, like many SE Asian languages, Khmer shows a tremendous amount of part-of-speech polyfunctionality, with words being free to assume different syntactic functions.

The presence of a large admixture of unassimilated Indic words results in the existence of two canonical word structure types, and even the presence of (suffixing) Pali morphology and Modifier # Head Pali syntax. As the language has been written for over 1300 years, and even fully assimilated Indic words are transliterated from their original forms, this means that literate speakers have a fairly deep understanding of the foreign sources of much of their vocabulary.

    Finally, it must be stressed that Khmer seems to exhibit considerably greater derivational richness than many other languages of the region.

References

Bisang, W. 1992. *Das Verb im Chinesischen, Hmong, Vietnamesischen, Thai, und Khmer*. Tübingen: Gunter Narr.
Bolinger, D. 1975. *Aspects of language*, 2nd ed. New York: Harcourt Brace Jovanovich.
Bréal, M. 1897. *Essai de sémantique*. Paris: Hachette.
Cun-Leuh. 2007. *Ve:jjakaw kmae* [Khmer grammar]. Phonm Penh: Pon Chaun & Tiang Ciat.
Ehrman, M. & K. Sos. 1972. *Contemporary Cambodian: A grammatical sketch*. Washington, DC: Foreign Services Institute.
Enfield, N. 2003. *Linguistic epidemiology*. London: Routledge-Curzon.
Gorgoniev, Yu. 1966. *Grammatika Khmerskogo jazyka*. Moscow: Akademia Nauk.
Haiman, J. 1998. *Possible origins of infixation in Khmer*. Studies in Language 22. 597–617.
Haiman, J. 2011. Cambodian/Khmer. Amsterdam: John Benjamins.
Haiman, J. & N. Ourn. 2003. Nouns, verbs, and syntactic backsliding in Khmer. *Studies in Language* 27. 505–28.
Headley, R. & K. Neou. 1991. *English/Khmer phrase book*. New York: Field Operations Division, Office of General Services, United Nations.
Headley, R., Kylin Chor, Lam Kheng Lim, Lim Hak kheang & Chen Chun. 1977. *Cambodian-English dictionary*. Washington, DC: The Catholic University of America Press.
Henderson, E. 1952. The main features of Cambodian pronunciation. *Bulletin of the School of Oriental and African Studies* 14. 149–74.
Huffman, F. Charan Promchan & Chhom-Rak Thong Lambert. 1970. Modern spoken Cambodian. New Haven & London: Yale University Press.
Humphrey, Chny-Sak. 1995. Serial and completive verbs in Khmer. In M. Alves (ed.), Southeast Asian Linguistics Society III, 171–204. Tempe: Arizona State University Press.
Iwasaki, S. & P. Ingkapirom. 2005. *A reference grammar of Thai*. Cambridge: Cambridge University Press.
Jenner, P. 1969. *Affixation in modern Khmer*. Unpublished PhD dissertation, University of Hawai'i.
Jenner, P. 1974. Observations on the Surin dialect of Khmer. *Southeast Asian Linguistic Studies* 1. 61–73.
Jenner, P. & S. Pou. 1982. *A lexicon of Khmer morphology*. Honolulu: University of Hawai'i Press.
Jespersen, O. 1964. *Language: Its nature, origin, and development*. New York: Norton.
Li, C. & S. Thompson. 1981. *Mandarin Chinese: A functional reference grammar*. Berkeley & Los Angeles: University of California Press.
Lim, H. & D. Purtle (edited, annotated, and supplemented by M. Ehrman & K. Sos). 1972. *Contemporary Cambodian: Introduction*. Washington, DC: Foreign Service Institute.
Martin, M. 1975. Le dialecte cambodgien parlé à Tatey, Massif des Cardamomes. *Asie du sudest et mode insulindien* 6. 71–79.
Ménétrier, E. 1933. *Le vocabulaire cambodgien dans ses rapports avec le Sanscrit et le Pali*. Phnom Penh: Imprimerie du Protectorat.
Nacaskul, K. 1976. Types of elaboration in some Southeast Asian languages. In P. Jenner et al. (ed.), *Austroasiatic studies* 2, 873–90. Honolulu: University of Hawai'i Press.
Nguyen, D. H. 1974. *Colloquial Vietnamese*. Carbondale: Southern Illinois University Press.
Noss, P. & I. Proum (with the assistance of D. Purtle & K. Sos). 1966. *Cambodian: Basic course*, vol. 1. Washington, DC: Foreign Service Institute.
Ourn, N. & J. Haiman. 2000. Symmetrical compounds in Khmer. *Studies in Language* 24. 483–513.

Pou, S. 2004. La derivation en cambodgien moderne. In S. Pou (ed.), *Selected papers on Khmerology*, 22–41. Phnom Penh: Reyum Publishing.

Prakorb, Phon-Ngam. 1992. The problem of aspirates in Central Khmer and Northern Khmer. *Mon-Khmer Studies* 22. 251–256.

Ross, J. 1967. Constrains on variables in syntax. PhD dissertation, MIT.

Schmidt, P. W. 1916. Einiges über das Infix -*mn* und dessen Stellvertreter in den austroasiatischen Sprachen. In L. Scherman & C. Bezold (eds.), Aufsätze zum Geburtstag am 7. Februar gewidmet von Freunden und Schülern. Breslau: M. & H. Marcus.

Sidwell, P. 2010. *Classifying the Austroasiatic languages: History and state of the art*. Munich: Lincom.

Sisovat, P. 1972. *Bo'ri'va: sap knong phiasa: kmae* [Servant words in Khmer]. Phnom Penh: privately printed.

Stolz, T. 2008. Total reduplication versus echo-word formation in language contact situations. In P. Siemund & N. Kintana (eds.), *Language contact and contact languages*, 107–32. Amsterdam: John Benjamins.

Thach, Ngoc Minh. 1999. The phenomenon of monosyllabization in the Kiengiang dialect of Khmer. *Mon-Khmer Studies* 5. 81–95.

Vickery, M. 1990. Loan words and devoicing in Khmer. *Mon-Khmer Studies* 18 (9). 240–50.

Wayland, R. & S. Guion. 2007. Tonogenesis in Khmer. *Journal of the Southeast Asian Linguistics Society* (SEALS) 12. 145–52. Canberra: Pacific Linguistics

Appendix 1: Summary of linguistic features

Legend
+++ the feature is pervasive or used obligatorily in the language
++ the feature is normal but selectively distributed in the language
+ the feature is merely possible or observable in the language
− the feature is impossible or absent in the language

	Feature	+++/++/+/−	§ ref. in this chapter
Phonetics	Lexical tone or register	+	§1.1.1, p.321
Phonetics	Back unrounded vowels	+++	§1.2.2, p.322–23
Phonetics	Initial velar nasal	+++	§1.2.1, p.322
Phonetics	Implosive consonants	+++	§1.2.1, p.322
Phonetics	Sesquisyllabic structures	++	§1.3, p.323 & §1.3.1, p.326
Morphology	Tendency towards monosyllabicity	++	§1.3.1, p.326
Morphology	Tendency to form compounds	+++	§2.1, p.327 & §2.1.4, p.333
Morphology	Tendency towards isolating (rather than affixation)	++	§2.1, p.327
Morphology	Psycho-collocations	++	§2.2, p.335

	Feature	+++/++/+/−	§ ref. in this chapter
Morphology	Elaborate expressions (e.g. four-syllable or other set patterns)	+++	§2.3, p.336
Morphology	Reduplication generally	+	§2.3, p.340
Morphology	Reduplication of nouns	−	−
Morphology	Reduplication of verbs	−	−
Grammar	Use of classifiers	++	§3.1.1, p.344
Grammar	Classifiers used in counting	+	§3.1.1, p.344–45
Grammar	Classifiers used with demonstratives	+	not discussed explicitly, but see §3.3, p.350
Grammar	Adjectival verbs	+++	§4.2.2, p.360
Grammar	Grammatical number	+++	not discussed explicitly, but see §2.1.2, p.329
Grammar	Inflection of verbs	−	−
Grammar	Use of tense/aspect markers	++	§4, p.352
Grammar	Use of verb plural markers	++	§4, p.352
Grammar	Grammaticalization of GET/OBTAIN (potential mod. resultative/perfect aspect)	+++	§4.1.2, p.355, see also §4.2.9, p.367
Grammar	Grammaticalization of PUT, SET (completed/resultative aspect)	−	−
Grammar	Grammaticalization of GIVE (causative, benefactive; preposition)	++	not discussed explicitly, but see §4.2.9, p.368
Grammar	Grammaticalization of FINISH (perfective/ complete aspect; conjunction/temporal subordinator)	+	§4.1.2, p.358
Grammar	Grammaticalization of directional verbs e.g. GO / COME (allative, venitive)	+++	§4.1.2, p.357
Grammar	Grammaticalization of SEE, WATCH (temptative)	++	not discussed explictly
Grammar	Grammaticalization of STAY, REMAIN (progressive and continuous, durative aspects)	+++	§4.2.2, p.360 & see also §4.2.6, p.363
Grammar	Serial verb constructions	++	§4, p.352
Syntax	Verb precedes object (VO)	++	§4.2, p.359
Syntax	Auxiliary precedes verb	+	§4, p.352
Syntax	Preposition precedes noun	++	not discussed explicitly
Syntax	Noun precedes adjective	+++	§3.1.1, p.344, see also §4.2.3, p.360

	Feature	+++/++/+/–	§ ref. in this chapter
Syntax	Noun precedes demonstrative	+++	§3.1.1, p.344
Syntax	Noun precedes genitive	++	not discussed explicitly
Syntax	Noun precedes relative clause	+++	not discussed explicitly
Syntax	Use of topic-comment structures	++	§4.2.8, p.365
Syntax	Ellipsis of arguments known from context	++	not discussed explicitly
Lexical Semantics	Specific terms for forms of rice	+++	not discussed explicitly
Lexical Semantics	Use of utterance-final pragmatic particles	+++	§5.2.1
Lexical Semantics	Encoding of politeness	++	§5.2, p.370 & §3.2.1, p.347
Lexical Semantics	Encoding of honorifics	+	not discussed explicitly

Appendix 2: Text interlinearized

រឿងទាក់ទងនិងប្រាសាទភូមិពោន(ខេត្តសុរិន្ទ្រ)
Rwang   teak   tau:ng   nwng   pra:s   a:t   Phu:m   Pau:n   (Khet Suri:n)
Tale   connected with   the   temple of   Phum   Pun   (province S.)[3]

ព្រះមហាក្សត្រខ្មែរបានសាងរាជធានីមួយនៅកណ្តាលព្រៃសំរាប់រាជវង្ស
Preah   mha: ksat   kmae   ba:n   sa:ng   riac   thiani: muaj   nev   kanda:l
HON   great   king   Khmer PAST   build   royal   city   one   be.at center

prej   samrap   riac   vaung
forest   for   king   family
"A great Khmer king built a royal capital in the middle of the forest as his family residential palace"

លាក់បំពួនអាត្មានៅពេលមានអាសន្ន ឬកើតសឹកសង្គ្រាម
Leak   bampuan   atma: nev   pee:l   mian   asawn   rw: kaeut   seuk   sangkriam.
Hide   hide   self   at   time   exist   emergency   or   arise   war   war
"as a refuge in times of war or turmoil"

---

[3] Excerpted from រឿងព្រេងខ្មែរទាក់ទងនិងប្រាសាទ *Rwang Pree:ng kmae teak tau:ng nwng prasa:t*, (ed. M. Tra: Nee:) : Ministry of Culture and Science & Unesco: Phnom Penh.

រាជធានីនោះហៅថាប្រាសាទភូមិពាន ជាជ័យភូមិអាចរក្សាសេចក្តីសុខ
Riac thiani: nuh hav tha: prasa:t Phu:m Pu:n kw: cia cej phu:m
Royal city that call say temple P.P. that is be –⁴ P.

a:c reaksa: seckdej sok
can preserve NOM safe
"This royal capital, called the temple of P:hu:m (the village) of Pu:n was the village that would be able to preserve the safety [of the royal family]"

ហើយបិតនៅឆ្ងាយពីទីក្រុងសំខាន់ៗទៀតផង
Haeuj theut nev cṅga:j pi: tikrong (sam kha:n) 2 tiat phaw:ng
and stand be.at far from city (important) 2 more also/PLU⁵
"and was located far from the important cities"

រាជធានីនោះមិនទាន់មានស្រះទឹកទេ
Riac thiani: nuh mwn toan mian srah teuk tee:
royal city that not yet have reservoir water no
"There were no water reservoirs yet in that royal capital"

ចំណែកផ្លូវថ្នល់
camnaek plav tnawl
as.for road street
"and as for streets,"

ក៏មិនទាន់មានដែរ
kaw: mwn toan mian dae.
So⁶ not yet have also
"there were also none."

---

4 The combination ជាជ័យ *cia cej* is an unusually occurring symmetrical compound in which the second element "victory" has been conscripted as a phonetic match for the copula *cia* and is semantically empty.
5 The word ផង *phaw:ng* in modern Khmer is usually glossable as "also". Here it could still have it earlier meaning as a plural or collective marker.
6 The coordinate clitic ក៏ *kaw:* has as its basic meaning "and (so)", but is multiply polysemous. Here it is functioning with one of its associated meanings, to introduce a "listed" parallel predication, cf. Haiman 2011: chapter 10.

គេគ្រាន់តែធ្វើផ្លូវលំជរៈស្មៅ
Kee: kroan tae tveu: plav lum cumreah smav
3 just make road narrow clear grass
"Just a narrow path was made, by clearing away the undergrowth"

បន្តិចបន្តួចល្មមដើរបាន ដើម្បីបិទបាំងគ្មប្រាសាទនឹង
bantec bantuac lmau:m daeu ba:n daeumbej bwt bang tua
a.bit – easy walk manage in.order close hide body

prasa:t nwng
temple the
"a bit, so that one could walk there easily, but the temple remained hidden"

រាជធានីអោយផុតពីភ្នែកសត្រូវប៉ុណ្ណោះ
riac thiani: aoj phot pi: pne:k satrev ponno:h.
royal city so.that beyond from eye enemy that.much
"from enemy eyes."

តមកអាណាចក្រ ខមបូរាណ
Taw: mau:k a'na'cak khawm bora:n
continue DIR empire Khawm[7] ancient
"Thereafter, with the rise of the ancient Khawm empire"

កើតចលាចលក្នុងប្រទេសព្រោះមានខ្មាំងសត្រូវលុកលុយរហូតដល់ទីក្រុង
kaeut cawla:cawl knong pratee:h pro:h mian kmang satrev luk
arise war.activity in country because exist enemy enemy invade

luj raho:t dawl tikrong.
invade up.to until city
"war came to the country because there were enemy invasions all the way up to the [capital] city"

ដើម្បីរក្សាសេចក្ដីសុខដល់រាជវង្សានុវង្សព្រះមហាក្សត្រ
daeumbej reaksa: seckdej sok dawl riac vaungsa'nu'vaung preah
in.order.to preserve NOM safe to royal family.all.kinds HON

---

7 A Khmer tribe.

mha:	ksat
great	king

"In order to protect the safety of his extended family, the king"

បានបញ្ជូនព្រះរាជធីតាព្រះនាមសិរិចន្ទ

ba:n	banjcu:n	preah	riac	Thi: Ta:	preah	niam	niang	Sej'rej'can
PAST	send	HON	royal	TT	HON	name	young.lady	S.

"sent [to] the king Thi: Ta: the [royal princess] named Sejrejcan"

ប៉ុន្តែមនុស្សទូទៅហៅព្រះនាងថានាងដោះធំព្រមទាំងមាន

pontae	mnuh	tu: tev	hav	preah	niang	tha:	niang	dawh	thom
but	people	generally	call	HON	missy	say	she	breast	big

prau:m	teang	mian
agree	all[8]	have

"but generally called by the people the young lady with the big breasts, together with"

សេនាភីលៀងចំនួន១០១នាក់ដែលមាននាយសេនាឈ្មោះពងចន្ទ

see:naa:	phi:liang	camnuan	101	neak	dael	mian	niaj	see:na:
retinue	bodyguard	number	101	CLF	which	have	leader	retinue

cmo:h	PonCan
name	PC

"a retinue of 101 guards, whose leader was called Pon Can"

ជាអ្នកមានចិត្តស្មោះត្រង់បំផុតចំពោះព្រះរាជវង្សានុវង្ស

cia	neak	mian	ceut	smawh	trawng	bamphot	campo:h	preah	riac
be	person	have	heart	loyal		extreme	towards	HON	king

vaungsa'nu'vaung
family.all.kinds

"a person extremely loyal to the king and his extended family"

---

8 The combination ព្រមទាំង *prau:m teang* has lost its literal meaning here and can be translated as "(together) with".

គាមព្រះនាងទៅដែរ
ta:m   preah   niang   tev   dae.
follow HON   missy   DIR   also
"and thus to her also."

កាលនោះមានស្ដេចមួយអង្គសោយរាជនៅនគរមួយ
Ka:l   nuh   mian   sdac   muaj   awng   saoj   riac nev   naukau: muaj
time   that exist king   one   CLF   rule   be.at   city   one
"At this time there was a king ruling in a city"

ឆ្ងាយដាច់ស្រយាលពីរាជធានីភូមិពួន
cnga:j   dac   sraja:l   pi: riac   thiani: Phu:m Pu:n
far   cut   removed   from   royal   capital   PP
"remote from the royal capital of PP"

បានចាត់ព្រានព្រៃ៧នាក់
ba:n   cat   prian   prej   7   neak
PAST   organize   hunter   forest   7   CLF
"who organized 7 hunters"

ព្រមទាំងដំរីមួយចំនួន
praw:m teang   damrej   muaj   camnuan
with   elephant   one   quantity
"together with a number of elephants"

ដើម្បីដេញចាប់សត្វព្រៃ
daeumbej   denj   cap   sat   prej
in.order.to   chase   catch   animal   forest
"to hunt wild animals"

ដែលកម្រមាន
dael   kamraw:[9]   mian
which   hard.to.find   exist
"that were rare."

---

[9] The word ក្រ *kraw*: "poor; hard to find" here takes on an infix ំ *-am-*, which, if it were meaningful, could be either a nominalizer or a causativizer. Here it seems to perform no semantic function, and could be called "decorative". See also footnote 10.

ហើយល្អរឆង
Haeuj	(l'aw)	2	phaw:ng
and	(good)	2	also/PLU

"and beautiful."

យកទៅចិញ្ចឹមក្នុងព្រះរាជវាំង
jau:k tev	cenjceum	knong	preah	riac	veang.
take go.to	raise	in	HON	royal	palace

"[These] were to be taken to be raised in the royal palace."

ព្រានព្រៃទាំង៧នាក់
Prian	prej	teang	7	neak
hunter	forest	all	7	CLF

"All 7 hunters"

បានធ្វើដំណើររហូតដល់ត្រពាំងព្រាន
ba:n	tveu:	damnaeu	raho:t	dawl	trapeang	Prian
PAST	make	journey	until	till	pond	P.

"traveled to Prian pond"

ដែលបិតនៅទិសខាង
dael	theut	nev	twh	kha:ng
which	stand	be.at	direction	side

"which is located"

ត្បូងភូមិតាព្រាហួណ៌
tbo:ng	Phu:m	Ta:	Priam
south	P.	T.	P.

"to the south of Phum Ta: Priam."

ស្រាប់តែ
Srap tae
suddenly

ព្រានបីនាក់
prian	3	neak
hunter	3	CLF

"three hunters"

ជួបប្រទះកន្លែងដានជើងមនុស្សដែលធ្វើដំណើរ
cuap prateah[10] kunlau:ng da:n ceu:ng mnuh dael tveu: damnaeu
meet encounter traces tracks foot person which make trip
"came on the footprints of the walkers"

រៀងរាល់ថ្ងៃ
riang roal[11] tngaj
– every day
"[who made these tracks] every day"

កណ្ដាលព្រៃព្រៅ
kanda:l prej crav.
middle forest deep
"in the middle of the forest"

ដោយការសង្ស័យ
Daoj ka: sangsaj
by NOM suspect
"Their suspicions aroused"

ព្រានព្រៃក៏ធ្វើដំណើរតាមដានជើងនោះ
prian prej kaw: tveu: damnaeu ta:m da:n ceu:ng nuh
hunter forest so make trip follow tracks foot that
"the hunters followed the trail of those footprints"

ហើយបានជួបប្រាសាទមួយនៅកណ្ដាលព្រៃ
haeuj ba:n cuap prasa:t muaj nev kanda:l prej
and get.to meet temple one be.at middle forest
"and so chanced upon the temple in the middle of the forest"

---

10 ជួប *cuap* usually means to "meet intentionally," while ប្រទះ *prateah* always means to "encounter by chance". This combination, which clearly has only the latter meaning, is a very mild example of the Khmer predilection for creating symmetrical compounds of (near) synonyms, where the quest for a symmetrical pair outweighs semantic accuracy.

11 The combination រៀងរាល់ *riang roal* "every" is a commonly occurring example of a decorative compound whose first member has been pressed into service to accompany a word with which it alliterates, losing all of its own meaning ("form") in the process.

ដោយមានពលសេនាយាមការពារជុំវិញផង
Daoj   mian   paul   see:na: jian   ka:pia   cumvenj   phaw:ng.
By   exist   force   retinue   guard   protect   around   also
"Because of the retinue standing guard all around the temple"

ព្រានព្រៃបានលាក់ធ្នូនិងឧបករណ៍បាញ់សត្វ
prian   prej   ba:n   leak   tnu: sna: nwng   o'pa'kaw: banj   sat
hunter   forest PAST   hide   bow   arrow   and   equipment   shoot   animal
"the hunters hid their bows, arrows and hunting gear"

ទុកមួយកន្លែង
tok   muaj   kanlaeng
keep   one   place
"keeping them in one place"

ហើយចូលទៅធ្វើទំនាក់ទំនងជាមួយអ្នកយាម
haeuj   co:l   tev   tveu: tumneak   tumnau:ng   cia muaj   neak   jiam
and   enter   go.to   make   connection   connection   together   person   guard
"and went in to make the acquaintance of the guards"

Danh Thành Do-Hurinville and Huy Linh Dao
Vietnamese[1]

Introduction

Vietnamese is the official language of Vietnam and the mother tongue of the Vietnamese people[2] (composed of about 85% of Vietnam's population, over 86 millions in 2008), and of about three million overseas Vietnamese, most of them in the United States, Canada, Europe, Australia, etc[3]. The Vietnamese language is also spoken as a second language by many ethnic minorities in Vietnam.

The origins of the Vietnamese language still remain an issue under debate. Currently, there are several hypotheses regarding its linguistic affiliation, hypotheses that place Vietnamese variously within the Austroasiatic, Austronesian, Chinese, or Tai-Kadai language families. Another approach views Vietnamese as a 'mixed' language in the sense that it cannot easily be demonstrated to pertain to any particular group, nor can it convincingly be argued to have an obvious linguistic substratum. According to the commonly held and most well supported position, which is based on solid lexical and phonological evidence, Vietnamese has been identified as part of the Mon-Khmer branch of the Austroasiatic language family[4], in which it represents by far the greatest proportion of speakers (several times larger than Khmer and the other Austroasiatic languages put together).

---

1 We would like to thank René-Joseph Lavie (MoDyCo 7114) and Jean Hurinville, who kindly proofread our article.
2 *Người Việt* or *người Kinh*.
3 According to the "Ethnologue: Languages of the World" (see *Wikipedia*), Vietnamese is spoken by a substantial number of people in Australia, Cambodia, Canada, China, Côte d'Ivoire, Finland, France, Germany, Laos, Martinique, the Netherlands, New Caledonia, Norway, the Philippines, Senegal, Thailand, the United Kingdom, the United States and Vanuatu. In Australia, Vietnamese is the sixth most widely spoken language; in the United States, it is the seventh most widely spoken language (3rd in Texas, 4th in Arkansas and Louisiana, and 5th in California) (see Wikipedia, cf. *Detailed List of Languages Spoken at Home for the Population 5 Years and Over by State: 2000*).
4 See Alves 2001, 2005, 2008 and references therein for further discussion on this issue.

Danh Thành Do-Hurinville: Université de Franche-Comté & ELLIADD, EA 4661
E-Mail: danh_thanh.do-hurinville@univ-fcomte.fr
Huy Linh Dao: INALCO & CRLAO, UMR 8563 (CNRS-EHESS-INALCO)
E-Mail: huy-linh.dao@inalco.fr

https://doi.org/10.1515/9783110401981-009

Vietnamese shares a large number of typological features with Thaï, Khmer, Lao, etc., concerning SVO and head-modifier orders, lack of morphological case marking, gender, number, tense, and, as a result, no finite and non-finite distinction. In other words, whereas the Indo-European languages tend to use inflectional morphology to express case, gender, number and tense, Southeast Asian languages resort to lexical words or syntactic constructions. As the result of one thousand years of contact with Chinese, a substantial part of the Vietnamese vocabulary comes from that language. Due to this intensive contact with its neighbour, which not only led to a dramatic restructuring of its lexicon (cf. Alves 2001) but also affected many aspects of its phonology, Vietnamese diverges in many respects from its Mon-Khmer sisters.

This article consists of four parts: phonology, morphology, syntax, and semantics-pragmatics in Vietnamese.

1 Phonology

After presenting the syllable structure, we will deal with the description of tones and registers (suprasegmentals), consonants and vowels (segmentals).

1.1 Syllable structure

The study of the Vietnamese syllable structure can be divided into three points: the characteristics, the components, and the two-level structure.

Most of the Vietnamese basic vocabulary is monosyllabic: the syllable boundary coincides with the morpheme boundary[5]; the syllable is the basic unit.

Phonologically, a monosyllabic word contains a maximum of the **five** following components: the onset (C_1), the glide (w), the nucleus (V), the coda (C_2), and the tone (T)[6].

Let's take ***thuyền*** 'boat' as example: / t^h-w-ie-n-2/. The onset is: /t^h/ <th>, the glide is: /w/ <u>, the nucleus is: /ie/ <yê>, the coda is: /n/ <n>, and the basically flat and long tone (tone 2, see below) is indicated by a grave accent in the spelling. The syllable structure of the above monosyllabic lexeme is: **C_1wVC_2 + T**.

---

5 Cf. section *Morphology* (Simplex words).
6 The onset, the nucleus and the tone are obligatory, the glide and the coda being optional.

A syllable is organized by a hierarchy of two distinct levels (cf. Đoàn *et al.*, 2003) as follows:

Table 1: Vietnamese syllable structure

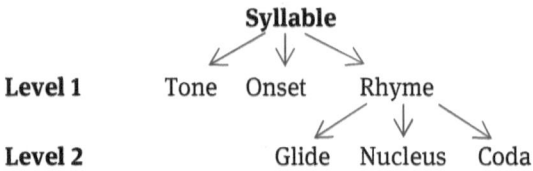

1.2 Tone and register (suprasegmentals)

North Vietnamese has a six-tone paradigm for sonorant-final syllables and a two-tone paradigm for obstruent-final syllables. According to Michaud (2004), the Vietnamese tone can be described as a complex bundle of pitch contour and voice quality characteristics (see also Brunelle 2009a, 2009b for further discussion).

In Đoàn *et al.*'s (2003) classification, the tone contour can be simple (flat) or complex (non flat).

Tone 1: *thanh ngang*, e.g. *ma* 'ghost' is high and flat throughout.
Tone 2: *thanh huyền*, e.g. *mà* 'relativizer' starts mid-level, falls gently. It is basically flat and long.
Tone 3: *thanh ngã*, e.g. *mã* 'horse, appearance', glottalized, starts mid-level, falls steep then rises steep above the height where it started.
Tone 4: *thanh hỏi*, e.g. *mả* 'tomb) starts mid-level, falls gently then rises gently to recover the level where it started.
Tone 5: *thanh sắc*, e.g. *má* 'mother, cheek) starts high, rises quickly to a very high pitch.
Tone 6: *thanh nặng*, e.g. *mạ* 'rice seedling, plate), glottalized, starts mid-level then falls to low level.

Table 2: Vietnamese tone system

Register / Pitch	Thanh bằng (tones flat)	Thanh trắc (tones non-flat)	
		Gãy (broken)	Không gãy (non-broken)
High	Tone 1	Tone 3	Tone 5
Low	Tone 2	Tone 4	Tone 6

The tones (classified in terms of register and in terms of pitch) are presented in the summary table above.

Tones 3 and 4 are performed with a fall at the start, then a rise, which forms a break. Therefore, they are named « broken tones ». As for tones 5 and 6, they are performed respectively with a rise and a fall. They are non-broken contours.

1.3 Consonants and vowels (segmentals)

The segmental phoneme consists of the onset, the medial glide, the nucleus and the coda.

1.3.1 The onset

There are 22 onsets in all, 18 in the northern Vietnamese, plus three in the central and southern dialects: /tʂ, ʂ, ʐ /. The glottal stop /ʔ/ is inserted into the initial position of a syllable beginning with a vowel in all three dialects, but it is not represented by any letter in the written language. The following table shows the onsets in the three dialects[7]:

INVENTORY OF VIETNAMESE ONSETS (cf. Đoàn et al.)

Table 3: Vietnamese onsets

Manner			Place Labial		Tip of tongue			Blade of tongue	Back of tongue	Glottal
			labial	dental	dental	alveolar	Palatal			
Stop	Aspirate				tʰ					
	Un-aspirate	Voiceless			t		tʂ	c	k	ʔ
		Voiced	b		d					
	Sonant (nasal)		m		n			ɲ	ŋ	
Fricative	Voiceless			f	s		ʂ		x	h
	Voiced			v	z		ʐ		ɣ	
	Sonant (lateral)				l					

---

7 The 22 Vietnamese consonants are transcribed by the use of Roman letters as follows: /b/ <b>; /m/ <m>; /f/ <ph>; /v/ <v>; /tʰ/ <th>; /t/ <t>; /d/ <đ>; /n/ <n>; /s/ <x>; /z/ <d>, <gi>; /l/ <l>; /tʂ/ <tr>; /ʐ/ <s>; /ʂ/ <r>; /c/ <ch>; /ɲ/ <nh>; /k/ <c>, <k>, <q>; /ŋ/ <ng>, <ngh>; /x/ <kh>; /ɣ/ <g>; /h/ <h>; /ʔ/ <Ø>.
In modern Vietnamese, the phoneme /p/ does not appear in the initial position of a syllable, except in some borrowings, or foreign person and geography names.

1.3.2 The medial glide

The medial glide /w/ occurs between the onset and the nucleus. It lowers the timbre of the syllable at the start, and makes one word distinct from another: **toán** /twan5/ has a lower timbre compared with **tán** /tan5/ (cf. Đoàn et al. 2003). This glide has two allophonic variants: [ɥ] before front vowels and [w] before other vowels.

1.3.3 The nucleus

Table 4: Vietnamese simple vowels

	Front	Back, unrounded	Back, rounded
Close	i	ɯ	u
Half-open	e	ɤ	o
Open	ɛ	a	ɔ

There are 13 vowels, out of which 9 are long[8] (see table above), and 4 are short[9]; there are 3 diphthongs[10]. That amounts to a total of 16 phonemes (cf. Đoàn et al.).

1.3.4 The coda

Vietnamese has 6 final consonants, 3 nasals and 3 stops, presented in the following table[11], and 2 final glides[12] (cf. Đoàn et al.).

Table 5: Vietnamese codas

	Labial	Palatal	Velar
Nasal	m	n	ŋ
Stop	p	t	k
Glide	w	j	

---

8 /i/ <i>, <y>; /e/ <ê>; /ɛ/ <e>; /ɯ/ <ư>; /ɤ/ <ơ>; /a/ <a>; /u/ <u>; /o/ <ô>; /ɔ/ <o>.
9 /ɤ̆/ <â>; /ă/ <ă>; /ɔ̆/ <o>; /ɛ̆/ <a>.
10 /ie/ <iê>, <yê>, <ia>; /uo/ <uô>, <ua>; /ɯɤ/ <ươ>, <ưa>.
11 /m/ <m>; /n/ <n>; /ŋ/ <nh>, <ng>; /p/ <p>; /t/ <t>; /k/ <ch>, <c>.
12 /w/ <u>, <o>; /j/ <i>, <y>.

2 Morphology

Vietnamese has no inflectional morphology and in this section on morphology, we will deal with word structure and morphological processes used in word formation such as reduplication and compounding.

2.1 Word structure

Vietnamese is often considered to be a monosyllabic language. Statistically, the majority of Vietnamese words are monosyllabic, and a significant number of morphemes have the status of words. However, Nguyen P. P. (1976: 7) states that Vietnamese words are not all monosyllabic. A minority of words have two syllables, and some of them three or four. Several polysyllabic words are formed by reduplicative derivation.

Concerning their structure Vietnamese words are divided into three groups: simplex words, complex words and compound words.

2.1.1 Simplex words

Simplex words cannot be decomposed any further into smaller meaningful units but only into sound segments (cf. Booij, 2007: 7), and they belong to the following subgroups: monosyllabic monomorphemic words and polysyllabic monomorphemic words.

- **Monosyllabic monomorphemic words**

Words like the following consist of one morpheme or one syllable and are the majority of the Vietnamese vocabulary[13].

(1) *nói* 'speak'; *ăn* 'eat'; *chạy* 'run'; *viết* 'write'; *cơm* 'cooked rice'; *gạo* 'rice'; *muối* 'salt'; *đường* 'sugar', etc.

- **Polysyllabic monomorphemic words**

Monomorphemic words consisting of two or three syllables can be divided as follows in two groups: (a) borrowings and (b) real polysyllables.

---

13 Nguyễn P. P. (*ibid.*) has counted 213 monosyllabic monomorphemic words in an excerpt including 326 words in the *Vietnamese Declaration of Independence* of 1945.

a. The first group consists of borrowings, mainly French words[14]. The following words are mentally segmented in quasi-syllables which are replaced by phonetically similar Vietnamese syllables:

(2) *áp-xe* 'abcès'; *cu-li* 'coolie'; *đi-văng* 'divan'; *ra-đi-ô* 'radio'; *xà-phòng* 'savon'; *xi-măng* 'ciment'; *xi-nê* 'ciné'; *ô-kê* 'okay'; *ra-đa* 'radar', etc.

b. The second sub-group of simplex words contains words of two syllables which cannot occurred separated from each other: These words are formed through reduplication of a meaningless (partially) reduplicated syllable.

b1. Reduplication of the whole syllable (mainly ideophones)
(3) *ồ ồ* 'sound of a hollow voice'; *rào rào* 'sound of the rain', etc.

b2. Reduplication of the initial consonant
(4) *bình bịch* 'sound of a motorcycle'; *vo ve* 'sound of a flying mosquito', etc. *rầm rì* 'sound of a conversation in a meeting room';

b3. Reduplication of the rhyme
(5) *bâng khuâng* 'be melancholy'; *cằn nhằn* 'groan'; *thình lình* 'suddenly', etc.

2.1.2 Complex words with reduplication

Complex words consist of (at least) two syllables (disyllabic bimorphemic words) one of which at least being a morpheme, i.e. being meaningful, whereas the other one has no morpheme status and is simply added via either total or partial reduplication. The syllables in boldface type are lexemes: they are "simplex words" (monosyllabic monomorphemic words). As for the morphemes in normal types, they can on no account be separated from the bold ones.

(6) *a.* **dịu** *dàng* 'be lovable';   *b.* *đo* **đỏ** 'be reddish';

(7) *a.* **lạnh** *lùng* 'be unfriendly';   *b.* **cây** *cối* 'trees and plants, vegetation'; **bắt** *bớ* 'arrest'; **mát** *mẻ* 'be fresh' ; **vui** *vẻ* 'be lively', etc.,

---

14 This can be explained by the historic relations between France and Vietnam.

They are formed either by
- reduplication of the initial consonant: **dịu** *dàng* 'be lovable' (cf. 6a), or by complete reduplication with a change of tone: *đo* **đỏ** 'be reddish' (cf. 6b).

From the semantic viewpoint, reduplication is used to:
- weaken the meaning of the morpheme in boldface type[15]: *đo* **đỏ** (be red + be red) 'be reddish',
- modify metaphorically the meaning of the morpheme in boldface type: **lạnh** *lùng* (be cold + *lùng*) 'be unfriendly' (cf. 7a),
- transform a count noun into a mass noun: **cây** *cối* (tree + *cối*) 'vegetation' (cf. 7b). It is a process of mass noun formation, commonly used in Vietnamese.

2.1.3 Compound words

Compound words are made up of two lexemes and can be divided into three subgroups (cf. Nguyễn P. P., 1976: 26).

- **Compound words consisting of "quasi-bound" lexemes**

The following words are Chinese borrowings, which constituents cannot stand alone as independent words while carrying their original meanings

(8) a. *phong phú* (be prosperous + be rich) 'be prosperous, be rich'
   b. *đế quốc* (emperor + nation) 'imperialism'
   c. *quốc gia* (nation + family) 'nation'

- **Compound words containing a "quasi-bound" lexeme and a lexeme**

In the following words, the lexemes in boldface type are free morphemes, the others which are Chinese borrowings, are "quasi-bound" morphemes:

(9) *thuỷ* **quân** (water + troops) 'marines'
   ái **tình** (love + feeling) 'love'

- **Compound words consisting of two lexemes**

The constituent of these compound words are free; their combination expresses a new or figurative meaning, or a larger and more general meaning than the one

---

[15] Only the lexemes in boldface type are stressed.

conveyed by each constituent. To illustrate the formation of compound words, let us examine a few compound verbs according to the classification of Nguyễn P. P. (1976: 30–36).

a. **From a part of speech viewpoint**

a1. Dynamic verb + dynamic verb –> dynamic verb
The two constituent verbs are dynamic and form a dynamic verb as follows:

(10) *đụng chạm* (touch + hurt) 'harm, wound'
   bao bọc (envelop + cover) 'enclose, protect'

a2. Stative verb + stative verb –> stative verb
The two constituent verbs are not dynamic and constitue a stative verb as follows:

(11) *béo mập* (be fat + be fat) 'be fat, be chubby'
   trong trắng (be clear + be white) 'be pure'

a3. Noun + noun –> dynamic verb
The two constituents are substantival and form a dynamic verb:

(12) *trai gái* (boy + girl) 'woo, go looking for a bit of skirt'
   đèn sách (lamp + book) 'study'

a4. Noun + noun –> stative verb
The two constituents are substantival and form a stative verb:

(13) *bướm hoa* (butterfly + flower) 'be gallant, be romantic'
   sắt đá (iron + stone) 'have an iron will'

b. **From a semantic viewpoint**

b1. Quasi-synonym lexemes
The two lexical constituents can be verbal or substantival:

(14) *bồng bế* (carry + carry) 'carry a baby in one's arms'
   miệng mồm (mouth + mouth) 'be very talkative'

b2. Semantically close lexemes
The two lexical constituents can be verbal:

(15) *cày bừa* (plough + rake) 'farm'
      mềm yếu (be soft + be weak) 'be characterless'

b3. Antonymous lexemes
Lexical constituents are generally verbal:

(16) *buôn bán* (trade + sell) 'trade'
      ăn thua (win + lose) 'compete with'

b4. Semantically complementary lexemes
The second verb completes the meaning of the first one:

(17) *bán rao* (sell + announce publicly) 'auction'
      hỏi thăm (ask + visit) 'inquire after somebody's health'

2.1.4 Affixation

Vietnamese has about twenty affixes most of them sino-vietnamese. They are bound morphemes in boldface type. Here are a few examples.

- **Prefixes**
(18) **bất** *động* (**not** + motion) 'be still or motionless'
      vô *lý* (**not** + be reasonable) 'be unreasonable or absurd'

- **Suffixes**
(19) *khoa học* **gia** (science + **expert**) 'scientist'
      ngôn ngữ **học** (language + **field of study**) 'linguistics'

2.2 Reduplication

Reduplication, which aims at creating new words by repeating either a whole word (full reduplication) or part of a word (partial reduplication), is very productive in Vietnamese. This section deals with the two following kinds of reduplication: reduplication of monosyllabic words into disyllabic words, and reduplication of disyllabic words into quadrisyllabic words.

2.2.1 Reduplication of monosyllabic words into disyllabic words

There are two possibilities:

- **Lexeme + lexeme (A => AA)**
(20) sáng 'morning' → **sáng sáng** 'every morning'
    tối 'evening' → **tối tối** 'every evening'

In the above examples, the reduplication is complete as it includes the initial consonant, the rhyme and the tone. The two constituent syllables in boldface type are stressed, and express the iterative aspect.

- **Bound morpheme + lexeme (A => A'A)**
(21) sáng 'morning' → sang **sáng** 'early morning'
    tối 'evening' → tôi **tối** 'slightly dark'

In the above examples, the reduplication is not complete because of the difference of tones. The syllables in boldface type are root lexemes, therefore they must be stressed. The syllables in normal type are bound morphemes and are unstressed. This kind of reduplication decreases the meaning of root lexemes.

(22) trắng 'be white' → trăng **trắng** 'be whitish'
    đỏ 'be red' → đo **đỏ** 'be reddish'

The partial reduplication in the above examples decreases the intensity of colours.

2.2.2 Reduplication of disyllabic words into quadrisyllabic words

There are several ways of forming quadrisyllabic words from disyllabic words.

- **Reduplication of the initial consonant (AB => ABAB')**
(23) nu na → **nu na** nu nống 'a children's game'

The quadrisyllabic word shares the same initial consonant as the disyllabic word. In this quadrisyllabic morpheme, the third syllable is the identical reproduction of the first syllable. The rhyme and the tone of the fourth syllable are different from those of the second syllable.

- **Reduplication of the rhyme (AB => A'AB'B)**
(24) kh<u>ênh</u> kh<u>ang</u> → l<u>ênh</u> **kh<u>ênh</u>** l<u>ang</u> **kh<u>ang</u>** 'to walk with difficulty'

First, the two syllables in the morpheme *khênh khang* are separated like *khênh – khang*, then the rhyme of each of those syllables is reduplicated as follows: *l<u>ênh</u> kh<u>ênh</u> – l<u>ang</u> kh<u>ang</u>*. In this quadrisyllabic morpheme, the first and the second syllables share the rhyme "ênh"; the third and the fourth syllables share the rhyme "ang".

- **Quasi-complete reduplication**

There can be four patterns.

a. **The pattern AB => ABA'B'**
(25) cong queo → **cong queo** còng quèo 'to be winding'

In the above quadrisyllabic morpheme, the original disyllabic morpheme (AB) in boldface type is in the initial position and its reproduction (A'B') in normal type is in final position. The tones of AB are different from those of A'B'.

b. **The pattern AB => A'B'AB**
(26) càu nhàu → cảu nhảu **càu nhàu** 'to grumble, to grunt'

In the above quadrisyllabic morpheme, the original disyllabic morpheme (AB) in boldface type is in the final position and its reproduction (A'B') in normal type is in initial position. The tones of AB are different from those of A'B'.

c. **The pattern AB => AABB**
(27) hăm hở → **hăm** hăm **hở** hở 'to enthuse'

Each of the two syllables in the original disyllabic morpheme (A = *hăm*, B = *hở*) is reduplicated according to the pattern AABB.

d. **The pattern AB => AB'AB**
(28) khập khiễng → khập <u>khà</u> **khập khiễng** 'to be lame'

The two syllables in the original disyllabic morpheme (AB) are in final position; they come third and fourth in the above quadrisyllabic morpheme (AB'AB). The first syllable is the identical reproduction of the third syllable (A). Only the initial consonant of the second syllable resembles the one of the other syllables, but the rhyme of that second syllable is quite different.

The meaning of the quadrisyllabic morphemes in the above four patterns is stronger than the one of the original disyllabic morphemes.

2.3 Psycho-collocation

"Psycho-collocation" is another essential characteristic of many languages in Southeast-Asia after the pioneering work of Matisoff (1986), followed by the studies of Jaisser (1990), Oey (1990), Vanbik (1998). Matisoff defines it as:

> A polymorphemic expression referring as a whole to a mental process, quality, or state, one of whose constituents is a psycho-noun, i.e., a noun with explicit psychological reference (translatable by English words like heart, mind, spirit, soul, temper, nature, disposition, mood). The rest of the psycho-collocation contains morphemes (usually action verbs or adjectives) that complete the meaning.

The psycho-collocation can be represented by the following equation: **Psycho-noun (noted PN) + Psycho-mate (noted PM) = Psycho-collocation**.

In Vietnamese, the majority of psycho-mates are stative verbs such as *đau* 'to be aching', *nát* 'to be crushed', *đứt* 'to be broken', etc., and the psycho-nouns can be *lòng* 'entrails, heart, bosom, palm', *dạ* 'stomach, belly, heart', *ruột* 'intestine, entrails', *gan* 'liver', *tâm* 'heart, mind', *đầu* 'head', *mật* 'bile', *bụng* 'belly', etc.

Among the above body parts, *lòng* meaning 'entrails, stomach, heart, bosom, palm' is virtually the most frequently used psycho-noun. It is metaphorically considered to be the core of the human feelings. We present below several commonly used psycho-collocations including *lòng*.

2.3.1 Psycho-mates + *lòng*

(29) *đau* **lòng**   (be aching + **long**)   'be heartbroken'
     nóng **lòng**   (be hot + **long**)   'be impatient, be anxious'
     vui **lòng**   (be joyful + **long**)   'be happy'

All the above psycho-mates are stative verbs; with lòng they form psycho-collocations which are verb phrases.

(30) (a) đau   lòng   (b) đau   tim[16]
       be aching **long**   be aching   heart
       'be heartbroken'   'have a heart disease'

Example (30a) is a psycho-collocation: the psycho-mate and the psycho-noun in boldface type are stressed. Example (30b) indicates a disease: only the noun in boldface type is stressed.

2.3.2 *Lòng* + psycho-mates

(31) **lòng** *dạ*   (**lòng** + stomach)   'heart'
     lòng *tham*   (**lòng** + be greedy)   'avarice, miserliness'

In this set of psycho-collocations, lòng is placed before a noun or a stative verb to form a noun phrase, as shown in the examples above.

2.3.3 Quadrimorphemic psycho-collocations

Quadrimorphemic psycho-collocations are abundant in Vietnamese. We briefly present below some psycho-collocations including *lòng* and other psycho-nouns.

(32) **lòng** *ngay* **dạ** *thẳng* (**lòng** + be straight + **dạ** + be frank) 'be sincere, be genuine'
     lòng *son* **dạ** *sắt*   (**lòng** + vermillon + **dạ** + iron)   'be extremely faithful'

Being virtually synonymic the psycho-nouns (PN) lòng and dạ are frequently put together to form proverbs, adages, sayings, etc., such as the examples above according to the pattern: $PN_1 + PM_1 + PN_2 + PM_2$.

(33) *ghi* **lòng** *tạc* **dạ**   (engrave + **lòng** + carve + **dạ**)   'remember forever a good deed'
     một **lòng** *một* **dạ**   (one + **lòng** + one + **dạ**)   'be wholehearted'

In the examples above the order of the psycho-nouns (PN) and the psycho-mates (PM) is: $PM_1 + PN_1 + PM_2 + PN_2$. The psycho-mates can be verbal or nominal.

---

[16] The noun *tim* denotes the organ "heart", *lòng* metaphorically designates the core of the human feelings.

Vietnamese

(34) (a) *xa **mặt** cách **lòng***   (be far + **face** + be separated + **long**)   'out of sight, out of mind'

Thai

(b) *klaj **taa** klaj **caj***   *(be far + **eye** + be far + **heart**)*   'out of sight, out of mind'

Semantically, the psycho-nouns and the psycho-mates in Vietnamese and in Thaï in (34) are virtually similar. Syntactically, their order is exactly identical.

3 Syntax

This section, devoted to the presentation of a summary of the Vietnamese syntax, consists of the three following points: noun phrase, verb phrase, and clausal and sentential organization.

3.1 Noun phrase

The noun phrase consists of a noun nucleus and of one or several subordinate modifiers which belong to two types: the pre-noun modifiers standing before the nucleus and the post-noun modifiers standing after the nucleus, as shown in the table 6 below (cf. Đoàn *et al.*, 2003).

Table 6: components of Vietnamese noun phrase

Pre-noun modifiers		Noun nucleus	Post-noun modifiers			
Totalisation phrases = A	Quantity phrases = B	$N_1 + N_2$	subclass = C	Qualifying phrases = D		Demonstratives = E
−2	−1	0	+1	+2 +3 +4 +5		+6
tất cả, cả, toàn bộ, toàn thể	1, 2, 3, 4… những, các, mấy, vài	N_1 = count noun (classifier) N_2 = mass noun		D_1 D_2 D_3 D_4		này, đó, kia, đấy, nọ…

We will study respectively the noun nucleus, the pre-nominal modifiers and the post-nominal modifiers.

3.1.1 Noun nucleus

Cao (2000) notes that there are two main kinds of nouns[17] in Vietnamese:
- **count nouns** (N_1) which are names of objects,
- **mass nouns** (N_2), which constitute the overwhelming majority of Vietnamese nouns, are names of species, properties, substances or qualities,

According to Cao, the classifier (count noun) is the head noun, and the mass noun is the modifier, depending on the modified-modifier order. As for Nguyen T. C. (1975), he specifies that the count noun (classifier) and the mass noun, noted respectively N_1N_2, form the noun nucleus: N_1 is the syntactic center, N_2 being the semantic center.

(35) Ba   **con**   mèo
     three CLF(animate)   cat
     'Three cats'

(36) Ba   **cái**   chai
     three CLF(inanimate) bottle
     'Three bottles'

(37) Ba   **quả**   cam
     three CLF(fruit)   orange
     'Three oranges'

In examples (35–37), *mèo* 'cat', *chai* 'bottle', *cam* 'orange' are mass nouns; they express respectively a species of animal, object and fruit. The nouns *con*, *cái*, *quả*, which are count nouns and traditionally called "classifiers", must be placed before those mass nouns in order to individuate them, thereby making them countable.

(38) Ba   **lít**   nước
     three litre   water
     'Three litres of water'

---

17 Certain mass nouns can function as count nouns.

(39) Ba **kí** đường
three kilo sugar
'Three kilograms of sugar'

Nouns such as *lít* 'litre' and *kí* 'kilogram' are "measure phrases" devoted to measure out a specific amount of the mass nouns in (38–39).

(40) Ba **chai** nước
three bottle water
'Three bottles of water'

Depending on the context, *chai* 'bottle' functions as a mass noun in (36), but as a count noun, more precisely as a "measure phrase" in (40).

(41) Ba **loại** mèo (chai, cam, đường…)
three kind cat (bottle, orange, sugar)
'Three kinds of cats (bottles, oranges, sugar)'

"Kind-classifiers" (cf. Nguyen H. T. 2004) such as *loại* 'kind, type' individuate mass nouns as shown in (41).

(42) Ba **cơn** gió
three gust wind
'Three gusts of wind'

In example (42), the "event-classifier" *cơn* (used for a sudden violent state) (cf. Nguyen H. T.) is placed before the mass noun *gió* 'wind' to individuate it.

(43) Ba **trận** đấu
three CLF fight
'Three fights/battles'

(44) Ba **cuộc** họp
three CLF meet
'Three meetings'

"Event-classifiers" such as *trận* (for a combat or outburst), *cuộc* (for an interaction), etc., individuate and nominalize the dynamic verbs in (43 and 44).

In short the nouns *con, cái, quả, lít, kí, chai, loại, cơn, trận, cuộc* in examples (35–44) share the same feature: they are count nouns (N₁) used to individuate the mass nouns (N₂) in those examples. In other terms, the count nouns and the mass nouns form the noun nucleus.

3.1.2 Pre-noun modifiers

The pre-noun modifiers include "totalization phrases", "quantity phrases" and the focus marker *cái*.

- **Totalization phrases (A)**

(45) **Tất cả** **ba** cuốn sách này
     all   three CLF book DEM
     'All these three books'

(46) **Tất cả** **các** cuốn sách này
     all   PL   CLF book DEM
     'All these books'

"Totalization phrases" such as *tất cả, cả, toàn bộ, toàn thể* 'all' occur before cardinal numerals (example 45), or plural markers (example 46). "Totalization phrases" cannot be preceded by a front modifier; they are in position A.

- **Quantity phrases (B)**

(47) Tôi có **một** căn nhà
     1SG have SG CLF maison
     'I have a house'

"Quantity phrases" can be
- cardinal numerals such as *một* 'one', *hai* 'two', *ba* 'three', *bốn* 'four',
- plural markers such as *những* (which is indefinite), and *các* (which is definite),
- the indefinite singular marker *một* as in (47).

"Quantity phrases" are in position B.

- **The focus marker *Cái* (B)**

(48) **Cái** cuốn sách này
 FOC CLF book DEM
 'This very book'

(49) Tất cả ba **cái** cuốn sách này
 all three FOC CLF book DEM
 'All these very three books'

(50) ***Cái** cái bàn này
 FOC CLF table DEM

Nguyen H. T. notes that *cái* can function as a focus marker, and that it occurs directly before the classifier *cuốn* as in (48 and 49). *Cái* can be preceded by no front modifier as in (48); but this focus marker can be preceded by a numeral and a totalization phrase as in (49). This marker always co-occurs with a classifier as in (48–49), but never with the classifier *cái* as in (50) which is ill-formed. Syntactically, the focus marker *cái* is in the position of quantity phrases (B).

3.1.3 Post-noun modifiers

The noun nucleus can be followed by the two main post-noun modifiers: **qualifying phrases** and **demonstratives**.

- **Qualifying phrases**

Qualifying phrases include adjunct phrases (C), phrases or clauses (D).

a. **Adjunct phrases (C)**

(51) Ba cái bàn **học**
 three CLF table study
 'Three desks'

(52) Ba cuốn sách **toán**
 three CLF book mathematics
 'Three books of mathematics'

(53) Ba   người   thợ   **dệt**
    three   CLF   workman   weave
    'Three weavers'

(54) Ba   con   gà   **trống**
    three   CLF   fowl   male
    'Three cocks'

In the examples above, the nuclei are: *cái bàn, cuốn sách, người thợ, con gà*. The adjunct phrases, corresponding to the position C (table 6) denote a subclass of those noun nucleus and restrict their meaning by specifying a type of table, book or workman (51, 52, 53), or an animal gender (54). The adjunct phrases, in boldface type, can be verbal (51, 53) or nominal (52, 54).

b. Qualifier phrases (D_1)

(55) Ba   cuốn   sách   toán   **to**
    three   CLF   book   maths   be big
    'Three **big** maths books'

(56) Ba   cuốn   sách   toán   to   **màu**   **xanh**
    three   CLF   book   maths   be big   color   be blue
    'Three big **blue** maths books'

Noun nucleus can be modified by qualifier phrases (B_1) (table 1), as shown in (21 and 22), used to express: sizes such as *to* 'be big', *nhỏ* 'be small'; states such as *cũ* 'be old', *mới* 'be new'; shapes such as *tròn* 'be round', *vuông* 'be square'; colours such as *màu xanh* 'blue colour', *màu trắng* 'white colour', etc.

c. Prepositional phrases (D_2) expressing the material

(57) Ba   cuốn   sách   toán   to   màu   xanh
    Three   CLF   book   maths   be big   colour   be blue

    bằng   **giấy**   **cao cấp**
    PREP   paper   high-grade
    'Three big blue **high-grade paper** maths books'

The material of an object can be indicated by the prepositional phrase: **[*bằng* + noun]** (position D_2) such as *bằng giấy cao cấp* 'made of high-grade paper' as in (57).

d. **Prepositional phrases (D₃) expressing the location or the possession**

(58) Ba   cuốn   sách   toán   to   màu   xanh
     three   CLF   book   maths   be big   colour   be blue

     bằng   giấy   cao cấp   **ở**   **trên kệ sách**
     PREP   paper   high-grade   LOC   on bookshelf
     'The three big blue high-grade paper maths books **on the bookshelf**'

(59) Ba   cuốn   sách   toán   to   màu   xanh
     three   CLF   book   maths   be big   colour   be blue

     bằng   giấy   cao cấp   **của**   **thư viện**
     PREP   paper   high-grade   POSS   library
     'The three big blue high-grade paper maths books **of the library**'

The location or the possession of an object are expressed respectively by the prepositional phrases [*ở* + noun] or [*của* + noun], corresponding to the position D₃, as shown in (58 and 59).

e. **Relative clauses (D₄)**

(60) Ba   cuốn   sách   toán   to   màu   xanh   bằng   giấy   cao cấp
     Three   CLF   book   maths   be big   colour   be blue PREP   paper   high-grade

     ở   trên   kệ sách   **mà**   tôi   mua   hôm qua
     LOC   on   bookshelf   REL   1SG   buy   yesterday
     'The three big blue high-grade paper maths books on the bookshelf **which I bought yesterday**'

The noun nucleus *cuốn sách* 'book' is identified by the relative clause introduced by the relativizer *mà* as in (60).

- **Demonstratives (E)**

(61) Ba   cuốn   sách   toán   to   màu   xanh   bằng   giấy   cao cấp
     three   CLF   book   maths   be big   colour   be blue PREP   paper   high-grade

     ở   trên   kệ sách   mà   tôi   mua   hôm qua   **đó**
     LOC   on   bookshelf   REL   1SG   buy   yesterday   DEM
     '**Those** three big blue high-grade paper maths books on the bookshelf which I bought yesterday'

In (61) the demonstrative *đó*[18] which is the last modifier used to make definite the noun nucleus *cuốn sách* 'book' and marks the end of the subject (or topic).

(62) Tất cả   ba   cuốn   sách   toán   to   màu   xanh
     all   three   CLF   book   maths   be big colour be blue

     bằng   giấy   cao cấp   ở   trên kệ   sách
     PREP   paper   high-grade   LOC   on   bookshelf

     mà   tôi   mua   hôm qua   đó // rất   hay.
     REL   1SG   buy   yesterday   DEM   very   be interesting
     'Those three big blue high-grade paper maths books on the bookshelf, which I bought yesterday, are very interesting'

The subject of example (62) presents a largest noun phrase with the following constituents:
- The **front** modifiers: the quantifier *tất cả* 'all' and the cardinal numeral *ba* 'three',
- The **noun nucleus**: *cuốn sách* 'book',
- The **end** modifiers: the adjunct phrase *toán* 'math' specifying a type of book; the qualifier phrases *to* 'be big' and *màu xanh* 'blue colour' showing respectively the state and the colour of the noun nucleus; the prepositional phrases indicating respectively the material *bằng giấy cao cấp* 'made of high-grade paper' and the site *ở trên kệ sách* 'on the bookshelf' of the noun nucleus; the relative clause introduced by the relativizer *mà*; the demonstrative *đó*, which is the last modifier used to make definite the noun nucleus and marks the end of the subject (or topic).
- Therefore all that follows is the predicate.

3.2 Verb phrase

The verb phrase consists of a verb nucleus and of one or several subordinate modifiers which are pre-verb modifiers that stand before the verb nucleus, and post-verb modifiers that stand after the verb nucleus, as shown in the table 7 below.

---

18 Demonstratives are divided into three groups according to their degrees of distance: proximal (*này, nầy*); medial (*đó, đấy, ấy*); distal (*kia*) (cf. Nguyen P.P. 1992)

Table 7: components of Vietnamese verb phrase

Pre-verb modifiers	Verb nucleus	Post-verb modifiers

We will study respectively the verb nucleus, the pre-verb modifiers and the post-verb modifiers.

3.2.1 Verb nucleus

The verb nucleus can be a verb or a series of verbs, called "serial verb construction", which is an areal characteristic of SEA languages (cf. Vittrant, 2006).

- **Nucleus as a simple verb**

(63) John   đang   **ăn**   cơm.
     John   PROG   eat   rice
     'John is eating rice'

(64) John   rất   **cao.**
     John   very   be tall
     'John is very tall'

(65) John   **định**   đi   chợ.
     John   plan   go   market
     'John is planning to go to the market'

The verb nucleus can be a dynamic verb (63), a stative verb (64) or a modal verb (65).

- **Nucleus as a serial verb construction**

According to Aikhenvald (2006: 1), serial verb constructions (SVC) are one of the main features in Southeast Asian, West African, Creole, Amazonian and Oceanian languages. This phenomenon is defined by this author as follows:

> "A serial verb construction (SVC) is a sequence of verbs which act together as a single predicate, without any overt marker of coordination, subordination, or syntactic dependency of any other sort. Serial verb constructions describe what is conceptualized as a single event. They are monoclausal; their intonational properties are the same as those of a monoverbal clause, and they have just one tense, aspect, and polarity value. SVCs may also share core and other arguments. [...]"

SVCs, very frequently met in Vietnamese, are illustrated in the examples below:

(66) John **cười** **nói** suốt cả ngày.
John laugh talk through all day
'John talks and laughs all day long'

(67) John đang **ngồi** **xem** phim.
John PROG sit watch film
'John sits watching a film'

(68) John đang **ăn** **đứng**.
John PROG eat stand
'John eats standing'

(69) John đã **đánh** **vỡ** cái bát.
John PERF beat be broken CLF bowl
'John has broken the bowl'

(70) John đã **đi** **vào** (**đi** **ra**).
John PERF go in (go out)
'John has gone in (gone out)'

(71) John đã **đi** **học** **về**.
John PERF go study return
'John has come home from school'

Examples (66 to 71) are perfect SVCs in the sense that the verbs in boldface type in each clause form a single event; there are neither marker of coordination nor of subordination. The SVCs share the same subject (*John*) and are preceded by the TAM markers *đã* or *đang*.

From the semantic viewpoint, the two dynamic verbs *cười* 'laugh' and *nói* 'talk' occur simultaneously in (66). In (67), the second verb *xem* 'watch' indicates the aim of the first verb *ngồi* 'sit'. In (68), the second verb *đứng* 'stand' shows in what manner the first verb *ăn* 'eat' occurs. In (69), the second verb *vỡ* 'be broken', which is a stative verb, indicates the result of the first verb *đánh* 'beat', which is a dynamic verb. In (70), the first verb *đi* 'go' expresses a centrifugal motion, the second verbs *vào* 'in' and *ra* 'out' indicate the direction of the motion. In (71), the first verb *đi* 'go' expresses a centrifugal motion, the second verb *học* 'study' determines the aim of this motion, and the third verb *về* 'return' indicates a centripetal motion. The order of those three verbs is chronological or "iconic" (cf. Aikhenvald and Dixon 2006).

3.2.2 Pre-verb modifiers

Pre-verb modifiers can be divided into the main following groups.

- **The first group**

The first group contains TAM markers such as *đang* (progressive aspect), *đã* (perfect aspect), *sắp* (imminential aspect), *vừa* (recent aspect), etc., which express primarily aspect and secondarily tense, as shown in (67–71).

- **The second group**

(72) John **vẫn còn** làm việc.
John still still work
'John is still working'

The second group includes *vẫn, còn, vẫn còn*, etc., which express the continuity of a state of affairs, as shown in (72).

- **The third group**

(73) John **thường** thức dậy lúc 7 giờ sáng.
John often wake up moment 7 hour morning
'John often wakes up at 7 a.m.'

The third group consists of *thường, luôn luôn, ít, hiếm*, etc., which indicate the frequency of a state of affairs, as shown in (73).

- **The fourth group**

(74) John **không** thích cuốn sách này.
John NEG like CLF book DEM
'John does not like this book'

The fourth group contains the negative markers *không, chưa*, the affirmative marker *có*, and the imperative markers *hãy, đừng, chớ*.

- **The fifth group**

(75) John **quá** tử tế.
John too be kind
'John is too kind'

The fifth group includes *quá* 'too', *rất* 'very', *khá* 'rather', *hơi* 'a little, a bit', etc., which express different degrees of stative verbs, as shown in (75).

3.2.3 Post-verb modifiers

Post-verb modifiers can be divided into the main following groups.

- **The first group**
(76) John ăn **xong** rồi.
 John eat finish CRS
 'John has finished eating'

The first group contains verbs such as *xong*, *hết* 'finish', which denote the end of an activity; they often combine with the marker *rồi* (which describes a currently relevant state 'CRS') as in (76).

- **The second group**
(77) John nói **được** tiếng Việt.
 John speak obtain Vietnamese
 'John can speak Vietnamese'

(78) John đã tìm **thấy** cuốn sách.
 John PERF look for see CLF book
 'John has found the book'

In the second group, the verbs *được* 'obtain, get, gain' or *thấy* 'see' placed after the verb nucleus, indicate the result of the activity expressed by the nucleus. In (77), *được* denotes the ability to speak Vietnamese. In (78), the use of *thấy* transforms the atelic verb *tìm* 'look for' into the telic verb *tìm thấy* 'find'.

- **The third group**
(79) Họ yêu **nhau**.
 3PL love RECIP
 'They love each other'

The word *nhau* in (79), always placed after the nucleus, is used to denote reciprocal activities.

- **The fourth group**
(80) John tử tế **lắm**.
 John be kind very
 'John is very kind'

(81) John   tử tế   **quá**!
     John   be kind too
     'How kind is John!'

Unlike *rất* 'very', *khá* 'rather', *hơi* 'a little, a bit', which are always placed before a stative verb, the word *lắm* 'very' is always placed after a stative verb. As for *quá* 'too', it can be placed before or after a stative verb as in (75 and 81). When this word is after a stative verb, as in (81), it functions as an exclamative particle.

3.3 Clausal and sentential organization

Most Vietnamese grammarians and linguists have been influenced by Indo-European language patterns: they have studied Vietnamese sentences according to the pattern subject-predicate. In reaction to this europocentric stance and in accordance with the view supported by Li Ch. and Thompson (1976), Cao (2004) states that Vietnamese is a "topic prominent language", and that *thì*, *là*, *mà*, which are pragmatic markers, can be used to separate the topic from the comment. In certain cases, the subject coincides with the topic and the predicate with the comment; but in spoken Vietnamese such an equivalence does not always hold.

3.3.1 Information structure of spoken Vietnamese

Examples (48 to 53) illustrate topic-comment structures in spoken Vietnamese.

(82) **Hôm qua,** **ở**   **đây**   trời   rất   đẹp.
     yesterday   LOC   here   sky   very   be fine
     'The weather was very fine here yesterday'

(83) **Ở**   **đây,**   vui   quá   nhỉ!
     LOC   here   be joyful   too   FP
     'What a joyful atmosphere in here!'

In (82), *hôm qua* 'yesterday' and *ở đây* 'here' are respectively a temporal and a spatial framework within which the main predication holds. They are a temporal and a spatial topic. The subject *trời* 'sky' and the predicate *đẹp* 'be beautiful' are the comment. In (83), there is only a spatial framework (topic). The subject *không khí* 'atmosphere' of the predicate *vui* 'be joyful' is tacit.

(84) **Anh   chàng   này**   tóc tai   bờm xờm   quá!
     CLF   man   DEM   hair   be shaggy   EXCLA
     'This man's hair is very shaggy!'

(85) **Chim**   thì   có   chim sẻ,   chim họa mi...
     bird   TOP   have   sparrow   nightingale
     'As for birds, there are sparrows, nightingales...'

In (84), the semantic relationship between the two initial noun phrases, NP₁: *anh chàng này* 'this man' and NP₂: *tóc tai* 'hair', is an inalienable possession. NP₁ represents the whole and NP₂, the part. The communicative function of this type of topic-comment construction[19] is to characterize a person or the "whole" by means of a predication referring to the "part". In (85), after choosing an animal class in the topic (noted by the topicalizer *thì*), the speaker presents the subclasses in the comment.

(86) **Tem**   (anh)   mua   ở   đâu   vậy?
     stamp   (2SG)   buy   LOC   where   FP
     'Those stamps, where did you get them?'

(87) **Bàn**   (tôi)   lau   sạch   rồi!
     table   (1SG)   wipe   be clean   CRS
     'The table has been cleaned (by me)'

In (86) and (87), the patients *tem* 'stamp' and *bàn* 'table' are placed in the topic position; they are salient. The agent can be dropped if it coincides with the addressee (86) or the speaker (87). If the agent refers to a third person, it is necessary to name him (her) clearly in the utterance.

3.3.2 Pragmatical markers *Thì* and *Là*

In this section, we will sum up the use of *thì* and *là*, which derive from lexemes: *thì* is a noun meaning "time", *là* is a verb-copula. From the syntactic viewpoint, they connect two constituents X and Y, which can be a phrase or a clause. From the pragmatic viewpoint, *thì* functions as a topic marker, *là* as a focus marker.

---

[19] Also called "double subject" constructions (cf. Li & Thompson, 1976, 1981)

- **The marker *Thì***

The grammaticalization process of the lexeme *thì* is as follows: time > temporal anaphoric conjunction > topic marker.

(88) **Thì**   giờ   là   vàng   bạc.
     time   hour   COP   gold   silver
     'Time is money'

According to Đào Duy Anh's dictionary (1950: 431), *thì* is a noun which derives from the chinese noun *shí* meaning 'time', as shown in (88).

(89) Nếu   trời   đẹp   **thì**   ta   sẽ   đi dạo.
     if   sky   be beautiful   TOP   1PL   FUT   go for a walk
     'If the weather is beautiful, then we'll go for a walk'

The noun *thì* 'time' has been grammaticalized to become a conjunction with the temporal anaphoric value 'at that time'[20] and the aspectual inchoative value. In other terms, the conjunction *thì* still retains some lexical meaning in accordance with the principle of "persistence" (cf. Hopper, 1991). In (89), *thì* is used in the clause level to link the subordinate clause, which expresses a condition, to the main clause, which indicates a consequence. Moreover, *thì* topicalizes the conditional clause, which is the topic (cf. Haiman, 1978), the main clause being the comment.

(90) Bà ấy   có   hai   cô   con gái,
     3SG   have   two   CLF   daughter

   cô   chị   **thì**   đẹp,   cô   em   thì   ngoan.
   CLF   elder   TOP   be beautiful   CLF   younger   TOP   be well-behaved
   "She has two daughters, the elder is beautiful, the younger is well-behaved"

(91) Tôi1   **thì**   tôi2   thích   đọc   Balzac.
     1SG   TOP   1SG   like   read   Balzac
     'As for me, I like reading Balzac'

---

20 We note an equivalence between the Vietnamese conjunction *thì*, the French conjunction *alors* and the English conjunction *then* which have the temporal meaning 'at that time'.

In (90) and (91), *thì* is used in the phrase level. Semantically, *thì* has virtually lost its lexical meaning, but it has gained a new more abstract grammatical meaning. From the syntactic and the pragmatic viewpoint, *thì* does not work as a conjunction, but as a topic marker used to create a contrast effect between two subjects such as *cô chị* 'the elder' and *cô em* 'the younger' as in (90), or between the speaker who likes reading Balzac and the other people who may like reading another author as in (91).

- **The marker *Là***

The grammaticalization process of *là*, copula > consecutive conjunction > focus marker, complies with the path of grammaticalization shown in Heine and Kuteva (2002: 95).

(92) Hà Nội **là** thủ đô của Việt Nam.
HaNoi COP capital POSS Vietnam
'Ha Noi is the capital of Vietnam'

In (92), the copula *là* links two noun phrases: the subject (*Hà Nội*) and the predicate (*thủ đô của Việt Nam*). This example sets up the topic plus comment structure in the form of an equation, where the topic, which coincides with the subject, equals the comment, which coincides with the predicate.

(93) Hễ trời mưa **là** tôi ho.
whenever sky rain FOC 1SG cough
'Whenever it rains, I cough'

In (93), *là* functions as a consecutive marker linking the subordinate clause *hễ trời mưa* 'whenever it rains' to the main clause *tôi ho* 'I cough'. Pragmatically, this particle focuses the main clause.

(94) Cuốn sách này **là** của thư viện.
CLF book DEM FOC POSS library
'This book belongs to the library'

In (94), *là* is not obligatory, but its use focuses on the prepositional predicate *của thư viện* 'belong to the library'.

(95) Tôi nghĩ **là** anh ấy có lý.
1SG think COMPLR 3SG have reason
'I think that he is right'

Like (94), *là* in (95) is not necessary, but this particle, which connects the verb *nghĩ* 'think' to its complement clause *anh ấy có lý* 'he is right', focuses on that clause. In this context, *là* functions as a complementizer.

3.3.3 Ellipsis

Argument ellipsis, which is a frequent phenomenon in Vietnamese, can affect the subject, the predicate, the object, or the subject and the object, as illustrated below.

- **Subject ellipsis**

(96) **(Tôi)** Cám ơn anh.
    1SG   thank   2SG
    'Thank you'

(97) **(Anh)** Khoẻ   không?
    2SG   be in shape   NEG
    'How are you?'

In spoken Vietnamese, indexical pronouns such as *tôi* '1SG' and *anh* '2SG', which occupy the subject function as in (96) and (97), can be dropped.

- **Predicate ellipsis**

(98) Ai   đã   mua   cuốn sách này? **Tôi**
    who PERF buy   CLF   book DEM   1SG
    'Who has bought this book?'   'Me'

In the context of (98), the answer contains only the pronoun *tôi* '1SG', the predicate is not necessary.

- **Object ellipsis**

(99) (Anh) Để   tôi   làm **(việc này)** cho   (anh).
    2SG   let 1SG   do   task DEM   BEF   2SG
    'Let me do it for you'

When the context is not ambiguous, the direct object *việc này* 'this task' and the second person *anh* '2SG' in the subject and the recipient function can be dropped, as shown in (99).

- **Ellipsis of subject and object**

(100) **(Tôi)** Đã bảo mà **(anh)** không nghe
     1SG PERF tell but 2SG NEG listen

     thì **(anh)** còn kêu ca gì nữa.
     TOP 2SG still complain what more
     "I told you, but you did not listen to me, why are you grumbing?"

In the case of (100), the ellipsis of the speaker *tôi* '1SG' and the addressee *anh* '2SG' is quite frequent in spoken Vietnamese.

3.3.4 Nominalization of verbs and clauses

The nominalization can affect a verb or a clause, as shown in examples below.

(101) mua   **người** mua
     'buy'   'buyer'

Example (101) illustrates an agent nominalization (V → $N_{agent\,of\,V}$). The noun *người* 'person' is placed before the dynamic verb *mua* 'buyer' to transform it into an agentive noun.

(102) đẹp   **người** đẹp   **cái** đẹp
     'be beautiful'   'beautiful woman'   'beauty'

The stative verb *đẹp* 'be beautiful' in (102) can be nominalized by the noun *người* 'person', which indicates a beautiful woman, or by the inanimate classifier *cái*, which denotes a notion.

(103) Gà gáy.
     cock crow
     'Cocks crow'

(104) **Tiếng** gà gáy
     sound cock crow
     'The crowing of cocks'

Example (103) is a minimal clause including the noun *gà* 'cock' and the predicate *gáy* 'crow'. The use of the noun *tiếng* 'sound' nominalizes this clause as in (104).

3.3.5 Yes-no questions

(105) Anh **có** khoẻ **không**?
      2SG AFFIR be in shape NEG
      'Are you fine (in good shape)?'

(106) Anh **đã** khoẻ **chưa**?
      2SG PERF be in shape NEG$_{PERF}$
      'Have you recovered?'

Examples (105) and (106) constitute two main types of yes-no questions in Vietnamese, according to the following patterns: Subject + (**có** / **đã**) + verb + (**không** / **chưa**)? Vietnamese uses two pairs of antonymous markers: *có* (affirmative marker) and *không* (negative marker); *đã* (perfect marker) and *chưa* (negative perfect marker)[21]. In (105) and (106), they surround the same verb to form yes-no questions. These examples do not mean the same thing: (105) is used when two persons meet each other, while (106) is used when the speaker knows that the addressee was ill and wants to hear if the latter has recovered at T_0.

4 Semantics and pragmatics

After presenting some usual semantic domains, we will describe a few Vietnamese particles expressing "propositional attitudes, emotions, and politeness of the speaker".

4.1 Usual semantic domains

As mentioned by Matisoff (1983: 79), there is a domain which needs to be investigated concerning comparative semantics in the SEA languages, given that these languages seem to share basically similar conceptual frameworks about man and nature. Therefore, we will briefly present food terminology and expressions of "cutting", "carrying", and "direction".

---

[21] *Chưa* has the meaning of "have not... yet", unlike *không* which signifies "not".

4.1.1 Food terminology

Vietnamese presents a rich paradigm of names to describe rice at different stages. The noun *mạ (cây lúa non)* designates 'rice seedlings' (young seedlings); the action *gieo mạ* is 'to sow rice seeds'. The product of the rice plant is *thóc* 'grain with its husk', called 'paddy' or 'unhusked rice'. Rice husk is *trấu*. The lexeme *gạo lứt* 'brown rice' or 'hulled rice' is unmilled or partly milled rice; it is natural grain. As for *gạo trắng* 'white rice', it is the name given to milled rice that has had its husk (*trấu*) and bran (*cám*) removed. There are two types of rice: *gạo tẻ* and *gạo nếp*. Once cooked, the former becomes *cơm* 'cooked rice' and the latter *xôi* 'cooked sticky rice'.

4.1.2 Expressions of "cutting", "carrying" and "direction"

There is an abundant vocabulary in Vietnamese concerning expressions of "cutting" and "carrying", as shown in the tables below.

- **Expressions of "cutting"**

Table 8: sample expressions of "cutting"

Verbs	Tools	Objects
băm 'mince, chop'	*con dao* 'knife'	*thịt* 'meat'
cắt 'cut'	*cái kéo* 'scissors', *con dao* 'knife'	*giấy* 'paper', *vải* 'cloth'
chặt 'cut, chop'	*con dao* 'knife'	*cành cây* 'branch'
chém 'cut off, guillotine'	*cái kiếm* 'sword', *máy chém* 'guillotine'	*đầu* 'head'
đốn 'cut down'	*cái rìu* 'axe'	*củi* 'wood'
hớt 'cut'	*máy cắt tóc* 'hair clipper'	*tóc* 'hair'
rọc 'cut by following a crease'	*cái kéo* 'scissors', *con dao* 'knife'	*vải* 'cloth', *giấy* 'paper'
thái 'cut in slices'	*con dao* 'knife'	*thịt* 'meat'
xén 'cut, trim'	*máy xén giấy* 'paper cutter'	*giấy* 'paper'
xẻo 'cut'	*con dao* 'knife'	*thịt* 'meat'
xẻ 'saw'	*cái cưa* 'saw'	*gỗ* 'wood', *thân cây* 'tree trunk'

- **Expressions of "carrying"**

Table 9: sample expressions of "carrying"

Verbs	Agent	Objects
ẵm (bế, bồng) 'carry in one's arms'	người lớn 'adult'	em bé 'baby'
chở 'carry'	tàu 'train', xe tải 'lorry'	hành khách 'passenger', hàng hóa 'goods'
đeo 'wear'	người 'person'	chain, earring
đội 'carry on one's head'	người 'person'	hat, basket
khuân 'carry with arms'	người 'person'	Furniture
mang 'wear, bear'	người 'person'	clothes, foetus
vác 'carry on one's shoulder'	người 'person'	bundle of clothes, luggage

- **Expressions of "direction"**

The table below presents serial verb constructions in which the first verb is *đẩy* "push"

Table 10: sample expressions of "direction"

Motion verb	Directional verb	SVC
đẩy 'push'	lên 'go up'	đẩy lên 'push up'
đẩy 'push'	xuống 'go down'	đẩy xuống 'push down'
đẩy 'push'	tới 'arrive'	đẩy tới 'push forward'
đẩy 'push'	lui 'move back'	đẩy lui 'push back, push away'
đẩy 'push'	ngang 'across'	đẩy ngang 'push across'
đẩy 'push'	dọc 'along'	đẩy dọc 'push along'
đẩy 'push'	vào 'enter'	đẩy vào 'push into'
đẩy 'push'	ra 'go out'	đẩy ra 'push out'

4.2 Pragmatics and Discourse

Particles are an important part of speech in Vietnamese; they can be modal and exclamative.

4.2.1 Modal particles

The modal particles are divided into the two following groups (cf. Đoàn *et al.*, *op. cit.*):

- **Modal particles used to form questions, orders and exclamations**

(107) Anh   đi   bây giờ   **à**?
      2SG   leave   now   INTERJ
      'You are leaving now, aren't you?'

(108) Ăn   **đi**!
      eat   IMP
      'Eat!'

(109) Hay   **thật**!
      be interesting   EXCLA
      'Really interesting!'

The particles *à, ư, nhỉ, nhé, hả, chứ, chăng*..., are used to form questions as in (107). Particles such as *đi, thôi, nhé, nào, với*..., express orders as in (108). As for *thật, thay, ghê*..., they are used as exclamations (109). Those particles are placed at the end of the sentences.

- **Modal particles that express the speaker's attitude**

(110) Cháu   chào   ông   **ạ**!
      1SG   salute   grandfather   MP
      'Good morning grandfather!'

(111) Đừng   nghịch   nữa,   mẹ   đã   bảo   **mà**!
      IMP   be a fool   more   mum   PERF   tell   MP
      'Don't play the fool, mum has already told you so!'

(112) Ôi,   cá   cháy   khét   hết   rồi   **đây**   **này**!
      EXCLA   fish   burn   be burnt   finish   CRS   MP   MP
      'Oh, no! The fish is burning!'

(113) Anh   đang   làm   gì   **vậy**?
      2SG   PROG   do   what   MP
      'What are you doing now?'

Modal particles such as *ạ, mà, đây, này, vậy* which reflect the attitude of the speaker toward his discourse like politeness, respect (110), warning (111, 112), asking about a fact (113), are placed at the end of the sentences.

4.2.2 Exclamative particles

(114) **A**!   Mẹ   đã   về!
      EXCLA mum PERF come back
      'Ah! Mum has come back!'

(115) **Trời** **ơi**!   Sao   nó   dại   thế!
      heaven EXCLA why 3SG be stupid MP
      'Heavens! How stupid he is!'

Exclamatives particles such as *a, á, ái, ái chà, chao ôi, eo ôi, ồ, ôi, ối, úi*, etc., lack lexical meaning. Those particles can combine with lexemes to form particles like *trời ơi* ('sky' + ơi), *cha mẹ ơi* ('father mother' + ơi), *làng nước ơi* ('village' + ơi), *tội nghiệp* 'poor', *hoan hô* 'cheer', etc. They are placed at the beginning of the sentences as in (114 and 115).

Conclusion

Vietnamese presents the primary features of an isolating language from the phonological, morphological, syntactic and pragmatic points of view.

Phonologically, most of the Vietnamese basic vocabulary is monosyllabic. The syllable boundary which coincides with the morpheme boundary, is the basic unit. A monosyllabic word contains to the maximum the five following components: the onset, the glide, the nucleus, the coda, and the tone. Among these five components, the tone and the onset are obligatory, whereas the glide and the coda are optional. Vietnamese has six tones which have a critical function in morpheme distinction.

Morphologically Vietnamese has no inflectional morphology, but has a lexical morphology illustrated by the word structure (simplex words, complex words and compound words), the reduplication (full reduplication and partial reduplication), and the psycho-collocation (psycho-noun + psycho-mate).

Syntactically the Vietnamese noun phrase consists of a noun nucleus and several subordinate modifiers which are pre-noun modifiers placed before the nucleus, and post-noun modifiers placed after the nucleus. The Vietnamese verb phrase includes a verb nucleus and several subordinate modifiers which are pre-verb modifiers that stand before the verb nucleus, and post-verb modifiers that stand after the verb nucleus. Serial verb constructions are the main feature of the Vietnamese verb phrase.

Pragmatically Vietnamese is a topic prominent language in which the markers *thì* (topicalizer) and *là* (rhematizer) are used to point out the topic or the rheme (or comment) of a sentence. Vietnamese has several particles placed at the end of sentences to form questions, orders, exclamations, or to express the speaker's attitude.

Abbreviations

AFFIR	affirmative
ASRT	assertive
BEF	benefactive
CLF	classifier
COMPLR	complementizer
COP	copula
CRS	currently relevant state
DEICT	deictic
DEM	demonstrative
EXCLA	exclamative
EXIST	existence verb
FP	final particle
1-2-3SG/PL	first, second, third person singular/plural
FOC	focus
FUT	future
IMP	imperative
INTERJ	interjection
LOC	locative
MP	modal particle
NEG	negative
NOM	nominalizer
NUM	numeral
PART	particle
PERF	perfective
PL	plural
POSS	possessive
PREP	preposition
PROG	progressive
RECIP	reciprocal
REFL	reflexive
REL	relativizer

SG   singular
TOP   topic

References

Alves, Mark J. 2001. What's so Chinese about Vietnamese?. In Th. Graham (ed.), *Papers from the Ninth Annual Meeting of the Southeast Asian Linguistics Society*, Tempe: Arizona State University, 221–241.

Alves, Mark J. 2005. The Vieto-Katuic Hypothesis: Lexical Evidence. In P. Sidwell (ed.), *SEALS XV: Papers from the 15th Meeting of the Southeast Asian Linguistics Society*, 169–176. The Australian National University, Research School of Pacific and Asian Studies, Canberra: Pacific Linguistics Publishers.

Alves, Mark J. 2008. Khái quát các nghiên cứu ngôn ngữ học về nguồn gốc của tiếng Việt [Linguistic research on the origins of the Vietnamese language: an overview]. *Tạp chí Khoa học ĐHQGHN, Khoa học Xã hội và Nhân văn* 24. 187–202.

Booij, Geert. 2007. *The grammar of word*. Oxford: Oxford University Press.

Brunelle, Marc. 2009a. Northern and Southern Vietnamese Tone Coarticulation: A Comparative Case Study. *Journal of the Southeast Asian Linguistics Society* 1. 49–62.

Brunelle, Marc. 2009b. Tone Perception in Northern and Southern Vietnamese. *Journal of Phonetics* 37 (1). 79–96.

Cao, Xuan Hao. 2000. Nghĩa của *loại từ* (The meaning of 'classifiers'). In Hà Nôi, KHXH (ed.), *Loại từ trong các ngôn ngữ ở Việt Nam* [Classifiers in the languages of Vietnam], 32–87.

Cao, Xuan Hao. 2004. *Tiếng Việt, sơ thảo Ngữ pháp chức năng* [Vietnamese, a sketch of Functional Grammar]. Vietnam, GD (ed.).

Chappell, Hilary. 2008. Variation in the grammaticalization of complementizers from *verba dicendi* in Sinitic languages. *Linguistic Typology* 12 (1). 45–98.

Clark, Marybeth. 1985. Asking questions in Hmong and other southeast Asian languages. *Linguistics of the Tibeto-Burman Area* 8 (2). 60–67.

Do-Hurinville, Danh Thành. 2010. Etude du topicalisateur *Thi* en vietnamien. *Bulletin de la Société Linguistique de Paris*, 411–443. Paris: Peeters.

Do-Hurinville, Danh Thành. 2009. *Temps, aspect et modalité. Etude contrastive avec le français*. Paris: L'Harmattan.

Đoàn, T. T., K. H. Nguyễn & N. Q. Phạm. 2003. *A Concise Vietnamese Grammar*. Hà Nôi: Hanoi National University.

Enfield, Nick J. 2005. Areal Linguistics and Mainland Southeast Asia. *Annual Review Anthropology* 34. 181–206.

Hengeveld, Kees. 1992. *Non-verbal predication: Theory, typology, diachrony*, Berlin & New York: Mouton de Gruyter.

Hopper, P. J. 1991. On some principles of grammaticization. In E. C. Traugott & B. Heine (eds.), *Approaches of Grammaticalization*, vol. 1, 17–35. Amsterdam: John Benjamins.

Jaisser, Annie C. 1990. Delivering an introduction to psycho-collocations with SIAB in Hmong. *Linguistics of the Tibeto-Burman Area* 13 (1). 159–178.

Li, Charles N. & S. A. Thompson. 1976. Subject and topic: A new typology of languages. In Charles N. Li (ed.), *Subject and Topic*, 457–490, New York, San Francisco & London: Academic Press.

Li, Charles N. & S. A. Thompson. 1981. *Mandarin Chinese: A functional reference grammar*. Berkeley: University of California Press.

Matisoff, James A. 1983. Linguistic diversity and language contact in Thailand. In John McKinnon & Wanat Bhruksasri (eds.), *Highlanders of Thailand*, 56–86. Kuala Lumpur & New York: Oxford University Press.

Matisoff, James A. 1986. Hearts and Minds in South-East Asian languages and English: An essay in the comparative lexical semantics of psycho-collocation. *Cahiers de Linguistique d'Asie Orientale* 15 (1). 5–57. http://www.persee.fr/authority/67272 (accessed 1 June 2018).

Michaud, Alexis. 2004. Final Consonants and Glottalization: New Perspectives from Hanoi Vietnamese. *Phonetica* 61. 119–146.

Nguyen, H. T. 2004. *The structure of the Vietnamese noun phrase*. PhD dissertation, Boston University, Graduate School of Arts and Sciences.

Nguyen, P. P. 1976. *Le syntagme verbal en vietnamien*. La Haye & Paris: Mouton.

Nguyen, P. P. 1992. Vietnamese demonstratives revisited. *The Mon-Khmer Studies Journal* 20. 127–136.

Nguyen, T. C. 1975. *Ngữ Pháp Tiếng Việt* [Vietnamese Grammar]. Vietnam: DHQG (ed.).

Oey, Eric. 1990. Psycho-collocations in Malay. *Linguistics of the Tibeto-Burman Area* 13 (1). 141–158.

Thompson, L. 1965. *A Vietnamese grammar*. Seattle: University of Washington Press.

Van-Bik, Kenneth. 1998. Lai psycho-collocation. *Linguistics of the Tibeto-Burman Area* 21 (1). 201–232.

Vittrant, Alice. 2006. Les constructions verbales en série, une nouvelle approche du syntagme verbal birman. *Bulletin de la Société Linguistique de Paris* 101 (1). 305–367. Paris: Peeters.

Appendix 1: Summary of linguistic features

Legend
+++ the feature is pervasive or used obligatorily in the language
++ the feature is normal but selectively distributed in the language
+ the feature is merely possible or observable in the language
− the feature is impossible or absent in the language

	Feature	+++/++/+/−	§ ref. in this chapter
Phonetics	Lexical tone or register	+++	§1.2, p.386
Phonetics	Back unrounded vowels	+++	§1.3.3, p.388
Phonetics	Initial velar nasal	+++	§1.3.1, p.387
Phonetics	Implosive consonants	+	not discussed explicitly
Phonetics	Sesquisyllabic structures	−	−
Morphology	Tendency towards monosyllabicity	++	§2.1, p.289
Morphology	Tendency to form compounds	+++	§2.1.3, p.391
Morphology	Tendency towards isolating (rather than affixation)	+++	§2.1.4, p.393
Morphology	Psycho-collocations	+++	§2.3, p.396

	Feature	+++/++/+/−	§ ref. in this chapter
Morphology	Elaborate expressions (e.g. four-syllable or other set patterns)	+++	§2.2.2, p.394 & §2.3.3, p.397
Morphology	Reduplication generally	+++	§2.2, p.393
Morphology	Reduplication of nouns	++	§2.2, p.393
Morphology	Reduplication of verbs	++	§2.2, p.303 & §2.1.2, p.390
Grammar	Use of classifiers	+++	§3.1, p.398
Grammar	Classifiers used in counting	+++	§3.1.1, p.399, see also §3.1.2, p.401
Grammar	Classifiers used with demonstratives	+++	§3.1.3, p.404
Grammar	Adjectival verbs	+++	§3.2.1, p.406
Grammar	Grammatical number	+	not discussed explicitly
Grammar	Inflection of verbs	−	−
Grammar	Use of tense/aspect markers	++	§3.2.2, p.408
Grammar	Use of verb plural markers	−	−
Grammar	Grammaticalization of GET/OBTAIN (potential mod. resultative/perfect aspect)	+++	§3.2.3, p.409
Grammar	Grammaticalization of PUT, SET (completed/resultative aspect)	−	−
Grammar	Grammaticalization of GIVE (causative, benefactive; preposition)	+++	not discussed explicitly
Grammar	Grammaticalization of FINISH (perfective/ complete aspect; conjunction/temporal subordinator)	+++	§3.2.3, p.409
Grammar	Grammaticalization of directional verbs e.g. GO / COME (allative, venitive)	+	§3.2.1, p.407, see also §4.2.2, p.418
Grammar	Grammaticalization of SEE, WATCH (temptative)	+	§3.2.1, p.407
Grammar	Grammaticalization of STAY, REMAIN (progressive and continuous, durative aspects)	+	§3.2.2, p.408
Grammar	Serial verb constructions	+++	§3.2.1, p.406
Syntax	Verb precedes object (VO)	+++	§3.2, p.405
Syntax	Auxiliary precedes verb	++	§3.2.2, p.408
Syntax	Preposition precedes noun	+++	§3.1.3, p.402
Syntax	Noun precedes adjective	+++	§ 3.1.3, p.402

	Feature	+++/++/+/−	§ ref. in this chapter
Syntax	Noun preceds demonstrative	+++	§3.1.3, p.404
Syntax	Noun precedes genitive	+++	§3.1.3, p.404
Syntax	Noun precedes relative clause	+++	§3.1.3, p.404
Syntax	Use of topic-comment structures	+++	§3.3.1, p.410
Syntax	Ellipsis of arguments known from context	+++	§3.3.3, p.414
Lexical semantics	Specific terms for forms of rice	+++	§4.1.1, p.417
Pragmatics	Use of utterance-final pragmatic particles	+++	§4.2, p.418
Pragmatics	Encoding of politeness	+++	§4.2.1, p.419–20
Pragmatics	Encoding of honorifics	++	not discussed explicitly

Appendix 2: Text interlinearized

Source:

Excerpt from an interview conducted by an online news channel Phô Bolsa TV (PhoBolsaTV), 2012, in Hanoi. The interviewer was a male journalist aged 35–45, a speaker of the southern dialect. The interviewee was a female student at Phuong Dông University, aged 21, a speaker of the northern dialect. (Link: https://www.youtube.com/watch?v=42vkukVxTao)

Title:

A female student of the Orient University of Hanoi, selling balloons on the New Year's Eve night

+ Total length of the video: 3'56
+ Length of the excerpt transcribed: 2' [0:30–2:30]

Transcription:

Interviewer:

Euh,	*sau*	*lễ giao thừa*		*ở*	*Hồ Gươm*[22],
INTERJ	after	New Year's Eve celebration		LOC	Sword Lake

Euh, after the New Year's Eve celebration at the Sword Lake,

---

[22] Also known as *Hồ Hoàn Kiếm*, which literally means "Lake of the Restored Sword" or "Lake of the Returned Sword"

chúng	tôi	rất	là	ngạc nhiên	thấy	nhiều	bạn	trẻ
PL	1SG	very	COP	surprise	see	many	person	young

we were very surprised to see many young people

đứng	lòng vòng	ở	khu vực	đền	Ngọc Sơn	bán	nhiều
stand	around	LOC	area	temple	Jade Moutain	sell	many

standing around the area of the temple of the Jade Moutain and selling various

thứ	quà	khác	nhau.	Có	bạn	thì	bán	những
stuff	thing	different	RECIP	EXIST	person	TOP	sell	PL

different kinds of stuff. Some were selling things

cái	loại	như	là	diêm	và	muối,	rồi	những	thứ	khác.
CLF	kind	as	COP	match	and	salt	then	PL	stuff	different

such as matches and salt, and then some other things too.

Và	đây	trước	mặt	chúng	tôi	là	một	bạn	tên	là
And	here	before	face	PL	1SG	COP	one	person	name	COP

And right here, in front of us, is a girl named

Huyền,	đang	bán	những	cái	bong bóng	rất	là	lớn,
Huyen	PROG	sell	PL	CLF	balloon	very	COP	big

Huyen, who is selling really big balloons.

Huyền	có thể	cho	biết	trước	hết	là	Huyền	hiện nay
Huyen	can	give	know	before	all	COP	Huyen	now

Huyen, could you please tell us, first of all, whether you are currently

là	đang	còn	đi	học	hay	là	đi	làm	rồi?
COP	PROG	still	go	study	or	COP	go	work	already

still a student or whether you are already in work?

Interviewee:

Dạ,	hiện tại	thì	em	vẫn	đang	là	sinh viên	năm
Yes	now	TOP	1SG	still	PROG	COP	student	year

Yes, right now, I'm a third year student

thứ	ba	trường đại học	Phương Đông	ạ.
order	three	university	Orient	PART

at the Orient University of Hanoi.

Interviewer:

Uhm,	*như*	*vậy*	*thì*	*ngày*	*Tết*[23]	*như*	*thế*	*này*	*thì*
INTERJ	as	such	TOP	New Year's Day		as	so	DEICT	TOP

Uhm, so, in such occasions like today (like New Year's Eve),

cũng	*có*	*nhiều*	*người*	*đi*	*chơi,*	*nhưng*	*những*	*người*
also	EXIST	many	people	go	play	but	PL	CLF

there are also many people who go out to have fun together, but yet

bạn	*trẻ*	*như*	*bạn*	*thì*	*lại*	*lựa*	*cái*	*công việc*
person	young	as	2SG	TOP	still	choose	CLF	work/job

young people like you choose, instead,

đi	*bán*	*thì*	*có thể*	*cho*	*biết*	*nó*	*như thế nào*	*không?*
go	sell	TOP	can	give	know	3SG	how	NEG

to go out selling things like that. So could you let us know what you feel about it/how things work out (are)?

Interviewee:

Dạ,	*lí do*	*mà*	*hôm nay*	*em*	*đi*	*bán*	*ạ,*	*thì*	*có*
Yes	reason	REL	today	1SG	go	sell	PART	TOP	EXIST

Yes, there are loads of reasons why I went out selling things today.

rất	*là*	*nhiều.*		*Nhưng*	*lí do*	*đầu tiên*	*là*
very	COP	multiple/numerous		but	reason	first	COP

But the first one is

tại vì	*năm*	*nay*	*em*	*không*	*có*	*ai*	*đi*	*chơi*	*cùng*	*và*
because because/that	year	now	1SG	NEG	have	someone	go	play	with	and

this year, I have no one to go out with/hang out with and

bạn bè	*của*	*em*	*rủ*	*em*	*đi*	*bán*	*bóng*	*và*
friend	POSS	1SG	ask	1SG	go	sell	balloon	and

my friends asked me to go selling balloons with them and

---

23 Vietnamese New Year's Festival

em	thấy	đây	là	một	điều	khá	là	thú vị.	Nó	có thể
1SG	see	this	COP	one	thing	quite	COP	interesting	3SG	can

I find this to be quite interesting. It can

giúp	em	có	một	cái	Tết		khác	so		với
help	1SG	have	one	CLF	New Year's Festival		different	compared		with

help me to have a wholly different New Year's Festival

mọi	năm	ạ.	Ngày mai	thì	em	vẫn	có thể	đón
every	year	PART	Tomorrow	TOP	1SG	still	can	attend

(compared with previous years). Tomorrow, I still can attend

giao thừa		cùng	với cả	bố mẹ	và	gia đình,	và
New Year's Eve		with	together	parents	and	family	and

New Year's Festival together with my parents and my family, and

em	nghĩ	là	ngày mai	có thể	dành	trọn vẹn	thời gian,
1SG	think	COP	tomorrow	can	reserve	entirely	time

I think that I can spend the whole day tomorrow with them.

còn	giao thừa		này	thì	em	có thể	đi	bán	bóng,
as for	New Year's Eve		DEICT	TOP	1SG	can		go	sell	balloon

As for this New Year's Eve, I can go out selling balloons,

em	có thể,	em	nghĩ	là	những	trái	bóng	đỏ	này
1SG	can	1SG	think	COP	PL	CLF	balloon	red	DEICT

I can, I think that those red balloons

có thể	mang	may mắn	đến	cho	mọi	người	ạ.
can	bring	good luck	come	give	every	person	PART

will/can bring good luck to everyone.

Interviewer:

Còn	vấn đề	tài chính,	nó	có	phải	là
As for	matter/issue	financial	3SG	ASRT	right/true	COP

As for money issue/matter, is it true that it (alone) is

một	cái	yếu tố	quyết định	để	năm	nay	gọi	là	đi	bán
one	CLF	factor	determine	for	year	now	call	COP	go	sell

one of the main reasons for you going out, say/I mean, to sell

bong bóng	*ngay*		*đêm*	*Giao Thừa*	*không?*
balloon	immediately/right		night	New Year's Eve	NEG
balloons	on the very night of the New Year's Eve ?				

Interviewee:

Dạ	*không,*	*tại vì*	*em*	*nghĩ*	*là*	*kiếm*	*tiền*	*thì*	*có*
RESP	no	because	1SG	think	COP	earn	money	TOP	EXIST

No, because I think that we can find time to make money (we can have many opportunities to

nhiều	*thời gian,*	*cái*	*thời gian*	*này*	*thì*	*nếu mà*	*mình*
many	time	CLF	time	DEICT	TOP	if	REFL

earn money), and it's good to spend this time with family too.

dành	*cho*	*gia đình*	*cũng*	*tốt.*	*Và*	*thứ hai*	*là*	*em*	*nghĩ*	*là*
reserve	for	family	also	good	And	second	COP	1SG	think	COP

And the second reason is that, for me,

những	*trái*	*bóng*	*đỏ*	*này*	*có thể*	*mang*	*may mắn*	*cho*	*những*
PL	CLF	balloon	red	DEICT	can	bring	good luck	give	PL

those red balloons can bring good luck to

người	*khác*	*và*	*em*	*cũng*	*có*	*một*	*cái*	*trải nghiệm*	*mới*
person	different	and	1SG	also	have	one	CLF	experience	new

other people and I can also gain a new experience

cho	*cái*	*Tết*		*của*	*mình.*	*Năm*	*nay*	*đã*
for	CLF	New Year's Festival		POSS	REFL	Year	now	ACCOMP

for my own New Year's Festival. This year, I've already

là	*hai mươi mốt*	*tuổi*	*rồi*	*ạ.*	*Em*	*muốn*	*đánh dấu*
COP	twenty one	age	already	PART	1SG	want	mark

turned twenty one. I want to mark

một	*năm*	*mới*	*với*	*những*	*sự*	*khác biệt*	*khác.*
one	year	new	with	PL	NOM	different	other

this new year with many other different things.

Em   nghĩ   là   đây   là   một   điều   khá   thú vị   và   em   rất
1SG   think COP   this COP   one   thing quite interesting and   1SG   very
I think this is quite exciting   and I truly

là   thích   ạ.
COP   like   PART
like it.

Interviewer:

Nhưng mà   trên   thực tế   thì   coi như là   thu nhập   từ   cái   bong bóng
But/yet   on   reality   TOP   consider   income   from CLF   balloon
But, in reality, I mean, is the money you get from selling those balloons

này   nó   có,   có   đáng kể   không?
DEICT 3SG   ASRT   ASRT   significant NEG
                            significant enough to you?

Interviewee:

Em   nghĩ   là   không   ạ.   Tại vì   là   euh   nếu mà
1SG   think   COP   NEG   PART   Because   COP   INTERJ   if
I don't think so.   Because   if

em   không   nhầm   thì   tính   đến   bây giờ   thì   bọn   em   vẫn
1SG   NEG   mistake   TOP   count   until now   TOP   PL   1SG   still
I'm not mistaken, so far, we still haven't

chưa   thu hồi   được   cái   số   tiền   mà   bọn   em
yet   retrieve   obtain   CLF   amount   money   REL   PL   1SG
recovered the initial outlay yet.

đã   bỏ ra.   Nhưng mà   em   thấy   rất   là   vui   ạ.
ACCOMP   outlay/spend   But   1SG   find   very   COP   happy   PART
                          But I feel really happy.

Em   học   được   rất   nhiều   điều   từ   đêm   Giao Thừa
1SG   learn   obtain   very   many   thing   from   night New Year's Eve
I've learnt many things from this New Year's Eve night

này,	*em*	*thấy*	*rất*	*là*		*ý nghĩa.*	*Em*	*thực sự*	*là*
DEICT	1SG	find	very	COP		meaningful	1SG	true	COP

I find it really meaningful. I truly

thích	*nó*	*và*	*em*	*nghĩ*	*là*	*năm*	*sau*	*em*	*sẽ*	*tìm*
like	3SG	and	1SG	think	COP	year	after	1SG	FUT	search

like it and I think that I'll search for another job next year

một	*việc*	*khác*	*hoặc*	*là*	*tiếp tục*	*công việc*	*bán*	*bóng.*
one	job	different	or	COP	continue	work/job	sell	balloon

or continue selling balloons.

Em	*nghĩ*	*là*	*sẽ,*	*nó*	*sẽ*	*thành công*	*hơn*	*ạ.*
1SG	think	COP	FUT	3SG	FUT	succeed	more	PART

I think it will be more successful than this year.

Justin Watkins
Wa (Paraok)

Introduction

Location and number of speakers

The speakers of Wa are located in a geographical area referred to by Gérard Diffloth (1980) as the Waic corridor, situated between the Salween and Mekong rivers, an area which straddles the south-western Chinese province of Yúnnán, the Shan States of north-eastern Burma and Northern Thailand. The Wa are thought to be among the autochthonous inhabitants of the area they occupy. Luó (1995) writes that a group likely to have been the ancestors of the Wa was in Yúnnán as early as the Qín dynasty (3rd century BC). In any case, it seems likely that the speakers of Northern Mon-Khmer languages were settled in the present-day Wa-speaking area earlier than other groups which now make up the majority of the population of the area, primarily speakers of Tibeto-Burman and Tai-Kadai languages.

Speaker numbers and dialects

The language described here, also known as Paraok, is the dialect of Wa spoken in Aishuai (Yànshuāi 岩帅), which is the one most widely understood and viewed as standard. Speaker numbers in such a geographically remote, topographically diverse and politically disparate area can at best only be estimates, but a working figure from the latest edition of the SIL Ethnologue (Lewis 2009) puts the total number of speakers of Wa, including Paraok and other varieties, at just under 1.2 million, with two thirds in China and one third in Burma.

The sub-categorization of dialects within Waic languages is confusing – as is indeed typical for the area when describing languages with a high degree of dialect diversity. SIL's major groupings (Lewis 2009), and their alternative names, are Vo (Awa, Wa, K'awa, Kawa, Wa Pwi, Wakut), Paraok (Wa, Praok, Baraog, Baraoke) and Western Lawa (Wa, Wa proper, Pava, Luwa, Lua, L'wa, Lavua, Lavüa, Mountain Lawa). The suggested total speaker numbers for these three groups are Vo 618,000, Paraok 528,400 and Western Lawa 82,000. This yields the

---

Justin Watkins: SOAS, University of London
E-Mail: jw2@soas.ac.uk

most inclusive count of 1,228,400 speakers. The SIL database includes a further 27,000 speakers of Blang (Bulang, Pulang, Pula, Plang, Kawa, K'ala, Kontoi) and 7000 of Eastern Lawa (Wiang Papao Lua), bringing to about 1.25 million the estimated total population speaking any of the Wa languages included in Diffloth (1980). This figure may certainly involve a degree of speculation and/or overlap.

Outside the main Wa-speaking area, migrations in recent decades have seen Wa villages established in northern Thailand. The oldest settlements, up to fifty years old, are closely integrated into Thai society, though the majority have been established within the last two generations. Further afield, there is a detectable Wa presence in Yangon/Rangoon, Taunggyi and Mandalay in Burma. Small numbers of Wa reside in Kūnmíng and across Yúnnán province in China.

Wa within Mon-Khmer

Generally, Wa languages are placed in the Palaungic or Palaung-Wa branch of Northern Mon-Khmer. Gérard Diffloth (1980, 1989) sifts through the fragmentary and often contradictory information published on the Wa languages and develops further the classification of the Wa languages proposed by Michel Ferlus (1974). Diffloth (1980) uses the term Waic to refer to one section of the Palaungic branch of Mon-Khmer for which he posits a common reconstructable source, Proto Waic.

Broadly speaking, Diffloth (1980) identifies three distinct groups of Waic languages, namely Bulang (formerly 'Samtau'), Wa and Lawa, as mentioned above. The areas inhabited by the speakers of the three groups of Waic languages are geographically distinct. Lawa speakers are located for the most part in Northern Thailand, while speaker of Wa (including Paraok) inhabit areas further north in the 'Waic corridor' in the Shan States and into Yúnnán. The offshoots of Bulang are spoken mostly in smaller areas to the north and north east of Keng Tung and into Yúnnán.

Ethno-linguistic comments

The status of Wa as a viable language is threatened by the encroachment of Chinese, and to a lesser extent also Burmese. The Wa lexicon, in particular, is subject to a high rate of attrition from borrowed Chinese vocabulary. Wa speakers live interspersed with speakers of many other languages. In the experience of the author, speakers of other languages rarely learn Wa, sometimes even in mixed marriages, while Wa speakers are typically multilingual. Of the small sample of some two dozen Wa speakers recorded for a field study (Watkins

2002) in the late 1990s, all were able to speak Chinese or Burmese to some degree if they had lived in China or Burma, or in several cases both. Those who had settled in Thailand also spoke at least some Thai. About half of the group spoke Lahu and about half of those who lived or had lived in the Shan State spoke Shan. A quarter spoke five or more languages.

1 Phonology

1.1 Register

In Wa, as in other Mon-Khmer languages, each vowel can occur in either of two registers, 'clear' and 'breathy', analogous to the 'head' and 'chest' registers of Khmer or Mon. The register contrast in Wa, as in Mon-Khmer generally, has a complex of phonetic correlates, including fundamental frequency, vowel quality, phonation type and vowel duration: the particular blend of these in any individual speaker's production of the register complex may vary, but in general breathy register in Wa is associated with slightly lower fundamental frequency and slightly breathy phonation. The register contrast, described in detail in Watkins (2002, chapter 6), co-occurs with final laryngeal consonants, as illustrated by the set of six words in (1) below, but is neutralized in syllables with a laryngeal initial [ʔ h] or where there is an aspiration gesture in the initial consonant.[1]

(1) tɛ   tɛh   tɛʔ   tɛ̤   tɛ̤h   tɛ̤ʔ
    'peach'   'less'   'land'   'peach'   'turn'   'wager'

1.1.1 Consonants

The inventory of consonants in the Wa phoneme inventory is shown in (2) below. There is a four-way voicing contrast in initial stop consonants (voiced/ unvoiced and aspirated/ unaspirated). Initial consonant clusters are restricted to bilabial and velar stops followed by [l] or [r]. Final consonants are restricted to unreleased voiceless stops [p t c k], nasals [m n ɲ ŋ] and glottals [ʔ h]. Final –

---

[1] Wa language data are presented here in broad IPA transcription following the conventions set out in this section. Watkins (2002: 28 ff) gives a account of the phonetic detail of Wa pronunciation; Watkins (2002: 188–200) gives a comparative account of the various orthographies in existence for Wa, none of which are used in this chapter.

ih is the reflex of *s in proto-Waic, just as written Khmer –*s* is pronounced [h], and survives as final –*s* in certain Waic dialects (Diffloth 1980). Note especially the large number of breathy-aspirated voiced segments in Wa.

(2)

	Bilabial	Labio-dental	Alveolar	Post-alveolar	Palatal	Velar	Glottal
Plosive/affricate	p b pʰ bʰ		t d tʰ dʰ	c j cʰ jʰ		k g kʰ gʰ	ʔ
Nasal	m mʰ		n nʰ		ɲ ɲʰ		
Fricative		v vʰ/f	s				h
Approximant			r rʰ			y/ʐ yʰ/ʐʰ	
Lateral approximant			l lʰ				

Words illustrating the contrast between these consonants are shown in the table (3) below.

(3)

p	pɔ	'side of body'	m	mai	'and'	y	yaoŋ	'village'
pʰ	pʰao	'now'	mʰ	mʰai	'to mark'	yh	yha	'to give birth' (of animals)
b	ba	'thigh'	n	num	'root'	r	ra	'two'
bʰ	bʰauɲ	'wind'	nʰ	nʰam	'blood'	rʰ	rʰa	'tooth'
t	tau?	'vegetable'	ɲ	ɲɛ?	'house'	l	lai	'why?'
tʰ	tʰa	'to wait'	ɲʰ	ɲʰot	'to push over'	lʰ	lʰɛ?	'rain'
d	dai	'flower'	ŋ	ŋu	'fire'	v	vɤ	'be missing' (of teeth)
dʰ	dʰah	'long'	ŋʰ	ŋʰo?	'grain'	v	vʰac	'black'
c	cao	'reason'						
cʰ	cʰɯ	'sack'				s	so?	'dog'
j	jao	'to jump'				h	haok	'hair'
jʰ	jʰɯih	'mouth'				ʔ	ʔɤ?	'I' (1sg pronoun)
k	kao	'ten'						
kʰ	kʰa	'from'						
g	gɔŋ	'mountain'						
gʰ	gʰok	'collar'						

1.1.2 Vowels and diphthongs

The Wa vowel system makes use of the nine vowel contrasts and a range of diphthongs, including high back unrounded vowels [ɤ ɯ] typical of Mainland Southeast Asian languages. There is no duration contrast. Watkins (2002) gives phonological and historical arguments for an analysis which recognizes five phonologically unitary diphthongs in Wa, shown on the vowel quadrilateral in (4) and the table (5) below, though the number of diphthongs in other analyses varies. In any case, the surface phonetic detail of diphthongs is particularly subject to variation between speakers and dialects (Watkins 2002: 34).

The Chinese descriptions which largely inform the transcription used in this chapter transcribe final approximants [j] and [w] as glides *i* and *u*. Furthermore, final palatals /ŋ k/ merge with final palatals /ɲ c/ when preceded by /i/, consistent with the off-glides before palatals observed generally in Mon-Khmer languages.

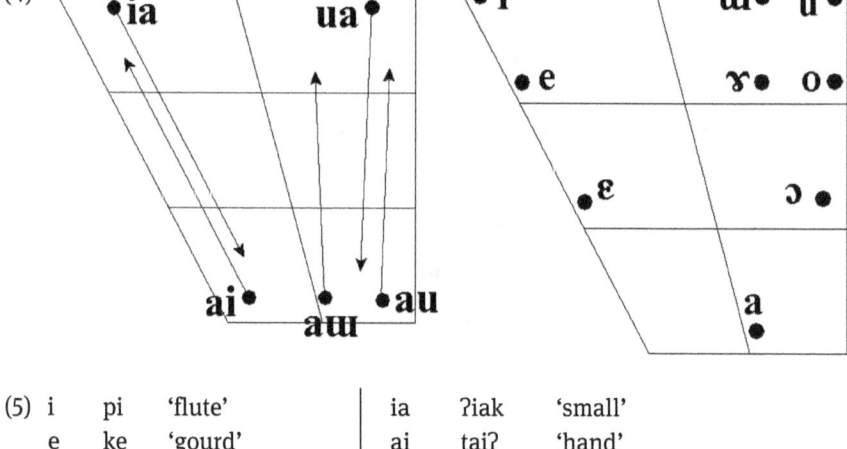

(5)	i	pi	'flute'	ia	ʔiak	'small'
	e	ke	'gourd'	ai	tai?	'hand'
	ɛ	kɛ	'sweet'	aɯ	haɯk	'hair'
	a	ka	'afterwards'	ao	haok	'to go up'
	ɔ	pɔ	'side (of body)'	ua	kuat	'cold'
	o	po	'mortar'			
	u	pu	'to fly'			
	ɤ	rɤ	'to pull'			
	ɯ	sɯ	'to pour'			

1.2 Syllable structure

Chinese analysts (Zhōu & Yán 1984; Wáng & Chén 1981) describe the segmental tier of the Wa syllable as a two-element object with an initial and a final, following the *fǎnqiè* syllable template of the Tāng dynasty Chinese rhyme dictionaries (Norman 1988: 24). According to the Chinese accounts, a Wa syllable must comprise an initial, a final and a register specification. The initial consists of one or two consonants; the final of at least one and up to three vowels plus an optional final consonant. This structure is expressed by Chinese analysts Wáng & Chén (1981: 40) as follows (ignoring register); optional elements are in parentheses.

initial   final
C_1 (C_2) (V_1) V_2 (V_3) (C_3)

In this very overpredictive framework, only C_1 and V_2 are unrestricted. C_2 is exclusively /r/ or /l/, V_1 and V_3 can often be analysed as consonant glides /y/ or /w/, which restricts the schema considerably, and the final consonant C_3 may be a plain stop, nasal or one of /ʔ/ or /h/, resulting in a syllable structure which is squarely consistent with the Mainland Southeast Asian stereotype as described by Henderson (1965) and Enfield (2005: 182).

1.2.1 Wa sesquisyllabicity and historical morphology

Henderson's (1952: 150–151) description of the phonological structure of Khmer is a good illustration of morphological affixation typically observed in the Mon-Khmer languages of Mainland Southeast Asia. Examples are given in (6). Henderson describes monosyllables in Khmer as 'extensile', capable of yielding 'extended monosyllable', or may have a 'minor syllable' with a tightly constrained structure added to it, yielding a 'minor disyllable' or 'sesquisyllable' in the terminology of Matisoff. The minor disyllable, a fourth structural type, has an initial syllable with restricted variation.

(6)
simple monosyllable		extended monosyllable		minor disyllable	
ចាំ	'wait'	ប្រចាំ	'watch one another'	បញ្ចាំ	'to pledge'
cam		prəcam		bɔŋcam	
កើត	'be born'	ខ្នើត	'waxing of moon'	បង្កើត	'give birth'
kaɤt		knaɤt		bɔŋkaɤt	
ដេក	'sleep'	ផ្ដេក	'put to bed'	បន្ទេក	'go to bed'
de:k		pde:k		bɔnde:k	

The Mon-Khmer extended monosyllable, called a sesquisyllable by Matisoff (1973), shows what remains of a morphologically rich disyllabic stage of Proto Mon-Khmer (Diffloth 1980), and points to the possibilities morphological complexity observed to a greater or lesser degree in the Mon-Khmer languages of Mainland Southeast Asia, including the Northern Mon-Khmer branch to which Wa belongs (see Shorto 1963 on Palaung and Riang-Lang; Svantesson 1983a on Kammu).

Within Northern Mon-Khmer, presyllables survive in varying stages of decay; in Wa the morphological system of prefixation has all but disappeared, leaving only a few prefixes with a broad, ill-defined range of functions. By far the most common presyllable in the Wa lexicon is *s.-* . According to Shorto (1963: 55), "In Praok [Wa], *s.-* probably results from the generalization in almost all prefixial contexts of a prefix which originally corresponded to those with an initial s- in [Palaung and Riang-Lang]." Shorto proposes that Wa *s.-* may be a vestige of a prefix *siC-, where C represents a stop. The second consonant of this prefix, or the single consonant of the other historical prefixes *b-* and *g-* which he describes, is preserved only when the initial consonant of the host syllable is *r-* or *l-*, permitting the formation of a morphologically complex consonant cluster. The prefixes *b-* and *g-* cannot form any other clusters; if they are prefixed to a morpheme with any other initial consonant, the stops are deleted, leaving behind only their voicing. Illustrative examples of these vestiges of Wa affixational morphology are given in (7) below, data from Wáng & Chén (1984).

(7) Wa affixational morphology

    g- prefixation and cluster formation:
    lah > glah   *lang > glaŋ*   *rɯʔ > grɯʔ*
    'burn' > 'hearth'   'long' > 'this long'   'deep' > 'this deep'

    Voicing of initial stop:
    pɯ > bɯ   *tiɲ > diɲ*
    'thick' > 'thickness'   'big' > 'size'

    s.- prefixation and voicing of stop:
    kiap > s.giap
    'thick' > 'thickness'

Whatever their provenance, these morphological processes are not productive in the modern language. Additionally, *s.-* may occur in some words as an optional and morphologically redundant prefix, as in (8).

(8) taiʔ ~ s.taiʔ   gaɯʔ ~ s.gaɯʔ
    'eight'   'happy'

In Wa the sesquisyllabic structure is not entirely restricted to the *s-* presyllable. In addition, the sesquisyllabic structure is sometimes observed when the first element of a bisyllabic (often partly reduplicative) sequence is reduced, as in (9). Reduction of this kind tends towards a consonant + indeterminate vowel, or maximally to the *s.-* presyllable, pronounced with or without an epenthetic vowel.

(9) Reduction of bisyllables to sesquisyllables. (Data from Wáng and Chén (1981)
    su so 'muddled up' > [su.so] ~ [sə.so] ~ [sʲ.so] ~ [s.so]
    ci kua 'smallpox' > [tɕi.kwa] ~ [ɕi.kwa] ~ [sʲ.kwa] ~ [s.kwa]
    ja̰ ra̰h 'frog' > [dʑa̰.ra̰h] ~ [dʑḭ.ra̰h] ~ [sʲ.ra̰h] ~ [s.ra̰h]

The difference in phonological structure between sesquisyllables and monosyllables with initial consonant clusters or initial ʔ, shown in (10) and (11), is evident from the fact that the two can occur together in single morpheme, albeit with morphologically complex etymology.

(10) *s.-* presyllables in conjunction with initial consonant clusters
     s.blap   s.prih   s.gluc   s.gʰrah
     'strike, kick' 'chapped'   'urge, hasten'   'rinse'

(11) *s.-* presyllables contrasted with initial *s-*
     s.ʔaŋ   saŋ
     'bone'   'want'
     s.ʔu   su
     'warm'   'intentionally'
     s.ʔut   sut
     'swollen'   'pick up'
     s.ʔoʔ   soʔ
     'rubber'   'dog'

2 Morphology

As is the case in many Southeast Asian languages, defining the word in Wa is not always a straightforward matter, so for the purposes of this section 'word' is interpreted as any cluster of morphemes which might usefully be considered to be a single lexeme. In the last section it was shown that Wa affixational morphology is entirely lexicalized and unanalyzable, such that the morphemes making up words are typically monosyllabic (or at most sesquisyllabic). The languages from which Wa has borrowed vocabulary—principally the varieties of Chinese and Tai languages found in areas adjacent to the Wa-speaking areas— also strongly favour monosyllables, though loans from other languages, for instance Indo-European ones, are not.

2.1 Morphological derivation by compounding

The Wa lexicon makes extensive use of compounding. The following examples (12)–(24) illustrate the way in which nouns and verbs can combine to complex polymorphemic noun phrases.

(12) N_1N_2 : synonyms (noun₁ = noun₂)
    krạuŋ   kʰrai
    clothes clothes
    'clothing, things, goods, possessions'

(13) $N_1N_2N_3N_4$: synonyms (noun₁ = noun₂), made up of (noun₃ and noun₄)
    krạuŋ   kʰrai   dai   tɕah
    clothes clothes skirt shirt
    'clothing, clothes'

(14) N_1N_2 : noun₁ associated with noun₂

    krạuŋ   nạɲ   pạoʔ   ɲiɛʔ   kạɲ   ɲiɛʔ   ɲiɛʔ   zʰia
    equipment   war   relatives house   work   house   house   bee
    'weapons'   'family member'   'housework'   'beehive'

    ɲiɛʔ   ʔaɲ
    house   shit
    'toilet'

(15) NV – noun which is verb (where verb is a stative/adjectival verb)
    dɯ   mʰɔm   dɯ   lɯt
    place   good   place   wrong
    'advantage'   'error, mistake'

(16) NV – noun which verbs

dɯ	s.dauh	tɕak	pih	tɕak	pu
place	finish	machine	suck	machine	fly
'ending'		'vacuum cleaner'		'aeroplane'	

(17) $(NV_1)(V_2A)$ – (noun which verb$_1$s) which (verb$_2$s adjectivally)
    tɕak   pu   haok   dzuŋ
    machine fly   climb vertical
    'helicopter'

(18) $N_1(VN_2)$ – noun$_1$ which verbs noun$_2$

tɕak	zuɯn	krauŋ	tɕak	tiəm	lai	tɕak	tɕaɲ	krauŋ
machine	press	clothes	machine	write	text	machine	sew	clothes
'iron'			'typewriter, computer'			'sewing machine'		

(19) NV – noun where one verbs

ɲiɛʔ	ʔit	dɯ	tum	ɲiɛʔ	ʔaɲ
house	sleep	place	rest	house	defecate
'bedroom'		'destintation'		'toilet'	

(20) $N_1(VN_2)$ – noun$_1$ where one verbs noun$_2$
    ɲiɛʔ   ʔah   lai
    house   read   text
    'school'

(21) $N_1(VN_2)$ – noun$_1$ where noun$_2$ verbs
    dɯ   pauŋ   lɔ li
    place rest   bus
    'bus station'

(22) $(N_1V_1)(N_2V_2)$ – (noun$_1$ which one verb$_1$s) and (noun$_2$ which one verb$_2$s)
    krauŋ   tɕup   ʔɯp   sɔm
    clothes wear   rice   eat
    'food and clothing'

(23) $(N_1V_1)(N_1V_2)$ – (noun$_1$ for verb$_1$ing) and synonym (noun$_1$ for verb$_2$ing)
    krauŋ   tɕup   krauŋ sɔm
    clothes wear   clothes wear
    'clothing'

(24) N₁(VN₂) – noun₁ which is verbed by noun₂
    krauŋ   muan   kɔn ɲɔm
    thing   play   child
    'toy'

A few nouns may serve as the head noun in compounds both with their original lexical meaning but also in a semantically bleached form. The higher the degree of semantic bleaching, the greater the productivity of the noun in morphological derivations. For instance, *kraʔ* 'road' may retain the meanings 'road' or 'way/method' as in (25):

(25) kraʔ   hɔ tɕʰɤ   kraʔ   ʔot
     road   train   way   live
     'railway'   'way of life'

or operate as a largely functional morpheme as in (26):

(26) kraʔ   tɕiʔ   blon   lʰaoŋ   kraʔ   gauʔ rʰɔm   kraʔ   s.bʰɔm
     road   can   much   high   road   happy   road   starve
     'technology'   'happiness'   'famine, starvation'

The relativizer *pa* is one of very few morphemes used in morphological derivations which is purely functional, or rather a grammatical morpheme whose source is obscure, yielding nouns such as (27) and (28) meaning 'that which is verbed' or 'that which verbs' (where the verb may be stative/adjectival):

(27) pa   pon
     REL   receive
     'income, earnings' < 'that which is received'

(28) pa   rauh   pa   suɯ
     REL   upright   REL   straight
     'righteousness' < 'that which is upright and straight'

A number of ethnic nationalities and clans, as in (29), are described using such formulations:

(29) pa   ʔauʔ   pa   raok   pa   rʰaʔ
     REL   ʔauʔ   REL   raok   REL   rʰaʔ
     Plang   Paraok, Wa   Pa Rhax (a Wa clan name)

2.2 Psycho-collocations

The only frequently encountered psycho-collocation in the sense of Matisoff (1986) in the Wa lexicon is rʰɔm 'heart', which appears in over 200 phrases in the Wa Dictionary database (Watkins 2013). This is consistent with Wa's geographical Mainland Southeast Asian linguistic neighbours which also use a 'heart/mind' morpheme to convey emotions, namely Chinese 心 xīn, Tai/Shan tsaɯ¹ ၸႂ် and Burmese seiʔ စိတ် (see Vittrant 2013). Overwhelmingly, such collocations in Wa take the form VERB + rʰɔm 'heart VERBS' – examples are given in (30). follow.

(30)	ʔa̱t	rʰɔm	heart is salty	'angry'
	ʔaoh	rʰɔm	heart is hot	'upset, irritated'
	praiʔ	rʰɔm	heart is spicy	'angry'
	tat	rʰɔm	heart cuts	'decide'
	ti̱ɲ	rʰɔm	heart is big	'bold'
	tṳk	rʰɔm	heart is asthmatic	'sad'
	kaoh	rʰɔm	heart stands up	'indignant, excited'
	haok	rʰɔm	heart climbs	'interested, envy'
	haʔ	rʰɔm	heart is hot, scorching	'rash, impetuous'
	lʰaoŋ	rʰɔm	heart is tall	'arrogant'
	nʰu̱k	rʰɔm	heart is asthmatic	'glum, depressed'
	nʰiən	rʰɔm	heart is hard, stiff	'stubborn'
	kʰriən	rʰɔm	heart is engaged	'obliged, embarrassed (cf. Burmese ʔaɜ-na²-dɛ²)'
	kʰriaŋ	rʰɔm	heart is seasoned, dried out	'cordial, polite'
	kʰrup	rʰɔm	heart is tired	'gloomy, disheartened'
	la̱c	rʰɔm	heart enters	'interested' (cf. Burmese seiʔ win²-zaɜ-dɛ²)
	lṳt	rʰɔm	heart is wrong	'cause offence'
	dṳt	rʰɔm	heart breaks	'die'
	bʰaŋ	rʰɔm	heart is wide open	'generous'
	dak	rʰɔm	heart retreats	'disgusted'
	saɯ	rʰɔm	uses heart	'engrossed'
	tʰɔ	rʰɔm	heart is shallow	'intolerant'

These collocations VERB + rʰɔm can be extended using the expressive doublet rʰɔm rʰi 'heart' to give VERB + rʰɔm rʰi or to form an ABAC expressive reduplicative form [VERB rʰɔm VERB rʰi], as in (31); see also section 3.3.2 below.

(31) gaɯʔ   rʰɔm   gaɯʔ   rʰi̯
    happy   heart   happy   heart
    'happy'

2.3 Elaborate expressions

2.3.1 Rhyming proverbs and sayings

Wang et al. (1992) is a major source of several thousand Wa proverbs and sayings. Proverbs and sayings in Wa typically pivot about a central rhyme, usually a near-exact one, which straddles the divide between two syntactic domains. The material either side of the divide may vary greatly in quantity and syntactical complexity. Often the syntax of the two halves of the whole phrase is symmetrical in structure. Elaborate sayings and proverbs of this kind frequently contain high-register Tai loans. The subject matter may be either pedestrian or lofty, sometimes with historical or legendary allusions. Some examples (32)–(34) follow, in which the third and fourth syllables rhyme or nearly rhyme.

(32) pa̯n   daɯʔ   ŋa̯c,   la̯c   daɯʔ   gru̯an.
    rest   place   fragrant,   enter   place   hunting hide
    'Rest in a fragrant place, enter a hunter's hide.' – Describes the joys of hunting.

(33) sɯ   nɔh   zɯt,   prɯt   nɔh   grai
    splash   3SG   extinguished,   smother   3SG   gone
    'Sprinkle it out, extinguish it till it's gone.' – A prayer to ward off fire.

(34) klɛh   ti̯ʔ   vo̯ŋ,   lṵŋ   ti̯ʔ   bɔ̯k.
    play   one   period,   act diligently   one   time
    'Be romantic for a while, make a true effort once.' (said between a courting man and woman.)

2.3.2 Expressive doublets and derived reduplicative forms

Wa makes use of expressive doublets as in (35), where an ordinary noun X is paired with an expressive synonym X*, which may be obscure or poetic and typically occurs nowhere else in the lexicon.

(35) rʰɔm + rʰi   > rʰɔm rʰi   'heart' + 'heart*'   > 'heart'
      prɛʔ   pruɨm   prɛʔ pruɨm   'food' + 'food*'   > 'food, grain'

X=X* doublets such as these can be used in combination with another pair of words to make four-syllable expressions, as in (36):

(36) X   X*
     prɛʔ   pruɨm   lai guɨ   >   prɛʔ pruɨm lai guɨ
     food/grain   trade   'grain produced to sell'

They can also be used as the base for part-reduplicated four-syllable nominal or verbal forms (37).

(37) NOUN   X   NOUN.REDUP   X*
     ŋɔ   prɛʔ   ŋɔ   pruɨm   >   ŋɔ prɛʔ ŋɔ pruɨm
     leftovers food   leftovers   food*   'leftovers'

     VERB   X   VERB.REDUP   X*
     yuɨh   prɛʔ   yuɨh   pruɨm   >   yuɨh prɛʔ yuɨh pruɨm
     make   food   make   food*   'cook food'

     loh   rʰɔm   loh   rʰi   >   loh rʰɔm loh rʰi
     change   heart   change   heart*   'start afresh'

     soŋ   rʰɔm   soŋ   rʰi   >   soŋ rʰɔm soŋ rʰi
     bitter   heart   bitter   heart*   'enraged'

Both the ABBC rhyme pattern and the expressive forms derived from doublets can be are used to form extended expressive forms of everyday words. For instance, the three bimorphemic compounds in (38) all mean 'neighbour':

(38) s.juɨn   plɔk   = paoʔ   nʰɔm   = paoʔ   plɔk
     close by   neighbourhood   friend plot of land   friend neighbourhood
     'neighbour'   'neighbour'   'neighbour'

Additionally, these can form an ABAC-type reduplicated phrase (39):

(39) paoʔ   plɔk   paoʔ   nʰɔm
     friend   neighbourhood   friend   plot of land
     'neighbour'

and also an ABBC-type elaborate partly reduplicated form (40):

(40) s.juɨn   plɔk   s.dzʰɔk   ɲiɛʔ
     close by   neighbourhood   pile up   house
     'nextdoor neighbour'

Alliterative partial reduplication is also used in Wa to form aesthetic ideophones. In (41), the initial consonant is used to form a pre-syllable with the vowel [u] in the register of the source syllable.

(41) kliən   >   ku kliən ~ klu kliən   dic   >   du dic
     'twist'   'twist repeatedly'   'trample'   'trample repeatedly'

This kind of pattern may simply be used to generate a number of alternative expressive forms in (42):

(42) pu praŋ ~ pru praŋ ~ puŋ praŋ ~ pruŋ praŋ
     'scatter, disperse'

We find also emphatic forms with euphonic chiming syllables – where the chime may precede or follow the simple unadorned source lexeme, as in (43):

(43) kloŋ   >   kloŋ kloc
     'drill'   'interrogate, question'

     bit   >   s.bit ~ s.biən ~ s.bit s.biən
     'sticky'   'miserly'

     s.kaoŋ   >   s.kaoŋ s.kiat
     'cold'   'freezing cold'

2.4 Loanwords

The Wa lexicon incorporates a large amount of loan vcabulary from a number of languages. The Wa speaking area lies on the boundary between the Chinese-speaking world and Mainland Southeast Asia. Predictably, words from the *lingue franche* of the area have found their way into the Wa lexicon, in particular Yunnanese Chinese and Tai/Shan languages spoken in Yunnan, China, and in Shan State, Burma. Only a small part of the Wa speaking people have come under the influence of Buddhism, and so the language has absorbed little vocabulary from Sanskrit or Pali.

Chinese loans are very large in number (at least 10% of the lexicon as documented in Watkins 2013), particularly in the domains of politics, science, agriculture, education and technology. Tai/Shan loans in Wa are fewer in number, and include the names of some plants, crops, crafts and materials, and larger numerals (which are themselves Tai/Shan borrowings from Chinese). Tai/Shan is also the source of some high-register ceremonial and formal language found in proverbs and sayings.

Loans from English, typically via Burmese, are found in varieties of Wa spoken on the Burmese side of the border, and include vocabulary to do with technology which was introduced to the Wa at the time of early colonial contact with the British. Loans from English include those in (44):

(44) Wa *pati*   < Burmese ပါတီ pa¹ti²   < English 'party'
     Wa *sai kɛ* < Burmese ဆိုင်ကယ် sʰaiN²-kɛ²   < English '[motor]cycle'

Certain words are likely to be borrowed from Chinese on the Chinese side of the border and from Burmese (or English via Burmese) on the Burmese side of the border, but there are also Chinese-Burmese hybrids which show the diversity of influences on Wa from both sides, as in n (45).

(45) *mɔʔ tʰɔʔ cʰɤ*   Burmese မော်တော် mɔ²tɔ² (< English 'motor')
     'car'   + Chinese 车 *chē* 'vehicle'
     cṵ yi pʰi ɲa   Chinese 主意 *zhǔyì* 'idea'
     'knowledge'   + Burmese ပညာ *pyiN²-ɲa²* (< Pali *paññā*) 'knowledge'

Many loanwords appear preceded by a Wa superordinary, as seen in (46) the following examples.

(46) classroom   *ɲɛʔ tʃaɔ sɯʔ*   < Wa *ɲɛʔ* 'house' + 教室 *jiàoshì* 'classroom'
     mango   *pliʔ mak mṵn*   < Wa *pliʔ* 'fruit' + Tai *maak² moŋ³* 'mango'
     Western suit   *krạɯŋ si tʃuaŋ* < Wa *krạɯŋ* 'clothes'
                                       + Chinese 西装 *xīzhuāng* 'Western suit'
     diesel oil   *bṵ di-sɛ*   < Wa *bṵ* 'oil' + Burmese ဒီဇယ် *diʔ-zɛ²*
                                       (< English 'diesel')

3 Grammar and Syntax

3.1 Nominal domain

This section describes some of the main features of noun phrases in Wa.

3.1.1 Noun phrases

The schema in (47) and the examples which follow it illustrate the structure of the Wa noun phrase. In general, the noun appears at the leftmost edge.

(47) NOUN   relative clause   numeral + CLF   possessive
                                          quantifier / plural   demonstrative

(48) jʰɔk   tiʔ   mu
       quail   one   CLF
       'a quail'

(49) pṵi   daɲ   tiɲ   taiʔ   tiʔ   kɑɯʔ
       person   very   big   hand   one   CLF
       'a very generous person'

(50) pa̰oʔ.grɔm   loi   kɑɯʔ   ʔan
       friend   three   CLF   that
       'Those three friends'

(51) Naŋ   Kṵai   pa   gra̰ɲ   yṵh.nan
       Nang   Kuai   REL   beautiful   like.that

       ci̤ʔ   khɔ   tiʔ   yṵh   pa̰oʔ.bḛ   kɔn   pḛʔ
       can   suit   CONJ   make   companion   child   sheep
       'Nang Kuai, who is that beautiful, can be the lamb's companion.'

The basic set of Wa pronouns is set out in (52) below. This type of pronoun system is found also in Palaung and other Northern Mon-Khmer languages, though in a Mainland Southeast Asian context it is unusual for a basic pronoun system to obligatorily contrast dual with plural number, and inclusivity with exclusivity in the 2nd person dual and plural.

(52) Wa pronouns

	singular	dual		plural	
1st person	ʔɤʔ	ʔaʔ	yɛʔ	ʔeʔ	yiʔ
	1SG	1DU.INCL	1DU.EXCL	1PL.INCL	1PL.EXCL
2nd person	maiʔ	paʔ		peʔ	
	2SG	2DU		2PL	
3rd person	nɔh	kɛʔ		kiʔ	
	3SG	3DU		3PL	

There is no obligatory marking of person or number, but a noun phrase may be marked as dual or plural using one of the 3rd person dual or plural pronouns as a noun-phrase suffix as in (53) and (54).

(53) ʔuc   gao̠ʔ rʰɔm   ʔɤʔ   kah   [Ø]   pa   kʰruɲ   ʔan   kiʔ
     very   nauseous   1SG   PREP   [Ø]   REL   filthy   that   PL
     'I feel revolted by those filthy [things].'

(54) mɛʔ   mɔɲ   ʔan   kɛʔ
     wife   husband   that   DUAL
     'that husband and wife couple.'

Empty-headed relative clauses such as *pa kʰruɲ* 'dirty [thing]' in (53) are very common indeed in Wa. They are explored further in section 4.3.3 below.

Like other Mainland Southeast Asian languages, Wa does not use articles to mark definiteness or indefiniteness. However, degrees of definiteness or indefiniteness can be expressed using the demonstratives or quantifiers such as those listed in (55), following the noun which they qualify.

(55) tit tiʔ / buh tiʔ   some, any
     (tiʔ) blah   some, a few
     mɔt tiʔ   a certain
     ʔin / ʔan   this / that

3.1.2 Classifiers

The position of classifiers in the noun phrase has been described above. There are few true classifiers in Wa, the notable exceptions being the classifiers *kauʔ* for people and *mu*, a general classifier. Besides these two, weights and quantities and a wide variety of countable nouns are used as measure words. A classifier or measure word occurs obligatorily with numbers, but need not be present with demonstratives.

3.2 Verbal domain

This section describes the main features of verbs and verb phrases in Wa.

3.2.1 Tense-mode-aspect particles

Like the vast majority of Mainland Southeast Asian languages, verbs in Wa lack inflection of any kind. The tense-mode-aspect system makes use of the preverbal morphemes such as in (56), and illustrated in the examples which follow.

(56) hɔc perfective marker
 ʔaŋ negative marker
 saʔ experiential, remote past marker ('ever')
 lai aspect marker ('after all'; 'not any more' in negative sentences)
 ɲaŋ aspect marker ('not yet' in negative sentence)

(57) nɔh   hɔc   ʔam   tiʔ,   ʔaŋ   lai   ciʔ   ɲe
 3SG   PERF   dumb   REFL, NEG   anymore   can   yell
 'He was dumbfounded and couldn't call out (anymore).'

(58) ʔup   ʔaŋ.ɲaŋ   sin,   bao?   ʔut   tiʔ   vut.
 rice not.yet   cooked,   again boil   one   while
 'The rice still isn't cooked, so boil it a while longer.'

(59) diʔ   nɛʔ   yiʔ   ʔaŋ   saʔ   kup   ʔih,
 formerly   family   2.PL.EXCL   NEG   ever   enough   eat,

 ŋai?   kah   ʔaŋ   lai   ʔuc   ʔih.
 today   but   NEG   anymore   finish   eat
 'In the past our family didn't have enough to eat, but nowadays we can't finish it all.'

Other time adverbs are commonly used additionally to express the temporal relations of actions and events, such as those listed in (60) and (61).

(60) kʰaiʔ   afterwards, later
     khaŋ   then
     nʰaoʔ   recently
     dị̇ʔ   previously
     kɔn   still

(61) **kʰaiʔ** hɔc   sɔm   ʔeʔ,   ʔɯp   **kɔn**   haoh   tɔm.nɛ
     after PERF   eat   2.PL.INCL rice   **still** much   somewhat
     'After we had eaten there was still a lot of rice left.'

3.2.2 Grammaticalization of verbs

The most common grammaticalized verbs in Wa are those which are commonly found in the language of the Mainland Southeast Asian area. As auxiliary verbs, they appear following the main verb in serial verb constructions, with the coordinating connection conjunction *tiʔ* between the two.

3.2.2.a *cịɛ* 'to own' > possessive (POSS)

When the possessor is a pronoun, *cịɛ* is not obligatory; it could be omitted from (62):

(62) saŋ   taʔ   chɤ   **cịɛ**   maiʔ   hu
     want   ride   car   **POSS**   2.SG   go
     'I want to go in your car.'

The head noun which is possessed can be elided. Prepositional phrases headed by possessive *cịɛ* appear frequently as complement of the copula *mɔ̣h*, as in (63) and (64).

(63) s.bẹiʔ   prẹ   mɔ̣h   **cịɛ**   ʔi   nap
     dress   silk   COP   **POSS**   I   Nap
     'The silk dress is I Nap's.'

(64) ʔaŋ   mɔ̣h   cịɛ   maiʔ,   kah   mɔ̣h   **cịɛ**   nɔh
     NEG   COP   POSS   2.SG,   then   COP   **POSS**   3.SG
     'If it's not yours, then it must be his.'

3.2.2.b *pɔn* 'to receive' > 'can', physical potentiality

Grammaticalized as a preverbal auxiliary, *pɔn* indicates physical capability (65), (66), rather than learned or chosen ability, which is expressed with the verb *ciʔ* 'able, possible'.

(65) kɛh ʔaŋ pɔn pai duɨih klɔt,
     if   NEG can heal return alive,

     kiʔ ciʔ mu̯k kaŋ ʔaʔ
     3.PL may chop head 2.DU.INCL
     'If we can't bring her back to life, they may cut off our heads.'

(66) ʔaŋ pɔn ju̯t kah kih tiʔ brɛ
     NEG can lack PREP salt one meal
     'I can't do without salt for a single meal'

However, like the grammaticalized forms of this verb in other Southeast Asian languages, the meaning can be hard to pin down, since in some contexts the meaning can veer towards 'gets to' or 'has the opportunity to', as in (67).

(67) kɔn yiʔ pu̯n lu̯c daɯʔ lɛn kah mɔh pak.ɲai yiʔ
     child 1PL.EXCL can join in army so is honour 1PL.EXCL
     'It is an honour for us that our son can serve in the army.'
     Or: '… that our son has the opportunity to…'

3.2.2.c *yɡoʔ* 'to see' > try

Following the main verb, *yɡoʔ* 'see' expresses actions undertaken speculatively or tentatively as in (68). In (69) *yɡoʔ* 'see' appears at the end of the sentence as a resultative complement.

(68) maiʔ cʰaŋ **yɡoʔ** kɔ ʔin
     2SG sing **see** song this
     'Try singing this song'

(69) ʔeʔ sum s.mɛ ŋʰoʔ kʰraoʔ nu̯m ʔin **yɡoʔ**
     1PL.INCL plant seed rice new year this **see**
     'We tried planting a new kind of rice this year.'

Unusually for Mainland Southeast Asian languages, the Wa verb *yɑoʔ* 'to see' also grammaticalizes as an auxiliary verb preceding the main verb to express potentiality, usually in negative contexts, as in (70) and (71).

(70) krɔʔ   kah   ʔaŋ   **yɑoʔ**   tiʔ   ʔih   prɛʔ
     thin   from   NEG   **see**   CONJ   eat   food
     'Thin from not being able to eat.'

(71) yɑm   ʔiak   ʔɤʔ   dị̂ʔ,   ʔaŋ   **yɑoʔ**   tiʔ   gɑɯ   lɑi
     thin   from   1SG   formerly,   NEG   **see**   CONJ   study   writing
     'When I was young, I didn't have the chance to go to school'

3.2.2.d *tɔʔ* 'to give' > causative / preposition

tɔʔ 'give' has causative and permissive senses as an auxiliary verb, as in (72) and (73). An interesting comparison can be made with the contrasting uses of auxiliary ေပး *pe³* 'give' in Burmese, which may have both permissive and causative meanings, usually when preceding and following the main verb, respectively (see Okano 2005).

(72) tɔʔ   nɔh   hu   khaŋ
     give   3SG   go   then
     'May he go!', 'Tell him to go!'

(73) maiʔ   lai   blɔk   tiʔ   tɔʔ   nɔh   gạc
     2SG   why   only   CONJ   give   3SG   watch
     'Why did you only let him see it?'

tɔʔ is used in a benefactive sense in (74).

(74) maiʔ   hoc   tɔʔ   yiʔ   ʔih   prɛʔ   tin
     2SG   come   give   2.PL.EX   eat   food   here
     'You bring food here for us to eat.'

3.2.2.e *ʔot* 'live' > progressive (PROG)

While *ʔot* seemingly does not occur with stative verbs with a continuous/durative meaning; it is frequently found with non-stative verbs to convey progressive aspect, as in (75) and (76).

(75) nɛ   kin   jʰɔm sauʔ   nɔh,   ʔot
     very   serious   illness   3SG   PROG

     tiʔ   s.kah   kah.gʰaok.kah.duŋ
     CONJ   talk   ramblingly
     'His illness is especially serious and he is rambling all over the place.'

(76) ʔai pao   ʔot   tiʔ   tot   sup
     Ai Pao   PROG   CONJ   smoke   tobacco
     'Ai Pao is smoking tobacco.'

3.2.2.f *ʔun* 'to put, to set' > completed/ resultative aspect

(77) kiʔ   liak   tiʔ   ʔun   krauŋ.
     3PL   buy   conj   RESULT   clothes
     'They've bought their clothes (and are all ready)'

(78) vaŋ   ʔeʔ   tiʔ   ʔun   khaoʔ   ʔin   kiʔ   sɔn   ʔaŋ   phrɔc
     preserve   2.PL.EX   CONJ   RESULT   tree   this   PL   so.that   NEG   chop
     'We preserve these trees in the forest so they are not cut down.'

3.2.2.g *kah* 'undo'

The high-frequency verb *kah* is of particular interest. As a transitive verb, it has meanings 'untie', 'solve', 'cure':

(79) yuh   buan son,   kah   maoʔ   mɔi
     do   favour,   untie   rope   cow
     'Please untie the rope tethering the cow.'

(80) s.dah   ʔin   kah   sawʔ   ʔaoh
    medicine   this   cure   illness   hear
    'This kind of medicine relieves heatstroke.'

(81) pa   kah   dṳ blwih   gum   loʔ   mai   lai   ka la
    REL   solve   meaning   phrase   short   and   speech   foreign
    'Explanation of the meaning of short phrases and foreign words.'

Grammaticalized, *kah* functions as a very high-frequency semantically versatile preposition which can express location ((82)(83)), instrumentality/causation ((84)(85)(86)) and location ((87),(88)), etc.:

Location:
(82) ʔot   nɔh   kah   kawŋ liam
    live   3SG   kah   Menglian
    'He lives in Menglian.'

(83) yum   lɛn   kah   naŋ
    die   soldier   in/from   battle
    'The soldier died in battle/from fighting.'

Causation/instrumentality:
(84) tawk   nɔh   kah   jʰɔm   sawʔ   tiʔ
    tired   3SG   kah   characteristic   illness   REFL
    'He is tired because of his illness.'

(85) sɔm   kah   tʰu
    eat_rice   kah   chopstick
    'eat using chopsticks'

(86) ʔɤʔ   mat   yṳh   taiʔ   tiʔ   kah   gɔn
    1SG   cut   do   hand   REFL   kah   knife
    'I cut my hand with a knife.'

Direction:
(87) la tha   ʔin   mɔh   pa   haok   kah   daw   mɤŋ tala
    train   this   is   REL   depart   kah   place   Mandalay
    'This train is the one which leaves for Mandalay.'

(88) ʔeʔ   hu   pian kraʔ kah plak laih
     2.PL.INCL go   on   road kah area market
     'We went along the road towards market.'

When information from an adverbial *kah*-headed prepositional phrase is fronted for topicalization or focus, *kah* may be stranded. The information thus fronted may be a noun phrase ((89)(90)), a (nominalized) verb phrase ((91),(92)), or a complete subordinate clause 'because his father scolded him' (93). The adverbial force of *kah* may sometimes be effectively translated with 'thereby'.

(89) [rɔm   s.gaoŋ ʔan]ᵢ koi   kaʔ   tiŋ   kaɲ   kah   []ᵢ
     [water   clear   that]ᵢ have   fish   big   head   **kah** []ᵢ
     'That clear water has big-headed fish in it.'

(90) [ŋɛʔ   prim]   ʔaŋ   pu̯i   ʔot   kah   []ᵢ
     [house   old]   NEG   people live   **kah** []ᵢ
     'People don't live in the old house.'

(91) [hoc   maiʔ]ᵢ ʔɤʔ   kɛt   gaɯʔ   rhɔm   kah   []ᵢ
     [come   2SG]ᵢ   1SG   vert   happy heart **kah** []ᵢ
     'I'm very pleased that you came.'

(92) [hɔc   koi   nat]ᵢ tit.tiʔ kɔʔ   ʔaŋ   lʰat   kah   []ᵢ
     [PERF   have   gun]ᵢ anything then   NEG   fear   **kah** []ᵢ
     'Once you have a gun, there is nothing to fear.'

(93) ja̯o   [ʔah   kɯɲ   nɔh   gah   nɔh]ᵢ kɯm   yi̯am kah   []ᵢ
     reason   [talk   father 3SGⱼ   to   3SGᵢ]ᵢ so   weep   **kah** []ᵢ
     'Because his father told him off, he cried (about it).'

3.2.3 Serial verb constructions (SVC)

Nuclear serial verb constructions in Wa are typical of Mainland Southeast Asian languages. Modals can combine freely in contiguous series with a main verb, as in (94) and (95).

(94) ʔaŋ   pu̯i   **ciʔ** sut   mu   koc   pian   tɛʔ
     NEG   person **can** pick.up   CLF   light on   earth
     'No one can pick up the sunlight on the ground.'

(95) ʔɤʔ   **taŋ**   yṳh   s.rṳ
     1SG   **must**   do   self
     'I must do [it] myself.'

Several modals can occur together, as in (96).

(96) s.mɛ̤   gat   **ciʔ**   saŋ   pɔ̤n   dɔc   tạ̄i   mhɔm   s.glṳm?
     seed   how   **can**   will   get   grow   flower   good   bunch
     'How could seeds like these be cultivated into fine flowers?'

3.2.4 Coordinating conjunction tiʔ

While 'asymmetrical' serial verb constructions of this type are common in Wa, 'symmetrical' SVCs are not found. If the additional verb is not a modal or a verb which has underdone grammaticalization to at least a partial extent, or optionally if it is, the coordinating conjunction *tiʔ* (glossed here as CONJ) is used to co-ordinate two verbs (one of which may be a modal) or verb phrases, which may be either two aspects of a single action or consecutive, discrete actions, or somewhere between the two. In this respect it is strikingly similar to the Burmese conjunction ပြီး *pyi³*, grammaticalized from the verb ပြီး *pyi³* 'finish'. In Burmese constructions VERB₁ *pyì* VERB₂, the two verbs may refer to two distinct actions, or two aspects of a single activity (see Romeo 2008: ch. 7; Vittrant, this volume, table 13, p. 99).

tiʔ is homonymous with a reflexive pronoun *tiʔ* and interrogative *tiʔ* 'what', but nonetheless it is not clear what the source lexeme for conjunctive *tiʔ* might be; there is certainly no obvious verbal candidate. The following sentences (97)–(100) illustrate the function of *tiʔ*, in which the verbs conjoined form part of a single event with the same subject and shared tense, aspect, modality and polarity.

(97) nɔh   ciʔ   tiʔ   plɛ̤   loʔ   mạn   khạn   loʔ   vaʔ
     3SG   can   CONJ   translate   speech   Burma   from   speech   Wa
     'He can translate from Wa into Burmese.'

(98) paih   tiʔ   phɛʔ   pliʔ
     peel   CONJ   eat   fruit
     'Peel and eat fruit [two activities co-occurring].'
     (Or also 'Peel fruit and [then] eat it.')

(99) lại   pa   mhaŋ mai? ti?   vại   ʔaŋ   koi
     book   REL   ask   2SG   CONJ borrow not   have
     'The book you asked to borrow isn't there.'

(100) gụn   ti?   yụh kạn
      endure CONJ do   work
      'work persistently.'

3.3 Clausal/sentential organization

It seems that word-order in Wa is VSO, although SVO is also common. It is difficult to know which of the two orders may be considered 'basic'. It may be on the one hand that VSO word-order is basic, but that the verb-initial order is disrupted due to the influence of SVO Chinese, and perhaps also of SOV Burmese. On the other hand, it may be that SVO is the basic word-order, but VSO is frequently preferred for reasons of emphasis or focus. In the absence of compelling evidence to sway the argument one way or the other, it remains the case that VSO word order is very common in Wa, and this is a feature worthy of note since it distinguishes Wa from the norm in Mainland Southeast Asian languages. Xiao Zegong (1981) observes that the difference between the two orders is a matter of focus and emphasis.

Looking in closer detail, it seems that rather than having a preference for VSO order *per se*, Wa likes the subject to be the second element, following the verb in (101), both the verb and the modal ((102) and (103)), or the negative *ʔaŋ* (104). In addition to the appearance of this word order, topicalized material may be fronted, as in (105).

(101) hoc   bʰauɯŋ tịn   kʰạn   plak   lʰaoŋ
      come   wind   big   from   side   north
      'a strong wind came from the north'

(102) cị?   gʰraoh ʔɤ?   gʰraoh kɔn.doi va?   ŋɛ
      can   dance   1SG   dance   orphan   Wa   only
      'I can only dance the Wa orphan dance'

(103) saŋ   gạc   ʔɤ?   ŋai   mai?   yạo?
      want   look.at   1SG   face   2SG   see
      'I want to have a look at your face.'

(104) ʔaŋ   ʔɤʔ   lai   pon   kan   jʰɔm   nɔh.
      NEG   1SG   anymore   can   tolerate attitude   3SG
      'I can no longer put up with his attitude.'

(105) lɔk.cɡoŋ   pa   ʔaŋ   ʔɤʔ   sum   cɯp
      leggings   which   NEG   1SG   want   wear
      'The leggings which I don't want to wear.'

3.3.1 Ellipsis of arguments

In slight contrast to many languages in the Mainland Southeast Asian area, definite arguments in Wa tend to be pronominalized and retained, rather than being ellided altogether, even if they are recoverable from the context. Similarly, as illustrated in section 4.2.2.g above, the *kah* of *kah*-headed prepositional phrases is often retained, even in contexts where information is recoverable from the context.

3.3.2 Topicalization

The organization of sentences in Wa very frequently follows the 'topic-prominent' tendency which is normal for Mainland Southeast Asian languages. The data in sentences (89)–(92) above are relevant examples of sentences where topicalized material has been fronted. Wa does not mark topics overtly with grammatical markers.

3.3.3 *Pa*-headed nominalized clauses

Wa makes very frequent use of focus-cleft constructions using relativizer *pa*, analagous to the Chinese 是...的 *shì...de* construction (Zimmerman et al. 2008). In such constructions, the material in focus is nominalized with the relativizer *pa*, as in (106) and may additionally be fronted, as in (107).

(106) [ŋhoʔ   gaoʔ]ᵢ mɔ̰h   pa   ʔui   ʔeʔ   ju̹   tiʔ   kah   [Ø]ᵢ   hɤi.
      [rice   rice]ᵢ is   REL   feed   we   life   REFL   by   [Ø]ᵢ   EXCL
      'Rice is the thing that we sustain our life with!'

(107) pa   daŋ   kɔɲ   pui   kah   [Ø]ᵢ   mɔh   [pui   pɛ]ᵢ
      REL   much   hate   people PREP   [Ø]ᵢ   is   people   deceive
      'What people despise most of all is liars.'

3.3.4 Question formation

The formation of questions in Wa follows the pattern observed by Clark (1985) to be typical of Mainland Southeast Asian languages. Yes-no questions can be formed using one of the sentence-final particles listed in (123), some of which are neutral interrogatives while others have certain attitudinal or pragmatic implications. *Wh*-questions are formed using an unremarkable set of *wh*-question words *in situ* with no sentence-final particle. In addition, questions may be formed using an tag-question particle, such as in (125).

4 Semantics and pragmatics

This section shows that Wa is predictably rich in those semantic domains which are expected to be so in Mainland Southeast Asian language.

4.1 Common semantic domains

4.1.1 Food

Wa has four terms for rice, shown in (108), but food is referred to in general terms using the three terms in (109).

(108) kla   rice seedling
      ŋʰoʔ   uncooked rice (husks on)
      gaoʔ   uncooked rice (husks off)
      ʔup   cooked rice

(109) ʔup   cooked rice
      prɛ̣ʔ   food and drink
      puan   food (other than grain)

Various basic words for eating are used, depending on what is being eaten, in addition to a good number of words for snacking. The verb *ih* is semantically broad, meaning 'use', but it is used generally for eating and drinking (as well as for wearing clothes, collecting, adhering to religion, etc). Some more restricted collocations are found in addition – see the examples in (110).

(110)
verb	example	translation
ʔih	ʔih prɛʔ	'consume food / drink.'
	ʔih s.dah	'take medicine.'
	ʔih s.bẹʔ	'wear clothes.'
	ʔih kʰɔ	'use a hoe.'
sɔm	sɔm ʔɯp	'eat rice.'
ŋɑɯʔ	ŋɑɯʔ plai	'drink alcohol.'
pʰɛʔ	pʰɛʔ pliʔ	'eat fruit.'
rʰɯp	rʰɯp	'drink tea, drink soup.'
yɔt	yɔt sɯp	'smoke tobacco.'
	yɔt plai	'drink alcohol.'

4.1.2 Washing

Another domain in the lexicon which is richly represented in Wa is that of washing, as illustrated in (111). The verbs in (111) all mean 'wash'or 'clean', but each is restricted to a specific semantic domain.

(111)
verb	semantic domain	example	
kʰoc	face/hands	kʰoc ŋai	wash face
pʰak	objects (also teeth)	pʰak ʔɔ	wash cooking pots
hɯm	child	hɯm kɔn ɲɔm	bathe a child
s.gʰrah	vegetables, food	s.gʰrah taɯʔ	rinse vegetables
s.daɯʔ	clothes	s.daɯʔ krɑɯŋ	wash clothes

4.1.3 Cutting

Like other Southeast Asian languages, the Wa lexicon caters very generously for the semantic domains of cutting, carrying and drying. (112) is a selection of cutting words from the Wa Dictionary (Watkins 2013), excluding those which seem to be derived from nouns (e.g. *sa* 'scythe > cut with a scythe').

(112) bɑ̰ɯʔ cut, sever.
gṳ cut, chop.
gam ~ gaɲ ~ grɑ̰ chop wildly, hack (meat)
gḛh hack, chop recklessly.
gʰlɔk carve, incise, cut.
ki̤ah peel, cut off rind (with a knife).
kip cut (with scissors).
kit ~ ki̤t cut, chop, hit, whack
krɑ̰k scratch, cut, abrade.
kʰak ~ kʰik cut, pare, peel
kʰloi chop, slash, hack, notch, gouge.
kʰluh cut off, chop off, break off
kʰrḛ cut, chop
lḛ ~ lɛk split off, cut off, pull away from
mak ~ mṳak ~ mṵk cut, cut off, sever
jʰia slit, slash, cut into strips
ŋe cut into sections
pat cut
pʰɔi chop, cut
piah slit, slash, cut into slices
pit cut off, dock, cut short
pɔ̰l cut, scratch
rʰip cut (with scissors)
rʰih cut, scratch
ri̤t saw, cut (planks)
s.gri̤h cut open, break, split
sit cut, slice, chop
tat cut, cut off, break off
tʰak cut, shovel
tʰah cut wood (with an adze)
tʰaŋ cut, chop
tʰum cut (large timber)
tuah cut off, cut, harvest
vit slice horizontally, cut off
vɔ̰k ~ vo̰c ~ s. vo̰c slice off, hack away, chop off

4.1.4 Carrying

Similarly, Wa verbs of carrying enable fine distinctions. Of particular interest is (113), a pair of back-carrying verbs *pɯih* and *kɔk*, which encode the gender of the carrier.

(113) *pɯih*   carry with strap on forehead supporting basket on back (women)
      kɔk   carry on back (firewood, etc. with ropes (men)

For other carrying verbs, the part of the body involved in the carrying or the method of lifting is specified, shown in (114).

(114) *pɯʔ*   carry (a load or person) on the back
      yaok   lift or carry between both hands
      kaŋ kao   carry on the shoulders
      gu   carry on the shoulder
      cah   drape over the shoulders, carry on or over head
      kʰɔp   carry (putting arms round)
      gao   carry on back
      gɯɲ   carry on back (e.g. a child)
      klɔm ~ s.grɔŋ carry (on shoulder, in the hands, between two people)

(115) lists a number of more general verbs of carrying or transportation.

(115) *giaŋ*   carry, bring, transport
      baʔ
      don
      vɛʔ
      tɯi
      tɔ
      taŋ   carry (using animals)

4.1.5 Drying

Drying verbs, shown in (116), distinguish between verbs of drying in the sun, by a fire or more generally.

(116) dʰa ~ da   dry in the sun
     piŋ
     toŋ
     yaŋ
     hok

     ka   dry by the fire, roast
     rẹŋ

     kroh   dry up, dry out
     hit
     kʰraɲ
     kʰriam
     gʰroh
     s.ʔoh

4.1.6 Pushing and manipulating objects

Verbs of pushing, shown in (117), allow for fine distinctions in meaning, according to the detail of the direction and force of the action being performed.

(117) pạc   shovel, push aside, scrape away (soil), scratch (face).
     pạm ~ pɯm ~ pɯ pạm ~ pɯ pạɲ   bump about, bang against
     tɯih ~ tɯɲ   bump into, bang (against, into, on), stub (toe).
     tx̌h   tap, touch, bump lightly
     tiah ~ tɯih   bump, bang, hit, strike, knock, beat, bump, smash, bang (into sth.)
     kɯ ~ kɯih   poke, butt, pile up
     krɯt   cram in, shove in.
     krɛ̥h   nudge, flick
     kuah ~ kuaih   push lightly, brush aside, pull up
     ɲʰɯn ~ ɲʰot   push, press on.
     cọt   push, push over
     kʰɯn   move aside, push to one side
     lɯih   bump, tap
     lɯ̣ih   roll away, push away
     jʰuih   poke, shove

pʰɛt	bump into, bang against, touch
riah	push aside, move away, spread out
s.ŋḛʔ	push, shove
tʰun ~ tʰuʔ	push
tʰeh	knock, bump
tʰui	push
tʰuʔ tʰiʔ	push and squeeze, jostle
viɲ	push aside, move away

4.1.7 Spatial deixis

Spatial deixis in Wa allows the conventional distinction common in Southeast Asian languages between here, there and far, as in (118). Beyond this three-way disctinction, further vowel alternations allow for a further 'far distant' disctinction, but these forms are probably not basic to the language and seem to be subject to some dialect variation.

(118) *tin* 'here'   *teh* 'over there'
  tan 'there'   *tiun* 'far away yonder'
  ten 'yonder'

There is also a set of terms to encode spatial relations in a way which has clearly become well adapted to the geographical context in which Wa is spoken, referring to direction up and down slopes, upstream and downstream and so on, listed in (119).

(119) *bla̰oŋ*   slope leading up, seen from bottom
  juɯ   slope leading down, seen from top

  la̰oŋ ~ loŋ ~ liɲ   upper side, uphill side
  seh ~ sḭuh ~ s.sḭh ~ s. sḭuh   lower side, downhill side
  sen   further down

  pḭaŋ   top, above, on
  grɯm   below, underneath

  ta̰oh   upstream
  cɔ̰   downstream

lʰɛʔ   lih   juɯ,   kɯ   haok   blaoŋ.
rain   descend   downhill,   gale   ascend   uphill.
'Rain goes downhill, a gale goes uphill.'

vuɯih plak   laoŋ mɔh plai,   vai   plak   seh   mɔh   prɛʔ.
face direction up   COP rice_beer, face direction down   COP   food.
'Looking up there's rice beer, looking down, there's food.' [An expression describing the abundance of a place or a festive occasion.]

4.2 Pragmatics & discourse

4.2.1 Final particles

As is the case in other Southeast Asian languages, the rich array of utterance-final particles is often the hardest syntactic category in the lexicon to describe adequately. The selection of phrase-final particles listed in (120), taken from Zhou and Yan (1984) and the Wa Dictionary (Watkins 2013), all await fine-grained analysis, but seem to fall into the broad categories shown.

(120) emphasis   pɔʔ, plɤi, tịt, ha, hɤi, lʰaoʔ, kʰɯ, kʰɤ
      supposition/suggestion   mai, nɛh, vai, ʔɔ ~ ʔɔʔ
      confirmation   lẹ
      declaration   ŋɛh

(121) jʰak   hɤi
      look   EMPH
      'Look!'

(122) kɛt   saɯʔ   ŋɛh
      very   hurt   EMPH
      'It really hurts!'

Interrogative particles are listed in (123) and tag-question particles in (125).

(123) interrogative particles   pah
                                 lah ~ laih ~ lɛ ~ lɛh ~ lʰɛʔ
                                 nɛ
                                 hɛh

(124) saŋ   hu   mai?   pa̠h
      want   go   2.SG   Q
      'Do you want to go?'

(125) tag question particles hɔ?, lɛ?

(126) pɔ̠   ge̠   mai?   yu̠h.nan   hɔ?
      NEG.IMP   play   2.SG   like.that   TAG.Q
      'Don't play around like that.'

4.2.2 Politeness

Like other northern Mon-Khmer languages, but in contrast to many other Southeast Asian languages, Wa pronouns, shown in (52) above, do not obligatorily encode hierarchy, formality or solidarity.

Much like other Southeast Asian languages, people address each other in Wa using forms of address based on birth-order names, kinship terms or relative generation rather than pronouns. Wa does not have an evolved system of honorific or humilific language, but (127) gives examples of resepctful terms of address.

(127)
	gloss	used to address
ta?	grandfather	older men
ya̠?	grandmother	older women
?ac	brother-in-law	man of same generation
pa?	you (2.DU)	married woman with children
giex	you (2.PL)	mature married woman with children

5 Conclusion/ summary

In conclusion, it can be said that Wa shares a large number of characteristics with other Mainland Southeast Asian languages, in particular Tai-Kadai and Mon-Khmer. There are, on the other hand, a number of typological features that are less typical in a Mainland Southeast Asian context, such as the rich inventory of initial consonants (especially aspirated voiced stops), preferred VSO word order, the placement of auxiliaries (or secondary verbs) in the preverbal position, etc. The influence of Wa's neighbours, both the culturally dominant Chinese to the north and the Tai/Shan with whom the Wa live in close proximity, is particularly marked. Apart from some lexical borrowing, Burmese has had relatively little influence on Wa.

References

Clark, Marybeth. 1985. Asking questions in Hmong and other southeast Asian languages. *Linguistics of the Tibeto-Burman Area* 8 (2). 60–67.
Diffloth, Gérard. 1980. The Wa languages. *Linguistics of the Tibeto-Burman Area* 5 (2). 1–182.
Diffloth, Gérard. 1989. On the Bulang (Blang, Phang) Languages. *Mon Khmer Studies* 18–19. 35–43.
Enfield, Nick J. 2005. Areal linguistics and mainland Southeast Asia. In *Annual Review of Anthropology* 34. 181–206.
Ferlus, Michel. 1974. Les langues du groupe austroasiatique-nord. *Asie du sud-est et monde insulindien* (ASEMI) 5 (1). 39–68.
Henderson, Eugénie J. A. 1952. The main features of Cambodian pronunciation. *Bulletin of the School of Oriental and African Studies* 14. 149–174.
Henderson, Eugénie J. A. 1965. The topography of certain phonetic and morphological characteristics of South-East Asian languages. *Lingua* 15. 400–434.
Lewis, M. Paul (ed.). 2009. *Ethnologue: Languages of the world*, 16th ed. Dallas, TX: SIL International. http://www.ethnologue.com (accessed 1 June 2018).
Luó, Zhījī 罗之基. 1995. *Wǎzú shèhuì lìshǐ yú wénhuà* 佤族社会历史与文化 [History and culture of Wa society]. Běijīng: Zhōngyāng mínzú dàxué chūbǎnshè.
Matisoff, James A. 1973. Tonogenesis in South East Asia. In Hyman (ed.), *Consonant types and tone*, 71–95. Southern California Occasional Papers in Linguistics No. 1.
Matisoff, James A. 1986. Hearts and minds in South-East Asian languages and English: An essay in the comparative lexical semantics of psycho-collocation. *Cahiers de Linguistique d'Asie Orientale* 15 (1). 5–57.
Norman, Jerry. 1988. *Chinese*. Cambridge: Cambridge University Press.
Okano, Kenji. 2005. The verb 'give' as a causativiser in colloquial Burmese. In Justin Watkins (ed.), *Studies in Burmese Linguistics*, 97–104. Canberra: Pacific Linguistics.
Romeo, Nicoletta. 2008. *Aspect in Burmese: Meaning and function*, vol. 96. Amsterdam: John Benjamins.
Shorto, Harry L. 1963. The structural patterns of the northern Mon-Khmer languages. In Harry L. Shorto (ed.), *Linguistic comparison in South East Asia and the Pacific*, 45–61. London: School of Oriental and African Studies.
Svantesson, Jan-Olof. 1983. *Kammu phonology and morphology*. Travaux de l'Institut de Linguistique de Lund 18. Lund: Gleerup.
Wáng, Jīngliú 王敬骝 & Chén Xiāngmù 陈相目 1981. Wǎyǔ Àishuāi huà de yīnwěi xìtǒng 佤语岩帅话的音位系统 [The sound system of Yaongsoi Wa]. *Mínzú xuébào* 民族学报 1981, reproduced in Wáng Jīngliú et al. (eds.), 1994: 39–57.
Wáng, Jīngliú 王敬骝 & Chén Xiāngmù 陈相目 1984. Wǎyǔ cí de xíngtài biànhuà 佤语词的形态变化 [Morphological alternations in Wa words]. *Mínzú diàochá yánjiū* 民族调查研究 [Nationalities Research]. Reprinted in Wáng Jīngliú et al. (eds.), 1994: 117–129.
Wáng Jīngliú 王敬骝, Zhāng Huàpéng 张化鹏, XiāoYùfēn 肖玉芬 & Wèi Ānxiáng 魏安祥 1992. *Loux Gāb Vax (Wǎyǔ shúyǔ huìshì)* 佤语熟语汇释. Kunming: Yunnan Minzu Chubanshe.

Wáng Jīngliú 王敬骝, Zhāng Huàpéng 张化鹏 & XiāoYùfēn 肖玉芬, (eds.). 1994. *Nbēen Loux. Vāx* / Wǎyǔ yánjiū 佤语研究 [Research on Wa]. Kūnmíng: Yúnnán mínzú chūbǎnshè.

Vittrant, Alice. 2013. 16 Psycho-collocational expressives in Burmese. *The aesthetics of grammar: Sound and meaning in the languages of Mainland Southeast Asia*, 255–279. New York: Cambridge University Press.

Watkins, Justin. 2002. *The phonetics of Wa*. Canberra: Pacific Linguistics 531.

Watkins, Justin. 2013. *Dictionary of Wa*. Leiden: Brill.

Xiāo, Zégōng 肖则贡. 1981. *Wǎyǔzhōng zhǔyǔ hé wèiyǔ de yǔxù* 佤语中主语和谓语的语 序 [Subject and predicate word-order in Wa]. Reprinted in Wáng et al. (eds.), 1992: 163. Kunming: Yunnan Minzu Chubanshe.

Zhōu, Zhízhì 周直志 & Yán Qíxiāng 颜其香. 1984. *Wǎyǔ jiǎnzhì* 佤语简志 [Handbook of Wa]. Běijīng: Mínzú chūbǎnshè.

Appendix 1: Summary of linguistic features

Legend
+++ the feature is pervasive or used obligatorily in the language
++ the feature is normal but selectively distributed in the language
+ the feature is merely possible or observable in the language
− the feature is impossible or absent in the language

	Feature	+++/++/+/−	§ ref. in this chapter
Phonetics	Lexical tone or register	+++	§1.1, p.434
Phonetics	Back unrounded vowels	+++	§1.1.2, p.436
Phonetics	Initial velar nasal	+++	§1.1.1, p.434–35
Phonetics	Implosive consonants	−	−
Phonetics	Sesquisyllabic structures	++	§1.2.1, p.437
Morphology	Tendency towards monosyllabicity	++	§1.2.1, p.437
Morphology	Tendency to form compounds	+++	§2.1, p.440
Morphology	Tendency towards isolating (rather than affixation)	+++	§1.2.1, p.437
Morphology	Psycho-collocations	++	§2.2, p.443
Morphology	Elaborate expressions (e.g. four-syllable or other set patterns)	+++	§2.3, p.444
Morphology	Reduplication generally	+	§2.3.2, p.444
Morphology	Reduplication of nouns	−	−
Morphology	Reduplication of verbs	−	−
Grammar	Use of classifiers	++	§3.1.2, p.449

	Feature	+++/++/+/−	§ ref. in this chapter
Grammar	Classifiers used in counting	+++	§3.1.2, p.449
Grammar	Classifiers used with demonstratives	++	§3.1.1, p.448
Grammar	Adjectival verbs	+++	not discussed explicitly
Grammar	Grammatical number	+	not discussed explicitly
Grammar	Inflection of verbs	−	§3.2.1, p.450
Grammar	Use of tense/aspect markers	++	§3.2.1, p.450
Grammar	Use of verb plural markers	−	−
Grammar	Grammaticalization of GET/OBTAIN (potential mod. resultative/perfect aspect)	+++	§3.2.2.b, p.452
Grammar	Grammaticalization of PUT, SET (completed/resultative aspect)	+	§3.2.2.f, p.454
Grammar	Grammaticalization of GIVE (causative, benefactive; preposition)	+	§3.2.2.d, p.453
Grammar	Grammaticalization of FINISH (perfective/ complete aspect; conjunction/temporal subordinator)	−	§3.2.1, p.450, see also §3.2.4, p.457
Grammar	Grammaticalization of directional verbs e.g. GO / COME (allative, venitive)	−	−
Grammar	Grammaticalization of SEE, WATCH (temptative)	++	§3.2.2.c, p.452
Grammar	Grammaticalization of STAY, REMAIN (progressive and continuous, durative aspects)	+++	§3.2.2.e, p.454
Grammar	Serial verb constructions	++	§3.2.3, p.456
Syntax	Verb precedes object (VO)	+	§3.3, p.458
Syntax	Auxiliary precedes verb	+	§3.2.2, p.451
Syntax	Preposition preceds noun	+	§3.2.2.g, p.454
Syntax	Noun precedes adjective	+++	§3.1.1, p.448
Syntax	Noun preceds demonstrative	+++	§3.1.1, p.448
Syntax	Noun precedes genitive		§3.1.1, p.448
Syntax	Noun precedes relative clause	+++	§3.1.1, p.448
Syntax	Use of topic-comment structures	++	§3.3, p.458–59

	Feature	+++/++/+/−	§ ref. in this chapter
Syntax	Ellipsis of arguments known from context	++	§3.3.1, p.460
Lexical semantics	Specific terms for forms of rice	+++	§4.1.1, p.460
Pragmatics	Use of utterance-final pragmatic particles	+++	§4.2.1, p.466
Pragmatics	Encoding of politeness	−	§4.2.2, p.467
Pragmatics	Encoding of honorifics	−	−

Appendix 2: Text interlinearized

The following passage in Wa is taken from Wang and Chen (1993).

dɯ   ʔot   grɔŋ   koi
place   live   situation   exist
'dwellings and living conditions'

hak.tɛʔ   ɲɛʔ   yauŋ   pa.rauk,   jiet   ʔot   kah   pian   gɔŋ,   ŋac
land   house village   Wa,   really   be.at   PREP   top   mountain, fragrant

gɔŋ   dɯ   s.dɔm
mountain   place   level
'Villages in the Wa lands are located in the mountains, on a level place high up in the mountains.'

yam   jauuh   pɯi   tiʔ   paŋ   laih   blaih   yauŋ
time   start   people   CONJ   grow   street   expand   village
'When people found a village'

pɯi   kɔn   pih   mɔc   yɯh   klɔŋ   s.vɣi
people   children   pray   spirit   make   river   before
'first of all the people pray to the river spirit'

tɔm   mɔc   mʰɔm,   pɯi   tɔm   sum   ɲɛʔ   saŋ   yauŋ.
advise   spirit   good,   people   then   build   house   build   village
'if the spirit gives good signs, people then put up their houses and build the village.'

ɲɛʔ   mọc   bian   kaŋ   ʔot   pian   yauŋ   plak   dɔm
house spirit place   head   be.at on   village side   right
'The spirit's tree (home) is at the top of the village on the right-hand side.'

pụi   taŋ   sɔk   dụu   ʔot   pak   gụaŋ   ɲɛʔ   yauŋ   tiʔ.
people oneself seek   place be.at open.up plot   house   village REFL
'People individually choose the plot to build their houses on.'

yạm   diʔ,   pụi   kɔn   taŋ   gụah   mɯ   lụk   rụ,   tiʔ   rụ
time   past,   people child oneself   allocate divide split   clan, one   clan

ʔot   tiʔ   baoh.
be.at one   area
'In the past, people were allocated a plot according to their clan, each clan in a separate area.'

hak.tɛʔ hɔc   pak   pụi,   pụi   ciʔ   tiʔ   siau ; ʔaŋ   ciʔ   tiʔ   cọih,
land   PERF open.up people, people can   CONJ   use,   not   can   CONJ   sell
'Once people have developed the land, they can make use of it but cannot sell it.'

ʒin   pụi   lɤi   suɨŋ   sɯm   ɲɛʔ   kah   hak.tɛʔ   s.bụm   pạuʔ.tiʔ
if   people then   want   put.up house   PREP   land   garden   RECIP
'If people then want to erect a house on someone else's land or garden'

pụi   kɔn   vɛʔ   lon   kịh,   gɛ   cʰaʔ,   blai   eeb
people child take   lump   salt,   packet   tea,   liquor   rice
'they take a block of salt, a packet of tea and some rice wine'

hu   cʰɔk.chɤɲ cau   ɲɛʔ   vɤi,   lɔm.lạu   mai   pạuʔ.tiʔ,
go   ask   master   house   before, discuss   with   RECIP
'and go to ask the head of the household first. They discuss with one another,'

tɔm   cau   ɲɛʔ   cụ   pụi   tɔm   tạɯk   pọn   sɯm   ɲɛʔ   kah.
then   master   house   allow   person then   only   can   put.up   house   PREP.
'and only then may the person build the house there.'

bụɯn   pa.rạuk,   ʔaŋ   pụi   saʔ   tʰian   gụaŋ   ɲɛʔ,
tradition   Wa,   NEG   person ever   argue   plot   house,
'In Wa tradition, people never argue over house plots,'

ca	hɔc	ciak	pui	saŋ	ʔot	guaŋ	ɲɛʔ	du	mɔʔ,
if	PERF	choose	person	want	be.at	plot	house	place	what

'once someone has decided where he wishes to locate his house,'

ca	hɔc	lɔm.lau	pui	nɔh	mai	pau? ti?	pui	mɔh	cu	pui	nɔh,
if	PERF	discuss	person	3SG	with	RECIP	person	is	allow	person	3SG

'once he has discussed it with others, people will allow him to do it.'

sin	cɔ	dauɯʔ	s.buɯm	pui,	sin	plauɯʔ	to	s.buɯm,
if	connect	place	garden	person,	if	destroy	body	garden,

'If it adjoins someone else's garden and damages the structure of their garden,'

plauɯʔ	khauʔ	pliʔ	paŋ	muah	pui,
destroy	tree	fruit	tree	banana	person,

'and harms their crops or trees,'

pui	duɯih	pʰɣiʔ	plut	pau?	cao	ʔan	ʔih	ŋɛ,
person	return	compensate	compensate	fellow	master	that	use	only

'then that person pays back to the owner in compensation only the amount used up.'

ʔaŋ	pui	doh kɛh	s.mah.s.mɔ	koi	kah.
NEG	person	at.all	bicker	envy	PREP

'People don't argue or feel resentment over it.'

ɲɛʔ	pa.rauʔ	sum	tiʔ	hɔt	kah	yuh	gɔŋ,
house	Wa	build	CONJ	follow	PREP	make	mountain

'Wa houses are built to suit the shape of the mountains'

kɔ	plak	lauŋ	hoc	plak	seh,	jiat	dia	tiʔ	hɔt	pauʔ,
start	side	high	come	side	low	just	lined.up	CONJ	follow	RECIP

'from high up to low down, lined up next to one another'

kok.buan	pui	nɔh	du	s.ɲai	jiat	s.du	mʰɔm	ɲɛ.
gaze.distance	person	3SG	place	far	just	equal	good	very

'If one looks at them from a distance they look very neat and tidy.'

cɣ	ɲɛʔ	ʔot	pa.rauʔ	koi	ra	cɣ	sum	tiʔ,
type	house	live	Wa	have	two	type	build	REFL,

'The are two types of building style of Wa houses.'

mɔh   ɲɛʔ   lʰauŋ   mai   ɲɛʔ   tɛʔ.
COP   house high   and   house earth
'which are "tall houses" and "earth houses".'

ɲɛʔ   lʰauŋ ʔot   pa.rɑuk, dẹʔ   ʔɔm   ɲɛʔ   lʰauŋ ʔot   siam nan.
house   tall   live Wa,   near   similar house tall   live Tai   like.that
'The tall houses which the Wa live closely resemble the tall houses inhabited by the Tai.'

plak   pịaŋ   mɔh   dṳ   ʔot   pṵi,
side   up   COP   place live   person
'The people live upstairs'

plak   grṳm   cị̌ʔ   tịʔ   plac   lịk   soʔ   ʔia   sim,   mɔi   krak
side   down   can   CONJ   contain pig   dog   chicken bird,   cattle, buffalo,

brɛ   kʰɔŋ,
animals   keep
'while downstairs they can keep pigs, dogs, chickens, birds, cattle, buffalo and livestock.'

ɟịʔ   tịʔ   ɣɾuʔ   khiʔ   kʰauʔ   kah.
can   CONJ   pile.up   wood   tree   PREP
'and they can store firewood.'

sum   ɲɛʔ   mɔh   sịau   pṵi   khauʔ, ʔoʔ,   ploŋ,
build   house   COP   use   person   wood,   bamboo, thatch,
'To build their houses, people use wood, bamboo, thatch,

mauʔ   dɔ.rɔn   mai   maux   mʰa ʔin kiʔ.
rope   Tripterygium.wilfordii and   rope   bamboo.strip
'vine-rope and bamboo binding strips.'

Hiroki Nomoto and Hooi Ling Soh
Malay

Introduction

Malay (*bahasa Melayu*) is a Western Malayo-Polynesian language in the Austronesian family. The standard varieties of Malay known as *bahasa Malaysia* and *bahasa Indonesia* are the national languages of Malaysia and Indonesia respectively. These two Malay varieties share a core grammar, with differences mainly in the phonology and lexicon. Besides Malaysia and Indonesia, Malay also enjoys official status in Brunei and Singapore, with different varieties being used in Thailand (mainly in the southern states where the ethnic Malays constitute the majority of the population), Timor-Leste (East Timor), Sri Lanka and Australia (Cocos and Christmas Islands).

In this article, we will focus on the standard variety of Malay spoken in Peninsular Malaysia, i.e. Standard Malay (see Appendix for a sample text). By Standard Malay we mean the variety used when conversing with people of various dialect backgrounds, but not the prescriptive language imposed by Dewan Bahasa dan Pustaka (DBP), an institution established by the Malaysian government to stardardize Malay and promote its use. Within Standard Malay, there exist two registers with considerable differences, viz. Formal Malay as the high variety and Colloquial Malay as the low variety in the sense of Ferguson (1959). As the high variety, Formal Malay enjoys high prestige, unlike Colloquial Malay which is sometimes described as 'broken' and 'lacking grammar'.[1] We will explicitly state which variety is in question when the relevant trait is characteristic of only one variety, but not both.

Peninsular Malaysia has been a multilingual society since at least when Malacca thrived as a centre of international trade in the 16th century. Malay was used in trade as a *lingua franca* for people from different parts of the world. It is

---

[1] See Nomoto and Shoho (2007) for other differences between Formal Malay and Colloquial Malay.

Hiroki Nomoto: Tokyo University of Foreign Studies
E-Mail: nomoto@tufs.ac.jp
Hooi Ling Soh: University of Minnesota
E-Mail: sohxx001@umn.edu

still a *lingua franca* for different ethnic groups within Malaysia, though nowadays English also serves the same function. Among the languages that have been influential as sources of new vocabulary are Sanskrit (before the arrival of Islam in the region in the 12th century), Arabic (after the arrival of Islam) and English (since the British colonization of Malacca in 1824). While contact between speakers of Malay and these languages occurred in limited settings and over limited periods of time (e.g. during trade), not all language contact situations share this characteristic. In particular, there was extended and consistent contact between Chinese and Malay in the context of mixed marriages between Chinese men and Malay women during the 15th and 16th centuries, which resulted in the emergence of a Malay-based creole Baba Malay (Lim 1988; Thurgood 1998). Direct encounters among speakers of different languages are not at all uncommon in the present-day Peninsular Malaysia, especially in medium and large-sized cities.

According to the Malaysia Department of Statistics, the total population of the country as of 2017 is approximately 32 million. It is estimated that about 65 per cent of the population speaks Malay as a first language whilst the rest of the population speaks it as a second language. Major languages spoken in Malaysia other than Malay include Chinese languages (especially Hokkien, Cantonese and Mandarin), Tamil and English.

1 Phonology

1.1 Suprasegmental phonology: tone and register

Distinct tones and registers (phonation types) do not exist in Malay. Lexical contrasts are made only segmentally. It is generally agreed that stress is not lexically distinctive in Malay in that it does not differentiate word meaning. However, there are discussions on whether the concept of 'word stress', namely that one or more syllable within a word is associated with a higher degree of prominence than the other syllables, is relevant for Malay. Some researchers assume the existence of word stress; a common characterization is that stress falls on the penultimate syllable of a word in the citation form, except when the penultimate syllable contains a schwa.[2] This observation dates back at least to

---

[2] It should be noted that there are other descriptions of word stress in Malay/Indonesian. In addition to the pattern described above, stress has also been described as falling on the final syllable, or sometimes on the penultimate syllable and sometimes on the final syllable. These

Winstedt (1920: 4). However, there are also authors who question the relevance of word stress in Malay/Indonesian. For example, Halim (1981: 86–88) claims that there is no word stress in Indonesian, and that the distribution of stress in words is of exactly the same pattern as the distribution of stress in units larger than words, which he refers to as 'pause-units'.[3] A recent acoustic study by Zuraidah et al. (2008), in our evaluation of it, confirms the validity of Halim's observation in Malay, though the authors attempt to draw rather different conclusions. Along a slightly different line, though also questioning the relevance of word stress, Gil (2007) argues that stress falls on a foot rather than on a syllable in Riau Indonesian.

1.2 Segmental phonemes: consonants and vowels

The consonant phonemes in Malay can be classified into two types: those native to Malay (summarized in Figure 1) and those borrowed from other languages, especially Arabic and English (summarized in Figure 2). Some borrowed consonants are often substituted by phonetically similar native consonants, which are given in parentheses.

p	b	t	d			k	g	(ʔ)[4]
	m		n		ɲ		ŋ	
		r						
			s				h	
			tʃ	dʒ				
		l						
w				j				

Figure 1: Native consonants in Malay

f (p)   v   z   ʃ   x (k, h)   ɣ (g)   q (k)

Figure 2: Borrowed consonants and their native substitutes in Malay

---

varying descriptions may be due in part to authors' describing different regional or social varieties of Malay/Indonesian (see Tadmor 2000).
3 In Halim's original generalization, the term 'accent' is used instead of 'stress'.
4 The glottal stop (ʔ) is in parentheses, as its phonemic status is unclear.

All consonants can occur in the word-initial position. The stops are usually realized without aspiration, though the presence or absence of aspiration does not lead to lexical contrast. The presence of phonemic prenasalized voiced obstruents has been reported in many Austronesian languages (Klamer 2002; Donohue 2004). However, where Malay is concerned, we are not aware of any variety in which prenasalized obstruents are phonemically distinguished from plain ones, except for Sri Lanka Malay, which acquired phonemic prenasalized stops /ᵐb, ⁿd, ᶮɟ, ᵑg/ as a result of contact with Sinhala (Nordhoff 2009: 96–99). Prenasalized obstruents appear to only occur as allophones in some varieties of Malay such as Sarolangun Malay spoken in Jambi, Indonesia (Cole et al. 2008). Most native roots in Malay are disyllabic, of the CV.CV(C) pattern. Initial consonant clusters are only found in loan words. Examples of loan words from Sanskrit and English are listed in (1).

(1) a. Loan words from Sanskrit
       *sw*asta 'private', *dw*ibahasa 'bilingual', *pr*asangka 'prejudice'
    b. Loan words from English
       *dr*ama 'drama', *kl*ausa 'clause', *kr*isis 'crisis', *sp*ek 'spectacles', *st*esen 'station', *tr*adisi 'tradition', *skr*ip 'script', *str*uktur 'structure'

Not all consonant phonemes can occur word-finally. Native Malay phonology allows only the following consonants in the word-final position: /p, t, k, m, n, ŋ, r, s, h, l/. Notice that the palatal nasal /ɲ/ is not included. In Peninsular Malaysia, there is a tendency to reduce final syllables in some way, either through the complete elimination of the coda or the elimination of the place feature of the final coda consonant.[5] This tendency is particularly evident in northern dialects. For example, in Kelantan Malay, final nasal consonants are dropped and the preceding vowel is nasalized as in (2a), and liquids are dropped as in (2b). Final stops lose their place features and are realized as a glottal stop as in (2c); /s/ is reduced to a glottal fricative as in (2d).

(2) Kelantan Malay
    a. /dalam/ → [dalɛ̃] 'inside'
    b. /mahal/ → [maha] 'expensive'
    c. /gəlap/ → [gəlaʔ] 'dark'
    d. /atas/ → [atah] 'top'

---

5 Sneddon (1993) points out a similar tendency towards final open syllables in languages in Sulawesi, Indonesia.

Some authors have noted that final voiced stops in loan words undergo devoicing to become voiceless (Farid 1980: 8–9; Teoh 1994: 53). However, Husni et al. (2006) claim that the devoicing is incomplete in that a final voiceless stop and a "devoiced" final voiced stop are not acoustically identical. Final consonant clusters are much more restricted than initial ones. No complex codas are allowed except in some loan words (e.g. se*ks* 'sex').

Standard Malay has six simple vowels /i, e, a, o, u, ə/ and three diphthongs /ai, au, oi/ (see Figure 3 for the inventory of simple vowels in Standard Malay). Vowel length is not distinctive.

Figure 3: The vowel system of Standard Malay

The vowel system in Standard Malay is thus considered simple compared to many Mainland Southeast Asian (MSEA) languages, which, according to Enfield (2005), commonly have nine simple vowel contrasts, often including a high central unrounded vowel (/ɨ/) and a number of complex vowel combinations. The Malay vowel system is perhaps more like Arakanese, which diverges from typical MSEA languages in having five simple vowel phonemes (the same ones as Standard Malay) and a diphthong /ai/ (Vittrant 2008). However, the number of vowel phonemes varies from dialect to dialect. It is common to find a vowel system with eight simple vowels consisting of the six vowels in Figure 3 and two additional half-open vowels /ɛ/ and /ɔ/ in northern dialects such as Kedah and Kelantan dialects (see Figure 4).

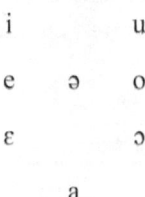

Figure 4: The vowel system of Kedah and Kelantan Malay

The vowel systems of these northern dialects are thus more in line with most MSEA languages such as Thai (Iwasaki and Ingkaphirom 2005), Lao, Vietnamese and Burmese, which have eight or nine simple vowels (Vittrant 2008). In fact, northern dialects of Malay share with Burmese the same eight simple vowels (Vittrant 2008). While the northern dialects generally have a vowel system that is more complex than Standard Malay, their consonant systems are usually reduced compared to Standard Malay, as mentioned above.

1.3 Syllable structure

Syllables in Malay consist of 0–3 onsets, a nucleus and 0–2 codas, i.e. (C)(C)(C)V(C)(C). However, as mentioned above, complex onsets and codas only occur in loan words. Thus, syllables in native words have one of the following structures: V, CV, VC, CVC. A sequence of two consonants at the syllable boundary, i.e. C_2 and C_3 in $C_1VC_2.C_3VC_4$, consist of either a /r/ (C_2) and another consonant (C_3) as in /pər.lu/ 'need', or a homorganic nasal + obstruent sequence, as in /sim.pan/ 'to save'. Sesquisyllables (Matisoff 1973), i.e. disyllabic words comprising a minor/atonal syllable followed by a full major syllable typically found in languages of MESA, have not been reported in Malay.

2 Morphology

2.1 Word structure

Malay is an agglutinating language, in which a word may consist of multiple morphemes. Thus, there is no particular tendency towards monosyllables in Malay, unlike many MSEA languages. Although there is no such tendency, many common words in Colloquial Malay have a reduced number of syllables in comparison with their Formal Malay counterparts. Some examples are given in Table 1.

Table 1: Reduced forms in Colloquial Malay

Formal Malay	Colloquial Malay	Meaning
tidak	tak	'not'
sudah	dah	'already'
hendak	nak	'will, to want'
sahaja, saja	aja, ja	'only'
ini	ni	'this'

Formal Malay	Colloquial Malay	Meaning
itu	tu	'that'
begitu	gitu	'like that'
sedikit	sikit	'a little, a few'
pergi	gi, pi	'to go'
perlahan	pelan	'slow'

Words in Malay may be formed through the attachment of affixes to roots. The number of productive affixes is relatively small in Malay. They can be categorized as (i) verbal, (ii) nominal, (iii) adjectival, and (iv) adverbial on the basis of the syntactic category of the affixed forms (Nik Safiah et al. 2008). A list of affixes and their functions (not exhaustive) are given in Table 2.

Table 2: Malay affixes and their functions

Category	Affix	Function(s)	Example(s)
(i) Verbal	meN-	active voice[6]	mem-baca 'to read' [baca 'to read']
		inchoative	mem-besar 'to grow' [besar 'big']
	di-	passive voice	di-besar-kan 'to be raised/enlarged' [besar 'big']
	ber-	possession	ber-makna 'to mean' [makna 'meaning']
		action	ber-doa 'to pray' [doa 'prayer']
	ter-	result state	ter-tutup 'to be closed' [tutup 'to close']
		accidental	ter-tidur 'to fall asleep' [tidur 'to sleep']
		ability	ter-kawal 'to be under control' [kawal 'to control']
	per-	to make more ...	(mem-)per-besar(-kan) 'to enlarge' [besar 'big']
	-kan	causative	(me-)naik-kan 'to raise (e.g. price)' [naik 'to rise']
	-i	locative	(me-)naik-i 'to climb (e.g. a mountain)' [naik 'to rise']
	ke- -an	adversative	ke-habis-an 'to run out of' [habis 'to finish']
(ii) Nominal	peN-	agent	peng-ajar 'teacher' [meng-ajar 'to teach']
	pe-	patient	pel-ajar 'student' [bel-ajar 'to learn']
	-an	result	ajar-an 'teaching, lesson' [di-ajar 'to be taught']
	peN- -an	action	peng-ajar-an 'teaching' [meng-ajar 'to teach']

---

6 The prefix meN- is standardly associated with active voice and is glossed as ACT throughout. However, this analysis of meN- is not uncontroversial, considering the aspectual effects of meN- discussed in recent works (Soh and Nomoto 2009, 2011; Soh 2013). See the discussion below and in section 3.2.1.

Category	Affix	Function(s)	Example(s)
	per- -an	action	pel-ajar-an 'learning, lesson' [bel-ajar 'to learn']
	ke- -an	abstract entity	ke-naik-an 'increase' [naik 'to rise']
(iii) Adjectival	se-	equative	se-besar 'as big as ...' [besar 'big']
	ter-	superlative	ter-besar 'biggest' [besar 'big']
(iv) Adverbial	se- -nya	as ... as possible, etc.	se-cepat-nya 'as quickly as possible' [cepat 'quick(ly)']

The verbal prefix *per-* is often preceded by the prefix *meN-* or *di-*. In Colloquial Malay, there is a tendency not to use the verbal prefix *meN-* (Benjamin 1993; Koh 1990: 153).

(3) a. Dia   sudah   mem-baca   novel   itu.   Formal Malay
       3SG   PFV   ACT-read   novel   that
       'S/he read the novel.'

    b. Dia   dah   baca   novel   tu.   Colloquial Malay
       3SG   PFV   read   novel   that
       'S/he read the novel.'

The reason for this tendency is arguably due to the fact that the denotation of a verb without *meN-* subsumes that of the corresponding *meN-* form (Soh and Nomoto 2011), and that colloquial speech may allow for more context-dependency. Degree achievement sentences like (4) illustrate this point most clearly. While a sentence with a verb without *meN-* can be used as either a telic or an atelic predicate, one with a *meN-* verb can be used only as an atelic one (Soh and Nomoto 2011, 2015).

(4) a. Harga   minyak   turun   selama/dalam   tiga   hari.
       price   oil   fall   for/in   three   day
       'The oil price fell for/in three days.'

    b. Harga   minyak   men-[t]urun   selama/*dalam   tiga   hari.
       price   oil   ACT-fall   for/in   three   day
       'The oil price was falling for three days.'

Besides affixation, compounding is also a productive morphological process in Malay. Compounds may be formed by the combination of two words of either the same or different syntactic categories. Examples are given below, with the syntactic category of each compound given in parentheses.

(5) N-N compounds
   a. *kereta api* 'train' (N)   [*kereta* 'car' + *api* 'fire']
   b. *matahari* 'sun' (N)   [*mata* 'eye' + *hari* 'day']

(6) A-A compounds
   a. *kurus kering* 'thin and haggard' (A)   [*kurus* 'thin' + *kering* 'dry']
   b. *kaya-raya* 'prosperous' (A)   [*kaya* 'rich' + *raya* 'great']

(7) V-V compounds
   a. *jual beli* 'trade' (N)   [*jual* 'to sell' + *beli* 'to buy']
   b. *temu bual* 'interview' (N)   [*temu* 'to meet' + *bual* 'to talk']

(8) P-P compounds
   a. *daripada* 'from (human, source)' (P)   [*dari* 'from' + *pada* 'at (human)']
   b. *kepada* 'to (human, target)' (P)   [*ke* 'to' + *pada* 'at (human)']

(9) N-A compounds
   a. *kerjasama* 'cooperation' (N)   [*kerja* 'work' + *sama* 'together']
   b. *kencing manis* 'diabetes' (N)   [*kencing* 'urine' + *manis* 'sweet']

(10) N-V compounds
   a. *bola sepak* 'football' (N)   [*bola* 'ball' + *sepak* 'to kick']
   b. *meja makan* 'dining table' (N) [*meja* 'table' + *makan* 'to eat']

(11) A-N compounds
   a. *setiausaha* 'secretary' (N)   [*setia* 'loyal' + *usaha* 'effort']
   b. *lebih masa* 'overtime (work)' (N)   [*lebih* 'more' + *masa* 'time']

(12) A-V compounds
   a. *salah guna* 'to misuse' (V)   [*salah* 'wrong' + *guna* 'to use']
   b. *kurang ajar* 'insolent' (A)   [*kurang* 'less' + *ajar* 'to teach']

(13) V-A compounds
   a. *kenal pasti* 'to identify' (V)   [*kenal* 'to recognize' + *pasti* 'certain']
   b. *(kerja) sukarela* 'voluntary (work)' (A)   [*suka* 'to like' + *rela* 'willing']

In standardized orthography, some compounds are written as two separate units demarcated by a hyphen or a space, while others are written as one unit.

As with other languages, Malay compounds may be categorized as endocentric or exocentric depending on how the elements of a compound relate to the compound with respect to their structure and meaning. Endocentric compounds are ones where one of the elements of the compound serves as the head of the compound. The meaning of an endocentric compound stands in a "type-of" relation with the meaning of the head of the compound. Examples of endocentric compounds are given in (14).

(14) Endocentric compounds
    a. *anak angkat* 'adoptee' (N)   [*anak* 'son/daughter' + *angkat* 'take']
    b. *harga mati* 'fixed price' (N)   [*harga* 'price' + *mati* 'dead']
    c. *ubi kayu* 'cassava' (N)   [*ubi* 'a kind of tuber' + *kayu* 'wood']
    d. *ibu jari* 'thumb' (N)   [*ibu* 'mother' + *jari* 'finger']

As shown in (14), endocentric nominal compounds in Malay may be left-headed or right-headed. (14a)–(14c) are left-headed in the sense that the left element of the compound determines the overall meaning and syntactic category of the compound. Thus, *anak angkat* 'adoptee' is a type of son/daughter, and *harga mati* 'fixed price' is a type of price, and so on. (14d) is right-headed in that *ibu jari* 'thumb' is a type of finger. Exocentric compounds on the other hand are ones without such a head. Examples are given below:

(15) Exocentric compounds
    a. *keras kepala* 'obstinate' (A)   [*keras* 'hard' + *kepala* 'head']
    b. *kecil hati* 'spiteful' (A)   [*kecil* 'small' + *hati* 'liver']
    c. *ibu bapa* 'parents' (N)   [*ibu* 'mother' + *bapa* 'father']
    d. *pergi balik* 'to travel back and forth' (V)   [*pergi* 'go' + *balik* 'return']

Compounds in Malay may also be categorized according to the semantic relationship that holds between the elements of the compound, in terms of whether the relation is one of coordination or subordination. Endocentric compounds involve a subordination relationship between the elements of the compound, as the elements of the compound do not have equal status. Some exocentric compounds such as (15c) and (15d) involve a coordinate relation between their constituent parts.

Being words rather than phrases (e.g. serial verb constructions), compounds can undergo further morphological processes such as affixation and reduplication.

(16) Affixation
    a. *ber-* + *kerjasama* 'cooperation' (N) = *bekerjasama* 'to cooperate' (V)
    b. *peN- -an* + *salah guna* 'to misuse' (V) = *penyalahgunaan* 'abuse' (N)
    c. *suka rela* 'voluntary' (A) + *-wan* = *sukarelawan* 'volunteer' (N)

(17) Reduplication
   a. *kakitangan-kakitangan* 'staffs' (N)
   b. *meja makan-meja makan* 'dining tables' (N)
   c. *sukarelawan-sukarelawan* 'volunteers' (N)

2.2 Psycho-collocations

Matisoff (1986: 9) defines a 'psycho-collocation' as "a polymorphemic expression referring as a whole to a mental process, quality, or state, one of whose constituents is a psycho-noun, i.e. a noun with explicit psychological reference (translatable by English words like HEART, MIND, SPIRIT, SOUL, TEMPER, NATURE, DISPOSITION, MOOD)." Many of the psycho-nouns are body-part terms. Psycho-collocations are common in Malay (Oey 1990). Examples are given below.

(18) *hati* 'heart, liver'[7]
   baik hati 'kind-hearted'   [*baik* 'good']
   besar hati 'glad, proud'   [*besar* 'big']
   hancur hati 'broken-hearted'   [*hancur* 'crushed']
   kecil hati 'narrow-minded'   [*kecil* 'small']
   keras hati 'persevering; obstinate' [*keras* 'hard']

(19) *kepala* 'head'
   kepala batu 'obstinate'   [*batu* 'stone']
   kepala berat, berat kepala 'stupid, dull'   [*berat* 'heavy']
   kepala besar 'proud'   [*besar* 'big']
   kepala dingin, dingin kepala 'cool-headed'   [*dingin* 'cold']
   ringan kepala 'clever, smart'   [*ringan* 'light']
   keras kepala 'stubborn'   [*keras* 'hard']

(20) *hidung* 'nose'
   hidung tinggi 'proud'   [*tinggi* 'high']
   keras hidung 'narrow-minded'   [*keras* 'hard']

(21) *mulut* 'mouth'
   berat mulut 'seldom talk, quiet'   [*berat* 'heavy']
   besar mulut 'brag'   [*besar* 'big']

---

7 See Goddard (2001) for other psycho-collocations with the noun *hati* 'heart, liver'.

(22) *muka* 'face'
    muka batu 'poker face'   [*batu* 'stone']
    muka manis 'sweetface'   [*manis* 'sweet']
    cari muka 'to brown-nose'   [*cari* 'to search']
    hilang muka 'to lose face'   [*hilang* 'to lose']
    tebal muka, muka tebal 'impudent'   [*tebal* 'thick']

(23) *telinga* 'ear'
    telinga nipis 'easily affronted'   [*nipis* 'thin']
    tebal telinga 'indifferent'   [*tebal* 'thick']

2.3 Elaborate expressions

Elaborate expressions usually have four syllables and are "rhyming/alliterative sound symbolic items" according to Enfield (2005). Their equivalents are referred to as 'pair-words' (in English) in Zainu'l-Abidin (1927).

Pair-words in Malay can be classified into three types. The first type is compounds comprising two distinct but phonologically similar words that convey related meanings. Examples are listed in (24).

(24) *kurus kering* 'thin and haggard' (= *kurus* 'thin' + *kering* 'dry')
    kaya-raya 'prosperous' (= *kaya* 'rich' + *raya* 'great')
    pecah belah 'disintegrated' (= *pecah* 'broken' + *belah* 'slit; side')

The second type can be analyzed as a type of rhythmic reduplication ('imitative reduplication' in Sneddon et al's (2010) term), whereby the base is repeated with changes in vowels and/or consonants. Examples of this type of pair-words are given in (25).

(25) a. Vowel alternation
       gunung-ganang 'mountain range' [*gunung* 'mountain']
       lenggak-lenggok 'to sway' [*lenggok* 'body movement when dancing']
       serba-serbi 'all sorts of' [*serba* 'all']
   b. Consonant alternation
       kuih-muih 'an assortment of cakes' [*kuih* 'cake']
       kacau-bilau 'chaotic' [*kacau* 'in disorder']
       saki-baki 'remainder' [*baki* 'remainder']
   c. Vowel and consonant alternation
       liang-liuk 'swaying' [*liuk* 'to turn to the left and right']

*beng**kang**-beng**kok*** 'winding' [*bengkok* 'crooked']
pi*ndah-**ra**ndah* 'to move constantly' [*pindah* 'to move']

The third type of pair-words involve neither compounding nor reduplication, and are referred to as 'inherently reduplicated words' in Nomoto (2012). While these "pair-words" appear to consist of two phonologically similar elements, neither of the apparent component parts cannot be considered the base. Examples are given in (26).

(26) *haru-biru* 'uproarious'
huru-hara 'clamourous'
dolak-dalik 'vacillating, uncertain'

Further information about Malay pair-words and their sound patterns can be found in Abdullah (1974: 71–72), Tham (1979), Mohd Yunus and Zaitul Azma (2011) and Nomoto (2012).

2.4 Reduplication

In addition to the rhythmic reduplication discussed in the last section, Malay also has full reduplication and partial reduplication. In full reduplication, the entire stem is repeated as in (27), while in partial reduplication only a part of the stem is repeated as in (28). Full reduplication of noun stems is associated with the explicit marking of plurality as will be elaborated further below.

(27) *pokok* 'tree(s)'   *pokok-pokok* 'trees'
buku 'book(s)'   *buku-buku* 'books'
pendapat 'opinion(s)' *pendapat-pendapat* 'opinions'

(28) *budak* 'kid(s)'   *be-budak* 'kids'
langit 'sky'   *le-langit* 'roof of the mouth'
berapa 'how many'   *be-berapa* 'several'

Stems of various syntactic categories can undergo full reduplication. The reduplication of different lexical categories is associated with different productive meanings. While full reduplication is in general productive in Malay, the productivity of partial reduplication is unclear. See Zaharani (2007: 59–60) for restrictions on partial reduplication in Malay.

The function of reduplication for noun stems is to express explicit plurality as mentioned in relation to (27) above. The plurality expressed is considered explicit because a bare NP such as *pokok* 'tree(s)' is number-neutral, and may refer to one or more trees, while its reduplicated form *pokok-pokok* 'trees' refers only to multiple trees. This use of reduplication is possible for all count nouns. The plural marking by reduplication here is considered 'ostensibly optional' in the sense that the denotation of the marked form (the reduplicated form) is a proper subset of the unmarked form (the bare NP). This is in contrast to 'genuinely optional' plural marking, where the denotations of the forms with and without marking are identical (see Nomoto 2013a). Because both a bare noun and a reduplicated noun can refer to plural entities, a question arises as to what governs the choice between the two. There is no clear answer to this question at the moment, though several factors have been offered in the literature. For example, Mintz (2002: 283) writes that a bare noun is used when the (plural) referents are seen as a unit, while a reduplicated form is used when they are seen as many individual parts. On the other hand, Nomoto (2013a) suggests that since bare NPs are vague with respect to singular and plural reference, when only multiple entities are intended as the referent, reduplication is obligatory. On a similar line, Sneddon et al. (2010: 20) state that in Indonesian, a noun is reduplicated only if the plurality of the referent is important to what the speaker wishes to convey, while Shiohara (2011, 2012) notes that the use of reduplicated nouns in Indonesian tends to occur when the referent is present visually.

Wh-words may be reduplicated in Malay. When they are reduplicated, they become indeterminates 'any X', as shown in (29).

(29) *apa* 'what' *apa-apa* 'anything'
 siapa 'who' *se-siapa/siapa-siapa* 'anybody'
 bila 'when' *bila-bila* 'anytime'

The reduplication of verbs has been associated with one of the following meanings: (i) repetitiveness, (ii) reciprocity and (iii) immediacy (see Mintz 2002: 295–297 and Asmah 1993: 203–210 for details). Examples are given in (30). Note that in V-V reduplication, only the stem is reduplicated.

(30) *muntah* 'to vomit'   *muntah-muntah* 'to keep on vomiting'
 ber- + *teriak* 'to shout'   *berteriak-teriak* 'to shout and shout'
 meN- + *tolong* 'to help'   *tolong-men-[t]olong* 'to help one another'
 meN- + *hormat* + *-i* 'to respect'   *hormat-menghormati* 'to respect each other'
 bangun 'to wake up'   *bangun-bangun* 'as soon as X wakes up'

The reduplication of adjectives and adverbs indicates intensity as shown below:

(31) *marah* 'angry'   *marah-marah* 'very angry'
     kecil 'small'   *kecil-kecil* 'very small'

(32) *jarang* 'rarely'   *jarang-jarang* 'very rarely'
     sering 'frequently' *sering-sering* 'very frequently'

Negation and auxiliaries may also be reduplicated. Reduplication does not appear to have a productive function in these cases.

(33) *bukan* 'not'   *bukan-bukan* 'unfounded'

(34) *sudah* 'have (perfect), already'   *sudah-sudah* 'that's enough'
     se-+boleh 'can'+*-nya*   *seboleh-bolehnya* 'as much as possible'

3 Grammar and Syntax

3.1 Nominal domain

3.1.1 Basic structure of the NP

The linear order of the elements composing NPs in Malay is as follows:

(35) **Quant Num   CLF N   Direct modifier   Poss   Relative clause Dem**
     semua tiga ekor kucing   berwarna hitam   saya   yang   comel   itu
     all   three CLF cat   coloured black   1SG   REL   cute   that
     'all those three cute black cats of mine'

In Colloquial Malay, the possessor can also occur prenominally, before N, followed by the possessive marker *punya*.

(36) dia   punya   mak   Colloquial Malay
     3SG   POSS   mother
     'his/her mother'

The emergence of *punya* as a productive possessive marker can be traced to around the middle of the 19th century, when a huge wave of Chinese immigrants were brought to work in the tin mining industry, though it is possible that they entered the language earlier, perhaps around the 15th century (Yap 2007). The immigrants spoke southern Chinese languages such as Hokkien, Cantonese, Hakka and Teochew. These Chinese languages have a form corresponding to *punya*, namely *e* in Hokkien, *ge* in Cantonese, *ke* in Hakka and *kai* in Teochew, and the nominal structure indicating possession in these languages are possessor-possessive marker-possessed, as shown in the Cantonese example in (37) (Yap 2007).

(37) nei   ge   dikjan
     2SG   POSS enemy
     'your enemy'

Malay does not use definite or indefinite articles. Bare NPs can be either definite or indefinite. However, there are devices to mark an NP as definite: the demonstrative *itu* 'that' and *ini* 'this', as well as determiners like *tersebut* 'mentioned', *berkenaan* 'relevant', *terbabit* 'involved', etc. These words all occur in the demonstrative position in (35). There are also words that bring about indefinite interpretations. They are the numeral *satu* 'one' and expressions containing its prefixal form *se-* such as *se-*CLF 'a', *(se-)suatu* 'some', *se-barang* 'any', etc. (see Shoho 2001 and Nomoto and Aznur Aisyah, to appear, for a description of indefinite expressions in Malay). For number marking in Malay, see section 2.4 on reduplication.

3.1.2 Classifier (CLF) device

Malay has numeral classifiers. Zainudin's (2000) classifier dictionary for primary school students lists 100 words that are considered classifiers. Among them, the most frequently used are *buah* (lit. 'fruit') for three-dimensional objects and abstract entities, *orang* (lit. 'human') for humans and *ekor* (lit. 'tail') for animals.

Classifiers are used when a numeral modifies a noun. However, numerals can modify nouns without the presence of numeral classifiers in Malay as shown in (38).

(38) tiga   (buah)   majalah
     three CLF   magazine
     'three magazines'

Nomoto (2013b) points out that an interpretive difference exists between expressions with and without a classifier: while both expressions can refer to particular instantiations of a kind, only expressions without a classifier can also refer to subclasses of a kind.[8] Thus, both the noun phrases with and without the classifier can be understood to refer to copies of a magazine (instantiations of the 'magazine' kind) as shown in (39a). Only the noun phrase without the classifier can be understood to refer to different titles (subkinds) of magazines as shown in (39b).

(39) a. *Masih tinggal {tiga buah majalah/ tiga majalah}. Semuanya*
still left three CLF magazine three magazine all

majalah Mastika.
magazine Mastika.
'We still have three (copies of) magazines. All of them are Mastika.'

b. *Masih tinggal {*tiga buah majalah/ tiga majalah}, iaitu*
still left three CLF magazine three magazine namely

majalah Mastika, Majalah PC dan Nona.
magazine Mastika magazine PC and Nona
'We still have three (titles of) magazines, namely Mastika, Majalah PC and Nona.'
(The sentence is acceptable with *tiga buah majalah* [three CLF magazine] if exactly one copy is left for each title.)

While numerals can modify nouns without classifiers, it is not possible to use classifiers without numerals as shown in (40).

(40) **Saya ingin mem-beli buah buku.*
1SG want ACT-buy CLF book

Malay is thus unlike some Chinese languages such as Cantonese, and some MSEA languages such as Vietnamese, where the classifier + noun sequence can occur without a numeral.

---

8 This interpretative difference between expressions with and without a classifier has also been reported in Thai for the sequences 'NP CLF Dem' versus 'NP Dem' (Piriyawiboon 2009).

(41) a. ngo   seung   maai   bun   syu.   Cantonese
       1SG   want   buy   CLF   book
       'I want to buy a book.'

   b. Tôi   muốn   mua   cuốn   sách.   Vietnamese
       1SG   want   buy   CLF   book
       'I want to buy a book.' (T. H. Nguyen, 2004: 17, cited in Tran 2011: 36)

Malay is also unlike some classifier languages (e.g. Mandarin) where the numeral *one* may be absent (or unpronounced) in the presence of a demonstrative (Tang 1990).

(42) *(se-/satu)   buah   buku   ini   Malay
      one   CLF   book   this

(43) zhe   (yi)   ben   shu   Mandarin
     this   one   CLF   book
     'this book'

The NP in the 'Num CLF NP' structure can be null in Malay. For example, an utterance like (44) is common at a local market when the seller and the buyer are clear on the referent intended. The classifier *biji* (lit. 'seed') is used for nouns denoting small objects.

(44) Bagi   dua   biji.
     give   two   CLF
     'Give me two.'

Such structures can also be used anaphorically, when a referent has been established in the prior linguistic context. This use of the 'Num CLF' sequence is also found in Thai (Haas 1942: 204).

3.2 Verbal domain

3.2.1 Inflection

Like many MSEA languages, verbs in Malay do not inflect for the person, gender or number of the subject, as shown in (45).

(45) Saya/kami/kamu/dia/mereka   mem-beli   surat khabar.
    1SG/1PL/2SG/3SG/3PL   ACT-buy   newspaper
    'I/we/he/she/they/you bought/buy/buys the newspapers.'

Tense is not overtly expressed in Malay either through verbal inflection or temporal auxiliaries. The temporal location of an event/state is determined contextually, or established by a temporal adverbial as in (46).

(46) Ali   berjumpa   Hassan   pada   pukul   sepuluh   semalam.
    Ali   meet   Hassan   at   o'clock ten   yesterday
    'Ali met Hassan at ten yesterday.'

Besides these strategies, the situation aspect (Akstionsart) and viewpoint aspect expressed by the sentence also contribute to temporal interpretation. According to Smith and Erbaugh (2005), unbounded situations receive a default present intepretation, while bounded events receive a default past interpretation in Mandarin Chinese. The same is found in Malay. (47), which describes a state (an unbounded situation), is interpreted as holding in the present, while (48), which describes an achievement (a bounded event), is interpreted as having occurred in the past.

(47) Mereka   berdua   berada   di   stesen   Kajang.
    3PL   both   be   at   station   Kajang
    'They are at the Kajang station (together).'

(48) Mereka   berdua   tiba   di   stesen   Kajang.
    3PL   both   arrive   at   station   Kajang
    'They arrived at the Kajang station (together).'

The default temporal interpretation can be overridden. For example, the presence of the temporal adverbial in (49) ensures a past interpretation, even though the sentence describes a state.

(49) Mereka   berdua   berada   di   stesen   Kajang   semalam.
    3PL   both   be   at   station   Kajang   yesterday
    'They were at the Kajang station (together) yesterday.'

Aspectual and modal information in Malay are not expressed through verbal inflection, but rather through auxiliaries. Aspectual/modal auxilairies typically occur between the subject and the predicate as in (50).

(50) *Ali* **pernah/boleh/sudah** *bermain gitar.*
Ali have.experienced/can/have.completed play guitar
'Ali has played guitar before/can play guitar/has played the guitar.'

While Malay verbs do not inflect for tense, aspect or mood information, they take affixes, with a variety of functions (see Table 2), some of which have been noted to have aspectual effects. For example, the prefix *ter-* has been noted to encode the completive aspect (e.g. Winstedt 1927; Asmah 2009: 146; Nik Safiah et al. 2008: 174; Soh 1994; Chung 2011). This is because the use of *ter-* indicates the completion of the event described and/or the result state as in (51).

(51) Completive/result state
Pencuri itu ter-tangkap oleh polis.
thief that TER-catch by police
'The thief has been caught by the police.'

However, the prefix *ter-* is also used to indicate that the event described by the sentence is accidental or not intended by the agent, or to express that the agent has the ability to carry out the activity/event described by the sentence.[9]

(52) Accidental
Dia ter-makan racun.
3SG TER-eat poison
'S/he drank poison accidentally.'

(53) Abilitative
Orang itu tidak ter-baca tulisan Cina.
person that not TER-read writing China
'That person could not read Chinese characters.'

Given that the same morpheme is associated with these different semantic effects, many authors have attempted to determine the basic meaning of *ter-* that explains its different semantic effects (see Soh 1994; Siraj 2010; Chung 2011; Nomoto 2011).

Another prefix that has been associated with an aspectual effect is the prefix *meN-* (Benjamin 1993; Soh and Nomoto 2009, 2011). Soh and Nomoto (2009,

---

9 The abilitative use is not as productive as the other two uses, which leads Nomoto (2011) to claim that the abilitative reading of *ter-* sentences is obtained by pragmatic inference.

2011) note that *meN-* has progressive-like aspectual effects; *meN-* does not occur in stative sentences like the progressive aspect.

(54) *Saya   suka/*meny-[s]uka   masakan   Jepun.*
　　　1SG   like/ACT-like   cuisine   Japan
　　　'I like Japanese cuisine.'

3.2.2 Verbal categories

Several morphemes in Malay have both lexical and functional uses. The functional use arguably evolved as a consequence of grammaticalization, as is often the case with many MSEA languages. We discuss two such morphemes in this section: *dapat* and *kena*. The word *dapat* is used as a verb meaning 'to get' as well as an auxiliary expressing ability/possibility/permission.

(55) a. *Aminah   **dapat**   hadiah   daripada   kekasih-nya.*
　　　　Aminah   get   present   from   lover-3SG
　　　　'Aminah got a present from her lover.'

　　 b. *Aminah   **dapat**   mem-beli   hadiah   untuk   kekasih-nya.*
　　　　Aminah   can   ACT-buy   present   for   lover-3SG
　　　　'Aminah could buy a present for her lover.'

The set of meanings associated with *dapat* 'to get' is similar to those expressed by the verbs meaning 'to acquire' in MSEA languages discussed in Enfield (2001) (e.g. Lao *dâj*, Northern Zhuang *dáy*, Cantonese *dak* and Mandarin *de*).

　　The word *kena* may be a verb expressing physical and abstract contact, meaning 'to touch, hit' (56a) or 'to incur' (56b). It may also be a modal verb that occurs in adversative passive and debitive ('have to') sentences, as shown in (56c) and (56d) respectively.

(56) a. *Tangan   saya   **kena**   pisau.*
　　　　hand   1SG   touch   knife
　　　　'My hand touched a knife.'

　　 b. *Gerai-gerai   kecil   pun   boleh   **kena**   cukai.*
　　　　stall-PL   small   even   can   incur   tax
　　　　'Even small stalls can get taxed.'

c. Ali **kena** *pukul* *oleh* *budak* *itu*.
   Ali get   hit   by   kid   that
   'Ali got hit by that kid.'

d. *Kita* **kena** *mem-baca* *lebih* *banyak* *buku*.
   1PL   have.to ACT-read   more   many   book
   'We have to read more books.'

Malay patterns like several MSEA languages such as Thai, Vietnamese (Prasithrathsint 2004), Hokkien (Bodman 1955), and Khmer (Hiromi Ueda, p. c.) in using the same morpheme for adversative passive and debitive sentences: *thùuk* (Thai), *bị* (Vietnamese), *tioq* (Hokkien) and *trəw* (Khmer). According to Nomoto and Kartini (2011), *kena* started its life as a transitive verb of physical contact meaning 'to hit, touch'. Then, the semantic domain expanded to subsume abstract contact to mean 'to get, incur'. An adversative passive use emerged as a result of a change in the verb's subcategorization frame; *kena* started to take a clausal complement in addition to a noun phrase. The debitive use arose because the modal meaning of *kena* led the speakers to reanalyze the verb as a member of a special predicate class, which involves ambiguity in terms of thematic role assignment.

3.2.3 Serial verb constructions

Serial verb constructions (SVCs) are monoclausal structures containing two or more verbs. The verbs/verb phrases present aspects of a single event and they are typically characterized as involving the sharing of arguments between or among verbs (see Muysken and Veenstra 2006 and Bril 2004 for further criteria). SVC-like structures are common in Malay. In (57), the subject serves as an external argument of both verbs, while in (58), the object serves as an internal argument of the first verb but the external argument of the second verb.[10]

(57) *Ali* **mem-[p]ekik** **me-minta** *tolong*.
     Ali   ACT-shout   ACT-ask   help
     'Ali shouted calling for help.'

(58) *Ali* **meng-hantar** *Siti* **pulang** *ke* *rumah-nya*.
     Ali   ACT-send   Siti   return   to   house-3SG
     'Ali took Siti back to her house.'

---

10 (57) and (58) are cited with modifications from Koh (1990).

As illustrated in (57) and (58), the verbs may be contiguous or non-continguous, exemplifying 'nuclear type SVC' and 'core type SVC' respectively (Foley and Olson 1985).

Both symmetrical and asymmetrical SVCs are attested in Malay. In symmetrical SVCs, the predicates involved are of equal rank, while in asymmetrical SVCs, the predicates are hierarchized and are headed, implying a modifier-head relation (Bril 2004). Thus, one of the participating verbs may be drawn from a grammatically or semantically restricted class in asymmetrical SVCs (e.g. verbs expressing direction, motion, posture, cause-effect, aspect, modality, etc.), while no such restriction exists for symmetrical SVCs (Bril 2004; Aikhenvald 2006). (59) is an example of a symmetrical SVC.

(59) Mereka **terkejut** **men-dengar** berita kematian-nya.
 3PL be.surprised ACT-hear news death-3SG
 'They were surprised, hearing the news about his death.'

(60)–(62) are examples of asymmetrical SVCs, expressing direction and motion, causative and aspect/modality respectively.

(60) a. Dia **pergi** meng-ambil songkok-nya segera.
 3SG go ACT-take Malay.cap-3SG immediately
 'He went to get his songkok immediately.' (Koh 1990: 292)

 b. Norisah **masuk** men-jatuh-kan diri-nya di atas sofa ...
 Norisah enter ACT-fall-CAUS self-3SG at top sofa
 'Norisah entered (and) dropped herself onto the sofa.' (Koh 1990: 293)

(61) a. Saya mem-**buat** adik me-nyanyi lagu.
 1SG ACT-make younger.sibling ACT-sing song
 'I made my younger brother/sister sing a song.'

 b. Emak **bagi/kasi** anak keluar bermain. Colloquial Malay
 mum give child go.out play
 'Mum let her child go out and play.'

(62) Ali **mula/habis/cuba/mahu** makan kari ayam.
 Ali begin/finish/try/want eat curry chicken
 'Ali began/finished/tried/wanted to eat chicken curry.'

3.3 Clausal/sentential organization

Malay is an SVO language. Other word orders are possible with information structure effects. (63a) is an SVO sentence used in unmarked contexts. (63b) and (63c) are respectively OSV and VOS sentences used in marked contexts, as reflected in their English translations.

(63) a. Siti   makan   sayur   saja.
       Siti   eat   vegetable   only
       'Siti only eats vegetables.'

  b. Sayur   saja   (yang)   Siti   makan.
     vegetable   only   REL   Siti   eat
     '(It is) only vegetables (that) Siti eats.'

  c. Makan   sayur   saja,   Siti.
     eat   vegetable   only   Siti
     '(She) only eats vegetables, Siti.'

3.3.1 Ellipsis of arguments

Argument ellipsis occurs in both Formal and Colloquial Malay. However, it is more frequent and less restricted in terms of possible ellipsis environments in Colloquial Malay than in Formal Malay (Koh 1990: 142). Eliding the subject of a subordinate or coordinate clause as in (64) is commonly found in both varieties.

(64) Sebelum   ___   men-[t]inggalkan   pejabat   tadi,   Formal Malay
     before   ACT-leave   office   just.now

     Lokman   kelihatan   gamam ...
     Lokman   appear   anxious
     'Just before (he) left the office, Lokman appeared anxious ...' (Koh 1990: 142)

By contrast, eliding a matrix subject as in (65) is virtually limited to Colloquial Malay.

(65) ... ini-lah   hari   terakhir   aku   bersekolah.   Colloquial Malay
          this-PART   day   last   1SG   go.to.school

___ sedih le   jugak, tapi apa   ___ boleh buat ...
     sad   PART also   but   what   can   do
'... this was my last day of school. (I) was sad, but what could (I) do ...' (Koh 1990: 143)

Colloquial Malay also allows an object argument to be elided, which makes the following sentence with a relative clause ambiguous.

(66) *Ada   yang tak   suka.*   Colloquial Malay
     exist REL   not   like
  a. 'There are people who don't like <something>.'
  b. 'There are people/things that <I/we/they> don't like.'

In interpretation (a), the object argument is elided. In interpretation (b), it is the subject argument that is elided.

While argument ellipsis is common, its occurrence is not without restrictions. In particular, prepositional objects cannot be elided in Malay as shown in (67) (cf. Fortin 2007; Sato 2007).

(67) a. *Dia   juga nak   pergi ke   *(sana).*   Colloquial Malay
        3SG   also want go   to   there
        'S/he doesn't want to go there either.'

   b. *Ali   tidak suka pada   *(mereka).*   Formal Malay
      Ali   not   like at/on 3PL
      'Ali doesn't like them.'

3.3.2 Information structure

In a Malay sentence, the topic can appear at the beginning or the end, separated from the rest of the sentence by a potential pause, which is more frequently realized when topics appear at the end of the sentence (Philips 1970).

(68) *Lelaki itu,   nama-nya   Hasan.*
     man   that   name-3SG   Hasan
     'That man, his name is Hasan.'

(69) *Nama-nya   Hasan,   lelaki   itu.*
     name-3SG   Hasan   man   that
     'His name is Hasan, that man.'

In the examples above, the topic NP anaphorically binds the possessor, which is the pronoun *-nya*. There are also topic constructions that do not involve a pronoun anaphorically bound by the topic (Philips 1970). In the examples below, the position in which the topic NP would occur in the corresponding non-topic construction is indicated by the underline.

(70) *Itu   semua   orang   sudah   tahu___.*
     that   all   person   PFV   know
     'That, everybody already knows.' (Utopia, October 2005, p. 51)

(71) *Berita   itu   kita   sudah   dengar   ___.*[11]
     news   that   1PL   PFV   hear
     'We have already heard the news.'

Furthermore, some topic NPs do not appear to be an argument of the predicate. For such topics, it may not be straightforward to identify the positions in the corresponding non-topic constructions in which they would occur. Examples are given below.

(72) *Kereta-kereta   itu,   ada   yang   berwarna   hitam.*
     car-PL   that   exist   REL   coloured   black
     '(Among) those cars, there are (ones) which are (coloured) black.' (Philips 1970: 561)

---

[11] There is a similar construction known as bare passives, also referred to as object-preposing constructions, passive type 2 and object voice. In bare passive sentences, the agent follows the auxiliary, adverb or negation and precedes the "bare" verb form, i.e. a form without the prefix *meN-* or *di-*. The bare passive counterpart of (71) is (i) below.

(i) Berita   itu   sudah   kita   dengar.
    news   that   PFV   1PL   hear
    'We have already heard the news.'

While bare passive sentences may appear to be an instance of topicalization, Chung (1976) shows that they are syntactically passive.

(73) Aduan   mengenai longkang tersumbat akan di-ambil tindakan
    complaint regarding drain   clogged   will PASS-take action

    pemulihan dalam tempoh 3 hari.
    remedy   within period 3 day
    '(Regarding) complaints on clogged drains, remedial actions will be taken within three days.' (Machang District Council's website)[12]

It may be possible to analyze these sentences as involving a prepositional phrase, but with the preposition not pronounced or dropped, a process that is common in Colloquial Malay. The relevant prepositions for (72) and (73) would be *antara* 'among' and *terhadap* 'on' respectively. The non-topic constructions for these sentences would thus be as follows:

(74) **Antara** kereta itu, ada   yang berwarna hitam.
     among   car   that exist REL coloured black
     'Among those cars, there are (ones) which are (coloured) black.'

(75) **Terhadap** aduan   mengenai longkang tersumbat akan di-ambil
     on   complaint regarding drain   clogged   will PASS-take

     tindakan pemulihan dalam tempoh 3 hari.
     action   remedy   within period 3 day
     'Regarding complaints on clogged drains, remedial actions will be taken within three days.'

Colloquial Malay has a topic marker, namely *kalau*, as shown in (76) (Nomoto 2009).

(76) Kalau tempat tu,   ramai pelancong Cina.   Colloquial Malay
     TOP   place that many tourist   China
     'Speaking of the place, there are lots of Chinese tourists there.'

Kalau as a topic marker is not available in Formal Malay, where it may only be used to mean 'if'.

---

12 Pencapaian Piagam pelanggan – PORTAL RASMI MAJLIS DAERAH MACHANG (http://www.mdmachang.gov.my/146?p_p_id=56_INSTANCE_h6eX&p_p_lifecycle=0&p_p_state=normal&p_p_mode=view&p_p_col_id=column-2&p_p_col_count=2&page=3, accessed 29/07/2011).

Focus constituents in Malay may be marked by focus morphemes such as *kah* and *lah*; the former is interrogative while the latter is not (Mashudi 1981: 303; Nomoto 2009; Cole et al., to appear; Fortin 2009; Nomoto and Aznur Aisyah 2016). Constituents in focus marked by *kah* and *lah* may be fronted as illustrated in (77) and (78) respectively.

(77) a. Dia   mem-baca **di perpustakaan-lah** kelmarin.
        3SG   ACT-read   in library-FOC   yesterday
        'It was in the library that he was reading yesterday.' (Mashudi 1981: 99)

   b. **Di perpustakaan-lah** dia   mem-baca   kelmarin.
       at   library-FOC   3SG   ACT-read   yesterday
       'It was in the library that he was reading yesterday.' (Mashudi 1981: 99)

(78) a. Guru   itu   pergi   **ke universiti-kah**   tadi?
        teacher that   go   to university-FOC   just.now
        'Was it to the university that the teacher went just now?' (Mashudi 1981: 100)

   b. **Ke universiti-kah**   guru   itu   pergi   tadi?
       to university-FOC   teacher   that   go   just.now
       'Was it to the university that the teacher went just now?' (Mashudi 1981: 100)

Besides *kah* and *lah*, *pun* 'also, too, even' may also be considered a focus morpheme (Mashudi 1981: 96–98; Goddard 2001).[13,14] (79a) is a neutral sentence while (79b) is a sentence where the verb phrase is in focus.

---

13 Mashudi (1981: 97) also includes *tah* as a focus morpheme. *Tah* together with a wh-word marks a rhetorical question.

(i) Aminah   itu   apa-tah   kurang-nya?
    Aminah   that   what-FOC   less-3SG
    'What is less pretty in Aminah?' ('Aminah is just as pretty') (Mashudi 1981: 97)

The extent to which *tah* patterns like other focus morphemes is not discussed in Mashudi (1981).

14 Nomoto (2006: 85) suggests that particles *pula* 'too' and *juga* 'also' are also focus markers.

(79) a. *Dia   tidak   mahu   mem-[p]andang.*
       3SG   not   want   ACT-look
       'S/he does not want to look.'

   b. **Mem-[p]andang**   *pun   dia   tidak   mahu.*
      ACT-look   FOC   3SG   not   want
      'He does not even want to look.'

3.3.3 Questions

Malay has several ways to form questions. In wh-questions, the wh-word may either stay in situ as in (80a) or occur in a sentence-initial position as in (80b). In addition, the wh-word can also occur in the initial position of an embedded clause as in (80c), showing that Malay has partial wh-movement (Cole and Hermon 2000). In all these sentences, the word *bila* 'when' may be associated with the embedded clause or the matrix clause, and hence may be questions about the time of the coming event or the time of the thinking event.

(80) a. *Awak   fikir   mereka   datang   ke   sini   **bila**?*
        2SG   think   3PL   come   to   here   when
        'When did you think they came here?'

   b. ***Bila***   *awak   fikir   mereka   datang   ke   sini?*
      when   2SG   think   3PL   come   to   here
      'When did you think they came here?'

   c. *Awak   fikir   **bila**   mereka   datang   ke   sini?*
      2SG   think   when   3PL   come   to   here
      'When did you think they came here?'

Yes-no questions are marked by a question intonation contour as in (81a)[15] and/or one of the following morphosyntactic devices: using the question particle *kah* (*ka*/*ke* in Colloquial Malay) at the end of the sentence (81b), adding the question marker *adakah* at the beginning of the sentence (81c), adding *ke t(id)ak/belum* 'or not/not yet' at the end of the sentence (81d), or adding *tak* 'not' after the aux-

---

[15] Not all intonation contours involve a clear rising contour. Further research is needed to provide an adequate description of question intonation contours in Malay.

iliary or the predicate (81e) or using the particle *kan* at the end of the sentence (81f).

(81) a. Question intonation
      Awak   boleh   datang?
      2SG   can   come
      'Can you come?'

  b. Yes/no question particle *kah (ka/ke)*
      Awak   boleh   datang-kah?
      2SG   can   come-Q
      'Can you come?'

  c. *Ada-kah* 'be + *kah*'
      Ada-kah   awak   boleh   datang?
      be-Q   2SG   can   come
      'Is it that you can come?'

  d. *Ke tak/belum* 'or not/not yet'   Colloquial Malay
      Awak   boleh   datang   ke   tak?
      2SG   can   come   or   not
      'Can you come or not?'

  e. *Tak* 'not'   Colloquial Malay
      Boleh   tak   awak   datang?
      can   not   2SG   come
      'Can you come?'

  f. Tag question with *kan*   Colloquial Malay
      Ali   dah   tahu   kan?
      Ali   already know   right
      'Ali already knew it, didn't he?'

Strategies exemplified in (80d)–(80f) are only found in Colloquial Malay.

4 Semantics and pragmatics

4.1 Common semantic domains

4.1.1 Food terminology

According to Matisoff (1983: 79), languages in Thailand are "unanimous in dividing food into two basic categories: rice and that which one eats with rice (e.g. Thai *khâaw* 'rice' and *kabkhâaw* 'with rice')," and this may serve as a semantic feature characterizing languages of Southeast Asia. Malay does so too, with distinct words for rice (i.e. *nasi*) and things eaten with rice (i.e. *lauk*).

Like most languages spoken in Thailand, Lahu and Mandarin (Matisoff 1983: 25), Malay has separate words for rice in the fields (i.e. *padi*) versus cooked rice ready to be eaten (i.e. *nasi*). In fact, Malay also has a word referring to uncooked rice, i.e. *beras*.

4.1.2 Expressions of "cutting", "carrying", "drying", "directional" (upper ~ lower, from ~ toward ...)

According to Matisoff (2004), Southeast Asian languages are rich in verbs of manipulation (e.g. CARRY, CUT), which reflect the physical lifestyle of the region. These verbs are in common use and are not specialized in a particular domain. Malay seems to fit this description. For example, there are many verbs for CARRY depending on the parts of the body involved in the act of carrying. Examples are given with the prefix *meN-*.

(82) CARRY
    membawa 'to carry along'
    mengangkat, mendukung 'to carry astride the back or waist'
    menggendong 'to carry on the back or hip'
    mengusung 'to carry on a stretcher'
    menjinjing 'to carry in hand'
    menanai 'to carry in hands'
    memikul 'to carry on shoulder'
    menanggung, menjulang 'to carry on shoulders'
    menjunjung 'to carry on head'
    membimbit/mengelek 'to carry under arm'

There are also a number of verbs for CUT and DRY, depending on how the action is carried out.

(83) CUT
memotong 'to cut'
menggunting 'to cut with scissors'
menggergaji 'to cut with saw'
mengapak 'to cut with axe'
mencukur 'to cut with razor'
menghiris 'to cut by slicing'
membelah 'to cut by splitting/halving'
mengerat 'to cut into pieces'
mencencang 'to cut into very small pieces'
menetak 'to chop'

(84) DRY
mengeringkan 'to dry'
menjemurkan 'to dry in the sun'
mengelap 'to dry using a towel, piece of cloth, etc.'

Different verbs exist for PUSH, depending on whether or not an object moves as a result of being pushed.

(85) PUSH
menekan 'to push down, press'
menolak 'to push away'

4.2 Pragmatics & discourse

4.2.1 Final particles

Malay has a number of final particles, which may be broadly categorized into two types: (i) interrogative particles and (ii) discourse particles. Interogative particles are discussed in section 3.3.3 above. Discourse particles indicate the speaker's attitude or belief about the propositional content of the utterance or his attitude or belief about other participants' attitude or belief on the relevant proposition. They include, but are not limited to, *kot/kut*, *punya*, *dah* and *lah/la/le*. *Kot* is an epistemic particle used to express uncertainty with respect to the propositional content of the utterance (Koh 1990: 78).

(86) *Ali   dah   tahu   **kot**.* Colloquial Malay
     Ali   PFV   know   I.guess
     'Ali knew it (but I may be wrong).'

Punya, on the other hand, indicates that the speaker is certain about the propositional content of the utterance (Koh 1990: 78; Yap 2007). Soh (2016) shows that in addition to expressing the attitude holder's certainty about the truth of the propositional content of the utterance, the use of *punya* also signals the source of the information presented as of the inferential type. The attitude holder may be the speaker or the external argument of verbs of saying and believing.

(87) *Ali   dah   tahu   **punya**.* Colloquial Malay
     Ali   PFV   know   for.sure
     'Ali knew it (I can assure you).'

The use of final *dah* may indicate the speaker's belief that one or more of the discourse participants hold a belief that is contrary to what is being asserted. Thus, the use of final *dah* in (88) indicates that the speaker believes that one or more of the discourse participants believe that Ali does not have knowledge of the matter (Soh 2017). This use of the final *dah* is comparable to the use of *already* in English (Soh 2011).

(88) *Ali   dah   tahu   **dah**.* Colloquial Malay
     Ali   PFV   know   already
     'Ali already knew it.'

The discourse particle *lah* is to be distinguished from the focus *lah* (cf. section 3.3.2). Depending on the intonation, the particle *lah* may convey either a "light-heartedness" or an "ill-tempered" effect in declaratives, and it may either "soften" or "harden" a request (Goddard 1994). According to Goddard (1994: 154), the different uses of *lah* can be explained by the fact that *lah* "offers an explanation of the speaker's illocutionary purpose, which is roughly to correct or preempt a misapprehension or misunderstanding of some kind." An example of the use of the discourse particle *lah* is given in (89).

(89) *Ali   dah   tahu   **lah**.* Colloquial Malay
     Ali   PFV   know   LAH
     'Ali already knew it (though you might have thought otherwise).'

It is possible for multiple final particles to co-occur. The order of multiple particles is not free, though a comprehensive description of it awaits further research. The interrogative particles must follow discourse particles as in (90) (Soh 2011).

(90) Kau sampai kat KLCC {**dah ke**/ ***ke dah**}?   Colloquial Malay
     2SG arrive at KLCC already Q   Q already
     'Have you arrived at KLCC?'

Within the discourse particles, Aoki (2012) notes that *punya* must precede *la(h)* as in (91).

(91) Aku tak lari ke stesen {**punya la**/ ***la punya**}.   Colloquial Malay
     1SG not run to station for.sure LA LA for.sure
     'I won't run to the station.'

4.2.2 Politeness

In Malay, different pronouns are used in settings of different formality which require different levels of 'politeness' or 'closeness'. Singular pronouns in Malay have forms that differ in their degrees of politeness or closeness, as shown below.

(92)   polite/distant ⟵⎯⎯⎯⎯⟶ non-polite/close
     1SG   saya   aku
     2SG   anda   awak   kamu   engkau/kau
     3SG   beliau   dia

As Koh (1990: 111) notes, non-polite/close pronouns "do not indicate impoliteness when used correctly." In addition to these pronouns, titles (e.g. *Dato', Haji, Prof., Dr., Tuan, Encik*) and kin terms (e.g. *mak cik* 'aunt', *kakak* 'older sister', *adik* 'younger brother/sister', *abang* 'older brother') are also used as address terms and to encode different levels of politeness or closeness. For instance, a waiter would address his male customer as *abang* at a neighbourhood restaurant, but he would switch to *tuan* 'Sir (lit. master)' if he worked at a restaurant in a five-star hotel.

(93) *Abang/Tuan   nak   makan   apa?*
     older.brother/Sir want eat   what
     'What would you like?'

See Mintz (2002: 86–94) for a detailed description of different pronouns as well as titles and kin terms as pronoun substitutes.

5 Conclusion/ summary

Vittrant (2008) and Enfield (2005: 186–187) have hypothesized that the languages of the MSEA linguistic area share specific features in different components of the grammar. For example, the phonological systems of the languages in the area are rich in vowel phonemes, with suprasegmental phenomena such as tones or registers (Vittrant 2008). The vowel system of Standard Malay is considered small compared to many MSEA languages, while the vowel systems of northern Malay dialects are more in line with most MSEA languages. Unlike many MSEA languages, Malay does not have distinct tones and registers, nor is there evidence of the development of sesquisyllables. Like many Southeast Asian languages, consonant phonemes that may appear in word-final position in Malay represent a reduced set compared to those that may appear in word-initial position. However, it should be noted that this feature is also shared by many of the world's languages, including languages genetically related to Malay that are not spoken in Mainland Southeast Asia such as Mantauran (Rukai) (Zeitoun 2007: 21), and other Austronesian languages in Indonesia and Borneo such as Toba Batak (Percival 1970: 31) and Iban (Asmah 1981: 17). In this connection, Prince and Smolensky (2004: 188) put forward the following generalization relating to the asymmetry of onset/coda licensing: "There are languages in which some possible onsets are not possible codas, but no language in which some possible codas are not possible onsets."

In terms of morphosyntactic features, languages in the area have been described as exhibiting a tendency towards monosyllabicity, with extensive use of compounding (as opposed to derivational morphology), and showing common use of numeral classifiers, psycho-collocations and elaboratives (Vittrant 2008). There is no particular tendency towards monosyllabicity in Malay, as it is an agglutinating language, with many words consisting of multiple morphemes. Malay makes extensive use of compounding and derivation, as well as reduplication. It employs numeral classifiers in numeral modification, but direct numeral modification is also possible, unlike many MSEA languages. The use of psycho-collocations and elaboratives is common. It is relevant to note that the use of psycho-collocations is also common in other Austronesian languages, such as Tsou (Formosan, Taiwan), Gayo (Western Malayo-Polynesian, northern Sumatra) and Kambera (Central Malayo-Polynesian, Sumba Island, eastern Indonesia). The use of psycho-collocations is so extensive that Musgrave (2006: 233) argues that "it could have already been present in Proto-Austronesian and inherited wherever it occurs in the family." In terms of their syntax, MSEA languages are considered mainly SVO, with argument ellipsis, serial verb constructions and the lack of grammatical marking of tense. Malay shares these features with MSEA languages. However, unlike some MSEA languages such as Vietnamese, where wh-question words may only stay in situ (Bruening and Tran 2006), Malay wh-question words may either stay in situ or occur in the initial position of a clause, whether matrix or embedded. Like many MSEA languages, Malay has many verbs of manipulation such as CARRY and CUT. It also has a number of final particles that may be broadly categorized as interrogative or discourse-related. In addition, Malay has pronouns that differ in terms of levels of politeness or closeness.

It is possible that some of these features that Malay shares with MSEA languages have resulted from contacts with the latter languages. Needless to say, however, there are other possible reasons for the resemblance, including contact with non-MSEA languages (notably Chinese languages, which happened to share the relevant features with MSEA languages), genetic inheritance (only relevant under the Austric superfamily hypothesis, which claims that Austronesian and Austro-Asiatic languages developed from a common proto-language and hence genetically related), parallel development, and universals (see Campbell 2006; Tosco 2008). All of these possibilities must be taken into account when evaluating the extent to which a particular common feature in Malay and MSEA languages is due to contact between the two aided by the geographic contiguity.

Abbreviations

1	first person
2	second person
3	third person
A	adjective
ACT	active
C	consonant
CAUS	causative
CLF	classifier
DEM	demonstrative
FOC	focus
N	noun
NP	noun phrase
P	preposition

PART	particle
PASS	passive
PFV	perfective
PL	plural
POSS	possessive
PROG	progressive
Q	question
REL	relativizer
SG	singular
TOP	topic
V	verb
V	vowel

References

Abdullah Hassan. 1974. *The morphology of Malay*. Kuala Lumpur: Dewan Bahasa dan Pustaka.

Aikhenvald, Alexandra Y. 2006. Serial verb constructions in typological perspective. in Alexandra Y. Aikhenvald & R. M. W. Dixon (eds.), *Serial verb constructions: A cross-linguistic typology*, 1–68. Oxford: Oxford University Press.

Aoki, Rina. 2012. *Kougo Mareego no danwashouji punya no tougoronteki kenkyuu*. [A syntactic study of the discourse particle *punya* in Colloquial Malay] BA Thesis, Tokyo University of Foreign Studies.

Asmah Haji Omar. 1981. *The Iban language of Sarawak: A grammatical description*. Kuala Lumpur: Dewan Bahasa dan Pustaka.

Asmah Haji Omar. 1993. *Essays on Malay linguistics*, 2nd ed. Kuala Lumpur: Dewan Bahasa dan Pustaka.

Asmah Haji Omar. 2009. *Nahu Melayu mutakhir (edisi kelima)*. Kuala Lumpur: Dewan Bahasa dan Pustaka.

Benjamin, Geoffrey. 1993. Grammar and polity: The cultural and political background to Standard Malay. In William A. Foley (ed.), *The role of theory in language description*, 341–392. Berlin & New York: Mouton de Gruyter.

Bodman, Nicholas C. 1955. *Spoken Amoy Hokkien*. Kuala Lumpur: Charles Grenier & Company.

Bril, Isabelle. 2004. Complex nuclei in Oceanic languages: Contribution to an areal typology. In Isabelle Bril & Françoise Ozanne-Rivierre (eds.), *Complex predicates in Oceanic languages: Studies in the dynamics of binding and boundedness*, 1–48. Berlin & New York: Mouton de Gruyter.

Bruening, Benjamin & Thuan Tran. 2006. Wh-questions in Vietnamese. *Journal of East Asian Linguistics* 15. 319–347.

Campbell, Lyle. 2006. Areal linguistics: A closer scrutiny. In Yaron Matras, April McMahon & Nigel Vincent (eds.), *Linguistic areas: Convergence in historical and typological perspective*, 1–31. Hampshire: Palgrave Macmillan.

Chung, Sandra. 1976. On the subject of two passives in Indonesian. In Charles N. Li (ed.), *Subject and topic*, 57–99. New York: Academic Press.

Chung, Siaw-Fong. 2011. Uses of *ter-* in Malay: A corpus-based study. *Journal of Pragmatics* 43. 799–813.
Cole, Peter & Gabriella Hermon. 2000. Partial wh-movement: Evidence from Malay. In Uli Lutz, Gereon Müller & Arnim Stechow (eds.), *Wh-scope marking*, 85–114. Amsterdam: John Benjamins.
Cole, Peter, Gabriella Hermon & Norhaida Aman. To appear. Clefted questions in Malay. In David Gil & James Collins (eds.), *Malay/Indonesian linguistics*. London: Curzon Press.
Cole, Peter, Gabriella Hermon & Yanti. 2008. Voice in Malay/Indonesian. *Lingua* 118. 1500–1553.
Donohue, Mark. 2004. Typology and linguistic areas. *Oceanic Linguistics* 43. 221–239.
Enfield, Nick J. 2001. On genetic and areal linguistics in Mainland South-East Asia: Parallel polyfunctionality of 'acquire'. In Alexandra Y. Aikhenvald & R. M. W. Dixon (eds.), *Areal diffusion and genetic inheritance: Problems in comparative linguistics*, 255–290. Oxford: Oxford University Press.
Enfield, Nick J. 2005. Areal linguistics and Mainland Southeast Asia. *Annual Review of Anthropology* 34. 181–206.Farid M. Onn. 1980. *Aspects of Malay phonology and morphology: A generative approach*. Bangi: Universiti Kebangsaan Malaysia.
Farid M. Onn. 1980. *Aspects of Malay phonology and morphology: A generative approach*. Bangi: Universiti Kebangsaan Malaysia.
Ferguson, Charles A. 1959. Diglossia. *Word* 15. 325–340.
Foley, William A. & Mike Olson. 1985. Clausehood and verb serialization. In Johanna Nichols & Anthony C. Woodbury (eds.), *Grammar inside and outside the clause: Some approaches to theory from the field*, 17–60. Cambridge: Cambridge University Press.
Fortin, Catherine R. 2007. *Indonesian sluicing and verb phrase ellipsis: Description and explanation in a Minimalist framework*. PhD thesis, University of Michigan.
Fortin, Catherine. 2009. On the left periphery in Indonesian. In Sandy Chung, Daniel Finer, Ileana Paul & Eric Potsdam (eds.), *Proceedings of the Sixteenth Meeting of the Austronesian Formal Linguistics Association*, 29–43. Santa Cruz: University of California.
Gil, David. 2007. Intonation and thematic roles in Riau Indonesian. In Chungmin Lee, Matthew Gordon & Daniel Büring (eds.), *Topic and focus: Cross-linguistic perspectives on meaning and intonation*, 41–68. Dordrecht: Springer.
Goddard, Cliff. 1994. The meaning of *lah*: Understanding 'emphasis' in Malay (Bahasa Melayu). *Oceanic Linguistics* 33. 145–165.
Goddard, Cliff. 2001. The polyfunctional Malay focus particle *pun*. *Multilingua* 20. 27–59.
Haas, Mary R. 1942. The use of numeral classifiers in Thai. *Language* 18. 201–205.
Halim, Amran. 1981. *Intonation in relation to syntax in Bahasa Indonesia*. Canberra: Pacific Linguistics.
Husni Abu Bakar, Karthik Durvasula, Nadya Pincus & Tim McKinnon. 2006. Incomplete laryngeal neutralization in KL Malay. Paper presented at the 11th International Symposium on Malay/Indonesian Linguistics (ISMIL).
Iwasaki, Shoichi & Preeya Ingkaphirom. 2005. *A reference grammar of Thai*. Cambridge: Cambridge University Press.
Klamer, Marian. 2002. Typical features of Austronesian languages in Central/Eastern Indonesia. *Oceanic Linguistics* 41. 363–383.
Koh, Ann Sweesun. 1990. *Topics in colloquial Malay*. PhD thesis, University of Melbourne.
Lim, Sonny. 1988. Baba Malay: The language of the 'Straits-born' Chinese. In Hein Steinhauer (ed.), *Papers in Western Austronesian linguistics* 3, 1–61. Canberra: Pacific Linguistics.

Mashudi Kader. 1981. *The syntax of Malay interrogatives*. Kuala Lumpur: Dewan Bahasa dan Pustaka.
Matisoff, James. 1973. Tonogenesis in Southeast Asia. In Larry M. Hyman (ed.), *Consonant types & tones*, 71–95. Los Angeles, CA: The Linguistic Program, University of Southern California.
Matisoff, James. 1983. Linguistic diversity and language contact in Thailand. In John McKinnon & Wanat Bhruksasri (eds.), *Highlanders of Thailand*, 56–86. Kuala Lumpur: Oxford University Press.
Matisoff, James. 1986. Hearts and minds in Southeast Asian languages and English: An essay in the comparative lexical semantics of psycho-collocations. *Cahiers de Lingustique – Asie Orientale* 15. 5–57.
Matisoff, James. 2004. Areal semantics – Is there such a thing? In Anju Saxena (ed.), *Himalayan languages, past and present*, 347–395. Berlin & New York: Mouton de Gruyter.
Mintz, Malcolm W. 2002. *An Indonesian & Malay grammar for students*. Perth: Indonesian/Malay Texts and Resources.
Mohd Yunus Sharum & Zaitul Azma Zainon Hamzah. 2011. Golongan dan rumus kata gandaan berima. *Jurnal Bahasa* 11. 27–47.
Musgrave, Simon. 2006. Complex emotion predicates in Eastern Indonesia: Evidence for language contact? In Yaron Matras, April McMahon & Nigel Vincent (eds.), *Linguistic areas: Convergence in historical and typological perspective*, 227–243. Hampshire: Palgrave Macmillan.
Muysken, Pieter & Tonjes Veenstra. 2006. Serial verbs. In Martin Everaert, Henk van Riemsdijk, Rob Goedemans & Bart Hollebrandse (eds.), *The Blackwell companion to syntax*, 234–270. Oxford: Blackwell.
Nguyen, Tuong Hung. 2004. *The structure of the Vietnamese noun phrase*. PhD thesis, Boston University.
Nik Safiah Karim, Farid M. Onn, Hashim Haji Musa & Abdul Hamid Mahmood. 2008. *Tatabahasa Dewan (edisi ketiga)*. Kuala Lumpur: Dewan Bahasa dan Pustaka.
Nomoto, Hiroki. 2006. *A study on complex existential sentences in Malay*. Master's thesis, Tokyo University of Foreign Studies.
Nomoto, Hiroki. 2009. On indefinite subjects of pivot verbs in Malay. *International Journal of Corpus Linguistics* 14. 221–254.
Nomoto, Hiroki. 2011. Mareeshiago no modariti no gaiyou [Modality in Malay: An overview]. *Gogaku Kenkyuujo Ronshuu* 16. 130–150.
Nomoto, Hiroki. 2012. Consonant-changing rhythmic reduplication in Malay as identity avoidance. Paper presented at the 19th Annual Meeting of the Austronesian Formal Linguistics Association (AFLA).
Nomoto, Hiroki. 2013a. On the optionality of grammatical markers: A case study of voice marking in Malay/Indonesian. In Alexander Adelaar (ed.), *Voice variation in Austronesian languages of Indonesia*, 123–145. Jakarta & Tokyo: Universitas Katolik Indonesia Atma Jaya & Tokyo University of Foreign Studies.
Nomoto, Hiroki. 2013b. *Number in classifier languages*. PhD thesis, University of Minnesota.
Nomoto, Hiroki & Aznur Aisyah Abdullah. 2016. Mareeshiago no shouten hyougen to meishi-jutsugobun [Focus expressions and nominal predicate sentences in Malay]. *Gogaku Kenkyuujo Ronshuu* 21. 171–189.

Nomoto, Hiroki & Aznur Aisyah Abdullah. To appear. Mareeshiago no toritate joshi to hutei hyougen [Focus-sensitive particles and indefinites in Malay]. *Gogaku Kenkyuujo Ronshuu* 22.

Nomoto, Hiroki & Kartini Abd. Wahab. 2011. Konstruksi *kena* dalam bahasa Indonesia: Perbandingan dengan bahasa Melayu. *Linguistik Indonesia* 29. 111–131.

Nomoto, Hiroki & Isamu Shoho. 2007. Voice in relative clauses in Malay: A comparison of written and spoken language. In Yuji Kawaguchi, Toshihiro Takagaki, Nobuo Tomimori & Yoichiro Tsuruga (eds.), *Corpus-based perspectives in linguistics*, 353–370. Amsterdam: John Benjamins.

Nordhoff, Sebastian. 2009. *A grammar of upcountry Sri Lanka Malay*. PhD thesis, University of Amsterdam.

Oey, Eric. 1990. Psycho-collocations in Malay: A Southeast Asian areal feature. *Linguistics of the Tibeto-Burman Area* 13. 141–158.

Percival, W. Keith. 1964. *A grammar of the Toba Batak*. PhD thesis, University of Michigan.

Philips, N. G. 1970. Topic clauses in Malay. *Bulletin of the School of Oriental and African Studies, University of London* 33. 560–572.

Piriyawiboon, Nattaya. 2009. The role of classifiers in N + Dem in Thai. Paper presented at the 19th annual meeting of the Southeast Asian Linguistics Society (SEALS).

Prasithrathsint, Amara. 2004. The adversative passive markers as a prominent areal feature of Southeast Asian languages. In Somsonge Buruphat (ed.), *Paper from the 11th Annual Meeting of Southeast Asian Linguistics Society 2001*, 583–598.

Prince, Alan & Paul Smolensky. 2004. *Optimality Theory: Constraint Interaction in Generative Grammar*. Malden, MA: Blackwell.

Shoho, Isamu. 2001. Mareeshiago no hutei hyougen. [A research into Malay indefinite expressions] *Gogaku Kenkyuujo Ronshuu* 6. 71–91.

Sato, Yosuke. 2007. P-stranding generalization and Bahasa Indonesia: A myth? *Snippets* 16. 17–18.

Shiohara, Asako. 2011. Reduplication and indication of plurality in Indonesian. Paper presented at the 15th International Symposium on Malay/Indonesian Linguistics (ISMIL).

Shiohara, Asako. 2012. Indication of plurality in Indonesian as observed in Indonesian school textbooks. Paper presented at the 15th International Symposium on Malay/Indonesian Linguistics (ISMIL).

Siraj, Pasha. 2010. 'Accidental' *ter-* in Malay as an anti-bouletic modifier. Paper presented at the 17th meeting of the Austronesian Formal Linguistics Association (AFLA).

Smith, Carlota S. & Mary S. Erbaugh. 2005. Temporal interpretation in Mandarin Chinese. *Linguistics* 43. 713–756.

Sneddon, James N. 1993. The drift towards final open syllables in Sulawesi languages. *Oceanic Linguistics* 32. 1–44.

Sneddon, James N. S., Alexander K. Adelaar, Dwi N. Djenar & Michael Ewing. 2010. *Indonesian: A comprehensive grammar*, 2nd ed. London: Routledge.

Soh, Hooi Ling. 1994. *Aspect and the organization of argument structure and phrase structure: Evidence from Malay*. Master's thesis, University of Calgary.

Soh, Hooi Ling. 2011. The syntax of *dah* in Colloquial Malay. Paper presented at the 15th international symposium on Malay/Indonesian linguistics (ISMIL).

Soh, Hooi Ling. 2013. Voice and aspect: Some notes from Malay. In Alexander Adelaar (ed.), *Voice variation in Austronesian languages of Indonesia*, 159–173. Jakarta & Tokyo: Universitas Katolik Indonesia Atma Jaya & Tokyo University of Foreign Studies.

Soh, Hooi Ling. 2016. Evidentiality, modality, focus and presupposition: The case of the discourse particle *punya* in Colloquial Malay. Paper presented at the 23rd annual meeting of the Austronesian Formal Linguistics Association (AFLA).

Soh, Hooi Ling. 2017. The syntax and semantics of the aspectual particle *dah* in colloquial Malay. Manuscript, University of Minnesota.

Soh, Hooi Ling & Hiroki Nomoto. 2009. Progressive aspect, the verbal prefix *meN-*, and the stative sentences in Malay. *Oceanic Linguistics* 48. 148–171.

Soh, Hooi Ling & Hiroki Nomoto. 2011. The Malay verbal prefix *meN-* and the unergative/unaccusative distinction. *Journal of East Asian Linguistics* 20. 77–106.

Soh, Hooi Ling & Hiroki Nomoto. 2015. Degree achievements, telicity and the verbal prefix *meN-* in Malay. *Journal of Linguistics* 51. 147–183.

Tadmor, Uri. 2000. Rekonstruksi aksen kata bahasa Melayu. In Yassir Nasanius & Bambang Kaswanti Purwo (eds.), *PELBBA 13: Pertemuan Linguistik (Pusat Kajian) Bahasa dan Budaya Atma Jaya: Ketiga Belas,* 153–167. Pusat Kajian Bahasa dan Budaya, Unika Atma. Jaya, Jakarta.

Tang, C. C. Jane. 1990. *Chinese phrase structure and the extended X-bar theory*. PhD thesis, Cornell University.

Teoh, Boon Seong. 1994. *The sound system of Malay revisited*. Kuala Lumpur: Dewan Bahasa dan Pustaka.

Tham, Seong Chee. 1979. Vowel patterning and meaning in Malay pair-words. In Nguyen Dang Liem (ed.), *South-East Asian Linguistic Studies*, 365–377. Canberra: Pacific Linguistics.

Thurgood, Elzbieta A. 1998. *A description of nineteenth century Baba Malay: A Malay variety influenced by language shift*. PhD thesis, University of Hawai'i.

Tosco, Mauro. 2008. What to do when you are unhappy with language areas but you do not want to quit. *Journal of Language Contact* THEMA 2. 112–123.

Tran, Jennie. 2011. *The acquisition of Vietnamese classifiers*. PhD thesis (pre-defence version), University of Hawai'i.

Vittrant, Alice. 2008. Burmese as a language of the Mainland South-East Asian *Sprachbund*. Paper presented at the 21st International Conference on Sino-Tibetan Languages and Linguistics (ICSTLL).

Yap, Foong Ha. 2007. On native and contact-induced grammaticalization: The case of Malay *empunya*. Manuscript, Department of Linguistics and Modern Languages, Chinese University of Hong Kong.

Winstedt, Richard O. 1920. *Colloquial Malay: A simple grammar with conversations*, 2nd ed. Singapore: Kelly & Walsh.

Winstedt, Richard O. 1927. *Malay grammar*. Oxford: Clarendon Press.

Zaharani Ahmad. 2007. *Pembentukan kata ganda separa bahasa Melayu*. Kuala Lumpur: Dewan Bahasa dan Pustaka.

Zainudin Dirin. 2000. *Kamus penjodoh bilangan untuk KBSR*. Shah Alam: Fajar Bakti.

Zainu'l-Abidin bin Ahmad (Za'ba). 1927. Pair-words in Malay. *Journal of the Malaysian Branch of the Royal Asiatic Society* 5. 324–338.

Zeitoun, Elizabeth. 2007. *A Grammar of Mantauran (Rukai)*. Taipei: Institute of Linguistics, Academia Sinica.

Zuraidah Mohd Don, Gerry Knowles & Janet Yong. 2008. How words can be misleading: A study of syllable timing and 'stress' in Malay. *The Linguistics Journal* 3. 66–81.

Appendix 1: Summary of linguistic features

Legend
+++ the feature is pervasive or used obligatorily in the language
++ the feature is normal but selectively distributed in the language
+ the feature is merely possible or observable in the language
− the feature is impossible or absent in the language

	Feature	+++/++/+/−	§ ref. in this chapter
Phonetics	Lexical tone or register	−	§1.1, p.476
Phonetics	Back unrounded vowels	−	§1.2, p.479
Phonetics	Initial velar nasal	+	§1.2, p.477
Phonetics	Implosive consonants	−	−
Phonetics	Sesquisyllabic structures	−	§1.3, p.480
Morphology	Tendency towards monosyllabicity	++	§2.1, p.480
Morphology	Tendency to form compounds	+++	§2.1, p.482–85
Morphology	Tendency towards isolating (rather than affixation)	++	§2.1, p.481–82, see also §3.2.1, p.492–95
Morphology	Psycho-collocations	+++	§2.2, p.485
Morphology	Elaborate expressions (e.g. four-syllable or other set patterns)	+++	§2.3, p.486
Morphology	Reduplication generally	+++	§2.4, p.487
Morphology	Reduplication of nouns	+++	§2.4, p.487
Morphology	Reduplication of verbs	+++	§2.4, p.488–89
Grammar	Use of classifiers	++	§3.1.2, p.490
Grammar	Classifiers used in counting	++	§3.1.2, p.490
Grammar	Classifiers used with demonstratives	−	§3.1.2, p.492
Grammar	Adjectival verbs	+	not discussed explicitly
Grammar	Grammatical number	−	§3.2.1, p.492
Grammar	Inflection of verbs	−	§3.2.1, p.492
Grammar	Use of tense/aspect markers	+++	§3.2.1, p.492–94
Grammar	Use of verb plural markers	−	not discussed explicitly
Grammar	Grammaticalization of GET/OBTAIN (potential mod. resultative/perfect aspect)	+++	§3.2.2, p.495

	Feature	+++/++/+/−	§ ref. in this chapter
Grammar	Grammaticalization of PUT, SET (completed/resultative aspect)	−	−
Grammar	Grammaticalization of GIVE (causative, benefactive; preposition)	+++	not discussed, though an example is given in (61b), §3.2.3
Grammar	Grammaticalization of FINISH (perfective/ complete aspect; conjunction/temporal subordinator)	−	−
Grammar	Grammaticalization of directional verbs e.g. GO / COME (allative, venitive)	−	−
Grammar	Grammaticalization of SEE, WATCH (temptative)	−	−
Grammar	Grammaticalization of STAY, REMAIN (progressive and continuous, durative aspects)	−	−
Grammar	Serial verb constructions	+++	§3.2.3, p.496
Syntax	Verb precedes object (VO)	+++	§3.3, p.498
Syntax	Auxiliary precedes verb	+++	§3.3, p.498, see also §3.2.1, p.492–95
Syntax	Preposition precedes noun	+++	not discussed explicitly
Syntax	Noun precedes adjective	+++	§3.1.1, p.489
Syntax	Noun precedes demonstrative	+++	§3.1.1, p.489
Syntax	Noun precedes genitive	+++	§3.1.1, p.489
Syntax	Noun precedes relative clause	+++	§3.1.1, p.489
Syntax	Use of topic-comment structures	+++	§3.3.2, p.499
Syntax	Ellipsis of arguments known from context	+++	§3.3.1, p.498
Lexical semantics	Specific terms for forms of rice	+++	§4.1.1, p.505
Pragmatics	Use of utterance-final pragmatic particles	+++	§4.2.1, p.506
Pragmatics	Encoding of politeness	+++	§4.2.2, p.508
Pragmatics	Encoding of honorifics	+++	§4.2.2, p.508

Appendix 2: Text interlinearized

'Mujur   tak   kena   tikam'   (Harian Metro, 11/08/2011)
fortunate not   get   stab
'Fortunate not getting stabbed'

KUALA LUMPUR: "Orang kata saya turut di-tikam, tapi mujur   tak kena.
Kuala Lumpur   person say 1SG too PASS-stab but fortunate not get

Saya tak nampak pisau, tapi orang di flat berdekatan memberitahu
1SG not see   knife but person at flat nearby   tell

kelompok   perusuh itu   bersenjatakan   pisau," kata
group   rioter   that   use.as.weapon   knife   say

Muhammed Asyraf Haziq Rossli,   20.
Muhammed Asyraf Haziq Rossli   20

'KUALA LUMPUR: "People have been saying that I was stabbed too, but fortunately I wasn't. I didn't see a knife, but people living in a nearby flat said that the rioters used knives as their weapon," said Muhammed Asyraf Haziq Rossli, 20.'

Dia yang cedera   di mulut   akibat di-serang   dan di-rompak perusuh
3SG REL   injured at mouth   result PASS-attack and PASS-rob   rioter

ketika melalui satu kawasan rusuhan di timur London, terpaksa
when   pass   one   area   riot   at east   London   have.to

menjalani pembedahan membetulkan rahang-nya yang patah dan
undergo   surgery   fix   jaw-3SG   REL   break and

kini menerima rawatan   di Royal London Hospital.
now   receive   treatment at Royal London Hospital.

'He, who suffered an injury to his mouth as a result of having been attacked and robbed by rioters while passing through a riot area in east London, had to undergo surgery to fix his broken jaw and is currently receiving treatment at Royal London Hospital.'

Dalam	temubual	di-rakam	wakil	Kelab	Umno	London
in	interview	PASS-record	representative	club	Umno	London

kelmarin,	penuntut	perakaunan	tajaan	Mara	di	Kolej
day.before.yesterday	student	accounting	sponsorship	Mara	at	college

Kaplan,	London	itu	memberitahu,	kejadian	berlaku	pantas	dan	dia
Kaplan	London	that	tell	incident	happen	quick	and	3SG

tidak	dapat	melarikan	diri	ketika	di-kerumuni	kumpulan	berkenaan.
not	can	run	self	when	PASS-surround	group	relevant

'In an interview recorded by the representative of Kelab Umno London the day before yesterday, the accounting student sponsored by Mara at Kaplan College, London, said that the incident occurred so quickly that he could not run away when surrounded by the group of rioters.'

"Saya	sedang	mengayuh	basikal	ketika	itu	dan	memang	tak
1SG	PROG	pedal	bicycle	time	that	and	really	not

boleh	buat	apa-apa	kerana	mereka	ramai,	(ketika	di-kerumuni)
can	do	anything	because	3PL	many	when	PASS-surround

ada	yang	seluk	belakang	baju	sejuk	ber-hud	yang	saya
exist	REL	grab	back	clothes	cold	with-hood	REL	1SG

pakai	dan	ada	ambil	telefon.
wear	and	exist	take	telephone

'"I was riding my bicycle then and really couldn't do anything because there were many of them, (when I was surrounded by them) one grabbed the back of the hooded sweater I was wearing and another took my phone.'

"Mereka	juga	tarik	basikal	yang	saya	tunggang	menyebabkan	saya
3PL	also	pull	bicycle	REL	1SG	ride	cause	1SG

jatuh	dan	mulut	berdarah.	Masa	jatuh	itu-lah	saya	rasa	rahang
fall	and	mouth	bleed	time	fall	that-PART	1SG	feel	jaw

saya	sudah	patah	dan	mereka	semua	lari	apabila	nampak	saya
1SG	PFV	break	and	3PL	all	flee	when	see	1SG

berdarah," kata-nya dalam nada berhati-hati menahan sakit.
bleed say-3SG in tone careful withstand pain

'They also pulled the bicycle I was riding, which made me fall and my mouth bleed. It was when I fell that I felt my jaw was broken and they all fled seeing me bleeding," he said in a careful tone, withstanding the pain.'

Muhammed Asyraf Haziq berkata, selepas di-serang, dia di-sapa pula
Muhammed Asyraf Haziq say after PASS-attack 3SG PASS-greet then

beberapa lelaki lain yang menawarkan pertolongan, tapi dalam masa
a.few man other REL offer help but in time

sama ada orang di belakang-nya menyelongkar beg sandang
same exist person at back-3SG rummage bag sling

di-pakai.
PASS-wear

'Muhammed Asyraf Haziq said, after he was attacked, he was then greeted by a few other men who offered help, but at the same time there were also people behind him rummaging in his backpack.'

"*Ketika rusuhan berlaku semua warga kulit hitam saja yang saya*
when riot happen all citizen skin black only REL 1SG

nampak, cuma ada dua orang saja kulit putih. Orang yang
see just exist two CLF only skin white person REL

menyerang dan merompak itu daripada kumpulan sama juga.
attack and rob that from group same also

'"When the riot happened, the people that I could see were all black-skinned citizens, there were only two white-skinned ones. The people who attacked and robbed me were also from that group.'

"*Dia macam ada satu kumpulan yang pergi, kemudian datang orang*
3SG like exist one group REL go then come person

lain dari belakang... jadi saya nak lari pun tak boleh
other from back so 1SG want flee even not can

dah,"   kata-nya.
already   say-3SG
'"It was like there was a group going and another group of people coming from behind ... so even though I wanted to get away, I couldn't do so already," he said.'

Dia	memberitahu,	ada	kanak-kanak	kecil	di-percayai	murid
3SG	tell	exist	child	small	PASS-believe	pupil

sekolah rendah terbabit dalam kumpulan merusuh itu, malah kanak-kanak
primary.school involved in   group   riot   that even child

terbabit   yang mengetuk dan menginginkan basikal-nya.
involved   REL knock   and want   bicycle-3SG
'He said that there was a small child, who was believed to be a primary school student, involved in the riot group, and, in fact, it was this child who knocked his bicycle and asked for it.'

Namun,   kata-nya dia tidak pasti   sama ada kanak-kanak terbabit
however   say-3SG   3SG not   certain whether child   involved

mendapat apa   yang di-inginkan kerana   dia terus   beredar
get   what   REL   PASS-want   because 3SG immediately leave

menyeberangi jalan berdekatan sebelum di-bantu   dua wanita ber-kulit
cross   street nearby   before PASS-help two woman   with-skin

hitam yang memberi-nya tisu   (bagi mengelap darah).
black REL give   tissue for   wipe   blood
'However, he said, he was not certain whether the child got what he wanted because he immediately moved away to cross the nearby street, when he was given help by two black-skinned women, who gave him tissue paper (to wipe the blood).'

"Budak kecil itu memang ada.   Dia yang ketuk-ketuk basikal
kid   small that really exist 3SG REL   knock   bicycle

saya tanda mahukan. Tapi, selepas apa yang berlaku, saya tak tahu
1SG sign want   but   after   what REL happen   1SG not know

dia	*dapat*	*atau*	*tidak*	*(basikal),*	*rasanya*	*orang*	*lain*	*yang*	*ambil*
3SG	get	or	not	bicycle	seemingly	person	other	REL	take

sebab	*dalam*	*video*	*pun*	*nampak*	*orang*	*lain*	*yang*	*kayuh,"*	*kata-nya.*
because	in	video	too	see	person	other	REL	pedal	say-3SG

'"The small kid was really there. It is s/he who knocked my bicycle to show that s/he wants it. But, after the incident that happened to me, I don't know if s/he got (the bicycle) or not. It seems another person had taken it because in the video too another person was seen riding it," he said.'

Marc Brunelle and Phú Văn Hẳn
Colloquial Eastern Cham

Eastern Cham is an Austronesian language spoken by about 100,000 people in the provinces of Ninh Thuận and Bình Thuận, in south-central Vietnam (Vietnamese census 2009). Eastern Cham communities are scattered throughout these two provinces and are interspersed with Vietnamese communities. As a result, all Eastern Cham speakers are now at least fluent in Vietnamese and younger speakers usually speak it natively (alongside with Cham). Until the 19th century, Cham (along with other Chamic languages and possible some Mon-Khmer languages) was the language of the "confederation" of Champa, a mandala-type kingdom located on the central coast of Vietnam that was gradually absorbed by the Vietnamese state from the 10th to the 19th century. As a former state language, Cham has a long written tradition, but its script is now barely used (Brunelle 2008).

Although there have been a number of descriptions of Eastern Cham, most of them have focused on the written language or on the formal language that is usually volunteered by speakers in data elicitation sessions (Aymonier 1889; Aymonier and Cabaton 1906; Moussay 1971; Bùi 1995; 1996a; b; Thurgood 2005; Moussay 2006). However, the differences between the colloquial and formal languages and the contexts of functional use of each variety strongly suggest that Eastern Cham is now in a diglossic situation (Brunelle 2008; 2009). The two varieties show marked differences, especially in their phonologies and in the degree to which they have been affected by Vietnamese. The goal of this article is to complement previous work by presenting a basic description of the colloquial language, which, as a living and quickly evolving language, is the locus of language convergence. The data provided in this paper are therefore entirely given in their colloquial form. We are well aware that this is controversial and that many Cham intellectuals oppose any scholarly description of what they consider a corrupt form of speech. However, as the colloquial variety is de facto the real language of the community, we believe it deserves to be described.

Marc Brunelle: Dept. of Linguistics, University of Ottawa,
E-Mail: marc.brunelle@uottawa.ca
Phú Văn Hẳn: Viện Khoa học xã hội vùng Nam Bộ (Institute of Social Sciences of southern Vietnam), E-Mail: phuvanhan@gmail.com

The data presented in this paper have been collected from a large number of consultants living in Ninh Thuận province and Hồ Chí Minh City over the past few years. They have been complemented and double-checked against the intuitions of the second author, who is a native speaker of Eastern Cham born in the village of Vụ Bổn, in Ninh Thuận. The reader should keep in mind that grammaticality judgments are difficult to elicit in a language that shows substantial sociolectal and dialectal diversity, does not have clear standards and is barely taught in schools. Overall, Cham speakers have much less rigid grammaticality judgments than speakers of large written languages like English, French or Vietnamese. Widespread bilingualism in Vietnamese further increases the tolerance of speakers to forms that would probably have been judged ungrammatical a few generations ago.

1 Phonology

Our phonology section slightly departs from the basic organization found in other chapters of this book. Since the basic word template plays a crucial role in the phonotactic restrictions found in Eastern Cham, it will be addressed first (§1.1) and will be followed by descriptions of segmental (§1.2) and suprasegmental phoneme inventories (§1.3).

1.1 Basic word template and syllable structure

The formal variety of Eastern Cham has two main types of word templates: monosyllables and sesquisyllables (Blood 1967; Thurgood 1996; 1999). Sesquisyllables are words made up of "a syllable and a half" (Matisoff 1973), i.e. disyllabic words with a major syllable and a reduced minor syllable. The main final syllable of a sesquisyllable is stressed and exhibits the entire array of possible phonological contrasts, while its minor syllable (or presyllable) only contains a subset of the vowels, onsets and codas found in the main syllable. This is shown schematically in (1a).

(1) Word shapes in the formal (a) and colloquial (b) varieties
    a.   σ   σ
        (C) (V) (C) **C (G/L) V (C)**
    b.   σ
        (C) C (G) V (C)

By contrast, the colloquial variety (1b) has lost most of its presyllables, due to a diachronic process of monosyllabization (Trung-tâm Văn-hoá Chàm 197?; Alieva 1991; 1994; Brunelle 2005b; 2009). Exceptions include religious and learned vocabulary items, which could be considered as inherently formal. A few sesquisyllables are also preserved to avoid homophony. The best example is the contrast between *ṭapăn* 'eight' and *tʰampăn* 'nine', which would both be realized as [păn] if they were monosyllabized.

Monosyllabization has taken place either through the loss of the entire presyllable, or through the elision of its vowel and the formation of an onset cluster composed of the onset of the presyllable and the onset of the main syllable. The complete loss of the presyllable or the formation of an onset cluster, and the exact realization of clusters (if clusters are formed), greatly vary across villages, age groups and genders. Without a full sociolinguistic survey, it is difficult to lay out precise rules, but two general principles seem to constrain the outcome of monosyllabization:
1) Clusters usually follow the sonority hierarchy, although some clusters consisting of a nasal and a stop can violate it, as in *mta* 'eye'.
2) If the onset of the main syllable was originally a liquid [l] or [r], a cluster is usually formed (as in *plěj* or *mlěj* 'village' < *palěj*).

An important point regarding the syllable structure given in (1) is that there are no words without onsets. Several dictionaries and grammars omit to mark onset glottal stops or choose not to do it for convenience (Moussay 1971; Bùi 1995; 1996a), but the presence of the onset glottal stop is carefully marked elsewhere (Blood 1967).

1.2 Segmental phonemes: consonants and vowels

Two factors constrain the phonotactic distribution of segments in Eastern Cham: the syllable in which they stand and their position in the syllable. As the colloquial variety is now almost entirely monosyllabic, the segments found in presyllables could be omitted. However, some words related to religion or other cultural activities are inherently formal and are therefore sesquisyllabic even in the colloquial language. We thus give the segmental inventory of presyllables, even if they are relatively uncommon.

1.2.1 Consonants

- **Main syllable onsets**

The full inventory of consonants, given in (2), surfaces in the onset of the main syllable. There are five places of articulation: labial, dental, palatal, velar and laryngeal. In addition to three series of stops (plain voiceless, voiceless aspirated and voiced implosive), there are voiceless fricatives, nasals, liquids and glides.

(2)	lab.	dent.	pal.	vel.	lar.
plain stops	p	t	c	k	ʔ
asp. stops	pʰ	tʰ	cʰ	kʰ	
implosives	ɓ	ɗ	ʄ		
fricatives		s			h
nasals	m	n	ɲ	ŋ	
liquids		l, r			
glides			j	w	
preglottalized glides			ʔj	ʔw	

This inventory is fairly consensual. The only divergence between authors is that Moussay treats the preglottalized glides /ʔw-/ and /ʔj-/ as simplex phonemes (Moussay 1971) whereas other scholars analyze them as sequences of glottal stops plus glides (Blood 1967; Bùi 1996a; Phú 2003). The distribution of medial glides suggests that the second solution is preferable: all onsets can be followed by the medial glides /-j-, -w-/ except the contentious preglottalized glides themselves. Another interesting fact about glides is that onset /w-/ cannot form a cluster with medial /-j-/, but that the cluster /jw-/ is possible, as in *jwa*, 'because'. The liquids /r/ and /l/ can also be found in medial position. They never form clusters with sonorants in the formal variety, but often combine with /m-/ in the colloquial variety.

Some onsets have several possible realizations. The aspirated /pʰ, kʰ/ can be realized as [f, x] respectively. The sonorant /w/ frequently alternates with [v] and [ʋ], while /r/ can be pronounced as [r], [z], [j] or [ʒ]. The voiced fricative [z] is also a common surface form of /j/. Combinations of onsets and medial glides or liquids have an even wider array of possible realizations. For example, /tr-/ can be realized as [tr-], [tʃ-] or [c-] and /tl-/ is often changed to [kl-]. These variants are largely determined by sociolinguistic factors, but since many of them are also idiosyncratic, they will not be discussed in detail here. What is interesting is that a number of them, like the realization of /w/ as [v] rather than [ʋ] and the spirantization of aspirated stops into fricatives seem to bring the Cham inventory closer to Vietnamese. The fact that [tʰ] is the only Eastern Cham aspirate that does not spirantize seems to support this claim, as it is also the only aspirated stop in modern Vietnamese.

- **Main syllable codas**

As in most Mainland Southeast Asian languages, the coda consonant inventory of Eastern Cham is a subset of onset consonants. It is given in (3).

(3)
	lab.	dent.	pal./vel.	lar.
plain stops	p [p~wʔ]	t	c [jʔ]	ʔ
fricatives		s [jh]		h
nasals	m	n	ŋ	
glides			j/w	

Several authors mention that the coda stops of Eastern Cham are debuccalized (Aymonier 1889; Blood 1967; Moussay 1971; Hoàng 1987; Bùi 1996a). This has led other researchers to posit a process of place neutralization in codas (Phú, Edmondson and Gregerson 1992; Thurgood 1999), but there is good evidence that contrasts are still maintained. While coda /-p/ is realized as either [-p] or [-wʔ] and coda /-c/ is systematically reduced to [-jʔ], coda /-t/ is still preserved everywhere, except in the word ke̯ʔ 'what' (historically hakĕ̯t). It has also been claimed that coda /-h/ is dropped (Phú, Edmondson and Gregerson 1992), but acoustic evidence does not support this (Brunelle 2005b; 2006).

A type of coda neutralization that is not controversial is the merger of the dental sonorants /-l, -r/ (Bùi 1996a). They are usually realized as [-n] in Ninh Thuận and as [-j] in Bình Thuận (the location of the exact isogloss is unclear). In formal speech, [-r] and [-l] are still found, although the relatively high proportion of hypercorrect forms in which [-l] is used for an etymological /-n/ suggests that this is not a regular alternation.

- **Presyllable onsets**

Presyllable onsets are a subset of main syllable onsets, as shown in (4). Two of the classes of onsets found in main syllables are not found in presyllables: implosive stops and aspirated stops. There is one exception to this generalization: the aspirated stop /tʰ/ was recently reintroduced in the inventory because a diachronic change turned most instances of onset /s/ into /tʰ/, thus creating an asymmetry in the distribution (Proto-Chamic *sălipăn > colloquial Eastern Cham tʰampăn). A final observation is that velar nasals are never found in presyllable onsets.

(4)		lab.	dent.	pal.	vel.	lar.
plain stops		p	t	c	k	ʔ
asp. stops			tʰ		
fricatives			s			h
nasals		m	n	ɲ	
liquids			l, r		
glides				j	w

- **Presyllable codas**

Presyllables codas can only be /h/, as in ṭăhla? 'I – formal' or nasals homorganic with the following main syllable onset, as in tănrăn 'plain'. They are given in (5).

(5) laryngeal   h
    nasals   homorganic nasal

1.2.2 Vowels

The best description of the modern vowel inventory of Eastern Cham is found in Bùi (1996). We will therefore use Bùi's grammar as a basis for comparison with other descriptions.

- **Main syllables**

In main syllables, there are nine vowel qualities. Seven of these nine vowels have a length contrast; the front and back mid vowels /e/ and /o/ only occur as long vowels. Long vowels are much longer than short vowels in wordlist reading (2:1 ratio), but this ratio seems smaller in running speech. The complete inventory is given in (6).

(6) ĭ/i   ɨ̆/ɨ   ŭ/u
    e   ə̆/ə   o
    ĕ/ɛ   ă/a   ɔ̆/ɔ

Contrastive length is overlooked by Blood, who writes that: "there are neither vowel clusters nor length contrast in the predominant syllable pattern" (Blood 1967), but it is accurately reported in other sources (Moussay 1971; Bùi 1996a). It is subject to two phonotactic constraints: open syllable vowels are always long and vowels closed by /-h/ or /-c/ [-jʔ] are always short.

There are two diphthongs, /ie/ and /uo/. They are treated as separate phonemes in all environments by some authors (Moussay 1971; Bùi 1996a). However, since they are frequently realized as the monophthongs [i] and [u] in closed syllables, they could be treated as free variants of the long vowels /i/ and /u/ in that environment. On the other hand, /ie/ and /uo/ occasionally contrast with the long vowels /i/ and /u/ in open syllables (Blood 1967), a contrast that is restricted to a handful of minimal pairs.

There is some allophonic variation in vowel realization. For example, /o/ is frequently raised to [u] before nasals. Since that type of allophony tends to vary from village to village and between gender and age groups, we will not attempt to describe it. Part of this variation could perhaps be attributable to contact with Vietnamese: some vowel changes are common to both Eastern Cham and south-central Vietnamese dialects (for example, /e/ often centralizes to /ə/ in closed syllables in both languages).

- **Presyllables**

To our knowledge, there are only two explicit descriptions of the vowel sub-inventory of presyllables (Bùi 1996a; Thurgood 2003). The vowels found in presyllables are a subset of the main syllable vowel inventory, as shown in (7).

(7) ĭ   ɨ̆   ŭ
    ə̆
    ă

There is no length contrast in presyllables, but vowels tend to be very short in this environment; they are usually shorter than short vowels in main syllables and are often centralized to schwa, even in relatively formal speech.

1.3 Suprasegmental phonology: register and tone

Phonological register originates from the loss of the voicing contrast in onset stops after the break-up of Proto-Chamic (Blood 1962; Bùi 1996a; Thurgood 1996; 1999). The basic pattern is given in (8). Voiceless and voiced aspirates underwent the same process as plain voiceless and voiced stops. Implosives, on the other end, maintained their voicing. Following previous work, we mark the low register as a subscript dot under the onset consonant (Moussay 1971). The choice of an open dot rather than the full one used by Moussay has been made to avoid confusion with the retroflex subscript.

(8) Proto-Chamic   Cham   Gloss
    păk   >   pă?   'at'
    băk   >   pă̰?   'full'

Phonetically, register is realized on the rhyme through a combination of pitch, intensity, vowel quality, voice quality and duration, but pitch and voice quality are its most robust correlates (Phú, Edmondson and Gregerson 1992; Brunelle 2005b; 2006). The high register, that stems from Proto-Chamic voiceless stops, voiceless aspirated stops and sonorants, is characterized by a relatively high pitch and a modal voice. The low register, which is the reflex of voiced stops and voiced aspirated stops, has a lower pitch, a breathier voice, and tends to be associated with longer vowels. The register contrast is neutralized in implosives and preglottalized glides. Phonetically, syllables headed by these consonants have a high pitch and a modal phonation.

1.3.1 Register spreading and monosyllabization

Historically, register spread rightwards through sonorants, but was blocked by stops. Examples of register spreading are given in (9).

(9) Written Cham   Gloss   Formal variety   Colloquial variety
    jalan   'road'   çalan [ça̤lan]   kl̥an~l̰an
    da?a   'to invite'   ṭa?a [ṭa̰?a]   ?a̰

Because of the monosyllabization process described above, presyllables were dropped in casual speech, which lead to the extension of the register contrast to sonorants in minimal pairs such as *ni* 'here' and *ṇi* (< *ṇani*) 'follower of nativized Islam'. As a result, the register contrast is now found in monosyllabic words headed by all consonants, except implosives and preglottalized glides.

1.3.2 Tonal developments?

It is tempting to analyze the Eastern Cham register contrast as a two-tone system (Blood 1967). There is limited evidence for or against such an analysis, but word game data suggest that register is a segmental property of onsets rather than a suprasegmental property of the rhyme (Brunelle 2005a). If this is correct, we have to adopt the position that Eastern Cham is still a relatively conservative Southeast Asian register language, despite intensive contact with tonal Vietnamese.

It has long been observed that the two registers of Eastern Cham are subject to allophonic pitch variations conditioned by codas (Blood 1967; Moussay 1971; Bùi 1996a). Recently, some authors have made a stronger claim, proposing that coda consonants are either lost or reanalyzed as suprasegmental elements, shifting the phonemic burden to the pitch curve itself and thus leading to the formation of a complex tone system (Hoàng 1987; Phú, Edmondson and Gregerson 1992; Thurgood 1993). However, careful recordings and phonetic analysis reveal that although codas are often debuccalized (§1.2.1), they are not dropped and maintain their patterns of contrast (Brunelle 2005b; 2006). Further, the pattern of allophonic pitch variation is not the same in all speakers, making it impossible to distinguish more than a two-way contrast in pitch (Brunelle 2005b; 2006). A final piece of evidence that suggests that Eastern Cham does not have a complex tone system is the important role of intonation in information structure (assuming that languages with complex tone systems limit the role of intonation for functional reasons). Intonation often distinguishes sentences types and accompanies sentence-final particles (Blood, DL 1977; Blood, DW 1977).

2 Morphology

A few aspects of Eastern Cham morphology will be discussed in this section. We will start with the loss of morphological affixes in Cham and the central role of compounding in word formation (§2.1). We will then assess the role of a few types of morphological processes that are common in Mainland Southeast Asia: psycho-collocations (§2.2), elaborative expressions (§2.3) and productive reduplication (§2.4).

2.1 Word structure

While Cham originally had a small set of prefixes and infixes (Aymonier 1889; Bùi 1996a; Moussay 2006), modern colloquial Eastern Cham has lost them. Their functions have now been taken over by periphrastic structures. For example, classical Cham *paɓăŋ* 'to feed' (causative *pa-* + *ɓăŋ* 'eat') is now rendered as *prěj ɓăŋ*, literally 'to give to eat'.

Compounding is now the most frequent word formation strategy. Types of compounds are reviewed and classified in detail in Bùi (1996a, §4.4.1). For the sake of brevity, only a few examples will be given here. Compounds can include identical or different parts of speech. In (10), examples of all possible types of compounds are given. In the first three pairs of examples (10a–c), a coordinative compound (without a semantic head) and a subordinative compound are given. All other examples (10d–i) are headed. Almost all these compounds belong to the same word category as their first element.

(10) a. N+N
- plěj ķan — village + country — 'hometown'
- ṭeh mɔ — vehicle + cow — 'oxcart or, by ext., any other vehicle'

b. A¹+A
- ṭah krah — bright + beautiful — 'luminous'
- ʔjaʔ plŏw — sunny + hot — 'sultry'

c. V+V
- ɗom klaw — talk + laugh — 'to joke'
- tɔŋ poh — hit + beat — 'to maltreat'

d. N+V
- ʔja mɲum — water + drink — 'drinking water'
- ṭaj tăm — rice plant + transplant — 'transplanted rice'

e. V+N
- wăn ķlaj — forget + forest — 'confused'
- ķwah çin — search + money — 'to earn a living'

f. N + A
- ṭaj çuʔ — rice + black — 'high-quality rice'
- ça klɔh — guy + blind — 'incorrigible person'

g. V + A
- ɗom kəh — speak + vulgar — 'to utter obscenities'
- ʔjŏʔ lap — look + cheap — 'to despise'

h. A + N
- sam kěj — beautiful + male — 'handsome'
- sĭt sɛʔ — small + body — 'small-bodied'

i. A + V
- ɓŏn ʔjŏʔ — easy + watch — 'good-looking'
- kan pac — difficult + study — 'hard to learn'

These compounds are not all lexicalized to the same degree. While *plěj ķan* 'hometown' (10a) is highly lexicalized (*ķan* 'country' is now relatively rare in the

---

1 Note that Eastern Cham distinguishes adjectives (or perhaps more accurately, stative verbs) and active verbs. A stative verb can be preceded by pjăʔ 'very', while an action verb cannot. For instance, *lăʔ pjăʔ sĭt* 'I am very short' is grammatical, but *lăʔ pjăʔ ɓăŋ* 'I eat a lot' is not.

spoken language), the decompositionality of *kan ɲac* 'hard to learn' (10i) is much greater and new compounds can be productively created by combining *kan* 'difficult' with other verbs.

2.2 Psycho-collocations

Psycho-collocations are a type of expression in which a psycho-noun, a noun referring to a body part, is combined to a 'psycho-mate', typically an adjective, to express personal qualities or mental states (Matisoff 1986). Psycho-collocations are common in all language families of Southeast Asia (Matisoff 1986; Jaisser 1990; Oey 1990). Colloquial Eastern Cham also has them, although they seem far less common than in Jingpho, Thai, Malay or Hmong.

Our non-exhaustive list of psycho-nouns includes half a dozen body parts, illustrated by the examples in (11). There is about the same number of psycho-mates, *prɔ̆ŋ* 'large' being the most common one. Note that contrary to Thai, it is not possible to reverse the order of the psycho-noun and its mate (Matisoff 1986).

(11a) kʰəh ŋĭn   beautiful + hand   'skillful'
       kl̥ɛh kl̥aj   tired + penis   'exhausted (men)'
       prɔ̆ŋ taj   large + liver   'reckless, foolhardy'
       prɔ̆ŋ rup   large + body   'self-important'
       prɔ̆ŋ kɔʔ   large + head   'arrogant'
       prɔ̆ŋ tjan   large + belly   'generous'

Reduplicated psycho-nouns with coupled mates are not common in Cham. The only example our consultants could come up with is in (11b). Finally, we found one example of a psycho-noun with antonymic mates (11c).

(11b) t̥ah bɔʔ t̥ah mta   bright + face + bright + eye   'proud'

(11c) sam taj   beautiful + liver   'good hearted'
       cʰaʔ taj   ugly + liver   'evil, bad (of a person)'

To sum up, psycho-collocations are attested in Cham, but do not seem to be much more common than in Western languages. It is unclear if the examples that we found are remnants of a previously much larger set or if the number of Cham psycho-collocations has always been relatively small.

2.3 Elaborative expressions

An elaborative expression is a form of reduplication based on rhyming or alliteration (Enfield 2005). Elaborative processes are not productive in the sense that they do not obey regular rules of segmental transformations. Like other Southeast Asian languages, Eastern Cham has an extremely large number of elaborative expressions. In the examples given in (12), the base is bolded.

(12) cɔh **rɔh** (cwah rwah in Bui 1996a) 'choose'   from rɔh 'choose'
     sup lup   'pitch dark' from sup 'dark'
     mi **măn**   'very fast'   from măn 'fast'
     lăŋ loi   'clear'   from lăŋ 'to explain.

Interestingly, the base of Cham elaborative expressions can be either the right or the left element, which further exemplifies their non-regular shape. As in other Mainland Southeast Asian languages, elaborative expressions can sometimes be quadrisyllabic, but this seems limited to the two examples in (13).

(13) ɓan ḳlaj ɓan klɔ   'pell-mell, meaningless'   ḳlaj 'forest'
     lin pin lan pan   'pell-mell, meaningless'   Not decomposable

2.4 Productive reduplication

Contrary to other Mainland Southeast Asian languages that have a number of reduplication templates following relatively transparent phonological and semantic rules, the only form of regular reduplication found in Eastern Cham is full reduplication. Contrary to Bùi (1996a), who claims that reduplication can have either an intensifying meaning or an attenuative meaning, our speakers' judgments (including the second author) only support the latter, which mirrors Vietnamese. A few examples of attenuative reduplication are given in (14).

(14) sam sam   'cute'   from sam   'beautiful'
     ɓʰoŋ ɓʰoŋ   'redish'   from ɓʰoŋ   'red'
     kʰăŋ kʰăŋ   'hardish'   from kʰăŋ   'hard'

3 Grammar and syntax

In this section, we will introduce a few basic facts about the noun phrase (§3.1) and the verb phrase (§3.2), and will then move on to the basic sentence structure (§3.3).

3.1 Nominal domain

3.1.1 Basic structure of the NP

The basic structure of the NP has already been described for conservative varieties of the language (Bui 1996, Thurgood 2003). The colloquial variety has the same basic template:

(15) (Qt) (Clf) (N) (Mod) (Dem)

For example:

(16) klɔ̃w   nǐʔ   paj   sĭt   ni
     three   CLF   rabbit   small   DEM
     'These three small rabbits.'

Qt can be a numeral (16) or quantifier (17), a sequence of two quantifiers (18) or a combination of both (19)

(17) tom   nǐʔ   paj   sĭt   ni
     some   CLF   rabbit   small   DEM
     'These few small rabbits.'

(18) pih   tom   nǐʔ   paj   sĭt   ni
     all   some   CLF   rabbit   small   DEM
     'All of these few small rabbits.'

(19) pih   klɔ̃w   nǐʔ   paj   sĭt   ni
     all   three   CLF   rabbit   small   DEM
     'All three of these small rabbits.'

A classifier can be either a sortal classifier (20) or a measure term (21) (Grinevald 1999, 2000).

(20) klɔ̃w   pɔh   ɲĭn   năn
     three CLF   bowls   DEM
     'Those three bowls.'

(21) klɔ̃w   ɲĭn   tʰɛ̆j   năn
     three bowls   rice   DEM
     'Those three bowls of rice.'

The noun that heads the NP can be omitted and replaced by its classifier if it consists of old information, as in (22).

(22) klɔ̃w   nɨʔ   paj   sĭt   ɓăn   ka-rot,   mĭn   ha   nɨʔ   çɔh   kɛ̆j.
     three CLF   rabbit   small   eat   carrot,   but   one   CLF   break   tooth
     'Three small rabbits eat carrots, but one breaks a tooth.'

Finally, Mod can be a stative verb, a possessive or a subordinate clause. The latter are not normally introduced by a complementizer, but optionally can, perhaps because of Vietnamese influence. This optionality is illustrated in sentence (23).

(23) kru   (lac)   lăʔ   kɔʔ   sɛ̆j   ɳroj   tʰɔ̃w   (lac)   nɨʔ   sɛh
     Teacher   COMP   I   meet   day   yesterday   know   COMP   CLF   pupil

     păŋ   o.
     listen   NEG
     'The teacher(s) I met yesterday know(s) that the pupils do not listen.'

3.1.2 Classifier device

As pointed out by Bùi (1996a), there are relatively few sortal classifiers in Cham. They include pɔh, which is used for fruits and vegetables, most objects and a few abstract nouns, kah, which is used for objects that come in pairs, ɓɛ̆ʔ, which is used for long objects, plah, which is used for flat objects, raŋ/nɨʔ which are used for people and ʈrɛ̆j/nɨʔ, which are used for animals. Overall, there seems to be fewer sortal classifiers in modern colloquial Cham than in the written variety described by Moussay (2006). Besides classifiers proper, a number of nouns that refer to the category to which an object belongs can also be used as sortal classifiers (Thurgood 2003): *pʰŭn* 'tree', *hla* 'leaf', *kan* 'fish'... Containers and units of quantity can be used as mensural classifiers. Syntactically, sortal and mensural classifiers behave identically, as shown in (20–21).

Classifiers are used to individualize mass nouns, which constitute the large majority of the Cham lexicon. When referring to one or several specific units of a mass (like *ɲuj*, the mass noun denoting pigs in general), one must single them out, just as English speakers must talk about containers of water instead of 'waters'. The contrast between a mass noun and singled out instances of that mass noun is illustrated in (24–25).

(24) mɔ   mɨ   tʰaŋ.
     cow   enter house
     'A cow walks into the courtyard. / Cows walk into the courtyard.'

(25) nɨʔ   mɔ   tɔʔ   ɓăn   hrŝʔ   ʈrĕj.
     CLF   cow   PROG   eat   grass   1pp
     'The cow is eating our plants. / The cows are eating our plants.'

However, some nouns are intrinsically count nouns and do not require classifiers. This includes most nouns denoting time spans, like *hrĕj* 'day', kinship terms, like *mɛʔ* 'mother' or *wa* 'older uncle/aunt', and many abstracts nouns like *ilimo* 'culture'. An example is given in (26).

(26) hḷăʔ   ɲac   ɲaj kɔn   ʈwa   thŭn.
     I   study Saigon   two   year
     'I studied in Saigon for two years.'

As in Vietnamese, classifiers can be omitted when listing set of objects (*ʈwa căm, klăw kŭn, paʔ jon...* 'two Chams, three Cambodians, four Vietnamese...').

3.2 Verbal domain

3.2.1 No inflection

Eastern Cham verbs are never inflected. Aspect is marked through a set of markers that can either precede the verb or follow the VP (Bùi 1996a; Thurgood 2003; Moussay 2006). The list of aspect markers given in (27) is not exhaustive but illustrates the most common aspectual distinctions.

(27) Aspect markers
 a. Progressive: tɔʔ V (gramm. from tɔʔ 'to sit')
 b. Near prospective: çɛʔ V (gramm. from çɛʔ 'to be near')
 c. Completive: plɔh/çəh]ᵥₚ
 d. Completive emphatic: hu V (gramm. from hu 'to have, to get')
 e. Incompletive: ka V ... (ʔo)]ᵥₚ
 f. Negative: ʔo]ᵥₚ
 g. Iterative: ʊš̆ʔ]ᵥₚ
 h. Attemptive: ʔjɔ̆ʔ]ᵥₚ (gramm. from ʔjɔ̆ʔ 'to watch')

<u>Examples (letters as above):</u>
Base sentence: kɔ̆w bă̆ŋ ʄă̆m
      I eat vegetables
 a. kɔ̆w tɔʔ ɓă̆ŋ ʄă̆m: I am eating vegetables.
 b. kɔ̆w çɛʔ ɓă̆ŋ ʄă̆m: I am on the verge of eating vegetables.
 c. kɔ̆w ɓă̆ŋ ʄă̆m plɔh/çəh: I have eaten vegetables already.
 d. kɔ̆w hu ɓă̆ŋ ʄă̆m: I did eat vegetables.
 e. kɔ̆w ka ɓă̆ŋ ʄă̆m (ʔo): I haven't eaten vegetables yet.
 f. kɔ̆w ɓă̆ŋ ʄă̆m ʔo: I don't eat vegetables (YN question if intonation rises)
 g. kɔ̆w ɓă̆ŋ ʄă̆m ʊš̆ʔ: I eat the vegetables again.
 h. kɔ̆w ɓă̆ŋ ʄă̆m ʔjɔ̆ʔ: I try out the vegetable.

Verbal modifiers seem exclusively aspectual (Thurgood 2003), with one exception. The preverbal future marker *tʰi* V (also *si*) seems to be a tense marker in the sense that it refers to the action as taking place in the future, regardless of its internal unfolding or aspectual structure. This is similar to the Vietnamese future marker *sẽ*.

3.2.2 Verbal categories

Southeast Asian languages tend to follow similar paths of grammaticalization. Most of the time, lexical verbs are grammaticalized as aspect markers or prepositions. Colloquial Eastern Cham also follows this trend, but much less systematically than other languages of the region.

 The best described case of this phenomenon in Southeast Asia is the grammaticalization of the verb 'acquire' into an aspecto-modal marker expressing possibility, permission or result (Enfield 2001; 2003). An almost identical scenario, the grammaticalization of *hu* 'to have, to get', has already been described for formal Eastern Cham and for Tsat, a related language (Thurgood and Li 2003). Thurgood and Li propose that *hu* has followed three paths of grammaticalization in Chamic languages. Their scenario is mostly based on Tsat and only partially illustrated with Cham data, but it does seem to apply to colloquial Eastern Cham, where two of the three paths are attested, while the third is borderline.

The original meaning of *hu* 'to have' is preserved in Eastern Cham, as in (28) although the second meaning of 'to receive or to acquire' is not found.

(28)   ɲu   hu   ṭwa   ṭrĕj   ɓaw.
       3ps   have   two   CLF   buffalo
       'He owns two buffaloes.'

The first path of grammaticalization found by Thurgood and Li is the transformation of *hu* into an existential copula that is used to introduce new information (Thurgood 2003; Thurgood and Li 2003). It is attested in Eastern Cham, as shown in (29).

(29)   hu   ṭwa   nĭʔ   sɛh   naw   ɓac.
       COP   two   CLF   pupils go   study
       'There are two pupils who go to school.'

The second path of grammaticalization of *hu* closely follows the path described by Enfield. According to Thurgood and Li, the steps along this path are the following:

> *Deontic ability > Physical enabling by an external agent > Social enabling by an external agent > Permission*

To the exception of the first step, deontic ability, these steps are all synchronically attested in colloquial Eastern Cham, as demonstrated in (30–32).

(30)   Agent-external, physical enabling:
       Kḷan   nĭʔ   lo,   ṭeh   pa   hu   ʔo.
       road   narrow   very   vehicle go.through   HU   NEG
       'The road is too narrow, the car cannot go through.'

(31)   Agent-external, social enabling:
       tʰɔ̆t   çiŋ   naw   ɓac   hu.
       poor   also   go   study   HU
       'The poor can also study.'

(32) Permission
    kɔw   naw   mʔĭn   tʰaŋ   jŭt   hu   lĕj?
    1ps   go   play   house   friend HU   Q
    'Can I go play at your house?'

The third path of grammaticalization of *hu*, found in Tsat by Thurgood and Li, ends in a resultative meaning. Resultatives with *hu* are not perfectly grammatical in colloquial Eastern Cham, but elicit mixed judgments, as shown in (33) and (34).

(33) ? ʔoŋ   tha   klɛh   hu   ŋă?   ke?   ʔo.
     grandfather   old   tired   HU   do   nothing NEG
     'The old man is so tired that he doesn't do anything.'

(34) ? naj   năn   ɳac   kʰăn   ʔăn   soj   hu   dom   sam.
     aunt   DEM   study   language   English long   HU   speak beautiful
     'She studied English a long time so she speaks it well.'

Although these examples do not attest the existence of a resultative structure, their borderline status does highlight the naturalness of the path followed by Tsat.

Two other Cham verbs have been grammaticalized into aspectual markers. The first one, *ʔjɔ̆ʔ* 'watch', has become a VP-final aspect marker meaning 'to try'. Note that this aspect marker can be used regardless of the success or failure of the attempt. The full verb is given in (35), while its grammaticalized form is given in (36)[2].

(35) lă?   ʔjɔ̆ʔ   tivi.
     1ps   watch   television
     'I watch television.'

(36) lă?   wă?   ră?   ʔjɔ̆ʔ.
     1ps   write   letter   watch
     'I try to write a letter.'

The last grammaticalized verb, *tɔʔ*, seems to have followed a slightly more complicated path. Its original meaning is 'to sit' (37), but it has also taken the

---

[2] See parallel grammaticalization in Khumi (p. 37), Burmese verb (p. 98) and Pwo Karen (p. 157).

meaning of 'to stay' or even 'to be at' (38). It has also evolved into a preverbal progressive aspectual marker (39). The grammaticalization of 'sit' as a progressive marker is common cross-linguistically (Heine and Kuteva 2005: 209, 213) and especially well-represented in Southeast Asia. In Eastern Cham, however, as pointed out in Thurgood (2005), tɔʔ has also taken on an adverbial function (40). Thurgood proposes to translate it as 'meanwhile', but in colloquial Eastern Cham, it seems to be a contrastive topicalizer that could be roughly translated as 'as for'.

(37) ʔoŋ năn klɛh lo jɔ̃w năn jə naw tɔʔ păʔ tʰaŋ.
grandfather DEM tired much so DEM so go sit at house
'That old men is very tired so he goes sit in the house.'

(38) kɔ̃w tɔʔ ti panraŋ.
1ps stay at Phan.Rang.
'I live in Phan Rang.'/'I am in Phan Rang.'

(39) kɔ̃w tɔʔ wăʔ răʔ.
1ps PROG write letter
'I am writing a letter.'

(40) tɔʔ kɔ̃w naw pɛ̆j kɔn.
as.for 1ps go Saigon
'As for myself, I go to Saigon.'

The second type of function word that is often derived from verbs in Southeast Asia is prepositions. In this respect, Eastern Cham is different from its immediate neighbours in that almost all of its prepositions are distinct from verbs. The only preposition that derives from a verb is *pjɛh* 'in order to', which is a grammaticalized version of the verb *pjɛh* 'to put'.

(41) hɨ pjɛh telefɔn ŋɔ̃ʔ pan.
2ps put phone on table
'You put the phone on the table.'

(42) lăʔ pac săp ʔaŋklɛ pjɛh naw pac ʔja ɲiw.
1ps study language English in.order.to go study country out
'I study English to go study abroad.'

3.2.3 Serial verb constructions

To our knowledge, Thurgood (2005) is the only explicit discussion of serial verb constructions in Eastern Cham. Although his paper is based on a more conservative variety of the language, Thurgood's generalizations hold in colloquial Eastern Cham as well. A full discussion of serial verb construction is beyond the scope of this chapter, but it is clear that some Cham verb sequences obey the criteria proposed elsewhere (Durie 1997; Vittrant 2006): Cham serial verb constructions 1) capture a single event, 2) share their subject, 3) are not syntactic arguments of one another and 4) have the intonation of a single phrase. While most examples spontaneously produced in everyday life involve directional verbs (as in 43), others are perfectly symmetric and express complex actions (as in 44).

(43) kŏw   mɨʔ   kiʔ   naw   tɔʔ   păʔ   năŋ.
     1sg   take   chair   go   sit   at   DEM
     'I take the chair and go sit over there.'

(44) ça   klu   mɨʔ   kan   hniʔ   ɓăŋ.
     boy   name   take   fish   cook   eat
     'Klu catches the fish, cooks it and eat it'

3.3 Clausal organization

The basic clause structure of Eastern Cham is SV(O), where V can be either an action or a stative verb, as in (45) and (46) respectively.

(45) l̥ăʔ   ṇuj
     I   happy
     'I am happy'

(46) l̥ăʔ   hwăʔ
     I   eat
     'I eat'

Like Classical Cham (Moussay 2006), colloquial Eastern Cham does not have an attributive copula and simply juxtaposes the subject and the predicate in attributive constructions, as in (47). However, colloquial Eastern Cham increasingly tolerates the Vietnamese copula là, adapted as l̥a, as in (48).

(47) ɲu   nɨʔ   sɛh
    he   CLF   pupil
    'He is a pupil.'

(48) ɲu   la̰   nɨʔ   sɛh
    he   COP   CLF   pupil
    'He is a pupil.'

Eastern Cham marks indirect objects with prepositions.

3.3.1 Ellipsis of arguments

Like many languages of the area, colloquial Eastern Cham readily allows ellipsis of arguments. The subject and the object can both be omitted if they are recoverable from the context. In the short paragraph in (49), optional elements are in parentheses.

(49) п̰roj   ça   klu   naw   mu.
    Yesterday   boy   name   go   ricefield
    'Yesterday, Klu went to the field.'

   (ɲu)   wah   kan   prɔ̃ŋ.
    3ps   fish.v   fish.n   big
    'He caught a big fish.'

   (ɲu)   ɓăŋ   (ɲu)
    3ps   eat   3ps
    'He ate it.'

The subject of the second sentence, which is easily recoverable from the context, can be dropped. Finally, in the third sentence, both subject and object can be omitted. Note that the use of two third person singular pronouns in the same sentence would be awkward. If neither the subject nor the object are dropped, the object is likely to be fully realized as the noun *kan*.

3.3.2 Information structure

Topicalization is a common way to highlight important information. As noted by Thurgood (2005: 8), topics are often, but not always, marked with the topic marker *năn* (or *ʔăn* in fast speech), which is derived from the proximate demonstrative. The functional split in the use of *năn* can be illustrated by sentences like (50), where its demonstrative and topicalizer functions co-occur:

(50) ɲan   năn   năn   tɔʔ   loj.
     guy   DEM   TOP   PROG   swin
     'That guy is swimming.'

We show in examples (51–54) that various parts of a sentence can be topicalized. The topicalized clause always ends on a rising intonation, even if the topicalizer *năn* is omitted.

(51) klu   (năn) wah   kan   prɔ̆ŋ   tɔʔ   loj   tlăm   ʔja   krɔŋ.
     name   TOP   fish.v   fish.n   large   PROG   swim   in   water river
     'Klu, (he) caught a big fish that was swimming in the river.'

(52) kan   prɔ̆ŋ   tɔʔ   loj   (năn) klu   wah   tlăm   ʔja   krɔŋ.
     fish.n   large   PROG   swim   TOP   name   fish.v   in   water river
     'A large fish that was swimming, Klu caught (it) in the river.'

(53) kan   prɔ̆ŋ   tɔʔ   loj   tlăm   ʔja   krɔŋ   (năn) klu   wah.
     fish.n   large   PROG   swim   in   water river   TOP   name   caught
     'A large fish that was swimming in the river, Klu caught (it).'

(54) ʔtɔʔ   loj   tlăm   ʔja   krɔŋ   (năn) klu   wah   kan   prɔ̆ŋ.
     PROG   swim   in   water river   TOP   name   fish.v   fish.n   large
     'Swimming in the river, Klu caught a big fish'
     (ambiguous: not clear who is swimming)

3.3.3 Other

Two additional questions need to be addressed. First, yes/no questions can be marked with a simple rising intonation, or more commonly with the sentence final particle *lĕj* or *ʔo*, again with a rising intonation. The particle *ʔo*, originally a negative particle, seems to be a calque from Vietnamese *không*, which can also be either a negative particle (when preverbal) or an interrogative particle (when sentence-final). This is similar to open questions, which are marked with sentence final question markers, without wh-raising, and have the same rising intonation (Blood, DW 1977). Intonation can be contrastive: when realized with a level intonation, the final particle ʔo turns a declarative sentence into a negative sentence.

(55) k̥ru   ni   naw   lĕj?   (Rising intonation)
     teacher DEM   go   Q
     'Does this teacher go?'

(56) k̥ru   ni   naw   ʔo?   (Rising intonation)
     teacher DEM   go   Q
     'Does this teacher go?'

(57) k̥ru   ni   naw   ʔo.
     teacher DEM   go   NEG
     'This teacher doesn't go.'

Secondly, entire sentences can be nominalized by adjoining them to the noun p̥rŭʔ 'work'. They can then be used like basic NPs. This is very similar to the corresponding Vietnamese strategy in which the nominalizer is việc 'work, business' and to Burmese, in which there is a nominalizer ye³ meaning 'affair, matter, business' (this volume, p. 106).

(58) p̥rŭʔ klu   wah   kan   ʔoh   fɔ̃wʔ jwa   ɲu tɔʔ   ti tʰaŋ.
     NMLZ name fish.v   fish.n EMPH.NEG exact because he PROG in house
     'That Klu caught a fish cannot be true because he was at home.'

4 Semantics and pragmatics

In this section, we will discuss a few semantic domains that are typically very rich in Southeast Asian languages (§4.1) and will discuss some pragmatic properties of the language (§4.2).

4.1 Common semantic domains

4.1.1 Food terminology

The distinction in Thai and Burmese noun between *rice* and *what is eaten with rice* is not reflected in Cham nouns, but is expressed verbally. The verb *hwăʔ* refers to the action of eating rice (with or without other types of food), while *ɓăŋ* refers to the fact of eating without rice.

As in other Southeast languages, rice is designated by a number of lexical items, which depend on the stage in the process of cultivation or preparation for consumption. Rice seedlings are referred to as *n̥ih*, rice plants and unhusked rice as *ʈaj*, husked rice as *pr̥ah/pjah* and cooked rice as *tʰɛ̆j*. Sticky rice, on the other hand, is called *ɗewʔ*.

4.1.2 Fine lexical distinctions in verbs

As in other Southeast Asian languages, some actions are rendered by a wide range of verbs with fine-grained semantic nuances. We will focus on the same set of lexical fields as the other chapters.

- **Cutting**

A variety of verbs express the idea of cutting in Cham. Most languages, as illustrated by the English glosses in (59), have wide range of terms to express the idea of cutting, but this seems to be especially true in Southeast Asia. Verbs for *cutting* are not associated to specific instruments, even if some co-occurrences are more frequent than others.

(59) Cut : kăʔ   Split : pl̥ah   Mince : tʰiʔ
     Slice : căʔ   Chop : cʰɔh   Saw : kĕʔ
     Cut off : tăʔ Chop down : kɔh

- **Carrying**

The concept of carrying is more interesting in that Cham, like other Mainland Southeast Asian languages, has a surprising number of verbs to express it.

(60) Bring: p̥a
     Carry under one's arm: k̥im   Carry on one's shoulder: k̥uj
     Carry on a vehicle: cɨŋ   Carry on the body, wear: p̥ăʔ

Carry in one basket tied to a perch held on shoulder: k̥lăm
Carry in two baskets tied to a perch held on shoulder: nɔŋ

- **Drying**

Cham only has three verbs for the concept of drying. The general action of drying something is expressed by either *ɓu* or *praŋ*, while the action of drying something on a fire is expressed by the verb *k̥ʰan*.

- **Directional verbs**

In order to add directionality to a Cham verb, an adverb of direction is added after the verb (*ŋɔʔ* 'up', *trŭn* 'down'...). The verb itself remains identical. Some verbs are also intrinsically directional like *ɗĭʔ* 'to go up'.

4.2 Pragmatics and discourse

4.2.1 Final particles

Eastern Cham has a wealth of final particles that have been extensively described by Doris Blood (Blood, DW 1977). She classifies them into eight discrete categories, which could be reorganized depending on one's theoretical framework. We provide below one example of each of these categories, appended to the same basic clause.

(61) Base sentence: ça   ka   naw   p̥ac.
                     boy   name go   study
                     'Ka goes to school.'

Negatives:	ça ka naw p̥ac ʔo. (flat int.)	'Ka does not go to school.'
Limitives:	ça ka naw p̥ac mĭn.	'Ka goes to school first/only.'
Interrogatives:	ça ka naw p̥ac lĕj?	'Does Ka go to school?'
Imperatives:	ça ka naw p̥ac mĕʔ!	'Go to school, Ka!'
Prohibitives:	ça ka naw p̥ac çoj!	'Do not go to school, Ka!'
Emphasizers:	ça ka naw p̥ac ɗa!	'Ka went to school, I'm afraid!'
Responses:	ça ka naw p̥ac ke. (rare)	'Ka does not go to school at all'
Vocatives:	ça ka ləj!	'Hey, Ka!'

Negatives and limitives are clause-final, while all other categories are sentence-final. As such, negatives and limitives can be combined with particles of the other categories. Example (62) illustrates this type of combination.

(62) ça   ka   naw   ɓac   wɛ̆ʔ   haj!
     boy   name   go   study   again   IMP
     'Ka, please go back to school!'

Note that the intonation associated with final particles can be contrastive. For example, the negative sentence given in (57) becomes interrogative if associated to a rising intonation (cf. §3.3.3). In most cases, however, the intonation associated to final particles seems largely fixed; variation in intonation can at most express subtle nuances of doubt, surprise, annoyance, etc.

4.2.2 Politeness

Politeness is often marked through address forms. In Eastern Cham, as in many Southeast Asian languages, kinship terms are the default terms of address. A common way of expressing politeness is to treat one's interlocutor as if they were much older than their actual age. For example, old women might address middle aged men as *ʔaj* 'older brother'.

Besides kinship terms, some pronouns are specifically used for politeness purposes. For example, the first person singular pronoun has an unmarked variant (*kɔ̆w*) and a variant that is used with social superiors in formal contexts (*lăʔ*). In some families, *lăʔ* is even the default first person pronoun when addressing older relatives, replacing kinship terms. The first person plural pronoun *trĕj* can also be used as a first person singular pronoun when talking to a social equal or inferior in a respectful way. Finally, the second person singular pronoun *hɨ* is used to address social equals or inferiors, while social superiors are addressed with kinship terms. All other pronouns are neutral with respect to politeness. All pronouns are gender-neutral.

Another way of expressing politeness is to start sentences with the verb *likɔ̆w* 'request, ask' followed by the term of address normally used with the interlocutor. This device, which seems to mirror Vietnamese *xin* (same meaning), is quite formal and could be translated as 'allow me to ask you…' or 'allow me to address you…'.

5 Conclusion

We have seen in this paper that Eastern Cham shares a number of grammatical features with other languages of Mainland Southeast Asia, more specially with

Vietnamese, a language with which it has been in contact for centuries and in which the entire language community is now bilingual. Cham is perhaps the most compelling case of language convergence in the area because, as convincingly demonstrated by Thurgood (1996, 1999) more than a decade ago, it has replaced so many of its Austronesian features with Vietnamese and other Mon-Khmer features. It is difficult to disagree with Thurgood's claim that internal change in Chamic languages has been channeled and oriented by the familiar properties of neighboring languages, but we must underline that we still have to explain why some features of Cham have been so dramatically modified, while others seem to have resisted convergence. While areal surveys give us a detailed snapshot of the work that has to be done and diachronic linguistics informs us on steps in which convergence gradually unfolds, the underpinnings of language convergence will only be fully understood with in-depth studies of bilingualism, language use and language change at the micro-sociolinguistic level.

Acknowledgements

Special thanks to our Eastern Cham consultants (and especially to Thanh Thị Hồng Cẩm) for providing us with their intuitions and grammaticality judgments.

Abbreviations

A	adjective
CLF	classifier
COMP	complementizer
COP	copula
DEM	demonstrative
FOC	focus
IMP	imperative
INTRJ	interjection
MOD	Modifier
N	noun
NEG	negative
NMLZ	nominalizer
OS	older sibling
PROG	progressive
Q	wh-word
QT	Quantifier
QUOT	quotative

RED	reduplication
TOP	topicalizer
V	verb
YS	younger sibling

References

Alieva, Natalia F. 1991. Morphemes in Contemporary Spoken Cham: Qualitative and Quantitative Alternations. *Cahiers de Linguistique Asie Orientale* 20 (2). 219–229.

Alieva, Natalia F. 1994. The progress of monosyllabization in Cham as testified by field materials. In Cecilia Ode & Wim Stokhof (ed.), *Proceedings of the Seventh International Conference on Austronesian Linguistics (ICAL)*. 541–549. Amsterdam: Rodopi.

Aymonier, Étienne François. 1889. *Grammaire de la langue chame*. Saigon: Imprimerie coloniale.

Aymonier, Étienne François & Antoine Cabaton. 1906. *Dictionnaire čam-francais*. Paris: E. Leroux.

Blood, David L. 1977. A three-dimensional analysis of Cham sentences. In David Thomas, Ernest W. Lee & Nguyễn Đăng Liêm (ed.), *Papers in Southeast Asian Linguistics, no. 4: Chamic Studies*, 53–76. Canberra: Pacific Linguistics.

Blood, David L. 1967. Phonological Units in Cham. *Anthropological Linguistics* 9 (8). 15–32.

Blood, Doris W. 1977. Clause and Sentence Final Particles in Cham. In David D. Thomas, Ernest W. Lee & Nguyễn Đăng Liêm (ed.), *Papers in Southeast Asian Linguistics, no. 4: Chamic Studies*. 39–51. Canberra: Pacific Linguistics Series A.

Blood, Doris Walker. 1962. Reflexes of Proto-Malayo-Polynesian in Cham. *Anthropological Linguistics* 4 (9). 11–20.

Brunelle, Marc. 2005a. Register and tone in Eastern Cham: Evidence from a word game. *Mon-Khmer Studies* 35. 121–131.

Brunelle, Marc. 2005b. *Register in Eastern Cham: Phonological, phonetic and sociolinguistic approaches*. PhD thesis, Cornell University.

Brunelle, Marc. 2006. A phonetic study of Eastern Cham register. In Paul Sidwell & Anthony Grant (ed.), *Chamic and Beyond*. 1–36. Sidney: Pacific Linguistics.

Brunelle, Marc. 2008. Diglossia, Bilingualism, and the revitalization of written Eastern Cham. *Language Documentation and Conservation* 2 (1). 28–46.

Brunelle, Marc. 2009. Diglossia and Monosyllabization in Eastern Cham: a Sociolinguistic Study. In James Stanford & Dennis Preston (ed.), *Variation in Indigenous Minority Languages*, 47–75. Amsterdam: John Benjamins.

Bùi, Khánh Thế. 1995. *Từ điển Chăm-Việt*. TP. Hồ Chí Minh: Khoa học xã hội.

Bùi, Khánh Thế. 1996a. *Ngữ Pháp Tiếng Chăm*. Hà Nội: Nhà Xuất Bản Giáo Dục.

Bùi, Khánh Thế. 1996b. *Từ điện Việt-Chăm*. TP. Hồ Chí Minh: Nhà xuất bản Khoa học xã hội.

Durie, Mark. 1997. Grammatical structures in verb serialization. In Alex Alsina, Joan Bresnan & Peter Sells (ed.), *Complex Predicates*, 289–354. Stanford: CSLI Publications.

Enfield, Nick J. 2001. On genetic and areal linguistics in Mainland South-East Asian: Parallel polyfunctionality of 'acquire'. In Alexandra Y. Aikhenvald & Robert M. W. Dixon (eds.), *Are-

al diffusion and genetic inheritance: Problems in comparative linguistics, 255–290. Oxford: Oxford University Press.

Enfield, Nick J. 2003. *Linguistic epidemiology: semantics and grammar of language contact in Mainland Southeast Asia*. London: Routledge/Curzon.

Enfield, Nick J. 2005. Areal Linguistics and Mainland Southeast Asia. *Annual Review of Anthropology* 34. 181–206.

Grinevald, Colette. 1999. Typologie des systèmes de classification nominale. *Faits de Langue* 7 (14). 101–122.

Grinevald, Colette. 2000. A morphosyntactic typology of classifiers. In G. Senft (ed.), *Nominal classification*, 50–92. Cambridge: Cambridge University Press.

Heine, Bernd & Tania Kuteva. 2005. Language contact and grammatical change. Cambridge: Cambridge University Press.

Hoàng, Thị Châu. 1987. Hệ thống thanh điệu tiếng Chàm và các kí hiệu. *Ngôn Ngữ* 1 (2). 31–35.

Jaisser, Annie. 1990. DeLIVERing an introduction to psycho-collocations with SIAB in Hmong. *Linguistics of the Tibeto-Burman Area* 13 (1). 159–178.

Matisoff, James. 1973. Tonogenesis in Southeast Asia. In Larry Hyman (ed.), *Consonant types and tone*. 71–96. Los Angeles: University of Southern California.

Matisoff, James. 1986. Hearts and minds in South-East Asian languages and English: An essay in the comparative lexical semantics of psycho-collocations. *Cahiers de linguistique – Asie orientale* 15 (1). 5–57.

Moussay, Gérard. 1971. *Dictionnaire cam-vietnamien-français*. Phan Rang: Trung-tâm Văn hoá Chăm.

Moussay, Gérard. 2006. *Grammaire de la langue Cam*. Paris: Les Indes Savantes.

Oey, Eric M. 1990. Psycho-collocations in Malay. *Linguistics of the Tibeto-Burman Area* 13 (1). 141–158.

Phú, Văn Hẳn. 2003. *Cơ cấu ngữ âm và chữ viết tiếng Chăm Việt Nam và tiếng Melayu Malaysia*. PhD dissertation, Viện Khoa Học Xã Hội.

Phú, Văn Hẳn, Jerold Edmondson & Kenneth Gregerson. 1992. Eastern Cham as a tone language. *Mon Khmer Studies* 20. 31–43.

Thurgood, Graham. 1993. Phan Rang Cham and Utsat: Tonogenetic themes and variants. In Jerold Edmondson & Kenneth Gregerson (eds.), *Tonality in Austronesian Languages*, 91–106. Honolulu: University of Hawai'i Press.

Thurgood, Graham. 1996. Language contact and the directionality of internal drift: The development of tones and registers in Chamic. *Language* 72 (1). 1–31.

Thurgood, Graham. 1999. *From Ancient Cham to modern dialects: Two thousand years of language contact and change*. Honolulu: University of Hawai'i Press.

Thurgood, Graham. 2005. A preliminary sketch of Phan Rang Cham. In K. Alexander Adelaar & Nikolaus Himmelman (ed.), *The Austronesian languages of Asia and Madagascar*: Curzon Press.

Thurgood, Graham & Fengxiang Li. 2003. The grammaticalization paths of Proto-Chamic *hu 'receive'. *Proceedings from the Annual Meeting of the Chicago Linguistic Society* 39 (1). 205–214.

Trung-tâm Văn-hoá Chàm. 197?. Số Đặc-biệt về Ngôn-ngữ Chàm. *Roh twah sưu-tầm* 28.

Vittrant, Alice. 2006. Les constructions verbales en série, une nouvelle approche du syntagme verbal birman. *Bulletin de la Société Linguistique de Paris* 1. 305–368.

Appendix 1: Summary of linguistic features

Legend
+++ the feature is pervasive or used obligatorily in the language
++ the feature is normal but selectively distributed in the language
+ the feature is merely possible or observable in the language
− the feature is impossible or absent in the language

	Feature	+++/++/+/−	§ ref. in this chapter
Phonetics	Lexical tone or register	+++	§1.3
Phonetics	Back unrounded vowels	++	§1.2.2, p.528
Phonetics	Initial velar nasal	++	§1.2.1, p.526
Phonetics	Implosive consonants	++	§1.2.1, p.526
Phonetics	Sesquisyllabic structures	+	§1.1, p.524
Morphology	Tendency towards monosyllabicity	++	§1.1, p.524
Morphology	Tendency to form compounds	++	§2.1, p.531
Morphology	Tendency towards isolating (rather than affixation)	+++	§2.1, p.531
Morphology	Psycho-collocations	+	§2.2, p.533
Morphology	Elaborate expressions (e.g. four-syllable or other set patterns)	+	§2.3, p.534
Morphology	Reduplication generally	+	§2.4, p.534
Morphology	Reduplication of nouns	+	§2.4, p.534
Morphology	Reduplication of verbs	+	§2.4, p.534
Grammar	Use of classifiers	++	§3.1.1, p.535 & §3.1.2, p.536–37
Grammar	Classifiers used in counting	+	§3.2.1, p.536–37
Grammar	Classifiers used with demonstratives	++	§3.1.1, p.535
Grammar	Adjectival verbs	+++	§2.1, p.531–32 & §3.3 p.542
Grammar	Grammatical number	−	−
Grammar	Inflection of verbs	−	§3.2.1, p.537
Grammar	Use of tense/aspect markers	++	§3.2.1, p.537 & §3.2.2, p.538–41
Grammar	Use of verb plural markers	−	§3.2.1, p.537
Grammar	Grammaticalization of GET/OBTAIN (potential mod. resultative/perfect aspect)	++	§3.2.2, p.538

	Feature	+++/++/+/−	§ ref. in this chapter
Grammar	Grammaticalization of PUT, SET (completed/resultative aspect)	−	§3.2.2, p.541
Grammar	Grammaticalization of GIVE (causative, benefactive; preposition)	+	§2.1, p.531
Grammar	Grammaticalization of FINISH (perfective/ complete aspect; conjunction/temporal subordinator)	−	−
Grammar	Grammaticalization of directional verbs e.g. GO / COME (allative, venitive)	−	§3.2.3, p.542
Grammar	Grammaticalization of SEE, WATCH (temptative)	+	§3.2.2, p.540
Grammar	Grammaticalization of STAY, REMAIN (progressive and continuous, durative aspects)	+	§3.2.2, p.540–41
Grammar	Serial verb constructions	++	§3.2.3, p.542
Syntax	Verb precedes object (VO)	+++	§3.3, p.542
Syntax	Auxiliary precedes verb	+	§3.2.1, p.537
Syntax	Preposition precedes noun	+++	§3.3, p.543
Syntax	Noun precedes adjective	+++	§3.1.1, p.535
Syntax	Noun precedes demonstrative	+++	§3.1.1, p.535–36
Syntax	Noun precedes genitive	+++	§3.1.1, p.535–36
Syntax	Noun precedes relative clause	+++	§3.1.1, p.535–36
Syntax	Use of topic-comment structures	++	§3.3.2, p.544
Syntax	Ellipsis of arguments known from context	++	§3.3.1, p.543
Lexical semantics	Specific terms for forms of rice	+	§4.1.1, p.546
Pragmatics	Use of utterance-final pragmatic particles	++	§4.2.1, p.547
Pragmatics	Encoding of politeness	+	§4.2.2, p.548
Pragmatics	Encoding of honorifics	+	§4.2.2, p.548

Appendix 2: Text interlinearized

'The story of the male buffalo that gave birth, excerpts (narrator : Nguyễn Văn Tỷ)

ʈankan	ɓaw	mnɔ	mnɨʔ
tale	buffalo	male	give.birth

<u>Underlined words</u> are borrowed from Vietnamese and transcribed in *quốc ngữ*.

hu	ƫwa	ʈɛ̌j	ʔaj	năn,	plɔh	ʔaj	jə	mʈa,	nɨʔ	ʈɛ̌j
COP	two	ygr.sibling	older.sibling	TOP	then	OS	COP	rich,	CLF	YS

jə	tʰɔ̌t.
COP	poor

'There were two brothers. The oldest was rich and the youngest was poor.'

ʈɛ̌j	năn	<u>là</u>	hu	tʰa	ʈrɛ̌j	ɓaw	mɲaj,	ɓa	jwa	păʔ	tʰaŋ	ʔaj
YS	TOP	COP	COP	one	CLF	buffalo	female	bring	send	at	house	OS

'The younger brother had a female buffalo that he brought to his brother's house...'

ka	ʔaj	klaŋ	<u>luôn</u>	năn.
give	OS	keep	at.the.same.time	TOP

'so that he would look after it.'

ʔaj	hu	ʈo	ɓaw	mnɔ	mɪ̆n,	mɪ̆n	tăn	tʰa	tʰŭn	ƫwa	tʰŭn	năn,
OS	COP	some	buff.	male	only	but	arrive	one	year	two	year	TOP

'The older brother only had male buffaloes, but after one or two years, ...'

ɓaw	mɲaj	ʈɛ̌j	ni	năn	mtjan	mnɨʔ.	ʈɛ̌j	iŋ	mɨʔ	ɓaw
buff.	female	YS	this	TOP	give.birth	give.birth	YS	want	take	buff.

maj	tʰaŋ.
return	home

'the female buffalo gave birth. The younger brother wanted his buffaloes back.'

tăn	naw	ɗom	ʔaj	năn	hl̥ăʔ	mɨʔ	ɓaw	maj	tʰaŋ	ɛ̌ʔ.
arrive	go	speak	OS	TOP	I	take	buff.	return	home	IMP

'He went to tell his brother: "I want to take the buffaloes home."'

ʔaj năn hə,   ka   mɨʔ ɓaw mɛʔ,   ɓaw   nɨʔ là   kŏw mɨʔ.
OS TOP QUOT give take buff. mother buffalo child COP   I   take.
'The older brother said : "Take the mother buffalo, I take the calf."'

ʈĕj lac hə?,   ɓaw   hḷăʔ mɨn   mnɨʔ,   ɓaw   hḷăʔ mŋaj,
YS   say QUOT   buffalo I   just give.birth buffalo I   female
'The younger brother said: "My buffalo just gave birth, it's female."'

ɓaw   ʔaj vẫn   mnɨʔ,   çɨŋ   mnɨʔ   ʔo. ɓaw   mnɔ   mɨn   mnɨʔ.
buffalo OS still give.birth able give.birth NEG buffalo male COP   give.birth
'"Your buffalo can't have given birth. Only male buffaloes give birth."'

ɓaw   mŋaj   mɨn mnɨʔ   ʔo.
buffalo female   COP give.birth NEG
'"Female buffaloes don't give birth."'

lac ʈĕj năn oan,   tức   quá   đây, naw jăʔ   păʔ plĕj   ka
say YS   TOP slander   angry much   now   go   compl. at   village give

lý klən   năn xử.
vill.head   DEM rule
'The younger brother was very angry, so he went to complain to the village chief.'

ʔaj ɲu   hu   çen   ɓa   wŏʔ   çen   ka   lý klən   ɓăŋ.
OS   he   COP money   bring   again money   give village.head eat
'The older brother had money and brought some to bribe the village chief.'

lý klən   xử   lac ɓaw mnɔ   mnɨʔ,   fɔ̆wʔ   ɓaw   mŋaj   ʔo.
village.head rule say buff male give.birth correct buff.   female NEG
'The village chief ruled that the male buffalo had given birth, not the female.'

ʈĕj năn lac là   thật   thua. naw jaʔ   wŏʔ   păʔ tổng,
YS   TOP say COP   truly lose   go   complain again at   commune.head
'The younger brother had really lost. He went to complaint to the commune chief'

tổng   çaŋ   lac jə   năn, ɓaw   mnɔ   mɨn mnɨʔ   trừ   fɔ̆wʔ   ɓaw
comm.hd   also say like DEM   buff. male COP g.birth   except correct buff

mɲaj ʔo.
fem. NEG
'The commune chief said the same; the male buffalo had given birth, not the male.'

[...] plɔh,   ɲan   tɕĕj   năn   ɲă?   kḙ?   çaŋ   o.
      then   boy   YS   TOP   do   what   able NEG
'So the younger brother couldn't do anything about it anymore.'

naw   jă?   pă?   <u>huyên</u>,   jă?   pă?   <u>huyên</u>   <u>xử</u>   jə   năn.
go   complain   at   district   complain at   district   rule   like   DEM
'He went to the district to complain, but the ruling was the same.'

tăn   tɕĕj   wăn kl̥aj   maj   pă?   tʰaŋ   hja   rah   kl̥an   naw,   kɔ̭?
arrive   OS   forget-forest return   at   house   cry   entire   road   go   meet

ʔaj   paj.
OS   rabbit
'The younger brother, upset, was going home crying, when he met brother rabbit.'

ʔaj paj   năn   ɲi   lac   fɔ̃w?   kḙ?   hɨ   hja?   hu   tʰa   kḙ?   năn?   [...]
OS rabbit TOP hear say   correct what   2PS   cry   COP   story   what   TOP
'Brother rabbit asked: "Why do you cry? What's happening?"'
(*Missing part: the younger brother tells him the whole story*)

ʔaj   paj   ɲu   dom   lac: <u>lo</u>   çoj,   <u>lo</u>   çoj.
OS   rabbit 3   speak   say   worry   IMP.NEG worry   IMP.NEG
'Brother rabbit said: "Don't worry, don't worry."'

koh   kḙ   hăj,   koh   ke,   hɨ   naw   pă?   <u>huyên</u>   naw,
tomorrow   morning INTRJ tomorrow   morning 2PS   go   at   district   go
'"Tomorrow morning, you go to the district..."'

hɨ   mi̭?   ɲi̭?   lŭ?   pah   ɓɔ?   pah   mta.
you   take   turmeric coat   spread   face   spread   eye
'"you take turmeric and you spread it on your face."'
(Cham women spread turmeric on their bodies after giving birth.)

[...] hɨ naw ŋa? tɔ? kɔh pă? nă? huyện, hɨ tš? wah ŋut ŋut naw.
      2PS go do sit quiet at front district 2PS nod ideophone go
"'You go sit quietly in front of the district office and you nod as if you're sleepy.'"

plɔh hẽ   po   huyện   ŋi   năn hɨ   phải trả lời. hɨ   trả lời: paj
then when lord district ask TOP 2PS must reply   2PS reply   rabbit

ɲu ptɔ   těj   ɗom.
3   teach YS   speak
"'When the district chief asks, you must answer". And he taught him what to say.'

tăn   kɔh   ke   năn těj ŋă? jăw   năn   mɨ?   ɲi?   lŭ?   ɓɔ?   mɨ?
arr. tom. morn. TOP YS   do   like DEM   take turn   coat   face take

taŋ   kɔ? lŭ?   ɓɔ?
coal pot coat   face

'The next morning, the younger brother did that. He took turmeric and coal from a cooking pot and coated his face with it.'

naw çaŋ   haw   wš?   plɔh   tɔ? pă? hlaw   huyện.
go   also   veil   again   then   sit at   front district.
'He also wore a veil (to look like a woman) and sat in front of the district office.'

tăn   oŋ   huyện   maj   ŋă? prŭ?, ɓoh ɲu çaŋ   ŋut ŋut   naw lac :
arrive old.man   district   come   do   work   see he also ideophone go say
'When the district chief came to work, he saw him sobbing and said :'

hɨ   tɔ?   ŋă?   ke?   pă? ni?   plɔh tɔ?   tš? wah ti   ni?
you   sit   do   what   at   here   then sit   nod   at   here
"'What are you doing here? You came here to sleep?'"

lac   oh!   hlă?   ʔiw   hlă?   maj   caŋ   huyện   hlă?   tš? wah   mlo.
say   NEG   I   call I   come   wait   district I   nod   much
"'No, I came here to talk to the district chief. I'm very sleepy.'"

mklăm   ni   hlă?   rɔŋ   mɨ   hlă?   mnɨ?.
night   this   I   take.care   father   I   give.birth
"'Last night, I helped my father give birth.'"

tổng huyện	ɗom	lac	hapăn	mɨ	hɨ	mnɨʔ	çaŋ.
district.head	speak	say	how	father	2PS	give.birth	able

'The district head said: "How can your father give birth?"'

mɛʔ	hɨ	ɲə	mnɨʔ	lac	mɨ	mnɨʔ	ʔo.
mother	2PS	COP	give.birth	say	father	give.birth	NEG

'"Your mother gave birth, not your father."'

mɨ	hḭ̆ăʔ	mnɨʔ	fɔ̃wʔ	mɛʔ	ʔo.	mɨ	hḭ̆ăʔ	I
father	I	give.birth	correct	mnɨʔ.	mother	NEG	father	give.birth

'"My father gave birth, not my mother. My father gave birth."'

lac	hɨ	ɗom	pjăʔ	ni	năn,	ɗom	bậy	ɗom	ba.	kăw
say	2PS	speak	go.out	this	FOC	speak	non-sense	speak	RED.	I

hwa	naw	krɔ̆ʔ!
pull	go	lock.up

'You're speaking non-sense. I'll have you locked up!'

lac	hăʔ?!	mɨ̆ŋ	hrĕj	năn	po	huyện	xử	lac	ɳaw	mnɔ	mɨ̆n
say	INTJ	since	day	DEM	lord	district	rule	say	buffalo	male	COP

mn [...]
give.birth

'"Uh? The other day, you ruled that the male buffalo gave birth..."'

mɨ	hḭ̆ăʔ	mnɨʔ	fɔ̃wʔ	k̰eʔ.	Huyện	năn	wăn	k̰laj.
father	I	given.birth	correct	what	district	TOP	forget	forest

'"so why can't my father give birth?" The district chief was confused.'

jɔ̃w	năn	jə	là	mlăw,	ploh	ɳjaj	lac	plĕj	ɳaw	nɨʔ	ʔoj
like	DEM	COP	COP	ashamed	then	tell	say	give	buff.	class	calf

năn	ka	ɲu	wɔ̆ʔ
TOP	give	3	back

'He was ashamed, so he ordered the calf to be returned to him.'

lac	ɳaw	mɳaj	mɨ̆n	mnɨʔ	fɔ̃wʔ	ɳaw	mnɔ	ʔo.
say	buff.	female	COP	give.birth	correct	buff.	male	NEG

'And said that females buffaloes give birth, but not male ones.'

Mathias Jenny
Thai

Thai (ภาษาไทย *phaasǎa thay*) is the official language of the Kingdom of Thailand. It is the medium of instruction at all levels of state and most private schools and the main language used in the mass media throughout the kingdom. The native speaker population is given at 20 million in the Ethnologue, but Standard Thai, based on the Central Thai dialect spoken in Bangkok, is spoken to at least some degree by all 64 million inhabitants of Thailand. Thai is used in all aspects of daily life, including culture, religion, commerce and entertainment. Apart from a vast native literature, many pieces of world literature, classical as well as popular and scholarly, have been translated into Thai. Thai script is included in standard Windows and Macintosh applications, and most major mobile telephone companies produce localized mobile phones with Thai script and keypad, making Thai the only Southeast Asian language written in non-Roman script to have fully kept pace with the digital era.

Thai has existed in written form since the late 13th or early 14th century,[1] and is the earliest member of the Tai-Kadai language family to be written. Thai is also the largest language of the family in terms of native speakers, followed by Lao or North-Eastern Thai, the only other member Tai-Kadai language family with official status at the national level (ca. 15 million speakers in Laos and north-eastern Thailand), and Zhuang with some 14 million speakers in the Guangxi Zhuang Autonomous Region in China. Other important languages belonging to the same family are Shan, spoken in northern Myanmar, Black and White Tai in Vietnam and Lue, spoken in the Xishuangbanna Dai Autonomous Prefecture in Yunnan. All these languages belong to the Tai branch of the Tai-Kadai language family. The most westernmost branch of the family includes Aiton and Phake, as well as the now extinct Ahom, known from chronicles and ritual texts, in Assam. The members of the Kadai or Kam-Sui branch are scattered throughout south-eastern

---

1 There is some discussion among Thai and Western scholars concerning the authenticity of the first inscription in Thai, viz. the Ramkhamhaeng inscription, traditionally dated to 1292 CE (s. Chamberlain 1991).

Mathias Jenny: Department of Comparative Linguistics, University of Zurich
E-Mail: mathias.jenny@uzh.ch

China, Hainan, and North Vietnam and are spoken by minority groups in these regions. For a detailed overview of the family see Diller (2008).

The position of of the Tai-Kadai languages relative to other language families is unclear. While the family was traditionally seen as a member of the Sinitic branch of the Sino-Tibetan family, more recently an alignment with Austronesian languages has been favored especially by Western scholars (see Benedict 1975). The many correspondences between Tai-Kadai and Sinitic in lexicon and phonology have been explained as being contact-induced rather than inherited from a common parent language.

Throughout its documented history Thai has been profoundly influenced by the classical languages of Indian culture, namely Sanskrit and Pali, as well as by Khmer, formerly the politically dominant language in central Mainland Southeast Asia. From the 14th century C.E., the royal court of Ayudhya saw itself as heir to the declining Khmer kingdom of Angkor Wat, and so most of the royal vocabulary (see section 3.1.3) in present day Thai is derived from Khmer. Less obvious, but none the less present, are loans from Mon. Words of Chinese origin can be found in all areas of the lexicon, bearing witness to a long history of linguistic and cultural contact. Loans from ethnic minority languages spoken in the hills of northern and north-eastern Thailand are mostly restricted to terms for local flora and fauna and some special cultural items and practices. Similarly, Thai has borrowed only few words in current use from Malay, spoken to the south of Thailand. Javanese and Indonesian words are found especially in the literary style, introduced by translations of famous Javanese and Indonesian works, such as the story of Inao. Neologisms used to be created based on Pali and Sanskrit words, but more recently English loans have played a major part in creating new vocabulary, especially in the field of modern technology. The vocabulary of modern Thai presents itself as a mixture of many different elements, all well integrated and adapted to Thai phonology.

In the second half of the 19th century, Thai underwent a process of standardization, which to some degree also meant Westernization, initiated mainly by King Rama IV, a scholar educated in western languages like English and Latin (Diller 1993). The resulting formal style (Diller's H for "high") shows some important differences from the colloquial language (Diller's L for "low"). A set of rules similar to Western models was promulgated, with the intention of making Thai syntax less ambiguous. Differences in pronunciation are seen mainly in the merger of /r/ and /l/ and the simplification of clusters in colloquial Thai, but not in the formal register. Differences in vocabulary are seen as different degrees of politeness, rather than different registers, although there is some overlap between the two.

1 Phonology

Thai is written in an Indian type script, which was developed in the 13th or 14th century based on a Khmer model. The major innovation in Thai script was the introduction of tone markers, the use of which, however, became consistent only a few centuries later. With forty four consonants and a large number of vowel signs and combinations thereof, the Thai script represents the phonology of the language rather well, although some ambiguities remain. The present Thai phonological system is the outcome of a series of changes that occurred during the development from Old Thai (Sukhothai, from the 13th century) to Modern Thai. At some point, probably after the 10th century,[2] voiced stops and fricatives became voiceless in many other languages across a vast area of China and Mainland Southeast Asia. This devoicing resulted in changes in vowels in some languages, in distinctive phonation types (registers) in others, and in the reorganization of the tone systems in languages that possessed them, like Thai and other Tai languages. The reorganization of tone systems was called "the great tone split" by Brown (1985: 18 ff).

Canonically, as part of these trends, voiced stops became unvoiced aspirated stops (as in Table 1), while voiced fricatives became unvoiced. The original voiced stops thus merged with the unvoiced-aspirated stops, often giving rise to phonemic tonal distinctions. It is possible that even before the split, tones came in allophonic variants according to the initial consonant. With the voicing distinctions lost, tones became the only distinctive feature for many otherwise identical syllables. Thai orthography did not change substantially after the devoicing and tone split, such that the marking of tones today is not transparent, as the same tone marker marks different tones according to the initial consonant. The examples below illustrate the development of Thai phonology.[3]

Table 1: Sound changes

Sukhothai	Orthography	Modern Thai	Gloss
gwāy	gwāy	khwaay	water buffalo
ba khun phā mɯaṅ	bɔ̀ khun phā mɯaṅ	phɔ̀ɔ khŭn phǎa mɯaŋ	name of ruler of Sukhothai
phû	phû	phûu	person
mláṅ	láṅ	láaŋ	clean, wash
bà	bɔ̀	phɔ̂ɔ	father

---

[2] The exact date and the origin of the devoicing are subject of dispute among linguists. It is likely that the change happened at different times in different languages.
[3] Sukhothai examples are taken from the Wat Si Chum inscription, ca. 1360 CE.

1.1 Segmental phonemes

The Thai language uses 21 consonantal phonemes in initial position, with a restricted set of consonants occurring in syllable final position.

Initial consonants: k, kh, ŋ, c, ch, d, t, th, n, b, p, ph, f, m, y, r, l, w, s, h, ʔ
Final consonants: k, t, p, ŋ, n, m, y, w, ʔ

The aspirated velar stop /kh/ is variously pronounced as [kʰ] or [kx], depending on the phonetic environment as well as on the speaker's dialect. The implosives [ɗ] and [ɓ] found in an earlier stage of the language are now usually pronounced as fully voiced stops in standard Thai and in most (urban) dialects of central and southern Thailand. The pronunciation of /c/ and /ch/ varies among speakers and dialects between palatal stops [c/cʰ] and affricates [tɕ/tɕʰ]. The pronunciation of /r/ is in formal Thai, and the language taught in school, a flap [ɾ], but for most speakers it merges with /l/ as [l]. The southern dialects are more conservative in retaining [ɾ] as a flap, while in the northern and north-eastern dialects (Lanna, Lao), /r/ is realized as [h]. The glottal stop /ʔ/ is always pronounced as such, both in initial and final position. Final /y/ and /w/ are analyzed as forming a diphthong together with the preceding vowel by some authors, but are usually analysed as a final approximant consonant in phonological accounts..

Final consonants, both sonorants and stops, are unreleased in all cases.

The vowel inventory of Thai is rather rich with high, mid and low vowels, occurring both as front and back, rounded and unrounded varieties. Vowel length is synchronically distinctive for almost all vowels, although historically the length distinction was relevant probably only for /a/ vs. /aa/.

Table 2: Vowels

i ii			ɯ ɯɯ	u uu
e ee			ɤ ɤɤ	o oo
ɛ ɛɛ				ɔ ɔɔ
	ə[4]			
	a aa			

There are three diphthongs in Thai, all starting with a high vowel and falling towards /ə/: /iə, ɯə, uə/. The first part of the diphthong is somewhat long, i.e.

---

4 The schwa sound in Thai is rather low, close to [ɐ].

longer than a phonologically short vowel but not quite as long as a long ones. As mentioned above, some authors describe final glides as parts of diphthongs, i.e. /ay/ as /ai/, /aw/ as /au/, etc. This analysis results in two types of diphthongs, namely one group that can take a final consonant (the diphthongs ending in /ə/) and another that cannot (the diphthongs ending in /i/ and /u/).

1.2 Suprasegmental phonology

Stress in Thai is predictable and falls on the last syllable of polysyllabic words. It is phonemic inasmuch as it may distinguish polymorphemic words (with one main stress) from phrases (with more than one stress), as in

'náam 'yen 'the water is cold' vs. nám-'yen 'cold water'.

This example also shows the typical shortening of the pretonic syllable in polysyllabic expressions, i.e. náam is shortened to nám.

Apart from stress, the main suprasegmental feature of Thai is the tone system comprising five tones. Basically each syllable receives a tone, with the exception of pretonic weak syllables (presyllables, see section 1.3). The five tones are, in the traditional Thai order:

Table 3: Descriptive names and conventional transcription of Thai tones

mid level	(sĭəŋ săaman 'normal tone')	no marker:	a
low level	(sĭəŋ ʔèek 'first tone')	grave:	à
falling	(sĭəŋ thoo 'second tone')	circumflex:	â
high level	(sĭəŋ trii 'third tone')	acute:	á
rising	(sĭəŋ càttəwaa 'fourth tone')	inverted circumflex (háček):	ǎ

There is hardly any mutual influence between the tones of neighboring syllables (tone sandhi) in Thai. In a few instances the second of two consecutive falling tones becomes low falling instead of high falling, but this phenomenon appears to be restricted to some fixed expressions like khɔ̀ɔp khun mâak khâʔ 'thank you very much', where mâak 'much' is high falling and the female politeness particle khâʔ is low falling.

Tones in Thai are characterized by glottal features as well as pitch and contour. The high level tone ends in a glottal constriction, while the mid level, low level and falling tones are more lax. The rising tone very often shows glottalization in the initial phase.

1.3 Syllable structure

The syllable in Thai is confined by restrictions both on the onset and coda. Counting the glottal stop /ʔ/ as a consonant, each syllable consists of at least an initial consonant and a rhyme. The rhyme consists of two morae, and may comprise either a long vowel (including diphthongs) or a short vowel and a final consonant.

A restricted set of consonant clusters are possible in the onset of the syllable. They invariably involve a voiceless stop (plain or aspirated) and a liquid (r, l or w). Not all combinations are permitted, though. There is /tr/ and /thr/, but not /tl/ or /thl/. The bilabial glide /w/ combines only with the velars /k/ and /kh/. In foreign loans, mostly from English, combinations like /br/, /fr/ or /fl/ occur, though they are usually reduced to [b] and [f] respectively in colloquial speech. Consonant clusters in native Thai words undergo simplification to various degrees in normal speech. Velar plus /r/l/ combinations are mostly pronounced as simple velar stop, while especially in Bangkok and its surroundings velar stop + w becomes [f]. The rare combination /tr/ is often pronounced like /k/, while /thr/ becomes [th].[5]

In the coda, only one of a restricted set of consonants /k, t, p, ŋ, n, m, y w, ʔ/ is possible, and no final consonant clusters are permitted. Other consonants may appear in the coda in Thai orthography, in many cases also more than one, but the pronunciation is always one of the codas permitted in Thai words. Thus a word written with final <-s> is pronounced with [-t], as are words orthographically ending in palatal stops. There is thus no one-to-one correspondence between the written final and the pronunciation. Syllables ending in a stop (unreleased) are called 'dead words' (*kham taay*) in Thai. They occur with a restricted set of tones, viz. low, falling or high. The mid level and the rising tone are excluded from dead syllables, while 'live words' (*kham pen*) can carry any of the five tones.

As in many other languages of Southeast Asia, there are in Thai words consisting of a weak presyllable followed by a main syllable, i.e. sesquisyllabic words. These are mostly loans from foreign languages, but a few can be traced back to Proto-Tai. The pre-syllable is either the result of a weakened element in a compound or of vocalic epenthesis in non-permitted initial clusters. Presyllables consist of a simple consonant or consonant cluster in the onset, and are pronounced with /ə/. The pre-syllable can receive full syllable stress, including vowel, coda and tone, in very careful formal speech, but it is usually pro-

---

5 In some words, the orthographic combination <thr-> is pronounced as [s].

nounced with a schwa and is not phonologically tone-bearing. In Thai orthography, pre-syllables are sometimes written with the visarga ะ <ḥ>, which stands for the short vowel *a* with following glottal stop, sometimes with no overt vowel:

Table 4: minor syllables

Thai	Transliteration	Usual (careful) Pronunciation	Gloss
สบาย	<sbāy>	səbaay (sà?baay)	comfortable
สนุก	<snuk>	sənùk (sà?nùk)	have fun
มะพร้าว	<maḥbrā́w>	məphráaw (má?phráaw)	coconut
ประตู	<praḥtū>	prətuu (prà?tuu)	door

The following syllable types thus occur in Thai (C = consonant, V = short simple vowel, VV = long vowel of diphthong, ^{T} = tone):[6]

CVC^T	CəCVC^T	CCəCVC^T
CCVC^T	CəCCVC^T	CCəCCVC^T
CVV^T	CəCVV^T	CCəCVV^T
CVVC^T	CəCVVC^T	CCəCVVC^T
CCVVC^T	CəCCVVC^T	CCəCCVVC^T

2 Word structure

Indigenous Thai words are typically monomorphemic, i.e. not analyzable as consisting of different morphemes. In other words, Thai does not show anything like productive morphological processes in its indigenous vocabulary. Derivational morphology has entered the Thai language mostly from Khmer. Originally restricted to Khmer loans, some morphological processes have become independent and productive at some stage of Thai. This is true especially for the infix /-am-, -amn-/, which can be added to indigenous Thai roots or to roots which in Khmer do not take the infix. One example of a non-Khmer word taking the Khmer derivational infix is the pair *sǐəŋ* 'sound, voice' – *sǎmnǐəŋ* 'accent, pronunciation'. The base word *sǐəŋ* itself may be an early loan from Chinese, cognate with Mandarin *shēng* 'sound, voice' (Schuessler 2007: 460). The Thai derivation may have been indirectly influenced by the Khmer word *sɔmleːŋ* 'sound'. Apart from the Khmer derivational affixes, which obviously gained some degree

---

6 For restrictions on medial and final consonants see above.

of productivity at some point, there are a few frozen examples of Austroasiatic-type affixes, especially the widespread causative prefix /p-/. Examples which seem to illustrate this very old process are *loŋ* 'move down' – *ploŋ* 'let down, abandon' and *lɔɔy* 'float' – *plɔy* 'let go', the latter with a change in tone. If these examples are valid, they may be evidence of a very early period of Tai-Austroasiatic contact.

2.1 Derivation or compounding?

A few very productive morphemes in modern Thai can be seen as derivational prefixes, although an alternative analysis as lexical compounding is more appropriate for less productive morphemes.. There are a handful of nominalizing prefixes, viz. *kaan*, *khwaam* and *kham*, as illustrated in (1).

(1)	เรียน	*riən*	'learn'	การเรียน	*kaan-riən*	'learning'
	รู้	*rúu*	'know'	ความรู้	*khwaam-rúu*	'knowledge'
	ถาม	*thǎam*	'ask'	คำถาม	*kham-thǎam*	'question'

The word *kaan* (from Pali *kāra* 'act') turns an activity verb into a *nomen actionis*, focusing on the activity or process described by the base verb. As a lexical item, *khwaam* means '(abstract) matter, thing, affair, state of affairs' and is rarely used on its own. It forms verbal nouns focusing on the state of affairs or characteristics expressed by the base verb rather than on an ongoing process. The word *kham* means 'a mouthful, word' and is used to form nouns from *verba dicendi* (speak, ask, beg, etc.).

The prefix *nâa-*, from the modal verb *nâa* 'ought, should, would be good to' forms derived verbs from verbal bases with what might be called 'passive-modal' meaning:

(2)	กิน	*kin*	'eat'	น่ากิน	*nâa-kin*	'appetizing'
	รัก	*rák*	'love'	น่ารัก	*nâa-rák*	'lovely'
	เกลียด	*klìət*	'hate'	น่าเกลียด	*nâa-klìət*	'disgusting'

As with the nominalizers above, an analysis as compound or phrasal construction is possible as well, and might be preferable historically, although synchronically *nâa-* behaves like a real derivational prefix. It is easy to demonstrate, though, how a sentence like the following can be reanalyzed, giving rise to *nâa-* as prefix.

(3) a. ลูกหมาตัวนี้(เรา)น่ารัก
   lûuk   măa   tuə   níi   (raw)   nâa   rák.
   offspring dog   CLF   PROX   (1PL)   ought   love
   'This puppy, we should love.'

b. ลูกหมาตัวนี้(*เรา)น่ารักน่าก
   lûuk   măa   tuə   níi   (*raw)   nâa.rák   mâak.
   offspring dog   CLF   PROX   (*1PL)   lovely   much
   'This puppy is very lovely.'

While the phrase 'this puppy' in (3a) is a topical object NP, it is reanalyzed as subject in (3b). This is shown by the impossibility to add another subject NP in (3b) and the scope of the adverbial V2 *mâak* 'be much' over *nâa.rák*, not only *rák*.

Another grammaticalized derivational prefix is *khîi-*, from the verb/noun *khîi* 'defecate; excrement, unusable left-over'. It is used to form verbs from active verbal bases, expressing that the subject performs the activity described by the base verb in excess, always with a negative connotation. Although the lexical noun/verb *khîi* is considered taboo and avoided in polite speech, it is commonly used (without taboo) in compounds and as verbal prefix. The expressions in (4) illustrate the use of this productive prefix:

(4) เล่น   *lên*   'play'   ขี้เล่น   *khîi-lên*   'playful, unserious'
    เหนียว   *niăw*   'sticky'   ขี้เหนียว *khîi-niăw*   'stingy'
    คุย   *khuy*   'chat'   ขี้คุย   *khîi-khuy*   '(given to) brag'

Other nominal and verbal compounds will be treated in the next section and in section 4.2.

2.2 "Psycho-collocations" and generic/logical V-O expressions

Like other languages of Southeast Asia, Thai makes vast use of what Matisoff calls "psycho-collocations" (Matisoff 1986). Psycho-collocations are conventionalized compounds involving a noun expressing the physical seat or centre of mental or emotional processes and states and a stative verb describing the process or state. The most common noun used in this type of compound in Thai is *cay* 'heart'[7]. In

---

[7] The same etymon is found as a psycho-noun in other Southeast languages such as Burmese or Khmer. See Vittrant (2014: 269–70).

elaborate expressions (see section 2.3), *cay* often co-occurs with *ʔòk* 'breast' in the formula [V-*ʔòk* V-*cay*]. Two basic structures are available for psycho-collocations involving *cay*, viz. [V-*cay*] and [*cay*-V]. In some cases the same verb can occur in both structures with a difference in meaning. In general, [V-*cay*] expresses a temporary state of mind, whereas [*cay*-V] expresses a more permanent trait of character. There are exceptions to this rule, though, e.g. *cay-hăay* 'be devastated' ('heart-disappear'), which denotes a temporary state of mind. The pairs are not necessarily semantically related, as seen in the examples This difference is illustrated by the following examples:

(5) ดีใจ *dii-cay* 'happy' ('good heart') ใจดี *cay-dii* 'kind' ('heart good')

น้อยใจ *nɔ́ɔy-cay* 'sad, disappointed' ('little heart') ใจน้อย *cay-nɔ́ɔy* 'easily offended' ('heart little')

ร้อนใจ *rɔ́ɔn-cay* 'anxious' ('hot heart') ใจร้อน *cay-rɔ́ɔn* 'impatient' ('heart hot')

In other cases, only one of the two formulas is common:

(6) a. ใจเย็น *cay-yen* 'patient' ('heart-cool')
ใจดำ *cay-dam* 'unkind, stingy' ('heart-black')
ใจกว้าง *cay-kwâaŋ* 'generous' ('heart-wide')
ใจแข็ง *cay-khĕŋ* 'unyielding' ('heart-hard')
ใจง่าย *cay-ŋâay* 'easily seduced, easily convinced' ('heart-easy')

b. อุ่นใจ *ʔùn-cay* 'appeased' ('warm-heart')
เจ็บใจ *cèp-cay* 'feel hurt' ('hurt-heart')
เสียใจ *sǐa-cay* 'sad, unhappy' ('waste-heart')
แปลกใจ *plɛ̀ɛk-cay* 'astonished, surprised' ('strange-heart')
ชื่นใจ *chûɯn-cay* 'delighted' ('moist-heart')

If the verb in a V-*cay*-construction denotes an activity, the compound meaning is usually 'V in reaction to someone else's feelings', as seen in the following examples.

(7) ปลอบใจ *plɔ̀ɔp-cay* 'comfort s.o.' ('appease-heart')
เกรงใจ *kreeŋ-cay* 'not want to impose on s.o.' ('fear-heart')
เอาใจ *ʔaw-cay* 'take care of s.o.' ('take-heart')
ให้ใจ *hây-cay* 'give in to s.o.' ('give-heart')

รู้ใจ	rúu-cay	'understand s.o.'s feelings' ('know-heart')
เข้าใจ	khâw-cay	'understand' ('enter-heart')
ไว้ใจ	wáy-cay	'trust s.o.' ('keep-heart')

In most of these expressions involving *cay* 'heart', the meaning is idiomatic and not predictable from the component parts of the compound.

Another type of conventional phrasal expression involves a transitive verb and a generic object which occurs natually with the verb. Many transitive verbs *require* a generic object, if no referential object is present, either overtly or understood from the linguistic or extra-linguistic context. The choice of generic object is conventionalized in Thai, and always denotes a referent that is typically associated with the activity expressed by the verb. In a few cases the generic object contributes a semantic component to the verb, as in the case of *kin-khâaw* 'eat' ('consume rice') vs. *kin-náam* 'drink' ('consume water'), where the generic object specifies the meaning of *kin* 'consume'. In (8), the generic object *phleeŋ* 'song' logically occurs with the verb *rɔ́ɔŋ* 'sing'.[8] The generic object is usually expressed only once in a given paragraph or conversational exchange. After its first mention, it is considered present in the context and is therefore dropped. The following examples illustrate the generic V-O collocations.

(8)
กินข้าว	kin-khâaw	'eat' ('consume-rice')
กินน้ำ	kin-náam	'drink' ('consume-liquid')
ซื้อของ	súɯ-khɔ̌ɔŋ	'shop' ('buy-thing')
อ่านหนังสือ	ʔàan-nǎŋsɯ̌ɯ	'read' ('read-book')
เขียนหนังสือ	khǐən-nǎŋsɯ̌ɯ	'write' ('write-book')
เรียนหนังสือ	riən-nǎŋsɯ̌ɯ	'study' ('learn-book')
ร้องเพลง	rɔ́ɔŋ-phleeŋ	'sing' ('sing-song')
ทอผ้า	thɔɔ-phâa	'weave' ('weave-cloth')
ซักผ้า	sák-phâa	'wash' ('wash-cloth')

The generic object has no semantic content and merely serves as "dummy" object, as can be seen in the following short conversation.

(9) A: ไปกินข้าวไหม B: ป๊ะ ไปกินอะไรดี
    pay kin khâaw mǎy?   pá?, pay kin ʔəray dii?
    go eat rice   Q   ADH go eat what good
    'Shall we go to eat?'   'Let's go. What shall we eat?'

---

8 The verb *rɔ́ɔŋ* also has an intransitive sense, meaning 'shout, cry'. The object *phleeŋ* therefore also has disambiguating function here.

A:	กินก๋วยเตี๋ยวดีไหม				B:	ดี
	kin	kǔay-tǐəw	dii	mǎy?		dii.
	eat	noodles	good	Q		good
	'Should we go to eat noodles?'					'OK.'

In some cases, a generic 'object' is used with a usually intransitive verb, as in *dɤɤn-thaaŋ* 'travel' ('walk-way'). Again, as seen above in the example 'study', the relation between the verb and the noun is not necessarily one of object/patient, but rather a logical semantic connection. A similar phenomenon is the collocation of a verb expressing a mental or physical state and the body part affected by the state or some entity connected to the state:

(10) a. ปวด   *pùət*   'ache'
     ปวดหัว   *pùət-hǔə*   'have a headache' ('ache-head')
     ปวดฟัน   *pùət-fan*   'have a toothache' ('ache-tooth')
     ปวดท้อง   *pùət-thɔ́ɔŋ*   'have a stomach ache' ('ache-stomach')

   b. คัน   *khan*   'itch'
     คันหัว   *khan-hǔə*   'have an itchy head' ('itch-head')
     คันมือ   *khan-mɯɯ*   'have itchy hands' ('itch-hand')
     คันหลัง   *khan-lǎŋ*   'have an itchy back' ('itch-back')

   c. สบาย   *səbaay*   'be comfortable'
     สบายใจ   *səbaay-cay*   'feel comfortable' ('comfortable-heart')
     สบายเท้า   *səbaay-tháaw*   'comfortable to wear (shoes)' ('comfortable-foot')
     สบายตัว   *səbaay-tuə*   'feel comfortable all over' ('comfortable-body')

   d. เก่ง   *kèŋ*   'skilled'
     เก่งเลข   *kèŋ-lêek*   'good at mathematics' ('skilled-number')
     เก่งอังกฤษ   *kèŋ-ʔaŋkrìt*   'good at English' ('skilled-English')
     เก่งบอล   *kèŋ-bɔɔn*   'good at soccer' ('skilled-ball')

2.3 Expressions, ideophones and euphonic compounds

"Elaborate expressions" are extensions of mostly conventionalized phrases generally involving a verb and an object. Being used very frequently in literary and poetic style, elaborate expressions also find their way into the colloquial language. The extent to which these expressions are used in everyday language is very much a matter of the individual style of a speaker. Elaborate expressions can be formed according to a variety of patterns. In colloquial Thai they are productive to some degree. Elaborate expressions typically consist of four syllables, two of which either share the initial consonant or the rhyme (nucleus and coda). Another possibility is that one word, usually the verb, is repeated with different but semantically related objects. Very often the objects occur as euphonic compounds in other contexts. The quadrisyllabic elaborate expressions can be lexical compounds, nominal or verbal, or phrases. In many cases the word added to the base expression does not have meaning on its own and merely has euphonic function (11a). In other cases the word added is part of a common compound (11b), while in still other cases the word added does have a meaning, but its connection to the normal object is merely phonetic, as in (11c). The following examples illustrate some common elaborate expressions.

(11) a. สนุกสนาน
       sənùk-sənăan   'have fun' ('have.fun-EUPH')
       วีซุ่มวีซ่า
       wiisûm-wiisâa   'visa' ('EUPH-visa')
       เสียดุมเสียดาย
       sĭədum-sĭədaay   'regret' ('EUPH-regret')

   b. สะดวกสบาย
       sədùək-səbaay   'convenient' ('convenient-comfortable')
       อาบน้ำอาบท่า
       ʔàap-náam-ʔàap-thâa   'take a shower' ('bathe-water-bathe-jetty')
       กินข้าวกินปลา
       kin-khâaw-kin-plaa   'eat' ('consume-rice-consume-fish')
       ล้างหน้าล้างตา
       láaŋ-nâa-láaŋ-taa   'wash one's face' ('wash-face-wash-eye')
       กลับบ้านกลับช่อง
       klàp-bâan-klàp-chɔ̂ŋ   'go home' ('return-house-return-channel')

   c. ยกไม้ยกมือ
       yók-máay-yók-mɯɯ   'raise one's hands' ('lift-wood-lift-hand')

Some elaborate expressions have idiomatic status, as example (12) shows.

(12) ข้าวยากหมากแพง
    khâaw-yâak-màak-phɛɛŋ   'bad days' ('rice-difficult-betel-expensive')

Ideophones are words that imitate a sound or describe a sensation. They are used in Thai not only in literary style, but also in everyday speech. As with the elaborate expressions, the usage of ideophones is a question of personal speech style and register. Ideophones are usually bisyllabic lexemes, formally made up of a base syllable and its reduplication, sometimes with a change in one or more vowel or consonant. Syntactically ideophones usually function as adverbials, but some predicative verbs look rather like ideophones and can be seen as the result of lexicalization, as seen in (14).

(13) หัวใจเต้นตุบๆ
    hǔacay tên tùp-tùp   'The heart is beating *tup-tup*.' ('heart dance *tup-tup*')
    ปวดหัวตุบๆ
    pùat-hǔa tùp-tùp   'Have a pulsating headache.' ('ache-head *tup-tup*')
    คันยิกๆ
    khan yík-yík   'itch a little bit' ('itch *yik-yik*')
    มืดตึ๊ดตื๋อ
    mûɯt tuít-tuɯ   'pitch dark' ('dark *tut-tuɯ*')[9]

(14) จุ้นจ้าน   *cùn-câan*   'meddle'
    จู้จี้   *cûu-cîi*   'fussy, meticulous'
    โผงผาง   *phǒoŋ-phǎaŋ*   'outspoken, tactless'

Euphonic compounds are another means of adding poetic flavour to the Thai language, both written and spoken. In euphonic compounds, an empty or semantically unrelated morpheme is added to a base lexeme. The choice of the added word is conventionalized: usually it shares the onset or the rhyme with the base word, or it is the reduplication thereof with a change in vowel. These vowel changes show some regularity in that there are fixed pairs of vowels occurring together in euphonic compounds, e.g. *u-i, o-e, ɔ-ɛ, a-ɤ, ua-ia*. Either the first or the second syllable of a euphonic compound can be the bearer of the semantics, as illustrated in (15). The difference between the expressions in (14) and the euphonic compounds in (15) is that the component parts of the former cannot occur alone, whereas one part of the compounds in (15) occurs as a free

---

[9] The quasi-ideophonic expression *tuít-tuɯ* is one of a number of lexeme-specific reinforcing elements, i.e. intensifiers that ocur with only a very limited number of base lexemes. Other examples are *khǎaw-cúa* 'snow white', *dɛɛŋ-kàm* 'intense red', *rɔ́ɔn-cǐi* 'burning hot'.

lexeme. The dividing line is not clear, though, as euphonic compounds tend to become conventionalized, which may result in the components losing their independence.

(15) ซุบซิบ   súp-síp   'gossip' ('EUPH-whisper')
     โซเซ   soo-see   'stagger' ('EUPH-stagger')
     มอมแมม   mɔɔm-mɛɛm   'dirty' ('make dirty-EUPH')

Sometimes the added word is semantically related to the base word, or the joined words together make up a new meaning. In this case, too, the phonetic similarity is important, i.e. the members of the compound are at least partially chosen for their phonetic shape.

(16) เรียบร้อย   rîəp-rɔ́ɔy   'tidy, orderly' ('even-hundred')
     เคร่งเครียด   khrêŋ-khrîət   'serious' ('strict-tense')
     ราบรื่น   râap-ruîɯn   'smooth, easy' ('flat-joyful')
     รู้เรื่อง   rúu-ruîəŋ   'be informed' ('know-story')
     ข้าวของ   khâaw-khɔ̌ɔŋ   'belongings' ('rice-thing')

2.4 Reduplication

Reduplication in Thai (indicated in Thai script by the doubling sign ๆ) is frequent and serves various functions, depending on the syntactic class and the semantics of the repeated word. Reduplication of nouns with human referents is sometimes used to indicate a group of individuals, though this use is rather restricted. Thus dèk-dèk (from dèk 'child') means 'children', phîi-phîi-nɔ́ɔŋ-nɔ́ɔŋ is 'brothers and sisters'. In a few cases the repetition of a measure word leads to an iterative reading, e.g. wan-wan 'day after day' from wan 'day'. Much more widespread is the use of reduplicated verbs, especially stative verbs. The meaning can be attributive or adverbial, either reinforcing or attenuating. Reduplicated verbs can be used both predicatively and attributively. Reduplication of stative verbs with the tone pattern [high tone-original tone] (e.g. díi-dii 'so good!', ʔərɔ́y-ʔərɔ̀y 'so delicious!') has an affective reinforcing function and is used almost exclusively by female speakers.

(17) ที่บ้านเขามีหมาตัวใหญ่ๆ สองตัว
     thîi   bâan   khǎw   mii   mǎa   tuə   yày-yày   sɔ̌ɔŋ   tuə.
     LOC   house   3HUM   exist   dog   CLF   big-RDPL   two   CLF
     'There are two rather big dogs at his house.'

(18) ถ้าออกต่างจังหวัด ขับรถดีๆ นะ
    thâa ʔɔ̀ɔk tàaŋ   caŋwàt   khàp   rót   dii-dii   ná?.
    if   exit different province drive car   good-RED   EMPH
    'If you go to the provinces, drive carefully, won't you?'

Reduplication of quantifiers leads to a reinforcement of the quantifier, putting emphasis on the quantity expressed.

(19) เขามาขายขนมหน้าบ้านทุกๆ วัน
    khǎw   maa   khǎay   khanǒm   nâa   bâan   thúk-thúk   wan.
    3HUM   come   sell   sweets   face   house   every-RED   day
    'He comes selling sweets in front of the house every single day.'

(20) รถคันนี้แพงมากๆ
    rót   khan   níi   phɛɛŋ   mâak-mâak.
    car   CLF   this   expensive   very-RED
    'This car is really very expensive.'

3 Syntactic structure

3.1 Nominal phrase

The nominal phrase in Thai can consist of either a simple or compound noun or pronoun, or it can exhibit a more complex structure, made up of various components, including modifiers such as relative clauses, determiners, numerals and quantifiers, and classifiers. Each of these categories will be described separately in the following sections. Noun phrases can be complements of verbs or prepositions, two categories that are not always clearly separable in Thai, as will be shown in section 3.1.5.

The maximal complexity of a noun phrase is illustrated in (21).

(21) ลูก   หมา   น้อย   น่ารักๆ   สอง   ตัว   ที่   ซื้อมา   นั้น
    lûuk   mǎa   nɔ́ɔy   nâa.rák-nâa.rák sɔ̌ɔŋ   tua   thîi   súɯ maa   nán
    offspring dog   small lovely-RED   two   CLF   REL   buy COME   MEDL
    head |MDF |MDF |MDF |QUANT |MDF |DET
    'Those two little lovely puppies that I have bought.'

3.1.1 Classifiers

Thai makes extensive use of nominal classifiers, not only in connection with numeral expressions, but also in other contexts where individuation of a referent is required. This includes the collocation of a noun with a modifier, quantifier, or a determiner. Classifiers can also be used to express anaphoric reference without a head noun, but always in combination with a modifier, quantifier or determiner. The choice of classifier with a specific head noun is highly conventionalized and (at least in theory) based on semantic or functional similarities, although there are a few rather idiosyncratic cases. A number of classifiers and their usage are set out in Table 5 below. Spoons and forks, for example, use the classifier *khan*, which is also used for umbrellas and land vehicles (but not ox-carts), while knives, not part of the traditional Thai cutlery, use *lêm*, which they share with books, candles, ox carts and needles. Most animals (and pieces of clothing, letters of the alphabet, among some other inanimate things) occur with the classifier *tuə*, literally 'body', but elephants use *chuîək*, literally 'rope'. While some classifiers cover a wide range of nouns, like *ʔan*, which is used for non-classified, smallish objects, others are very specific, being applicable to only to a few nouns, like *puîiun*, which occurs only with saws. Human referents receive different classifiers according to social status, *tuə* being derogatory, *khon* neutral, *thân* polite/respectful, *ʔoŋ* and *phraʔ.ʔoŋ* for different levels of royalty and *rûup*, literally 'image', for monks. The correct choice of classifier is fixed in the standard language and is a subject of learning up to high school level.

Table 5: Some Thai classifiers and their usage

	Classifier form	Used with nouns meaning:
คัน	khan	Spoons, forks, umbrellas, land vehicles (except ox carts)
เล่ม	lêm	knives, books, candles, ox carts, needles
ตัว	tuə	animals, pieces of clothing, letters of the alphabet, inanimate things, human (derogatory)
เชือก	chuîək	elephant
อัน	ʔan	small objects
ปื้น	puîiun	saws
คน	khon	human (neutral)
ท่าน	thân	human (polite)
องค์ พระองค์	ʔoŋ, (phraʔ.ʔoŋ)	human (royal persons)

The word order in nominal phrases including a classifier is always as in (22)

    head – numeral – classifier – determiner

(22) a. บ้านสองหลังนี้
        bâan   sɔ̌ɔŋ   lǎŋ   níi
        house two   CLF   this
        'these two houses'

    b. เพื่อนกี่คน
        phɯ̂an kìi   khon
        friend   how.many CLF
        'how many friends'

Nouns expressing measurements of time, space, or volume do not require a classifier and can be combined directly with modifying elements.

(23) a. จะอยู่ที่นี่หลายวัน
        càʔ   yùu   thîi   nîi   lǎay   wan.
        PROS stay LOC   PROX many   day
        'I will stay here many days.'

    b. เขาวิ่งไปสี่ร้อยเมตร
        khǎw wîŋ   pay   sìi   rɔ́ɔy   méet.
        3HUM run   GO   four hundred meter
        'He ran four hundred meters.'

Some nouns can function as measure words in one context and as objects with their own classifiers in others, as seen in (24).

(24) a. น้ำหนึ่งแก้ว   b. แก้วหนึ่งใบ
        náam nɯ̀ŋ   kɛ̂ɛw   kɛ̂ɛw nɯ̀ŋ   bay
        water one   glass   glass one   CLF
        'one glass of water'   'one glass'

3.1.2 Determiners

Determiners in Thai comprise demonstratives and interrogatives, the latter also used as indefinites. Determiners usually occur after a classifier, but are sometimes directly attached to a head noun.

(25) a. บ้าน(หลัง)นั้น
      bâan   *(lăŋ)*   *nán*
      house   (CLF)   MEDL
      'that house'

b. ครู(คน)ไหน
   khruu   *(khon)*   *năy*
   teacher   (CLF)   which
   'which teacher'

The demonstratives in Thai indicate three levels of distance from the *origo*, viz. *níi* 'this, PROXIMAL', *nán* 'that, MEDIAL', and *nóon* 'that, DISTAL'. The distance expressed is not only spatial, but also temporal and emotional. While EGO (the speaker) and NUNC (the time of speaking) are the prototypical origo, the medial demonstrative can co-occur with first person pronouns to indicate emotional distance from one self or one's behavior at a certain time. Similarly, the proximal demonstrative *níi* can occur with second or, more rarely, third person pronouns to express special emotional closeness to the referent. The proximal and medial demonstratives can be combined, either as *níi-nán* PROX-MEDL or as *nán-nán* MEDL-MEDL, with the final *nán* expressing anaphoric topicality of the referent.

The interrogative determiners are *năy* or *day* 'which'[10] and *ʔəray* 'what (kind of)'. As *ʔəray* is originally a compound of the general inanimate classifier *ʔan* and an obsolete form *ray* of the interrogative determiner, it does not usually occur with classifiers but is attached directly to the head noun. Notice the difference between *rót khan năy* 'which car' and *rót ʔəray* 'what kind of car'. In negative and interrogative contexts, the interrogative determiners receive indefinite reading.

The combination of a classifier and postponed (unstressed) numeral *nùŋ* (or *nɯŋ*) 'one' functions like an indefinite article. Compare the expressions in (26a) and (26b) below.

(26) a. บ้านหนึ่งหลัง
      bâan   *nùŋ*   *lăŋ*
      house   one   CLF
      'one house'

b. บ้านหลังหนึ่ง
   bâan   *lăŋ*   *nùŋ*
   house   CLF   one
   'a house'

---

10 Of the two forms, *day* is used only in literary style.

Nouns in Thai are underspecified as to number, i.e. *rót* can be 'a/the car' or '(the) cars'. The use of a determiner has a strong singularizing effect, so that *rót khan níi* can only be understood as 'this car', not 'these cars' (see section 4.1.3 for more details on number).

3.1.3 Number and quantifiers

As stated above (section 2), number is not necessarily expressed in Thai. If the number of referents of a noun phrase is recoverable from the context or not relevant to the current discourse, it is left unmarked. There are, however, various possibilities for expressing plurality of nouns, including group classifiers used in combination with determiners. These are semantically less restricted than individuating classifiers. In common use are *phûək* for human or highly animate referents, and *làw* for general referents, including human/animate and, more commonly, inanimate objects. The singular/plural distinction of the nominal expression therefore lies in the classifier, rather than in the noun.

(27) a. เพื่อนคนไหน
      phûən khon năy
      friend CLF which
      'which friend'

    b. เพื่อนพวกไหน
      phûən phûək năy
      friend CLF.GROUP which
      'which friends'

(28) a. รถคันนี้
      rót khan níi
      car CLF PROX
      'this car'

    b. รถเหล่านี้
      rót làw níi
      car CLF.GROUP PROX
      'these cars'

The Thai numerals are early loans from Chinese, with the exception of *sǔun* 'zero', which is from Sanskrit *śūnya* 'center, empty, zero', and the higher numerals like *rɔ́ɔy* 'hundred' (from the verb *rɔ́ɔy* 'put on a string') and *phan* 'thousand' (from *phan* 'bind together').

    Compound numbers are formed from the basic numerals in regular fashion, with lower numeral before higher numeral meaning multiplication, and lower numeral after higher numeral meaning addition. The only irregularities are the use of *ʔèt* after multiples of ten (and sometimes hundred and thousand), and *yîi* instead of *sɔ̌ɔŋ* in the word *yîi-sìp* 'twenty'. The compound numerals are illustrated in example (30).

(29) The Thai numerals

๑ หนึ่ง, -เอ็ด	nɯ̀ŋ, -ʔèt	1	๐ ศูนย์	sǔun	0
๒ สอง, ยี่-	sɔ̌ɔŋ, yîi-	2	ร้อย	rɔ́ɔy	100
๓ สาม	sǎam	3	พัน	phan	1000
๔ สี่	sìi	4	หมื่น	mɯ̀ɯn	10,000
๕ ห้า	hâa	5	แสน	sɛ̌ɛn	100,000
๖ หก	hòk	6	ล้าน	láan	1,000,000
๗ เจ็ด	cèt	7			
๘ แปด	pɛ̀ɛt	8	ห้าสิบเอ็ด	hâa-sìp-ʔèt	51
๙ เก้า	kâaw	9	ยี่สิบสอง	yîi-sìp-sɔ̌ɔŋ	22
๑๐ สิบ	sìp	10	สองร้อย	sɔ̌ɔŋ-rɔ́ɔy	200

(30) ๓๖,๔๙๘
sǎam-mɯ̀ɯn-hòk-phan-sìi-rɔ́ɔy-kâaw-sìp-pɛ̀ɛt
3 × 10,000 + 6 × 1,000 + 4 × 100 + 9 × 10 + 8 = 36,498

While numerals are used to indicate an exact amount of referents, there are more general quantifiers in Thai, which behave syntactically like numerals, occurring before a classifier or a measure word. The general quantifier indicating plurality is *lǎay* 'many, numerous', the indefinite quantifier *baaŋ* means 'some', and the interrogative quantifier is *kìi* 'how many'.

(31) a. หมาบางตัว b. หมาหลายตัว c. หมากี่ตัว

mǎa	baaŋ	tuə	mǎa	lǎay	tuə	mǎa	kìi	tuə
dog	some	CLF	dog	many	CLF	dog	how.many	CLF
'some dogs'			'many dogs'			'how many dogs'		

Focal particles can occur between the head noun and the quantifier phrase, indicating a subjective feeling of a small (*khɛ̂ɛ*) or a big (*tâŋ*) amount.

(32) a. มีเงินแค่สิบบาท b. มีเงินตั้งสิบบาท

mii	ŋɤn	**khɛ̂ɛ**	sìp	bàat.	mii	ŋɤn	**tâŋ**	sìp	bàat.
have	money	FOC	ten	baht	have	money	FOC	ten	baht
'I have only ten baht.'					'I have as much as ten baht.'				

If the inclusive marker *tháŋ* is used in combination with a quantifier, the classifier may be dropped. An expression like N *tháŋ* QF means 'all QF Ns'. In combination with a classifier or a measure word, *tháŋ* means 'the whole'.

(33) a. เพื่อนทั้งหก (คน)
   phûɯan tháŋ hòk (khon)
   friend INCL six (CLF)
   'all six friends'

b. เด็กทั้งหลาย
 dèk tháŋ lǎay
 child INCL many
 'all the (many) children'

(34) a. ทั้งวัน ทั้งคืน
   tháŋ wan tháŋ khɯɯn
   INCL day INCL night
   'all day and all night'

b. บ้านทั้งหลัง
 bâan tháŋ lǎŋ
 house INCL CLF
 'the whole house'

3.1.4 Other modifiers

Like determiners and quantifiers, other modifiers of nouns always follow the modified noun. They can consist of a simple (usually stative or adjectival) verb or a marked relative/attributive clause. The most common relativizer in colloquial Thai is *thîi*. In more formal speech, *ʔan* and *sûŋ* are also used. There are no restrictions on the relativized grammatical or semantic function of the head noun, but for most oblique functions, requiring the use of a preposition, a resumptive pronoun is used.

(35) a. คนดี
   khon dii
   man good
   'a good man'

b. คนไม่ดี
 khon mây dii
 man NEG good
 'a bad man'

(36) a. คนที่เขียนหนังสือเรื่องนี้
   khon thîi khǐan nǎŋsɯɯ rɯ̂aŋ níi
   man REL write book story PROX
   'the man who wrote this story'

  b. เพื่อน (คน) ที่เราไปกินข้าวกับเขา
   phɯ̂an (khon) thîi raw pay kin khâaw kàp khǎw
   friend (CLF) REL 1PL go eat rice with 3HUM
   'the friend we went to eat with'

A noun can also be modified by another noun (phrase) or a pronoun. In this case, the modification is either possession or specification. No clear line can be drawn between nominal compounds and nouns modified by other nouns.

(37) a. บ้าน (ของ) ผม　　　　b. ประตู (*ของ) บ้าน
　　　 bâan　(khɔ̌ɔŋ)　phǒm　　　 pratuu　(*khɔ̌ɔŋ)　bâan
　　　 house　(POSS)　　1M　　　　 door　　(POSS)　　　house
　　　 'my house'　　　　　　　　　 'the/a door into the house'

If the possessum is a modified noun, the possessive marker khɔ̌ɔŋ 'of' (lit. 'thing') obligatorily occurs between possessum and possessor, as in bâan lǎŋ mày khɔ̌ɔŋ phǒm 'my new house'. The possessive marker optionally also occurs with plain nouns as possessum.

A special case of nominal modifiers are expressions consisting of a generic head noun expressing a class followed by the specific name of a member of this class.

(38) a. ต้นมะม่วง　　　　　 b. นกกระจอก
　　　 tôn　　məmûaŋ　　　　 nók　　kracɔ̀ɔk
　　　 tree　 mango　　　　　　bird　 sparrow
　　　 'mango tree'　　　　　　'sparrow'

Some of these 'class noun' – 'specific name' expressions are typically more lexicalized than others. Bird names usually take the class noun nók, resulting in a phonetic linker in many cases, as exemplified in (38b) above (See parallel examples in Burmese chapter p. 71, 72). The original name of the sparrow was cɔ̀ɔk, which, in close connection with nók became nók-ka-cɔ̀ɔk. This was reanalysed (and respelled) as nók and kracɔ̀ɔk (krà?cɔ̀ɔk in formal speech). For this reason, many birds' names have the "prefix" kra-/krà?- in modern Thai.

3.1.5 Prepositions

Although relator nouns like khâaŋ 'side; beside', and serialized verbs often cover functions of prepositions in other languages (the "coverbs" of Bisang 1992, and section 3.2.2 below), there are some original prepositions in Thai which cannot be synchronically analysed as having the grammatical function of verbs or nouns in modern Thai. The most frequent of these is probably the COMITATIVE kàp, which merges with the formal DATIVE marker kɛ̀ɛ in colloquial Thai, becoming ka (stressed form kà?). This preposition is frequently used not only with a comitative function, but also to indicate indirect objects, as in bɔ̀ɔk ka khǎw 'tell him'. Beneficiaries are either marked by the verbs hây 'give' (RECIPIENT and general BENEFACTIVE) or phùa 'set aside'(ADDITIONAL BENEFACTIVE), or by the

PURPOSIVE marker *phûǝ* 'for (the sake of)'.[11] This marker functions as a preposition before nominal expressions and as a subordinator before clauses. The INSTRUMENTAL preposition *dûǝy* is also used as adverb, meaning 'also, too, as well'. Unlike verbal prepositions (coverbs), true prepositions (and relator nouns) always need an overt nominal expression following them, i.e. they cannot be stranded.[12] If the noun phrase is for some reason not adjacent to the preposition, as in some relative expressions, a resumptive pronoun must be used, as seen in (36b) above.

3.2 Verbal domain

The verbal phrase[13] in Thai consists minimally of a single verb and maximally of a number of verbs, secondary verbs and verbal particles. A single verb can form a complete utterance in Thai, with the interpretation depending on the discourse context. No verbal morphology exists in Thai, either derivative or inflectional, apart from some fully Khmer infixes, not productive and better seen as phenomena of lexicalization than morphology (see above, section 2). Secondary verbs (V2s) can occur before of after the main verb, indicating various categories including tense, mode and aspect (TAM), and directionality. Verbal particles function mainly to express polarity and number. They can be separated from the main verb by V2s or objects, which shows their status as free forms rather than affixes.

3.2.1 Verbal categories (polarity, number, TAM, directionality, etc.)

Polarity in Thai is expressed by the pre-verbal NEGATION particle *mây*, which always occurs directly before the verbal element to be negated; it is a narrow focus negation marker. Only verbal elements can be negated by this particle. If a nominal or adverbial phrase is to be negated, a dummy verb *chây* 'be so, be the case that' must be used. This construction can also be used to extend the focus of negation over a whole clause. The narrow focus of the negation marker al-

---

11 This preposition is not cognate with the (co-)verb *phuìǝ*, in spite of the phonetic similarity in modern Thai.
12 A stranded preposition is one that is separated from its NP, as in the English phrase 'the book I am looking for'.
13 I use 'verbal phrase' in the sense of Dixon (2010: 108 ff) 'verb phrase', which is different from 'verb phrase' (including object NPs) in some syntactic theories.

lows for fine distinctions in negative expressions, as seen in the following examples.

(39) a. คุณไม่มา (ก็) ได้
 khun **mây** maa (kɔ̂) dây.
 2 NEG come (TCL) GET
 'You don't have to come.'

b. คุณมาไม่ได้
 khun maa **mây** dây.
 2 come NEG GET
 'You cannot come.'

c. ไม่ใช่คุณมาได้
 mây chây khun maa dây.
 NEG be.so 2 come GET
 'It is not the case that you can come.'

d. คุณไม่มาไม่ได้
 khun **mây** maa **mây** dây.
 2 NEG come NEG GET
 'You have to come.
 (You can't not come)'

The negation *mây* can occur by itself as short answer to a polar question. Extended negation scope is expressed by the preverbal phrase *mây dây* 'NEG GET'. Modified negation can be made by *mây khɤɤy* V 'never', *yaŋ mây* V 'not yet' and *mây* V *lɛ́ɛw* 'not any more'. Attenuated negation is expressed by *mây khɔ̂y* V 'not very, hardly'. Emphatic negation is made by *mây* V *lɤɤy* 'not V at all' or the COUNTEREXPECTATIVE *mây* V *rɔ̀ɔk* 'not V, contrary to what you said/thought'.

If the subject of a verb has a human or highly animate plural referent, the verb may be followed by the RECIPROCAL particle *kan*, often translatable as 'together, each other', but sometimes merely indicating the plurality of the subject. This use is not possible with stative verbs, but natural with verbs denoting actions. Plurality without reciprocity or 'togetherness' is seen in example (40a), where there is no implication that the people in question have gone somewhere together, while (40b), referring to a group of animals, is ambiguous and *kan* in (40c) is understood as reciprocal if no object is present in the discourse context. If the discussion has been about children and sweets, the normal interpretation of (40c) would be 'they like them (i.e. sweets)', with *kan* expressing the plural of the subject, rather than reciprocity. If an act is performed by the subject alone, the marker *ʔeeŋ* 'self' can be added after the verb and the object, as in *kháw kin ʔeeŋ* 'he eats it by himself'.

(40) a. เขาไปไหนกันหมด
 khǎw pay nǎy kan mòt?
 3HUM go where PL/REC all
 'Where have they all gone?'

b. มันกินกันอยู่
   man   kin   kan   yùu.
   3   eat   PL/REC   STAY
   'They are eating (together/each other).'

c. เขาชอบกัน
   khǎw   chɔ̂ɔp   kan.
   3HUM   like   REC/PL
   'They like each other.'

Another non-verbal morpheme which appears in the verbal phrase is the PROSPECTIVE marker cə (full form càʔ), grammaticalized from the obsolete verb càk 'know', which occurs in standard Thai only in the bound compound rúu.càk 'know'. The prospective marker is placed before the verb and the negation marker mây. It indicates realis, i.e. future and hypothetical, as well as expected but not actually confirmed events like generic statements. It occurs after some modal verbs like yàak 'want to' and khuən 'ought to', but not others like tɔ̂ŋ 'must'. Although cə can be used to describe future events, it is not a future marker as such. Tense as grammatical category does not exist in Thai, positioning in time of an event being implied by the context, or expressed explicitly by adverbs or other lexical means.

Aspectual distinctions are expressed mainly by secondary verbs (V2s). Some are semantically concrete, like post-verbal tɔ̀ɔ 'continue', or the phasal verbs rɤ̂ɤm 'begin' and lɤ̂ɤk 'end, stop', both in pre-verbal position. Others, like the directionals, have been semantically bleached through grammaticalization into mainly functional rather than lexical verbs (see below). A rather recent aspectual marker, rarely used in colloquial speech, is the originally nominal Khmer loan kamlaŋ 'strength, power', which is used to indicate progressive events. It serves as translation equivalent of English V-ing forms, after which it was calqued.

3.2.2 Serial verb constructions

A serial verb construction (SVC) is a single clause containing two or more lexically full verbs expressing a single event. Various definitions of SVCs (Bril (2004), Aikhenvald and Dixon (2006), Vittrant (2006), among others), mention other features such as argument sharing, common TAM and polarity, as well as equal syntactic status of all verbs involved: no verb is subordinate to or dependent on the other(s). Two major types of SVCs can be distinguished, namely root serialization and core serialization (Bril, 2004: 2). In root serialization (also called nuclear serialization), all verbs in a predicate are adjacent, preceded or followed by the arguments. In core serialization, two or more cores, each consisting of a verb and its arguments, are conjoined to form a complex predicate, with identical arguments expressed overtly only once. Unlike root serialization, core serialization allows the verbs to be separated by arguments (but not adverbial elements). In this type of serialization, the object of V_1 often functions as subject of V_2.

Verb serialization in Thai is of the second type: the verbs in a SVC are not necessarily adjacent, even if the serialization consists of a main verb and one or two grammaticalized secondary verbs (see section 3). The object NP always follows the first verb it logically complements, as seen in (41a), where the noun *khənŏm* 'sweets' is the object of both *súɯ* 'buy' and *kin* 'eat', but appears only after the former.

(41) a. ผมซื้อขนมมากิน
 phŏm **súɯ** *khənŏm* *maa* **kin**.
 1M buy sweets come eat
 'I bought in some sweets to eat.'

That the serial verb construction is a syntactic unit is shown by the impossibility of peripheral elements like prepositional phrases intervening in the expression, even if they belong after one of the verbs logically, as seen in (41b) and (41c).

b. *ผมซื้อขนมมาจากตลาดกิน
 *phŏm *súɯ* *khənŏm* *maa* *càak* *təlàat* *kin*.
 1M buy sweets come from market eat

c. ผมซื้อขนมมากินจากตลาด
 phŏm **súɯ** *khənŏm* *maa* **kin** *càak* *təlàat*.
 1M buy sweets come eat from market
 'I bought sweets at the market.'

SVCs can have various interpretations, with either the first or the second verbs, or both, carrying the main semantics of the expression. In (42) and (43), both verbs retain their full lexical meaning,.

(42) เขานั่งกินข้าว
 khǎw **nâŋ** **kin** *khâaw*.
 3HUM sit eat rice
 'He is sitting and eating.'

(43) โจรวิ่งหนีตำรวจ
    coon **wîŋ** **nǐi** tamrùət.
    thief run flee police
    'The thief ran away from the police.'

In some cases, only prosodic stress (indicated by ') and context determine which verb is the full lexical verb and which the secondary verb, as in (44a-b).

(44) a. เราไปอยู่
    raw **pay** 'yùu.
    1PL go stay
    'We go to live there.'

   b. เราไปอยู่
    raw '**pay** yùu.
    1PL go STAY
    'We still go there.'

All verbs in an SVC share polarity: it is possible to negate only the whole expression, not one of its parts. If in a sentence like (41a) above only the second verb is negated, the expression is receives a biclausal interpretation, as in (41a´). In this case, there usually is a pause between the two clauses, which are not a single intonation unit.

(41) a´. ผมซื้อขนมมา ไม่กิน
    phǒm **súɯ** khənǒm maa [...] mây **kin**.
    1M buy sweets come NEG eat
    'I bought some sweets in but I/you/they are not eating them.'

3.2.3 Secondary verbs

Verbs in SVCs can easily be grammaticalized, losing their full lexical semantics and acquiring grammatical functions. Unlike grammaticalization elsewhere in the language, the process of grammaticalization into secondary verbs in Thai does not involve phonetic reduction: the secondary verb has the same shape as the full lexical verb, with which it coexists in the language in many cases. These grammaticalized secondary verbs (V2) occur in fixed positions relative to the main verb and to each other, if more than one is present in a construction. The function of many V2s depends on their position; the same verb may occur in different positions with different functions. The functions covered by V2s range from valence to TAM, resultative (success), manner, speaker attitude, the expression of emotions, and clause linking.

Unlike main verbs in SVCs, some V2s can be negated independently, with the scope of the negation extending only over the verb directly following it. The following table shows the main grammaticalized V2s with their lexical meaning, position relative to the main verb (V) or a clause (C), and their grammatical functions.

Table 6: Secondary verbs

Form and lexical meaning	Position	Grammatical function
ให้ *hây* 'give'	_ V	CAUSATIVE (permissive, jussive)
	V _	benefactive
	_ C	so that (PURPOSIVE, DIFFERENT SUBJECT)
ได้ *dây* 'receive, get'	_ V	get to V, really V
	V _	have the opportunity to V
เป็น *pen* 'be'	V _	able, know how to V
ไหว *wǎy* 'move'	V _	capable (physically, mentally)
ต้อง *tɔ̂ŋ* 'touch' (obsolete)	_ V	must, have to
อยาก *yàak* 'desire' (obsolete)	_ V	want to
ถูก *thùuk* 'come into contact'	_ V, _ C	be affected by (quasi PASSIVE)
	V _	V correctly
ไว้ *wáy* 'keep, deposit'	_ V	do for later use (resultative)
เลย *ləəy* 'go past'	_ V	V right away, spontaneously
กว่า *kwàa* 'go beyond'	V _	more than (COMPARATIVE)
ว่า *wâa* 'say'	V _ C	that (COMPLEMENTIZER)
แล้ว *lɛ́ɛw* 'finish'[14]	_ V	SEQUENTIAL (and then)

---

14 As full verb, *lɛ́ɛw* has been replaced in Thai by the Khmer loanword *sèt*.

Form and lexical meaning	Position	Grammatical function
อยู่ yùu 'stay, remain'	V _	NEW SITUATION (NSIT)[15]
	_ V	stay and/to V
	V _	be still V-ing (TEMPORARY)
	V _	DIRECTIONAL (away from center of interest)
ขึ้น khɯ̂n 'go up'	V _	more than before; succeed
ลง loŋ 'go down'	V _	less than before; succeed
เข้า khâw 'enter'	V _	succeed
ออก ʔɔ̀ɔk 'exit'	V _	succeed
ต่อ tɔ̀ɔ 'follow'	V _	keep V-ing (CONTINUOUS)

V2s expressing manner include, besides common modifiers like *rew* 'be.fast', *cháa* 'be.slow', also more idiosyncratic verbs like *lên* 'play', which marks an activity executed for pleasure, as in *kin lên* 'eat for fun' (i.e. without being hungry or without the aim of becoming full. This V2 is fully productive and can be attached to any activity if semantically compatible.

The directions are a special class of V2s, which Bisang (1992: 67) divides into two subcategories, namely "verbs of direction" (*Richtungsverben*) and "verbs of orientation" (*Orientierungsverben*). Verbs of direction include V2s like 'move up', 'move down', 'move in' and 'move out', verbs of orientation are 'towards the center of interest' and 'away from the center of interest'. In Thai, a verb indicating the manner of movement, e.g. *dɤɤn* 'walk' can be combined with a verb of direction and a verb of orientaion, resulting in the complex structure *dɤɤn khâw maa* 'walk in' (lit. 'walk – enter – come'). Directionals function as modifiers of the main verb and cannot be negated independently.

The verbs of orientation *maa* 'come' and *pay* 'go' operate in the three different but sometimes inter-related dimensions of space, time and emotion. In essence, whenever the main verb includes motion, the spatial reading is domi-

---

[15] NSIT is widespread category in Southeast Asian languages, indicating that a new (but somehow expected) situation has started now. Its interpretation depends on the context and the presence of other V2s and ranges from 'is V-ing now', 'has started V-ing now' to 'has V-ed', 'has finished V-ing now' (s. Jenny 2001: 125ff). See for instance Burmese verb final particle ပြီ *pyi²* (Burmese chapter, § 3.3.1, table 12 p. 97).

nant, otherwise the interpretation can be temporal or emotional. In the temporal domain, *maa* 'come' expresses an event that has started some time in the past and extends towards the present, while *pay* 'go' indicates that the event goes on from now into the future (continuative aspect). In the emotional domain, *maa* expresses ongoing involvement of the speaker in events that may be reversible, and are often positive, while *pay* denotes events that are removed from the interest of the speaker, usually irreversible, and often negative. The different domains overlap to some extent, and a mixture of the three interpretations in a single expression is frequent. Depending on the semantics not all verbs are compatible with both, e.g. *taay* 'die' can normally only be combined with *pay*, not with *maa*. Others, like *phûut* 'speak, say' and *tham* 'do' are compatible with both, resulting in different meanings. Specific interpretations are hightly dependent on context.

(45) พูดมา *phûut maa* 'he told me; I/you/he said; tell me (I will listen)'
 พูดไป *phûut pay* 'he told so.; he goes on talking; just talk (I won't listen)'
 ทำมา *tham maa* 'I/you/he did, has been doing; I/you/he did it (and it's good)'
 ทำไป *tham pay* 'I/you/he will go on doing; I/you/he did it (I don't like it)'

3.2.4 Valence

Thai does not have any morphological means to change the valency of a predicate. Many verbs van be used either transitively or intransitively, with the transitive reading usually involving causation: *pìt* 'close sth.' ~ 'be closed', *ʔɔ̀ɔk* 'issue, put out' ~ 'leave, go out'.

Causative function can be periphrastically expressed by placing the purposive marker *hây* (lit. 'give') before the predicate indicating the action caused and the causee, as in (46) (See parallel functions of 'give' in Mon and Burmese). The meaning is either permissive or jussive, depending on the discourse context. The reading can be disambiguated by adding a verb expressing permission (e.g. *ʔanúʔyâat* 'allow') or command (e.g. *sàŋ* 'order', *bɔ̀ɔk* 'tell') before *hây*. Unlike the lexical (unmarked) transitives/causatives like *pìt* and *ʔɔ̀ɔk*, the periphrastic constructions do not express direct causation, i.e. the caused event is not necessarily carried out. A more neutral causative is expressed by *tham hây* 'make GIVE', which normally is interpreted as direct causation, as in (46b) and does not require an animate causer.

(46) a. แม่ (อนุญาต/บอก) ให้เด็กไปเล่นข้างนอก
    mêε   (ʔənúʔyâat/bɔ̀ɔk) **hây** dèk   pay   lên   khâaŋ-nɔ̀ɔk.
    mother (allow/tell)   GIVE   child go   play side-out
    'The mother let/made the child go and play outside.'

b. ลมพัดทำให้บ้านพังหลายหลัง
    lom   phát   rεεŋ   **tham** **hây** bâan   phaŋ   lǎay   lǎŋ.
    wind   blow   strong   make   give   house collapse many   CLF
    'The wind blew hard causing many houses to collapse.'

The *hây* causative construction is also used to indicate subject switch in desiderative expressions. The changed subject ("causee") does not have to be overtly expressed.

(47) a. ผมอยากไป   b. ผมอยากให้ไป
    phǒm   yàak   pay.   phǒm   yàak   **hây**   X   pay.
    1M   DES   go   1M   DES   GIVE   X   go
    'I want to go.'   'I want X to go.'

There is no straightforward passive construction in Thai, although the Westernization of Thai grammar which started in the mid 19th century has led to an originally adversative construction being extended to more neutral contexts, developing into a quasi-passive form. The construction 'X *thùuk* Y' literally means 'X is affected by Y', usually in a negative way. As full verb *thùuk* means 'hit, come into contact with', which has led to a wide range of semantic and grammatical extensions, including 'correct' (derived from an idiom like 'hit the mark'), 'cheap', and adversative passive-like expressions. Unlike morphosyntactic passives in other languages, the adversative *thùuk* construction is biclausal and does not lead to a reduction of arguments or a necessary demotion of the agent, although this is possible in formal style. In colloquial Thai, the argument preceding *thùuk* is the entity affected by the (usually clausal) argument following it (See the cat in example (48)). While the former argument is typically (but not necessarily) animate or construed as animate (e.g. in metonymical or metaphorical extensions), the latter argument usually is a situation or, rarely, a nominal referent.

(48) แมวถูกหมาไล่รอบสวน
    mεεw   thùuk   mǎa   lây   rɔ̂ɔp   sǔən.
    cat   HIT   dog   chase   surround   garden
    'The cat was chased by the dog around the garden.'

(49) a. (formal Thai)
หนังสือเล่มนี้ถูกเขียนโดย ก.

năŋ.sɯ̌ɯ	lêm	níi	thùuk	khĭǝn	dooy	X.
book	CLF	PROX	HIT	write	by	X

'This book was written by X.'

In spoken Thai, the more recent Khmer loan *dooy* 'hit, come into contact with' is taking over the function of *thùuk* as a full verb as well as pre-clausal adversative auxiliary. While in the formal register *thùuk* is developing into a neutral passive marker (49), *dooy* retains its adversative connotation.

In most cases, equivalents of English passive are expressed in Thai by simply fronting the undergoer to the preclausal topic position, usually separated from the clause by a short intonation pause. In a kind of mixed structure, the agent can be expressed as oblique in formal Thai also with fronted undergoers, but without intonation pause, resulting in an unmarked passive reading of the verb:

(49) b. (formal Thai)
หนังสือเล่มนี้เขียนโดย ก.

năŋ.sɯ̌ɯ	lêm	níi	khĭǝn	dooy	X.
book	CLF	PROX	write	by	X

'This book was written by X.'

3.3 Clause structure

Clause structure in Thai is governed by pragmatic as well as syntactic factors. While the basic word order can be described as Subject Verb (Object), it is more useful to speak of a TOPIC-COMMENT clause structure. Just about any constituent of the clause can function as topic and thus be placed before the comment, although it is much more common for verbs to function as part of the comment (usually the predication) than as topics. The verb is also the only obligatory element in most clauses, arguments being freely omitted if they are retrievable from the linguistic or extra-linguistic context.

While pragmatics plays an important role in the structure of the clause in Thai, there are syntactic restrictions on the ordering of constituents. Multiple topics are allowed in Thai, but the object and the subject cannot be simultaneously topicalized. This leads to the ungrammaticality of SOV (or AOV) word order, i.e. with both fronted subject and object (50). Other word orders, i.e. OSV (51) and SVO (52) are allowed. The other syntactic restriction is that subjects do not occur in postverbal position, except as antitopics or 'afterthoughts', where they are not part of the clause *per se* and separated from it by an intonation pause. The different possible and impossible constituent orders are illustrated in the following examples.

(50) *เขา หมาไม่ชอบ
 **khǎw   mǎa   mây   chɔ̂ɔp.*   SOV
 3HUM   dog   NEG   like

(51) หมา เขาไม่ชอบ
 mǎa,   khǎw   mây   chɔ̂ɔp.   O-SV
 dog   3HUM   NEG   like
 'Dogs, he doesn't like.'

(52) เขาไม่ชอบหมา
 khǎw   mây   chɔ̂ɔp   mǎa.   SVO
 3HUM   NEG   like   dog
 'He doesn't like dogs.'

(53) ไม่ชอบหมา คนนั้น
 mây   chɔ̂ɔp   mǎa,   khon   nán.   VO – A
 NEG   like   dog   person   MEDL
 'He doesn't like dogs, that guy.'

In ditransitive clauses, the theme (object) precedes the recipient (beneficiary). In actual language use, ditransitive clauses with both theme and recipient overtly expressed are avoided, though, or the theme is fronted in a serial verb construction of the type *ʔaw* X *hây* Y 'take X give Y'. The recipient may be marked by the prepositional verb *hây* or the preposition *kàp/kɛ̀ɛ* 'to'.

3.3.1 Clause linkage

Complete sentences or clauses can be linked by juxtaposition or by the use of a marker, such as *lɛ́ʔ* 'and', *lɛ́ɛw* 'and then', and *tɛ̀ɛ* 'but'. There is no morphosyntactic marker of finiteness in Thai, nor is there a syntactic difference between matrix and subordinate clauses. This means that no clear-cut syntactic distinction can be made between coordinate and subordinate clauses. Coordination and subordination can thus be defined only functionally and by the presence of an overt linkage marker, which always occurs clause initially in one of the conjoined clauses. While the above mentioned linkers are traditionally described as coordinators, there are a number of subordinators in Thai as well.

Besides functionally specific subordination markers like *thâa* 'if', *tháŋ-tháŋ thîi* 'although' and *muâ* 'when' etc., Thai also has linkage markers with broader functions, some of which are not restricted to subordinate clauses but can also appear as linker between nouns and modifiers, such as *wâa* 'that', lit. 'say' (56) (57), or as prepositions, like *phuâ* 'in order to, for the sake of', *thîi* 'that, at'. The latter also serves to introduce relative clauses in postnominal position (54) (55) and to nominalize complete sentences, often with the dummy head noun *kaan* 'the fact'. Many of the morphemes used to mark subordination are transparently derived from lexical verbs or nouns, some of which are still in common (in some cases only in dialectal or literary) use. Subordinate clauses in Thai usually follow the matrix clause (58), but this order can be reversed for pragmatic reasons except in relative clauses, which always follow their head noun. The following examples illustrate the use of some of these morphemes in different functions.

(54) ผมดีใจที่คุณมาได้
phǒm   dii-cay   **thîi**   khun   maa   dây.
1M   good-heart   REL   2   come   GET
'I'm glad that you could come.'

(55) หนังสือที่อ่านแล้ว เก็บในตู้
năŋ.sɯ̌ɯ   **thîi**   ʔàan   lɛ́ɛw   kèp   nay   tûu.
book   REL   read   NSIT   collect   in   cupboard
'He put the book which he had read in the cupboard.'

(56) เขาบอกว่าจะมา
kháw   bɔ̀ɔk   **wâa**   cə   maa.
3HUM   tell   SAY   PROS   come
'He said that he would come.'

(57) คำว่าอร่อย แปลว่าอะไร
kham   **wâa**   ʔərɔ̀y   plɛɛ   **wâa**   ʔəray?
word   SAY   'aroy'   translate   SAY   what
'What does *aroy* mean?'

(58) เขาไม่ได้มา เพราะ (ว่า) ไม่มีเวลา
kháw   mây   dây   maa   **phrɔ́ʔ**   (wâa)   mây   mii   weelaa.
3HUM   NEG   GET   come   because   (SAY)   NEG   have   time
'He didn't come because he had no time.'

(59) เขาทะเลาะกันเพราะลูก
    kháw   thəló?   kan   **phró?**   lûuk.
    3HUM   quarrel REC   because   child
    'They quarreled because of their children.'

A special form of clause linkage can be seen in expressions involving the TOPIC-COMMENT LINKER (TCL) *kɔ̂*. In constructions of the type C1 *kɔ̂* C2, its function can be consecutive, sequential or concessive.

(60) มีเงินก็ไปได้
    mii   ŋɤn   kɔ̂   pay   dây.
    have   money   TCL   go   GET
    'If you have money, you can go.'

(61) ไม่มีเงินก็ไปได้
    mây   mii   ŋɤn   kɔ̂   pay   dây.
    NEG   have   money TCL   go   GET
    'Even if you don't have money, you can go.'

(62) ทำงาน (แล้ว) ก็ได้เงิน
    tham   ŋaan   (lɛ́ɛw)   kɔ̂   dây   ŋɤn.
    do   work   (FINISH) TCL   get   money
    'I work and then I'll get money.'

This linker is also used in other constructions, such as NP *kɔ̂* VP, where it is translated as 'NP VPs too', 'even NP VPs', or similar, depending on the semantics of the verbs and NPs involved, as well as on the context.

3.3.2 Questions

Content questions (wh-questions) in Thai are formed with an interrogative (attributive, pronominal, adverbial), which occurs *in situ*, occupying the place where the constituent asked about normally occurs in the sentence. There is no change in constituent order or other morphosynyactic means indicating the interrogative force besides the question word itself. Common interrogative words are *khray* 'who', *ʔəray* 'what', *thammay* 'why', *thîi-nǎy* 'where', *yaŋŋay* 'how', *mûə-ray* 'when', etc. (See Table 7). The addition of the particle *bâaŋ* at the end of the sentence pluralizes the question, i.e. more than one answer is expected.

Table 7: Common interrogative words

	Thai form	Meaning	Origin
ใคร	khray	'who'	from khon-ray 'which person'
อะไร	ʔaray	'what'	from ʔan-ray 'which thing'
ทำไม	thammay	'why'	from tham-ray 'do what'
ที่ไหน	thîi-nǎy	'where'	'which place'
ยังไง	yaŋŋay '	'how'	from yàaŋ-ray 'which manner'
เมื่อไร	mûɨa-ray	'when'	'which time'

Polar (yes/no) questions are formed by adding an interrogative sentence final particle to a complete sentence or a part of a sentence. Three interrogative particles are in common use in Thai, covering different functions.

The particle *mǎy* (supposedly from *rɨ̌ɨ mây* 'or not') is placed after affirmative verbal expressions to form a yes/no-question. This form has a connotation of an invitation or an expected positive answer. It cannot be used with negated sentences or with nominal or adverbial predicates.

The morpheme *rɨ̌ɨ* 'or' can be used to form alternative questions (*chaa rɨ̌ɨ kaafɛɛ* 'tea or coffee?') or polar questions if placed at the end of an utterance, either verbal or non-verbal. It is the only construction available in negative questions (*mây pay rɨ̌ɨ?* 'aren't you going?') and with non-verbal predicates (*phǒm rɨ̌ɨ?* '(did you mean) me?'). In affirmative questions *rɨ̌ɨ* marks surprise or disbelief, expecting a negative answer, as in *pay rɨ̌ɨ?* 'are you really going?'.

The most connotationally neutral form of polar question in colloquial Thai is by adding the sentence final particle *(rɨ̌ɨ) plàaw* '(or) not' (lit. 'empty'). This is also the form preferred in indirect speech, as in (63).

(63) ไม่รู้ว่า เขาจะไปหรือเปล่า
 mây rúu wâa khǎw cə pay rɨ̌ɨ plàaw.
 NEG know SAY 3HUM PROS go or not
 'I don't know whether he is going.'

Both content and polar questions can be "passed on" to a new addressee or referent with the formula (*lɛ́ɛw*) *X lâʔ*, where X is the new addressee to who, or the new referent about which, the question is asked.

(64) เขาไปไหน แล้วคุณล่ะ
 khǎw pay nǎy? *lɛ́ɛw khun lâʔ?*
 3HUM go where FINISH 2 Q
 'Where is he going?' 'And what about you?'

3.3.3 Imperatives

No special morphosyntactic means are necessary to form an imperative. The bare verb is sufficient, though this sounds rather abrupt and impolite in many contexts. To attenuate the abruptness of an imperative, a softening particle such as preverbal *chûay* 'help' and/or sentence final *nɔ̀y* 'a bit' is added. Other possibilities are to express the imperative by an indirect speech act, such as *khɔ̌ɔ hây* C 'I wish that C', *chɤɤn C* 'I invite you to C' or *C nɔ̀y dây mǎy?* 'could you C a bit?'. A stronger form of command ends in *síʔ*, probably a shortened version of the V2 *sǐa*, lit. 'waste', used to express a perfective event with a connotation of irreversibility and absoluteness.

Hortative expressions usually take the sentence final particle *thɤ́ʔ/hɤ́ʔ*, which expresses a mild request or wish for someone to do something.

The prohibitive is expressed by preverbal *yàa*, which may be modified by postverbal *ʔìik* 'again' to express 'don't C anymore' or preverbal *phûŋ* for 'don't C yet'. Third person prohibitive (or negative optative) uses preclausal *yàa hây* 'may not C'.

3.3.4 Other clause particles

Thai makes frequent use of clause or sentence final particles (SFP) to express different notions, including speaker's attitude, modality, etc. Among the most common of these SFPs are emphatic *náʔ* and *sìʔ*, and the counter-expectative *rɔ̀ɔk*, which occurs mostly, but not exclusively, in negative statements.

Sentence-final honorific particles form a category of their own, the use of which depends on the social status and gender of the speaker and the social status of the hearer. The normal forms used in polite speech are *khráp* for male speakers to equals or superiors, *khâʔ/kháʔ* for female speakers to equals or superiors, *câʔ/cáʔ* to intimate friends and children,[16] and *wáʔ* expressing contempt, intimacy or dismissiveness (i.e. a kind of anti-honorific).

---

[16] The falling tone variant is used in statements, the high tone in questions and imperatives.

4 Semantics

4.1 Pronouns

The Thai pronoun system makes elaborate distinctions based on the gender and social status of speech-act participants and third person referents. The following table lists some of the most common pronouns with an indication of the social status thus implied.

Table 8: Pronouns

1. PERS.		2. PERS.		3. PERS.	
กู *kuu*	intimate, impolite	มึง *mɯŋ*	intimate, impolite	มัน *man*	objects; hum ref. contemptuous
ข้า *khâa*	intimate	เอ็ง *ʔeŋ*	intimate	เขา *khǎw*	neutral
ฉัน *chǎn*	informal, intimate	แก *kɛɛ*	informal, contemptuous	เธอ *thɤɤ*	female referents
ผม *phǒm*	m. speaker, neutral	เธอ *thɤɤ*	familiar, intimate	หล่อน *lɔ̀ɔn*	female referents
กระผม *kràʔphǒm*	m. speaker, formal	คุณ *khun*	neutral, polite	ท่าน *thân*	formal
ดิฉัน *dìʔchǎn*	f. speaker, formal	ท่าน *thân*	formal		
ข้าพเจ้า *khâaphaɕâaw*	formal	เจ้า *câaw*	literary		
เรา *raw*	plural				

In everyday speech, pronouns are frequently replaced by kinship terms (see § 4.2.2), personal names (especially for female speakers also in the first person) or professional terms such as 'teacher', 'doctor', 'market seller', etc., in all persons.

4.2 Semantic domains

According to the socio-cultural context and history of the Thai language, some semantic domains are very elaborate while others are less well equipped or loaded with foreign loans. As can be expected in a mainly agricultural society, there is a wide array of terms for edible and useful plants and animals, both domesticated and wild. One surprising lacuna in the vocabulary of Thai is the distinction between different stages of rice, which is present in other languages in Southeast Asia. Thai uses the generic term *khâaw* not only for rice in all stages of production (rice plant, unhusked rice, husked rice, cooked rice), but also for other kinds of cereals. It has also come to mean 'food' in general, serving as generic object of *kin* 'eat'.

4.2.1 Elaborate vocabulary

More elaborate is the vocabulary in activities involving the human body, especially different types of carrying objects, as the following table illustrates.

Table 9: Verbs for 'carry'

ถือ	thɯ̌ɯ	carry on hands
หิ้ว	hîw	carry hanging down from hand (e.g. a handbag)
แบก	bɛ̀ɛk	carry on back
หอบ	hɔ̀ɔp	carry with both arms
อุ้ม	ʔûm	carry with both arms close to body (e.g. a child)
หาบ	hàap	carry on pole across shoulder
หาม	hǎam	carry on pole between two people
เทิน	thɤɤn	carry on head
สะพาย	səphaay	carry suspended on back
คาบ	khâap	carry in mouth (as a dog)

As seen in 2.1.4, nouns belonging to certain semantic domains usually take a class indicator proclitic, such as *tôn* for trees and other plants, *nók* for birds, *plaa* for fishes, *prəthêet* for countries, *mɯəŋ* for towns and cities, etc. This class indicator can be dropped in some cases, especially if the referent is well known or present in the discourse.

Basic colour terms are syntactically stative verbs; they can be directly negated and combine with aspectual markers where semantically appropriate. The basic colour terms are etymologically opaque; they can not be semantically linked to other lexemes, while secondary colour terms are mostly transparently derived from nouns and do not have verbal features. All colour terms can take the class indicator proclitic *sǐi* 'colour'. The basic colour terms are listed in the following table. Notice the absence of a basic verbal term for 'blue' (*sǐi nám-ŋɤn* 'silver-water colour', *sǐi fáa* 'sky colour') and 'brown' (*sǐi nám-taan* 'sugar colour') from the list.

Table 10: Basic colour terms

ขาว	khǎaw	'white'	เหลือง	lǔəŋ	'yellow'
ดำ	dam	'black'	เขียว	khǐəw	'green'
แดง	dɛɛŋ	'red'	ม่วง	mûəŋ	'purple'
แสด	sɛ̀ɛt	'orange'	เทา	thaw	'grey'

4.2.2 Kinship terms

Kinship terms in Thai make an obligatory gender distinction from 'mother' and 'father' up. The gender of other kinship terms can be specified by adding *chaay* 'man' for male and *sǎaw* 'young woman, virgin' for female. Words referring to relatives younger than one's parents are not specified for gender but for relative age. In compound expressions like 'parents' the older, and where applicable the male part, precedes the younger/female part, as in *phɔ̂ɔ-mɛ̂ɛ* 'parents', *phîi-nɔ́ɔŋ* 'siblings', *pùu-yâa-taa-yaay* 'grandparents'. One interesting feature of the Thai kinship system is that there are no reciprocal terms like 'brother' and 'sister' apart from the recent (and rarely used) compound *lûuk-phîi-lûuk-nɔ́ɔŋ* 'cousin' (male or female, not specified for relative age), lit. 'child-elder.sibling-child-younger.sibling'. Another typologically unusual feature, which is nonetheless common in Southeast Asian languages, is the greater elaboration of generations below self than those above self. The main kinship terms are given in the following table.

Table 11: Kinship terms

พี่	phîi	elder sibling	อา	ʔaa	younger sibling of father
น้อง	nɔ́ɔŋ	younger sibling	น้า	náa	younger sibling of mother
ลูก	lûuk	son, daughter	ป้า	pâa	elder sister of father or mother
หลาน	lǎan	grand-child, niece, nephew	ลุง	luŋ	elder brother of father or mother
เหลน	lěen	son/daughter of *lǎan*	ปู่	pùu	father's father
ลื่อ	lɯ̂ɯ	son/daughter of *lěen*	ย่า	yâa	father's mother
ลืบ	lɯ̂ɯp	son/daughter of *lɯ̂ɯ*	ตา	taa	mother's father
ลืด	lɯ̂ɯt	son/daughter of *lɯ̂ɯp*	ยาย	yaay	mother's mother
พ่อ	phɔ̂ɔ	father	ทวด	thûat	great grandparent (and above)
แม่	mɛ̂ɛ	mother			

4.3 "Royal speech": raachaasàp

One important aspect of the Thai language is the existence of special lexical items reserved for members of the monk order and royalty, the so-called *raachaasàp*. There is a number of different sets of vocabulary, each appropriate for speaking with or about a specific set of referents (Fry & al 2013: 344). The use of the appropriate lexical set is part of the formal education in Thailand, and is adhered to in all public and official contexts. While the monastic vocabulary consists of only few lexical items, such as *chǎn* for 'eat' (standard Thai *kin*) and *cam wát* for 'sleep' (lit. 'stay in the temple', standard Thai *nɔɔn*), the royal vocabulary consists of a complete set of nouns and verbs, including affixes to change 'common talk' into 'royal speech', viz. *soŋ*, literally 'maintain', as verbal prefix and *phráʔ-thîi-nâŋ*, literally 'royal seat', as nominal suffix. Different lexemes are used for different levels of royalty and other segments of society, actually forming a continuum from the highest levels of the royal family down to the lowest 'market slang' (*phaasǎa talàat*). Most of the high level vocabulary is derived from Khmer and Sanskrit sources, an inheritance of the Angkorian Khmer empire, while the monastic vocabulary is mostly Pali. The following table illustrates some of the differences between common and royal speech (see Diller 2006 for more details).

Table 12: Royal speech

Common		Royal		Gloss
กิน	kin	เสวย	sǎwɤ̌ɤy	eat
ไป	pay	เสด็จ	sadèt	go
นอน	nɔɔn	บรรทม	banthom	sleep
ป่วย	pùay	ประชวร	prachuan	be sick
น้ำ	náam	พระสุธารส	phráʔ sùʔthaarót	water
ประตู	pratuu	พระทวาร	phráʔ thawaan	door
คอ	khɔɔ	พระศอ	phráʔ sɔ̌ɔ	neck
แว่นตา	wên taa	ฉลองพระเนตร	chalɔ̌ɔŋ phráʔ nêet	glasses

5 Conclusion

In this chapter I have described the workings of the Thai language with an emphasis on the characteristics it shares, in various domains, with other languages in the region. Accordingly, it can be observed that the Thai lexicon has, in common with neighbouring languages Mon and Burmese, a system of psycho-collocations formed from the same Pali etymon *citta* 'mind', a developed classifier system. Serial constructions and TOPIC-COMMENT type sentences are common. It is noted further that, like the languages of other neighbouring hierarchical societies such as Burmese, Mon and Khmer, Thai has a pronominal system which encodes social relationships and a system of honorific vocabulary used in royal and religious contexts.

In general, it has been shown that Thai occupies a central position within the Mainland Southeast Asian linguistic area, possessing as it does the great majority of the properties which are characteristic of the languages in the area.

Abbreviations

ADH	adhortative
CLF	classifier
DEM	demonstrative
DES	desiderative
DET	determiner
EMPH	emphatic
EUPH	euphonic
FOC	focus
HON	honorific
HUM	human
INCL	inclusive marker
LOC	locative
MDF	modifier
NEG	negation
NSIT	new situation
PL	plural
PROB	probability
PROS	prospective
PROX	proximal
Q	question
QUANT	quantifier
RED	reduplication
REC	reciprocal
REL	relativizer
SUB	subordinator
SG	singular
TCL	topic-comment linker

References

Aikhenvald, Alexandra Y. & R. M. W. Dixon. (eds.). 2006. *Serial Verb Constructions: A cross-linguistic typology*. Oxford: Oxford University Press.

Benedict, Paul K. 1975. *Austro-Thai. Language and culture*. New Haven: HRAF Press.

Bisang, Walter. 1992. *Das Verb im Chinesischen, Hmong, Vietnamesischen, Thai und Khmer*. Tübingen: Gunter Narr Verlag.

Bril, Isabelle. 2004. Complex nuclei in Oceanic languages: Contribution to an areal typology. In I. Bril & F. Ozanne-Rivierre (eds.), *Complex predicates in Oceanic language: Studies in the dynamics of binding and boundness*, 1–48. Berlin: Mouton de Gruyter.

Brown, Marvin. 1985. *From ancient Thai to modern dialects. And other writings on historical Thai linguistics*. Bangkok: White Lotus.

Chamberlain, James R. (ed.). 1991. *The Ramkhamhaeng controversy*. Bangkok: The Siam Society.

Diller, Anthony. 1993. Diglossic grammaticality in Thai. In William A. Foley (ed.), *The role of the theory in language description*, 393–420. Berlin & New York: Mouton de Gruyter.

Diller, Anthony. 2006. Polylectal grammar and Royal Thai. In Felix K. Ameka, Alan Dench & Nichilas Evans (eds.), *Catching language. The challenge of grammar writing*, 565–607. Berlin & New York: Mouton de Gruyter.

Diller, Anthony, Jerold A. Edmondson & Yongxian Luo (eds.). 2008. *The Tai-Kadai languages*. London & New York: Routledge.

Dixon, R. M. W. 2010. *Basic linguistic theory. Vol. 1: Methodology*. Oxford: Oxford University Press.

Fry, Gerald W., Gayla S. Nieminen & Harold E. Smith. 2013 [2005]. *Historical Dictionary of Thailand*. (Revised 3rd version). Lanhma, Toronto & Oxford: The Scarecrow Press.

Jenny, Mathias. 2001. The aspect system of Thai. In Karen H. Ebert & Fernando Zúñiga (eds.), *Aktionsart and aspectotemporality in non-European languages*, 97–140. Zurich: Arbeiten des Seminars für Allgemeine Sprachwissenschaft (ASAS).

Matisoff, James A. 2001. Prosodic diffusibility in South-East Asia. In Alexandra Y. Aikhenvald & R. M. W. Dixon (eds.), 2006, *Areal diffusion and genetic inheritance*, 291–327. Oxford: University Press.

Schuessler, Axel. 2007. *ABC Etymological dictionary of Old Chinese*. Honolulu: University of Hawai'i Press.

Vittrant, Alice. 2006. Les constructions des verbes en série. Une autre approche du syntagme verbal en birman. *Bulletin de la Société de Linguistique de Paris* 101 (1). 305–367.

Vittrant, Alice. 2014. Psycho-collocational expressives in Burmese, In Jeffrey P. Williams (ed.), *The aesthetics of grammar, sound and meaning in the languages of Mainland Southeast Asia*, 255–279. New York: Cambridge University Press.

Appendix 1: Summary of linguistic features

Legend
+++ the feature is pervasive or used obligatorily in the language
++ the feature is normal but selectively distributed in the language
+ the feature is merely possible or observable in the language
− the feature is impossible or absent in the language

	Feature	+++/++/+/−	§ ref. in this chapter
Phonetics	Lexical tone or register	+++	§1.2, p.563
Phonetics	Back unrounded vowels	+++	§1.1, p.562
Phonetics	Initial velar nasal	+++	§1.1, p.562
Phonetics	Implosive consonants	+	§1.1, p.562
Phonetics	Sesquisyllabic structures	+++	§1.3, p.564
Morphology	Tendency towards monosyllabicity	+++	§1.3, p.564
Morphology	Tendency to form compounds	+++	§2.1, p.566
Morphology	Tendency towards isolating (rather than affixation)	+++	§2, p.566
Morphology	Psycho-collocations	+++	§2.2, p.567
Morphology	Elaborate expressions (e.g. four-syllable or other set patterns)	+++	§2.3, p.571–73
Morphology	Reduplication generally	+++	§2.3, p.572, §2.4, p.573
Morphology	Reduplication of nouns	+++	§2.4, p.573
Morphology	Reduplication of verbs	+++	§2.4, p.573
Grammar	Use of classifiers	+++	§3.1.1, p.575
Grammar	Classifiers used in counting	+++	§3.1.1, p.575, §3.3.1, p.578
Grammar	Classifiers used with demonstratives	++	§3.1.2, p.577
Grammar	Adjectival verbs	+++	§3.2, p.582
Grammar	Grammatical number	++	§3.2.1, p.582
Grammar	Inflection of verbs	−	§3.2.1, p.582
Grammar	Use of tense/aspect markers	++	§3.2.1 & 3.2.2, p.582
Grammar	Use of verb plural markers	++	§3.2.1, p.582
Grammar	Grammaticalization of GET/OBTAIN (potential mod. resultative/perfect aspect)	+++	§3.2.3, p.586–89
Grammar	Grammaticalization of PUT, SET See the verb 'keep, deposit' (Burm $t^h\grave{a}$) +++	+++	§3.2.3, p.587
Grammar	Grammaticalization of GIVE (causative, benefactive; preposition)	+++	§3.2.3, pp.586–89, §3.2.4, p.589
Grammar	Grammaticalization of FINISH (perfective/ complete aspect; conjunction/temporal subordinator)	+	§3.2.3, p.587

	Feature	+++/++/+/−	§ ref. in this chapter
Grammar	Grammaticalization of directional verbs e.g. GO / COME (allative, venitive)	+++	§3.2.2, p.584
Grammar	Grammaticalization of SEE, WATCH (temptative)	+	not discussed explicitly
Grammar	Grammaticalization of STAY, REMAIN (progressive and continuous, durative aspects)	+++	§3.2.2, p.588
Grammar	Serial verb constructions	+++	§3.2.2, p.588
Syntax	Verb precedes object (VO)	+++	§3.3, p.591
Syntax	Auxiliary precedes verb	++	§3.2, p.582–84
Syntax	Preposition precedes noun	+++	§3.1.5, p.582
Syntax	Noun precedes adjective	+++	§3.1, p.574
Syntax	Noun preceds demonstrative	+++	§3.1, p.574, §3.1.2, p.577
Syntax	Noun precedes genitive	+++	§3.1, p.574
Syntax	Noun precedes relative clause	+++	§3.1.4, p.580
Syntax	Use of topic-comment structures	+++	§3.3, p.591
Syntax	Ellipsis of arguments known from context	+++	§3.3, p.591
Lexical semantics	Specific terms for forms of rice	−	§4.2, p.598
Pragmatics	Use of utterance-final pragmatic particles	+++	§3.3.4, p.596 & §3.3.2, p.594
Pragmatics	Encoding of politeness	+++	§3.3.4, p.596
Pragmatics	Encoding of honorifics	+++	§4.1, p.597

Appendix 2: Text interlinearized

ตอนนั้น เขาว่าพนมเพลิงน่าจะเป็นเมรุสำหรับเผาศพของราชวงศ์ ส่วนไอ้เตาข้างล่างเนี่ย น่าจะเป็นของไอ้บริวาร

tɔɔn	nán	khăw	wâa	phənom-phlɤɤŋ	nâa	cə	pen	meen
period	MEDL	3HUM	say	Phanom-Phloeng	ought	PROS	be	funeral.pyre

sămràp	phăw	sòp	khɔ̌ɔŋ	râatchəwoŋ.	sùən	ʔây	taw	khâaŋ	lâaŋ
for	burn	corpse	POSS	royal.family	part	REF	oven	side	below

nîə   nâa   cə   pen   khɔ̌ɔŋ   bɔɔríʔwaan.
PROX.EMPH ought   PROS be   POSS   retinue

'They say that back then Phanom Phloeng probably was the [place of the] funeral pyre where the bodies of the royal family were cremated. The kilns down here probably were [the places] of the servants.'

มีอยู่วันหนึ่งนะ วันหนึ่งยามที่อยู่ที่นั่นนะฮะ เขาได้ยินเสียงคล้ายๆ กับคนตีระนาดเนี่ย เป็นดนตรีไทยนี่นะครับ

wan   nɯ̀ŋ   náʔ,   wan   nɯ̀ŋ   yaam   thîi   yùu   thîi   nân   náʔ   háʔ
day   one   EMPH   day   one   guard REL   stay LOC   MEDL   EMPH   HON
khǎw dây.yin sǐəŋ   khláay-khláay kàp   khon tii   rənâat   nîə
3HUM hear   sound   similar-RED   with man   beat xylophone PROX.EMPH

pen   dontrii thay   níi   náʔ   khráp.
be   music   Thai   PROX EMPH   HON

'One day the guard who was [on duty] there heard a sound quite like someone playing the xylophone, it was [traditional] Thai music.'

เวลาประมาณตีสอง จะเป็นเฉพาะวันพระ วันอื่นจะไม่มี เวลาตีสองเขาจะเห็นแสงนะ ลักษณะแบบเป็นเหมือนกับคล้ายๆ แสงที่ออกจากพลุยังงี้เนี่ย ออกจากกลางๆ ครับ ออกจากเจดีย์บนเขา แต่ไม่รู้ออกจากองค์พระ หรือออกจากตรงไหน

weelaa prəmaan   tii.sɔ̌ɔŋ, cə   pen   chəphɔ́ʔ wan   phráʔ, wan
time   exclusive about   two.am PROS be   day   holy   day

ʔɯ̀ɯn   cə   mây   mii,   weelaa tii.sɔ̌ɔŋ khǎw cə   hěn   sɛ̌ɛŋ   náʔ,
other PROS NEG   have   time   two.am   3HUM PROS see   light EMPH

láksənàʔ   bɛ̀ɛp pen   mɯ̌ən kàp   khláay-khláay sɛ̌ɛŋ thîi ʔɔ̀ɔk   càak
characteristics style be   same with similar-RED   light REL   go.out from

phlúʔ   yaŋŋíi   nîə.   ʔɔ̀ɔk   càak klaaŋ-klaaŋ khráp, ʔɔ̀ɔk   càak
fireworks like.this   PROX.EMPH go.out from middle-RED   HON   go.out from

ceedii bon khǎw,   tɛ̀ɛ   mây rúu   ʔɔ̀ɔk   càak ʔoŋ phráʔ rɯ̌ɯ
pagoda on   mountain but   NEG know go.out from CL   holy   or

ʔɔ̀ɔk   càak troŋ   nǎy.
go.out from straight where

'At about 2 am, this happens only on Buddhist holy days, it does not happen on other days, at 2 am he would see a light, quite similar to the kind of light that comes from fireworks, like this, coming out from the middle there, from the pagoda on the hill, but it is not known whether it comes out from the Buddha image or from what place exactly.'

แล้วทีนี้ เขาก็สงสัย เอ๊ะใครตีหรือไปจุดไฟตรงนั้น ก็ขึ้นไป ปรากฏว่ามันก็ไม่มีอะไร
lɛ́ɛw	thii	níi	kháw	kɔ̂	sǒŋsǎy,	ʔéʔ	khray	tii	rɯ̌ɯ	pay
FINISH	time	PROX	3HUM	TCL	suspect	INTERJ	who	beat	or	go

cùt	fay	troŋ	nán.	kɔ̂	khɯ̂n	pay,	praakòt	wâa	man	kɔ̂	mây
light	fire	straight	MEDL	TCL	go.up	go	appear	SAY	3	TCL	NEG

mii	ʔəray.
have	what

'And now he became suspicious, who is there playing [the xylophone] or lighting a fire? So he went up there, but it turned out that there was nothing.'

ทีนี้ วันรุ่งขึ้นอีกวันหนึ่ง มันเป็นกลางวัน เขาก็เห็นว่ามีคนมาเดินขึ้นไป ตัวใหญ่มาก แต่ทีนี้เนี่ย เดินๆ ไปแล้วหายตรงหลังเจดีย์

thii	níi,	wan	rûŋ	khɯ̂n	ʔìik	wan	nɯ̀ŋ,	man	pen	klaaŋ
time	PROX	day	dawn	go.up	in.addition	day	one	3	be	middle

wan,	kháw	kɔ̂	hěn	wâu	mii	khon	maa	dɤɤn	khɯ̂n	pay,	tua
day	3HUM	TCL	see	SAY	have	man	come	walk	go.up	go	body

yày	mâak,	tɛ̀ɛ	thii	níi	nîə,	dɤɤn-dɤɤn	pay	lɛ́ɛw	hǎay
big	much	but	time	PROX	PROX.EMPH	walk-RED	go	FINISH	disappear

troŋ	lǎŋ	ceedii.
straight	back	pagoda

'Now, the next day, it was during the day, he saw a man walking up there, a very big man. But now, as he walked there, he disappeared behind the pagoda.'

เขาก็หากันอยู่เป็นครึ่งวันแล้ว ไอ้คนนั้นมันไปทำอะไรในเจดีย์ ไปขุดของหรืออะไรยังงี้ ปรากฏว่ามันก็ไม่มี

kháw	kɔ̂	hǎa	kan	yùu	pen	khrɯ̂ŋ	wan	lɛ́ɛw,	ʔây	khon	nán
3HUM	TCL	seek	PL	STAY	be	half	day	FINISH	REF	man	MEDL

man	pay	tham	ʔəray	nay	ceedii,	pay	khùt	khɔ̌ɔŋ	rɯ̌ɯ	ʔəray
3	go	do	what	in	pagoda	go	dig	thing	or	what

yaŋŋíi?	*praakòt*	*wâa*	*man*	*kɔ̂*	*mây*	*mii.*
like.this	appear	SAY	3	TCL	NEG	have

'They looked for him half a day, [asking] "what is that guy doing in the pagoda? Is he digging for [antique] stuff or something like this?" But it turned out that there was no one [to be found].'

ก็จู่ๆ มีคนมาจากกรุงเทพฯ เขานำของมาบวงสรวง มีผู้ใหญ่เขาบอกว่ามีพระเขาฝันเห็นพระที่นี่อะไรยังงี้

kɔ̂	*cùu-cùu*	*mii*	*khon*	*maa*	*càak*	*kruŋ.thêep,*	*kháw*	*nam*	*khɔ̌ŋ*
TCL	unexpected-RED	have	man	come	from	Bangkok	3HUM	lead	thing

maa	*buəŋsǔəŋ.*	*mii*	*phûu*	*yày*	*kháw*	*bɔ̀ɔk*	*wâa*	*mii*	*phráʔ,*
come	make.offering	have	person	big	3HUM	tell	say	have	holy

kháw	*fǎn*	*hěn*	*phráʔ*	*thîi*	*nîi*	*ʔəray*	*yaŋŋíi.*
3HUM	dream	see	holy	LOC	PROX	what	like.this

'Then all of a sudden there were people coming from Bangkok, they brought things to make offerings. There was an important person, he said that there was a monk, that he had seen a monk here in his dreams or something like this.'

หลังจากนั้น เมื่อประมาณปี ๒๕๓๕ เท่าที่ผมจำได้นะครับ มีไก๊ด์เป็นไก๊ด์ของบริษัทฝรั่งเศส มานอนนอนที่รีสอร์ท

lǎŋ	*càak*	*nán,*	*mûə*	*prəmaan*	*pii*	*sɔ̌ɔŋ-phan-hâa-rɔ́ɔy-sǎam-sìp-*
back	from	MEDL	when	about	year	two-thousand-five-hundred-three-ten-

hâa	*thâw*	*thîi*	*phǒm*	*cam*	*dây*	*náʔ*	*khráp,*	*mii*	*káy,*
five	as.much	REL	1M	remember	GET	EMPH	HON	have	guide

pen	*káy*	*khɔ̌ŋ*	*bɔɔriʔsàt*	*fəràŋsèet,*	*maa*	*nɔɔn*	*thîi*	*riisɔ̀ɔt.*
be	guide	POSS	company	French	come	sleep	LOC	resort

'After that, in about 2535 [BE], as far as I remember, there was a tour guide, he was a tour guide of a French company, who came to stay at the resort.'

ก็มันนึกยังไงไม่รู้ประมาณตีสองนะ มันให้เด็กที่ร้านไปเป็นเพื่อน อยากจะไปเขาพนมเพลิง

kɔ̂	*man*	*núk*	*yaŋŋay*	*mây*	*rúu*	*prəmaan*	*tii.sɔ̌ɔŋ*	*náʔ*	*man*	*hây*
TCL	3	think	how	NEG	know	about	two.am	EMPH	3	GIVE

dèk	*thîi*	*ráan*	*pay*	*pen*	*phûən,*	*yàak*	*cə*	*pay*	*kháw*	*phənom-*
child	LOC	shop	go	be	friend	DES	PROS	go	mountain	Phanom-

phlɤɤŋ.
Phoeng
'Then, I don't know what came over him, about two o'clock that night, he asked an employee of the hotel to accompany him. He wanted to go to the Phanom Phloeng hill [he said].'

เขาบอกว่าจะฝังตัวเองมาอยู่ที่นี่ เขาขุดหลุมฝัง

kháw	bɔ̀ɔk	wâa	cə	făŋ	tuə	ʔeeŋ	maa	yùu	thîi	níi.	kháw
3HUM	tell	SAY	PROS	bury	body	self	come	stay	LOC	PROX	3HUM

khùt	lŭm	făŋ.
dig	hole	bury

'He said he was going to bury himself and come to stay here. He started digging a hole to bury [himself].'

ทีนี้ยามไม่ให้ขุด ขุดที่นี่ไม่ได้ เขาบอกว่าอยากจะอยู่เขาพนมเพลิง อยากจะรับใช้เขาพนมเพลิง

thii	níi	yaam	mây	hây	khùt.	khùt	thîi	níi	mây	dây.
time	PROX	guard	NEG	GIVE	dig	dig	LOC	PROX	NEG	GET

kháw	bɔ̀ɔk	wâa	cə	yùu	thîi	kháw	phənom-phlɤɤŋ,	yàak	cə
3HUM	tell	SAY	PROS	stay	LOC	mountain	Phanom-Phloeng	DES	PROS

ráp	cháy	kháw	phenom-phlɤɤŋ.
receive	use	mountain	Phanom-Phloeng

'He said he was going to stay at Phanom Phloeng hill, he wanted to serve the Phanom Phloeng hill.'

ก็คงจะก่อนหน้านั้นคงจะไปทำอะไรไม่ดีสักอย่างหนึ่ง

kɔ̂	khoŋ	cə	kɔ̀ɔn	nâa	nán	khoŋ	cə	tham	ʔəray	mây	dii
TCL	PROB	PROS	before	face	MEDL	PROB	PROS	do	what	NEG	good

sák	yàaŋ.
just	kind

'It must have been at some time in the past, he must have done something bad [to the hill spirits].'

David Mortensen
Hmong (Mong Leng)

This chapter presents a description of Mong Leng, also known as Mong Njua, Hmong Njua, "Green Hmong" or "Blue Hmong," as it is spoken in parts of Laos and by Lao Hmong expatriates living in the United States, France, and Australia. Mong Leng varieties are also spoken, with considerable variation, in Southern China, Vietnam, and Laos. The total population is difficult to estimate because of the lack of reliable numbers from Vietnam. However, the total population in Laos, China, Thailand, and Burma is estimated as 210,000 (Lewis 2009). There are probably not more than four million speakers of closely related dialects (Lemoine 2005).

Mong Leng is in the Far Western Hmongic branch of Western Hmongic within the Hmong-Mien (Miao-Yao) language family. It is structurally identical to Hmong Daw (White Hmong) in most respects and the term "Hmong" will be used when statements apply to both dialects. Except where otherwise noted, data are from the author's field materials. All glosses and translations are the author's. IPA transcriptions are used in the phonology section and in interlinear examples. The RPA (Romanized Popular Alphabet) orthography is used elsewhere.

The RPA is a missionary orthography developed by Linwood G. Barney, William A. Smalley, and Yves Bertrais (Barney and Smalley 1953). Prior to its development there was no widely used orthography for writing Mong Leng. This orthography was initially intended as a unified orthography for Mong Leng and Hmong Daw in which the same word would be spelled the same for both dialects. However, this proved impractical and instead Mong Leng users have modified the original Barney, Smalley, and Bertrais orthography to be more suitable for writing their language. The orthography represents the phonemic inventory of Mong Leng adequately, albeit with symbols that a linguist is not inclined to expect. Particularly confusing for many is the use of final "consonant" symbols to represent tonal categories. In §1 on phonology, below, equivalencies between an IPA transcription and RPA are given.

David Mortensen: Language Technologies Institute, Carnegie Mellon University
E-Mail: davidmortensen@gmail.com

Mong Leng is not as well described as its sister, Hmong Daw or White Hmong. Past grammatical descriptions include Lyman (1979) and Harriehausen (1990). Lexicons include Lyman (1974) and Xiong, Xiong & Xiong (1983).

1 Phonology

1.1 Suprasegmental phonology: tone and register

Mong Leng has a complex tonal system where both pitch and voice quality cues play a role in distinguishing tonal categories (Andruski and Ratliff 2000). Mong Leng has seven tonal categories. More conservative Hmong dialects have eight distinct tones (Wang 1985), but two of these (the two historical tones characterized by breathy voice) have merged in Mong Leng.

Table 1: Mong Leng tones

Pitch contour	Transcription	RPA	Description
[45]	x́	-b	very high rising
[52]	x̂	-j	falling
[35]	x̌	-v	rising
[21] (M)	x̣	-g	low falling breathy in male speech;
[42] (F)			high falling breathy in female speech
[44]	x	-0	high-mid level, "chanted" voice quality
[22]	x̀	-s	low-mid level
[21]	x̱	-m	low falling creaky, sometimes with final glottal stop

It has been shown by Andruski and Ratliff (2000) that Mong Leng speakers use both pitch and voice quality in distinguishing tonal categories. However, the cues provided by breathy voice are far more robust that those provided by creaky voice.

1.2 Segmental phonemes : consonants and vowels

In order to maintain a neutral stance on a controversy to be discussed below, the consonant and vowel inventories will be discussed in terms of inventories of onsets and rhymes. Earlier discussions of the Mong Leng phonological inventory include Lyman (1974; 1979) and Mortensen (2004).

Like other Hmongic languages, Hmong has a large number of possible consonant onsets. Unlike Hmong Daw, or White Hmong (Ratliff 1992: 9), Mong Leng does not have a series of voiceless nasals.

Table 2: Mong Leng onsets

		labial	labial cluster	dental	dental cluster	dental	postalveolar	palatal	retroflex	velar	uvular	glottal
oral stop/ affric	plain	p <p>	pl <pl>	t <t>	tl <dl>	ts <tx>	tʃ <ts>	c <c>	tʂ <r>	k <k>	q <q>	ʔ <Ø>
	asp	pʰ <ph>	pʰl <plh>	tʰ <th>	tʰl <dlh>	tsʰ <txh>	tʃʰ <tsh>	cʰ <ch>	tʂʰ <rh>	kʰ <kh>	qʰ <qh>	
prenas stop/ affric	plain	ⁿp <ⁿp>	ⁿpl <ⁿpl>	ⁿt <ⁿt>	ⁿtl <ⁿdl>	ⁿts <ⁿtx>	ⁿtʃ <ⁿts>	ⁿc <ⁿc>	ⁿtʂ <ⁿr>	ⁿk <ⁿk>	ⁿq <ⁿq>	
	asp	ⁿpʰ <nph>	ⁿpʰl <nplh>	ⁿtʰ <nth>	ⁿtʰl <ndlh>	ⁿtsʰ <ntxh>	ⁿtʃʰ <ntsh>	ⁿcʰ <nch>	ⁿtʂʰ <nrh>	ⁿkʰ <nkh>	ⁿqʰ <nqh>	
nasal		m <m>		n <n>				ɲ <ny>		(ŋ) <g>		
fricative	vless	f <f>				s <x>	ʃ <s>	ç <xy>				h <h>
	vcd	v <v>				ʒ <z>	ʝ <y>					
lateral	vless			ɬ <hl>								
	vcd			l <l>								

Of the onsets, /ŋ-/ very rare and only occurs in borrowed words and expressives. Also, for many speakers, the retroflex series has merged with the post-alveolar series. In some subdialects, the dorsal, palatal, and retroflex series have all merged with the dental series.

Hmong has a mid-sized rhyme inventory, with a contrast between oral and "nasal" vowels (it is not clear if these vowels inherently nasalized and a secondary nasal coda is sometimes inserted after them or if there is an underlying nasal coda which is sometimes deleted, leaving only nasalization behind). Aside from these nasalized vowels, it has six monophthongs and four diphthongs:

Table 3: Mong Leng rhymes

	\multicolumn{3}{c}{*monophthongal rhymes*}	
	front	central	back
high	i <i>	ɨ <w>	u <u>
mid	ẽ [ẽŋ ~ ẽ] <ee>		õ [õŋ ~ õ] <oo>
	e <e>		o [ɔ] <o>
low		ã [ã] <aa>	
		a <a>	
	\multicolumn{3}{c}{*diphthongal rhymes*}	
high nucleus		ua [uə] <ua>	
low nucleus	ai [aj] <ai>	aɨ [aɰ] <aw>	au [aw] <au>

All Mong Leng diphthongs fall in sonority.

1.3 Syllable structure

The syllable structure of Mong Leng is very simple. Depending on the analysis given of [ã], [ẽŋ ~ ẽ], and [õŋ ~ õ], Mong Leng allows either no codas or a single, nasal coda /ŋ/. Likewise, [tl tʰl ⁿtl ⁿtʰl] and [pl pʰl ⁿpl ⁿpʰl] have been analyzed either as unit phonemes—stops with a "lateral release" (Golston and Yang, 2001, Golston and Fulop 2008)—or as consonant clusters (Wang 1985, Johnson 2002, Mortensen 2004). If the propositions that Mong Leng has final nasals and lateral clusters are accepted, the set of Mong Leng syllables may be described as C(l)V(ŋ). If neither of these are accepted, Mong Leng syllables are strictly CV.

Many Hmongic languages have sesquisyllabic words, that is, words with pretonic minor syllables (Li 2002) . Mong Leng preserves this pattern in vestigial form, but allows only three such reduced pre-syllables, qùa [qò̤], pì, [pì̤] and túa [tṳ́] and only allows them in a limited number of verbs, nouns, and expressives. For examples, see (1) below. These pre-syllables are shorter than normal syllables but not as short as the minor syllables in truly sesquisyllabic languages. Pre-syllables occur only in native vocabulary. Except for these words and compounds, Mong Leng words are mostly monosyllabic.

2 Morphology

2.1 Word structure

The minor syllable prefixes of Mong Leng are largely devoid of predictable semantic content, but they do distinguish lexical items and show some regular patterns in their semantics and distribution. To the extent that they are grammatical at all, they serve derivational functions. The most common prefix is the highly productive reciprocal marker sis- [ʃĩ], as show in example (1a). Two other affixes, quas- [qŏ] and pis- [pĩ] are attached to nouns (1d–g), and a few verbs (1b–c), and may be prefixed to or infixed into expressives (Xiong, Xiong, and Xiong 1983). They are used nonproductively to distinguish related lexical items. To the extent that they are productive, their effect is usually more stylistic than semantic or grammatical. I refer to them here as euphonic affixes (EUPH) because they are usually optional and their presence seems to be motivated by the sound of the expression rather than semantic or grammatical factors. As shown most clearly by (1h–i), quas and pis now act as infixes with expressives and are inserted before the ultimate syllable in a verb-expressive sequence.

(1) a. *sis-hlub*   RECIP-love   'love each other'
    b. *tsawg*   be_few   'be few'
    c. *pis-tsawg*   PIS-be_few   'how many?'
    d. *yawg*   adult_male   'adult male'
    e. *quas-yawg*   QUAS-adult_male   'man; husband'
    f. *puj*   adult_female   'grandmother'
    g. *quas-puj*   QUAS-adult_female   'woman; wife'
    h. *nyob<quas>tsawg*   sit EXP<EUPH>   'sit down! (as on a stool)'
    i. *ua dlog<pis>dlig*   do EXP<EUPH>   'do a slapdash job'

Most morphologically complex words in Hmong are compounds. These can be divided into compounds with a morphological and semantic head (hierarchical compounds) and compounds with parallel elements and no single head (coordinative compounds). Each of these categories can be divided, in turn, into a number of types.

2.1.1 Coordinative compounds

Hmong coordinative (parallel) compounds must consist of two constituents that are semantically related, either by synonymy (2), semantic proximity (3), or antonymy (4). In all of these cases, the semantic relation between the parts and the whole is clear: the whole construction refers to a natural category to which both of the members belong. For compounds of synonyms, this is the category to which both members refer; for coordinative compounds of near-synonyms or antonyms, this is the semantic category of which both members are representative members.

(2) a. *fuab-txeeb*   seize-seize   'seize'
    b. *naj-xyoo*   year-year   'year'
    c. *dlaag-zug*   strength-strength   'strength'

(3) a. *dlej-cawv*   water-liquor   'beverages'
    b. *num-tswv*   leader-lord   'rulers'
    c. *xyoob-ntoo*   bamboo-tree   'woody vegetation'

(4) a. *nkauj-nraug* young woman-young man 'romance'
    b. *nam-txiv*   mother-father   'parents; married couple'
    c. *dlaab-neeg*   deity-human   'beings; stories'

As illustrated by (4a, c), these compounds often develop non-compositional meanings following lexicalization.

2.1.2 Hierarchical compounds

Hmong hierarchical compounds are usually head initial. Their constituents may be N-N, N-V, V-N, and V-V and may act either as nouns or (stative) verbs, depending on their type. The most common type of hierarchical compound in Hmong is attributive. That is, the head determines the general type of the referent and the modifier specifies attributes of the referent. A few lexicalized examples are given in (5–6):

(5) a. *kua-muag*   liquid-eye   'tear'
    b. *mov-nplej*   cooked grain-rice plant   'cooked grain made from rice (rather than corn or beans)'

	c.	plaub-noog	hair-bird	'bird feathers (bird hair)'
	d.	zib-muv	honey-bee	'bee honey'
(6)	a.	qob-lab	tuber-be_red	'sweet potato'
	b.	qhovchaw-mog	place-soft	'genitals (soft place)'
	c.	puj-laug	adult_woman-old	'old woman'

A significant body of N-N attributive compounds are of the "class noun + specific noun" type, where the complement is a hyponym of (semantically subordinate to) the head. These compounds are particularly common in descriptions of humans and varieties of plants and animals:

(7)	a.	txiv-dluaj	fruit-peach	'peach'
	b.	txiv-kaabtxwv	fruit-orange	'orange'
	c.	txiv-lwg	fruit-eggplant	'eggplant'
	d.	txiv-zuaj	fruit-pear	'pear'
(8)	a.	hluas-nkauj	youth-young woman	'young woman'
	b.	hluas-nraug	youth-young man	'young man'

The modifiers in these compounds often behave as bound morphemes that do not occur without a class noun. Thus, dluaj occurs in txiv-dluaj 'peach' but does not appear as a monomorphemic word dluaj 'peach'. The heads may be viewed as class terms in the sense of Grinevald (1999) and Vittrant (2005).

Another subset of these compounds are effectively nominalizations and are headed by kev 'way', tub 'boy', and qhov 'thing'. Examples of this type of compound appear in (9):

(9)	a.	kev-kaaj	way-bright	'brightness'
	b.	kev-zoo	way-good	'goodness'
	c.	tub-saab	boy-steal	'thief'
	d.	qhov-zoo	thing-good	'that which is good'

Noun-VP compounds are also quite common in Hmong, but are difficult to distinguish from NPs where a stative verb is functioning as a modifier. These compounds are frequently nominalized by compounding them with kev or tub, yielding a rough equivalent of synthetic compounds (e.g. dogcatcher) in English. Event and abstract nominalizations are formed with kev 'way'. Likewise, agent (and some patient) nominalizations are formed by compounding verbs with tub 'boy':

(10) a. kawm-ntawv   study-paper   'study; become educated'
     b. kev-kawm-ntawv   way-study-paper   'studying; education'
     c. tub-kawm-ntawv   boy-study-paper   'student'

Hmong has a class of endocentric N-V compounds which function as nouns, but also function as stative verbs. The majority of these are "psycho-collocations" referring to a quality of character, as seen in (11):

(11) sab-phem
     liver-be_bad
     'evil heart' (endocentric)
     'be evil-hearted' (exocentric)

For additional examples of this type of compound, see section 2.2 on psycho-collocations. Note, however, that there are also examples, like moov-zoo meaning 'good fortune' or 'be fortunate', which do not involve psychological states or ethical qualities:

(12) moov-zoo
     fortune-be_good
     'good fortune' (endocentric)
     'be fortunate' (exocentric)

While many instances of this type of compound exist, this construction is no longer productive.

Hmong has many lexicalized phrases consisting of a transitive verb plus a noun:

(13) a. tua-phom
        kill-gun
        'shoot'

     b. ntaus-phoojywg
        strike-friend
        '"forge" a friendship'

The morphological status of these idioms as compounds is unclear. They may be compounds or may be products of the phrasal syntax. The Mong Leng lexicon also includes a considerable body of constructions consisting of an intransitive verb followed by a non-core argument. The resulting compound verb is intransitive:

(14) a. *luv-ceg*   broken-leg   'to have a broken leg'
     b. *tu-sav*   be broken-life   'die'
     c. *tuag-teg*   die-hand   'have paralyzed hands'
     d. *lug-ntshaav* come-blood   'bleed'

(15) a. *moog-tsheb*   go-car   'to travel by car'
     b. *moog-kev*   go-road   'to travel by road'
     c. *dhla-qeej*   leap-lusheng   'to dance with a lusheng'
     d. *taag-caij*   finish-time   'to be out of time'

There are a number of reasons one might believe these are compounds rather than simple phrases (where the verbs display valency alternations) (Clark 1995: 541ff). For example, expressives modifying these constructions do not occur directly after the verb root, but after the whole construction:

(16) a. kuv   tu   sab   nrho.
        kǔ   tu   ʃá   ⁿtʂʰo
        1SG   be_severed   liver   EXP
        'I'm deeply offended.'

     b. *kuv   tu   nrho   sab
        kǔ   tu   ⁿtʂʰo   ʃá
        1SG   be_severed   EXP   liver

Expressives are normally inseparable from the verb root. Clark argues that these compounds represent a type of noun-incorporation (Type I noun incorporation, on which, see Mithun 1984). Note that Clark only discusses the cases where the noun has a part-whole relationship to the undergoer, as exemplified in (14). However, as show in (15), "incorporated" nouns may have other roles in the event including means, indications of manner, and undergoers. Problematically for Clark's hypothesis, these constructions do not satisfy either the inseparability or the integrity criterion, as shown in (17):

(17) a. nwg   luv   ceg   lawm.
        nɨ̧   lǔ   cḛ   lai̧
        3SG   be_broken   leg   COMPL
        'His leg is broken (he is leg-broken)'

b. nwg   luv   saab   ceg   xis   lawm.
   nɨ   lŭ   ʃáŋ   cę   sì   lạɨ
   3SG   be_broken   CLF   leg   right COMPL
   'His right leg is broken (he is right leg-broken).'

c. nwg   txawm   luv   ceg_i   lawm   los   mom   yeej
   nɨ   tsạɨ   lŭ   cę   lạɨ   lo   mọ   jêŋ
   3SG   thus   be_broken   leg   COMPL   even   doctor always

   khu   tau   pro_i.
   kʰu   tau
   fix   can   pro
   'Even if his leg_i is broken, the doctor can always fix it_i (his leg)'

In (13b), a classifier intervenes between the verb and noun. A modifier (xis 'right') also modifies the noun, violating the integrity criterion. Example (13c) shows that the noun can be referred to by a pronoun outside of the construction, another violation of the integrity criterion. For these reasons, it is probably best to treat these constructions as lexicalized collocations and not proper compounds or instances of noun incorporation (but see Mithun 1984 on loose versus tight incorporation).

Many phrases of this type are psycho-collocations—compounds or collocations that express a psychological state in relation to a "psycho-noun."

2.2 Psycho-collocations

As in many SEA languages, psychological states, sensations, and properties in Hmong are often expressed in relation to body parts (Matisoff 1986, Jaisser 1990, Clark 1996, Vittrant to appear). These are of two types: verb-noun compounds, which usually express a psychological state or sensation (18), and noun verb compounds, which generally express a psychological or ethical property (19). Both of these compound types function as stative verbs:

(18) a. *zoo-sab*   'good-liver > be happy'
     b. *chim-sab*   'angry-liver > be angry'
     c. *khua-sab*   'wistful-liver > be wistful, nostalgic'
     d. *taag-sab-taag-ntsws*   'finish-liver-finish-lung > with all one's heart'
     e. *txhawj xeeb*   'worry-heart > be worried'

(19) a. *sab-zoo*   'liver-good; be good hearted'
     b. *sab-phem*   'liver-ugly; be evil hearted'
     c. *sab-luj-sab-dlaav* 'liver-big-liver-wide; be generous, brave'
     d. *plaab-plawv-luj*   'stomach-heart-large; be intelligent'

2.3 Elaborate expressions

In certain styles of Mong Leng discourse—story telling, formal speeches, impassioned tirades, and so on—elaborate expressions are extremely frequent. This construction is productive and skilled speakers are able to coin new elaborate expressions extemporaneously. These typically have the form ABAC, where AB and AC are both well-formed compounds and BC is a possible (and most frequently, already existing) coordinative compound:

(20) a. *xyoob-ntoo*
         çóŋ-ⁿtoŋ
         bamboo-tree
         'woody vegetation'

     b. *nplooj-xyoob-npooj-ntoo*
         ⁿplôŋ-çóŋ-ⁿplôŋ-ⁿtoŋ
         leaf-bamboo-leaf-tree
         'leaves of woody vegetation.

There are also "pseudo-elaborate expressions" having the form ABCD where AB and CE are well formed compounds and both AC and BD are possible coordinative compounds:

(21) a. *kaab-kev*
         káŋ-kě
         path-way
         'ritual'

     b. *tshoob-kʉg*
         tʃʰóŋ-kʉ
         wedding-wedding
         'wedding'

c. *kaab-tshoob-kev-kug*
 káŋ-tʃʰóŋ-kĕ-ku̯
 path-wedding-way-wedding
 'wedding rituals'

2.4 Expressives

In Hmong, expressives are distinct from elaborate expressions, though both are used in colorful or forceful speech. Hmong expressives, referred to as "postverbal intensifiers" by Heimbach (1969), do modify clauses, but do more than just intensify them. They communicate very subtle impressions of sound, motion, color, and affect, which are often difficult to characterize in purely propositional terms. Thus *ntsuav* indicates that the activity signified by the verb is judged to be unsavory by the speaker:

(22) koj   dlaim   ntawv   ntub   quas   ntsuav.
     kô   tlai̯   ⁿtăɨ   ⁿtú   qùa   ⁿtʃŭa
     2SG   CLF   paper   wet   EUPH   EXP
     'Your paper is wet (in some bad way)!'

Plawg indicates that an action is taken with surprising suddenness:

(23) nwg   tawm   plawg   tuaj
     nɨ̯   tai̯   plai̯   tûa
     3SG   exit   EXP   come
     'He came out suddenly.'

Lab pliv 'red-EXPRESSIVE' indicates, according to Xiong, Xiong, and Xiong (1983), a pale red like the light of a flashlight with weak batteries:

(24) lub   nub   tawm   lab   pliv   tim   npoo   ntuj
     lú   nú   tai̯   lá   plĭ   tḭ   ⁿpoŋ   ⁿtû
     CLF   sun   emerge red   EXP   over_at rim   sky
     'The sun emerged, a weak red, at the horizon.'

Many Hmong expressives are onomatopoetic (25), or otherwise iconic, but others are more or less arbitrary (26):

(25) a. *ndlibndleeb* /ⁿtlíⁿtléŋ/ 'of the sound of cowbells'
     b. *qimqog* /qḭqo̰/ 'of a chicken's clucks of protest'

(26) a. *ntshufwv* /ⁿtʃʰufɨ̰/ 'of feasting with energy and gusto'
     b. *tsawg* /tʃa̰ɨ/ 'of sitting upright as on a stool'

Ratliff (1992: 141–163) showed that (even) the iconic expressives are part of a highly patterned, language specific system. She demonstrated through a series of experiments that it was possible to predict the approximate meaning of two-syllable expressives based on their phonological properties (for example, the sequence of tones). While many expressives are "reduplicative" in that they involve the repetition of the onset, rhyme, or tone, they are not reduplication in the prototypical sense, since there is usually no "base" from which the reduplicated form can be derived. For exceptions in White Hmong, see Ratliff (1992: 143–146).

2.5 Reduplication

Verb reduplication is common and productive in Mong Leng. If a stative verb is reduplicated, the result is intensification (27):

(27) a. *phem* 'bad'   *phem~phem*   'very bad'
     b. *zoo-sab* 'happy (good-liver)' *zoo~zoo-sab* 'very happy'
     c. *txomnyem* 'unfortunate' *txom~txomnyem*   'very unfortunate'

In orthography, the reduplicated syllable is simply repeated twice, but phonetically, there is considerable phonological reduction of the initial "copy." The vowel in these initial repetitions is often schwa-like in quality and is very short. The second repetition often bears a super-high tone and is often lengthened:

(28) a. nwg   zoo   nkauj.
        [nɨ̰   ʒoŋ   ⁿkâu]
        3SG   good   maiden
        'She is beautiful too.'

     b. nwg   zoo~zoo   nkauj
        [nɨ̰   ʒə~ʒő:ŋ   ⁿkâu]
        3SG   INT~GOOD   maiden
        'She is very beautiful!'

Non-stative verbs can also be reduplicated, and this sometimes indicates intensity, but can also mark durative aspect:

(29) noog   -w   quaj~quaj   tim   taj   tuaj
     nɔŋ   ɨ   qua~qua   tḭ   tâ   tûa
     bird   quail DUR~cry   way_over_at   plain   come
     'Quail cried and cried from the plain.'

Nominal reduplication is not widely attested.

3 Grammar and Syntax

3.1 Nominal domain

3.1.1 Basic structure of the NP

For clarity, I will divide the Hmong NP into three portions: the pre-noun complex, the noun (including compounded morphemes), and the post-noun complex. These complexes are strictly ordered relative to one another.

In the pre-noun complex, possessors precede numerals and quantifiers (e.g. 'every'), which precede classifiers:

(30) kuv   ob   lub   tsev
     kŭ   ó   lú   tʃě
     1SG   two   CLF   house
     'my two houses'

Finally, between the classifier position and the noun, a single member of a closed class of adjectival modifiers may appear. Examples include *tuam* 'great; large', *nam* 'large, contemptible', and *nyuas* 'small'. These are not to be confused with stative verbs, which act as adjectival modifiers when they appear post-nominally. However, these pre-nominal modifiers are unlike adjectives in many languages in that they cannot be used predicatively. The presence of one of these closed-class adjectives in a nominal phrase allows various possibilities that would otherwise require the presence of a classifier. For example, nouns with an adjective but no classifier can be possessed and quantified:

(31) a. *kuv   ob   lub   nam   pobzeb*
     kŭ   ó   lú   na̰   pózé
     1SG   two   CLF   large   stones
     'my two great stones'

   b. *ob   nam   pobzeb*
      ó   na̰   pózé
      two   large   stones
      'two great stones'

   c. *kuv   nam   pobzeb   nuav*
      kŭ   na̰   pózé   hŏ
      1SG   large   stone   DEM:1
      'this large stone of mine.'

In the post-noun complex, stative verbs modifying the phrase occur closest to the noun. Relative clauses come after any stative verbs modifying the NP, but before the demonstratives:

(32) *lub   tsev   lab   kws   kuv   ua   hov*
     lú   tʃẽ   lá   kɨ   kŭ   ua   hŏ
     CLF   house   red   REL   1SG   make   DEM:3
     'that red house that I built'

The demonstrative cluster has up to two parts: a spatial locative and a person based demonstrative (in that order). The spatial deictics are discussed at greater length in §4.1.2. The person-based demonstratives are discussed in §3.1.3 on pronouns. The following example illustrates the two types of deictic together:

(33) *Nwg   tuaj   saab   peg   nuav.*
     nɨ̰   tûa   ʃá   pḛ   nŭa
     3SG   come   CLF(side)   up_there   DEM:1
     'He came to the side (of the country) up here.'

In summary, the nominal complex has the following structure:

(34) poss ≺ quant ≺ clf ≺ adj ≺ N ≺ stative verb ≺ relative clause ≺ spatial deictic ≺ person-based demonstrative

The co-occurrence requirements and dependencies among the various elements in the noun phrase are quite complex. A simplified summary is given below in table form:

Table 4: Co-occurrence restrictions in the Mong Leng NP

Item type	Implies the presence of
noun	–
classifier	numeral, noun, or deictic
adjective	noun
relative clause	classifier
deictic	classifier
modifier	classifier or noun
possessor	adjective or classifier
numeral/quantifier	adjective or classifier

A maximal NP is given in example ():

(35) ob   lub   nyuas   pobzeb   dlawb   kws   wb   pum   hov   muaj
     ó   lú   ɲùa   pó ́ʒé   tláɨ   kɨ   ɨ   pu̯   ho   mûa
     two   clf   little   stone   white   rel   1du   see   dem:3 exist

fwjchim.
fɨcʰɨ̯
power
'Those two little white stones that we saw have power.'

Nouns can be omitted from NPs if they can be recovered from the discourse context.

3.1.2 Classifier (CLF) device

Classifiers play a prominent role in Hmong grammar. Certain items in an NP (like demonstratives) can only occur if a classifier is present. Others (e.g. numerals) require either a classifier or an adjective:

(36) a.   dlev
          tlě
          dog
          'dog; dogs'

b. *ob   dlev
    ó   tlĕ
    two dog
    'two dogs'

c. ob   tug   dlev
   ó   tṵ   tlĕ
   two CLF   dog
   'two dogs'

d. ob   (tug)   nyuas   dlev
   ó   (tṵ)   ɲùa   tlĕ
   two (CLF) little   dog
   'two little dogs'

These relationships are summarized in Table 4. Classifiers also play a role in indicating definiteness and specificity. Noun phrases with a bare noun are non-specific and indefinite. This means that its referent has not be introduced in discourse previously (indefinite) and that it cannot be identified with a specific entity or group of entities. See (37a). When a classifier alone is added, as in (37b), the noun phrase is both definite and specific. When a numeral and a classifier are added, the noun phrases is marked as indefinite and specific, as long as no demonstrative is present (37c). If a demonstrative is present, as in (37d), then the noun phrase receives a definite and specific reading.

(37) a. kuv   pum   dlev.
       kŭ   pṵ   tlĕ
       1SG   see   dog
       'I saw dogs/a dog' (indefinite and non-specific)

b. kuv   pum   tug   dlev.
   kŭ   pṵ   tṵ   tlĕ
   1SG   see   CLF   dog
   'I saw the dog.' (definite and specific)

c. kuv   pum   ib   tug   dlev.
   kŭ   pṵ   í   tṵ   tlĕ
   1SG   see   one CLF   dog
   'I saw a (specific) dog.' (indefinite and specific)

	d.	kuv	pum	ob	tug	dlev	hov
		kŭ	pu̱	ó	tu̱	tlě	hŏ
		1sg	see	two	CLF	dog	DEM:3

'I saw those two dogs' (definite and specific)

The classifier system is quite extensive—Xiong, Xiong, and Xiong (1983) list 19 classifiers in Mong Leng and Heimach (1969) lists 72 for the closely related Hmong Daw dialect—but only a few classifiers are common. Some classifiers are used only for a single noun (e.g. tsaab 'CLF for letters' which occurs only with ntawv 'paper). Hmong has both quantificational and sortal classifiers. Quantificational (or mensural) classifiers are classifiers that signify a quantity of a noun with low countability. One example is thooj 'CLF for pieces or sections' in thooj nqaij 'the piece of meat.' Sortal classifiers are classifiers that group nouns into classes by sort. There is no single basis for classification, but the most important criteria seem to be shape, function, and collectivity. By way of illustration, here are some of the most important classes and approximate definitions:

Table 5: Examples of Mong Leng classifiers

sortal	lub	round objects, bulky objects, and some abstract concepts
	tug	humans, animals, long slender objects, and some abstract concepts (strength, ideas)
	txuj	thread-like objects (ropes, roads); narratives
	tsob	plants (including trees)
	raab	things wielded with the hands; tools
	dlaim	flat things
quantificational	pob	packets
	cov	masses; collections
	nkawm	pairs

There is some degree of arbitrariness to noun class assignment in Hmong (e.g. pencils (cwjmem) belong to the same noun class as dlaagzug 'strength' and tswvyim 'idea'), but the classifiers have enough semantic content that a noun may have different meanings depending on the item acting as its classifier:

(38) a. tug qau   'penis (as a body part)'
     b. raab qau   'penis (as an instrument)'

(39) a. dlaim ntawv   'sheet of paper'
     b. cov ntawv   '(collection of) paper'
     c. tug ntawv   'written character'

d. tsaab ntawv   'letter'
e. phau ntawv   'book'

The classifier *cov*, for masses and collections (40a), is used to indicate plurality (40b–c) and can be used with any noun. It may be evolving into a general marker of plurality (Ratliff 1991), as suggested by examples like (40c), where *cov* occurs with another classifier. However, as (40d) shows, when *cov* occurs with a numeral, it receives a "collection" or "mass" rather than a "plural" interpretation.

(40) a. *cov   dlej*
        cŏ   tlê
        COV   water
        'The water'

   b. *cov   ntawv*
        cŏ   ⁿtăɨ
        COV   paper
        'The papers'

   c. *cov   phau   ntawv*
        cŏ   pʰau   ⁿtăɨ
        COV   CLF(books) paper
        'The books'

   d. *peb   co   ntawv*
        pé   co   ⁿtăɨ
        three COV   paper
        'Three collections of papers'

3.1.3 Pronouns

Among personal pronouns, Hmong distinguishes three persons and three numbers:

Table 6: Hmong personal pronouns

	SG	DU	PL
1	kuv	wb	peb
2	koj	meb	mej
3	nwg	obtug	puab

The third person dual pronoun is transparently derived from a numeral-classifier sequence ('two-CLF(animals, people, cylindrical objects)'). It displays some regional variation; for example, *ob-leeg* ('two-CLF(people)') is sometimes encountered as '3DU'. Hmong also has two impersonal pronouns, *yug* 'IMP.SG' and *luag* 'IMP.PL', which are approximately equivalent to English impersonal *one* and *they*.

Hmong has a complex system of deixis that includes both a spatial system and a person-based system of demonstrative pronouns. The following person-based demonstratives exist: *nuav* 'DEM:1', *ko* 'DEM:2', *hov* 'DEM:3', *i* 'DEM:3.RECENT', *u* 'DEM:3.REMOTE.' The first person demonstrative refers to things in the proximity of the speaker, literally or metaphorically. The second person demonstrative, transparently derived from the second person singular pronoun *koj*, refers to things at the immediate person of the interlocutor. The third person demonstratives refer to things proximal to neither the speaker nor the interlocutor.

3.2 Verbal domain

3.2.1 No inflection

Mong Leng has no verbal inflection. Tense is not encoded grammatically. Aspect, mood, and polarity are marked either by particles (see Section 3.2.2) or grammaticalized verbs (see section 3.2.3).

3.2.2 Verbal Categories

In the following section, the non-verbal verb particles will be discussed in the order in which they occur (preceding the verb): discourse relatedness, modality, aspect, and status. The verbal complex has the structure seen in (41):

(41) Structure of the verbal complex

$$\left(\left\{ \begin{array}{c} \text{dis rel} \\ \text{txha (le)} \\ \text{txawm} \\ \text{maam(le)} \\ \text{tsua} \\ \text{etc.} \end{array} \right\} \right) + \left(\begin{array}{c} \text{modalP} \\ \text{tub} \end{array} \right) + \left(\begin{array}{c} \text{modalV1} \\ \text{yuav} \end{array} \right) + \left(\left\{ \begin{array}{c} \text{aspectP} \\ \text{yeej} \\ \text{pheej} \\ \text{tseem} \\ \text{taabtom} \end{array} \right\} \right) + \left(\left\{ \begin{array}{c} \text{status} \\ \text{tsi} \\ \text{xob} \\ \text{puas} \end{array} \right\} \right) +$$

$$\left(\begin{array}{c} \text{aspectV} \\ \text{tau} \end{array} \right) + V_h + \left(\left(\left\{ \begin{array}{c} \text{status} \\ \text{tsi} \\ \text{puas} \end{array} \right\} \right) + \left(\begin{array}{c} \text{modalV2} \\ \text{tau} \end{array} \right) \right)$$

A closed class of *discourse relatedness* markers occur at the left edge of the VP which indicate that the current clause is related to, or a consequence of, the preceding clause. A partial list of these particles is given in (42):

(42) *txha/txhaj/xam (le)* 'therefore'
  txawm 'so; though'
  ho 'thus, then'
  rua 'thus, then'
  kuj 'also'
  maam/maav (le) indicates that the event to which the clause refers will occur only after the event or condition specified in the previous clause comes about.

Following these is a modal marker, *tub* which encodes speaker surety regarding the truth of the proposition expressed by the clause, as shown in (43).

(43) Kuv   tub   ncu   koj   heev.
    kŭ   tú   ⁿcu   kô   hĕŋ
    1SG   truly remember   2SG   very
    'I really do miss you.'

In the following position, the aspect marker *tseem* occurs, meaning 'still', followed by a group of aspect markers: e.g. *pheej* 'iterative' and *taabtom/sawbsim* 'continuous'.

The status markers follow these aspect particles. They consist of the unmarked (realis) negative particle *tsi*, the irrealis negative particle *xob*, and the question particle *puas*. These occur before the modal verb *tau* (see §3.2.3), but after all other particles. *Tsi* occurs in ordinary negative clauses; *xob*, by contrast, occurs in commands, hypothetical clauses, and other unrealized negative clauses:

(44) a. Koj   xob   moog!
       kô   só   mǫŋ
       2sg   NEG.IRR   go
       'Don't go!'

   b. Koj   xob   moog,   zoo   dlua!
      kô   só   mǫŋ   ʒoŋ   tlua
      2sg   NEG.IRR   go   good   comparative
      'It would be better were you to not go!'

Xob frequently co-occurs with *tsi* 'NEG' (particularly in negative commands).

The question particle *puas* actually marks a kind of indeterminate status—where the truth of a proposition is underdetermined. Like the "wh-words" in Hmong, which have the same indeterminate property, it is used in both questions and statements of doubt or agnosticism:

(45) a. *Nwg   puas   tuaj?*
       nɨ   pùa   tûa
       3sg   Q   come
       'Did/will he come?'

   b. *Sov   nwg   puas   tuaj!*
       ʃŏ   nɨ   pùa   tûa
       DUBATIVE   3sg   Q   come
       'I doubt he will come!'

The construction *V tsi V* (V NEG V), is also used to mark the same kind of status, and thus can be used both to ask questions and to discuss indeterminate states of affairs. Take the following examples:

(46) a. Hawj (1986: 11)
       Tua   nyog   tsi   nyog   los   cale   tua   lauj.
       tua   ɲɔ   tʃi   ɲɔ   lò   cale   tua   lâu
       kill   appropriate   NEG   appropriate   FOC   procede   kill   FP
       'Whether or not its appropriate to kill her, go ahead and do it!'

   b. *Tua   nyog   tsi   nyog?*
       tua   ɲɔ   tʃi   ɲɔ
       kill   appropriate   NEG   appropriate
       'Is it appropriate to kill her?'

Other modal and aspectual markers will be discussed in the following section on serial verb constructions.

3.2.3 Serial verb constructions (SVCs)[1]

SVCs of both the symmetrical and asymmetrical types are extremely common in Hmong discourse. Symmetrical SVCs are used primary to express complex events where components vary in temporal or logical precedence but only where the components can be seen as a single event. See, for example, the following sentences:

(47) a. Thoj (1987)

Cais	ob	saab	nam	haavdlej	cale
cài	ó	ʃáŋ	na̰	hăŋtlê	cale
Then	two	side	great	ravine	precede

tu-nrho	ndlwg	nrov-<quas>voog	taug	haav	lawm.
tu-ⁿtsʰo	ⁿtlḭ	ⁿtsŏ-<EUPH>vo̰ŋ	ta̰u	hăŋ	la̰ḭ
broken-EXP	flow	sound-EXP<EUPH>	follow	valley	COMPL

'Then the two sides of the great ravine split and flowed with a booming sound through the valley.'

b. Thoj (1985)

Ntxawm	hab	Yob	obtug	pum	Yawm	Xeev	Txwjlaug
ⁿtsa̰ḭ	há	yó	ótṵ	pṵ	ja̰ḭ	sěŋ	tsîla̰u
PN	and	PN	3DL	see	Mister	Provincial	Elder

nkaag-plawg	lug	sawv	xaam-<quas>nuv...
ⁿka̰ŋ-pla̰ḭ	lṵ	ʃăḭ	sa̰ŋ-<qua>nuv
crawl-EXP	come	stand	survey-EXP<EUPH>

'Ntxawm and Yob Nraug Ntsuag saw Mister Provincial Elder enter (into the house), stand, and survey it...'

Asymmetrical SVCs can provide modal, aspectual, and directional information about an event. For example the verb *yuav* 'want, intend' can mark desiderative, deontic, and epistemic modality, as show in example (48):

---

[1] For a different analysis of Hmong SVCs, presented with greater nuance and detail, see Jarkey (1991).

(48) a. Desiderative modality (Thoj 1987: 10)
Kuv   yuav   tuaj   moog   thaam   hluas-nkauj.
kŭ   yŭa   tûa   mɔŋ   tʰa̤   l̥ùa-ⁿkâu
1sg   YUAV   come   go   chat   girl
'I intend to go chat up girls.'

b. Deontic modality (Hawj 1985: 9)
Puab   yuav   lug   noj   tshais,   puab   maamle   moog   tsev.
púa   jŭa   lṳ   nô   tsʰài   púa   maŋle   mɔŋ   tʃě
3PL   YUAV   come   eat   breakfast 3PL   then   go   house
'They had to have eaten breakfast before they could go home.'

c. Epistemic modality (Thoj 1985)
Ua   caag   los   yuav   tau   tuag   quas-tag
ua   caŋ   lò   jŭa   tau   tṳa   qùa-ta̤
Do   what   FOC   YUAV   TAU   die   EUPH-real
'Come what may, they must surely die.'

Yuav's use in serial verb constructions has moved far beyond its lexical meaning.

Similarly, the verb *tau* 'get', seen in (48c), has developed different grammatical meanings depending on its position relative to the main verb. This common Southeast Asian pattern is explored at greatest depth by Enfield (2003), who includes Hmong as one of his example languages. However, the polysemy of *tau* both as a grammatical marker and a lexical verb was noticed as early as Heimbach (1969: 307). If *tau* occurs before the main verb, it usually indicates that the state of affairs expressed by the verb is achieved, as shown in (49):

(49) Thoj (1987: 15)
Obtug   tau   lug   nyob   uake   thaam   hluas-nkauj.
ótṳ   tau   lṳ   ɲó   uake   tʰa̤   l̥ùa-ⁿkâu
3DL   TAU   come   exist   together   chat   girl
'They came to chat up girls together.'

However, it can also be used to express the notion 'get to', as shown in (50). See also Enfield (2003: 299).

(50) Kuv   tau   moog   noj   peb-caug.
    kŭ   tau   mǫŋ   nô   pé-cạu
    1SG   TAU   go   eat   three-ten
    'I got to go eat thirty (celebrate the New Year).'
    'I went and ate thirty (celebrated the New Year).'

If tau occurs after the verb, it usually expresses potential mood:

(51) Thoj (1987: 17)
    Yog   *koj*   *khu*   *tau*   *nwg*   *zoo*...
    jǫ   kô   kʰu   tau   nɨ   ʒoŋ
    Is   2SG   fix   get   3SG   good
    'If you can heal her...'

However, it can still occur in an SVC after another verb the meaning 'V and succeed' (52). See also Enfield (2003: 237).

(52) Hawj (1985: 8)
    Faabkis   *kuj*   *txeeb*   *tau*   *puab*   *tug*   *chij*   *lawm*   *hab*
    fáŋkì   kû   tséŋ   tau   púa   tụ   cʰî   lạɨ   há
    French   too   seize   TAU   3PL   CLF   flag   PRF   also
    'The French had also seized their flag (seized and obtained their flag).'

Verbs of motion occur frequently in SVCs, both as main verbs and as auxiliary verbs. The most important of these are *lug* 'to come to point of reference/point of origin', *tuaj* 'to come (out); to come towards reference point', and *moog* 'to go (away from reference point). All of these have less concrete functions. Most importantly, they specify the path through space of a participant in an event:

(53) a. Thoj (1985: 8)
        kuv   *lemaam*   *coj*   *koj*   *moog*   *tu.*
        kŭ   lemaŋ   cô   kô   mǫŋ   tu
        1SG   then   lead   2SG   go   tend
        '...then I'll take you away and care for you.'

    b. Thoj (1987: 8)
        Thov   *koj*   *tawm*   *lug*   *rua*   *kuv*   *pum*   *koj*   *ib*
        tʰŏ   kô   tạɨ   lụ   tṣua   kŭ   pụ   kô   í
        beg   2SG   exit   come   for   1SG   see   2SG   one

plag.
plȧ
moment
'Please come out so I may see you a moment.'

More abstractly, these verbs can be used as to indicate paths through time (that is, aspectual distinctions). Moog 'go' indicates an event continuing on beyond the reference time; lug 'to come to point of reference/point of origin' indicates an event that persists up to the reference time (and thus acts as a PERFECT marker):

(54) a. Yaaj and Vaaj (1985: 16)
Peb	yuavtsum	txaus	sab	tu	kuas	zoo	moog.
pé	jŭatʂɨ	tsàu	ʃá	tu	kùa	zoo	mɔŋ
1PL	must	enough	liver	tend	cause	good	MOOG

'We must be content to care for him so that he'll be fine from here on out'

b. Hawj (1985: 7)
Puab	txhajle	tawg	taag,	hab	tsiv	ntawd	lug	lawd.
púa	tsʰâle	taɨ	taŋ	há	tʃĭ	ⁿtăɨ	lɨ	lăɨ
3PL	thus	disperse	finish	and	flee	there	PRF	COMPL

'So they all scattered, and have abandoned that place up to the present.'

The comparative is an SVC construction that deserves special treatment. The comparative marker is the verb *dlua* 'to pass' occurs post-verbally. The preverbal argument acts as the thing compared and the postverbal argument acts as the standard of comparison:

(55)
Nwg	txawj	dlua	kuv.
nɨ	tsâɨ	tlua	kŭ
3SG	able	pass	1SG

'She is more skilled than I.'

While this construction is fixed, the verb that is used as a marker of comparison is not. In addition to *dlua*, *tshaaj* 'exceed', *dlhau* 'cross', and probably other verbs may be used to express comparisons. Thus, the same comparison as in (55) can be expressed as in (56a, b):

(56) a. *Nwg   txawj   dlhau   kuv.*
      nɨ̰   tsâɨ   tʰlhau   kŭ
      3SG   able   cross   1SG
      'She is more skilled than I.'

   b. *Nwg   txawj   tshaaj   kuv.*
      nɨ̰   tsâɨ   tʃʰâŋ   kŭ
      3SG   able   exceed   1SG
      'She is more skilled than I.'

There is regional and individual variation in which formulation is preferred. However, it is difficult to identify specific pragmatic differences between them.

The majority of asymmetrical SVCs contain one of the verbs that carries grammatical or spatial (rather than purely lexical) meaning. A non-exhaustive list is given in Table 7.

Table 7: Grammaticalized verbs in SVCs

	Main verb meaning	Grammaticalized serial verb meanings
moog	'go'	'direction away from speaker; on into future'
lug	'come; come back'	'direction towards arguments's abode; PERFECT'
tuaj	'come'	'direction towards speaker'
tawm	'exit'	'ELATIVE'
nkaag	'enter'	'ILLATIVE'
tau	'get'	'POTENTIAL mood; "achieved" aspect'
lawm	'leave'	'COMPLETIVE'
yuav	'want'	'DESIDERATIVE, OBLIGATORY, and EPISTEMIC modality. FUTURE?'
taag	'be complete'	'COMPLETIVE'
dlua	'pass'	'COMPARATIVE degree; REPETITIVE aspect'
dlhau	'cross'	'COMPARATIVE degree; SUPERLATIVE degree'

However, the set of verbs that can occupy this grammatical role is not fixed—stative verbs as a class can provide manner or evaluative information about the event to which the SVC refers:

(57) Yaaj and Vaaj (1985: 15)
     Koj   lemaam   rov-qaab   tau   zoo   lawv   le   koj   thov.
     kô   lemaŋ   tʂŏ-qáŋ   tau   ʒoŋ   lăɨ   le   kô   tʰŏ
     2SG   then   return-back   get   good   follow as   2SG   beg
     'Then you will get again a good fortune (get well) as you ask.'

3.2.4 Clausal/sentential organization

Sentences are verb-medial (VO). Adpositional phrases are also head-initial. Topic arguments are initial except in pragmatically marked constructions.

3.2.5 Ellipsis of arguments

Both topic and non-topic arguments can be elided. Zero-reference is most common for inanimate nouns, possibly because of a tendency to use personal pronouns only for humans and animals.

3.2.6 Information Structure

Hmong is topic-prominent. The topical element is fronted and may be marked with a topic marker such as mas (58a) or may be left unmarked (58b):

(58) a. Yaaj and Vaaj (1985: 9)
       Luas   tej   mas   nim   ua   zaam   lab-<quas>vog.
       lùa   tê   mà   nị   ua   ʒaŋ   lá-<qùa>vǫ
       IMP.PL PL   TOP   EMPH do   clothing red-EXP<EUPH>
       'The others, they wore clothes of the reddest red.'

    b. Yaaj and Vaaj (1985: 8)
       Moov   tsi   muaj.
       mǒŋ   tʃi   mûa
       fortune NEG exist
       'Luck, it did not exist (for them)'

Other particles that can serve as topic markers in Mong Leng include *tes* and *cais*:

(59) a. Kuv   tes   (kuv) yeej   has   le   hov.
       kǔ   tè   kǔ   jêŋ   hà   le   hǒ
       1SG   TES   1SG   always say as   DEM:3
       'Me, (I've) always said that.'

b. *Kuv   cais   (kuv)   yeej   has   le   hov.*
   kŭ   cài   kŭ   jêŋ   hà   le   hŏ
   1SG   CAIS   1SG   always say   as   DEM:3
   'Me, (I've) always said that.'

Both of these particles also appear in other contexts with the meaning 'then' or 'so'. It is not yet clear how these particles differ in function when serving as topic markers.

Hmong also has an explicitly marked focus construction. Focused constituents can marked with the particle *los* 'FOC':

(60) *tug   twg   los   nyam   Pov.*
     tṳ   tḭ   lò   ɲa̰   pŏ
     CLF   Q   FOC   like   PN
     'ANYONE would like Pao.'

There is also a cleft-like construction:

(61) *yog   kuv   txhaj   tsi   paub   xwb.*
     jɔ̰   kŭ   tsʰâ   tʃi   páu   xɨ́
     be   1SG   thus   NEG   know   just
     'It's just ME who doesn't know.'

For more specific information on the topic of information structure in Hmong, see Fuller (1987, 1988).

3.2.7 Others

In addition to *puas V* questions and the less common *V not V* questions, yes-no questions requesting affirmation of a supposition can be formed by adding the final particle *los* or *lov*:

(62) a. *Koj   puas   moog?*
        kô   pùa   mɔŋ
        2SG   Q   go
        'Are you going?'

b. *Koj   moog   tsi   moog?*
   kô   mɔ̰ŋ   tʃĭ   mɔ̰ŋ
   2SG   go   NEG   go
   'Are you going?'

c. *Koj   moog   lov?*
   kô   mɔ̰ŋ   lŏ
   2SG   go   Q
   'You're going, huh?'

Mong Leng is a "wh-in-situ" language. Content questions are formed by replaceing a noun phrase, quantifier, etc., with a wh-marker.

(63) a. *Koj   ua   num.*
        kô   ua   nṵ
        2SG   do   work
        'You are doing work?'

   b. *Koj   ua   dlaabtsi?*
      kô   ua   tláŋtʃĭ
      2SG   do   what
      'What are you doing?'

Most frequently, these phrases consist of a noun classifier and the wh-marker *twg* (occurring in isolation as 'what' or 'where'):

(64) a. *Nwg   dlua   twg   lawm?*
        nɨ̰   tlua   tɨ̰   laɨ̰
        3SG   pass   Q   COMPL
        'Where has she gone?'

   b. *Leej   twg   tuaj?*
      lêŋ   tɨ̰   tûa
      CLF(person)   Q   come
      'Who has come?'

   c. *Nwg   nyob   qhov   twg?*
      nɨ̰   ɲó   qʰŏ   tɨ̰
      3SG   be_a_place   CLF(place)   Q
      'Where is she?'

"Manner" questions are formed by placing *(le) caag* ('as' + 'what manner?') after a verb.

(65) Tebchaws   Lostsuas   zoo   le   caag?
     téc^hàɨ   lòtʃùa   ʒoŋ   le   cạ
     country   Lao   good   as   what_manner
     'What is Laos like?'

4 Semantics and Pragmatics

4.1 Common semantic domains

4.1.1 Food terminology

The generic word for food in Hmong, *mov*, actually means 'cooked rice'. An even more general word for food is *zaub-mov*, a coordinate compound of *mov* and *zaub* 'vegetables; dishes other than rice'. Rice vocabulary is quite rich: the rice plant, and unprocessed rice is called *nplej*. After the rice hulls are removed, the product is called *ntsab*. *Ntsab* may be cooked, producing *mov*, or ground into rice flour (*moov*) which can be made into cakes called *ncuav*.

4.1.2 Expressions of "cutting", "carrying", "drying", and "direction"

Hmong has a relatively large number of terms for carrying and similar concepts. These include, but are not limited to, those given in **Table 8**:

Table 8: Mong Leng verbs of carrying

nqaa	'to carry; to bear'
ris	'to bear a burden'
coj	'to lead somewhere; to take something, whether by leading or carrying.'
kwv	'to carry on the shoulders'
aub	'to carry on the back (e.g. a child).' (impolite)
ev	'to carry on the back (e.g. a child).' (polite)
thauj	'to haul (of animals, motor vehicles)'

In contrast, Hmong is relatively poor in verbs of cutting: *hlais* 'to slice', *txav* 'to chop (as with a knife)', *ntuv* 'to chop, as with an axe', *kaw* 'to cut with a back and forth motion, as with a saw'. Likewise, the vocabulary for drying is modest: *qhuav* 'be dry', *nqhuab* 'to dry', *zab* 'to dry in the sun or by a fire'.

Hmong has a rich lexicon for spatial deixis, both for describing paths and locations. Directional paths are described using motion verbs as described in section 3.2.3. Static locations are specified by a closed class of locative words which may function either like prepositions or demonstratives, depending on their syntactic position. These are listed in **Table 9**. The temporal deictic *thaus* displays the same grammatical behavior as the spatial deictics and is therefore listed with them.

Table 9: Mong Leng spatial and temporal deictics

ntawm	'by; that there'
tom	'over there; that over there'
tim	'way over there; that way over there'
peg	'up there; that up there'
nraag	'down there; that down there'
sau	'on top; that on top'
nrau	'outside; that outside'
huv	'inside; underneath; that inside or underneath'
thaus	'when, then'

4.2 Pragmatics and discourse

4.2.1 Final particles

Mong Leng has a great variety of final particles. For the most part these fulfill two functions:
1. Indicate what speech act the utterance represents (an assertion, question, address, command, etc.)
2. Indicate the speaker's attitude toward the utterance (surety, doubt, belief that it is self-evident, intention of force or politeness, and so on).

For example, someone who is eating as a guest in a Hmong home is likely to hear the phrase below:

(66) *Hais   mov   ntxiv   mag!*
    hài   mǒ   ⁿtsǐ   mạ
    dish   rice   add   FP
    'Dish up more rice!' (Polite.)

The final particle *mag* signals polite insistence that the guest dish up more rice. It also "genders" the command female. A male would be likely to use the more forceful particle *nawb* in the same context. In a different context, where there is a dispute about whether a third party will come with them or not, one of the participants might issue the following complaint:

(67) Nwg   yeej   tsi   xaaw   tawm   huv   tsev   li   las.as!
     nɨ̧   jêŋ   tʃĭ   săŋ   tạɨ   hŭ   tʃĕ   li   là.ʔà
     3SG   always   NEG   think   exit   in   house   at_all   FP
     'He never wants to leave his house at all!'

In this utterance, *las as* expresses irritation that the interlocutor has not yet come around the the speaker's way of thinking, when, in the view of the speaker it is obviously correct. As was mentioned in §3.2.7 above, final particles may also be used to form particular types of questions, including the common greeting given in (66):

(68) Koj   tuaj   lov?
     kô   tûa   lŏ
     2SG   come   FP
     'You've come, have you?'

The particle *lov* may even occur as a single word utterance meaning 'Is that so?' This type of question particle is in complementary distribution with the other question formation strategies introduced in §3.2.7:

(69) a. Koj   puas   tuaj?
         kô   pùa   tûa
         2SG   Q   come
         'Will you come?'

     b. Koj   tuaj   tsi   tuaj?
         kô   tûa   tʃĭ   tûa
         2SG   come   NEG   come
         'Will you come?'

     a'. *Koj   puas   tuaj   lov?
         kô   pùa   tûa   lŏ
         2SG   Q   come   FP
         'Will you come?'

b'. *Koj   tuaj   tsi   tuaj   lov?
    kô   tûa   tʃi   tûa   lŏ
    2SG   come NEG   come FP
    'Will you come?'

The particle *lov* is best viewed not as a generic question marker, but a marker of a very specific type of tag-like question.

In (68), some of the more common particles are listed, along with approximate characterizations of their functions:

(70) a. *os*   'polite assertion'
     b. *es*   'complaint; firm assertion; vocative'
     c. *huas*   'counter assertion'
     d. *las as*   'counter assertion; indicates speaker frustration'
     e. *kaj*   'conjecture; speculation'
     f. *nev*   'reminder'
     g. *mag*   'polite request or assertion; used primarily by females; only occurs in verbal sentences'
     h. *nawb*   'emphatic request, command, or assertion'
     i. *nas has*   'command; indicates speaker frustration'
     j. *lov, los* 'question with presupposition'
     k. *aw*   'address; vocative'
     l. *xwb*   'judgment of triviality or simplicity'
     m. *lauj, laub* 'exclamation'

4.2.2 Politeness

Unlike some other Southeast Asian languages (Vietnamese, Thai, Khmer), the primary terms of personal address and references in Hmong are ordinary pronouns, unmarked for age or status (see §3.1.3 on pronouns). While it is possible to refer to other (even unrelated) persons using kinship terms (e.g. *yawmtxwv* 'father in law'), pronouns encoding person and number are more common than terms encoding age, gender, or status.

5 Conclusion

While Hmong differs from the "prototypical" SEA language in several respects—it has more consonants, fewer vowels, and a less articulated vocabulary for certain semantic fields, to name a few deviations—Hmong is, in most typological respects, like its eastern SEA neighbors. It has numerous tonal contrasts, which are correlated with voice quality differences. The morphology is highly isolating, and word formation depends largely on compounding and reduplication. Noun classifiers play an important role in the syntax. Serial verb constructions and their grammaticalized reflexes serve as the primary means of encoding complex events. Subtleties of color, sound, movement, and evaluation are expressed through a rich system of expressives. Furthermore, a large set of final particles communicate the force of, and the speaker's attitude toward, an utterance.

Abbreviations

EMPH	emphatic
EUPH	euphonic affix
EXP	expressive
FP	final particle
PN	personal name

References

Andruski, Jean E. & Martha Ratliff. 2000. Phonation types in production of phonological tone: The case of Green Mong. *Journal of the International Phonetic Association* 30 (1–2). 37–61.

Barney, Linwood G. & William A. Smalley. 1953. Third Report on Meo (Miao): Orthography and grammar. Unpublished report.

Clark, Marybeth. 1996. Where do you feel? Stative verbs and body-part terms in Mainland Southeast Asia. In Hilary Chappell & William McGregor (eds.), *The grammar of inalienability. A typological perspective on body part terms and the part-whole relation*, 529–563. Berlin & New York: Mouton de Gruyter.

Enfield, Nick J. 2003. *Linguistic epidemiology: Semantics and grammar of language contact in mainland Southeast Asia*. London: RoutledgeCurzon.

Fuller, Judith Wheaton. 1988. *Topic and comment in Hmong*, Bloomington, Indiana: Indiana University Linguistics Club.

Fuller, Judith Wheaton. 1987. Topic markers in Hmong. *Linguistics of the Tibeto-Burman Area* 10 (2). 113–127.

Fulop, Sean & Chris Golston. 2008. Breathy and whispery voicing in White Hmong. *Journal of the Acoustical Society of America* 123 (5). 3883–3883.

Golston, Chris & Yang, Phong. 2001. White Hmong loanword phonology. In Caroline Féry, Antony Green, Ruben Florentius Hendricus Eduardus van de Vijver (eds.), *Proceedings of HILP 5*, 40–57. (Linguistics in Potsdam 12). Potsdam: Universitätsbibliothek.

Grinevald, Collette. 1999. Typologie des systèmes de classification nominale. *Fait de Langue* 14. 101–122.

Hawj, Khu Ntxawg. 1986. *Lug Nruag Moob: Lug Nruag Dlaab* [Mong Stories: Diety Stories], Winfield, Illinois: Mong Volunteer Literacy, Inc.

Hawj, Khu Ntxawg. 1985. *Moob Ua Rog Vwm* [Mong Wage the Insane War], Winfield, Illinois: Mong Volunteer Literacy, Inc.

Harriehausen, Bettina. 1990. *Hmong Njua: Syntaktische Analyse einer gesprochenen Sprache mithilfe datenverarbeitungstechnischer Mittel und sprachvergleichende Beschreibung des südostasiatischen Sprachraumes*. Tübingen: Niemeyer.

Heimbach, Earnetst E. 1969. *White Meo-English Dictionary*. Ithaca & New York: Southeast Asia Program, Cornell University.

Jaisser, Annie C. 1990. DeLIVERing an introduction to psycho-collocations with SIAB in White Hmong. *Linguistics of the Tibeto-Burman Area* 3. 159–178.

Jarkey, Nerida. 1991. Serial verb constructions in White Hmong: A functional approach. PhD dissertation, University of Sidney.

Jarkey, Nerida. 2006. Complement Clause Types and Complementation Strategy in White Hmong. In R. M. W. Dixon & Alexandra Y. Aikhenvald (eds.), *Complementation: A cross-linguistic typology*, 115–136.

Johnson, Michael. 2002. The reconstruction of labial stop+ sonorant clusters in proto-far Western Hmongic. *Transactions of the Philological Society* 100 (1). 25–58.

Lemoine, Jacque. 2005. What is the actual number of the (H)mong in the World? *Hmong Studies Journal* 6. 1–8.

Lewis, M. Paul (ed.). 2009. *Ethnologue: Languages of the world*, 16th edition. Dallas: SIL International. http://www.ethnologue.com.

Li, Yunbing. 2002. Lun Miaoyu mingci qianzhui de gongneng [On the function of nominal prefixes in the Miao language]. *Minzu Yuwen* 2002 (3).

Lyman, Thomas A. 1974. Dictionary of Mong Njua: A Miao (Meo) Language of Southeast Asia. La Haye & Paris: Mouton.

Lyman, Thomas A. 1979. Grammar of Mong Njua (Green Miao): A descriptive linguistic study. Sattley, CA: Blue Oak Press.

Mithun, Marianne. 1984. The evolution of noun incorporation. *Language* 60 (4). 847–894.

Matisoff, James A. 1986. Hearts and minds in South-East Asian languages and English: an essay in the comparative lexical semantics of psycho-collocation. *Cahiers de Linguistique d'Asie Orientale* 15 (1). 5–57.

Mortensen, David R. 2004. Preliminaries to Mong Leng (Hmong Njua) phonology. Manuscript, UC Berkeley.

Ratliff, Martha. 1991. Cov, the underspecified noun, and syntactic flexibility in Hmong. *Journal of the American Oriental Society* 111 (4). 694–703.

Ratliff, Martha. 1992. Meaningful tone: A study of tonal morphology in compounds, form classes, and expressive phrases in White Hmong. DeKalb, IL: Northern Illinois University, Center for Southeast Asian Studies.

Thoj, Ntsuab Vaaj. 1987. *Nkauj Zaab* [Maiden Jang], Winfield, IL: Mong Volunteer Literacy.
Thoj, Xeev Pov. 1985. *Yob Nraug Ntsuag hab Noog Yaajqawg Poob Qaabnraag* [Yob Nraug Ntsuag and the Swallow that Fell Down], Winfield, IL: Mong Volunteer Literacy.
Vittrant, Alice. 2005. Classifier systems and noun categorization devices in Burmese. In Patrick Chew (ed.), *Proceedings of the 28th annual meeting of the Berkeley Linguistics Society: Special Session on Tibeto-Burman and Southeast Asian Linguistics*, 129–148. Berkeley: Berkeley Linguistics Society.
Wang, Fushi. 1985. *Miaoyu Jianzhi* [A Sketch of the Miao Language]. Beijing: Minzu Chubanshe [Nationalities Press].
Xiong, Lang, William J. Xiong & Nao Leng Xiong. 1983. *English-Mong-English dictionary: Phoo Txhais Lug Aakiv-Moob-Aakiv*. Milwaukee, WI: Xiong Partnership Productions.
Yaaj, Ntxhoo Xub. 1985. *Ceebpov* [Chengpao (personal name)], Winfield, IL: Mong Volunteer Literacy.
Yaaj, Ntxhoo Xub & Nom Tooj Vaaj. 1985. *Nuj Sis Loob* [Nou Shi Long (personal name)]. Winfield, IL: Mong Volunteer Literacy.

Appendix 1: Summary of linguistic features

Legend
+++ the feature is pervasive or used obligatorily in the language
++ the feature is normal but selectively distributed in the language
+ the feature is merely possible or observable in the language
− the feature is impossible or absent in the language

	Feature	+++/++/+/−	§ ref. in this chapter
Phonetics	Lexical tone or register	+++	§1.1, p.610
Phonetics	Back unrounded vowels	−	§1.2
Phonetics	Initial velar nasal	+	§1.2, p.611
Phonetics	Implosive consonants	−	−
Phonetics	Sesquisyllabic structures	−	§1.3, p.612
Morphology	Tendency towards monosyllabicity	+++	§1.3, p.612
Morphology	Tendency to form compounds	+++	§2.1.1 & §2.1.2, p.614
Morphology	Tendency towards isolating (rather than affixation)	+++	§2.1, p.613
Morphology	Psycho-collocations	+++	§2.2, p.618
Morphology	Elaborate expressions (e.g. four-syllable or other set patterns)	+++	§2.3, p.619

	Feature	+++/++/+/−	§ ref. in this chapter
Morphology	Reduplication generally	++	§2.5, p.621
Morphology	Reduplication of nouns	−	§2.5, p.622
Morphology	Reduplication of verbs	++	§2.5, p.621
Grammar	Use of classifiers	+++	§3.1.1 & § 3.1.2, p.622–27
Grammar	Classifiers used in counting	++	§3.1.2, p.624–26
Grammar	Classifiers used with demonstratives	++	§3.1.2, p.624–26
Grammar	Adjectival verbs	+++	−
Grammar	Grammatical number	−	−
Grammar	Inflection of verbs	−	§3.2.1, p.628
Grammar	Use of tense/aspect markers	++	§3.2.2, p.628
Grammar	Use of verb plural markers	−	−
Grammar	Grammaticalization of GET/ OBTAIN (potential mod. resultative/perfect aspect)	+++	§3.2.3, p.632
Grammar	Grammaticalization of PUT, SET (completed/resultative aspect)	−	−
Grammar	Grammaticalization of GIVE (causative, benefactive; preposition)	+++	−
Grammar	Grammaticalization of FINISH (perfective/ complete aspect; conjunction/temporal subordinator)	++	§3.2.3, p.634
Grammar	Grammaticalization of directional verbs e.g. GO / COME (allative, venitive)	+++	§3.2.3, p.633–35
Grammar	Grammaticalization of SEE, WATCH (temptative)	−	−
Grammar	Grammaticalization of STAY, REMAIN (progressive and continuous, durative aspects)	+	not discussed explicitly
Grammar	Serial verb constructions	+++	§2.3.2 & §3.2.3, p.631
Syntax	Verb precedes object (VO)	+++	§3.2.4, p.636
Syntax	Auxiliary precedes verb	+++	§3.2.2, p.628 & §3.2.3, p.635
Syntax	Preposition precedes noun	+++	−
Syntax	Noun precedes adjective	++	§3.1.1, p.622
Syntax	Noun preceds demonstrative	+++	−

	Feature	+++/++/+/−	§ ref. in this chapter
Syntax	Noun precedes genitive	−	−
Syntax	Noun precedes relative clause	+++	−
Syntax	Use of topic-comment structures	+++	§3.2.6, p.636
Syntax	Ellipsis of arguments known from context	+++	§3.2.5, p.636
Lexical semantics	Specific terms for forms of rice	+++	§4.1.1, p.639
Pragmatics	Use of utterance-final pragmatic particles	+++	§4.2.1, p.640
Pragmatics	Encoding of politeness	+	§4.2.1, p.642
Pragmatics	Encoding of honorifics	−	−

Appendix 2: Text interlinearized

The following text is excerpted from Yaaj and Vaaj (1985). It represents the opening scenes of a Hmong folktale about Nou Shi Long, a Hmong folk hero. All phonemic transcriptions, translations, and glosses have been added by the chapter author.

Noob   caaj   thaus   u,   muaj   ob   tug
nóŋ   cáŋ   tʰàw   u   mûa   ó   tṳ
day   branch   at_time   DEM:3.REMOTE   exist   two   CLF

kwv-tij
kɨ̌-tî
younger_brother-older_brother
'In the old days, there were two brothers,…'

NujSisLoob   hab   nwg   tug   kwv,   nyob   ua   ntsuag.
nûʃilóŋ   há   nɨ̌   tṳ   kɨ̌   ɲó   ua   ⁿtʃṳa
PN   and   3SG   CLF   younger_brother   live   do   orphan
'Nuj Sis Loob and his younger brother, living as orphans.'

Obtug   nam   hab   txiv   tub   tuag   taag   ntsuag.
ótṳ   na̠   há   tsɨ̌   tú   tṳa   ta̠ŋ   ⁿtʃṳa
3DU   mother   and   father   EMPH   die   finish   orphan
'Their mother and father had died, leaving them fully orphaned.'

Obtug	nam	hab	txiv	tub	tuag	lawm	ntxuv.
ótṳ	nạ	há	tsɨ̌	tú	tṳa	lạɨ	ⁿtsǔ
3DU	mother	and	father	EMPH	die	COMPL	be_early

'Their mother and father had already died early.'

Obtug	ua	neej	lug	tav	nraug,
ótṳ	ua	nêŋ	lṳ	tǎ	ntsạu
3DU	do	human	come	finish	youth

'They lived to adolescence,'

cais	NujSisLoob	tug	kwv		cale	mob	ntuj
cai	nûʃíloŋ	tṳ̌	kɨ̌		cale	mó	ⁿtû
then	PN	CLF	younger_brother		proceed	be_sick	heaven

mob	teb	tuag<pis>kag		lawm	hab.
mó	té	tṳa<pì>kạ		lạɨ	há
be_sick	earth	die-abrupt<EUPH>		COMPL	also

'then Nuj Sis Loob's brother became very sick and suddenly died as well.'

Zagnua,	tsuas	yog	tshuav	NujSisLoob	ib	leeg	nrug
ʒạnua	tʃùa	jọ	tsʰǔa	nûʃílóŋ	í	lẹŋ	ⁿtsṳ
now	only	be	remain	PN	one	CLF	accompany

luas	ua	neej	xwb.
lùa	ua	nêŋ	sɨ́
IMP.PL	do	human	just

'Now, it was only Nuj Sis Loob alone who remained to live with other people.'

Nwg	ua	ntsuag-nam	ntsuag-txiv	ntsuag-kwv
nɨ̀	ua	ntʃṳa-nạ	ntʃṳa-tsɨ̌	ntʃṳa-kɨ̌
3SG	do	orphan-mother	orphan-father	orphan-younger_brother

ntsuag-tij		taag-nrho.
ntʃṳa-tî		tạŋ-ⁿtsʰo
orphan-older_brother		finish-EXP

'He was utterly bereft of mother, father, younger brother, and older brother.'

Nwg	naj<quas>nub	moog	hlawv	xyaab	hlawv	ntawv	thov
nɨ̀	nâ<qùa>nú	mọŋ	lǎɨ	çáɲ	lǎɨ	ⁿtǎɨ	tʰǒ
3SG	daily<EUPH>	go	burn	incence	burn	paper	beg

kuas	Yawm	Nyoog	hab	Yawm	Saub	obtug	paab	coj	puab
kùa	ja̠ɨ	ɲɔŋ	ha	ja̠ɨ	ʃáu	ótṵ	páŋ	cô	púa
cause	Mister	PN	and	Mister	PN	3DU	help	lead	3PL

rov	qaab	lug	nrug		nwg	nyob.
tʂŏ	qáŋ	lṵ	ntʂṵ		nɨ̠	ɲó
return	back	come	accompany		3SG	live

'He daily went to burn incese and paper, asking that Yawm Nyoog and Yawm Saub to bring them back to live with him.'

Nkauj	MimSee	yog	Yawm	Xeev	Txwjlaug	tug	ntxhais
ⁿkâu	mi-mʃeŋ	jɔ̠	ja̠ɨ	sĕŋ	tsîla̠u	tṵ	ⁿtsʰài
Maid	PN	be	Mister	Provincial	Elder	CLF	daughter

nraab	kws	zoo	nkauj	dlua	lwm	leej	lwm	tug
ⁿtʂa̠ŋ	kɨ̠	ʒoŋ	ⁿkâu	tlua	lɨ̠	lêŋ	lɨ̠	tṵ
middle	REL	good	maiden	pass	other	CLF	other	CLF

huv-tuabsi.
hŭ-túaʃi
clean- altogether

'Maid Mim See was Mister Provincial Elder's middle daughter who was more beautiful than all others.'

Yawm	Xeev	Txwjlaug	paab	nam	ntxhais	najnub	taug	kev
ja̠ɨ	sĕŋ	tsîla̠u	páŋ	na̠	ⁿtsʰài	nânú	ta̠u	kĕ
Mister	Provincial	Elder	CLF	great	daughter	daily	follow	way

dlhau	NujSisLoob	lub	tsev	moog	kaav	kab	nraag	moos.
tʰlau	nûʃlóŋ	lú	tʃĕ	mɔ̠ŋ	kăŋ	ká	ⁿtʂa̠ŋ	mòŋ
cross	PN	CLF	house	go	govern	shop	down_at	town

'Mister Provincial Elder's great band of daughters daily followed the road past Nuj Sis Loob's house to go set up shop down in the town.'

Puab	pheej	uake	tuaj	pum	NujSisLoob	najnub
púa	pʰêŋ	uake	tûa	pṵ	nûʃlóŋ	nânú
3PL	repeatedly	be_together	come	see	PN	daily

hlawv	xyaab	hlawv	ntawv	thov	ntawm	toj	ntxaas.
l̥ăɨ	çáŋ	l̥ăɨ	ⁿtăɨ	tʰɔ̌	ⁿtaɨ	tô	ⁿtsàŋ
burn	incense	burn	paper	beg	by	hill	grave

'They repeated came together and saw that Nuj Sis Loob burnt incense and paper in petition by the graves daily.'

Muaj	ib	nub,	thaus	kws	Nkauj	MimSee	puab	moog	kaav
mûa	í	nú	tʰàu	kɨ̀	ⁿkâu	miʃeŋ	púa	mǫŋ	kăŋ
exist	one	day	at_time	REL	Maid	PN	3PL	go	govern

kab	lug	txug	tsev,	Nkauj	MimSee	txhaj	moog	nug	txiv,
ká	lṳ	tsṳ	tsě	ⁿkâu	miʃeŋ	tsʰâ	mǫŋ	nṳ	tsǐ
shop	come	arrive	house	Maid	PN	then	go	ask	father

Yawm	Xeev	Txwjlaug	tas:
ja̤ɨ	sěŋ	tsɨ̂la̤u	tà
Mister	Provincial	Elder	COMP

'So one day, when Maid Mim See and company returned from market and arrived home, Maid Mim See went and asked her father, Mister Provincial Elder,...'

"Txiv!	Luas	pheej	ua	xyaab	ua	ntawv	moog	hlawv	rua
tsǐ	lùa	pʰêŋ	ua	çáŋ	ua	ⁿtăɨ	mǫŋ	l̥ăɨ	tɕua
Father	IMP.PL	repeatedly	do	incese	do	paper	go	burn	to

ntawm	tej	toj	ntxaas,	hab	thov	nam	thov	txiv	paab	nua,
ⁿtaɨ	tê	tô	ⁿtsàŋ	há	tʰɔ̌	na̤	tʰɔ̌	tsǐ	páŋ	nua
at	PL	hill	grave	and	beg	mother	beg	father	help	DEM:1

luas	nam	hab	luas	txiv	puas	rov	qaab	lug	paab
lùa	na̤	há	lùa	tsǐ	pùa	tʂǒ	qáŋ	lṳ	páŋ
IMP.PL	mother	and	IMP.PL	father	Q	return	back	come	help

quas-tag?"
qùa-ta̤
EUPH-real

'"Father, if people repeatedly burn incense and paper by the graves, and ask their mother and father to help, will their mother and father really return to help them?"'

Yawm	Xeev	Txwjlaug	kuj	qha	ncaaj		tas:
jɑ̰ɨ	seŋ	tsɨ̂lɑ̰u	kû	qʰa	ⁿcâŋ		tà
Mister	Provincial	Elder	also	tell	be_straight		COMP

'Mister Provincial Elder answered directly, saying...'

"Nkauj	MimSee!	Kev	muab	xyaab	muab	ntawv	hlawv	thov
ⁿkâu	mḭseŋ	kě	múa	çáŋ	múa	ⁿtǎɨ	lǎɨ	tʰǒ
Maid	PN	way	take	incese	take	paper	burn	beg

yeej	yog	txuj	kev	zoo	kawg	kws	tsimnyog	suavdlaawg
jêŋ	jo̰	tsû	kě	ʒoŋ	kɑ̰ɨ	kɨ	tsḭɲo̰	sŭatlɑ̰ɨ
always	be	CLF	way	good	end	REL	worthy	everybody

ua	huas!
ua	hùa
do	FP

'Maid Mim See, petitioning by burning incense and paper is always a good practice that ought to be performed by everyone!'

Yog	tug	twg	tau	ua	lawm,	tug	ntawd	yeej	yuav
jo̰	tṵ	tɨ̰	tau	ua	lɑ̰ɨ	tṵ	ⁿtǎɨ	jêŋ	jŭa
be	clf	Q	ACHEIVED	do	COMPL	CLF	that	always	want

tau	zoo	neej	ib	nub	yaav	tom	ntej."
tau	ʒoŋ	nêŋ	í	nú	jăŋ	to̰	ⁿtê
get	good	human	one	day	time_period	there_at	front

'Should anyone have done this, that person will definitely obtain a good estate one day in the future.'

Thaus	Nkauj	MimSee	nov	nwg	txiv	has	qha	le	nuav,
tʰàu	ⁿkâu	mḭseŋ	nǒ	nɨ̰	tsɨ̌	hà	qʰa	le	nŭa
at_time	Maid	PN	hear	3SG	father	speak	tell	as	DEM:1

nwg	txawm	txaus	sab,	hab	xaav	tas
nɨ	tsɑ̰ɨ	tsàu	ʃá	há	săŋ	tà
3SG	thus	be_enough	liver	and	think	COMP

'When Maid Mim See heard her father say this, she was satisfied and thought that:'

ua	caag	los	yawm	tuabneeg	kws	puab	pheej	taug	kev
ua	caŋ	lò	jaɨ	túaneŋ	kɨ	púa	pʰêŋ	tau̯	kĕ
do	how	FOC	man	person	REL	3PL	repeatedly	follow	road

moog	pum	nyob	nraag	qaab	zog	yuav	zoo	neej
mɔŋ	pṵ	ɲó	ⁿtsa̰ŋ	qa̰ŋ	ʒo̰	jŭa	ʒoŋ	nêŋ
go	see	be	down_at	bottom	village	want	good	human

ib	nub	xwb.
í	nṵ́	sɨ́
one	day	just

'…come what may, the man which they always saw at the bottom of the village while following the road must one day obtain a good estate.'

Cais	nwg	txawm	moog	nrhav,	hab	yuav	yuav	NujSisLoob
cài	nɨ̰	tsa̰ɨ	mɔŋ	ⁿtʂʰǎ	há	jŭa	jŭa	nûʃlóŋ
Then	3SG	thus	go	seek	and	want	marry	PN

ua	quasyawg.
ua	qùaja̰ɨ
do	husband

'So she went seeking him, and wanted to marry Nuj Sis Loob as her husband.'

Alice Vittrant and Justin Watkins
Guidelines for the description of Mainland Southeast Asian languages

Each author who contributed to the volume was provided with a suggested plan covering the following comprehensive overview of the linguistic features which form the basis for considering Mainland Southeast Asia (hereafter MSEA) to be a linguistic area. From the outset, we hoped that chapters with similarly organized content would make for better comparison between languages and allow common linguistic features to appear more prominently.

Enfield (2005) is a useful summary of the linguistic features of the Mainland Southeast Asian linguistic area, as is Matisoff (1986b). Much of the data upon which Matisoff and Enfield base their accounts was presented in an earlier comparative typological survey by Eugénie Henderson (1965) which catalogues a wide range of linguistic features in 59 languages including languages of Mainland Southeast Asia and further afield in the region. Henderson includes all the languages represented in this volume, with the exception Min Chinese and Khumi, though she does include other Chinese languages (Cantonese, Mandarin and Hakka) and other Chin languages (Tiddim and Lushai).

Henderson (1965: 401) notes: 'In the course of investigations extending over many years into the present phonological and grammatical structure of a variety of languages in the Southeast Asian mainland, my attention has, however, inescapably been drawn to a number of features which suggest themselves as characteristic of the area.'

1 Phonology

The common phonological features observed in languages of the MSEA area are complex vowel systems (such as diphthongs, a large number of contrasting vowel qualities, contrastive vowel length), tone or register (or mixed) systems,

---

Alice Vittrant: Aix-Marseille Université/CNRS
E-Mail: alice.vittrant@cnrs.fr
Justin Watkins: SOAS, University of London
E-Mail: jw2@soas.ac.uk

particular syllabification patterns (restricted set of final consonants, restrictions on syllable-intial consonant clusters, 'minor' and 'major' syllables) (Henderson 1965: 401–402, Enfield 2005: 186 ff).

Henderson (1965) catalogues a number of phonological features in her typological survey, and she notes the following ways in which these shared phonological features may be correlated and associated with some grammatical functions (p. 406). She, for instance, reports correlations between pitch, phonation and the morphological use of the tone for languages such as Burmese, Southern Vietnamese and Boro (p. 412).

1.1 Suprasegmental phonology: tone and register

Henderson (1965) also notes correlations between the presence or absence of tone, initial and final consonant patterns, vowel quality and phonation type, all phenomena that have become well known from studies on tonogenesis[1].

> "In the beginning was the Sino-Tibetan monosyllable, arrayed in its full consonantal and vocalic splendor. And the syllable was without tone and devoid of pitch. And monotony was on the face and the mora. And the Spirit of Change hovered over the segments flanking the syllabic nucleus. And Change said: 'Let the consonant guarding the vowel to the left and the right contribute some of the phonetic features to the vowel in the name of selfless intersegmental love, even if the consonants thereby be themselves diminished and lose some of their own substance. For their decay or loss will be the sacrifice through which Tone will be brought into the worlds, that linguists in some future time may rejoice. And it was so. And the Language saw it was good, and gradually began to exploit tonal differences for distinguishing utterances [...] And the tones were fruitful and multiplied, and diffused from tongue to tongue in the Babel of Southeast Asia." Matisoff (1973: 73)

In many languages of the area, contrastive pitches (tone) and phonation types (register) must be examined together. For instance, in Northern Vietnamese the *hỏi* tone is realized with breathy phonation whereas *ngã* and *nặng* tones are re-

---

1 The interaction of initials, syllable-types, and tones in Asian languages and within the Tibeto-Burman linguistic family has been described by Haudricourt 1961, Matisoff 1973, 1990, Bradley 1978, Brunelle & Kirby 2015 *inter alia*. To summarize, diachronic sources for lexical tones in Asian languages are essentially final and initial consonants, with some loss of vocalic phonemes (Michaud 2011).

alized with creaky phonation, sometimes described as glottalization (see Do-Hurinville & Dao, this volume). The Mong Leng tone system also shows the interaction of pitch and phonation.

Table 1: Mong Leng Tone system
Adapted from Mortensen (2004) and Mortensen (this volume)

(1) tib [ti55] 'to pile' /(M)H/ very high rising
    tij [ti52] 'older brother' /HL/ high falling
    tiv [ti35] 'to endure' /MH/ (high) rising
    tig [tʰi̤21] 'to turn' /MLɦ/ low falling breathy
    ti   [ti44] 'close' /M/ high-mid level, 'chanted voice quality'
    tis [ti22] 'wing' /L/ low-mid level
    tim [tḭʔ21] 'because' /MLʔ/ low falling creaky, sometimes with final stop

The Burmese tone system is another good illustration of a system which mixes tonal and phonation type features.

Table 2: Description of the Burmese tone system (adapted from Bradley 1982: 160)

Traditional Name	Pitch contour	Length	Phonation	Duration
'creaky'	high	short	creaky	less long
'even'	low-growing	long	clear (or normal voice)	fairly long
'heavy'	low (or middle)	long (or longer)	slightly breathy	very long
'killed' (with glottal constriction)	very high	very short	normal	short

1.2 Segmental phonemes: consonants and vowels

1.2.1 Consonants

We find in MSEA languages that certain patterns prevail in the inventory of initial consonants: the presence or absence of aspiration, patterns of voicing contrasts in consonants, including pre-glottalization and prenasalization, and the presence or absence of velar vs. uvular consonants. For instance, the Mon initial consonant inventory contains aspirated consonants beside plain stops, but no phonemic voicing contrast; the implosives ɗ and ɓ are pronounced as fully voiced implosive or preglottalized stops.

Table 3a: Initial consonant in Mon
Adapted from Jenny (this volume)

	k	kh	ŋ	
ɕ	c	ch	ɲ	hɲ
ɗ	t	th	n	hn
ɓ	p	ph	m	hm
y	r	l	hl	w
hw	s	ʃ	h	ʔ

Table 3b: Possible clusters in Mon

ky	kr	kl	kw
khy	khr	khl	khw
py	pr	pl	
phy	phr	phl	

As for prenasalized consonants, the Mong Leng set of initial consonants includes plain and aspirated ones, contrasting also velar and uvular consonants.

Table 4: Mong Leng consonant onset – from Mortensen (this volume)

		labial	labial cluster	dental	dental cluster	dental	postalveolar	palatal	retroflex	velar	uvular	glottal
Oral	plain	p	pl	t	tl	ts	tʃ	c	tṣ	k	q	ʔ
	asp	pʰ	pʰl	tʰ	tʰl	tsʰ	tʃʰ	cʰ	tṣʰ	kʰ	qʰ	
prenasal	plain	ⁿp	ⁿpl	ⁿt	ⁿtl	ⁿts	ⁿtʃ	ⁿc	ⁿtṣ	ⁿk	ⁿq	
	asp	ⁿpʰ	ⁿpʰl	ⁿtʰ	ⁿtʰl	ⁿtsʰ	ⁿtʃʰ	ⁿcʰ	ⁿtṣʰ	ⁿkʰ	ⁿqʰ	
nasal		m				n		ɲ		(ŋ)		
fricative	vless	f				s	ʃ	ç				h
	vcd						ʒ	ʝ				
lateral	vless				ɬ							
	vcd				l							

In general, we find highly constrained patterns of initial consonant clusters. In Mon (Table 3b), initial clusters are allowed only with a velar or labial stop in first position and a liquid in second position. Whereas in Pwo-Karen, the C2 inventory is reduced to liquid consonants only (table 5).

Table 5: Possible combinations of C1 and C2 in Pwo-Karen – From Kato (this volume)

		p	θ	t	c	k	ʔ	ph	th	ch	kh	b	d	x	h	m	n	j	l
C2	w	+	+	+	+	+	+		+	+	+	+	+	+	+	+	+	+	+
	l	+		+	+				+	+				+					
	r	+		+															
	j	+			+						+					+			+

Final consonants are also highly restricted and final consonant clusters are extremely rare in the area. In Pwo-Karen, only the uvular nasal /ɴ/ can occur syllable-finally, whereas in Burmese the final consonants p, t, k are all realized as a glottal stop together with a change in the vowel quality (2) and the nasal final consonants m, n, ɲ, ŋ nasalize the vowel of the rhyme or become a homorganic consonant (3).

Burmese
(2)   a. တပ်   b. တတ်   c. တက်   d. လပ်   e. လတ်   f. လက်
WB   <tap>   <tat>   <tak>   <lap>   <lat>   <lak>
Transc.   taʔ   taʔ   tɛʔ   laʔ   laʔ   lɛʔ
            'fix, attach'   'be skilled'   'go up'   'be vacant'   'be fresh'   'hand'

(3)   ဆင်း   [sʰiːn⁵²]   /shiɴ³/   'to go down, descend'
       ဆင်းပါ   [sʰiːm⁵² ba²²]   /shiɴ³ Paʔ/   'Please go down'
       ဆင်းတာ   [sʰiːn⁵² da²²]   /shiɴ³ Taʔ/   '(the fact) X go/went down'
       ဆင်းခဲ့   [sʰiːŋ⁵² gɛ⁵⁵]   /shiɴ³ Khɛ¹/   'went down (+ change of situation)'

To summarize, final consonants generally form a smaller set, with an absence or a neutralization of contrasts, although Mon-Khmer languages may show a higher and unusual number of contrastive and distinctive final consonants. For instance, Kri syllables show a three-way contrast for oral sonorant finals (cf. (4)a,b,c) and distinguishes between phonetically similar checked palatal stop final [c̚] and post-glottalized palatal glide [jʔ] (Enfield & Diffloth 2009: 18).

Kri (Mon-Khmer Language, Laos) – from Enfield and Diffloth (2009)
(4)   Voiced   Checked   Voiceless
     a.   tˀɔːj   'tail'   tˀɔːjʔ   'bowl'   tˀɔːj̥   'to follow, to chase'
     b.   camaːl   'shiny'   ʔumaːlʔ   'to hunt'   da̤l   'to bounce'
     c.   kaʋər   'stir'   kaʋˀərʔ   'embrace'   tar̥   'to run out of workspace'
     d.   kʰaːj   'tree sp.'   kʰa̰ːjʔ   '1SG.'   kʰaːj̥   'to escape'

e. ɓa:cʼ   mushroom   ɓa:jʔ   salt
f. ʔə:cʼ   go   kə:jʔ   head hair
g. ha:cʼ   slippery   ha:jʔ   To strip

1.2.2 On vowel systems

In the vowel systems of MSEA languages, languages have generally large inventories of contrasting vowel qualities as in Khmer (see Haiman, this volume), in some cases including back unrounded vowels [ɯ] and contrastive vowel length — as in Thai (table 7) —, in addition to characteristic diphthongs.

Vowel contrasts may correlate with tone and register systems as in Burmese where the creaky and killed tones despite their similarities in terms of duration, pitch and phonation type, are not easily confused thanks to the vowel realization (Watkins 2000: 144 ff).

Table 6: Phonetic realizations of the vowels /i/ and /ɔ/ according to tone in Burmese

	low tone	high tone	creaky tone	'killed' tone
/i/	[mi:²²]	[mi:⁵²]	[mḭ⁵⁵]	[mjɪʔ]
	မိ (Name)	မီး 'fire'	မိ 'mother'	မြစ် 'river'

/ɔ/	[mɔ:²²]	[mɔ:⁵²]	[mɔ̰⁵⁵]	[mauʔ]
	မော့ 'look up'	မော 'tired'	မော့ 'tilt up'	မောက် 'haughty'

Table 7 provides a comparison of the vowel systems of some languages in and outside the MSEA area. Thai and Burmese show a four-way distinction in vowel height, and are part of the MSEA *Sprachbund*. Arakanese — a Burmese dialect spoken in the western part of Burma, therefore on the edge of the MSEA *Sprachbund* — has fewer vowel-height distinctions than Standard (or Central) Burmese.

Interestingly, comparing Burmese dialects with other Tibeto-Burman languages such as Central Tibetan or Meitei shows that there are fewer vowel-height distinctions in the latter languages. Thus, apart from Kham dialects which have rich vowel systems and are spoken on the edge of the MSEA area, Amdo dialects and other Tibetic dialects such as Balti (5 vowels), Sherpa (7 vowels) and Ladhaki, have generally fewer vowels. Generally speaking, the further west these languages are spoken, the fewer vowels they have.

Table 7: Comparison of simple vowel systems

Thai[2] (Tai-Kadai)			Burmese[3] (Tibeto-Burman, within MSEA)			Arakanese (Tibeto-Burman, west of MSEA)			Standard Tibetan[4] (Tibeto-Burman, outside MSEA)			Meithei[5] (Tibeto-Burman, outside MSEA)		
i	ɯ	u	i		u	i		u	i/y		u	i		u
e	ɤ	o	e		o	e	ə	o	e/ø		o	e	ə	o
ɛ		ɔ	ɛ		ɔ			ɔ	ɛ					
	ə			ə			a			a			a	
	a			a										

1.3 Syllable structure

In general, the languages of the MSEA have monosyllabic morphemes; additionally, sesquisyllabic syllable structures — i.e. a prevocalic consonant or consonant cluster considered as a half syllable (Henderson 1952: 170, Matisoff 1973: 86)— are a characteristic feature of many languages.

Some authors define a sesquisyllabe as any disyllabic word with a reduced number of contrasts in the initial syllable, while a more restrictive definition of sesquisyllabes describes them as 'one and half syllables', comprising an initial minor syllable with a neutral vowel or a syllabic consonant. The examples in (5) are from Stieng.

Stieng (from Bon 2014: 87)
(5) a. [gə.naː]   often reduced to   [gnaː]   *'together'*
    c. [mə.rac]   often reduced to   [mrac]   *'chilly'*
    b. [trə.saj]   often reduced to   [təsaj]   *'vein'*
    d. [kən.cian] often reduced to   [ncian]   *'ring'*
    e. [kə-sɔw]   reduced to   [kʰsɔw]   *'to show'*

---

2 From Jenny (this volume, chapter on Thai). Note that the Thai vowel system shows also a length distinction, leading to a larger set of vowels.
3 From Vittrant (this volume, chapter on Burmese).
4 From Tournadre (1996: 57).
5 From Chelliah (1997: 21).

Many languages contrast major vs. minor syllables in some way (Butler 2015); often minor syllables have greater restrictions on initial consonant clusters (Pittayaporn 2015), and may make use of a smaller subset of vowels. Henderson (1952) described Khmer as having a class of monosyllables with extended onsets which was distinct from a class of disyllables consisting of a 'minor' syllable followed by a major one, as shown in (6).

Khmer word structure (from Henderson 1952)
(6) a. simple monosyllable   ដេក [deːk]   'sleep'
    b. extended monosyllable   ផ្ដេក [pʰdeːk]   'to put to bed'
    c. minor disyllable   បន្ដេក [bɔn.deːk] 'go to bed'

2 Morphology

2.1 Word structure

The generally monosyllabic morphemes of MSEA languages can rarely be extended with affixational morphology; derivational compounding prevails. One exception is the Mon-Khmer family where most languages make use of prefixes (or infixes) —although few of them are productive. Examples of Mon-Khmer affixational morphology are given in (7).

Tibeto-Burman languages spoken in the Indosphere[6] area have extensive suffixing as shown by Khumi sentence in (8).

(7) a. Wa (Mon-Khmer)[7]: g- prefixation
        lang   > g-lang   raɯʔ   > g-raɯʔ
        'long' > 'this long' 'deep' > 'this deep'

---

6 The labels *Indosphere* and *Sinosphere*, coined by Matisoff 1991, encapsulate the view that Tibeto-Burman languages can be divided into two types according to their grammatical features, a typological classification correlating with geography. Languages of the first type (complex morphology, extensive suffixing, polysyllabic words) are found mainly in South Asia, while languages of the second type (simpler morphology, verb serialization, prefixation, compounding, occasional onset clustering (sesquisyllabism)) are more commonly found in Mainland Southeast Asia.
7 From Watkins, this volume.

b. Stieng (Mon-Khmer)[8]: nominalizing infix -n-
 pu:s   > p-ən-u:s   cɛ:h   > c-ən-ɛ:h   par   > p-ən-ar
 'sweep' > 'broom'   'old'   > 'old age'   'fly'   > 'feather'

Khumi (Tibeto-burman), from Peterson (2005 [2002])
(8) kaay   móey=loe   phayloeeyng=moe   ang-ke-tlaw-noe-te-ba
    1S   eye=TOP   ant=DEF   1/2O-bite-LARGEO-NMZL-EVID-EVAL

noe=piee-te
QUOT=say-EVID
'"The ant bit me in the eye!" he said to her.'

The following types of nominal compounding listed by Suriya (1988), are found in most languages of the area — as well as other types of compounds. Adjective compounds (for those languages that have a distinct syntactic adjective category) or verbal compounds are also common.

Table 8: Compounding in three Southeast Asian languages

	Stieng[9]	Vietnamese	Yongning Na (Mosuo)[10]
N-N compounds with antonyms	• [mej-moəm] 'parents' *father-mother*	• nắng mưa 'bad weather' *sunlight-rain*	• zɔ³³-mu³³ 'child' *son-daughter*
	• [dəəh-ŋa:j] 'distance' *close-far*	• may rủi 'chance' *luck – misfortune*	• kʰɯ³¹.tsʰɯ¹³-lɔ⁵⁵-kʰɤ³³ 'limbs' *foot – hand*
N-N compounds with quasi-synonyms	• [miar-srej] 'land' *field-paddy*	• miệng mồm 'be very talkative' *mouth-mouth*	
	• [ʔuɲ-mbul] 'lamp' *fire- bulb*	• kiểu cách 'affected" *manner-way*	
N-N compounds comprising	• [təəm-pa:s] 'coton tree' *trunk-coton*	• cây cam 'orange tree' *tree-orange*	• sɯ³³-dzɯ³¹ 'tree' 'tree' *wood-CLF.tree*

---

8 Adapted from Bon (2014).
9 Adapted from Bon (2014).
10 Adapted from Lidz (2010).

	Stieng[11]	Vietnamese	Yongning Na (Mosuo)[12]
generic N + specific N	• [təm-pret] 'banana tree' *trunk-banana*	• cây táo 'apple tree' *tree-apple*	• nɤ³¹-lɯ³³ 'soybean' *soy-CLF.kernel*
V-V compounds / Adj-Adj compounds	• [boək-sʔuəc] 'kindness' *white-black*	• béo mập 'be fat' *greasy-fat*	• lɔ³¹-yĩ³³-ʐu³¹-yĩ³³ 'to work' *to labor-to work*
	• [roək-saː] 'earn one's living' *look.for-eat*	• bao bọc 'to enclose' *to cover-support*	

2.2 Psycho-collocations

Psycho-collocations are a semantic field in which many MSEA languages can form distinctive compounds. These compounds typically pair a part of the body with a stative verb to express an emotion or feeling. They were termed 'psycho-collocations' by Matisoff (1986a).

The following authors have described psycho-collocations in particular languages: VanBik (1998) for Hakha Lai; Oey (1990) for Malay, Jaisser (1990) for White Hmong, Vittrant (2014) for Burmese.

Malay, from Nomoto & Soh, this volume
(9) a. besar hati   'glad, big heart'
        big – liver
    b. kepala besar   'proud'
        head – big
    c. besar *mulut*   'brag'
        big-mouth

Cham, from Brunelle & Phu, this volume
(10) a. prɔ̃ŋ taj   'reckless, foolhardy'
        large-liver
     b. prɔ̃ŋ kɔʔ   'arrogant'
        large-head
     c. sam taj   'good hearted'
        beautiful-liver

---

11 Adapted from Bon (2014).
12 Adapted from Lidz (2010).

2.3 Elaborate expressions

'Elaborate expressions' are a characteristic feature of many MSEA languages. They are structures – often quadrisyllabic – with an aesthetic component typically involving patterns of symmetry, rhyme, alliteration, repetition and so-on. General accounts of the phenomenon can be found in Enfield (2005: 189) and Matisoff (1986b: 76–77). Williams (2014) is collection of accounts of the use of phonaesthetics and sound symbolism in elaborate expressions in MSEA languages, including general overviews of the phenomenon in Austroasiatic (Sidwell 2014) and Tai (Hudak 2014). General overviews of the languages of this volume are also included in Williams (2014): Haiman's and Watkins' contributions are dedicated respectively to Khmer and Wa, two Mon-khmer languages, Wheatley and Peterson focus on Burmese and Khumi (Tibeto-Burman languages), and Wilaiwan's contribution describes the phenomenon in Thai. Mong Leng elaborate expressions are described in detail in Mortensen (2003).

This characteristic feature has been studied in other Mon-Khmer (Migliazza 2005), Tai-Kadai (Wayland 1996, Compton 2007) and Southeast Asian languages in general (Watson 2001).

Thai, from Jenny, this volume

(11) a. สะดวกสบาย 'convenient'
        sədùək-səbaay
        convenient-comfortable'
    b. กินข้าวกินปลา 'eat'
        kin-khâaw-kin-plaa
        consume-rice-consume-fish

Southern Min, from Chappell, this volume

(12) a. *chui³-chio³-bak⁸-chio³* 喙笑目笑 'beaming radiantly'
        mouth-smile-eye-smile
    b. *gong⁷-bin⁷-gong⁷-bin⁷* 憨面憨面 'kind of stupid-faced'
        simple-face (x 2)
    c. *ang⁵-ang⁵* 紅紅 'sort of red, reddish'
        red (x 2)
    d. *sui²-sui²* 美美 'beautiful'
        beautiful (x 2)

In part related to the grammatical function of aesthetics in MSEA languages, reduplication in particular plays a grammatical role in several languages of the area. See for instance Min example in (12)b where reduplication code the approximate meaning 'rather X', and Malay example, where reduplication plays many different functions according to the stem category.

Table 9: Reduplication in Indonesian; examples adapted from Grange (2006).

Reduplication function	Syntactic category reduplicated	Simple form	reduplicated form
plural of nouns	N	pokok 'tree'	pokok pokok 'trees'
		anak 'child'	anak anak 'children'
plurality of action (iterativity, continuation)	V	datang 'to come'	datang-datang 'to come all (of them)' [several event of coming]
		ber-lompat 'to jump'	berlompat-lompat 'to hop'
		mem-baca 'read'	membaca-baca 'to leaf through'
		ber-teriak 'shout'	berteriak-teriak 'shout several times'
formation of adverb	V (or V_{adj})	cepat 'quick'	cepat cepat 'quickly'
		betul 'be true'	betul-betul 'truly, really'
intensification	V (or V_{adj})	sakit 'ill'	sakit- sakit 'very ill'

3 Grammar and Syntax

In this section, we introduce a few basic facts about the noun phrase (§ 3.1) and the verb phrase (§ 3.2), and then move on to basic sentence structures (§ 3.3).

3.1 Nominal domain

This section sets out to describe some of the main features of noun phrases (NP) in the language studied, giving the basic structure of the NP, and how demonstratives, definiteness and number are expressed.

3.1.1 Basic structure of the NP

Figure 1 shows the basic structure of the Burmese NP. The big brackets represent the available ordered slots in the NP, while the small brackets represent optional items which may be expressed within each slot. In Burmese, which is a final verb language, modifiers of the noun precede it, whereas information about number, such as plurality, classifier phrase, quantifiers, follow it.

Figure 1: The structure of the noun phrase in Burmese

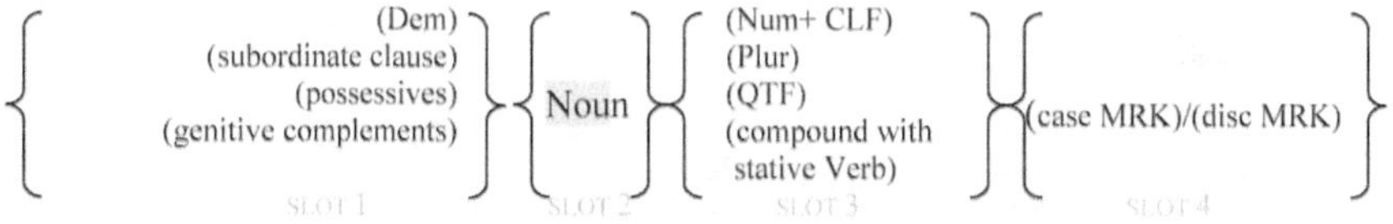

{ (Dem) / (subordinate clause) / (possessives) / (genitive complements) } { Noun } { (Num+ CLF) / (Plur) / (QTF) / (compound with stative Verb) } { (case MRK)/(disc MRK) }

SLOT 1   SLOT 2   SLOT 3   SLOT 4

In contrast, in the Mon-Khmer language Wa the noun always appears in the first slot, with modifiers following it.

Figure 2: The structure of Wa NP

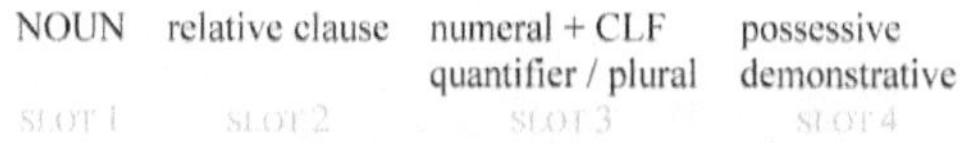

NOUN   relative clause   numeral + CLF   possessive
                         quantifier / plural   demonstrative
SLOT 1   SLOT 2   SLOT 3   SLOT 4

Related to the basic structure of the NP is a comparison of word order in languages of the area. The table (10) summarizes what is frequently found in the different linguistic families, or sub-groups[13].

Table 10: Constituents order (cf. Enfield 2003: 52)

	Mon-Khmer	Tai-Kadai	Hmong-Mien	Chinese languages	Tibeto-Burman
(S) VO	+	+	+	+	−
Prepositions	+	+	+	±	−
Comparative	+	+	+	±	−
Head-modifier	+	+	+	−	±
Noun-genitive	+	±	+	−	−
Possessee-possessor	+	+	−	−	−
Num-CLF-N	+		+	+	
N- Num-CLF	+	+			+

---

13 See also Pinnow (1960).

(13) a. Vietnamese
hai quyên sách lón này
2 CLF **book** big DEM
'These two big books.'

b. Thai
หนังสือใหญ่สองเล่มนี้
náŋsɯ̌ɯ yày sɔ̌ɔŋ lêm nîi
book big 2 CLF DEM
'These two big books.'

c. Burmese
အဒီစာအုပ်ကြီး နှစ်အုပ်
ʔɛ.dî² sa².ʔoʔ Cí³ n̥iə ʔoʔ
DEM.ANAPH **book** big 2 CLF
'These two big books.'

3.1.2 Classifier device

Classifier devices differ from one language to another, even in the Southeast Asian area where languages share so many structural features. The classifiers (sortal classifiers or measure term) may be obligatorily or optionally used with numeral, demonstrative or in genitive constructions.

Cham (from Brunelle & Phu, this volume)
(14) klɔ̆w ɓɔh ɲĭn năn
three CLF bowls DEM
'Those three bowls.'

(15) klɔ̆w ɲĭn thĕj năn
three bowls rice DEM
'Those three bowls of rice.'

The number of classifiers in a language's repertoire ranges from dozens of forms to less than ten. For instance, Min dialects (see Chappell, this volume) or Yongning Na (see Lidz, this volume) have around 40 true individuating classifiers, excluding measure words and collective nouns that may appear in the same slot. On the other side, Khumi speakers commonly use very few, lacking even a specific classifier for animals (see Peterson, this volume).

Some languages make extensive use of them, not only in quantifier phrases but also in contexts where individuation of the referent is required. Thus, classifiers may be required in nominal phrase containing a demonstrative, such as in (14) and (15).

They may also occur in bare classifier constructions without a numeral, expressing definiteness or indefiniteness (16) and finally they can have an anaphoric function (17), or be used to form indefinite expressions (18).

Chinese Wu (from Li & Bisang 2012: 336)
(16) kɣ   lɔpan   ma   lə   **bu**   tsʰotsʰɔ
     CLF   boss   buy   PFV   **CLF**   **car**
     'The boss [/*a boss] bought a car [/*the car.]'

Cham (from Brunelle & Phu, this volume)
(17) **klɔ̆w** **nɨʔ** paj sĭt ɓăŋ ka-rot, mĭn ha **nɨʔ** çɔh k̥ĕj.
     three CLF rabbit small eat carrot, but one **CLF** break tooth
     'Three small rabbits eat carrots, but one breaks a tooth.'

Burmese (from Vittrant, this volume)
(18) a. တစ်အုပ်အုပ် ယူပါ။   တစ်ယောက်ယောက် ဖြေနိုင်မလား။
     tə-ʔoʔ-ʔoʔ   yu² =Pa²   tə-yaɔʔ-yaɔʔ   phye² naiN² =mə la³
     one-CLF$_{book}$.REDUP take=POL one-CFL$_{human}$..REDUP answer CAN =IRR QST
     'Take **some** book or other.' 'Could **someone** answer [this question]?'

Grinevald (1999, 2000, 2007) and Aikhenvald (2000) give a general account of nominal classification devices. Jones (1970), Goral (1978), Bisang (1999), and Simpson (2005) write on Southeast Asian classifier systems. Language-specific accounts include Bisang (1993) on Hmong, Vogel (2002) on Khmer, Vittrant (2002 [2005]) on Burmese, or Somsonge (2007) on Tai-Kadai languages, *inter al.*

3.2 Verbal domain

3.2.1 No inflection

MSEA languages are well-known for their lack of inflection (see Enfield 2005: 188). They usually do not encode tense, that is to say tense is not a category which is obligatorily expressed in the VP. However, languages may be able to deploy non-obligatory morphemes to express tense and other aspectual/modal distinctions.

Similarly, number is frequently not obligatorily encoded or required in MSEA languages, although many languages do have a way to express number distinctions in the VP.

Burmese (from Vittrant, p.c.)
(19) ကလေးတွေ နားထောင်ကြ။
     kəle³   -Twe²   na² TɔɔN²   =Ca¹   Ø
     children   -PLUR   listen   =PLUR   (IMP)
     'Hey kids! Listen!'

Mon (from Jenny, this volume)
(20) ကောန်ဉာဴအာဘာအိုတ်ရ။
     kon.ɲàc   ʔa   phɛ̀ə   ʔɒt   raʔ
     child   go   school   all   FOC
     'The children have (all) gone to school.'

3.2.2 Verbal Categories

Aspect and mode are the categories most usually expressed inside the VP in MSEA languages, frequently by means of a pre- or post-verbal auxiliaries (Goddard 2005: 109, 119 ff).

Here are some current examples of grammaticalized verbs in MSEA languages, including the famous 'GET' auxiliary (see Enfield 2003, 2005; Van der Auwera et al. 2009) with a pre-verbal and a post-verbal meaning as in Stieng.

Stieng (from Bon 2014)
(21) a. paŋ   **ɓaːn**   laːn   muaj
         3   **get/obtain**   car   a
         'He got a car.'

     b. hej   ɲɔp   **ɓaːn**   muaj
         1SG   catch   ASP: RESULT   a
         'I got one.'

     c. **ɓaːn**   bəːh   gɔk   waŋ   Tɛːh-Dɔm
         MOD.DEONTIC   come   live   village   TD
         'I [got to/could] come to TD village.'

- to get, to obtain > potential modality, resultative/perfect aspect
- to put, to set > completed/ resultative aspect
- to give > causative, benefactive > preposition (see (22))
- to finish > perfective/ complete aspect > conjunction/temporal subordinator
- to go ~ to come (and other directional verbs) => allative/venitive, laudative/malefactive, aspect
- to see/ to watch > temptative & success, as in "she tries a skirt" vs. "she tries to wear a skirt" (without succeeding). See in (24) and (27).
- to stay, remain > progressive and continuous, durative aspects: different aspectual meanings depending on the category of verbs : stative vs. nonstative. See for instance Watanabe (2005), Romeo (2008 : 108ff).

Vietnamese (adapted from Do-Hurinville 2008).
(22) a. Paul mua **cho** Mary cuốn sách này.
       Paul buy **give** Mary CLF   book DEM
       'Paul bought this book and gave (it) to Mary.'

   b. Paul mua cuốn sách này **cho**   Mary ...
      Paul buy CLF   book DEM **give/BEN** Mary
      'Paul bought this book for Mary...'

   c. Paul mua cuốn sách này **cho**   Mary đọc.
      Paul buy CLF   book DEM **give/BEN** Mary read
      'Paul bought this book so that Mary read it.'

The verb ហើយ *haeuj* 'finish' in the Khmer example (23)a indicates the completion of an event. It also functions as a sequential clausal conjunction (see (23)b).

Khmer (from Haiman, this volume)
(23) a. វាខានជឹកទឹកត្នោតយូរណាស់មកហើយ។
       via kha:n pheuk teuk tnaot ju: nah mau:k   haeuj
       3   miss drink juice palm long.time very come:DIR finish:PERF
       'He had missed drinking palm syrup for a very long time already.'

   b. គាត់លូកដៃទៅក្នុងថង់យាមហើយដកលុយមួយរៀលមក។
      koat lu:k daj tev knong thawng jiam haeuj   daw:k
      3   reach hand go in   knapsack   finish:CONJ remove

luj muaj rial mau:k
money one rial come:DIR
'He reached into his knapsack and took out a one *riel* piece.'

Cham (from Brunelle & Phu, this volume)
(24) a. l̥ă? ʔjŏ̆? tivi.
   1PS watch television
   'I watch television.'

  b. l̥ă? wă? ră? ʔjŏ̆?.
   1PS write letter TAM:watch
   'I try to write a letter.'

Further accounts of these grammaticalizing processes may be read in Smeall (1975), Matisoff (1991), and Heine & Kuteva (2003).

3.2.3 Serial verb constructions (SVC)

Serial verb constructions (SVC) are a key feature of the verb systems of many MSEA languages. The key feature of SVCs is that two or more verbs combine to form, to a greater or lesser extent, a single verbal predicate. Aikhenvald & Dixon (2006) note that this is done "without any overt marker of coordination, subordination or syntactic dependency of any sort." See also Foley and Olson (1985), Durie (1997: 290).

The main features of a SVC are that the component verbs express a single event, sharing tense, aspect, modality and polarity. They must share at least one argument, and can have only one subject. None of the verbs of an SVC can be the syntactic argument of another verb of the SVC. A SVC comprises a single intonational phrase and the component elements may display other forms of phonological juncture. Frequently, SVCs are grammaticalized or lexicalized. Depending on the word order preferred in a language, certain elements in the SVC may become more prepositional and less verbal in their function.

However, in certain cases, an SVC may possess only some of the features just described.

While SVCs are clearly an areal characteristic of MSEA languages, the details vary from language to language.

Mon (from Jenny, this volume)
(25) ကၠိုဂြိပ်ဒတိတ်အာနှကိုကၠံ။
    klʋ   **krìp**   **tèə**   **tɛt**   ʔa   nù   kʋ   klɔʔ.
    dog   **run**   **run.away**   **go.out**   GO   SRC   OBL   garden
    'The dog ran away out of the garden.'

In general, it is possible to distinguish between 'symmetrical' SVCs which are time-iconic, and refer to sequential actions which constitute one event or the various phases of a single event (26) and 'asymmetrical' SVCs where a certain element or elements have undergone grammaticalization (27) or lexicalization (28).

The possibilities are further explored in Aikhenvald & Dixon (2006), Bisang (1991), Bisang (1996), Durie (1997), Vittrant (2006, 2012), Diller (2006).

Thai (from Jenny, this volume)
(26) เขานั่งกินข้าว
    kháw   **nâŋ**   **kin**   khâaw.
    3HUM   **sit**   **eat**   rice
    'He is sitting and eating.'

Wa (from Watkins, this volume)
(27) ʔeʔ   **sum**   **s.mɛ**   ŋʰoʔ   kʰraoʔ   nu̱m   ʔin   **ya̱oʔ**
    1PL.INCL   **plant**   **seed**   rice   new   year   this   **see**
    'We tried planting a new kind of rice this year.'

Burmese (from Vittrant 2012)
(28) ရှေးတုန်းက သားတစ်ယောက် မွေးစားဖူးတယ်။
    ʃe³.TouN³.Ka¹   θa³   tə-yauʔ   **mwe³.Sa³**   Phu³   =Te²
    In the past   son   one-CLFhum   **give birth.eat**   EXPER   =REAL
    'In the past, [he] had adopted a son.'

3.3 Clausal/sentential organization

For most MSEA languages, the basic word order is (S)VO, with the exception of most Tibeto-Burman languages of the area which are verb-final.

Stieng (Mon-Khmer, from Bon 2014)
(29) sədiaŋ-təklɔw   kɑl   cʰɨː
     human   cut.down   tree
     S   V   O
     'A man cuts down a tree.'

Khumi (Tibeto-burman language from Peterson, this volume)
(30) kay¹   h'ni³   ngo¹   abay¹=nö³   s'ra¹⁰=a¹   niw¹
     1S   [DEM   fish   cut=NMLZ   doctor=LOC]   see
     S   O   V
     'I saw the doctor who cut the fish.'

3.3.1 Ellipsis of arguments

In general, arguments already known from the context (or co-text) may be omitted. For instance, in (31) from a dialogue situation, the arguments are retrievable from the speech situation and are therefore not expressed by a linguistic mean. See Tamba-Mecz (1983), Kibrik (2001) on ellipsis of arguments.

Burmese
(31) ပြင်ပေးလိုက်မယ်။
     pyiN²   pe³   lai?   =mɛ²
     repear   give/BENEF   follow/ASP:TERM   =IRR
     '[I] will repair [it] for [you].'

3.3.2 Information Structure

In organizing information in the discourse, MSEA languages are known to be 'topic-prominent', rather than 'subject-prominent'. Unlike in, say, Indo-European languages, no emphasis is put on an argument (subject) by verbal agreement. Rather, MSEA languages give prominence to the topic of the sentence, the argument referred to in new information given by the speaker. Topical arguments are usually fronted as in (32)b, and sometimes external to the clause, but remain semantically connected to rest of the sentence, which can be considered a 'comment' on the topic. See Lambrecht (1984), Krifka (2006) and Goddard (2005: 128ff), *inter alia*.

Pwo Karen (from Kato, this volume)

(32) a. သာအ္စွာ ဒ္ယောဟ် သာခုင်း॥
    θàʔwà   dʊ́   θàkhléiɴ
    Thawa hit Thakhlein
    'Thawa hit Thakhlein.'

b. သာခုင်းကဒ် သာအ္စွာ ဒ္ယောဟ်॥
    θàkhléiɴ   nɔ́   θàʔwà   dʊ́
    Thakhlein TOP Thawa hit
    'As for Thakhlein, Thawa hit (him).'

Mong Leng (from Yaaj and Vaaj, 1985: 9)

(33) Luas   tej   mas   nim   ua   zaam   lab-<quas>vog
    lùa   tê   mà   nį   ua   ʒaŋ   lá-<qùa>vǫ
    IMP.PL PL TOP EMPH do clothing red-EXP<EUPH>
    'The others, they wore clothes of the reddest red.'

The grammaticalization of topic markers from conjunctions seems to be an areal feature observed in, for example, Vietnamese, Hmong, Black Thai (Clark, 1991: 87).

In (34), for instance, the noun *thì* 'time' has been grammaticalized to function as a conjunction and also a topic marker (35).

Vietnamese (from Do-Hurinville & Dao, this volume)

(34) Nếu   trời   đẹp   **thì**   ta   sẽ   đi dạo.
    if   sky   be beautiful CONJ 1PL FUT go for a walk
    'If the weather is beautiful, then we'll go for a walk.'

(35) Tôi   **thì**   tôi   thích   đọc   Balzac.
    1SG TOP 1SG like read Balzac
    'As for me, I like reading Balzac.'

3.3.3 Others

Clark (1985) notes that many SEA languages distinguish between polar 'yes-no' questions and *wh*-questions. Moreover, polar questions may in some cases be formed by the juxtaposition of two alternative positive and negative propositions of the same verb, as in Mandarin Chinese. See for instance Mong Leng questions in (36).

Mongleng (from Mortensen, this volume)
(36) a. Koj   puas   moog?
         kô   pùa   mɔŋ
         2SG   QST   go
         'Are you going?'

   b. Koj   moog   tsi   moog?
       kô   mɔŋ   tʃi   mɔŋ
       2SG   go   NEG   go
       'Are you going?'

   c. Koj   moog   lov?
       kô   mɔŋ   lŏ
       2SG   go   QST
       'You're going, are you?'

MSEA languages have "a penchant for nominalizing whole sentences without embedding them into any larger unit, typically via a particle, which is also used in citation-form verbs, and which has a relative/genitive function in other constructions." (Matisoff 1986b: 78).

In Thulung Rai, a language spoken by about a thousand people in Eastern Nepal (Lahaussois 2003), the morpheme ‹mu-› (and its allomorphs) is used with different functions including citation form, nominalizing and relativization.

Thulung Rai (from Lahaussois, 2003)
(37) a. si-**mu**   b. po-**mu**
         'to die'   'to eat'

(38) make   sinben-**mu**   hapa   much   kam bo-mu   basi
     grain   plant-NMLZ   much   work   make-NMLZ   OBL
     'Planting seed requires a lot of work.'

(39) go   khok-to-**m**   dzam   brɔpa   bai-ra
     1SG   cook-1SG/3SG.PST-NMZL   rice   good   be-3SG.PST
     'The food I cooked was good.'

Compare also the following examples. The particle တယ် *Tɛ²* which marks the citation form of the verb in Burmese, has also a quotative function. See (40). As predicted by Matisoff 1986, it also appears in relative clauses, and in nominalized or completive clauses, with a slight different form (allomorph တာ Ta^2).

Burmese (from Vittrant, this volume, and Vittrant 2002)
(40) အမ မသွားနိုင်ဘူး။ မသွားနဲ့တဲ့။ [A4/38]
 ʔəma¹   mə=   θma³   naiN²   =Phu³   mə=   θə=³   =nɛ¹   Tɛ¹
 older sister NEG go   can   NEG   NEG   go   IMP.NEG QUOT
 'You (sister) cannot go (there). Don't go there, they said.'

(41) a. ကြည့်တဲ့ ဗွီဒီယိုအခွေ။
    ci¹   =Tɛ¹   bi²di²yo².ʔəkwe²
    watch   REL.REALIS   video-tape
    '(the) video-tape that (I) watch'

 b. မည့်လွန်းတဲ့သရက်သီး မစားနဲ့။
    mɛ¹   lwuN³   =Tɛ²   θəyɛ³.θəi³   mə=   sa³   =nɛ¹
    ripe be in excess REL.REALIS mango   NEG   eat   IMP.NEG
    'Don't eat mangos that are too ripe'

(42) အိမ်ထောင်ကျတာက ထောင်ကျတာထက် မဆိုးဘူးလား။
 ʔeiN².thɔN².ca¹ =Ta² =Ka¹ thɔN².ca¹ =Ta² thɛʔ mə= sho³ =Phu³ la³
 be.married   NMZL   S   be.in.jail NMZL COMP NEG bad   NEG   QST
 'To be married isn't it worse than to be in jail?'

4 Semantics and pragmatics

4.1 Common semantic domains

MSEA languages typically share conceptual frameworks relating to certain semantic domains, mentioned by Matisoff (1986b: 79).

Among them are certain terms relating to food. Broadly, food is divided into two categories:

'rice' and 'what-is-eaten-with-rice'.

(43)   *Rice*   *With-rice*
   Burmese thəmiN³   ထမင်း   hiN³   ဟင်း
   Thai   khâaw   ข้าว   kàp-khâaw กับข้าว

Further, most languages have distinct terms for rice in various stages of its growth, production and preparation. The following table is adapted from L. Bernot (2000: 103).

Table 11: Words meaning rice

English	Vietnamese	Yao (Hmong-Mien)	Chinese	Burmese	Cham	Wa[14]
Rice seedlings	ma	yang	秧 yāng	pyo³ ပျိုး	ɲih	kla
Paddy, rice in field	lua	blau	稻 dào	zəba³ စပါး	ṭaj	–
Unhusked rice	thoc	tsu	谷 gǔ	kaɔʔ ကောက်	ṭaj	ŋʰoʔ
Husked rice	gao	hmei	米 mǐ	sʰāN² ဆန်	ɻrah/ɻjah	gaoʔ
Cooked rice	com	hnang	饭 fàn	thəmiN³ ထမင်း	thěj	ʔɯp

Frequently, MSEA languages encode fine lexical distinctions in the following semantic domains:
- Verbs of cutting: according to the nature of the object being cut, the tool, the type of motion involved, the size of the resultant pieces, etc. (see Wa data from Watkins, this volume)
- Verbs of carrying: according to the part of the body and the position used for carrying (hand, shoulder, back, arm(s), etc.)
- Verbs of drying: drying by fire, in the sun, etc.
- Verbs of pushing: according to the direction of the pushing (up, down, pressing, etc.)

Table 12: Words encompassing a 'carry' meaning (adapted from this volume[15])

English	Vietnamese	Thai	Malay	Khumi	Wa	Khmer
To carry (general) or to carry along	chở		membawa		klɔm ~ s.grɔŋ	ហា haa ដាក់ dək បា baa
To carry on back		แบก bɛ̀ɛk	menggendong	pho³	gao	ព្រូន prɔnɔɔ
To carry on/across shoulder	vác	หาบ hàap	menanggung, menjulang	tʼva¹, apu¹	gu, kaŋ kao	លី lii ពុន pun

---

14 See Brunelle & Phu on Cham; Watkins on Wa, this volume
15 See Do-Hurinville & Dao, Jenny, Nomoto & Soh, Peterson and Watkins chapters for fine-grained semantics of these terms. For Khmer, see Haiman's chapter and Khmer dictionary online <www.sealang.net>.

English	Vietnamese	Thai	Malay	Khumi	Wa	Khmer
To carry on or between hands		ถือ *thǔɯ*	*menanai*		*ygok*	
To carry in one hand, or hanging from one hand		หิ้ว *hîw*	*menjinjing*	*vä, süng³*		កាន់ kan យួរ yuə ទ្រ tro
To carry on head	*đội*	เทิน *thɤɤn*	*menjunjung*	*atläng⁴*	*cah*	ទូល tuul
To carry with/ in arms	*khuân*	หอบ *hɔ̀ɔp*		*t'pång⁴*		កាន់ kaaŋ ត្រកាន់ trakaaŋ
To carry close to body/astride the waist/in one's arm/on the back	*ẵm (bế, bồng)*	อุ้ม *ʔûm*	*mengangkat, mendukung*	*pew¹*	*kʰɔp*	បី bəy ពរ pɔɔ

Certain head nouns used in compounding are found across a range of MSEA languages, e.g. 'ankle' < 'foot-eye' in couple of languages. Further examples can be seen in Matisoff (1978 and 2004).

4.2 Pragmatics & discourse

4.2.1 Final particles

MSEA languages generally deploy systems of sentence-final particles as the basic means of expressing the illocutionary force of an utterance: requesting, questioning, persuading, advising, reminding, instructing, etc. Particles are also used to convey propositional attitudes, such as the emotions of the speaker: surprise, doubt, impatience, reluctance, hesitation, etc.

For instance, the Cham sentence in (44)a is a declarative sentence. The same propositional content appears modified by different final particles in the following sentences, changing the illocutionary force. Burmese example (45) shows final particles conveying attitudes of the speaker. Other examples may be found in Goddard (2005: 144) and Fischer (2006).

Cham, from Brunelle & Phu, this volume
(44) a. ça   ka   naw   pac
         boy   name   go   study
         'Ka goes to school.'

b. ça   ka   naw   pac   lĕj   Illocutionary force:
   boy   name   go   study   QST   > interrogative
   'Does Ka goes to school?'

b. ça   ka   naw   pac   mĕ?   > imperative
   boy   name   go   study   IMP
   'Go to school!' Ka.'

b. ça   ka   naw   pac   da!   > emphasizer
   boy   name   go   study   EMPH
   'Ka went to school, I'm afraid!'

Burmese, adapted from Hnin Tun (2006: 40)
(45) a. ဒီကိုလာနော်။   'Come here, OK?'
        di²=Ko²   la²   **nɔ²**   The request is softer, soliciting the addressee's agreement.

   b. ဒီကိုလာလေ။   'Please, come here. Come along!'
      di²=Ko²   la²   **le²**   The order while checking that the addressee is paying attention.

   c. ဒီကိုလာကွာ။   'Come on, won't you?'
      di²=Ko²   la²   **Kwa²** Compelling attention, signaling some exasperation, informal request.

   d. ဒီကိုလာစမ်း။   'Get over here!'
      di²=Ko²   la²   **SaN³** A sharp, abrupt command.

   e. ဒီကိုလာဆို။   'Come' (I already called you, so please do come!)
      di²=Ko²   la²   **sho²** Reiterating a request, impatiently.
      DEM=DIR   come DM

4.2.2 Politeness

In a number of languages, complex sets of pronouns are used to encode systems of honorifics and levels of politeness. Distinct lexical items may be used to express honorific, humilific, religious or royal contexts. Goddard (2005) gives an account of these phenomena.

Table 13 shows the Thai pronominal device, that encodes either gender distinction and social status. See also the Khmer pronominal device in table 14, that mainly encode social status for the three speech-act participants.

Table 13: Thai pronominal device, from Jenny, this volume

1. PERS.		2. PERS.		3. PERS.	
กู *kuu*	intimate, impolite	มึง *mɯŋ*	intimate, impolite	มัน *man*	objects; hum ref. contemptuous
ข้า *khâa*	intimate	เอ็ง *ʔeŋ*	intimate	เขา *khǎw*	neutral
ฉัน *chǎn*	informal, intimate	แก *kɛɛ*	informal, contemptuous	เธอ *thɤɤ*	female referents
ผม *phǒm*	m. speaker, neutral	เธอ *thɤɤ*	familiar, intimate	หล่อน *lɔ̀ɔn*	female referents
กระผม *kràʔphǒm*	m. speaker, formal	คุณ *khun*	neutral, polite	ท่าน *thân*	formal
ดิฉัน *dìʔchǎn*	f. speaker, formal	ท่าน *thân*	formal		
ข้าพเจ้า *khâaphacâaw*	formal	เจ้า *câaw*	literary		
เรา *raw*	plural				

Table 14: Khmer pronominal device, from Haiman, this volume

1. PERS.		2. PERS.		3. PERS.	
ខ្ញុំ *knjom*	speaker is acting humble or polite	អ្នក *neak*	addressee is younger or of lower status	គាត់ *koat*	referent is respected other
អញ (anj)	speaker is arrogant or on intimate terms with addressee	ឯង *aeng*	addressee is of much lower status	វា *via*	referent is unrespected other
អាត្មា *atma*	speaker is monk	លោក *lo:k*	addressee is older or of higher status	គេ *kee:*	referent may be any other
យើង *jeu:ng*	neutral (Plural)	ចាន់ *chan*	speaker and addressee are both monks	ទ្រង់ *truang*	referent is royalty

5 Summary

In conclusion, regarding the characteristics of MSEA languages, how typical or ordinary is the language examined?

Which of the shared features are present? Which are widespread; which are not found?

In general, how does the language in question match the norms of the MSEA linguistic area?

In these guidelines, we have described a number of grammatical features shared (to some extent/various degrees) by languages of Mainland Southeast Asia. These features are the ones which have to be investigated in an areally-orientated description of a language.

The pervasiveness of the features may vary according to language contact history and other linguistic and sociolinguistics factors (see Aikhenvald 2006). The language in question may have been in close contact with one or more languages of the area, resulting in a case of language convergence (such as Cham with Vietnamese, or Karen or Mon with Burmese).

The language may be spoken on the edge of the linguistic area, display fewer areal features (see Khumi or Yongning Na), and even be considered part of a different linguistic area (South Asia), or between two linguistic areas as for Tani, a Tibeto-Burman language spoken in Northeast India (see Post 2015).

In summary, the notion of linguistic area does not rely exclusively on linguistic criteria. It requires language communities to have shared culture and history. Thus, each language description, although following the same guidelines, will result in a different language sketch.

Abbreviations

1	first person
2	second person
3	third person
ADJ	adjective
ANAPH	anaphoric
ASP	aspect
BENEF	benefactive
CLF	classifier
COMP	comparative marker
CONJ	conjunction
DEF	definite
DEM	demonstrative
DIR	directional
DM	discourse marker
EMPH	emphatic
EUP	euphonic
EVID	evidential

EVAL	evaluation
EXPER	experimentative
EXP	expressive
FOC	focus
FUT	future
HUM	human
IMP	imperative
INCL	inclusive
IRR	irrealis
MOD	modality
LOC	locative
N	noun
NEG	negation
NMLZ	nominalizer
O	object
OBL	oblique
PERF	perfect
PL(UR)	plural
POL	politeness
PST	past
QST	question, interrogative
QUOT	quotative
REAL	realis
REDUP	reduplication
REL	relative marker
RESULT	resultative
S	subject
SG	singular
SRC	source
TAM	tense-aspect-modality
TERM	terminative
TOP	topic
V	verb

References

Aikhenvald, Alexandra Y. 2000. *Classifiers: a typology of noun categorization devices*: Oxford studies in Typology and Linguistic theory. Oxford: Oxford University Press.
Aikhenvald, Alexandra Y. 2006. Grammars in Contact: A Cross-linguistic Typology. Oxford: Oxford University Press.
Aikhenvald, Alexandra Y. & R. M. W. Dixon (eds.). 2001. *Areal Diffusion and Genetic Inheritance: Problems in Comparative Linguistics*. Oxford: Oxford University Press.
Aikhenvald, Alexandra Y. & R. M. W. Dixon (eds.). 2006. *Serial verb constructions: A crosslinguistic typology*. Oxford: Oxford University Press.

Bernot, Lucien. 2000. Riziculteurs. In *Voyage dans les sciences humaines. Qui sont les autres*, 101–142. Paris: Presses de l'Université de Paris-Sorbonne [1ere édition: 1975, in 'Éléments d'ethnologie'].

Bisang, Walter. 1991. Verb serialization, grammaticalization and attractor positions in Chinese, Hmong, Vietnamese, Thai and Khmer. In Hansjakob Seiler & Waldfried Premper (eds.), *Partizipation*, 509–562. Tübingen: Gunter Narr.

Bisang, Walter. 1993. Classifiers, quantifiers and class noun in Hmong. *Studies in Language* 17. 1–51.

Bisang, Walter. 1996. Areal typology and grammaticalization: Processes of grammaticalization based on nouns and verbs in East and mainland South East Asian languages. *Studies in Language* 20 (3). 517–597.

Bisang, Walter. 1999. Classifiers in East and Southeast Asian languages: Counting and beyond. In *Numeral Types and Changes Worldwide*, 113–185. Berlin & New York: Mouton de Gruyter.

Bon, Noëllie. 2014. Une grammaire de la langue Stieng, Langue en danger du Cambodge et du Vietnam. PhD thesis, Université Lyon 2.

Bradley, David. 1978. *Proto-loloish*. Copenhagen & London: Monograph Series 39, Scandinavian Institute of Asian Studies.

Bradley, David. 1982. Register in Burmese. In David Bradley (ed.), *Papers in Southeast Asian Linguistics No. 8, Tonation*, 117–132. Canberra: Pacific Linguistics, the Australian National University.

Butler, Becky. 2015. Approaching a phonological understanding of the sesquisyllable with phonetic evidence from Khmer and Bunong. In N. Enfield & B. Comrie (eds.), *Languages of Mainland Southeast Asia. The state of the art*, 443–499. Berlin & Boston: Mouton de Gruyter.

Brunelle, Marc & James Kirby. 2015. Re-assessing tonal diversity and geographical convergence in Mainland Southeast Asia. In N. Enfield & B. Comrie (eds.), *Languages of Mainland Southeast Asia. The state of the art*, 82–110. Berlin & Boston: Mouton de Gruyter.

Clark, Marybeth. 1985. Asking questions in Hmong and other southeast Asian languages. *Linguistics of the Tibeto-Burman Area* 8 (2). 60–67.

Clark, Marybeth. 1991. Conjunctions as topicalizers, More on Southeast Asian Languages. In Martha Ratliff & Eric Schiller (eds.), Papers from the First Annual Meeting of the Southeast Asian Linguistics Society (SEALS), 87–107.

Compton, Carol J. 2007. Four-word phrases in Lao discourse: yuu4 4 dii2 2 mii3 3 hEEN3 3. In *SEALS XII Papers from the 12th Annual Meeting of the Southeast Asian Linguistics Society 2002*, ed. R. Wayland et al., Canberra, Australia, 23-35. Pacific Linguistics, the Australian National University.

Chelliah, Shobhana L. 1997. *Metei Phonology*. Berlin & New York: Mouton de Gruyter.

Diller, A.V.N. 2006. Thai serial verbs: Cohesion and culture. In Alexandra Y. Aikhenvald & R.M.W. Dixon (eds.), *Serial Verb Constructions: A cross-linguistic typology*, 160–167. Oxford: Oxford University Press.

Durie, Mark. 1997. Grammatical structures in verb serialization. In Alex Alsina, Joan Bresnan & Peter Sells (eds.), *Complex Predicates*, 289–354. Stanford: CSLI Publications.

Do-Hurinville, Danh Thành. 2008. Nominalisation et construction du thème en vietnamien. *Faits de Langues – Nominalisations* 30. 209–216.

Enfield, Nick J. 2001. On genetic and areal linguistics in Mainland South-East Asian: Parallel polyfunctionality of 'acquire'. In A. Y. Aikhenvald & R. M. W. Dixon (eds.), *Areal diffusion and genetic inheritance: Problems in comparative linguistics*, 255–290. Oxford: Oxford University Press.

Enfield, Nick J. 2003. Linguistic epidemiology: Semantics and grammar of language contact in *Mainland Southeast Asia*. London: Routledge/Curzon.

Enfield, Nick J. 2005. Areal Linguistics and Mainland Southeast Asia. In *Annual Review Anthropology* 34. 181–206.

Enfield, N. J. & G. Diffloth. 2009. Phonology and sketch grammar of Kri, a Vietic language of Laos. *Cahiers de Linguistique – Asie Orientale* (CLAO) 38 (1). 3–69.

Fischer, Kerstin (ed.). 2006. *Approaches to discourse particles*. Oxford: Elsevier.

Foley, William & M. Olson. 1985. Clausehood and verb serialization. In Nichols, J. & A. Woodbury (eds.), *Grammar Inside and Outside the Clause*, 17–60. Cambridge: Cambridge University Press.

Goddard, Cliff. 2005. *The Languages of East and Southeast Asia: An Introduction*. Oxford & New York: Oxford University Press.

Goral, Donald R. 1978. Numerical Classifier Systems: A Southeast Asian Cross-linguistic Analysis. Linguistics of the Tibeto-Burman Area 4 (1). 1–72.

Grange, Philippe. 2006. *Temps et Aspect en Indonésien*. PhD thesis. Université de Poitiers, France.

Grinevald, Colette. 1999. Typologie des systèmes de classification nominale. *Faits de Langue* 14, La catégorisation dans les langues. 101–122.

Grinevald, Colette. 2000. A morphosyntactic typology of classifiers. In G. Senft (ed.), *Nominal classification*, 50–92. Cambridge: Cambridge University Press.

Grinevald, Colette. 2007. The linguistic categorization of spatial entities. Classifiers and other nominal classification systems. In Michel Aurnague, Maya Hickmann & Laure Vieu (eds.), *The categorization of spatial entities in language and cognition*, 93–122. Amsterdam: John Benjamins.

Haudricourt, André-Georges. 1961. Bipartition et tripartition des systèmes de tons dans quelques langues d'Extrême-orient. *Bulletin de la Société de Linguistique de Paris* 53. 257–267.

Heine, Bernd & Tania Kuteva. 2002. *World lexicon of grammaticalization*, Cambridge, UK: Cambridge University Press.

Henderson, Eugénie J. A. 1952. The main features of Cambodian pronunciation. *Bulletin of the School of Oriental and African Studies* 14 (1). 149–174.

Henderson, Eugénie J. A. 1965. The topography of certain phonetic and morphological characteristics of South East Asian language. *Lingua* 15. 400–434.

Hudak, Thomas J. 2014. Proverbs, proverbial elaboration, and poetic development in the Tai languages. In J. Williams (ed.), *The aesthetics of grammar*, 135–150. Cambridge: Cambridge University Press.

Jaisser, Annie C. 1990. DeLIVERing an introduction to psycho-collocations with SIAB in Hmong. *Linguistics of the Tibeto-Burman Area* 13 (1). 159–178.

Jones, Robert B. 1970. Classification in Southeast Asia. *Journal of the American Oriental Society* 90 (1). 1–13.

Kibrik, Andrej A. 2001. Reference maintenance in discourse. In M. Haspelmath, E. König, W. Oesterreicher & W. Raible (eds.), *Language typology and language universals: An international handbook,* vol. 2, 1123–1141 (Handbuecher Zur Sprach- und Kommunikationswissenschaft [Handbooks of Linguistics & Communication Science]). Berlin & New York: Mouton de Gruyter.

Krifka, Manfred. 2006. Basic notions of Informational Structure. In C. Fery & M. Krifka (eds.), *Interdisciplinary Studies of Information Structure 6*, Potsdam: Universitätsverlag. https://amor.cms.hu-berlin.de/~h2816i3x/Publications/Krifka_InformationStructure.pdf (accessed 1 June 2018).

Lahaussois, Aimée. 2003. Nominalisation and its various uses in Thulung Rai. Linguistics of the Tibeto-Burman Area 26 (1). 33–57.

Lambrecht, Knud. 1994. *Information structure and sentence form. Topic, focus, and mental representations of discourses referent.* Cambridge: Cambridge University Press.

Li, XuPing & Walter Bisang. 2012. Classifiers in Sinitic languages: From individuation to definiteness-marking. Lingua 122. 335–355.

Lidz, Liberty A. 2010. A descriptive grammar of Yongning Na (Mosuo). PhD dissertation, University of Texas, Austin.

Matisoff, James A. 1973. Tonogenesis in Southeast Asia. In Larry M. Hyman (ed.), *Consonant, types and tone, Southern California Occasional Papers in Linguistics*, no. 1, 71–95. Los Angeles: University of California.

Matisoff, James A. 1978. Variational semantics in Tibeto-burman: The 'organic' approach to linguistic comparison. Philadelphia: ISHI Publications.

Matisoff, James A. 1986a. Hearts and Minds in South-East Asian languages and English: An essay in the comparative lexical semantics of psycho-collocation. In *Cahiers de Linguistique d'Asie Orientale* 15 (1). 5–57. http://www.persee.fr/issue/clao_0153-3320_1986_num_15_1 (accessed 1 June 2018).

Matisoff, James A. 1986b. Linguistic Diversity and Language Contact. In *Highlanders of Thailand*. Singapore: Oxford University Press.

Matisoff, James A. 1991. Areal and Universal Dimensions of Grammatization in Lahu. In Elizabeth Closs Traugott & Bernd Heine (eds.), *Approaches to grammaticalization: Focus on Theorical and Methodological Issues*, vol. 2, 383–453. London: John Benjamins.

Matisoff, James A. 2001. Genetic versus contact relationship: Prosodic diffusibility in South-East Asian languages. In A. Y. Aikhenvald & R. M. W. Dixon (eds.), *Areal diffusion and genetic inheritance: Problems in comparative linguistics*, 291–327. Oxford: Oxford University Press.

Matisoff, James A. 2004. Areal semantics – Is there such a thing? In Anju Saxena (ed.), *Himalayan languages, past and present*, 347–395. Berlin & New York: Mouton de Gruyter.

Michaud, Alexis. 2011. Les systèmes de tons en Asie orientale: typologie, schémas évolutifs et modélisation. In L.-J. Boë & J.-L. Schwartz (eds.), *Faits de Langues* 37 (*La parole: Origine, développement, structures*). 247–261.

Migliazza, Brian. 2005. Some Expressives in So. *Ethnorêma* 1 (1). 1–18. http://www.ethnorema.it/pdf/numero%201/BRIAN%20MIGLIAZZA.pdf (accessed 1 June 2018).

Mortensen, David. 2003. *Hmong elaborate expressions are coordinate compounds.* Unpublished manuscript, UC Berkeley.

Mortensen, David. 2004. Preliminaries to Mong Leng (Hmong Njua) phonology. Manuscript. http://www.davidmortensen.org/papers/mong_leng_phonology.pdf (accessed 1 June 2018).

Oey, Eric. 1990. Psycho-collocations in Malay. *Linguistics of the Tibeto-Burman Area* 13 (1). 141–158.

Peterson, David. 2002 [published in 2005]. On Khumi verbal pronominal morphology. *Berkeley Linguistics Society* 28, special session.

Pinnow, H. J. 1960. Über den Ursprung der voneinander abweichenden Strukturen der Munda- und Khmer-Nikobar-Sprachen. *Indo-Iranian Journal* 4 (2–3). 81–103.

Pittayaporn, Pittayawat. 2015. Typologizing sesquisyllabicity. In N. Enfield & B. Comrie (eds.), *Languages of Mainland Southeast Asia. The state of the art*, 500–528. Berlin & Boston: Mouton de Gruyter.

Post, Mark. 2015. Morphosyntactic reconstruction in an areal-historical context: A pre-historical relationship between North East India and Mainland Southeast Asia? In N. Enfield & B. Comrie (eds.), *Languages of Mainland Southeast Asia. The state of the art*, 204–260. Berlin & Boston: Mouton de Gruyter.

Romeo, Nicoletta. 2008. *Aspect in Burmese*. Amsterdam: John Benjamins.

Sidwell, Paul. 2014. Expressives in Austroasiatic. In J. Williams (ed.), *The Aesthetics of Grammar*, 17–35. Cambridge: Cambridge University Press.

Simpson, Andrew. 2005. Classifiers and DP structure in Southeast Asia. In Guglielmo Cinque & Richard Kayne (eds.), *The Oxford handbook of comparative syntax*, 806–838. Oxford: Oxford University Press.

Smeall, Christopher. 1975. Grammaticalized verbs in Lolo-Burmese. *Linguistics of the Tibeto-Burman Area* 2. 273–287.

Somsonge, Burusphat. 2007. A comparison of general classifiers in Tai-Kadai languages. *Mon-Khmer Studies* 37. 129–153.

Suriya, Ratanakul. 1988. Languages in Southeast Asia: part I, Austroasiatic and Sino-Tibetan languages. (In Thai). Bangkok: Mahidol University, Research Center of Southeast Asian Cultures.

Tamba-Mecz, Irène. 1983. L'ellipse: Phénomène discursif et métalinguistique. In *Histoire Épistémologie Langage* 5 (1) (L'ellipse grammaticale: Études épistémologiques et historiques). 151–157.

Tournadre, Nicolas. 1996. *L'ergativité en tibétain*. Paris & Leuven: Peeters.

VanBik, Kenneth. 1998. Lai psycho-collocation. *Linguistics of the Tibeto-Burman Area* 21 (1). 201–232.

Van der Auwera, Johan, Peter Kehayov & Alice Vittrant. 2009. Acquisitive modals. In L. Hogeweg, H. De Hoop & A. Malchukov (eds.), *Cross-linguistic studies of tense, aspect, and modality*, 271–302. Amsterdam: Benjamins.

Vittrant, Alice. 2002 (published in 2005). Classifier Systems and Noun Categorization Devices in Burmese. *Proceedings of the 28th Annual Meeting of the Berkeley Linguistics Society* 28. 129–148.

Vittrant, Alice. 2004. *La modalité et ses corrélats en birman, dans une perspective comparative*. Doctoral dissertation, Université Paris 8, Saint-Denis.

Vittrant, Alice. 2005. Burmese as a modality-prominent language. In Justin Watkins (ed.), *Studies in Burmese linguistics*, 145–162. Canberra: Pacific Studies.

Vittrant, Alice. 2006. Les constructions verbales en série, une nouvelle approche du syntagme verbal birman. *Bulletin de la Société Linguistique de Paris* 101 (1). 305–367. Paris: Peeters.

Vittrant, Alice. 2012. How typology allows for a new analysis of the verb phrase in Burmese. Lidil 46 (Typologie et description linguistiques. Interfaces et interactions). 101–126.

Vittrant, Alice. 2014. Psycho-collocational expressives in Burmese. In J. Williams (ed.), *The aesthetics of grammar*, 255–279. Cambridge: Cambridge University Press.

Vittrant, Alice. 2015. Expressing motion: The contribution of Southeast Asian languages with reference to East Asian Languages. In N. Enfield & B. Comrie (eds.), *Languages of Mainland Southeast Asia. The state of the art*, 586–632. Berlin & Boston: Mouton de Gruyter.

Vogel, Sylvain. 2002. Détermination nominale, quantification et classification en Khmer contemporain. *Bulletin de l'École française d'Extrême-Orient* 89 (1). 183–201.

Watanabe, Kazuha. 2005. The development of continuous aspect. In Michael Fortescue, Eva Skafte Jensen, Jens Erik Mogensen & Lene Schøsler (eds.), *Historical Linguistics 2003 – Selected papers from the 16th International Conference on Historical Linguistics, Copenhagen, 11–15 August 2003*, 301–315. Amsterdam: John Benjamins.

Watkins, Justin. 2000. Notes on creaky and killed tone in Burmese. *SOAS Working papers in Linguisitics and Phonetics* 10. 139–149.

Watson Richard L. 2001. A comparison of some southeast Asian ideophones with some African ideophones. In F. K. E. Voeltz & C. Kilian-Hatz (eds.), *Ideophones*, 385–405. Amsterdam: John Benjamins.

Wayland Ratree. 1996. Lao expressives. *Mon Khmer Studies* 26. 217–231.

Williams, Jeffrey (ed.). 2013. *The aesthetics of grammar*. Cambridge, Cambridge University Press.

Maps

Map of language families

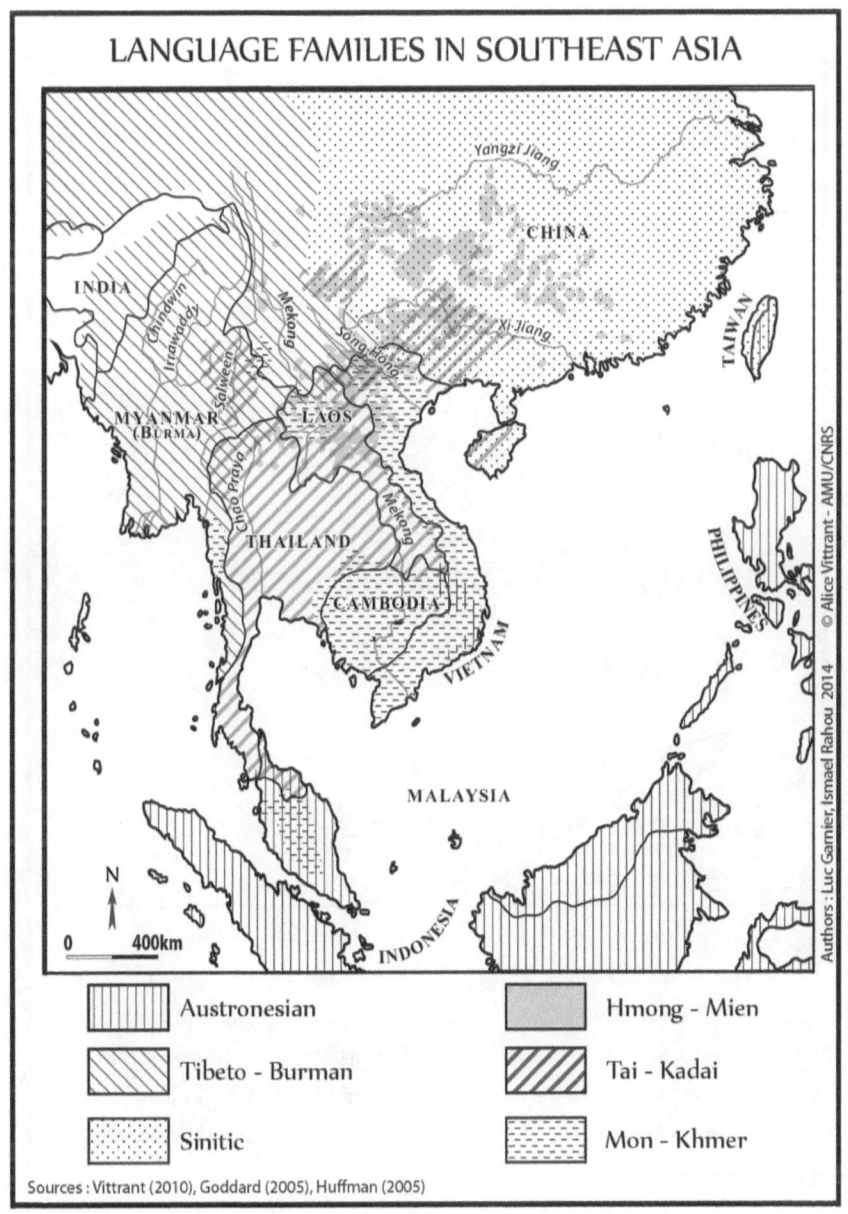

Map of fieldwork locations

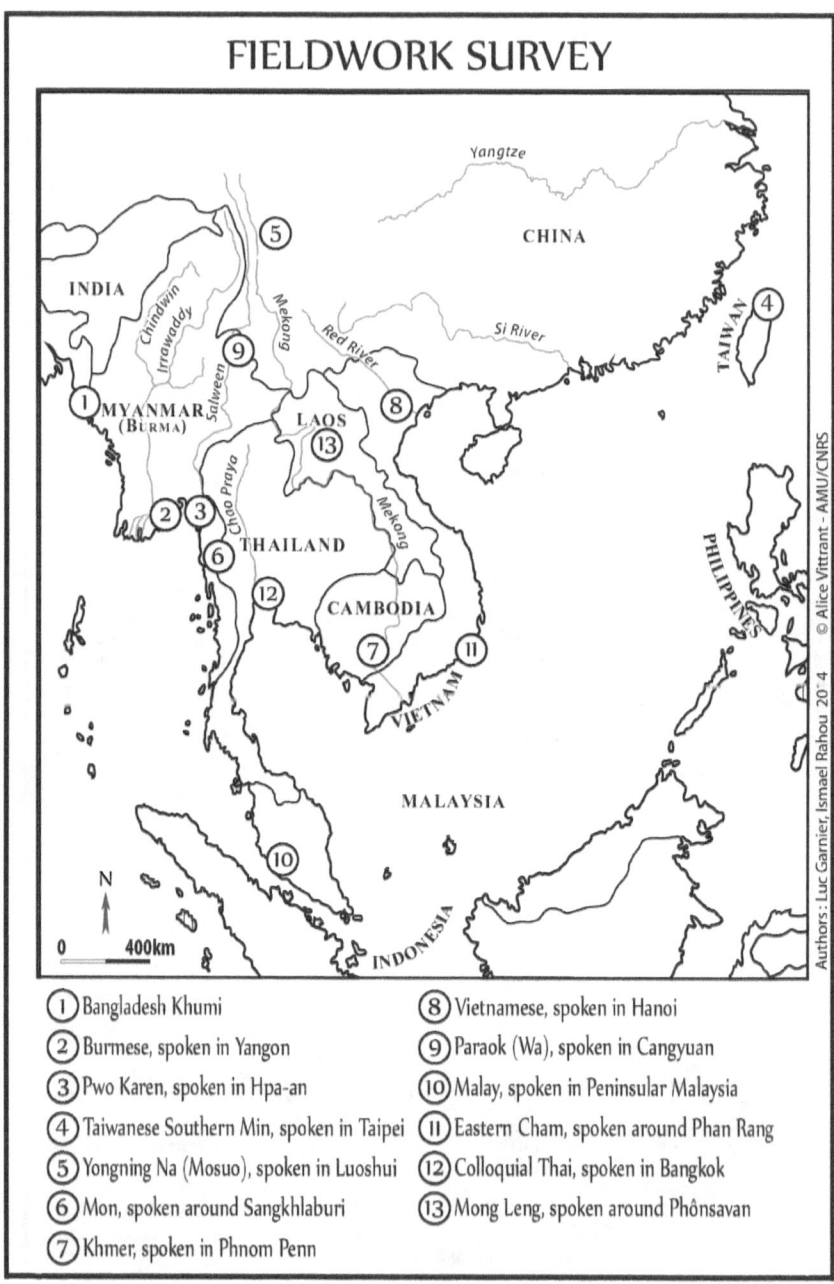

Maps of pervasiveness of the shared features

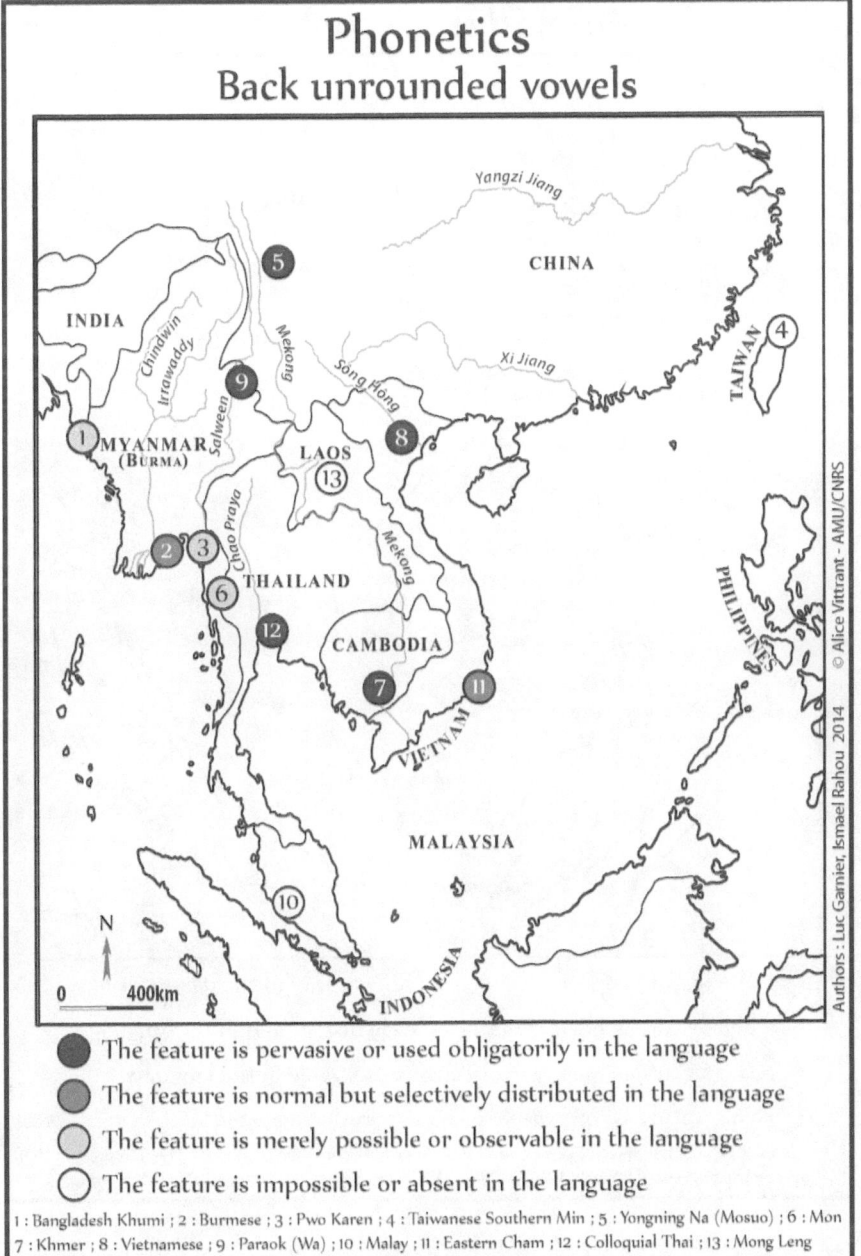

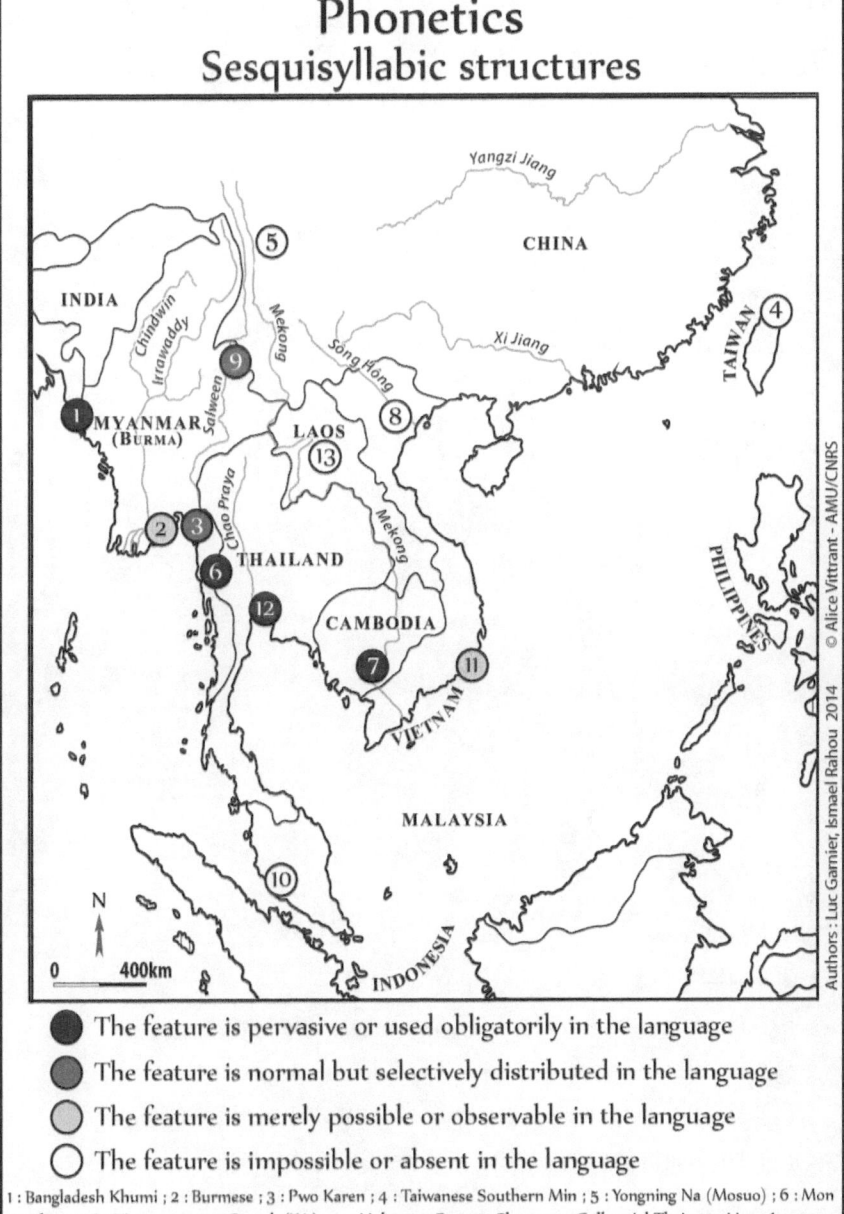

Phonetics
Sesquisyllabic structures

- ● The feature is pervasive or used obligatorily in the language
- ● The feature is normal but selectively distributed in the language
- ○ The feature is merely possible or observable in the language
- ○ The feature is impossible or absent in the language

1 : Bangladesh Khumi ; 2 : Burmese ; 3 : Pwo Karen ; 4 : Taiwanese Southern Min ; 5 : Yongning Na (Mosuo) ; 6 : Mon
7 : Khmer ; 8 : Vietnamese ; 9 : Paraok (Wa) ; 10 : Malay ; 11 : Eastern Cham ; 12 : Colloquial Thai ; 13 : Mong Leng

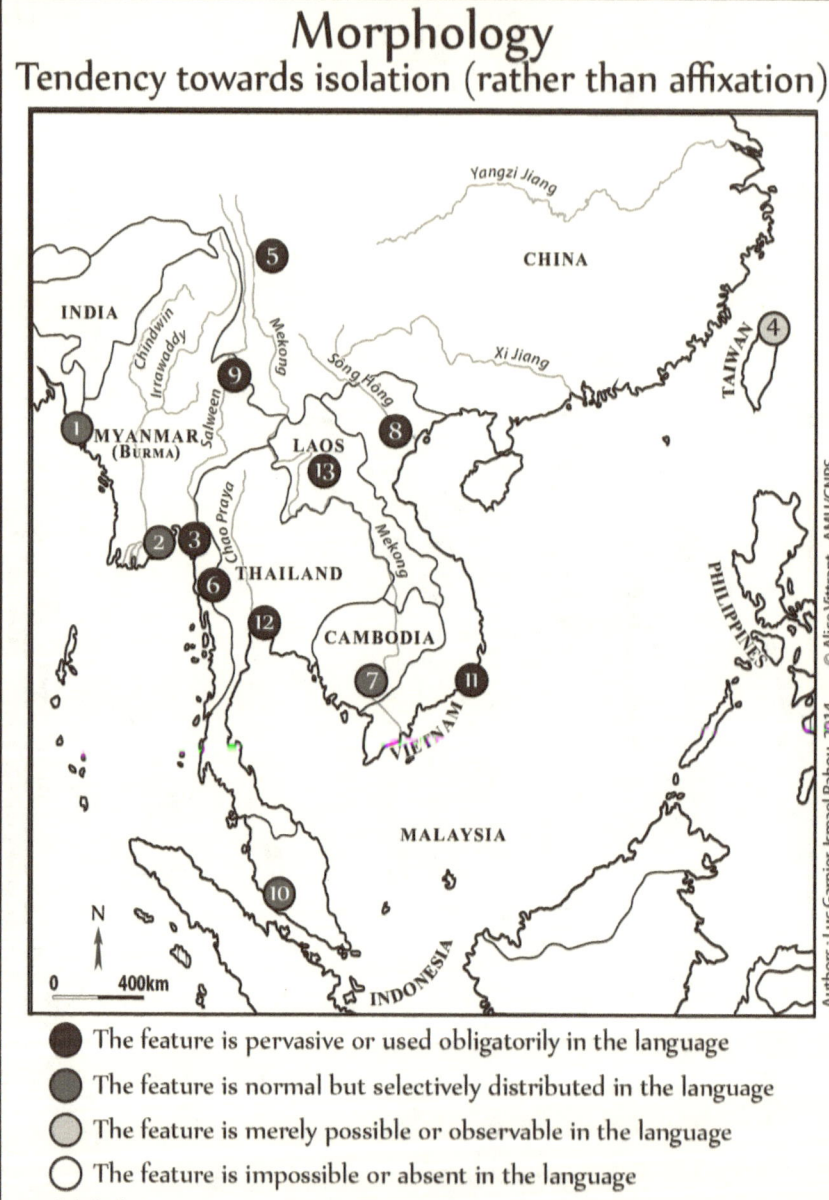

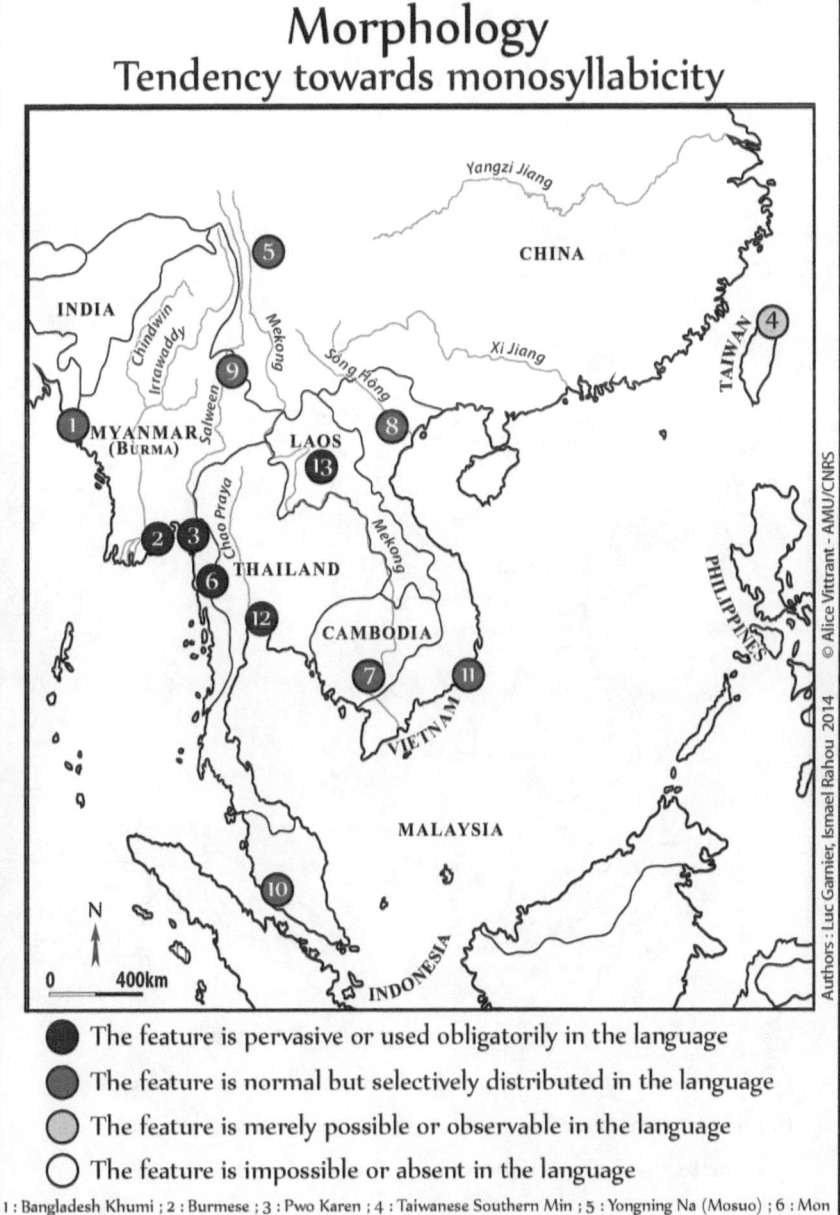

Morphology
Tendency towards monosyllabicity

- ● The feature is pervasive or used obligatorily in the language
- ● The feature is normal but selectively distributed in the language
- ○ The feature is merely possible or observable in the language
- ○ The feature is impossible or absent in the language

1 : Bangladesh Khumi ; 2 : Burmese ; 3 : Pwo Karen ; 4 : Taiwanese Southern Min ; 5 : Yongning Na (Mosuo) ; 6 : Mon
7 : Khmer ; 8 : Vietnamese ; 9 : Paraok (Wa) ; 10 : Malay ; 11 : Eastern Cham ; 12 : Colloquial Thai ; 13 : Mong Leng

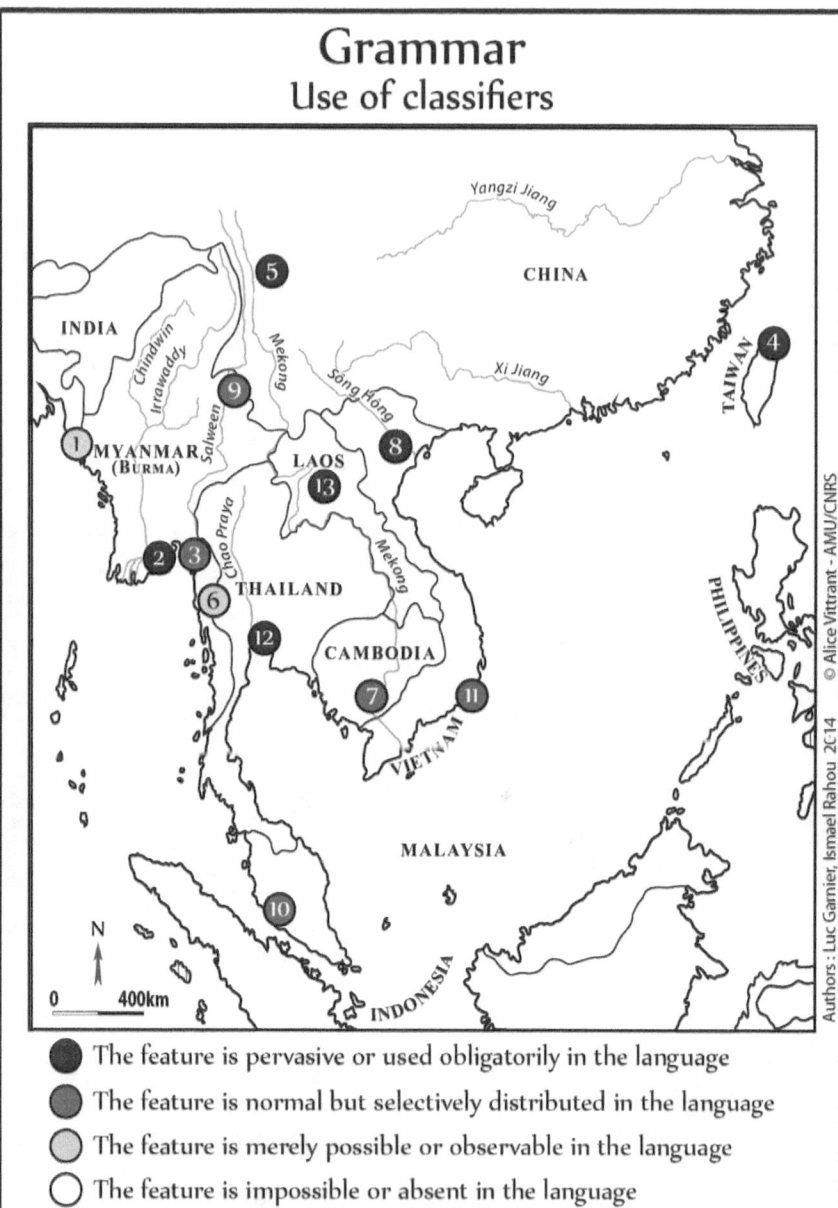

Grammar
Classifiers used in counting

- ● The feature is pervasive or used obligatorily in the language
- ● The feature is normal but selectively distributed in the language
- ○ The feature is merely possible or observable in the language
- ○ The feature is impossible or absent in the language

1 : Bangladesh Khumi ; 2 : Burmese ; 3 : Pwo Karen ; 4 : Taiwanese Southern Min ; 5 : Yongning Na (Mosuo) ; 6 : Mon 7 : Khmer ; 8 : Vietnamese ; 9 : Paraok (Wa) ; 10 : Malay ; 11 : Eastern Cham ; 12 : Colloquial Thai ; 13 : Mong Leng

Grammar
Classifiers used with demonstratives

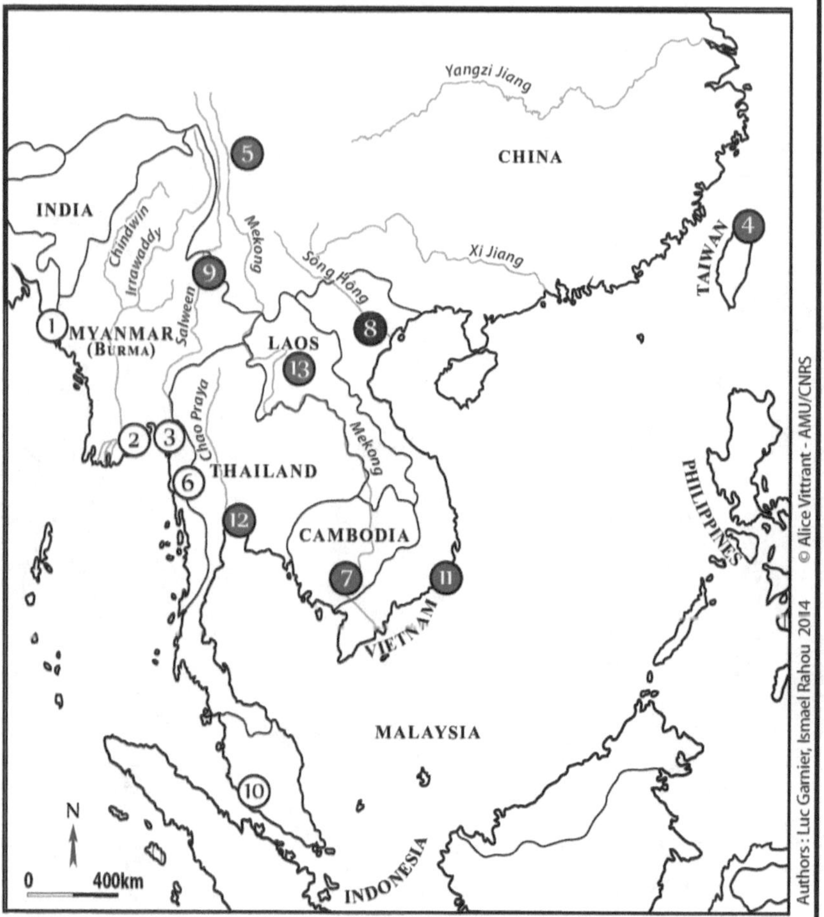

- ● The feature is pervasive or used obligatorily in the language
- ● The feature is normal but selectively distributed in the language
- ○ The feature is merely possible or observable in the language
- ○ The feature is impossible or absent in the language

1 : Bangladesh Khumi ; 2 : Burmese ; 3 : Pwo Karen ; 4 : Taiwanese Southern Min ; 5 : Yongning Na (Mosuo) ; 6 : Mon
7 : Khmer ; 8 : Vietnamese ; 9 : Paraok (Wa) ; 10 : Malay ; 11 : Eastern Cham ; 12 : Colloquial Thai ; 13 : Mong Leng

Grammar
Inflection of verbs

● The feature is pervasive or used obligatorily in the language
● The feature is normal but selectively distributed in the language
○ The feature is merely possible or observable in the language
○ The feature is impossible or absent in the language

1 : Bangladesh Khumi ; 2 : Burmese ; 3 : Pwo Karen ; 4 : Taiwanese Southern Min ; 5 : Yongning Na (Mosuo) ; 6 : Mon
7 : Khmer ; 8 : Vietnamese ; 9 : Paraok (Wa) ; 10 : Malay ; 11 : Eastern Cham ; 12 : Colloquial Thai ; 13 : Mong Leng

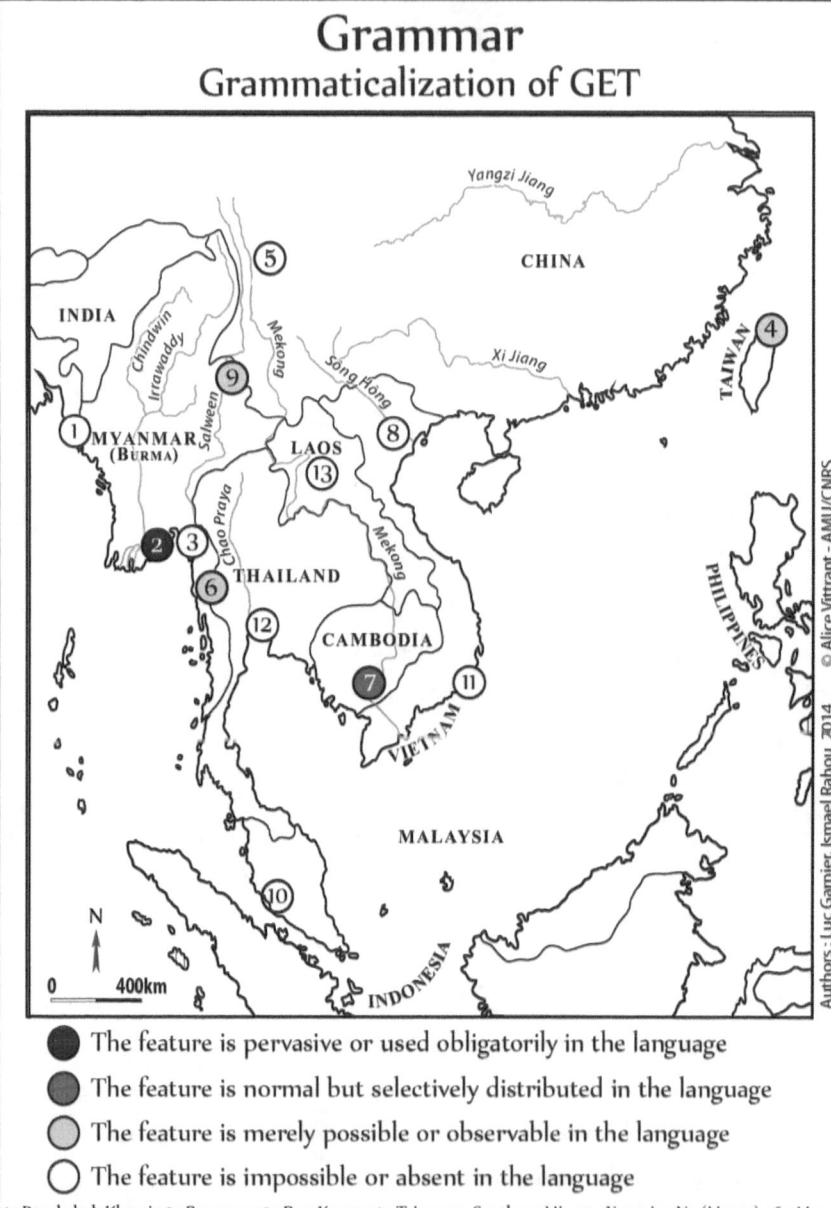

Grammar
Grammaticalization of GET

● The feature is pervasive or used obligatorily in the language
◉ The feature is normal but selectively distributed in the language
◎ The feature is merely possible or observable in the language
○ The feature is impossible or absent in the language

1 : Bangladesh Khumi ; 2 : Burmese ; 3 : Pwo Karen ; 4 : Taiwanese Southern Min ; 5 : Yongning Na (Mosuo) ; 6 : Mon
7 : Khmer ; 8 : Vietnamese ; 9 : Paraok (Wa) ; 10 : Malay ; 11 : Eastern Cham ; 12 : Colloquial Thai ; 13 : Mong Leng

Maps — 699

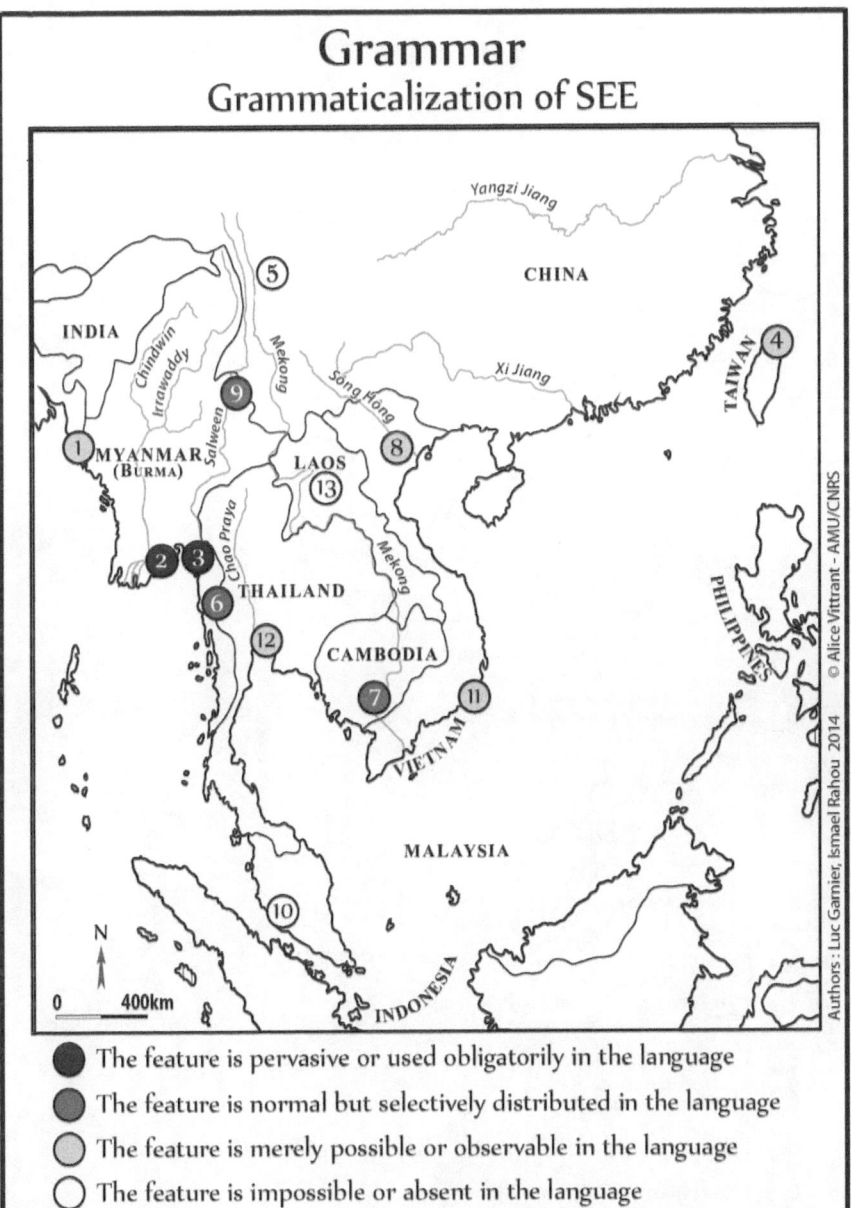

Grammar
Grammaticalization of SEE

● The feature is pervasive or used obligatorily in the language
● The feature is normal but selectively distributed in the language
○ The feature is merely possible or observable in the language
○ The feature is impossible or absent in the language

1 : Bangladesh Khumi ; 2 : Burmese ; 3 : Pwo Karen ; 4 : Taiwanese Southern Min ; 5 : Yongning Na (Mosuo) ; 6 : Mon
7 : Khmer ; 8 : Vietnamese ; 9 : Paraok (Wa) ; 10 : Malay ; 11 : Eastern Cham ; 12 : Colloquial Thai ; 13 : Mong Leng

Grammar
Serial verb constructions

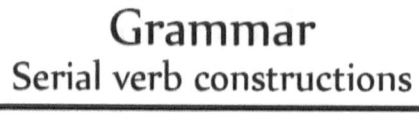

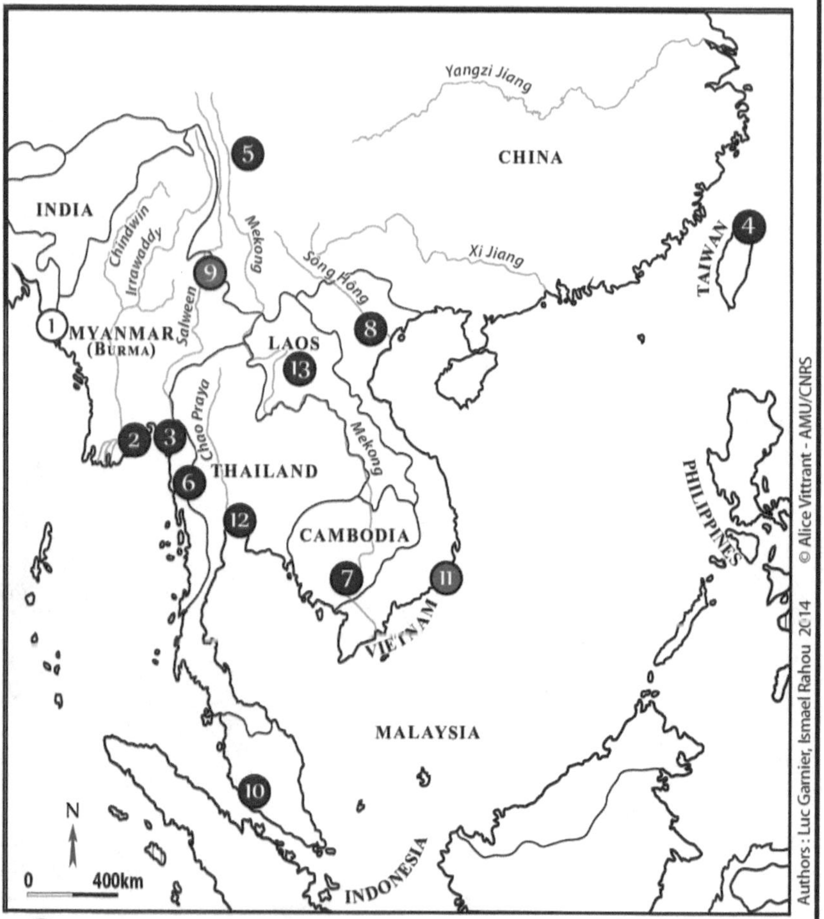

- ● The feature is pervasive or used obligatorily in the language
- ● The feature is normal but selectively distributed in the language
- ○ The feature is merely possible or observable in the language
- ○ The feature is impossible or absent in the language

1 : Bangladesh Khumi ; 2 : Burmese ; 3 : Pwo Karen ; 4 : Taiwanese Southern Min ; 5 : Yongning Na (Mosuo) ; 6 : Mon
7 : Khmer ; 8 : Vietnamese ; 9 : Paraok (Wa) ; 10 : Malay ; 11 : Eastern Cham ; 12 : Colloquial Thai ; 13 : Mong Leng

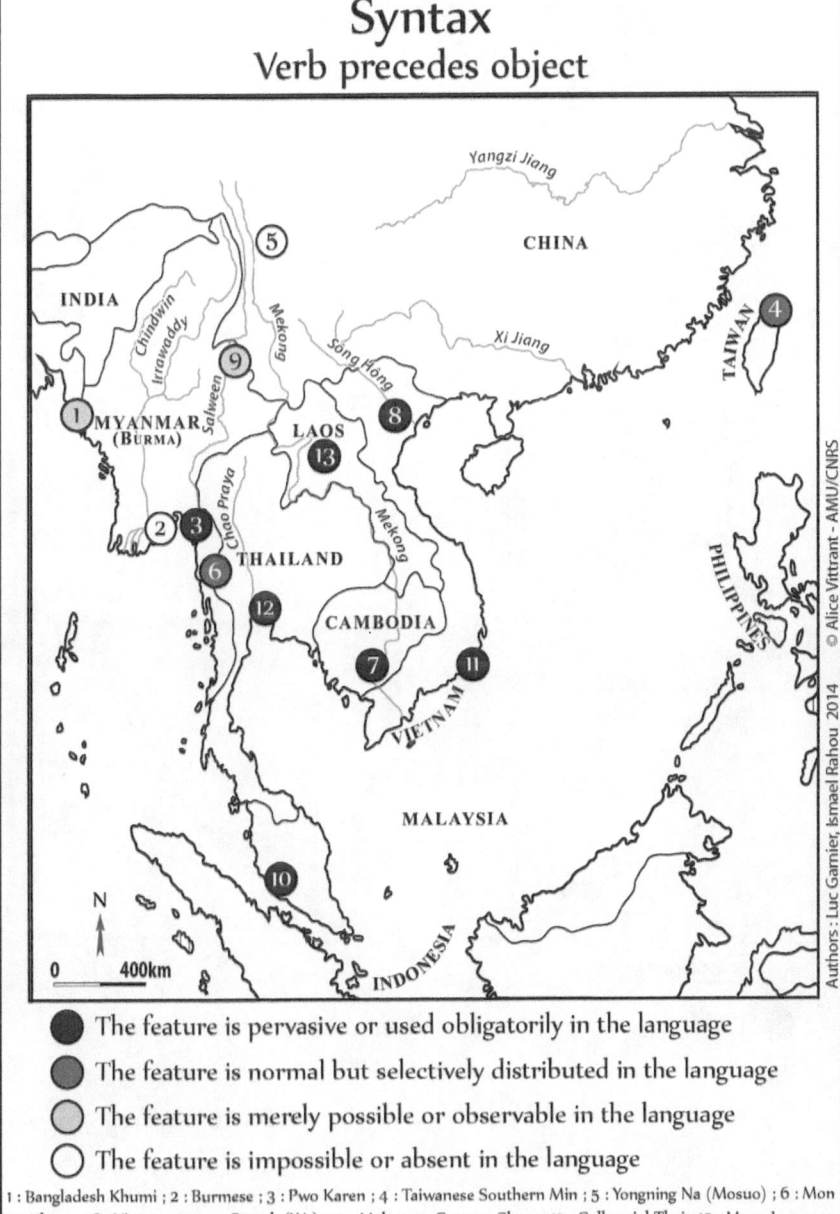

Maps of pervasiveness of the shared features

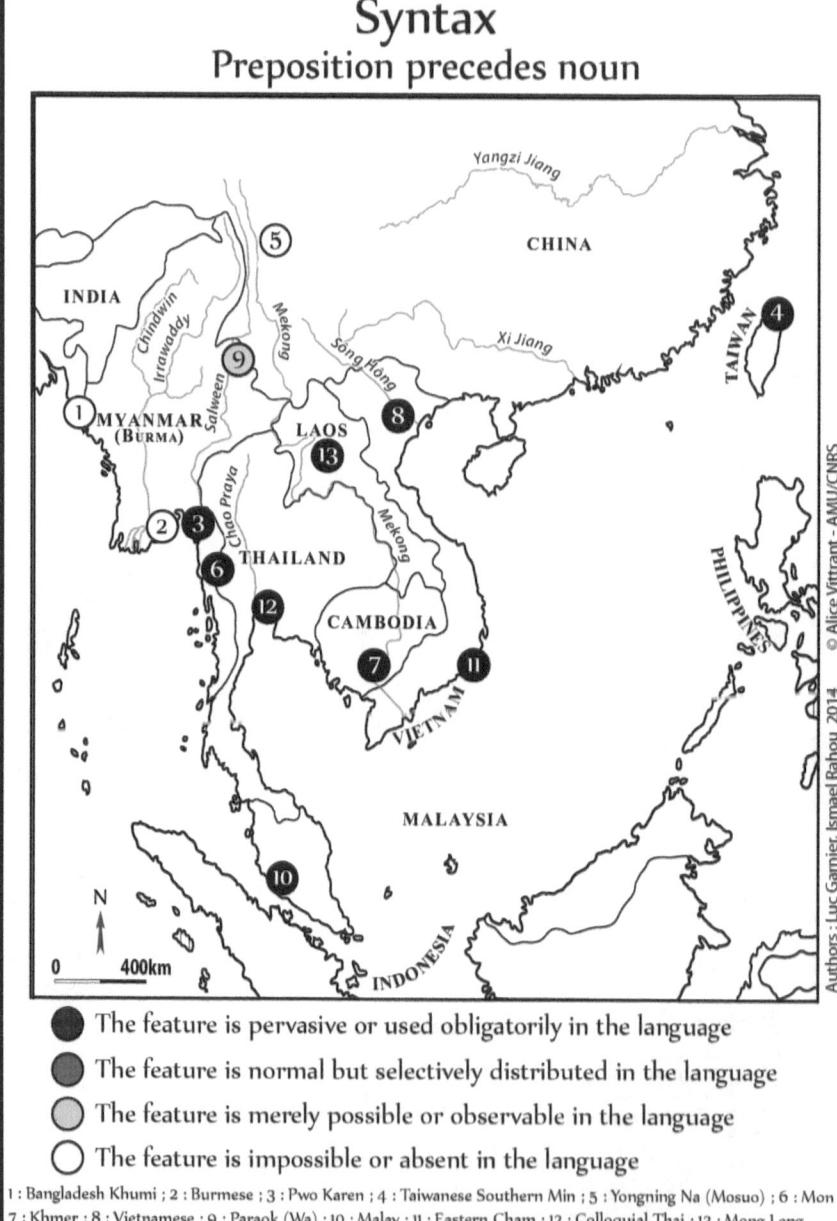

Maps — 705

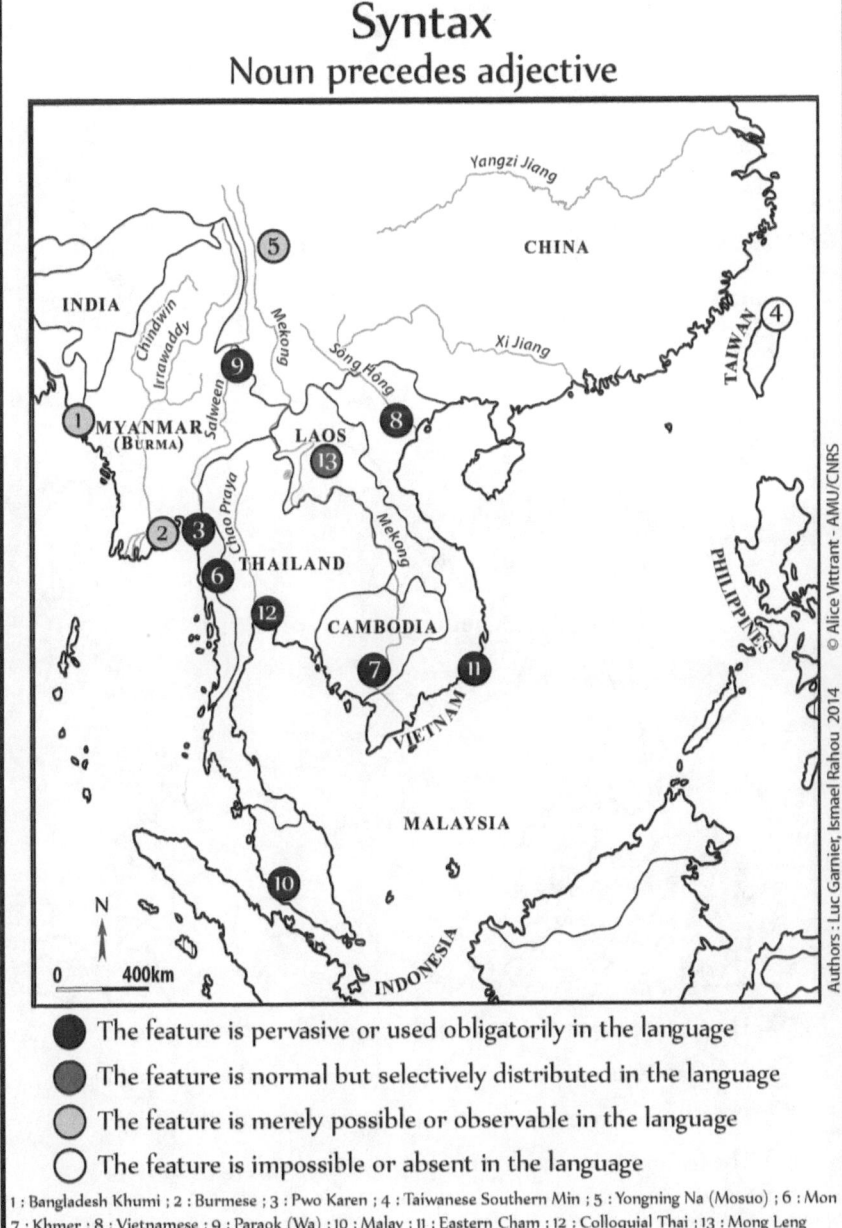

Syntax
Noun precedes adjective

- ● The feature is pervasive or used obligatorily in the language
- ● The feature is normal but selectively distributed in the language
- ○ The feature is merely possible or observable in the language
- ○ The feature is impossible or absent in the language

1 : Bangladesh Khumi ; 2 : Burmese ; 3 : Pwo Karen ; 4 : Taiwanese Southern Min ; 5 : Yongning Na (Mosuo) ; 6 : Mon
7 : Khmer ; 8 : Vietnamese ; 9 : Paraok (Wa) ; 10 : Malay ; 11 : Eastern Cham ; 12 : Colloquial Thai ; 13 : Mong Leng

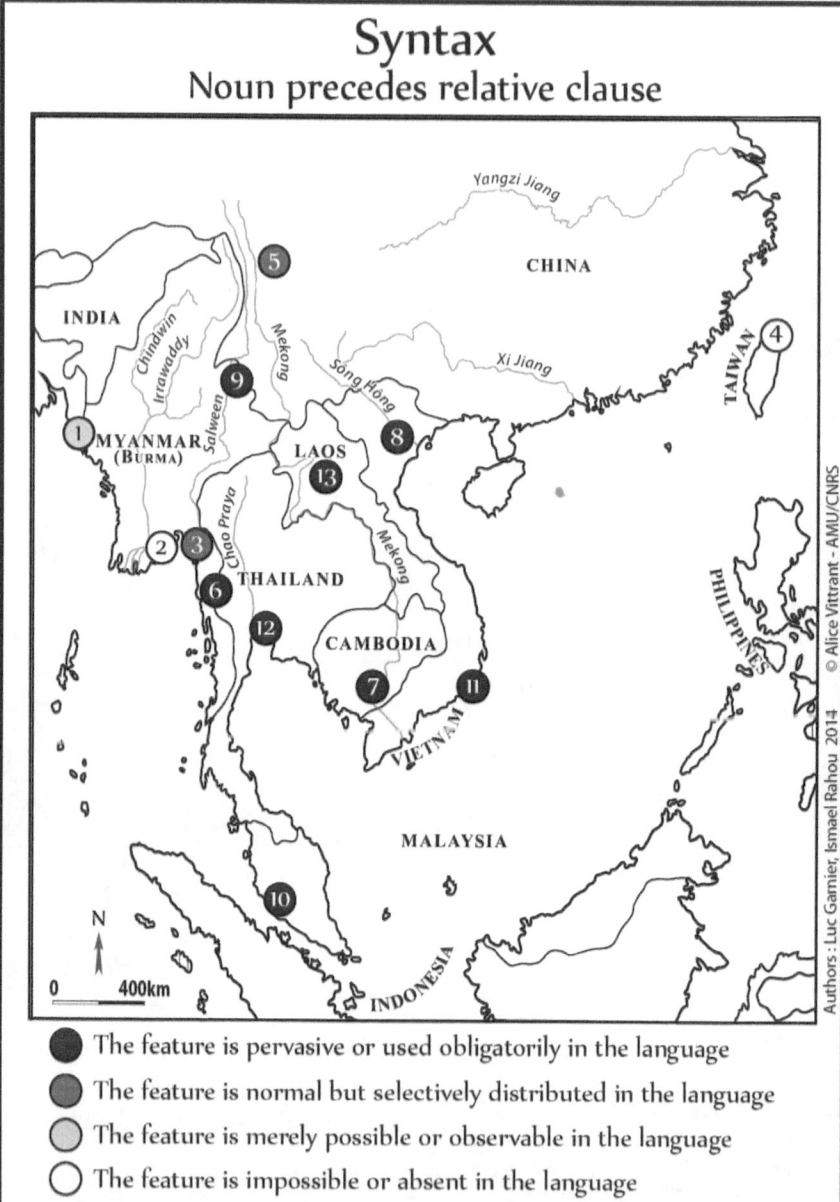

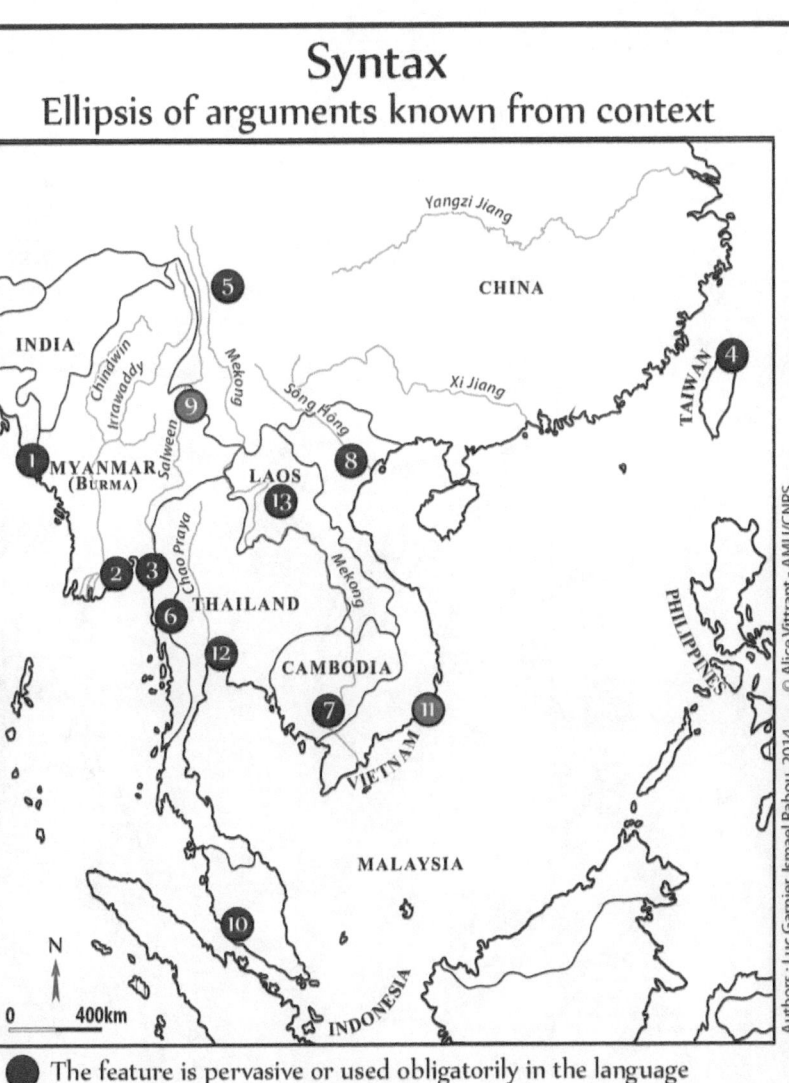

Syntax
Ellipsis of arguments known from context

- ● The feature is pervasive or used obligatorily in the language
- ◉ The feature is normal but selectively distributed in the language
- ○ The feature is merely possible or observable in the language
- ○ The feature is impossible or absent in the language

1 : Bangladesh Khumi ; 2 : Burmese ; 3 : Pwo Karen ; 4 : Taiwanese Southern Min ; 5 : Yongning Na (Mosuo) ; 6 : Mon ; 7 : Khmer ; 8 : Vietnamese ; 9 : Paraok (Wa) ; 10 : Malay ; 11 : Eastern Cham ; 12 : Colloquial Thai ; 13 : Mong Leng

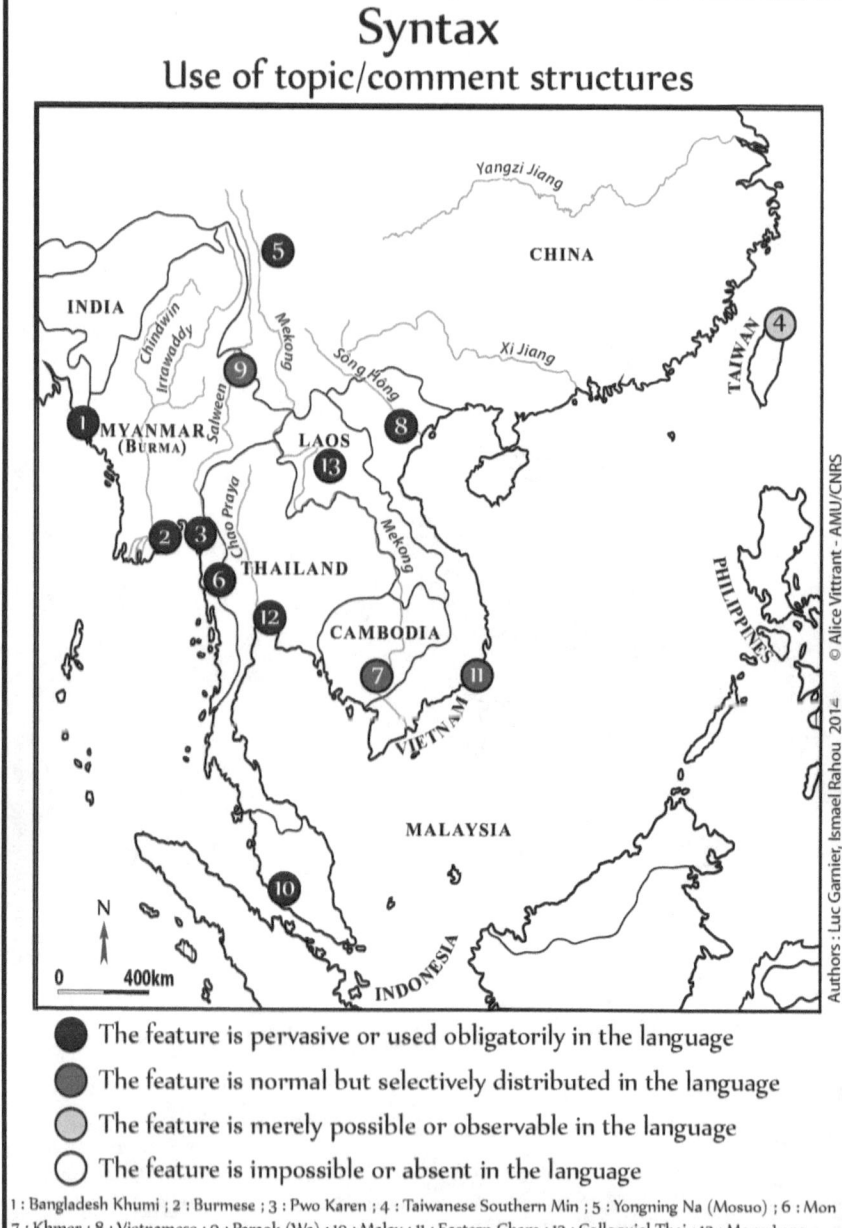

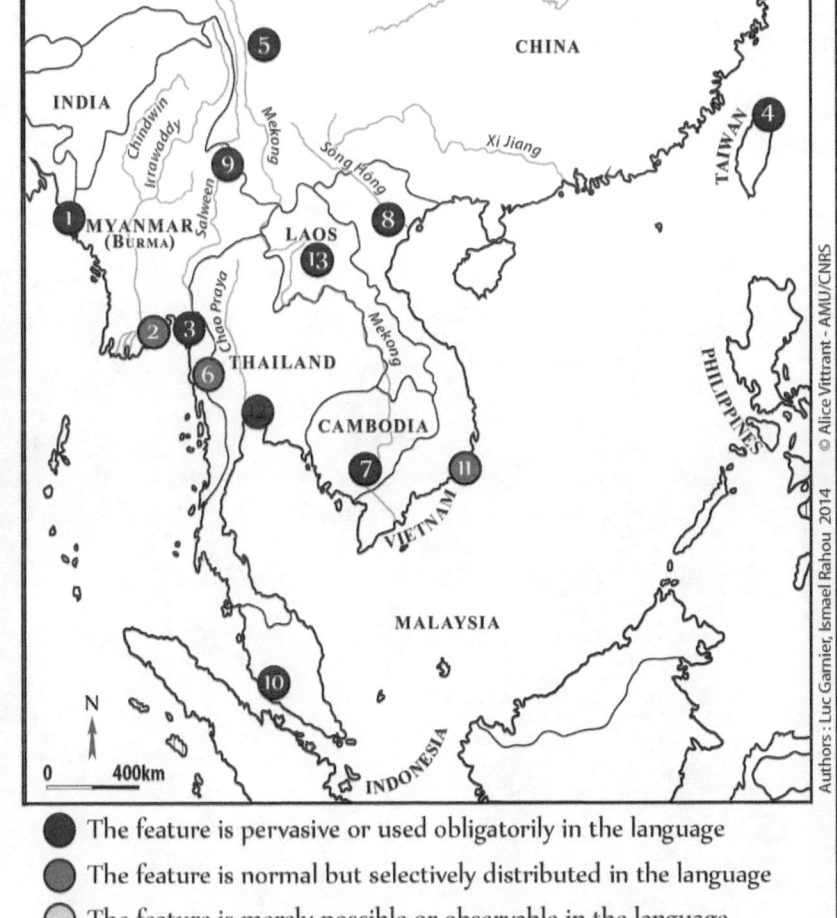

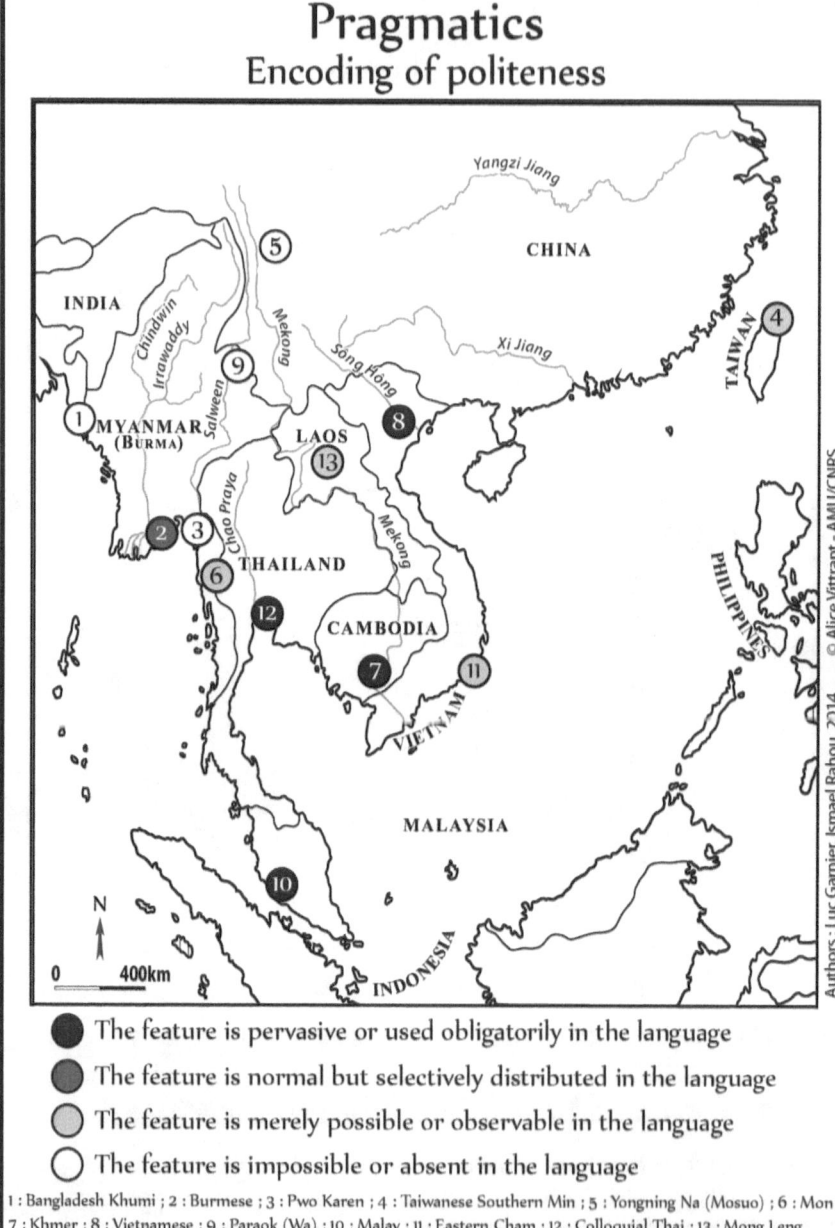

Language Index

Ahom 559
Aiton 559
Amoy/Xiamen (Min Chinese) 177–79, 183, 191
Arabic 73, 476–77
Arakanese/Rakhine 12, 56, 61, 115–16, 119, 479, 658–59
Athabaskan 30
Atsi/Zaiwa VII
Austroasiatic VI, X, 4, 7, 220, 384, 566, 663
Austronesian VI, X, 4, 7, 220, 384, 475, 478, 509–10, 521, 549, 560

Bai X, 235
Bawm 12
Burmese (Myanmar) XVII, 7, 56–122, 132–135, 148, 150, 157, 158, 161, 162, 168, 176, 280, 284–85, 291–92, 296, 298, 302, 305, 308, 310–12, 433–34, 443, 447, 453, 457, 545, 567, 588–89, 601, 654–59, 663–65, 668, 671, 674–75, 676, 680
Burmish VII
Bwe (Karen) 131–34, 161

Cantonese (Chinese) VIII, 177–78, 202–03, 204, 217, 220, 476, 490, 492, 495, 653
Cham (Eastern Cham) VI–XVIII, 1, 7, 523–553, 662, 666–67, 670, 676, 677, 680

Devanagari 57

Fuzhou/Foochow (Min Chinese) 178–79, 213

Geba (Karen) 131, 133–34, 163, 168
Gekho (Karen) 131

Hainanese (Min Chinese) 176, 179
Hakka 177, 217, 490, 653
Hindi 73
Hmong V, VI, XVIII, 4, 7, 61, 66, 75, 94, 110, 262, 342, 355, 609–647, 662, 667, 673
Hmong-Mien (Miao-Yao) 4, 7, 177, 220, 609, 665, 676

Hmongic 609, 611, 612
Hokkien (Min Chinese) XVI, 176, 177, 178, 180, 181, 182, 476, 490, 496

Indonesian 262, 476, 477, 488, 560, 664
Intha (Burmese) 56, 61

Japanese VII–IX, 40, 112, 221–22
Javanese VI, 264, 560
Jingpho/Jingpo/Jinghpaw VII, VIII, 56, 98, 533

Kachin – See Jingpho
Kam-Sui 559
Karen VII–XVII, 56, 98, 131–73, 540, 656–57, 673, 680
Kayah (Karen) 14, 56, 131, 153, 163
Kayin (Karen) 56
Kham 98, 658
Khmer V–XVII, 4, 7, 61, 75, 93, 262, 277, 310, 320–383, 434, 435, 437, 496, 560–61, 565, 567, 582, 584, 587, 591, 600, 658, 660, 663, 667, 669, 676–77, 679
Khumi IV–XVII, 5, 7, 12–50, 540, 653, 660–61, 663, 666, 672, 676–77, 680
Kuki-Chin 12–15, 17, 28, 35, 36, 45, 50

Lahu VIII–XIV, 22, 98, 237, 243–44, 262, 355, 434, 505
Lao VI, 355, 385, 480, 495, 559, 562
Lashi/Leqi VII
Laze 234
Lisu 235
Lolo-Burmese VIII, 57, 63–64, 220, 234
Lue (Lü) VII, 559

Malay VI, VIII, XII, XIII, XVI, XVII, 7, 75, 423, 475–517, 560, 662, 664, 676–77
Mandarin Chinese 177–79, 181, 183, 188–91, 194–96, 202–06, 209, 212–14, 217, 220, 235, 247, 355, 476, 492–93, 495, 565, 653, 673
Marma 12, 17, 56, 59
Maru/Langsu VII

Meithei/Manipuri VII, 57, 659
Min (Chinese) – See Southern Min and Hokkien
Mon V–XVII, 56–57, 67, 73, 75, 99, 131, 132, 134, 136, 166, 262, 277–316, 320, 560, 589, 601, 655–56, 668, 671, 680
Mon-Khmer 4, 7, 131, 220, 277, 281, 320, 327, 384–85, 432–34, 436–38, 448, 467, 523, 657, 660, 663, 665
Monebwa (Karen) 131, 133
Mong Leng (Hmong) VI–XVII, 609–647, 655, 656, 663, 673
Mongsen Ao 14, 20, 30, 37
Mopwa (Karen) 131
Mru 12
Munda X

Na (Yongning)/Mosuo VI, XI–XVII, 5, 136, 137, 139, 191, 221, 234–72, 661–62, 666, 680
Naxi 57, 234–36
Nepali VII
Newar/Newari 98, 258
Nyahkur (Mon) 277
Old Mon 278–79, 283, 293, 295, 296, 303, 308

Pa-O (Karen) 131
Paku (Karen) 131, 133
Pali VI, IX, XIII, XV, 57, 67, 72–73, 75, 82, 86, 277, 286, 291, 306, 310, 323, 326–27, 329–30, 335–37, 346, 372, 447, 560, 566, 600
Phake 559
Portuguese VIII, 177
Proto-Tibeto-Burman 13, 84, 96, 105, 138, 143, 238
Pumi 235
putonghua – See Mandarin Chinese 227
Pwo (Karen) VII–XVII, 131–171, 540, 656, 657, 673
Pyu 57, 277

Qiang 262

Sanskrit VI, 57, 82, 285, 310, 324, 326, 447, 476, 478, 560, 578, 600

Sgaw (Karen) 131, 143, 149–50, 161–63, 168
Shan VII–VIII, 56, 73, 432, 434, 443, 446–47, 467, 559
Shantou/Swatow (Min Chinese) 177–79, 203
Sinitic X, 176–221, 234, 306, 560
Sino-Tibetan V, 4, 7, 57, 176, 560, 654
Southern Min (Chinese) XVII, 5, 176–223, 653, 663
Stieng 320, 659, 661–62, 668, 672

Tai-Kadai V–XIII, 4, 7, 72, 220, 384, 432, 440, 444, 446–47, 467, 559–61, 564, 566, 659, 663, 665, 667
Taiwanese (Chinese) VIII, 177, 179–80, 184, 191, 195, 199, 205, 210, 213–14, 216, 218, 220
Tavoyan/Tavoyen (Burmese) 56, 61
Teochew /Chaozhou (Min Chinese) 176–79, 203, 490
Thai VI–IX, XIV–XVI, XVIII, 7, 22, 75, 93, 132, 150, 156, 164, 176, 262, 278, 279, 298, 308, 310, 342, 349, 355, 366, 385, 398, 417, 434, 480, 491–92, 496, 505, 533, 546, 559–601, 642, 658–59, 663, 666, 671, 673, 675–77, 679
Thalebwa (Karen) 131
Thangkul 98
Tibetan V, VII, 57, 98, 112, 234–35, 258, 265, 658–59
Tripura 12

Vietnamese VI–XVII, 7, 75, 87, 93, 94, 220, 342, 355, 384–425, 491–92, 496, 510, 523–24, 527, 529–30, 534, 536–38, 542, 544–45, 548–49, 654, 661–62, 666, 669, 673, 676–77

Wa (Paraok) VII–VIII, XI–XVII, 1, 7, 336, 342, 432–471, 660, 663, 665, 671, 676–77

Xumi/Shixing 234, 267

Yaw 56

Zhuang 495, 559

www.ingramcontent.com/pod-product-compliance
Lightning Source LLC
Chambersburg PA
CBHW021217300426
44111CB00007B/341